THE COLLECTED VERSE
OF MARY GILMORE

Two volumes

VOLUME TWO: 1930–1962

THE ACADEMY EDITIONS OF AUSTRALIAN LITERATURE

THE AUSTRALIAN ACADEMY OF THE HUMANITIES

THE COLLECTED VERSE
OF MARY GILMORE

Edited by
JENNIFER STRAUSS

Two volumes
VOLUME TWO: 1930–1962

UNIVERSITY OF QUEENSLAND PRESS

Published 2007 by the University of Queensland Press,
Box 6042, St Lucia, Queensland 4067, Australia

This, the Academy Edition of the texts of *The Collected Verse of Mary Gilmore*, established from the original sources is copyright
© Estate of Mary Gilmore, Jennifer Strauss, the Australian Academy of the Humanities, 2005.
The introductory matter and end matter are copyright
© Jennifer Strauss, the Australian Academy of the Humanities, 2005.

Adapted from a page design by Alec Bolton

Typeset by Caren Florance

Production and co-ordination:
Australian Scholarly Editions Centre Projects,
School of Humanities and Social Sciences,
University of New South Wales at ADFA,
Canberra ACT 2600, Australia

Printed in Australia by McPherson's Printing Group

Distributed in the USA and Canada by
International Specialized Book Services, Inc.,
5804 N.E. Hassalo Street, Portland, Oregon 97213-3640, USA

National Library of Australia Cataloguing-in-Publication entry

Gilmore, Mary, Dame, 1865–1962.
The collected verse of Mary Gilmore.

Academy ed.
Bibliography.
ISBN 978 0 7022 3591 7 (v. 2. 1930–1962).
ISBN 978 0 7022 3592 4 (v. 2. 1930–1962: pbk.).

1. Gilmore, Mary, Dame, 1865–1962 – Criticism and interpretation.
2. Australian poetry – History and criticism.
I. Strauss, Jennifer, 1933– . II. Title.
(Series: Academy editions of Australian literature).

A821.2

CONTENTS

GENERAL EDITOR'S FOREWORD

THE Academy Editions of Australian Literature is the first series of critical editions of major works of the nation's literature. The series provides reliable reading texts and contextual annotation based on rigorous scholarship and thorough textual collation. The term 'Literature' in the series title is interpreted broadly. It is taken to extend beyond the traditional literary genres and to encompass other forms, for instance, personal diaries and plays for the popular stage.

The project was initiated by the Australian Academy of the Humanities as a response to the unreliability of most currently available printings of Australian works dating from the nineteenth century and first half of the twentieth century. It is not generally appreciated that the normal circumstances of the transmission of the text of a literary work, say a full-length novel that undergoes several typesettings over a fifty- or hundred-year period, invariably lead to some thousands of textual changes. Most of these are variants of punctuation and other matters of detail, consequent on the publisher restyling each new edition for its intended audience (magazine or newspaper, Australian, British or American). However, a significant number of changes in wording inevitably occurs as each new typesetting is proofread, to whatever degree of accuracy the time permits, against its copy – typically the immediately previous printing. Rarely do publishers scrupulously check the new edition against the original one. Where photo-lithographic reprints of early editions have been decided upon, the choice has usually been determined by the modern one-volume format, whereas original printings of nineteenth-century novels were typically in two or three volumes.

The textual changes of new typesettings are not often sanctioned by the author, even if still alive: authors tend to have their eye on what they are writing at the moment rather than on the textual accuracy of reprintings of what they have written in the past. The accumulated changes are also historically misleading in that they do not represent exactly what the original audiences read and therefore distort our understanding of the relationship between those audiences and the version of the work that they read. This is particularly important in the case of Australian literary works, which were often written for publication or serialisation in a local magazine or newspaper, were revised by the author, and then reshaped by well-meaning but interventionist editors for first publication in book form. Further textual changes or abridgement often occurred in the course of first overseas publication and by the reissuing of the work in cheap, double-column or collected works formats. American editions usually varied from their British counterparts, and both contained departures from their Australian original. All this assumes that the works have actually remained available. In the case of plays for the commercial stage, poems published in fugitive broadsheets or in brief-lived newspapers, and privately kept diaries, our access is conditioned by the accidents of their collection by family, individual collectors and libraries.

The case for full-scale critical editions that would address these problems for major Australian works is overwhelming. The Academy Editions volumes clarify the often confusing textual histories of these works and establish reliable reading texts. Notation of textual variance in the different versions is provided, together with historical and other explanations of whatever in the texts may be no longer clear to the modern reader.

The Introduction gives a history of the writing, revision, production and reception of the work (or body of works), and will be found to contain much hitherto unknown information. A biographical context is provided where possible, focusing particularly on and around the time of writing and publication. The author's relevant dealings with amanuenses, editors, publishers and advisers, as revealed in letters, memoirs and publishers' archives, are canvassed for any effect they may have had on the work and on how the author saw his or her task and audience. All extant manuscript and other pre-publication material is described, as well as any serialisations and the early publications in book form. These have been consulted as a preliminary to the editing process, and variant readings in the printed tradition are recorded at the foot of the reading page. The historical account (supplemented in the present volume by the Preface) lays the groundwork for the description of the editorial principles adopted. Given the range of authors, genres and historical periods covered by the Academy Editions series, no uniform editorial approach has been prescribed in advance. Where previously unpublished material is extant in only one version, the choice of copy-text is straightforward. However, the editor must still decide how, in a myriad of ways, to balance the needs of a modern readership against the historical interest of the manuscript's peculiarities of presentation. In the case of prose fiction volumes, editors are obliged to make a difficult choice between a textual presentation that gives highest authority to authorial intention and one that has a documentary form of the text as its authority. As the Academy Editions series is intended to serve a predominantly Australian readership, both now and in the future, some editions will favour the form of the work read by its earliest Australian audiences before being reshaped overseas. Whatever the approach taken by the editor, original spellings and punctuation are respected wherever they would not actively mislead the modern reader, and unavoidable decisions to emend the copy-text are recorded. Errors in quotations left uncorrected are present in the original sources.

ACKNOWLEDGEMENTS

I AM grateful in the first instance to the Australian Academy of the Humanities for its acceptance of my proposal for a Collected Verse of Mary Gilmore as part of the Academy Editions series and for the contributions of the members of the Editorial Board. The Academy has been a generous supporter of the edition, especially in funding editorial assistance, and the Australian Research Council and the Arts Faculty of Monash University both provided much-needed research funds. The Department of English at Monash University has unquestioningly provided infrastructure support.

It is fourteen years since I first wrote on Mary Gilmore for the collection of essays entitled *The Time to Write: Australian Women Writers 1890–1930* (1993). In the intervening period many people and many institutions have contributed to the knowledge of Gilmore's life and writing, as well as to specific research into the poems themselves, their manuscripts and their publication history. This edition has benefited from their work. For a variety of research assistance in both areas over those years I have to thank Karen Cramer, Sue Foster, Dianne Heriot, Dunya Lindsey, John Lowe, Susan McDougall and Anne Olsen. Special thanks are due to Margaret Henderson, who was responsible for transferring the poems in Gilmore's collections to computer files, as well as searching out poems in the Mitchell and Fryer libraries. Kate Chadwick assisted in a preliminary proofreading of many of the uncollected poems. At the Australian Scholarly Editions Centre, Tessa Wooldridge helped with proofs and Caren Florance contributed far more than a typesetter would normally be expected to do.

This edition could not have come into existence without the resources of various libraries and archives. I am greatly indebted to the informed and enthusiastic assistance of the librarians and library staff at several institutions, especially at the major manuscript sites of the Mitchell Library (State Library of New South Wales) and the Manuscript Room of the National Library of Australia, as well as at the Special Collections sections of the libraries of the University of New York at Buffalo, the Australian Defence Force Academy and the Fryer Library of the University of Queensland. Access to rare printed material, journals and microfilm material was provided by the State Libraries of New South Wales, Queensland, South Australia and Victoria. Specific requests for information or material were met courteously and promptly by these libraries and by those of the Australian National University, Macquarie University, Monash University (Rare Book Room and the Centre for Australian Indigenous Studies), the University of Melbourne (Special Collections), the University of Western Sydney and Wagga Wagga City Library. Special thanks are due to the staff of the Biblioteca Nacional in both Buenos Aires and Montevideo for surmounting language difficulties to meet my requests.

Archives were also an important resource. I am grateful for the responsiveness of staff at the archives of Charles Sturt University at Wagga Wagga, the Australian War Memorial, the Catholic Archdiocese of Sydney, the City of Sydney Archives, the Regional History Room of the Goulburn Branch Library, the Casterton Historical Society and the Temora Rural Museum.

Among individuals who gave of their time to answer questions or give expert advice I must thank Gilmore's biographer, W. H. Wilde, Harry Heseltine, Conrad Hamann and Wallace Kirsop of Monash University, Isobel Moulinho of the Department of Romance Languages, La Trobe University, and my colleague Harold Love for wise words on problems of collating and annotating.

There are, however, two people whose contribution has been immeasurable. Meredith Sherlock's meticulous collating skills were the more valuable because of her grasp of editorial principles and her commitment to their application, while her apparently inexhaustible patience and cheerfulness shamed any suggestion of flagging editorial morale. As General Editor of the Academy Editions, Paul Eggert has given unstintingly of his editorial expertise, attending not only to large questions of content and presentation, but also to the most minute details in his constant determination that the edition should meet the highest possible standards of scholarly editing. If there is any falling short, the responsibility is entirely mine.

January 2007 *JS*

The Academy Editions of Australian Literature

The Academy Editions project was initiated under John Mulvaney's Secretaryship of the Australian Academy of the Humanities with an Institutional Grant from the Australian Research Council. The project has been housed at the Australian Scholarly Editions Centre, University of New South Wales at the Australian Defence Force Academy, Canberra, and has received continuing support from its host School of Humanities and Social Sciences and its Information, Communication and Technology Services. The co-operation of the National Library of Australia, the ADFA Library, and State and major university libraries, as well as that of libraries and scholars overseas, is also gratefully acknowledged.

Management Committee

Graeme Turner (chair), John Byron, Stuart Cunningham, Brian Denehy, Paul Eggert and Harry Heseltine.

Advisory Board

John Barnes, Bruce Bennett, Veronica Brady, Alan Brissenden, John Hardy, Margaret Harris, Laurie Hergenhan, Joy Hooton, Veronica Kelly, Wallace Kirsop, Ken Stewart and Chris Wallace-Crabbe.

CHRONOLOGY

ENTRIES refer to Mary Gilmore ('MG'; born Mary Jean Cameron) except if indicated.

16 August 1865	Born near Goulburn, first child of Donald Cameron and Mary Ann Beattie.
July 1878	Unpaid pupil teacher for her uncle, George Gray, at Cootamundra.
Early 1879	Accompanies Grays to school at Woomargama near Albury.
From mid-1880	Pupil teacher with uncle, John Beattie, at Yerong Creek, near Wagga Wagga.
January 1883	Probationary pupil teacher at Wagga Wagga Public School.
31 May 1886	Posted as 'Teacher of a Small School' to Beaconsfield.
12 March 1887	'After the Shipwreck' in *Bathurst Free Press and Mining Journal*.
22 September 1887	Posted to Silverton (near Broken Hill) as a provisionally qualified teacher, after passing classification examination.
19 November 1887	First issue in Brisbane of William Lane's radical journal, *Boomerang*.
January 1890	Appointed Assistant Teacher at Neutral Bay, Sydney.
From January 1890	Meets Henry Lawson, John Farrell and J. F. Archibald.

March 1890	William Lane becomes founding editor of Brisbane *Worker*.
From 16 August 1890	Maritime Strike involves seamen, coalminers, transport workers and shearers throughout s.e. Australia. MG active in Labour Defence Committee organised by Trades and Labour Council.
January–May 1891	First Queensland Shearers' Strike ends in trial and conviction of 12 union leaders.
October 1891	New Australia Co-operative Settlement Association announced in *Worker*.
17 September 1892	'A Spell Is on Me', first of poems (1892–93) in *Queenslander* as 'Em Jacey' or 'Emma Jacey'.
23 October 1892	Meets William Lane.
29 October 1892	First poem in *Worker*: 'The Dream-Mother Came to Me'.
November 1892	New Australia Association journal, *New Australia*, begins publication in Wagga Wagga.
March 1893	Association and journal move to Sydney. MG involved in its production and writing articles and poems as 'Rudione Calvert', 'M.J.C.', 'M.C.' and 'M.'.
July 1893	*Worker* becomes a separate publication in New South Wales.
16 July 1893	First colonists sail for Paraguay in the *Royal Tar*.
17 August 1895	'Mighty Easy, Ain't It', first of c. 35 poems (1893–1907) in *Hobart Clipper*.
Mid-November 1895	Leaves for second Paraguayan settlement (Colonia Cosme) to be its school teacher.
2 January 1896	Reaches Colonia Cosme via Wellington (New Zealand) and Montevideo (Uruguay).

January 1896 – December 1899	Active in production of *Cosme Evening Notes* and *Cosme Monthly*.
8 August 1896	First poem in *Bulletin*: 'The Outcast'.
29 May 1897	Marries William Alexander Gilmore, a shearer and farm labourer from Strathdownie, near Casterton, Victoria.
November 1897 – November 1899	Eight poems in *Cosme Monthly*.
21 August 1898	William Dysart Cameron Gilmore ('Billy') born at Villa Rica (*or* Villarrica).
25 March 1899	First poem in *Bookfellow*: 'Good-Night'.
12 August 1899	Gilmores resign from Cosme.
November 1900	Gilmores leave Paraguay for Patagonia (Argentina).
July 1902	Gilmores return to Australia.
Early 1903	Settles at Strathdownie. Correspondence with A. G. Stephens begins.
1 October 1903	14 poems published by Stephens on Red Page of *Bulletin*.
From 1904	Poems and articles in *New Idea* (to December 1910), *Worker* (to February 1931) and other journals.
1906	Included in Bertram Stevens's *An Anthology of Australian Verse*. Several of her Red Page poems set to music as 'Six Songs from the South'.
Early 1907	Moves to Casterton; active for local Labor Party till 1911.
7 February 1907	Invited to contribute to Stevens's *Native Companion*.
14 February 1907 – 30 November 1921	Poems published in A. G. Stephens's revived publication of *Bookfellow*.
November 1907	Suggests a Women's Page to NSW *Worker* editor Henry Lamond.

2 January 1908	First *Worker* Women's Page (salary £2 a week).
8 November 1909	Volume of poems accepted by George Robertson.
1910	*Marri'd and Other Verses* (Melbourne: George Robertson).
January 1910 – December 1917	Poems in *Lone Hand*.
June 1911	Family leaves Casterton: MG (with Billy) to Sydney, Will to farm in North Queensland.
July–November 1912	Campaigns for Maternity Allowance.
October 1913–1916	Involved in financing of *Bookfellow*.
February 1914	*The Worker Cook Book* (Sydney: Worker Trustees).
March 1914	Founding member of Sydney Lyceum Club.
15 May 1914	Billy leaves Sydney to join his father in Queensland.
15 July 1915	'Australia Marching On' (*Worker*) reflects initial support for war effort.
24 November 1915	First publication in *Sydney Morning Herald* ('Mother-Word'); last is 'The Proud', 3 August 1957.
September–October 1916	On sick leave from *Worker* during period of first conscription referendum.
1917	*The Tale of Tiddley Winks* (Sydney: Bookfellow).
November 1917	In second conscription referendum, opposes conscription for overseas service.
1918	First of surviving diaries.
November 1918	*The Passionate Heart* (Sydney: Angus & Robertson).
From November 1918	Campaigns in *Worker* for soldier settlement schemes.

August 1920	In hospital with blood pressure, heart and respiratory problems.
March 1921	To Goulburn for health reasons. Periods in St John of God's Hospital, otherwise living in Hotel Imperial.
After March 1921	Contemplates conversion to Catholicism.
12 May 1921	First publication in *Catholic Press*: 'So Great This Faith'.
1922	*Hound of the Road* (Sydney: Angus & Robertson) is first collection of essays recollecting pioneer days.
May–July 1922	As 'Hill 17' campaigns for Rocky Hill to be site of Goulburn war memorial.
2 September 1922	Henry Lawson dies.
15 December 1922	'The Dead Poet', among earliest of poems in *Goulburn Evening Penny Post*.
7 July 1923	'Song Immortal', first of poems in *Daily Telegraph* (last in mid-1927).
March or April 1924	Dictates her version of relationship with Lawson ('Henry Lawson & me') to Lawson's sister (Gertie) in Goulburn.
December 1924 – July 1927	Poems in *Spinner*.
July 1925	Returns permanently to Sydney.
December 1925	*The Tilted Cart* (Sydney: Worker Trustees).
May–June 1926	Articles on her life and work in *Australian Women's Mirror*, *New Zealand Tablet*, *Wentworth Magazine*.
October–November 1927	Essay series 'Literature: Our Lost Field' in *Sydney Morning Herald* begins MG's public involvement in Aboriginal issues.
23 November 1928	Chairs inaugural meeting of the Fellowship of Australian Writers (FAW); elected one of four Vice-Presidents.

January 1930	Appointed to Film Censorship Appeal Board.
August 1930	*The Wild Swan* (Melbourne: Robertson & Mullens).
From 1931	Manuscript reader for Angus & Robertson.
Early 1931	*The Rue Tree* (Melbourne: Robertson & Mullens).
6 February 1931	Resigns from *Worker* after period of strained relations with editor, Henry Boote; final column 11 February.
Mid-1932	*Under the Wilgas* (Melbourne: Robertson & Mullens).
Early 1933	Settles in Kings Cross flat, Sydney.
16 August 1933	Made Life Fellow of FAW at birthday celebration which becomes a regular feature of Sydney literary life.
January 1934	Begins keeping of diaries later presented to Mitchell Library, Sydney.
June 1934	*Old Days Old Ways* (Sydney: Angus and Robertson), a great popular success.
May 1935	Awarded King's Silver Jubilee Medal.
December 1935	*More Recollections* (Sydney: Angus & Robertson).
1 February 1937	Created Dame of the British Empire.
1938	Awarded Commonwealth Literary Fund (CLF) Fellowship.
9 April 1938	Correspondence begins friendship with R. D. FitzGerald.
2 August 1939	*Battlefields* (Sydney: Angus & Robertson).
29 June 1940	'No Foe Shall Gather our Harvest' in *Australian Women's Weekly*, a major popular success.
1941	'The Pear Tree' in first of Angus & Robertson's annual anthologies (*Australian Poetry 1941*).

December 1941	*The Disinherited* (Melbourne: Robertson & Mullens).
From 1942	Begins collecting biographical and literary material for donation to Mitchell Library.
14 March 1942	'Singapore', on the fall of Singapore, in *Australian Women's Weekly*.
November 1942	First approach to CLF for support for proposed *Fourteen Men*.
23 January 1943	Awarded CLF Scholarship.
1944	*Pro Patria Australia and Other Poems* (Sydney: W. H. Honey).
July 1944	Seeks assistance from CLF for publication of a volume of selected verse.
22 February 1945	Will Gilmore dies of septicaemia.
28 June 1945	Awarded CLF pension.
30 July 1945	Sudden death of Billy Gilmore.
Early 1946	CLF appoints R. D. FitzGerald and Tom Inglis Moore to assist with preparation of *Selected Verse*.
May 1947	In political dispute over award of CLF grants to left-wing writers.
20–25 October 1947	Official guest at Children's Book Week, in Wagga Wagga.
12 November 1947	Speaker at Eureka Youth League celebration of Children's Book Week.
28 July 1948	Again approaches CLF for support for a revised *Fourteen Men*.
16 August 1948	Receives advance copies of *Selected Verse* (Sydney: Angus & Robertson; 2nd revised edition 1969, re-issued as *The Passionate Heart and Other Poems*, 1979).
1949–51	Campaigns against Menzies's Suppression of Communism Bill.
March 1952	Offers regular column ('Arrows') to *Tribune*

	in protest against scare tactics of the Cold War; writes for *Tribune* till 1962.
12 September 1953	Memorial poem for W. M. ('Billy') Hughes in *Daily Telegraph*.
16 August 1954	Receives first copies of *Fourteen Men*.
November 1954	Prepares material for donation to Mitchell Library and Poetry Collection at State University of New York at Buffalo before entering hospital for tests and observation.
1955	*Verse for Children* (Sydney: Writers' Press).
24 February 1955	Operation for colon cancer.
June 1955	Special issue of *Overland* with tributes to MG.
18 August 1955	Controversy over MG's 'fictionalising' of Lambing Flat riots in the apparently auto-biographical title poem of *Fourteen Men*.
May 1956	Union movement endows Mary Gilmore Awards for Literature.
8 September 1956	Appears at National Assembly for Peace organised by Australian Peace Council.
September 1957	William Dobell portrait, commissioned by Australasian Book Society, proves controversial but MG defends it.
9 November 1958	Honorary member of the Australian Journalists' Association.
3 May 1959	Leads Sydney May Day pageant.
9 August 1959	Australian Broadcasting Commission screens 'Dame Mary Remembers'.
4 October 1960	Donates Dobell portrait to the Art Gallery of New South Wales.
December 1960	R. D. FitzGerald's article on MG, with a Louis Kahan portrait, in *Meanjin*.
May 1961	Wins union movement's Queen of the May competition as nomination of Building Workers' Industrial Union.

2 December 1962	Dies.
6 December 1962	State funeral, Sydney. Ashes later interred at Cloncurry, Queensland.
15 August 1965	Centenary of birth marked by special issue of *The Realist* and by Mary Gilmore Centenary Celebrations, including launch of *Mary Gilmore: A Tribute* – a celebration of her life and work, edited by Dymphna Cusack, Tom Inglis Moore and Barrie Ovenden for the Australasian Book Society.

LIST OF ABBREVIATIONS

'Gilmore' is used in text and 'MG' in notes. Gilmore's main publishers are abbreviated in notes as 'A&R' (Angus & Robertson) and 'R&M' (Robertson & Mullens). Individual poems are cross-referenced by the alphanumeric identifier (M1, R66 etc.) assigned in this edition (see p. 3). The companion volume ('volume 1') to the present one is *The Collected Verse of Mary Gilmore: Volume 1 1887–1929*, ed. Jennifer Strauss (St Lucia: University of Queensland Press, 2004). In addition, the following abbreviations are used:

Works by Mary Gilmore

Bat	*Battlefields* (Sydney: Angus & Robertson, 1939)
Dis	*The Disinherited* (Melbourne: Robertson & Mullens, 1941)
FM	*Fourteen Men* (Sydney: Angus & Robertson, 1954)
HR	*Hound of the Road* (Sydney: Angus & Robertson, 1922)
MR	*More Recollections* (Sydney: Angus & Robertson, 1935)
MV	*Marri'd and Other Verses* (Melbourne: George Robertson, 1910)
ODOW	*Old Days Old Ways: A Book of Recollections* (Sydney: Angus & Robertson, 1934)
PH	*The Passionate Heart* (Sydney: Angus & Robertson, 1918)
PPA	*Pro Patria Australia and Other Poems* (Sydney: W. H. Honey, [1944])
RT	*The Rue Tree* (Melbourne: Robertson & Mullens, 1931)
SV	*Selected Verse* (Sydney: Angus & Robertson, 1948)
TC	*The Tilted Cart: A Book of Recitations* (Sydney: The Worker Trustees, 1925)
TTW	*The Tale of Tiddley Winks* (Sydney: The Bookfellow, 1917)
UW	*Under the Wilgas* (Melbourne: Robertson & Mullens, 1932)
VC	*Verse for Children* (Sydney: The Writers' Press, [1955])
WS	*The Wild Swan* (Melbourne: Robertson & Mullens, 1930)

Anthologies

Anthologies are abbreviated by the name of the editor or the first named of multiple editors. Where an editor has been responsible for more than one anthology this is indicated by the addition of a numeral.

Dubois   *The High Light: A Souvenir Volume by the Adelaide Drawing and Sketch Club*, ed. Bernard Dubois (Adelaide: George Robertson, 1910)

Eldershaw   *The Peaceful Army*, ed. Flora Eldershaw (Sydney: Fellowship of Australian Writers, 1938)

Green   *Modern Australian Poetry*, ed. H. M. Green (Melbourne: Melbourne University Press, 1946)

Hansen   *An Austral Garden: An Anthology of Australian Verse*, ed. M. P. Hansen and D. McLachlan (Melbourne: Roberston & Mullens, 1912)

Ingamells   *New Song in an Old Land*, ed. Rex Ingamells (London: Longmans Green, 1943)

Lavater   *The Sonnet in Australia*, ed. Louis Lavater (Sydney: Angus & Robertson, 1926)

Lawson   *Australian Bush Songs and Ballads*, ed. Will Lawson (Sydney: Johnson, 1944)

Mackaness1   *The Wide Brown Land*, ed. George and Joan Mackaness (Sydney: Angus & Robertson, 1934)

Mackaness2   *Poets of Australia*, ed. George Mackaness (Sydney: Angus & Robertson, 1946)

Mackaness3   *An Anthology of Australian Verse*, ed. George Mackaness (Sydney: Angus & Robertson, 1952)

Moore   *Australia Writes*, ed. T. Inglis Moore (Melbourne: F. W. Cheshire, 1953)

Mudie   *Favourite Australian Poems*, ed. Ian Mudie (Adelaide: Rigby, 1963)

Murdoch1   *A Book of Australasian Verse*, ed. Walter Murdoch (London: Oxford University Press, 1924)

Murdoch2   *A Book of Australian and New Zealand Verse*, ed. Walter Murdoch and Alan Mulgan (Melbourne: Oxford University Press, 1949)

Pizer   *Freedom on the Wallaby*, ed. Marjorie Pizer (Sydney: Pinchgut Press, 1953)

Serle   *An Australasian Anthology*, ed. Percival Serle (London: Collins, 1927)

Stable   *The High Road of Australian Verse: An Anthology for Australian Schools*, ed. J. J. Stable (London: Oxford University Press, 1929)

Stephens   *Anzac Memorial 1916*, ed A. G. Stephens (Sydney: Returned Soldiers Association, 1916)

Stevens1	*An Anthology of Australian Verse*, ed. Bertram Stevens (Sydney: Angus & Robertson, 1906)
Stevens2	*The Golden Treasury of Australian Verse*, ed. Bertram Stevens (Sydney: Angus & Robertson, 1909)
Thompson	*Penguin Book of Australian Verse*, ed. John Thompson, Kenneth Slessor and R. G. Howarth (Mitcham, Vic: Penguin, 1958)
Wannan	*Treasury of Australian Frontier Tales*, ed. Bill Wannan (Melbourne: Lansdowne Press, 1944)
Wilkinson1	*Gleanings from Australasian Verse: Poems of Manhood*, ed. Mary Wilkinson (Melbourne: Whitcombe & Tombs, [1919])
Wilkinson2	*Gleanings from Australasian Verse: Love Poems*, ed. Mary Wilkinson (Melbourne: Whitcombe & Tombs, [1920])
Wilkinson3	*Gleanings from Australasian Verse: Nature Poems*, ed. Mary Wilkinson (Melbourne: Whitcombe & Tombs, [1920])
Wright1	*A Book of Australian Verse*, ed. Judith Wright (Melbourne: Oxford University Press, 1956)
Wright2	*New Land New Language*, ed. Judith Wright (Melbourne: Oxford University Press, 1957)

Periodical publications

AB	*Albury Banner*	BFP	*Bathurst Free Press and Mining Journal*
Adv	*Advocate*	Bkfw	*Bookfellow*
AinA	*Art in Australia*	BM	*Barrier Miner*
AJ	*Australasian Journalist*	Bn	*Bulletin*
AJSU	*Arts Journal of Sydney University*	Boh	*Bohemia*
Annals	*Annals of Our Lady of the Sacred Heart*	BPMag	*Burns Philp Magazine*
		Bth	*Birth*
ANR	*Australian National Review*	CEN	*Cosme Evening Notes*
AP[*year*]	*Australian Poetry* (Angus & Robertson Annual Anthology. Year [italicised] is included in title)	CFP	*Casterton Free Press*
		Clip	*Clipper*
		CL	*Country Life*
		CM	*Cosme Monthly*
APA	*Australian Poetry Annual*	CP	*Catholic Press*
Argus	*Argus*	CT	*Canberra Times*
ArgL	*Argyle Liberal*	Des	*Desiderata*
Aus	*Aussie*	DT	*Daily Telegraph*
AusH	*Australian Highway*	DTNP	*Daily Telegraph News Pictorial*
AV	*Adelaide Voice*		
AWA	*Australian Writers' Annual*	DTPS	*Daily Telegraph Pictorial Supplement*
AWM	*Australian Women's Mirror*		
AWW	*Australian Women's Weekly*	EJ	*Everylady's Journal*

FAdv	Farmers' Advocate	Quad	Quadrant
FAW	Fellowship (Journal of the Fellowship of Australian Writers)	RA	Red Ant
		Reveille	Reveille (Journal of the New South Wales Branch of the Returned Sailors, Soldiers and Airmen's Imperial League of Australia)
FJ	Freeman's Journal		
Fwp	Fellowship (Melbourne Free Religious Fellowship)		
GEPP	Goulburn Evening Penny Post		
HA	Home Annual	SMag	School Magazine (New South Wales)
Hermes	Hermes (Sydney University Medical Journal)	SMH	Sydney Morning Herald
		SmW	Smith's Weekly
Hesper	Hesper	SnMH	Southern Morning Herald
Ink	Ink (Annual Anthology of the Association of Women Writers, NSW)	Spin	Spinner
		ST	Sunday Times
		StW	Standard Weekly
Jindy	The Jindyworobak Anthology (Annual)	Sun	Sydney Sun
		Sy	Southerly
Junee	Junee Democrat and Southern Cross	T&C	Town and Country Journal
		TD	Tasmanian Democrat
KCT	Kings Cross Times	TemI	Temora Independent
LD	Labor Daily	TLS	Times Literary Supplement
LH	Lone Hand	Tri	Triad
LMag	Lilley's Magazine	Trib	Tribune
Mjn	Meanjin	TribM	Tribune (Melbourne)
MP	Murray Pioneer	Verse	Verse
NA	New Australia	WB	Woman's Budget
NC	Native Companion	WDA	Wagga Wagga Daily Advertiser
NewI	New Idea		
NZT	New Zealand Tablet	WMag	Wentworth Magazine
OL	Orange Leader	WmC	Wingham Chronicle
Ovld	Overland	Wr	Worker (also known as the Australian Worker)
Presb	New South Wales Presbyterian		
		WWE	Wagga Wagga Express
QD	Queensland Digger	WWld	Woman's World
Qlr	Queenslander		

Reference works and other abbreviations

CG   W. H. Wilde, *Courage a Grace: A Biography of Dame Mary Gilmore* (Carlton, Vic: Melbourne University Press, 1988)

Dixon   R. M. W. Dixon, W. S. Ransom and Mandy Thomas, *Australian*

	Aboriginal Words in English: Their Origin and Meaning (Melbourne: Oxford University Press, 1990)
Letters	*Letters of Mary Gilmore*, ed. W. H. Wilde and T. Inglis Moore (Carlton, Vic: Melbourne University Press, 1980)
Macquarie	*The Macquarie Dictionary*, ed. A. Delbridge, J. R. L. Bernard, D. Blair and W. S. Ransom, 2nd revision (Chatswood, NSW: Macquarie Library, 1987)
OCAH	*Oxford Companion to Australian History*, ed. Graeme Davison, John Hirst and Stuart Macintyre (Melbourne: Oxford University Press Australia, 1998)
OCAL	*The Oxford Companion to Australian Literature*, ed. William H. Wilde, Joy Hooton and Barry Andrews, 2nd edn (Melbourne: Oxford University Press Australia, 1994)
OED	*Oxford English Dictionary*, ed. James A. H. Murray, Henry Bradley, W. A. Craigie and C. T. Onions (Oxford: Clarendon Press, 1933)
Parker	K. Langloh Parker, *Australian Legendary Tales* and *More Australian Legendary Tales* (Melbourne: Melville, Mullen and Slade, 1896 and 1898). The Word Lists provided are identical in the two volumes.
Parker 1905	K. Langloh Parker, *The Euahlayi Tribe: A Study of Aboriginal Life in Australia* (London: Constable, 1905)
Reed	A. W. Reed, *Aboriginal Words and Place Names* (Adelaide: Rigby, 1965)
Ridley	William Ridley, *Kamilaroi and Other Australian Languages* (Sydney: Government Printer, 1875)
Thieberger	*Aboriginal Words*, ed. Nick Thieberger and William McGregor (Macquarie University, NSW: The Macquarie Library, 1994)
Webster	*Webster's Third New International Dictionary* (Springfield, Mass.: G. & C. Merriam Company, 1966)
ADFA	Australian Defence Force Academy Library
Buf	Library of State University of New York at Buffalo
CLF	Commonwealth Literary Fund
FAW	Fellowship of Australian Writers
Fryer	Fryer Library, University of Queensland (Hayes Collection)
ML	Mitchell Library, State Library of New South Wales
NLA	National Library of Australia
MS, MSS	Manuscript(s) (AMS: autograph MS; TMS: typescript)
n. d.	no date
n. t.	no title

For the abbreviation of references to the contents of manuscript collections, see volume 1, Appendix.

PREFACE

T<small>HIS</small> second volume of *The Collected Verse of Mary Gilmore* opens with the three collections that marked a new phase in her writing and in her public reputation: *The Wild Swan* (1930), *The Rue Tree* (1931) and *Under the Wilgas* (1932).[1] While the religious poems of *The Rue Tree* stand as something of an anomaly in Gilmore's oeuvre, *The Wild Swan* and *Under the Wilgas* not only demonstrated in their best poems a maturing and deepening of the lyrical powers that had pleased reviewers of *The Passionate Heart* (1918), but also introduced unpredictable preoccupations that were to be persistent in her future writing. New perceptions of the damage done by white settlement to Australia's natural environment and its Indigenous inhabitants, and a newly formed evaluation of Aboriginal culture, influenced and complicated her previous attitude to the pioneering enterprise. In her earlier writing the settlement of Australia had been a source of pride or of pathos, but never of shame. A new and disturbing note was struck in such lines as 'Like a blast of the desert we came, and we slew' from 'A Song of Swans' (I3).[2]

It was not that Gilmore surrendered all her admiration for the courage and hardiness of the pioneers. It would still find a voice in 'The Ringer' (M1) or 'Ode to the Pioneer Women' (M3) in *Battlefields* (1939), but it is heard in *Fourteen Men* (1954) only in her increasingly expansive author's notes. These develop the apotheosis of her father that had begun in the notes to *Under the Wilgas* and in the prose essays of *Old Days Old Ways* (1934) and *More Recollections*

---

[1] For a general overview of MG's life, see volume 1, Introduction; and see also Chronology.

[2] Poems are cited by their alphanumeric position: here, the third poem of Section I.

(1935).[3] As the socially and ecologically virtuous pioneer, Donald Cameron comes to represent the witness for the defence against the accusations heard in the Indigenous voices of 'The Lament of the Lubra' (I21), 'The Myall in Prison' (K15), 'Truganini' (M67) and 'Ichabod' (R63), or manifest in the silences and absences of a brutalised nature exemplified in 'A Song of Swans' (I3), 'Primeval Australia' (I27), 'The Wollundry Lagoon' (K17) and 'I Saw the Beauty Go' (M30).

The achievement of three major collections in as many years appears all the more impressive when one remembers that Gilmore spent several years of the period during which these poems were written in semi-seclusion in Goulburn for health reasons. Their publication also required a considerable degree of the formidable Gilmore determination, a quality that would be called upon twenty or so years later to bring *Fourteen Men* to the bookshops.[4] Although *The Passionate Heart* had been a publishing success for Angus & Robertson in 1918, sales of *Hound of the Road*, the first of Gilmore's collections of prose reminiscences, had been disappointing. The firm was not receptive to the idea of a new volume of verse. Approaching 65, and with a justifiable conviction of the worth of what she had to offer, Gilmore decided to look elsewhere.[5] She turned to her Melbourne publisher of *Marri'd and Other Verses* (1910). George Robertson & Co. had now become the firm of Robertson & Mullens, and its manager was Captain Charles H. Peters. He accepted all three volumes in rapid succession and published them promptly and with a high standard of production, although the cost was borne by Gilmore herself.

Nevertheless, her reputation was rising, and appropriate public figures were summoned to bear witness to it. The distinguished naturalist A. H. Chisholm provided the Introduction to *The Wild Swan*. *Battlefields* attracted a Foreword by Sir Donald Charles

---

[3] On Donald Cameron as a valuer and transmitter of Aboriginal culture and as a protector of the environment, see MG's notes to K12, K16, K20, M62, R53, R55, R72 and the additional notes for I26 and N1 supplied by MG in *SV*.

[4] See volume 1, Introduction, pp. lxvii–lxviii.

[5] There is no evidence of any falling out with George Robertson over A&R's unwillingness to publish. During the 1930s Robertson began to use her as a reader of manuscripts, a role that made a welcome contribution to an income depleted by her resignation from the *Worker* in 1931.

Cameron, ex-soldier, member of Parliament 1933–37 and head of the Clan Cameron in Australia. In 1941, Peters, a returned soldier, wrote the Introduction to *The Disinherited*, and the Foreword to *Selected Verse* (1948) was written by fellow poet and man of letters, Robert D. FitzGerald. In the case of *The Rue Tree* and *Under the Wilgas*, Gilmore herself provided introductory remarks that show considerable self-confidence. In the Foreword to the latter, for instance, she dismisses with contempt those who belittle Aboriginal language (along with the languages of the South Americans and Chinese) as 'gibberish' and concludes:

> I have attempted to write here in songs some of the emotions of a people once generous, once wise, once proud and free; and I have written them in words I think they might have used, had they spoken English instead of the language so unfortunately[6] theirs.

As a financial investment, the arrangement with Robertson & Mullens afforded only modest returns. As her letters and her biography show, Gilmore was never a wealthy woman, and at times her financial situation was precarious. In terms of her reputation, however, the returns were high. These three volumes, followed by the very popular *Old Days Old Ways* and *More Recollections*, confirmed her as a major figure in the literary landscape of Australia, with an appeal for a remarkably wide range of readers. It was a position intensified by the popularity of her World War II poems[7] and persisting until her death, and it was honoured in ways that reflected the diversity of her admirers. Her fellow writers made her a Life Member of the Fellowship of Australian Writers on her birthday in 1933, instituting a tradition of annual celebrations in her honour; politicians made her a Dame of the British Empire in 1938; and the trades union movement made her their May Queen in 1961.

---

[6] I.e. as helping to bring about their misfortunes (because of arrogant assumptions that English possessed an exclusive lien on civilisation).

[7] See volume 1, Introduction, pp. lxiv–lxv. See here Section O, numbers 3, 6, 8, 9, 15, 16 and 17 and Section R, numbers 37 and 38, but especially O10, R29 and R33.

The division of poems between the two volumes of this edition
required some deliberation. In terms of published collections,
The Tilted Cart (1925) can be seen as both the culmination and
the effective end of Gilmore's role as a *Bulletin*-style versifier of
bush themes and bush ballads. It might therefore have seemed an
appropriate place to end the first volume, but it was decided to
include in it, as Section H, the uncollected poems that followed *The
Tilted Cart* during 1925–29. Heterogeneous as these are in theme
and style, they have more affinity with either that collection or other,
earlier uncollected poems than with the three collections that would
follow. Some twenty can be seen as continuing in the thematic and
stylistic mode of *The Tilted Cart*,[8] while a number, usually published
in the *Worker*, are poems of social criticism based on urban life,
maintaining a strain also found in the poems of Section F. The
extent to which Section H represents the whole range of Gilmore's
composition over the period 1925 to 1929 is limited, however, by
the fact that Gilmore selected for the collections of 1930, 1931 and
1932 those poems from this transitional period that she considered
appropriate in theme and style.[9]

Of the collections published in the period covered by Volume
Two (1930–62), it is probably *The Wild Swan* that most consistently
and fully demonstrates her poetic powers. Gilmore herself elected
to give poems from this collection prominence in *Selected Verse* in
1948, placing them second only to those poems she chose from the
finest of her earlier volumes, *The Passionate Heart*. *The Wild Swan*,
then, makes a fitting point of entry to Volume Two and the second
phase of Gilmore's poetic career. In emphasising what is new in its
themes, however, there is a risk of overlooking important elements
of continuity. From the outset, Gilmore's work showed an unusual
combination of attitudes. It combined compassion for the weak and
the maimed with an admiration for energy and passion, a trust in the
forces of life that drew her towards vitalism; but she equally admired
personal stoicism, as witnessed in the cogent simplicity of 'Never

[8] See Section H, numbers 1, 3, 6, 9, 11, 13, 18, 21, 29, 38, 42, 48, 59, 63, 68, 72, 73, 87, 95 and 97.
[9] In such cases, these texts appear only as collated states within volume 2, since the editorial policy mandates preference for the collections as copy-texts: see volume 1, Introduction, pp. lxxiii–lxxv.

Admit the Pain' (I73), the poem that would supply the title for W.
H. Wilde's biography of Gilmore, *Courage a Grace* in 1988.

The more complex interplay of attitudes is better illustrated,
however, by 'Nurse No Long Grief' (I87):

> O, could we weep,
>   And weeping bring relief!
> But life asks more than tears
>   And falling leaf.
>
> Though year by year
>   Tears fall and leaves are shed,
> Spring bids new sap arise
>   And blood run red.
>
> Nurse no long grief,
>   Lest thy heart flower no more;
> Grief builds no barns; its plough
>   Rusts at the door.

Through a long life, until she joined 'the Army of the Dead,/
Stilled for a while, in camp' (I150), Mary Gilmore was always one
to put her hand to the plough, to create and capture through her
poetry the 'sheaf that my hand must bind' (R1).

Editorial rationale

The presentation and sequence of poems in this edition respects
the logic of their publication, as explained in more detail in
the Introduction to Volume One. Volume Two follows the same
chronological policy, placing the uncollected poems in dated sections
between the sections that present the published collections. Copy-
texts of collected poems are taken from their first appearance in a
collection.[10]

An Appendix to this volume lists the poems individually by their
date of composition, regardless of their groupings by section in this

---

[10] This explains the seeming oddity of why Section P (*PPA*, [1944]) contains only
one poem, the previously uncollected title poem: the remaining eight poems in this
booklet had all appeared in earlier collections and have been located accordingly,
with printings in *PPA* treated as collated states (see p. 607 n. 1). All poems in *SV*
had been published in earlier collections.

edition. This different ordering may assist literary, biographical and other interpretation.[11] Compositional sequence can help to reveal Gilmore's working methods as a poet and the rapid gestation of much of her verse. Her occasional poems, for instance, often followed hot on the heels of some event or encounter. This can be a source of strength of feeling but also of rough-and-ready art. Composition dates can shed light on the poet's development as a writer; they show peaks and troughs of productivity, the ebb and flow of preoccupations.

The dates also show that the coherence of the collections – something to which Gilmore gave considerable attention – can obscure the extent to which she was pursuing several lines of thought and of style simultaneously. The interlocking composition dates of the poems of Sections A and B, for instance, remind us that the radical and the womanly co-existed in a way obscured by the selection of poems in *Marri'd and Other Verses*. Composition dates of 1917 for J72 and J68 show that Gilmore's writing of religious poetry was not solely due to the influence of the nuns of Goulburn, where she lived during 1921–25, and that she did not simply tire of Aboriginal themes after *Under the Wilgas*, to return to them later in *Fourteen Men*. Rather, with the important exception of M62 ('Aboriginal Themes'), she chose different emphases for the poems selected for *Battlefields*.

Glossing Aboriginal words

This volume contains, mainly in Sections I, K and R, a number of poems with Aboriginal themes containing Aboriginal words that Gilmore glossed. Her motivation was partly nationalistic: in her notes, she argues for enriching a distinctive sense of Australian identity by culturally absorbing native elements, in the manner of New Zealand and America.[12] She also saw the practice as a process of restitution, as she explains in her Foreword to Keith McKeown's *The Land of Byamee: Australian Wild Life in Legend and Fact* (1938):

Thus to this poor, sad, dispossessed people, whose stories these

[11] E.g., the celebratory 'Marri'd' (B1) dates from 1896, whereas MG was not married until 1897.
[12] See, e.g., I22 author's note for line 5 and the collation entry for lines n1–22 in

are, is given back possession. We see them as they were before they were ruined and destroyed, and we realize that they had a lore that gives them an equal place in the world with those so long thought to be the only ones worth recording.[13]

The glosses that she provided for Aboriginal words in her poems were part of her attempt to transmit Aboriginal lore. For later readers they also raise questions as to how reliable they are and from what source she drew them.

In this edition an attempt has been made to corroborate Gilmore's use of Aboriginal words and her glossing of them, typically presented in her notes to the poems. This has been possible in many instances, but not all. When author's notes are described as 'uncorroborated' this means that the Aboriginal word she cites has not so far been confirmed. If the existence of the word is confirmed but the meaning given in her gloss is doubtful, this is noted.[14]

'Uncorroborated' does not necessarily imply error or fabrication, any more than local traditions that enshrine meanings not yet confirmed by scholarly research can be considered as other than not proven. Gilmore's glossing of 'Mirrabooka' as the Southern Cross in K1 and K4 agrees with local readings of that popular place name. But the claim of local authorities in the Queensland region of Capricorn that the town of Biloela is named for the cockatoo (or white cockatoo) – a claim that is reinforced by the Revd William Ridley's early word list – throws little light on 'The Song of Biloela' (I147), except to confirm the impression that the poem may draw on an unidentified Aboriginal legend or use an Aboriginal name for its associative value.[15]

Despite the sustained efforts of modern scholarship, we still do not possess a comprehensive knowledge of all the Aboriginal languages that existed in Australia before white settlement, nor has agreement been reached on how known material should be described. Dharuk and Dharug, Wiradjuri and Wiradhuri still compete as names for two of the best documented of New South

R64.

[13] (Sydney: Angus & Robertson), p. ix.

[14] Evidence has been drawn from Dixon, Parker, Parker 1905, Reed, Ridley and Thieberger (see Abbreviations for full citations). The word lists in Parker (unlike those of Parker 1905) and Reed do not identify particular Aboriginal languages.

Wales (NSW) languages. Early recorders of Aboriginal language were confronted with entirely oral languages that lacked certain sounds heard in English[16] and had distinctive sounds that had to be given ad hoc representation by English spelling. R. M. W. Dixon notes that there was considerable interest in Aboriginal customs and languages from the late nineteenth century up to World War I, but contributions to his compilation from that period are mainly local and linguistically limited.[17] He concludes: 'Despite this activity before the First World War, most Australians had little idea of the nature of Australian languages', and adds: 'Between 1920 and 1960 little work was done on Australian languages.' This context for Gilmore's writing must be appreciated.

One result of the resumed activity of the 1960s is that the written form of many words changed, rendering older forms outmoded. The name given in 1896 to the widely spread tribal people of central Australia and to their language, by the pioneering anthropologist W. B. Spencer, was Arunta. This form was confirmed in the 1910 edition of the *Encyclopaedia Britannica* and by Spencer and F. J. Gillen's *The Arunta: A Study of a Stone Age People* (1927). Gilmore uses 'Arunta' up to her composition of R54 in 1952. It was so well-established that she felt that it could stand as a general name for Aborigines and for Aboriginal Australia.[18] In the 1950s the transcription of the name changed to Aranda (also Aranta);[19] in the 1990s, as Dixon notes, Arrernte was claimed as a more accurate form.

Corroborated words used by Gilmore are drawn mainly from NSW languages.[20] These include Dharuk (also Dharug) from the vicinity of Sydney; Wiradjuri (also Wiradhuri) from the area of the Murrumbidgee and Lachlan Rivers in southern-central NSW; Kamilaroi, from the Liverpool Range (NSW) north to the

[15] Cf. the unidentified titular names in I20, K13 and K18.
[16] Cf. R65 author's note and n. 6.
[17] See Dixon 6–7; known to MG among those cited was William Ridley (see M62 author's note and n. 4).
[18] See K4 author's note for line 24 and cf. K2, where a similar significance is given to *churinga* (sacred tribal object), which also entered general usage through Spencer and Gillen's study of the Arunta.
[19] See citations in the on-line edition of the *OED*.
[20] Exceptions other than 'Arunta' and *churinga* (see note 18) are instances apparently from Gabi-Gabi (Queensland, see K19 n. 1) and Kaurna (vicinity of Adelaide,

Queensland border; Yuwaalaraay from northern NSW (regarded
as a dialect of Kamilaroi); and Wembawemba from southern NSW
and northern Victoria along the area of the Murray River between
Swan Hill and Echuca (Victoria). Gilmore might reasonably be
expected to have had access to surviving oral traditions from most
of these areas, either directly in her youth, or through her father,
or later during her years in Goulburn (1921–25).[21]

In the absence of any explicit references to written sources that
might have been available to Gilmore in the 1920s, other than to K.
Langloh Parker and William Ridley,[22] the probability that she drew
on oral traditions for words in *The Wild Swan* and *Under the Wilgas*
is strong. After 1932, her interest in Aboriginal culture largely found
expression in the prose reminiscences of pioneering history in *Old
Days Old Ways* and *More Recollections*, but in 1954 in *Fourteen Men*
she acknowledged two writers who had stimulated her interest in
Aboriginal narratives: Keith McKeown (noted above) and William
E. Harney.[23] The latter's knowledge of Aboriginal culture relates to
the Northern Territory and northern Queensland. Harney started
publishing poems and short stories in the 1940s in *Walkabout* and
the *Bulletin*, to which he was a prolific contributor during the
period 1951–53. Other works by him that would have been available
to Gilmore while she was preparing *Fourteen Men* were *Taboo*
(1943), *North of 23 Degrees: Ramblings in Northern Australia* (1946),
Brimming Billabongs: The Life Story of an Australian Aboriginal
(1947) and *Songs of the Songmen: Aboriginal Myths Retold* (1949).

see K4 n. 3).

[21] On MG's claim for direct childhood experience of Aboriginal life, see I19
author's note for line 44, K17 and author's notes, and further author's notes to
K20, M62 and R55. These also present her father as knowledgeable in Aboriginal
matters: cf. n. 3 above for further instances. On the Goulburn years, see volume
1, Introduction, pp. li and liii–liv.
[22] K. Langloh Parker was the publishing name of Catherine Langloh Parker (née
Field, 1856–1940). She grew up with Aboriginal children on her father's property
on the Darling River (NSW) but her Aboriginal legends were mostly collected while
living after marriage on pastoral properties in northern NSW and Queensland. On
MG's knowledge of Parker's work, see *CG* 267–8 and MG's acknowledgement of
it in the last of her 'Our Lost Field' articles (*SMH*, 29 October 1927). On Ridley
see M62 n. 4.
[23] (1895–1962). MG's first reference is in material added in *SV* (1948) to the
author's note to M62 (see entry for line n26); in *FM* he is referred to in R55,

From 1943 he was a regular visitor at Gilmore's Kings Cross flat and is several times referred to in her published correspondence.[24] Neither McKeown nor Harney were linguists or provided systematic listings of Aboriginal words; nor do the poems of *Fourteen Men* show other evidence (as might have been expected) of changes in Gilmore's knowledge of Aboriginal languages.[25] The expectation may, however, be unreasonable, given the gap in development of studies of Aboriginal languages between 1920 and 1960.

author's note for line 27.

[24] See *CG* 369–70 and *Letters* 191, 208, 219 and 252.

[25] The poems in the section 'Aboriginal Versions' all have composition dates earlier than 1950: R65, 1932; R63, 1938; R66, R69 and R70, 1940; R64, no date but published 1942; R72, 1947 and R71, 1948. R67 and R68 are annotated as revised in 1947, but their undated manuscripts in ML 4/3 are included with poems dated from 1920–29. See volume 1, Appendix for manuscript locations

THE POEMS

1930–1962

NOTE ON THE TEXTS

Copy-texts are of two kinds: for collected poems, the first printing in a published collection; for uncollected poems, the first verified printing in a newspaper, magazine, journal or anthology. The List of Abbreviations explains the acronyms employed throughout the edition, and the Appendix in Volume One gives the locations of manuscripts seen and examined for each poem.

Conventions of presentation

An *alphanumeric* (e.g. B2) indicating the alphabetical section of this edition (B) and the poem's place within that section (no. 2) precedes the *title*, and *subtitle* if present. Poems lacking titles in the copy-text source are given the first line as title, enclosed in square brackets. For an untitled poem with part headings, the title is supplied from the first of these. *Dedications*, *epigraphs* and any indication that a poem has been written especially for a particular journal are placed immediately before the text. *Authorial notes*, where present, are treated as part of the text and placed immediately after the last line of verse. Each note is indexed by an asterisk; square brackets indicate editorial provenance for the sign. *Editor's explanatory notes* are indicated by superscript numbers within the text.

The textual note, placed at the end of the text or at foot-of-page, contains, in sequence:

- *composition date* taken from the earliest available source (see volume 1, Introduction, p. lxxvii n. 98). Absence of composition date is indicated by (n. d.).
- *copy-text source*: For copy-texts taken from journals and annuals,

the date of publication and page numbers are given. (The List of Abbreviations gives dates for the anthologies and MG's collections.) Page numbers are also given for anthologies that do not have a list of contents.

- *generic headings* in journal-published poems (such as FOR THE BAIRNS).

- *signature for uncollected poems* where this is other than Mary Gilmore or forms thereof: for example, versions of her maiden name – Jeanie Cameron, M.J.C., M.C. – and pseudonyms such as Emma Jacey, Rudione Calvert, Smarty, Hill 17 are recorded. If there is no immediate contextual evidence for MG's authorship, then absence of signature is noted.

- *citation of collated states*: For uncollected poems, where the earliest published version is the copy-text, subsequent typesettings and reprints up to 1962 are listed in chronological order. For poems where the copy-text is drawn from the published collections, prior states, as well as subsequent ones to 1962, are listed. Only new typesettings are collated; each one is assigned an alphabetical symbol.

- *provenance of collated states* is as for the copy-text source. Any variant titles or subtitles are recorded in small capitals; absence of a title is indicated by (n. t.). Signatures and headings are treated as for the copy-text, except that the name Mary Gilmore (or any form of it) is included if it is contextualised, for example as part of an acknowledgement of prior or prospective publication.

THE LIST OF VARIANTS follows the textual note. Its completeness is qualified by the silent categories listed below and by any *Not otherwise recorded* category stated for the particular poem. An italicised line number indicates that the entry must be read in conjunction with the category. Parentheses around a line number or range of line numbers (e.g. '(16–18)') indicate that further variants located within the range are listed next. Authorial notes, if present, are referenced by a separate lineation (e.g. n20).

Square brackets indicate editorial provenance. In addition, the following symbols are used:

X	=	Copy-text
ˢ	=	Copy-text reading has been modified by a silent category
Om.	=	Omitted
Ed.	=	Editorially supplied reading
~	=	Same word as in the reading text in an entry recording a variant of punctuation, capitalisation or spelling
[. . .]	=	Missing or illegible text
/	=	Line-break
//	=	Stanza break
P	=	New paragraph

In each entry *the reading to the left of the square bracket* is from the reading text of the poem, based on its declared copy-text unless editorially emended. Emendation is signalled by the symbol for its source, or by *Ed.* or a preceding ˢ. *Variants follow* in alphabetical sequence; a range such as *A–D* indicates that the states assigned the symbols *A*, *B*, *C* and *D* share the variant reading. *Braces* { } are occasionally used to enclose a minor variant in a reading otherwise shared by another collated state.

Silent categories of emendation and recording

1. Titles of poems are presented in upper case, roman font (the most common usage in the collections). Subtitles are also standardised.

2. Variant titles in collated states are recorded in the textual note in small capitals. Following full stops are not recorded, but other punctuation is preserved and variants recorded. Collated-state subtitles follow the title in parentheses.

3. Epigraphs and dedications are standardised. They are placed immediately below the title in italics (for epigraphs) or roman (dedications). Enclosing brackets have not been preserved. Only substantive variants are listed.

4. Indications of poems having been written, for example '(For the Bulletin)', are silently standardised to small capitals, but formatting and style are preserved in collations.

5. Square brackets are treated as parentheses throughout. Brackets (square and round) enclosing MG's authorial notes are silently removed and variants not reported.

6. Poems are presented in roman font, but shifts for emphasis (to italic or bold) in copy-texts are preserved (as italic). The use of roman pointing in

such passages is not preserved, but collations otherwise record distinctions in the format of pointing. The printing of entire poems in italics (a once-common practice in some journals and newspapers) is not followed and is recorded only where there is a need for collation.

7. Initials (e.g. M.J.C.) are treated as unspaced throughout.

8. Words and initials in full capitals in the text and textual note (but not collations) are uniformly presented in small capitals.

9. Variance in spacing between text and part headings, numbers or breaks is ignored.

10. Authorial notes are placed immediately after the last line of verse; variant placements are not recorded.

11. Ornamental presentation of the initial word or letter of a text is not pre-served. If a variant requires its recording, the dropped capital is presented as an initial capital, with the rest of the word in small capitals.

12. Except where a prolonged pause or emphasis is apparently intended, the degree of spacing before and after punctuation marks is ignored in both copy-text and collated states.

13. The em dash without spacing is adopted throughout, ignoring variant presentations.

14. Variants in collated states are recorded for the following standardisations of the reading texts: the use of three dots to signify an ellipsis, with preserva-tion of a full stop if present; spacing and the position of the apostrophe in elided constructions such as 'isn't', 'don't', 'I've'; the presentation of part headings in small capitals; and of part numbers in roman small capitals till Section P, then in arabic (reflecting the shift in MG's practice after the publication of *Dis*, 1941).

15. Breaks within the text (other than stanza divisions) are uniformly indicated by a line of four asterisks. Variance in collated states is recorded; but the routine use of asterisks to indicate stanza divisions, as in some newspaper printings, is ignored in both texts and collations.

16. Consistency has been imposed on degrees of line indentation and the position of speech prefixes, and variants ignored.

17. The presence of a composition date, or of a place of composition, is not preserved but recorded in an editorial note if of special interest.

As a guide to accurate quotation, the List of Poems with Stanzas Broken at Foot of Page specifies those poems in Volumes One and Two where the last stanza on a page is completed on the following page.

SECTION I

The Wild Swan (1930)

I1   DEDICATORY

In Memory of My Father

I have known many men, and many men
   In the quick balance of the mind have weighed,
And even as Abram found his score was ten,
   His ten was one,[1] so was my hope betrayed.
But though the tale is told, and fallen, spent,   5
   Is the first fiction of a great man's name,
Eminent amid the uneminent
   He still stands tall, a lonely mark for fame.
Yet where Truth sweeps Time's mouldered, dusty floor
   I have seen fame, long swollen, flung out as naught,   10
And I have seen one, whom the world called poor,
   Walking amid the mountains of his thought.

(19 August 1929)   *Copy-text: WS*   *Collated states: SV (A)*   Wright1 (B)

2 weighed,] ~. *B*   **5** fallen, spent,] ~ ~ *A B*   **8** tall,] ~; *A B*   **9** Yet] So, too, *A B*   Truth] truth *A B*   sweeps] sweeps out *A B*   Time's] time's *A B* mouldered,] *Om. A B*   floor] ~, *B*   **10** fame] names *A B*   swollen] praised *A B* naught,] ~; *A B*

---

[1] In pleading against the destruction of Sodom, Abraham had to reduce the requirement of righteous men from twenty (a 'score'), to ten, to one (Genesis 18. 23–32).

BOOK I: *THE WOMAN OF FIVE FIELDS*

I2   THE ARGOSY

Mark now this argosy[1] which I set sail,
  A thousand ships, a thousand words,
Hoping that no contemptuous, lettered flail[2]
  Beat all my merchandise to sherds.[3]

Each word a hold, each hold a word, how small,   5
  How slight these carriers of freight!
Ah, even as we who are but breath to call,
  A sigh upraised to challenge fate.

My ships I loose, myself a sail unknown
  Except one clothe me with a word.   10
O little fleet, to what far coast art blown,
  Bear witness of this breath which stirred!

(8 May 1923)   *Copy-text: WS   Collated states: DT*, 21 February 1925, p. 10 (*A*)

1 sail,] ~— *A*   2 ships,] ~— *A*   3–4 Hoping . . . sherds.] Cargoed as though
with merchandise set bale/ On bale, and some few singing birds. *A*   6 slight]
frail *A*   7 call,] ~— *A*   9 loose,] ~: *A*   11 O] ~, *A*

[1] Strictly a single large freight-carrying merchant-vessel from Ragusa, here a fleet of
ships. *OED* regards as untraceable any connection with the ship *Argo* in which Jason
carried the treasure of the Golden Fleece.   [2] Erudite destructive critic.   [3] Variant
spelling of *shards*: broken pieces, fragments.

I3   A SONG OF SWANS

I   THE BLACK SWANS

O ye wild swans, that from your watery element
Rocked in the beating of ten thousand wings,
The winds declared ye to the stars in your ascent,
And the lone settler, closed within his narrow pent,[1]

(16 December 1925)   *Copy-text: WS   Collated states: DT*, 30 January 1926, p. 10 (*A*)
SV (*B*)

1 O] ~, *A*   2 Rocked] Rose *A*   beating] beating thunder *A*   3 ye] you *B*
your] their *A*   4 settler,] ~ *B*

Wakened upon the sound the night-air servant brings,   5
Whispered, "The birds are restless for far journeyings!"
And like a cloud above the lakes, and like a cloud
Above the river reaches and the long lagoons,
Mounted the wing that through eternities had ploughed
The plains of heaven, until each flight became a shroud   10
Of shadowy movement drawn beneath high-riding moons,
And faint in distance as the ghosts of lost galloons.[2]

II   THE WHITE SWAN

Once a child waking heard the beat of those great wings,
And, running, saw where like a shining angel rose
A glistening bird, bright in its moonlit silverings: 15
Saw the wing's curve and spread, and the white breast that
        springs
Round as the prow of cloud, that, at the evening's close,
Night slowly stalls above the sun that setting goes:
Saw where an army ranged in endless ranks that ran
On either hand as each dark fugler,[3] in his might,   20
Climbing upon the air moved out and led the van:[4]
Saw the vast mass up-soar and sail in widening fan:
And saw the snowy-breasted wanderer, gleaming white,
Lace in and out the host, and go with that great flight.

III   THE MURRUMBIDGEE[5] HEARD

O ye wild swans the Murrumbidgee yearning heard, afar,   25
Cry through the height, "To thee thy children come again!"

---

5 sound] sounds *A*   6 are] grow *A*   10 heaven,] ~ *A*   12 galloons] platoons *B*
13 child waking] ~, ~, *A*   15 silverings:] ~; *A*   16 springs] ~, *A*   17 cloud,]
~ *B*   18 stalls] stills *A*   goes:] ~; *A*   19 where] then *A*   ranged] rise *A*
20 as] where *A*   21 moved] sped *A*   van:] ~ *A*   22 Saw] As *A*   up-soar and
sail] upsoared and sailed *A*   fan:] ~; *A*   23 And saw] Saw there *A*   24 host,]
~ *A*   flight.] ~! *A*   25 swans] ~, *A*   yearning] *Om. B*   26 through] from *B*

---

[1] Confines (noun), possibly alluding to the smallness of a settler's hut.
[2] Galleons, in particular the large vessels used by the Spaniards in carrying on trade with
the Americas.   [3] A soldier who, because of his skill, led troops during drill exercises,
hence one who shows the way; cf. usage in E24 and J12.   [4] Vanguard.
[5] From Aboriginal *murrumbidga*, big water (Reed); cf. MG's more poetic translation in
M13 (line 14). See Preface for MG's use and glossing of Aboriginal words.

And, as ye came, felt all her bosom stir, as bar
By bar upon the mountain side, by cliff and scar,
She loosed the rising waters out till grey Ganmain[6]
Called to her reeds the white spoonbill and gentle crane—   30
And bid the old Deepwater Swamp set wide each gate,
And drink her swelling tide till every billabong
Ran flush, and all the summered marshes in the spate
Bloomed out again in green, while little birds, elate,
Dipped in the flood and sang—O ye wild wings, how long,   35
How long since last your mighty pinions beat in throng!

IV   NEVER AGAIN

Never again as of old shall we know the flight
Of the swans in their going; like petals they fell,
They are gone, they are dead; they have passed in the blight
Of our being! Never again will the day, or the night,   40
Hear, as they fly, the sound of their trumpeting bell
On the air till it dies like the lapse of a swell!
Never again shall the moonlight gleam on the wing!
Like a blast of the desert we came, and we slew;
We burned the reeds where the nestlings lingered, till
       Spring,   45
That sang in the bird, came in like a dull dead thing!
Now only the dreamer dreams of the hosts we knew,
That trembling died in the flame of our passing through.

27 And, as ye came] Who, as she heard. *A*   as] till *A*   29 out] ~, *A B*
30 crane—] ~; *A*   ~, *B*   31 And] Who *A*   Swamp] swamp *A*   gate,] ~ *B*
33 in] felt *A*   34 Bloomed out] And bloomed *A*   38 going; like] ~. Like *A*
they] that *A*   fell,] ~ *A*   ~; *B*   39 dead;] ~— *A*   40 will . . . night,] shall
day (or the night) *A*   41 Hear,] ~ *A*   fly,] ~ *A*   43 shall] will *B*   moonlight
gleam] moons shine out *A*   wing!] ~; *B*   44 came,] ~ *A*   slew;] ~, *A*
45 Spring,] spring *A*   spring, *B*   46 bird,] ~ *A*   dull dead] sad dumb *A*
thing!] ~. *A*   48 flame] wind *A*   through.] ~! *A*

[6] Not the small town of that name in the Coolamon Shire of the Riverina district, but
the wetlands of the property described in G12 as: 'Far Ganmain of swamp and sedge'
(line 12).

14   THE TRUMPETER*

Dulled is the glossy breast, heavy the wing;
  Slow beats the great heart naught could slacken;
Shimmers no more the back that once could fling
  A glinting sun-spar over hill and bracken!
    For now as earthward, where the shadows blacken,   5
      Drops slowly down his mighty pinion,
    Wakes not for him again the spring:
      The years have brought to end his old dominion.

Once like a king he rode the aery coast,
  And marked, below, the trackless ocean;   10
Or, lifting through the cloud his flagging host,
  Eased there the flight upon earth's windy motion.
    But none now call upon that old devotion,
      And slowly downward moves the pinion;
    Life has defined its uttermost: 15
      Fallen the sceptre from the old dominion.

The black man knew his path, and, star by star,
  Watched the timed route of his returning;
And named at night his trumpeting, afar,
  As toward the swamps he sloped in homeward yearning.   20
    Empty the forests now of eyes, discerning,
      That loved to greet that looked-for pinion:
    The reedy marges silent are,
      And at an end is all the old dominion.

His was the wisdom of the trumpeters,   25
  The father-wisdom born of power;
He made the fretful winds his ministers,
  And taught the young the way within the nower.[1]

[cont. overleaf

(n. d.)   *Copy-text: WS   Collated states: SV* (A)
Not otherwise recorded: MG's note is not signalled in A.
5 now] ~, A   **21** eyes,] ~ A

[1] Obsolete variant of *nowhere*; hence, here, uncharted space.

And time he knew; the season's clanging hour
　　Struck like a bell upon that pinion,   30
Which felt throughout its breadth, in spur,
　　The call to rise and lead in old dominion.

And they who held, as he, unwritten law,
　　Who heard Biami[2] in the thunder,
Who charted heaven by what on earth they saw,   35
　　Named the great trumpeters "The Wings of Wonder."
And these no hungry need might stalk and plunder;
　　Where spread each broad, upsoaring pinion,
No youthful pride the spear might draw. . . .
　　Alas! the end of that old wise dominion!   40

* When I was a child, "trumpeter" and "trumpeters" were familiar words. Not every swan was called a trumpeter. The aboriginals, regarding the wild birds and animals as their flocks and herds, had provision made for their preservation. The great old leaders of flight were known, and never killed. The wisdom of centuries was with them. And I remember   n5
well the disgust expressed by my own people when a man who was either a "new-chum" from overseas, or a "green-horn" from the city, shot, and boasted of shooting, a trumpeter. The act was reprobated by everybody. As my father said, he might as well have killed an albatross.[3] Everyone thought the bird should have been hung round his neck.   n10

29 clanging hour] change and stir *A*   36 Wonder."] ~". *A*   38 broad,] ~ *A*
39 draw. . . .] ~. *A*   n7 "new-chum"] ~ *A*   "green-horn"] ~ *A*

[2] Cf. *Bai-ame* (Ridley), *Byamee* (Parker, Reed), *Baiami* (Reed): creator god, All-Father, giver of tribal laws and customs; see also I22, I24, K2, M62 author's note, line 13 and R71 author's note, line 15.
[3] When the Ancient Mariner kills an albatross, traditional sign of good fortune, and his ship is becalmed, his fellow sailors hang the slaughtered bird around his neck to mark him as the cause of misfortune: see 'The Rime of the Ancient Mariner' (1798) by Samuel Taylor Coleridge (1772–1834).

I5   THE FLIGHT OF THE SWANS

Long, long ago I stood amid the thundrous rout
　　Where restless swans beat on the waters, in their might,
Till all the wash was foam: when suddenly from out
　　The waste one bird arose in orient for flight.

I marked his widening pinions cut upon the air,   5
In sound as though one whipped the wind and whispered
    there.

And as he swaying upward reared, his cry, far sent,
    Ran like a ribbon-length of clarion through space—
A call that floated out as if it could not die;
    Which, as the bird made on, hung lone in its high place   10
As might a man's loosed spirit hang, when, from the clay,
In first release it wavers toward its outward way.

Then, as full flight began, the forest heard, and heard
    The lakes, and every little cove and inlet woke,
And said, "Moves from our reaches now the gallant bird!"   15
    And from each linked recess the tides of movement broke,
As the first squadroned companies swept out and took
The forward way where death, alone, might backward look.

And from that urgent moil[1] of wings trail upon trail
    Out of the tangle of the rising turned to plane,   20
And upward through the sky swung out like wisps of veil,
    Smaller, yet smaller seen, and then not seen at all.
Thus in the void of night the milky star-dust shows,
In faint receding light, and ever passing goes.

Then as I watched where line by line the leaders flew,   25
    Roiled[2] from the marsh the mass till all the air with wings
Was tremulous and tumult-shaken through and through. . . .
    So sped the birds that there seemed mightier than kings:
And as they went a stillness fell upon the waste,
Stranger than sound, stranger than movement in its haste.*   30

[cont. overleaf

(n. d.)   *Copy-text:* WS   *Collated states:* SV (A)

Not otherwise recorded: MG's note is not signalled in A.

1 Long,] ~ A   3 foam: when] ~! When A   7 cry, far sent,] far sent cry A
9 die;] ~, A   10 place] ~. A   11 As] So A   13 Then,] ~ A   began,] ~ A
14 woke,] ~ A   17 out] ~, A   18 death, alone,] ~ ~ A   19 wings . . . trail]
~, . . . ~, A   20 rising] ~, A   22 at all] again A   23 star-dust] stardust A
shows,] ~ A   25 Then] ~, A   27 through. . . .] ~. A   28 kings:] ~, A

---

[1] Turmoil, confusion.   [2] Roll or flow vigorously (archaic, of a stream).

Now, when the moonlight drips in silver on the grass,
    And when each pendant leaf is hung with shining dew,
Sometimes I hear a wreath of lonely migrants pass,
    And dream of old things where late comers dream of new;
Then on the earth again that stillness seems to fall;   35
Then broods the widowed land o'er loss beyond recall.

* My husband has often told me how, when he was a boy, along the
Coorong[3] the swans would be in thousands, and that suddenly something
would stir them to meditate flight, and they would beat the waves with
their wings, with a sound like thunder, till all the waters whitened with
foam. Then in a mass they would rise and fly, and leave a silence itself   n5
as strange as thunder. And many a time in Riverina, as a child, I have
run to my mother in terror because I heard "thunder" when there were
"no clouds," and she would tell me it was swans in the distance beating
their wings as they readied for flight. Later on I learned to recognise
the sound, and to listen to it unafraid. The Bush learned in those days   n10
what it can never learn again.

32 pendant] pendent *A*   34 late comers] late-comers *A*   n1 has] *Om. A*
n4 wings,] ~ *A*   n5 silence] silence in *A*   n6 child,] ~ *A*   n8 "no clouds,"]
~ ~. *A*   and] And *A*   n9 recognise] recognize *A*   n10 Bush] bush *A*

[3] Wetland ecosystem at the mouth of the Murray River, South Australia.

16   THREE SWANS WENT BY

Whither, ye wanderers in the heights your wings still dare,
Crying as though forgotten things mourned in your keening?
Our hearts are broken as we hear you go,
    So few in flight, so slow.

Lone in the lonely verge, scarce can the ear ensnare   5
The thin, sad notes that downward fall; that leaning
On the shouldered air seem but a breath
    Of sound, haunted by death!

. . . Out of the land long swept away, from woods laid bare,
Surely the wonder of our youth went with them there.   10

(n. d.)   *Copy-text: WS   Collated states: SV* (*A*)
5 Lone] ~, *A*   6 thin,] ~ *A*   7 shouldered] shouldering *A*   9 . . . Out] ~ *A*

I7   SWANS AT NIGHT

Within the night, above the dark,
    I heard a host upon the air—
Upon the air they made no mark,
    For all that they went sailing there.

And from that host there came a cry,   5
    A note of calling strange and high;
I heard it blown against the sky,
    Till naught there seemed but it and I.

A long and lonely wraith of sound,
    It floated out in distance wide,   10
As though it knew another bound,
    A space wherein it never died.

I heard the swans, I heard the swans,
    I heard the swans that speed by night;
That ever, where the starlight wans,[1]   15
    Fly on unseen within the height.

I never knew how wide the dark,
    I never knew the depth of space,
I never knew how frail a bark—
    A speck—is man within his place,   20

Not till I heard the swans go by,
    Not till I marked their haunting cry,
Not till within the vague,[2] on high,
    I watched them pass across the sky.

                                        [*cont. overleaf*

(8 March 1924)   *Copy-text: WS*   *Collated states:* DT, 9 December 1924, p. 14 as THE
FLIGHT OF THE SWANS (*A*)   *GEPP*, 11 December 1924, p. 6 as THE FLIGHT OF THE SWANS
(*B*)   Green, stanzas 1–6 only, as *FROM* SWANS AT NIGHT (*C*)   *SV* (*D*)

2 air—] ~; *A B*   ~, *D*   **3** air] void *D*   mark,] ~ *A B*   **6** calling] keening *A B*
7 sky,] ~ *A B*   **8** Till . . . seemed] As though there were *A B*   I.] ~ *B*
11 bound,] ~— *A B*   **16** on unseen] ~, ~, *A B*   **19** bark—] ~, *D*
20 A speck—] How small *D*   place,] ~. *A B*   **21** swans] swan *B*   **22** haunting]
wailing *A B*   **23** till] ~, *D*   vague,] ~ *A B D*   high,] ~ *A B*   **24** watched]
heard *A B*   sky.] ~ . . . *C*

---

[1] Grows pale.   [2] Undefined expanse (rare usage); cf. I67 line 15.

O trackless birds, far-journeying,   25
    What guide have ye, or swift or slow,
To give ye trust in strength of wing
    That must upbear ye as ye go?

What mark is set before your way?
    What urging burns within the heart,   30
That bids ye, at the close of day,
    Uplift the wing of your depart?

What visions drawn from inner sight
    Declare to you the way ye go;
What power upholds you in your flight   35
    To that unknown ye cannot know?

I heard against the phantom sky
    The swans their hollow music cry,
I felt the loneliness on high,
    The dark where they went sailing by.   40

They say the swan sings but for death,
    They say he wans in height to die;
Has he no more than that sharp breath
    That whistles outward on his cry?

Is he but offspring of a vast³   45
    Where no Hand shaped but gusty chance?
That draws no future from the past?
    That goes unconscious of advance?

Nay, though we were but shaken dust,
    Nay, though in darkness still we went,   50

(25–60) O . . . cry.] *Om. C*   25 far-journeying] far journeying *D*   26 ye] you *D*
slow,] ~ *A B*   27 ye] you *D*   28 ye as ye] you as you *D*   30 heart,] ~ *A B*
31 ye] you *D*   33 visions] vision *A B*   34 Declare] Declares *A B*   ye] you *D*
36 ye] you *D*   38 cry,] ~; *A B*   42 die;] ~: *A*   43 Has] Hath *A B*   that] his *A B*
46 Hand] hand *D*   47 past?] ~, *A B*   48 goes] moves *D*   advance?] advance?// Is
he but child of will-less law/ That, moving, knows not that it moves;/ Has eyes, and yet
which never saw,/ And its own proof, itself, disproves? *A B*

³ Immense space (mainly poetic).

We still must measure by our trust
   The Power that lifting o'er us bent;

And He Who held within His Hand
   That trackless bird, by night and day,
Guided him out by sea and land,   55
   His Hand will never cast away.

I never knew how vast the sky,
   I never knew how small was I,
Until I heard, remote and high,
   The distant swans' far-floated cry.   60

51 We still must] Still do we *A B*   **52** bent;] ~. *A B*   **54** That] The *D*
56 Hand *A*] hand *X*   **57** I] . . . ~ *A B*   **58–9** I never . . . remote] Until I heard,
in broken cry,/ Upon its rim, far-thinned *A B*   **60** distant swans'] keening of the
swans *A B*   far-floated cry] go by *A B*   far floated cry *D*

18   THE MOPOKE

I heard the hautbois* of the solitude,
   And followed after that elusive sound,
Which, uttered from the shy bird's feathery hood,[1]
   Haunted all places, yet in none was found.
     For now on air it seemed,   5
     And now on tree,
     Muting and fluting over me.

How many a moonlit night—a girl—a child—
   I sought to trace that strange and wandering note,
Now running here, now there, till, half-beguiled,   10
   My will upon its movement seemed to float!
     Mopoke! Mopoke! it cried;
     Mopoke! Till all
     The chequered darkness held the call.

[cont. overleaf

(n. d.)   *Copy-text: WS   Collated states: SV (A)*
Not otherwise recorded: MG's note is not signalled in *A*.
9 trace] find *A*   **13** Till] till *A*

[1] Cf. I125, lines 22–3.

It is a lovely thing to hear a bird—   15
   And hear it through the shadowy places of
The night!—to seek a wing that goes unheard,
   And trace its flight through spaces far above!
     Ah, follows still my heart,
     And half afraid,   20
     The mopoke's note within the shade."

* There is no bird-voice in all the bush so like the sound of the hautbois[2]
as that of the mopoke. And I recollect, well, my father explaining to me,
as a child, how the aboriginals spoke of it as, "The tree speaks." Had
they known the hautbois, it is certain they would also have said, "The
wood speaks."   n5

15 bird—] ~, *A*   16 shadowy places] leafy shadow *A*   17 night!—] ~! *A*
18 spaces far] some dim place *A*   20 half afraid] half-afraid *A*   21 shade.] ~! *A*
n1 bird-voice] bird voice *A*   n2–3 And . . . as,] My father, showing the bird to
me, said the aboriginal name—with them one word, of course—was *A*
n3 speaks."] ~". *A*   n3–5 Had . . . speaks."] *Om. A*

[2] Oboe.

I9   THE FIRST THRUSH

IN THE TREES OF THE OLD CHISHOLM GARDEN
AT GOULBURN

Though leaves have fallen long since,
The wagtails flirt and flit,
Glad in the morning sun;
While, on the knotted quince,
The dewdrops, pearled on it,   5
Bead to a little run. . . .

Soft as a breathing air
There came a lovely sound
Out of the branches bare;
So rich it was, and round,   10

(n. d.)   *Copy-text: WS*   *Collated states:* Mackaness1 (no subtitle) (*A*)
6 run. . . .] ~ . . . . *A*

Sense stood, in listening bound,
Stilled to its sweetness there!

It was the thrush's note,
That seemed as though his heart
On some loved thing did dote;   15
As though he yearned apart,
Knowing some hidden smart,
Pain in the long sweet rote.[1]

There, as the spider hung
Grey-breasted 'gainst the brown   20
Skin of the quince, he sung
A song that, o'er the town,
Rose up as though to crown
The tree-tops whence it sprung.

And now, it seems to me,   25
That long full breath he drew,
Like perfume shed on air,
Still dwells within the tree,
Though long ago he flew,
And left it naked there.   30

[1] Repeated phrase.

I10   THE GREEN-LEEK[1]

Thou wast a leaf,
Thou wast the grass in sheen,
Thou wast the corn in spathe[2]
Ere yet the grain was seen:
Of all green loveliness that went on wing   5

(12 November 1923)   *Copy-text: WS   Collated states: SV (A)*
Not otherwise recorded: Wherever copy-text has 'Thou wast', *A* has 'You were'.
5 wing] ~, *A*

[1] One AMS of I10 in NLA 727 2/3/13 is annotated: 'To a cut pocket of an old wattle-tree by the house, the greenleeks used to come. We used to stand behind the bole, so small we were, & slipping the hand round it, catch the greenleeks as they came for

Thou wert the chief,
O emerald of the spring!

These hands, that held,
In memory hold again,
As when thy beating heart   10
Throbbed out its fear and pain!
Ah, though my will for thy detention stood,
Thou wast not celled
A prisoner from thy wood!

My hollow grasp   15
Thy slender body filled;
And thought, reminding, tells
How a child's startled wonder thrilled
To feel that thou, so small, shouldst be so warm,
Who in my clasp   20
Fluttered thy sharp alarm!

Now like a dart
Thrusts loneliness, as though
Something I loved was lost,
O long ago!   25
And longing asks, in spite of years of calm,
To feel a child's heart
Hoard thee, breast and palm.

---

6 Thou wert] You were *A*   10 thy] your *A*   12 thy] your *A*   13 celled] ~, *A*
14 thy] your *A*   16 Thy] Your *A*   19 thou] you *A*   shouldst] should *A*
20 Who] When *A*   21 Fluttered thy sharp] You fluttered in *A*   25 O] ~, *A*
28 thee,] you— *A*

the gum. Only sometimes, when the boys did not want it, was I allowed to hold one in
my hand; & though I was eldest too sensitive & suffering to ask for it often. Besides I
was always told "Girls should not want things": I think no child ever wanted things
withheld with more longing than I did. M.G.' See volume 1, Appendix for manuscript
locations and descriptions.

[2] The sheathing leaf enclosing the early inflorescence of plants such as corn, arums
and palms.

III   THE GODWIT*

So far it flew
Upon the distant verge of sight,
I saw (and scarcely knew
I saw, so small dimensions ran)
A bird that looked no larger than   5
A mote, and yet it held in view
Immeasurable flight!

Thou hadst no fear that thou shouldst come to naught,
O little living thing which Thought
The Slinger on the distance hurled—   10
O godwit, passing over all the world!

But thou, within thy heart, by day and night,
Held that which led thee safely through the height;
And we, who baffled stood and watched thee go,
Envied thy fortitude, thy power to know!   15

God-wit indeed art thou! His wisdom spoken
In thee, who makest flight, unbroken,
In conquest over land and sea.
But O, how small a thing thou art,
Sanctioned, and set with stars apart,   20
To breast infinity!

* The godwit leaves Australia in the morning and is well on its way to
Asia by evening. Wit, in the older use of the language, meant wisdom
or knowledge. The word godwit is beautiful, both in its own meaning
and in its burden of history.

(n. d.)   *Copy-text: WS   Collated states: SV (A)*

Not otherwise recorded: MG's note is not signalled in *A*.

4 ran)] ~), *A*   **12** night,] ~ *A*   **16** God-wit] Godwit *A*   **n1–2** to Asia] *Om. A*
n3 both] alike *A*

112   SWIFTS

Who has declared to them their powers,
    Their wings for flight;
Bid them where distance towers
    Attain the height;
Sustained them through the hours   5
    Of day and night?

Ye have not thought, O heedless man,
    How learned these eyes
Whose sight must ranging scan
    What forward lies,   10
And lift from earth's low span
    To search the skies!

Nor have ye thought (or ye had seen!)
    What wonders pleat
These wings of glistening sheen,   15
    That, bravely fleet,
Seek, over seas between,
    Their far retreat!

O little feathered float! O frail
    And tiny oars!   20
Ye do not fear to fail,
    Though tempest roars,
And icy winds impale
    These nether shores!

Ah, had man but your steadfast will!   25
    I watch you where

(n. d.)   *Copy-text: WS   Collated states: Wr*, 7 July 1926, p. 14 (*A*)

1 has] hath *A*   powers,] ~— *A*   2 flight;] ~? *A*   3 them] ~, *A*   towers] ~, *A*
4 height;] ~? *A*   5 Sustained] Or keeps *A*   8 How learned] What mean *A*
9 must] may, *A*   ranging] ~, *A*   11 And] Or *A*   12 To] And *A*   13 thought
(or] ~—~ *A*   seen!)] ~!— *A*   15 sheen,] ~ *A*   16 That,] (So *A*   fleet,] ~!) *A*
17 Seek, over] That seek, o'er *A*   19 little] tiny *A*   20 tiny] downy *A*   21 Ye
. . . fail,] Fearless you onward sail *A*   25 but] half *A*   will!] ~! . . . *A*

You mount in flight, until
Unseen you fare,
And dream I see you, still,
Who are not there.   30

27 flight,] ~ *A*   29 And dream] Thinking *A*   you,] ~ *A*

I13   THE SOLDIER-BIRD

How oft we stalked a leaf and thought it you,
Where, in a bush, you watched us, peering through—
We who as Indian braves had marked your flight,
And thought our eyes still kept you in their sight!

In greeny-gold and grey, a trace of black,   5
Surely for camouflage you did not lack,
As you, half wondering what was our intent,
Poised on your twig, awhile, before you went.

O wise, wise bird, whose grave considering look
Spoke learning deeper than in any book,   10
Surely your wit was ours! But ours (so young!)
Was less than yours as from your perch you swung,
Leaving us wrangling there, where each one claimed
The first to sight you—lost, the other blamed!

Alas, what lengthening years have passed between   15
Since first I saw you flit amid the green—

(n. d.)   *Copy-text: WS   Collated states: DT*, 9 January 1926, p. 10 as THE SOLDIER
BIRD (*A*)

Not otherwise recorded: A divides each pair of lines into a four-line stanza, and lines
5 and 6 follow 7 and 8.
1 and] And *A*   2 a] the *A*   us,] Us *A*   peering] peeping *A*   3 who] ~, *A*
braves had] ~,/ Had *A*   4 And thought] Thinking *A*   you] You *A*   4 sight!]
~, *A*   5 a] A *A*   trace] hint *A*   6 you] You *A*   7 As] While *A*   was] Was *A*
8 twig,] ~ *A*   awhile, before] ~/ Before *A*   went.] ~! *A*   9 O] ~, *A*
considering] Considering *A*   10 in] In *A*   book,] ~! *A*   11 ours! But] ~;/ ~ *A*
12 yours] ~, *A*   your] Your *A*   swung] sprung *A*   13 wrangling] ~, *A*
where] Where *A*   14 The . . . the] Pre-eminence of sight:/ The *A*   15 have]
Have *A*   16 amid] Amid *A*   green—] ~: *A*

I with my black-boy sling,[1] and John and Hugh[2]
As bow-and-arrow chiefs to follow you!

And oft, as now, I pause with wistful sigh,
Wondering if still within your trees you fly,   20
Wondering if in the old familiar ways
Children exploring go, as in our days,

Wondering, if one returned to his old place,
Would it be his would be the stranger's face . . .
Time gives us dreams; there you still fly o'erhead,   25
To nest amid the ghosts of trees long dead.

---

17 I] ~, *A*   and] And *A*   John] Jack *A*   **18** bow-and-arrow] bow and arrow *A*
to follow] To capture *A*   **19** And oft] Sometimes *A*   with] With *A*   **20** your]
Your *A*   fly,] ~; *A*   **21** if] ~, *A*   familiar] Familiar *A*   ways] ~, *A*
22 Children . . . go,] Any still wander *A*   in our] In other *A*   days,] ~; *A*
23 Wondering,] ~ *A*   to] To *A*   **24** the] The *A*   ˢface . . .] ~. *A*   **25** Time . . .
there] My day is done. But *A*   still] Still *A*   **26** To nest] Nesting *A*   of] Of *A*

---

[1] Slingshot or catapult seen as an Aboriginal weapon.
[2] Hugh and John Cameron, MG's brothers, b. 1866 and 1869, are her companions
in other childhood reminiscences (F122, G8 and H69). Hugh is the subject of M11,
John of Z6.

114   THE PEEWEE

When the dawn awakes, and the morning breaks,
Who cries as he flies,
Curulit! Curulit! Curulit!

Who but the bird that we call
The peewee—the mudlark—even pug-wall—   5
Who, bright as the point of a share[1]
In the sun laid bare,
Cries out as he flies—
      Flit-Flit—
Curulit! Curulit! Curulit!   10

(n. d.)   *Copy-text: WS   Collated states: SV* (*A*)
2 Who] What *A*   **4** Who] What *A*   **5** peewee—] ~, *A*   **6** Who] Which *A*
9 Flit-Flit] Flit-flit *A*

---

[1] Ploughshare (blade).

I₁5   THE SPOONBILL

Where yonder brooding spoonbill stands,
　　Once stood another by that pool;
And there two children, holding hands,
　　Saw him at evening in the cool.

Strange how the mind a scene retains!   5
　　The children, through long-sundered years,
Still keep, amid life's counted gains,
　　That memory—with tears, with tears!

(n. d.)   *Copy-text: WS*   *Collated states: SV (A)*
1 Where yonder] Here, where yon *A*   stands,] ~ *A*   **6** long-sundered] long
sundered *A*   years,] ~ *A*

I₁6   THE IBIS

All day he watched within the reedy flood,
　　All day the sickle of his bill
Pierced through the weed, and oozy mud,
　　Where the quick fled, the slow lay still.

He knew no title-deeds by which to hold   5
　　An idle land against his kind;
He knew his life's communal fold,
　　The law of fellowship defined.

Stately among the dredging weeds he walked,
　　Alert where most he seemed the slow;   10
He saw the spoonbill, where he stalked,
　　And the plumage that shined like snow;

He saw the egret that in silence stood
　　Like a demoiselle[1] in a dream,
And the black duck swim, with her brood   15
　　Trailed out like a kite at stream.

---

[1] Damsel, maiden.

And theirs was the water, his was the sedge,
　　While behind him the peewee ran;
Land, and water, and water's edge,
　　And freedom for each in its span.　　　　　　　　20

He drew his own full sustenance from earth,
　　He made none slave that he might reign;
He shut no plenty up till dearth
　　Starved for the blade that gave the grain.

Not his th' inquiet hunger of man's heart,—　　　25
　　The piercing doubt, hope's dark alloy;
Not his to feel the tears that start
　　Where pain yoke-fellow walks with joy.

No lord commanding bid him bend to toil,
　　No chain of time denied his wing;　　　　　　　30
He knew the marsh was his to spoil,[2]
　　And his the harvest of the Spring.

And all day long, within his beating heart,
　　He felt his fatherhood, elate,
As in his feathered nest, apart,　　　　　　　　　35
　　He saw his nurslings and his mate.

(n. d.)　　*Copy-text: WS*　　*Collated states:* None

---

[2] Plunder.

I17　THE KOALA:
A PLEA FOR THE SLAUGHTERED

Make now complaint all ye who love the forest things,
　　Cry it aloud and bid the distance heed,
And pray all swift and friendly feathered wings
　　To tell abroad what shame is in this deed—
How from the woodland and　　　　　　　　　　5
　　The hill, and from the happy vales are driven
The furry tribes, that found within this land
　　Their haven and their heaven.

And hear me, O ye trees, that through the kinder years
　　Sent out the shelter of your boughs, that fed　　　　　10
Through endless centuries the little bears
　　And in your fastness made for them a bed—
Tell how the carnage runs
　　By height and hollow, as to death are given
These helpless things that found, beneath our suns,　　15
　　Their haven and their heaven.

Ye crystal streams that ever mantling clothe the hills
　　With tender green, that dress the earth with moss,
And slake the fern-leaf that the noontide stills,
　　Do not your borders mourn to you, in loss,　　　　　20
As slaughter makes resound
　　That runs through every valley, where man's levin[1]
Strikes down to death these innocents, that found
　　With us their haven and their heaven?

Ye cliffs that hold the mountains up! Ye rocks　　　　　25
　　That guard! Will ye not backward fling to man,

(n. d.)　*Copy-text: WS*　*Collated states: DT*, 20 August 1927, p. 6 as A PLEA FOR THE SLAUGHTERED (*A*)

Not otherwise recorded: A has this note: 'BRISBANE. Thursday.—Hunters and trappers have taken early advantage of the open season for native bears. At the first fur-skin sale of the season no fewer than 23,510 skins of the koala were offered at auction.' *A*'s text is in italics throughout; the swung dash here means the repeated word is in italics.
1 Make now complaint] *Come now with me, A*　　forest] *woodland A*　　**2** Cry it aloud] *Gather ye in, A*　　bid] *from A*　　heed] *call A*　　**3** And . . . and] *That we may ask of A*　　**4** tell . . . deed—] *bear a message ere worse ill befall: A*　　**5** How] *Lest A*　　woodland] *forest A*　　**6** happy] *whisp'ring A*　　vales] ~, *A*　　**7** tribes,] ~ *A*　　that] *once A*　　this] *the A*　　**9** And . . . O] *Hearken, A*　　**10** Sent out] *Gave them A*　　boughs] *leaves A*　　**11** Through . . . little] *With blossom and with honey-dew the A*　　bears] ~, *A*　　**12** fastness] *hollows A*　　**13** Tell . . . carnage] *Hear now how ravage A*　　**14** height . . . as] *hill and valley, where A*　　**15** things] ~, *A*　　that] *once A*　　found,] ~ *A*　　suns,] ~, *A*　　**17** Ye crystal] *O, glistening A*　　streams] ~, *A*　　ever] *Om. A*　　**19** slake] *slaked A*　　fern-leaf] *fernleaf A*　　that . . . stills] *where the moonlight spills A*　　**20** Do . . . in] *Will not the trees about ye speak their A*　　loss,] ~? *A*　　**21** As . . . resound] *Hear ye not, too, the sound A*　　**22** valley,] ~ *A*　　**23** Strikes . . . that] *Cracks in the slaughter of the wild once A*　　**25** Ye] *O A*　　cliffs] ~, *A*　　**26** guard! . . . fling] *ever stand on guard, fling back A*

[1] Man's lightning, i.e. the flash of the hunter's gun.

In loud detaining thunder, till it shocks,
    The word by which this evil thing began?
O, bid the cities learn
    How these dear foresters to death are given,   30
Who, for so long, found in each wooded turn
    Their haven and their heaven!

O noble waratahs that paint the South, are these
    Not also of the tribes of old ye knew—
These little clinging things that through the trees   35
    Reached clambering forth to drink the morning dew?—
That now like children cry
    Within the night: mascots to murder given:
Who once found here, beneath this Austral sky,
    Their haven and their heaven.   40

27 detaining] *complaining A*   28 by] *with A*   began?] ~; *A*   29 O, bid] *Shout till A*   31 Who . . . long,] *Though once they A*   each] *every A*   32 heaven!] ~. *A* 33 noble] *Om. A*   waratahs] ~, *A*   paint] *clothe A*   South] *south A* 34 knew—] ~?— *A*   36 Reached] *Reach, A*   dew?—] ~: *A*   37 That] *Who A* now] ~, *A*   children] ~, *A*   38 night:] ~— *A*   given:] ~— *A*   39 once . . . beneath] *lived and once found 'neath A*   sky,] ~ *A*

118   THE LESSER BRETHREN*

They grave no living word in stone,
    Their hampered paws no record leave;
Only they know in pain to moan,
    Only they know in loss to grieve.

And yet they read our human eyes,   5
    Love's message in their deep look shown;
And longing speak in little cries,
    Almost in utterance our own.

(n. d.)   *Copy-text: WS*   *Collated states:* SMH, 24 September 1927, p. 11 as FAITHFUL DOGS (*A*)

Not otherwise recorded: MG's note is not signalled in *A*.
6 shown;] ~. *A*   7 And longing] ~, ~, *A*

The loyalties of life are theirs,
    And conscience lives where these are strong;   10
But we—unnumbered as our hairs
    The days we do these kind things wrong.

Ah, had we only thought how far
    Man stands from man, although we hear
A common speech that makes no bar,   15
    We might have held these friends more near!

* Cootamundra,[1] Wednesday.—While Mr. and Mrs. Edward Weissel, of Illawong, were absent from home, two of the children had a remarkable escape from death. A 6-ft. brown snake was about to spring at one of them when three of Mr. Weissel's dogs rushed in. A battle ensued, in which the snake was killed. Two of the dogs—one a valuable sheep dog   n5 and the other a fox terrier—died from bites. The fox terrier was found dead on top of the snake.—(*Sydney Morning Herald*, 22/9/'27).

---

10 lives] speaks *A*   **11** hairs] ~, *A*   **12** these] those *A*   **13** had] if *A*
14 man,] ~— *A*   **15** A common speech] And speak a tongue *A*   bar,] ~— *A*
n1 Cootamundra] COOTAMUNDRA *A*   **n2** home,] their home *A*   the] their *A*
n3 6-ft.] 6ft *A*   **n5** dogs] faithful dogs *A*   dog] dog, which had taken prizes at various shows, *A*   **n7** snake. *A*] ~." *X*   (*Sydney Morning Herald*, 22/9/'27)]
"Sydney Morning Herald," 22/9/'27 *A*

---

[1] From *gooramundra*: swamp, low-lying place; also breeding-place of turtles (Reed) but Thieberger gives Wiradjuri *guudhamang*: turtle, place of turtles; cf. R65 author's note, lines 53–4.

I19   THE ABORIGINALS[*]

Who is this that cometh here,
    Bent and bowed, and in the sere,[1]
Who is this whose ravaged frame
    Seems to speak of wrong and shame?

                          [cont. overleaf

(n. d.)   *Copy-text: WS*   *Collated states: DT*, 25 October 1925, p. 10 as THE ABORIGINES: A LAMENT (*A*)   Stable as THE ABORIGINES: A LAMENT (*B*)   *SV* (*C*)   Pizer as *FROM* "THE ABORIGINALS" (*D*)

Not otherwise recorded: Wherever copy-text has 'ye', *c* has 'you'. MG's note, omitted in *D*, is not signalled in *A–C*.

(1–59) Who . . . fern!] *Om. D*   **2** bowed,] ~ *C*   sere,] ~? *A B*

---

[1] Dry withered state of old age, decay.

Child of people we betrayed,   5
Name him man, and yet a shade.

Quick feet I no more know,
    Where are ye now?
Once ye were like the river's flow;
    Like leaves that thickened on the bough;   10
Like dust that, whirling hither, thither,
    Pillared upon the winds that lent
It height ere they had wandered on,
    Or fallen spent;
Now ye are gone as these are gone.   15
Ah, whither?

O friends whom I once knew,
    Where are ye now?—
Ye who were thick as grass that grew,
    Or as the ibis, when the prow   20
Of his far flight (turned hither, thither)
    Swept upward ere the fall of night,
And swung, borne his strong wing upon,
    Beyond our sight!
Now ye are gone as these are gone,   25
    And no man answers whither!

    O ye who were mine own,
        Where are ye now?
    What blighting wind was on ye blown
        That broke ye ere ye learned to bow?   30
    Ah, as the swans that, hither, thither,
        Made their blind way within the height,
    Where no star lit and no sun shone
        To give them light,

6 man,] ~ *A B*   **9** flow;] ~, *A B*   **10** thickened] quickened *A B*   bough;] ~. *A*
~, *B*   **12** winds] ~, *A B*   **13** It] Its *A*   on,] ~ *A B*   **14** fallen] ~, *A B*
spent;] ~. *A*   ~: *B*   **15** gone . . . gone.] ~, . . . ~; *A B*   **17** O friends] ~, ~, *A B*
I once] once I *B*   **18** now?—] ~? *A–C*   **19** Ye who] Once ye *A B*   You who
C   **21** thither)] ~), *A B*   ~,) *C*   **22** upward] ~, *A*   **25** ye are] are ye *B*
27 O ye] Ye *A B*   were] were once *A B*   **29** ye] you *A–C*   blown] ~, *A B*
30 broke ye] broke you *A–C*   **31** Ah] Now *C*   **32** height,] ~ *C*   **33** lit] ~, *C*
shone] ~, *A*   **34** light,] ~— *A B*

As they are gone, so ye are gone,   35
    And now none comes to tell us whither!

O, the lost tribes! . . .
He came a ghost,
Where once there walked a host.
O, the lost tribes!   40

O, the fern, the bonny, bonny fern! . . .
    With what shall we bind ye?
O scattered tribes, forsaken,
    Whither turn to find ye,
And from what darkness waken?   45
Down from your tree the blossom has been shaken.
O, the fern, the bonny, bonny fern!

When the snow delivers
    Of its burden to the sun,
Out along the rivers   50
    Cry the waters as they run,
"Where now are they to whom we once were givers?"
O, the fern, the bonny, bonny fern!

Where fled the quarry, leaping,
    By hill and creek and plain,   55
They lie together, sleeping,
    The hunter and the slain!
Now but the rain remembers them in weeping.
O, the fern, the bonny, bonny fern!

Never again from the night, the night that has taken,   60
    Shall ever the tribes return to tell us their tale;
They lie in a sleep, whence none shall ever awaken
    To mark the shadow at noon, or follow the quail.

35 gone, so] ~ ~ *c*   **37** O,] ~ *c*   **40** O,] ~ *c*   **41** O,] ~ *c*   fern! . . .] ~! . . . *A*
~! *c*   **42** ye?] ~, *A*   ~. *B*   you, *c*   **43** O] ~, *A B*   forsaken, *A*] ~? *X C*
46 shaken.] ~, *A B*   **47** O,] ~ *c*   fern!] ~. *A*   **52** "Where] '~ *B*   they] ~, *A B*
givers?"] ~?' *B*   **53** O,] ~ *c*   **57** slain!] ~. *A B*   **58** Now] ~, *A B*   weeping.]
~: *B*   **59** O,] ~ *c*   **62** whence] where *c*   awaken] ~, *A B*   **63** mark the]
mark a *A*   make a *B*

Never again shall be heard the sound of their calling,
  Through space sent out on a breath, in a cry blown thin; 65
Their forests are still; the pad of the soft foot, falling,
  Returns no more to the camp when the dusk draws in.

Fallen the flame and the spear, and fallen the hunter;
  The child's bones lie in the grass, by the weed o'ergrown;
The gunyah[2] once home is fallen like fallen Arunta,[3] 70
  Only a womerah[4] left, and a mouldered bone.

Burned in the ash of the fire the conqueror lighted,
  Driven to drown in the swamp—but the wind their dirge;
The hunted of the dogs: whom no man ever has righted;
  Their blood is black on our hands that nothing can purge. 75

> O, the lost tribes! . . .
> There came a ghost
> Where once there walked a host.
> O, the lost tribes!

[*] In Spring Street, Melbourne, in the winter of 1924, I heard an old blackfellow, sitting out of the wind in the sun, singing over and over again to himself the half-forgotten songs of his people. Once I was "sister" to the aboriginals; long ago when I was a child.

64 calling,] ~ *B*   65 space] ~, *A B*   out] forth *C*   70 gunyah] ~, *A B*   home] ~, *A B*   fallen like] ~, ~ *A*   fallen, like the *B*   72 fire] fires *A–C*   lighted,] ~; *A–C*   73 swamp—] ~; *C*   74 The hunted] Hunted *A B*   the] *Om. A B* dogs:] ~; *A–C*   righted;] ~—— *A B*   75 hands] ~, *A B*   76 O,] ~ *C* tribes! . . .] ~ . . . *A B*   ~! *C*   77 ghost] ~, *A B*   79 O,] ~ *C*   (n1–4) In . . . child.] *Om. D*   n1 In . . . 1924,] *Om. A B*   n2 out of the wind] in the sun *A B* in] and in *C*   out of *A B* '*A B*   sun] wind *A B*   singing] sing *A–C*   again] *Om. C* n3 to himself] *Om. A B*   people.] people. He sang outside my window in Spring Street, Melbourne, in the winter of 1924. *A*   people. . . . *B*   Once] When I was a child *A B*   "sister"] '~' *B*   n4 aboriginals;] ~. *A B*   long . . . child.] *Om. A B*

---

[2] From Dharuk *gunya/ gunyah*: hut of boughs and sheets of bark (Thieberger, Dixon).
[3] See Preface, p. xxxiv. Cf. K2 line 3, K4 line 24 and author's note, K6 line 12, K12 line 13 and R54 line 11.
[4] From Dharuk *wamara*, Wiradjuri *wamarr*: spear-thrower (Thieberger, Dixon).

120   WHERE NOW IS BRIBENABOOKA?*

Hear, O ye tribes, my words, my words!
   Like wind ye came, like wind ye go—
Ye are no more than passing birds
   That fly before the storms that blow;
The spear is sped, the lance is sprung,   5
The fire is dead, the song unsung.

Where now is Bribenabooka, he
Whose feet were swift to climb the tree?
Where now is Narrandierra, who
Out of its hole the adder drew?   10
Where is Kedarr whose pace outran
The white canoe a hundred span?
Where are the masters, where the seers?
Only the wind that passes hears.

Never again the mantling trees   15
That clothed the land will call the bees;
Tamed are the bees, that all their lives
Fly in and out their chambered hives!
Tamed are the bees and tamed the wild,
Charted and fenced and reconciled.   20

Who now sings Mirrabookarra's spear
That swifter flew from year to year—
Swift as a hawk in its hunting flight,
Swift as the star that fled by night?
Father to son it passing came,   25
Now is there none to name its name.

Great was Boondarra, but he is gone,
   Great was Bemboka, but he is dust;
Time in his passing took them on,
   Time is the judge, and time is just.   30

[cont. overleaf

(n. d.)   *Copy-text:* WS   *Collated states:* SMH, 23 February 1929, p. 13 as WHERE NOW
IS BRIBENABOOKA (*A*)

1 words!] ~—— *A*   2 go—] ~! *A*   30 judge,] ~ *A*   just.] ~; *A*

But, ah, where lies the page we scan
How spoiled the writing Time began!

Who now shall call the heroes' song,
Or shout the challenge from the strong?
Who hold tradition to the light   35
Lest it decay and fall to night?
Fathers and sons a thousand years
Chanted the names that now none hears;
The bones are dust, the songs are dead,
Like leaves a gust of wind has shed.   40

* The references are to aboriginal historical folk-lore stories. I remember
that my father constantly spoke of parallels with the Iliad and the
Odyssey; the great spear that no man but the right one could pull out
of the tree, being one.
_____

31–2 But . . . began!] Injustice dwells alone with man/ Who blots the page that time
began. *A*   34 from] of *A*   35 hold] holds *A*   38 hears;] ~— *A*
n1 folk-lore] and folklore *A*   n4 tree,] ~ *A*   one.] one.—M.G. *A*

I21   THE LAMENT OF THE LUBRA

What have we left of all the long, long years,
The untouched forest and the vanished tribes?
O eyes that seek, and seeking shall not find,
O lips would sing, and know not to what airs,
O hands would touch, and that find naught to touch,   5
And memory, within whose urn men keep
In childish disarray the record of
The past, now but from fragments shall ye shape
Anew the lore of this disvalued land!

The strange romances centuries handed down,   10
The aspirations of the race we had

(n. d.)   *Copy-text: WS   Collated states: DTNP*, 14 May 1927, p. 41 (*A*)   *SV* (*B*)
Not otherwise recorded: A's text is in italics throughout.

2 The untouched] Of ancient *B*   5 and that] but which *B*   8 past,] *past; A*
8 shall ye] can you *B*   9–10 land!// The] *land!! The A*   ~!/ ~ *B*

Not asked to know—their legends and their dreams—
These fallen blossoms of uncounted years,
These have we trampled in the dust, and these
Laid waste while yet the treasure filled our hands!   15
What wise philosophies are lost, where men,
Too ignorant to know the silk within
The stranger thread, despise, and then destroy!

Beside the riverbank the lubra mourned,
She mourned the child the stranger's hand had slain:—   20

    "Dear fledgling of the reeds,
        I hold thee
    Here at my heart whose needs
        Foretold thee!
    Now must the wilgas weep,   25
    Where lonely thou shalt sleep,
    Thou who hadst but an hour
    Ere fallen like a flower.

    "How like a broken leaf
        Art lying   30
    Slack in my arms of grief,
        While, flying,
    Time speeds hastening on!
    Soon, soon wilt thou be gone,
    All lonely in thy sleep,   35
    While o'er thee wilgas weep.

    "Yet my heart sees thee near,
        As standing
    With thy high-lifted spear
        Commanding,   40

12 know—] *know, A*   ~, *B*   13 years,] *years— A*   ~— *B*   15 hands!] *hands. A*
~. *B*   16 lost,] *lost A*   18 destroy!] *destroy. A*   19 riverbank] *river-bank A*
river-bank *B*   19 mourned,] ~; *B*   20–1 slain:—// "Dear] *slain:/ "Dear A*
~://"~ *B*   21 fledgling] fledgeling *B*   23 heart] *heart, A*   24 thee!] *thee; A*
25 wilgas] *wilga's A*   29 broken] *bruised A*   32 While, flying,] *While flying A*
35 All] So *B*   35 sleep,] ~ *B*   36 While] Where *B*   thee] *the A*   37 "Yet *B*]
~ *X*   "Yet *A*   38 As] *As, A*   ~, *B*   39 thy *B*] my *X*   *thy A*   39 high-lifted]
up-lifted *B*   spear] *spear, A*

I watched thee like a king,
Fresh from the Bora ring—[1]
Who now art but a flower,
Low fallen ere its hour.

"O nursling of my heart,   45
        Thy token
Declared thee as a dart
        Unbroken;
Among thy fellows none
Made mock of thee, my son!   50
Now must the wilgas weep,
Where thou, so lone, must sleep!"

. . . Here I, dreaming a dream of justice, bring
This thread of thought to twine from it a chord
To make my land a native harp, whereon   55
Some day the wind may blow, and one who hears
Draw from its slender note a song profound.

42 ring—] ~. *B*   *43* Who now] Now thou *B*   *43* flower,] ~ *B*   *51* weep,]
weep A   *52* so lone] alone *B*   must] *shalt A*   *53* ˢ. . . Here] ~ *B*   *54 thought*
to] thought, or A

[1] From Kamilaroi *buurra* (Dixon), *boorah* (Parker 1905): site where boys were initiated
into manhood in the ceremony of the same name; cf. K17 line 20. Ridley derives it
from *bor* or *bur*: the girdle investing the initiate with manhood.

I22   OUR LOST FIELD*

Moorangoo, the dove,[1] in her high place mourned,
And Mulloka, the Water Spirit, turned
In his shade as he heard her weep,
Sad as the lone Koala that cries in his sleep

(n. d.)   *Copy-text: WS   Collated states: SMH*, 29 October 1927, p. 11 (n. t.) (*A*)
SV (*B*)

Not otherwise recorded: MG's note, omitted in *A*, is not signalled in *B*.

1 Moorangoo] Moorango *A*   *2* Water Spirit] water spirit *A*   *4* Koala] koala *A B*

[1] Uncorroborated, as are Aboriginal words at lines 2, 7, 9 and 13.

At the sound of the gun, 5
Asking for pity where pity was none.

And Mulloka, looking up to the sky,
Raised to Mirrabooka, the Cross,[2] his cry;
Maipoona, the deep water, heard,
And old Pannamoona, the ocean,[3] stirred 10
To his depths, and the gilgais[4] shook to the sound
As it rang to the uttermost bound
Of Attunga, the height,
To Biami, All-Father of day and of night.[5]

* This stanza is taken from a series of articles called "Our Lost Field,"
which appeared in the "Sydney Morning Herald" in 1927.[6] In these I
tried to point out, more fully than in former pleas, what Australia has
lost in distinctive literature in not using the aboriginals and aboriginal
lore, with their native customs and words. I tried to show by the verse n5
quoted the use that could be made of the material even yet at hand. The
words I took without regard to difference in tribal language, applying
them as I found them, and purely as an example for others to follow,
and do better.

5 the gun,] a gun— A   6 pity where] ~—~ A   6–7 none.// And] ~./ ~ A
11 To his depths] At the call A   sound] ~, B   13 height] Height A
14 Biami A] Biama X   All-Father] All-father A   n1 Field,"] ~", B
n2 "Sydney Morning Herald"] Sydney Morning Herald B   n4 aboriginals] ~, B
n4 and aboriginal] their B   n5 with their] and B   n9 better.] better. I think Dr
John Dunmore Lang was the first to do this. B

[2] Cf. K1, K3 and K4, and see Preface, p. xxxiii.
[3] From panamuna: deep water (Reed).
[4] From Wiradjuri and Kamilaroi gilgaay: waterhole, or terrain characterised by the
presence of mounds, rims and hollows in which water might accumulate (Dixon).
[5] See I4 n. 2.
[6] Collated state A, part of the fourth SMH article, showed how schoolchildren might
be educated 'in the words belonging to our own country', just as New Zealand children
were with Maori language and culture. 'It will be objected here', MG added, 'that I
have taken words of mixed dialects and used them as if they were of one dialect and
kind . . . but better a bold attempt at something than a dumb acquiescence to silence
and nothing'.

I23   THE RING-BARKED TREE[1]

Come not again, lone wandering by the shore,
   The years have said farewell, and from their place
Have blotted out the names thy kindred bore!
   O come no more!—ask not again to trace,
With sad and wistful fingers,   5
      Where, upon the rocky face,
   Thy totem sign still lingers;
The happy days are gone and none them shall restore.

Yet for remembrance this one day remain,
   And from the box-tree strip thy last canoe;   10
Scorch hard the ends and dare the stream again,
   And, in thy brave courageous passing through,
Show us once more the steering
      That of old the fathers knew,
When, on the current veering,   15
They held a branch as fin in conquest over strain.

Gather the twigs to stay the swirling flow—
   The little hands the tree hangs down to part,
As thou the waters, all the winds that blow;
   And show the hard white man what ancient art   20
Thy worn and ravaged fingers
      Follow still through memory's chart,
As when the old Churingas,*
Guardians of the past, watched with thee long ago.

Pole outward to the stream's high crest, and let   25
   Thy lubra trail the sternward branch to steer,

(n. d.)   *Copy-text: WS   Collated states: SV (A)*

Not otherwise recorded: Except where noted, copy-text instances of 'thou', 'thee' and 'thy' are replaced by 'you' and 'your' in *A*. MG's note is not signalled in *A*.
4 more!—ask] ~! ~ *A*   **7** Thy] The *A*   **8** The] Your *A*   **12** thy] a *A*   brave] ~, *A*   **16** branch] ~, *A*   fin] ~, *A*   **18** part,] ~ *A*   **19** As] (~ *A*   waters,] ~) *A*

---

[1] A tree killed by cutting a circle of bark around the entire trunk, usually to clear land; here a metaphor for the destroyed Aboriginal way of life (line 36). Bark for canoe-making (line 10) was stripped lengthwise.

Moving the bodies' balance—easing yet—
  As currents, roiling,[2] touch the banks and veer;
And, lest thy frail craft flinder[3]
  In the midst, and no help near,   30
Where the stream angles hinder,
With hand and leaf diffuse what pressures toward thee set.

Then when thou comest to thy landing place,
  Who hast so used the stream it ferried thee,
Turn toward the setting sun thy lonely face,   35
  And read thy history in a ring-barked tree.
O shadowy wanderer on a twilit shore,
Return no more! Ask not again to trace,
  With sad and ravaged fingers,
Where upon the rocky face   40
  Thy totem sign still lingers.
The happy days are gone and none them shall restore.

* Churingas are sacred stones, or emblems of wood, intricately carved
and with hidden meanings in the carving.[4] Every tribe and family had
them. Great care was taken of them, and if my memory is not at fault
they were the title deeds of tribal land boundaries, together with rights
of hunting, fishing and safe conduct in travel. I do remember that a   n5
tribe or group without them could be treated as trespassers, and killed,
when passing through territory not their own when on their way from
the plains to the rivers; a migration in olden times made regularly for
the fish season. The tribe that lived nearest the Murrumbidgee, in the
case that I remember, would cross to the far side, leaving the other bank   n10
free to the strangers for the time of their stay. Riparian rights everywhere
were open to all, but they were regulated by inter-tribal law.[5] Further,
there was an interchange made in that when those near the rivers wanted
another kind of diet they were allowed to hunt unmolested for a fixed
period in certain parts of the territory of those on the plains, with a   n15

---

28 currents, roiling,] roiling currents *A*   30 midst] flood *A*   33 thou comest to]
at last you reach *A*   34 hast so used] bid *A*   it ferried thee] your ferry-hand to
be *A*   35 toward] to *A*   41 Thy] The *A*   lingers.] ~! *A*   42 gone] ~, *A*
n4 were] were in a way *A*   land] *Om. A*   n5 fishing] ~, *A*   n7 when passing]
if passing *A*   n8 in olden times] *Om. A*   n9–10 in . . . remember] when I was a
child *A*   n12 Further,] ~ *A*   n15 with] allowing *A*

---

[2] Cf. I5 n. 2.   [3] Rare verb meaning to break into flinders or pieces.
[4] Cf. Dixon: 'sacred ceremonial objects', from Arrernte (see Preface, p. xxxiv); see further
K1 author's note for line 26, K2, K3 line 4, R65 line 10 and R69 entry for n17–24. As

return right for those on the plains who needed fish and water-
fowl. It was conceded that when the tribal health required it, this
should be done. All this I heard at later times from my father, but I
quite well remember being taken as a little child to the bank of the
Murrumbidgee and having it explained to me, then, as showing how wise   n20
and just for the conservation of their people the aboriginal laws were.

n16–17 water-fowl] water fowl *A*   n17 it,] ~ *A*   n18–21 All . . . were.] *Om. A*

a name for Australia, see K1 line 26, K2 line 7 and P1 line 6, and for a bull-roarer see
I26 n. 2.

[5] In English Common Law, any person owning and occupying land on the bank of
a natural stream acquires rights to use its waters. In Aboriginal law the land was not
owned and access was communal, although tribal territorial occupation might modify
rights of usage.

I24   UNTO THEE, BIAMI,[1] UNTO THEE

> Unto Thee, Biami, unto Thee!
>   The woods call, and the stream
> Sings as of old, but we
>   Are but drift of a dream.
>
> The stranger came, and no more the shield   5
>   Is in the hand! The spear
> Lies broken in the field,
>   Like summer grass in sere.
>
> Fallen is the boomerang, and slow
>   The swift foot once so free,   10
> Homeless and lone we go,
>   O Biami, to Thee.
>
> Unto Thee, Biami! for in Thee
>   Hunger shall end, and thirst
> That wrung no longer be   15
>   Dry at the breast that nurst;

(n. d.)   *Copy-text: WS   Collated states: SV (A)*

Not otherwise recorded: A provides an unsignalled endnote gloss on Biami as 'God
the All-Father'.

7 field,] ~ *A*   10 free,] ~; *A*

[1] See I4 n. 2.

We shall not be afraid in the night;
    But the fire shall be lit,
And secure in the light
    Of it there we shall sit.   20

Unto Thee, Biami, unto Thee,
Ending we go.

16 nurst;] ~! *A*   17 night;] ~, *A*   22 go.] ~. *A*

I25   THE HUNTER OF THE BLACK*

Softly footed as a myall,[1] silently he walked,
All the methods of his calling learned from men he stalked;
Tall he was, and deeply chested, eagle-eyed and still,
Every muscle in his body subject to his will.

Dark and swarthy was his colour; somewhere Hampshire born; 5
Knew no pity for the hunted—weakness all his scorn;
Asked no friendship, shunned no meetings, took what life
    might bring;
Came and went among his fellows something like a king.

Paid each debt with strict exactness, what the debt might be;
Called no man employed him master; master's equal, he;   10
Yet there was not one who sought him, none who held his hand,
Never father, calling, bid him join the family band.

                                                    [*cont. overleaf*

(20 July 1925)   *Copy-text: WS   Collated states: Bn*, 17 September 1930, Red Page,
signed M<small>ARY</small> G<small>ILMORE</small> (in the "Wild Swan," just published by Robertson and Mullens)
(*A*)   *SV* (*B*) *Trib*, 26 November 1952, p. 8 (*C*)   Pizer (*D*)

Not otherwise recorded: C indicates omission of stanzas 4 and 5 with a line of four asterisks.
MG's note, omitted in *C*, is not signalled in *B*.

1 walked,] ~ *C*   2 stalked;] ~ *C*   3 was,] ~ *C*   5 colour] color *A C*
6 hunted—] ~, *B*   ~; *C*   all] met *B C*   7 friendship] friendships *C*   8 king.]
~; *B*   10 equal,] ~ *A C*   11 hand,] ~; *B C*   12 father,] ~ *B C*   calling,] ~ *C*
bid] bade *A*

[1] From Dharuk *mayal/ miyal*: a stranger (Dixon), thus an Aborigine living in a traditional
tribal way, outside European civilisation. Author's notes for K15 and K23 give it as
a general term for Aborigines. It also means native vegetation (cf. *myall*: a drooping
acacia, Parker 1905): see I37 line 26, K15 entry for n1, R55 author's note for line 4,
and R70.

Tales and tales were told about him, how, from dawn till dark,
Noiselessly he trailed his quarry, never missed a mark,
How the twigs beneath his footstep "moved but never broke,"   15
How the very fires he kindled "never made a smoke."

Men would tell, with puzzled wonder marked on voice and brow,
How he'd stand a moment talking, leave, and none knew how;
"He was there! . . ." and then had vanished, going as he came,
Like the passing of a shadow, like a falling flame.   20

Once (I heard it when it happened) word was sent, to him,
Of a lone black on Mamoosa—O, the hunting grim!
Through three days and nights he tracked him, never asking
        sleep;
Shot, for him who stole the country, him who killed a sheep.

Tomahawk in belt, as only adults needed shot,   25
No man knew how many notches totalled up his lot;
But old stockmen striking tallies, rough and ready made,
Reckoned on at least a thousand, naming camps decayed.

Time passed on, and years forgotten whitened with the dust;
He whose hands were red with slaughter sat among the just,   30
Kissed the children of his children, honoured in his place,
Turned and laid him down in quiet, asking God His grace.

* Called in those days a sharp-shooter; to-day he would be a sniper.
I remember this man well. I met one of his daughters lately, but I did
not mention that I had known her father, or knew what he had been.
He had a large family and many grandchildren, and as a paid killer of
the black, he was but one of many.   n5

(13–20) Tales . . . flame.] *Om.* C   13 till] to *A*   15 footstep] footsteps *A*
broke,"] ~", *B*   16 smoke."] ~". *B*   17 tell,] ~ *A B*   wonder] ~, *B*   brow,]
~ *A*   18 how;] ~. *A*   19 "He was there! . . ."] "~ ~ ~!" . . . . *A*   *"He was*
there!" B   20 the] a *D*   21 happened)] ~,) *B*   word was] words were *A*
sent,] ~ *A–C*   him,] ~ *A–C*   22 Mamoosa] Mimosa *B C*   O,] ~ *B C*
23 nights] night *A*   26 lot;] ~. *A*   31 honoured] honored *A C*   place,] ~. *C*
32 His] his *B C*   *n1* in] *Om.* D   *n1* sharp-shooter;] ~, *B*   *n1* to-day] today *B D*
(*n2–5*) I remember . . . many.] *Om.* B   *n2* this] the *D*   *n3* father,] ~ *D*
n5 black,] ~ *A*

I26   O, RACE THE FOREST KNEW

Blow, blow ye winds, and bid the mountains hear once more
    their call;
Echo again, ye streams, the rustle of a foot's light fall;
Mourn for them, hills, and O, ye grasses, cry,
Grieving for those whom we condemned to die!

Hunters no more, no more they stalk the quarry through
    the glade,   5
Passing like shadows through the trees, and shades within a
    shade;
No more the womerah[1] speeds the driving spear—
The tribes have fallen like the leaves of yester-year!

The Murrumbidgee whisp'ring at its banks cries, "Where
    are they
Whose thousand camp-fires drove the darkness of the night
    away?"   10
Silent the camps—the tawny embers cold,
No more to throw on night their scattered gold.

Climbing the sky the moon peers through each dusky tree:
"Were they not here," she says, "who month by month
    measured by me
The ceremonial and the feast, and sung   15
The waking life within the initiate young?

[cont. overleaf

(21 August 1925)   *Copy-text: WS   Collated states: SV* as O RACE THE FOREST KNEW (*A*)

Not otherwise recorded: In *A*, MG adds this unsignalled note, referring to lines 42–4:
'When a black twirled his spear, threw it up above his head, caught it again without
stopping the twirl, and then launched it forward while rotation was still in it, it meant
death. The spear was held in the middle for this tossing and twirling, and in its descent
caught farther back for the drive. The catch and drive had to be simultaneous, otherwise
the twirl was lost. As a child I used to stand in terror or run like lightning into the house
and shut the door when I saw this. Yet, because of father, I was always safe.'
1 mountains] mountain *A*   **3** them,] ~ *A*   and O,] ~, ~ *A*   grasses,] ~ *A*
9 whisp'ring] whispering *A*   **11** camps—] ~, *A*   **14** here,] ~ *A*   says] asks *A*

[1] See I19 n. 4.

"Were they not here who twined the hunter's belt of
       'possum fur,
Who loopd the snare, and edged the boy's spear with a
       plover's spur;
Who drew the lengthened sinew out, that bound
The whirling flint rolled silence in its sound?"[2]   20

Disconsolate and sad she wanders on, disconsolate
She moves through heaven; and as the wonga-wonga[3]
       mourns its mate,
She downward peers amid the trees to call
The lost of every creek and waterfall!

O race the forest knew in days gone by!   25
       O people of the wild!
As winds blow out the cloud against the sky,
So were ye rent and blown, so flung to die,
       The father slain beside the child.

The brolga[4] called you brother, and the swan   30
       Declared your name abroad;
The lizard wrote your shadow on
The rock at noon, and as the night came, wan,
       Your symbol in the sky was to'ard!

Now is there no one left to name the stars   35
       Whose constellations spake
For you the way your fathers trod, as Mars

---

17 Were] Came *A*   'possum] possum *A*   18 loopd] looped *A*   spur;] ~, *A*
19 out,] ~ *A*   22 and] ~, *A*   28 die,] ~— *A*   31 abroad] on high *A*
33 noon,] ~; *A*   as] when *A*   34 symbol . . . to'ard!] starry symbol lit the sky. *A*
35 is there] there is *A*

---

[2] Describes the making of a bull-roarer, a piece of flint or wood attached to a string and whirled in the air to make a roaring sound; used in ceremonies and rituals and therefore sometimes called a *churinga* (see I23 n. 4). On different kinds and functions of bull-roarers, see K1 line 19 and author's note, K9 author's note, and K17 lines 27–8 and author's note. MG's 'nurmi' or 'narmi' for the small bull-roarer she calls the 'woman-drawer' (see K1 author's note for line 19, K8, K9 and R69) is uncorroborated.
[3] From Dharuk *wanga wanga*: the wonga pigeon (Dixon).
[4] From Kamilaroi *burralga*: dancing bird (Dixon); cf. *bᵘralga* (Ridley), *brälgah* (Parker), *baralga* (Reed).

And Buddha speak the ancient avatars,[5]
    And, silent, still the silence break;

Now is there none to tell the hidden lore,   40
    To shape anew the bowl of stone,
To twirl the spear that, ere the rifle-bore,
Bid weaponed flight sail straight nor wasting soar,
    Death writ on every shaft so thrown!

We who destroyed denied the tribal law   45
    We who had not wit to read;
Upon a rock a flawed stone all we saw,
Where the unknown had put his hand to draw
    The emblem of his race and creed . . .

There is a star that shines at eve above the mountain edge,   50
And o'er the darkling verge of forest and of sedge,
Like a benignant face that turns in grief
Where life's poor blotted story stains a leaf:

There swims a moon within the sky, that hangs like some
      great tear,
A tear which, rounding out, yet may not fall (as set too near   55
The heart of God) lest it should once again
Flow forth, and drown the sinful race of men:

There is a Pity, infinite, wherein the slayer and
The slain lie in a sleep; and there the earth lays hand in hand:
There Death pleads up to God for brotherhood!   60
O ill deeds done, be yet man's plough for good!

---

40 Now] Nor *A*   none] one *A*   **41** anew the] the grinder's *A*   **42** spear] ~, *A*
46 who] *Om. A*   **49** ˢcreed . . .] ~. . . . *A*   **53** poor] ~, *A*   leaf:] ~; *A*
57 men:] ~; *A*   **59** hand:] ~, *A*   **60** There Death] While death *A*
61 good!] ~. *A*

---

[5] I.e. give names to past manifestations of the divine in physical form.

I27   PRIMEVAL AUSTRALIA

Lift up, ye Winds, and part the cloudy curtains of the sky
    That they may feel the sun, on whom has fallen the dark!
And, O ye lamps of Memory, that years gone by
    Must cling to for remembering, out of your spark
Send forth a ray to tell to later comers   5
All that has vanished with the far-off summers.

Tell of the tribes that once were many as the sands—
    Were many as the landward waves where storm-winds blow,
Bidding the white-caps leap till each a moment stands
    O'er watery wastes far seen, before it falling goes!   10
O Memory, tell of these to later comers,
Lest we forget them and their far-off summers!

Tell of the kangaroos, whose numbers none could name,
    Lifting above the grass their heads of stately mien;
They played as children play when dusk of evening came,   15
    They played again at dawn where now no play is seen!
Tell of them, Winds, to all the later comers,
Lest none remember them and their far summers!

Tell of the emu rising like a king of birds,
    His nesting place the earth, his pasture all the land;   20
Now where he led his flock deploy man's spreading herds,
    While where he with his young ones stalked great cities stand.
O Memory, wake and tell the later comers,
Lest he go unremembered with his summers!

(n. d.)   *Copy-text: WS   Collated states: DTPS*, 23 July 1926, p. 2 (*A*)   *SV* (*B*)

Not otherwise recorded: The division of stanzas in *A* (lines 17–22 grouped as stanza 4
and lines 23–30 as stanza 5) is corrected by MG in the clipping held in ML 17/9. *A*'s
text is in italics throughout.

1 ye] O *B*   Winds] *winds A*   *1* sky] ~, *B*   *2* sun,] ~ *B*   *3* O] *O, A*
lamps] *Lamps A*   *3* Memory,] ~ *B*   *8* Were many] Many *B*   storm-winds]
storm winds A   blow,] *blow A*   *9* Bidding] *And bid A*   leap] *leap, A*
9 stands] ~, *B*   *11* these] him *B*   *12* summers!] *summers. A*   ~. *B*   *16* seen!]
seen. A   *20* land;] ~! *B*   *21* Now] ~, *B*   *21* flock] ~, *B*   *22* While] ~, *B*
22 stalked] ~, *B*   *23* wake . . . the] *tell of him to A*   tell of him to *B*

Tell of the brolga and his ancient minuet 25
    Learned long before the race of man began to climb;
A scattered few there be that somewhere dance it, yet,
    As children whisper vaguely on a broken rhyme:
Tell of it, O ye Winds, to later comers,
Lest they forget these, too, and all their summers! 30

For centuries untold, at dawn the forest stirred
    To multitudinous voices chirping to the sky;
Saw the wing-stretching of the newly-wakened bird,
    And heard amid the down the hungry nestlings cry:
Now who is left to tell to later comers 35
All this, O Winds that knew the far-off summers?

Upon the earth a thousand wandering tracks enlaced,
Like rain-made rivulets that move towards a stream;
Here the echidna crept, and there the dingo paced,
    Yonder the quail set, trembling, at the eagle's scream. 40
O Memory, wake and tell to later comers
What wonder and what lore filled far-off summers!

Once all the whole year through the happy Bush was loud;
And, O, the singing and the chatter after rain!
Now on the plains the grass is like an empty shroud; 45
    The woods are silent—for the hand of man has slain:
And ye will never know, ye later comers,
What we, who pass, knew in the old far summers!

25 minuet] *minuet, A* ~, B   27 it,] *it A* ~ B   28 rhyme:] *rhyme. A*   29 it]
these B   30 these] them B   32 sky;] ~, B   34 cry:] *cry. A* ~. B
36 Winds] *Winds, A*   37 enlaced,] ~ B   38 Like *Ed.*] Lake X B *Like A*
40 set] sat B   40 trembling,] ~ B   43 Bush] *bush A* bush B   44 O,] ~ B
46 silent—] ~, B slain:] *slain. A*   47 ye . . . ye] *ye will never know, ye A* you
. . . you B   48 summers!] *summers. A*

I28   KOSCIUSKO AND CANBERRA[1]

Hear Kosciusko call his brother heights,
　　And breathe in icicles upon the wind!
And hear his henchmen shout each note, until,
　　Beyond the ranges borne—by distance thinned—
The mighty-sounded names seem but the breath   5
Of soft airs falling to their death!

Calls Kosciusko to the Kookbundoons,
　　Crookwell and Laggan answer him again,
And yet his cry, insistent, searches forth
　　Where bleak Taralga breeds her hardy men;   10
And there he piles the snow on fell and moor,
And writes in sleet on every door.

And still he calls, till all the drowsy vales
　　Of Pejar and lone Grabben Gullen wake,
And don for him the garment of the frost   15
　　Until the very grass-blades, trodden, break
And crackle like the twig that summer burns
Beneath the solstice ere it turns.

Then on through poplared Roslyn runs his voice,
　　And beats upon the golden Autumn leaves   20
His bannered words, which, to the listening ear,
　　Whisper of patterns that the hearth-fire weaves;
Of wood high-heaped upon the whitened hobs,
And flame that quivering leaps and throbs.

(3 May 1927)   *Copy-text: WS*   *Collated states: DTNP*, 7 May 1927, p. 22 (*A*)

Not otherwise recorded: A's text is in italics throughout; the swung dash in this collation
means the repeated word is in italics. MG's note is omitted in *A*.

3 hear . . . shout] *shouts his henchman there A*   **14** Pejar] *Pijar A*   **15** frost] ~, *A*
16 break] ~, *A*   **17** crackle] ~, *A*   **18** solstice] ~, *A*   **20** Autumn] *autumn A*
22 that] *th*[. . .] *A*   weaves;] ~ *A*   **23** Of wood] *In logs, A*   **24** that quivering]
~, ~, *A*

[1] In 1927 Canberra became the new home of the government of the Commonwealth of
Australia with the opening of the temporary Parliament House. The highest mountain
in Australia, now spelled Kosciuszko, was named in 1840 by explorer P. E. Strzelecki

Ainslie and Tidbimbilla[2] answer him,   25
   And from his heights Mount Campbell makes reply;
And, where a blue Sierra lifts its points,
   The Murrumbidgee Ranges hear his cry:
Which softly onward to the plains is borne,
Like the last note of some far horn.   30

. . . To-day* he calls upon his brother heights
   To greet Canberra, waking like a bride;
Old Father Dandenong has heard his voice,
   Mount Lofty answers from the Torrens' side;
The gaunt Coolgardie Ranges lift the head,   35
And hear again lost myriads tread!

The Barron Falls have lent a bridal veil,
   Tasmania knits a scarf of silver lace—
Behold she stands; whom nations yet shall hail,
   The sun of morning on her lovely face!   40
She comes, unhistoried 'mid her mountain walls,
Where Kosciusko waits and calls.

* The opening of Canberra as the capital of Australia.

27 a] *the* A   28 cry:] ~, A   29 Which] *That,* A   softly] ~, A   31 To-day*]
To-day A   heights] ~, A   36 myriads] *millions* A   tread!] ~. A   39 Behold]
See where A   stands;] ~, A   41 unhistoried] ~, A   42 Where] *Whom* A
waits] *hails* A   calls.] ~! A

after Polish patriot Tadeusz Kosciuszko (1746–1817). It and other places named up to
line 30 are in the Australian Capital Territory or nearby in NSW. From line 33 Victoria,
South Australia, Western Australia and Queensland are designated by a representative
mountain, while Tasmania is directly named.

[2] Standard spelling is now Tidbinbilla.

I29   CASTERTON[1] TO MOUNT GAMBIER

O, to go out once more and see the moon's clear shining
    Break on the waters into silver bars,
Hear the curlew and plover call, in lonely pining,
    Under the spear-points of ten thousand stars;
To stand where opening spaces show the heath's low level,   5
    And watch the gold of early morning rim the sedge;
Where, in the long lagoon, the rippling wavelets bevel,[2]
    As the black swan swings downward to the water's edge!

Once more to see the Blue Lake,[3] like a sapphire shimmer
    In the deep heart of steep descents of green;   10
To watch again in winter nights the stars' faint glimmer
    Tremble in waterpools where rain has been;
To feel across Strathdownie heaths,[4] in distance risen,
    The soft, susurrant wind climb upward to the hill,
And hear the sunny bees, in some fair flowering prison,   15
    Murmur of sweets where eucalyptine perfumes spill!

O, to pull rein on one clear height, and there, in wonder,
    Mark the far summit of Mount Gambier rise,
Above the faint and misty veils, the heavens under,
    Like some great finger pointing to the skies!   20
For there in quick, courageous hours of youth, high-hearted,
    Life stood immortal in its own immortal dreams,

(9–12 April 1924)   *Copy-text: WS   Collated states: DT,* 19 September 1925, p. 10
(*A*)   *SV* (*B*)

1 O,] ~ *B*   3 call,] ~ *B*   pining,] ~ *B*   4 spear-points] spearpoints *A B*
6 sedge;] ~, *A B*   7 bevel,] ~ *A*   9 Lake,] ~ *A B*   17 O,] ~ *B*   18 rise,]
~ *A B*

---

[1] Casterton is in s.w. Victoria where MG lived (1903–11) nearby on the Gilmore farm
or in the township itself (see volume 1, Introduction, p. xl).
[2] Go on the angle, normally used of hard surfaces.
[3] In a volcanic crater close to Mount Gambier, where poet and horseman Adam Lindsay
Gordon (1833–70) leapt his horse over the safety fence onto the narrow edge of the
crater. On Gordon, see I31 and n. 1.
[4] Strathdownie is a scrubland area of heath and marshes between Casterton and the
South Australian border area of which Mount Gambier is the main town.

E'en though it saw where from on high the falcon darted,
    And heard the dying leveret perish in its screams!

Once, there, through a night I rode with the moon high-sailing, 25
    Naught heard but the sound of the wheel, the hoof,
When came the cry of a child, like a ghostly wailing,
    From the pallid shield of a frost-bound roof;
Only that and the crackle of frore[5] in its breaking
    Under the firm strong shoes, and the turn of the wheel;   30
Only the click of ice as it sprang in the making,
    Where the splash of the waters lay under its seal!

. . . I dream I hear in Cawker's paddocks[6] the hoof-beats flying,
    Where the foals string out like pennons that sway behind;
I hear the whinnying mares make answer to their crying,   35
    And stirs, as of old, a thought long kept in mind;
And I have written it here that others may read it,
    And seal with the seal of love what all should keep;
For memory starves, if never comes one to feed it,
    When they whom the land first knew in its bosom sleep!   40

23 where] ~, _B_   high] ~, _B_   24 screams!] ~. _A_   25 rode] drove, _B_   high-sailing]
high sailing _A B_   26 wheel] trace _B_   29 that] ~, _B_   breaking] ~, _B_   30 shoes,]
~ _B_   36 mind;] ~. _A_   38 keep;] ~, _B_   40 they] ~, _B_   knew] ~, _B_

[5] I.e. frosty grass (neologism).
[6] Thomas Cawker (1837–1926) operated a livery stables in Casterton – which 'lost a
friend, a sportsman and a man' through his death (Mount Gambier _Border Watch_, 19
December 1927). See further I31, line 18 and n. 2.

I30   MALEBO*

There is a hill—I know it well;
    Sunlit it stands, and odorous of pine;
The river in the distance runs
    With many a rounding curve and twine;
And, there, in the heavy trees   5
    Is heard
    The low song of a bird,
And the bombinating[1] bees.

Bunched in the cool of dusky swales[2]
  That by the river lie, as huge black shapes   10
The cattle stand, darked by the sun
  Whose brilliance deeps what shadow drapes.
There, as wandering fancies cruise,
  They seem
  Like things half seen, in dream,   15
When the summer noons bemuse.

There, too, in days long, long gone by,
  My father set his mill, and the pit-saw
Sang like a greater bird its song,
  As it cut where a line was law.   20
How still the great plumbob[3] hung!
  How clear
  To the young listening ear
Steel teeth on the white logs rung!

Maybe on Malebo is still   25
  One who remembers how my father ran,
And with his bare hands held the log
  That, slambering[4] down, had nipped its man!
So little he thought the deed,
  Unheard   30
  It went, save one told, stirred,
How quick his mind to the need.

          *   *   *   *

What others played I know not; we
  In self-contained content, tradition-learned,

(n. d.)   *Copy-text: WS   Collated states: SV* (*A*)

Not otherwise recorded: MG's note is not signalled in *A*. There is a second note in *A* on
the Horse-stinger (line 43) as 'the dragonfly, also called "the devil's darning needle",
from the way it "darns" the air in flight.'

15 seen,] ~ *A*   **21** hung!] ~; *A*   **24** logs] slabs *A*   **31** save] till *A*
32.1 ˢ* . . . *] *Om. A*   **33** we] ~, *A*

[1] Buzzing, humming.   [2] Patches of shade.
[3] A metal bob attached to the end of a plumbline, used to determine perpendicularity.
[4] Portmanteau word from slamming and lumbering.

Dwelt in a world whose olden flame   35
    Beside our humbler hearth-fire burned;
So Roland to the Dark Tower came;
    There Ilium fell;
    There Merlin wove his spell;
There was proclaimed proud Iseult's fame.[5]   40

And when Spring brought the buttercup,
    And o'er the rushy coolamons[6] the grey
"Horse-stinger" poised in shining mail,
    Or like a spear sped on away,
Then as crusaders bold we flew,   45
    Banner and cross,
    A straddled stick for horse,
That haughty paynim[7] to pursue.

And in still nights, when o'er the Bush
    The moon moved like a ship that no man's hand   50
Drave on, as mystic, wonderful,
    Unshadowed she shadowed the land,
Held there enthralled, we watched her go,
    Racing the cloud,
    Or, calm and ample-prowed,   55
Sail lone, and white as the white snow.

There, the lamp lit, came bumbling in
    The beetle upward veering toward the height;
And a little moth, like a knot
    Of silk, slew itself in the light;   60

36 burned;] ~. *A*   38 fell;] ~, *A*   39 spell;] ~, *A*   40 There was proclaimed]
And there was told *A*   41 Spring] spring *A*   42 rushy] reedy *A*   43 "Horse-
stinger"] ~ *A*   44 on] far *A*   48 That] Some *A*   49 in] on *A*   Bush] bush *A*
54 cloud,] ~; *A*

---

[5] References are to the romantic narratives of Robert Browning's 'Childe Roland
to the Dark Tower Came' (*Men and Women*, 1855), Homer's *Iliad* and Sir Thomas
Malory's *Morte Darthur* (*c.* 1470), which includes the stories of the wizard Merlin and
the doomed lovers Tristan and Iseult. Cf. childhood reading and make-believe games
in G12, H69 and I97.
[6] From Kamilaroi *kuluman* (Ridley) or *gulaman* (Dixon): a wooden vessel for carrying
water, by extension a small lake or waterhole; cf. K4 author's note for line 12.
[7] Pagan.

While in the dark outside, the oak
  Stood sentinel,
  And in the sky's deep well
Star to star calling woke . . .

Odorous of pine is the hill,   65
  And the years nor lessen nor take away
That scent, nor the hush on the air
  Of a noon on a summer's day.
Beautiful is Malebo,
  Although   70
  Never again I go
Where the warm winds o'er it blow.

* A hill near Wagga Wagga.

64 woke . . .] ~. *A*   n1 A] Malebo: a *A*

131   THE GORDON FOX

We found the fox, we found the fox,
We found the fox at Dingley Dell![1]
I heard the hounds tongue out their cry,
I heard the huntsman pounding by,
I heard the heathcock rise and fly,   5
    As we went hunting the fox!
    As we went hunting the fox!
      The fox! The fox!

Away! Away! The fox! Away!
The fox we hunt at Dingley Dell!   10
The mare extends and pulls her head,
Her eyes are lit, her nostril red,

(n. d.) *Copy-text: WS* *Collated states: Bn*, 19 December 1928, Red Page as THE
GORDON FOX! (*A*)[2]

Not otherwise recorded: The collation for lines 23–4 and 31–2 is identical to 15–16.
4 huntsman] huntsmen *A*   9 Away! Away] ~! away *A*   fox! Away] ~!—away *A*
12 nostril] nostrils *A*

[1] Adam Lindsay Gordon's cottage near Mount Gambier. See also 129 n. 3.

She bites the bit as it were bread—
   As we go hunting the fox!
   As we go hunting the fox!   15
      The fox! The fox!

Jack Filgate lifts and cracks a fence,
And Cawker[3] flings the brush aside;
While o'er the hill, and down the dale,
The hounds and huntsmen string and trail   20
Like wind behind the rusty tail—
   As we go hunting the fox!
   As we go hunting the fox!
      The fox! The fox!

His pads he beats to save his brush,   25
The fox we hunt at Dingley Dell;
Four small round pads that carry him,
O'er hill and scarp, and valley rim,
Beyond the hounds and huntsmen grim—
   As we go hunting the fox!   30
   As we go hunting the fox!
      The fox! The fox!

Hola! Hola! Away! Away!
If lost the fox at Dingley Dell,
The huntsman lifts his glass and cries,   35
"Here's to the fox where'er he lies!
Here's to the hope that never dies!"
   As we go hunting the fox!
   As we go hunting the fox!
      The fox! The fox!   40

15–16 As . . . fox! The fox!] *Om. A*   **17** lifts] ~, *A*   **19** hill,] ~ *A*   dale,] ~ *A*
21 tail—] ~, *A*   **25** beats] heats *A*   brush] mask *A*   **27** small round] little *A*
that] to *A*   him,] ~ *A*   **28** scarp,] ~ *A*   rim,] ~ *A*   **33** Away! Away!] ~! ~!
. . . . *A*   **37** dies!"] ~"— *A*

[2] Printed in *Bn* to support MG's suggestion that the newly-formed FAW should 'make a new song every year in remembrance of the past, or in celebration of the present . . . It is written in memory of Gordon. Filgate and Cawker were friends of his; he was a rider, and if there had been a fox at Dingley Dell he could not have helped hunting it. If there were no fox, then that was the fault of the times and not of Gordon.'
[3] See I29 n. 6.

I32 THE WILD HORSES

Let the dark mountain shake to the thunder
  Where the wild horses trample the fern,
Let the deep vales re-echo and wonder,
    When, like an eddy, they circle and turn!
      Watch the lithe motion   5
      Run free as an ocean,
Never has man laid a hand on a head;
      Never a halter
      Has bid a step falter,
Never a crest bent down to be led!   10

Mark, in their starting, the pride of their bearing!
  Swift wheel the leaders, each in his place;
Snorting, they stare at us, timid and daring,
    Ere with a whirl they are off at a race.
      O, the wild sally,   15
      As, down through the valley,
Turn they again to the mountains they know;
      Chased and the chaser
      Outstretched like a racer,
Where, as the wind, unconquered they go!   20

Follow them, hunter, follow and follow—
  Let the heart pound its answering beat—
Over the top, and into the hollow,
    Where the loud echoes awake and repeat!
      On through the timber,   25
      Quick thew and limber,[1]
While the wide nostril drinks deep of the air;

(n. d.)   *Copy-text: WS*   *Collated states: DT*, 2 May 1925, p. 10 (*A*)   *SV* (*B*)
Mackaness1 (*C*)

2 fern,] ~; *A*   **3** wonder,] ~ *A*   **6** ocean,] ~— *A*   **7** head;] ~: *B*   **9** falter,]
~; *A*   **10** led!] ~. *A*   **11** bearing!] ~. *C*   **15** O,] ~ *B*   sally,] ~ *A*
16 through] *Om. A*   **21** follow—] ~! *A*   **23** top,] ~ *A*   hollow,] ~ *A*

[1] Speedy and supple muscle.

Never feet blunder
Where tree and rock sunder,
Never a balk,[2] but its conquest is there.   30

Lift, for your life, where the low logs are lying;
   Swing from the branches, sway from the brush;
Clamber the rocks—the hoof-beats are flying—
   Bend to the withers, and leap for the rush!
      O, the hard panting   35
      For breath that is wanting;
O, the drooped head, and the fallen-in flanks!
      Winded and shaken,
      Yet never o'ertaken,
Hear the shrill leader rally the ranks!   40

What though the pommel scarce keep you from reeling;
   What though the breath be almost a cry;
What though all turn in a dream that is stealing
   Sense from intention and light from the eye—
      Follow them, follow,   45
      By height and by hollow;
Follow them, follow, whatever the course!
      Soon will the wonder
      Die out with the thunder,
Soon will the mountain forget the wild horse.   50

29 sunder,] ~ *A*   **30** balk,] ~ *A*   **32** branches,] ~; *A*   **41** reeling;] ~, *B*
42 cry;] ~, *B*

---

[2] Obstacle, barrier.

I33   PEJAR CREEK[1]

Deep in the meadow grass
   Easy stand the cattle,
Lightly lock the young bulls
   In a mimic battle,
Pride gathers with each shock,   5
   Every break and rally—
That's where the Pejar runs,
   Runs like a slip of silver through the valley.

Softly as a thrush sings
   In the morning hushes,   10
Softly sing the waters
   Round the reedy rushes,
Softly at the sand-bar,
   Softly at the sally—
That's where the Pejar runs,   15
   Runs like a slip of silver through the valley.

Where awakes the morning
   To dapple all the hills,
Where the dewdrop, shaken,
   Pendent slides and spills,   20
Where with golden bugles
   Sunset calls reveille—
That's where the Pejar runs,
   Runs like a slip of silver through the valley.

Where the Springtime blossoms   25
   Like a mellow laughter,
Over all the grasses,
   Over ridge and rafter,

(n. d.)   *Copy-text: WS   Collated states: DT*, 5 September 1925, p. 10 as PEJAR CREEK
(GOULBURN) (*A*)   *SV* (*B*)   Mackaness1 (*C*)

2 cattle,] ~; *A*   **4** battle,] ~; *A*   **12** rushes,] ~; *A*   **17** Where] When *B*
18 hills,] ~; *A*   **19** the] *Om. C*   **20** Pendent slides] Pendant runs *A*   spills,]
~; *A*   **25** Springtime] springtime *A B*   **28** rafter,] ~. *A*

[1] The Pejar, like the Wollondilly (line 34, and see F58), rises in the mountains w. of

Over all the tree-tops,
    Down each ferny valley—   30
That's where the Pejar runs,
    Runs like a slip of silver through the valley.

Where the Pejar rises
    Springs the Wollondilly,
Twinned upon the mountains   35
    Babbling brook and ghyllie;[2]
Where the bridge-heads rumble
    Side by side they dally—
Out where the Pejar runs,
    Runs like a slip of silver through the valley.   40

30 valley] alley *A B*   **34** Springs] Runs *A*   **35** mountains] ~, *A*   **37** the]
their *A*   rumble] ~, *A B*

Goulburn. Both now run into the Pejar Dam, built 1980. Reed glosses the Aboriginal
name as 'water trickling over stone'.

[2] Variant spelling of *gill*, a small stream or rivulet. Cf. F27 line 1.

I34   AS THE BEAUTY OF SHIPS

Turn back ye ever passing hours! Once more
    A while bid Time in armistice to stand,
As when the moon her native course forebore
    And Gideon heard the chosen voice command![1]
        O turn again, ye hasting hours,   5
            And, to the fields restoring,
        Re-clothe with hue and scent the flowers,
            The sun to be adoring.

                                          [*cont. overleaf*

(n. d.)   *Copy-text: WS   Collated states: SV* (*A*)[2]

1 back] ~, *A*   **2** Time] time *A*   **3** forebore] ~, *A*   **4** chosen] mighty *A*
7 Re-clothe] Reclothe *A*

[1] Making the moon stand still is one of the exploits not of Gideon (Judges 6. 11–28)
but of Joshua (see Joshua 10. 12–13).
[2] The MS of *SV* sent to Angus & Robertson contained a stanza (its lines 49–56) omitted
in *WS* and marked for deletion for *SV*. They appeared in *SV* at the request of Angus
& Robertson's in-house editor, Beatrice Davis (letter to MG, 9 December 1947): line
49 helped to justify the poem's title. MG's autograph annotation of Davis's letter

Ye have taken away the beauty, the gay
  And gallant colour of the Spring's glad march,   10
That, marshalling on the earth as dawn on day,
    Broke in bright hosting 'neath the heavenly arch!
      Ye have stolen and taken away,
        And there is no restoring,
      Beauty that knew not to delay,   15
        The sun to be adoring.

Once bloomed a groundling herb, the moccasin,
  Which in the Springtime held its slipper up,
As though it asked that fairy feet step in!
    At dawn a dewdrop glinted in its cup,   20
      And there the early bee would stoop,
        And drink in full restoring,
      Ere he his upward way would loop,
        The sun to be adoring.

And once amid the grass, as far as eye   25
  Could reach, the blue-bell raised its slender stalk,
And told its joy to every breeze went by—
    A field of blue, clear as the azure balk[3]
      Where hung the curtains of the sky;
        And there, through distance soaring,   30
      Came the great eagle sailing high,
        The sun to be adoring.

There was a little cushioned flower—who now
  Remembers it?—which on its wiry stem
Raised from the clay a head drought could not bow,   35
    As it, from scant, repaid earth with a gem.
      And there the blue-winged butterfly
        Would light, as though, in-shoring,

---

10 Spring's] spring's *A*   **18** Which] ~, *A*   Springtime] springtime, *A*   up,] ~ *A*
26 blue-bell] bluebell *A*   **27** by—] ~; *A*   **29** sky;] ~! *A*   **31** eagle] ~, *A*

(held in ML 5/1) does not refer specifically to the lines' inclusion, but their appearance in *SV* shows she agreed.

[3] I.e. a space of blue between clouds ('the curtains of the sky', line 29) as in a strip of land left unploughed ('balk').

A ship with sails drew nigh,
    Beauty to be adoring.   40

And trees gave shade; and their foundations held
    Like hands the earth against the call of suns
Whose hot winds blew, or waters torrent-swelled;
    And axes ate as war eats men with guns.
        O, with what scent the ancient trees,   45
            From riper sap outpouring,
        Enriched still air and passing breeze,
            The sun to be adoring!

The hard, devouring destiny of man
    Bids him as chessman take earth's native hoard,   50
His their replace; yet, through what length time span,
    Above his moves sits Nature at the board,
        She, the All-Mother, watching lest
            He, in his hasty scoring,
        Dim the far vision, lose the quest,   55
            Beauty to be adoring.

42 Like . . . earth] The earth, like hands, *A*   43 or] and *A*   torrent-swelled;] ~. *A*
44 And] Then *A*   45 O] Oh *A*   48 adoring!] ~.// In the beauty of ships, and
wind-blown clout,/ Man conquered the earth and furrowed the waste;/ Yet the
conquered was beauty the plough put out/ In the buds turned down in the furrow's
haste./ So never more, through later hours,/ Come again here, restoring,/ Beauty
of sail, beauty of flowers,/ The sun to be adoring. *A*   50 him] ~, *A*   chessman]
~, *A*   51 their] to *A*   53 watching] ~, *A*

I35   THE BUSH-BORN CHILD

I

My mother's terrors wake in me,[1]
    And all her fears are mine;

(n. d.)   *Copy-text:* WS   *Collated states:* DT, 21 November 1925, p. 10 (*A*)   *SV* as THE
BUSH BORN CHILD (*B*)

2 mine;] ~! *A*

[1] In 1866, Donald Cameron's work on the mail run meant that his wife and Mary

She was so young where silence lay
Round her small world, like some great sea
    Which no man's measure might define!   5

There, 'mid the endless range of trees,
    Unspaced both land and time,
Home in the vast a tiny bay,
The unknown spoke in every breeze,
    And made each darkling bough its mime.   10

For in the tree-tops, at the dusk,
    Were formed strange caravans,
Which seemed, though shadow-shaped, to sway
'Neath ancient bales of silk and musk,
    Telling time's history, and man's.   15

There giant horsemen rode, and there
    The elephant's huge bulk
Rolled, mountainous, where the last ray
Of light died out upon the air,
    And left earth darkened like a hulk.   20

Then from the pines came whisperings,
    Low and mysterious;
Complaints night made, and even day
Held half-released! . . . What suffering clings
    Through other's pain asleep in us!   25

II

My mother's terrors wake in me,
    And all her fears are mine!
The hollow night that arching bends

3 lay] ~, *A B*   8 Home] ~, *A*   vast] ~, *A*   bay,] ~— *A*   9 breeze,] ~ *A*
10 mime] mine *B*   11 For] ~, *B*   tree-tops,] ~ *A*   dusk,] ~ *B*   12 Were
formed] She saw *A*   13 Which] ~, *A*   seemed . . . shadow-shaped,] shadow-
shaped, yet seemed *A*   14 'Neath ancient] Beneath the *A*   musk,] ~ *A*
15 Telling] That speak *A*   18 Rolled,] Rose, *A*   ~ *B*   where] as *B*   19 air,]
~ *A*   24 suffering] suff'ring *A*   25 other's] others' *A B*

(b. 1865) were often alone in an isolated two-room slab hut at Red Bank, near Crookwell:
here, this period is run together with the earlier pregnancy.

Above the earth, dark, though we see
   The stars that down upon us shine,   30

Seemed but to emphasise how small
   In its pavilion,
How lone where its grey curtain ends
Folded her round, was she whose call
   Broke on the boundless and was gone.   35

Yet there love built its house for her,
   And there with hovering wings
Life poised and smiled—who never lends
Save with the usury of a spur
   Upon each gift of joy he brings.   40

Now, as beneath her heart she bore—
   Me—her unconscious child,
So in my heart, while time ascends,
Sounds the deep spaces' murmuring roar,
   Shudder the tremors of the wild.   45

My mother's terrors wake in me,
And all her fears are mine.

31 emphasise] emphasize B   33 curtain ends] curtain-/ ends A   curtain-ends B
41 bore—] ~, B

I36   THE DEEP WATER

PANNAMOONA[1]

There is a spot,
And though my eyes may not
Upon it look again,
Yet would my full heart carry it,
As it were fain to marry it   5
With all things held in tender thought.

[1] Cf. Aboriginal names in I22, where 'Pannamoona' is the ocean, and the deep water
is 'Maipoona'.

Swans in its coves
Of quiet lay, and doves
Within its coasts made nest;
And the wild plover of the night,   10
In his unrest waning in flight,
Plaintively uttered there his loves.

And on the hill—
O that it stood there still!—
There was a quandong tree   15
To which the small bush bee would come,
In husbandry busy and dumb,
And of its nectar take his fill.

In blossoming time
The bee! . . . When the sun's climb   20
Spoke summer drawing near,
Then *Yarri** read in its bright fruit
Time o' th' year, and heard the bruit[2]
Of wild fowl crying, "Flight is near"!

And by it grew   25
A currajong, which who
Should see must love, its green
Shade havening the kangaroo,
When the fierce teen[3] of summer drew
From its retreat the very dew.   30

Once long ago,
Where now the wheat fields glow,
We flushed a curlew, where
It kept itself a secret place—
A tiny lair hid where no trace   35
Might to the prowling dingo show.

And there all day,
Only as children may,
We ran and busy played;

[2] Noise or sound conveying rumour or news.
[3] Affliction (archaic; cf. H90 line 7).

Built cubby-houses bough by bough,   40
Our stock-yards made, and with a plough
Of stick furrowed a yard of clay.

Now the flock sheep
Over that country sweep,
And there sleek cattle lie;   45
While never one remembered sound,
Or woodland cry, utters its round
Amid the paths we used to keep.

* The aboriginals. Yarri is a man's name among the tribes.[4]

(n. d.)   *Copy-text: WS   Collated states:* None

[4] Uncorroborated.

I37   THE WOMAN OF FIVE FIELDS

ANZAC DAY

The Woman of Five Fields she stood at the gate,
  And over the gate she leaned;
"For the tall sons who went," she said, "I wait,
  Though the soil they ploughed is gleaned."
She took the bonnet from off her head,   5
And she wept for her sons, her sons long dead.

The Woman of Five Fields looked out where the gulls
  Sailed up and over the sea;
"Long I followed," she said, "the darkened hulls
  That carried my sons from me.   10
They came not back" . . . And she bowed her head,
And wept for the sons, the sons long dead.

The Woman of Five Fields leaned over the gate,
  Her bonnet fell from her hand:

(n. d.)   *Copy-text: WS   Collated states:* DT, 25 April 1927, p. 6 (*A*)   *SV* (*B*)
4 soil] crop *B*   ploughed] sowed *B*   **8** sea;] ~: *A*   **9** said,] ~,. *A*
11 back" . . .] ~." . . . *A*   ~ . . . " *B*

"I loved my sons," she said, "yet, heart elate,   15
    I gave them all to the land:
I gave them all for the land," she said;
"I count them still, and they are not dead."

Then the Woman of Five Fields named, one by one,
    The homes where her sons were born: 20
"I loved them all alike, first son, last son,
    And each grew straight as the corn;
And the homes where they were born," she said,
"I loved . . ." She wrung her hands for her dead.

"My sons made dancing-time of the harvest home   25
    Till they swayed like the myall trees,
And they sang love sweet as the honeycomb,
    And the time of flowers and bees:
That was a long while ago," she said,
"Long ere in Flanders their bones lay dead.   30

"At shearing time, when the sheep were penned, the high
    Clip-clip of the flying shears
Made music as fine as when, passing by,
    Spring speaks and the young grass hears.
That, too, was long, long ago," she said,   35
"Or ever in France their youth lay dead."

Low and softly a far Voice whispering passed:
    "Death could not diminish them;
Now none shall see their glory overcast,
    Their flower fade upon its stem!"   40
Then the Woman of the Five Fields said,
"They died: but Death himself in them is dead."

And she said, "I weep but mother's tears: my sons
    Were my sons, bone of my bone:

16 land:] ~. *A*   18 "I *A*] ~ *X*   are] *are A*   20 born:] ~; *B*   24 loved . . .]
~. . . . *A*   25 harvest home] harvest-/ home *A*   26 myall trees] myall-trees *B*
28 bees:] ~. *A*   31 "At] ~ *A*   33 fine] sweet *A*   passing by] drawing nigh *B*
38 them;] ~. *A*   42 Death] death *A*   43 tears:] ~; *A*   44 bone:] ~; *A*

And, though in my heart I heard the guns,   45
    They went—and I made no moan."
She took her bonnet up in her hand;
Its silken folds hung over the land.

47 hand;] ~: *A*

138 "LEST WE FORGET"[1]

I heard the roll of the kettledrum beat,
    Rat-a-tan, rat-a-tan-tan, tan!
It sounded as though in a far-off street,
An empty, hollow, and echoing street,
    Like some lone place in the heart of a man.   5
And all on the air, as it throbbed and beat,
    The rap of the little drum said,
"Come out, all ye ghosts of the world, and meet;
    Come out and follow me, Shades of the Dead!"

So haunting and strange was the call, it seemed   10
    Like a note in the mind half-heard;
Yet never a man in his dark place dreamed,
But down where he slumbered the quick notes streamed,
    Till the dust of the grey flesh waked and stirred;
And as round by round ran the rhythmed repeat,   15

(n. d.)   *Copy-text: WS   Collated states: DT*, 26 March 1927, p. 6 (*A*)   *SV* (*B*)

Not otherwise recorded: The collation for lines 18, 26, 44, 53 and 62 is identical to 9.
2 Rat-a-tan] Ratatan *A*   rat-a-tan-tan, tan] rata-tan-tan, tan *A*   rat-a-tan-tan-
tan *B*   **7** rap] lilt *B*   **8** out,] ~ *B*   world,] ~ *A B*   **9** Come] "~ *A*
10 call,] ~ *A*   **13** But] ~, *A*   slumbered] ~, *A*   **14** stirred;] ~. *A*   **15** And]
~, *A B*   by round] ~ ~, *A*

---

[1] Originally in 'Recessional' by Rudyard Kipling (1865–1936), written for Jubilee Day
1898, the phrase had empire-wide significance. So MG refers in succession to World
War I battles in Egypt, the Middle East and France; the Scots in the Crimean War
(1853–56); the Irish contingents of both the War of Austrian Succession (1741–48)
and Wellington's Spanish campaigns during the Napoleonic Wars (1808–14); and
the sailors of Drake's naval victory over the Armada (1588). Australian participation
in the Gallipoli campaign of World War I completes the sequence. See also Z8 for an
Army of the Dead.

The call of the little drum said,
"Come out, ye ghosts of the war, and meet;
   Come out and follow me, Shades of the Dead!"

Loud, as from the turn of a street, it came,
   Loud as from the turn of a street,   20
The rattle of the sticks it leapt like flame,
And each rap-tap-tap was a dead man's name;[2]
The dead men rose and gathered for the meet,
   As the kettledrum rip-rap said,
"Come out of your graves, O men, like the wheat;   25
   Come out and follow me, Shades of the Dead!"

All up from the dark, then, the dead men marched,
   They gathered like a soundless wind;
Like locusts they came from where the sand parched,
And the sun burned red, and the dust storm arched,   30
   And the curtains of heaven fall down unpinned;
And, as each one came in his old array,
   The roll of the kettledrum said,
"Fall in, ye ghosts of the dust, as I play:
   Fall in, and follow me, Shades of the Dead!"   35

They came from the South, and the warm brown lands,
   Where the earth ran thick with their blood,
They came from the North, where the iron ice stands,
And the guns belched fire from their frost-bound hands,
   And the slow Somme covered their eyes with mud;   40
From out of their holes in the earth they came,
   They met as the kettledrum said,
"Was it for gold, or was it for a Name?
   Come out and follow me, Shades of the Dead!"

---

16 call] lilt *B*   **19** street,] ~ *A B*   **23** rose] ~, *A*   **27** dark,] ~ *A B*   then,] there *A* ~ *B*   marched,] rose; *A*   **29** parched] glows *A*   **30** burned] burns *A* red,] ~ *B*   dust storm arched] Khamsin blows *A*   **31** unpinned;] ~. *A* **34** play:] ~; *A*   **35** Fall] "~ *A*   **36** South] south *B*   warm] ~, *A*   **37** thick] red *A*   **38** North] north *B*   **40** mud;] ~. *A*   **41** came,] ~; *A*   **42** met] ~, *A*

[2] If stanza 3 is to agree in rhyme pattern and form with the other nine-line stanzas, a line is missing here, but there is no MS extant to provide it.

Then forth from the host stepped a kilted man,   45
    And his pipes played an old, old lay:
"We'll hae nane but Hielan' bonnets!" it ran,
    And it told the tale of a dark redan,[3]
        And the Heights of Alma won in a day.
And all through the lilt of the Highland air   50
    The cry of the kettledrum said,
"Lest their names should perish, and no man care,
    Come out and follow me, Shades of the Dead!"

Swift came the Wild Geese,[4] flying thick as rain,
    Back from the countries of the world;   55
O'Donnell, and O'Ruark, Shea, and Lehane,
    Singing out of France, singing out of Spain,
        The colours that they carried never furled.
There, as they gathered—regiment, platoon—
    The ruffle of the drumsticks said,   60
"Who would forget the Risin' of the Moon?[5]
    Come ye and follow me, Shades of the Dead!"

Now from the caverns of the sea there rose
    The roll of another drum-beat;
Its challenge rang out (O, the long tide knows!)   65
Till over the deep spake a Voice, "Who Goes?"
    And back came the answer, "The Dead of the Fleet!"
Loud called the drum of the Men of Devon,[6]
    As the rip of the little drum said,

---

46 lay:] ~, *A B*   **47** hae] ha'e *B*   **48** redan *A*] Redan *X*   **50** And] ~, *B*   air]
~, *B*   **51** cry] note *B*   **54** Swift] Then *A*   **56** O'Donnell] O'Donnel *A*
Shea,] ~ *A*   **57** O'Shea *B*   **57** Spain,] ~. *A*   **58** colours] colors *A*   **61** Risin']
risin' *A*   **63** Now] Then *A*   **65** O] Oh *A B*   **67** "The . . . Fleet!"] *"The Dead
of the Fleet!" B*   **68** Loud] Then *A*   of the] of *B*

---

[3] A form of ground fortification.
[4] First used of those eighteenth-century Irish troops who, during the War of Austrian
Succession, fought on both sides (for the Anglo–Dutch alliance or for the French). With
its alternative form 'the grey geese', it later came to be used generally for all the Irish
who left their homeland during the long period of Irish emigration (cf. W. B. Yeats,
'September 1913'). See also F24.   [5] See H5 n. 4.
[6] Francis Drake (*c.* 1540–96) came from the s.w. county of Devon, as did most of his
sailors.

"O, come ye from hell, or come ye from heaven,   70
    Rise up and follow me, Shades of the Dead!"

Though the earth was thick with the ghosts of men,
    Yet the kettledrum made no stay;
Boomeranged each stroke with the sound of ten,
As ripped through the air another call then,   75
    And Australia answered it, "Suvla Bay!"[7]
Then the drums of the world beat up, beat on,
    And the drums of the whole world said,
"We have remembered you, ye who are gone;
    We have remembered you, O ye dead!"   80

70 O,] Oh, *A*   ~ *B*   **71** Rise] "~ *A*   **72** Though] Then *A*   **73** Yet] But *A*
80 We] "~ *A*

[7] On the ill-fated Gallipoli campaign, which saw 27,000 Australian casualties, as well as massive New Zealand, French and British losses, see C38 n. 1. Suvla Bay and Anzac Cove were the two sites of the final withdrawal of some 80,000 Anzac and Allied troops in December 1915.

I39   A CHANT OF ANZAC

The Lord shall deliver us from our foes,[1]
    He shall scatter them in His might;
They shall be consumed as consume the snows
    When the sun rides out in the height.

They shall not behold the face of the sun—   5
    They shall be put out; and the dark
Shall write their day as a course that is run
    Where the runner knows not the mark.

(n. d.)   *Copy-text: WS   Collated states: DT*, 24 April 1926, p. 19 (*A*)

Not otherwise recorded: A places a stanza break between lines 9 and 10, not 8 and 9, but MG marks this as a typographical error in its print clipping held in ML 5/1.
3 snows] ~, *A*   **5** sun—] ~. *A*

[1] The poem conflates Old Testament passages such as: Ezekiel 14. 23, 'I will deliver my people out of your hand'; Hosea 10. 8, 'and they shall say to the mountains, Cover us'; Job 18. 5–6, 'the light of the wicked shall be put out, and the spark of his fire shall

The arm of the Lord shall be our right arm;
    In it we shall know no decay;   10
Nor wounds shall affright, nor terrors alarm,
    Nor death in his coming dismay.

We shall not fear the dark, for the Lord
    Shall be our Captain and our Light;
To us will He give the strength of His sword,   15
    Till the foe run scattered in flight.

From the terror that pursues them they shall cry
    To the mountains to cover them;
But from them even the waters shall fly,
    And the tree forbid them its stem.   20

The Lord shall deliver us from our foes;
    They shall be as shadows that pass;
They shall run as the leaves that the storm wind blows,
    And break as a strickle² of grass.

---

16 run] ~, *A*   **17** cry] ~, *A*   **19** But] ~, *A*   them] ~, *A*

not shine. The light shall be dark in his tabernacle, and his candle shall be put out with him'; and Psalm 9. 5, 'thou hast destroyed the wicked, thou hast put out their name for ever and ever'.

² Confuses *strick* (a bundle of broken hemp, jute or grass) with *strickle*, meaning a piece of flat wood used to strike off surplus grain at the rim of a measure.

140   AUSTRALIA

Here in the leisure
    Of this hour I write,
Who once must seize the hasty measure¹
    In its flight.

Now may I, dreaming,   5
    Dip into the deep,
And trawl the thought, that still broods teeming,
    From its sleep.

¹ Melody or rhythm.

O thou, my country,
    We, who were too young   10
To praise thee singing as the wintry
    Lands are sung,

Now leave the callow
    Rhythms of youth behind,
And sound thee from the ripened fallow   15
    Of the mind.

We were so young we
    Knew thee not, and feared
The fuller note we might have sung thee,
    And endeared.   20

And thou wast stranger,
    Too; where custom clung,
Thought lowly born in history's manger,
    O unsung!

(n. d.) *Copy-text: WS   Collated states: SMH*, 14 April 1928, p. 13 (*A*)   *SV* as THIS
AUSTRALIA (*B*)

9 O] And *A*   country,] ~! *A*   **10** We,] ~ *A*   **11** thee singing] ~, ~, *A*
15 sound] sing *A*   **16** mind.] ~! *A*   **19** sung] lent *B*   thee,] ~ *A*
20 endeared.] ~: *A*   **22** Too;] ~, *A*   where custom clung,] and young—how
young!— *A*   **23** Thought] ~—*A*

141   THE FIRST-FOOTERS

Whose be these bearded faces,
    And whose these weathered hands,
Which, from the outer spaces,
    Stand as on border lands?
Whose be these forms that gather,   5
    Eager and yet retreating,
Set to depart, yet loth
    In wistfulness of meeting?

These are the rude first-footers,
    Who, ere a road was marked,   10

Fiercely, and as free-booters,
    Took what no hand had clerked;
These are the men, who, grasping,
    Seized as the eyes commanded;
Nameless they are, and yet   15
    They made the land, fore-handed.

Hell had no power to hold them,
    These ghosts for Hades named;
Lucifer first enrolled them,
    Left them the still untamed;   20
Hither they came, earth-wandering,
    As beasts enchained—defiant—
Who broke their chains, as men,
    And faced the wild, reliant.[1]

They were the dread beleaguered,   25
    They were the black-defamed,
Who, though their gaunt frames meagred,[2]
    Mocked at what law acclaimed;
Ships held them not, nor prison,
    Nor stormy seas affrighted;   30
Death-driven they deemed death but
    A camp with fire unlighted.

Savage was all their going;
    Theirs was a brutal prime;
Dark are their faces showing,   35
    Yet darker still their time;
Dark were their deeds, but, hark ye,
    A road they made before us,
They were the pioneers,
    We follow as the chorus.   40

(n. d.)   *Copy-text: WS   Collated states: SV (A)*

15 and yet] ~, ~, *A*   **25** beleaguered *A*] beleaguer *X*   **31** Death-driven] ~, *A*

---

[1] Convicts permanently banished from England but free to take up land in the Australian colonies after the completion of their sentence. Until the 1830s land was often taken by squatting, i.e. occupying it without licence (lines 9–14).
[2] Grew thin.

142   THE LEGISLATORS

These are the men whom peace obeys,
　　War answers to their call;
Dynasties count through them their days,
　　And nations rise and fall.

And they are fellow-men, no more　　　　　　5
　　Than we, who give them power
To stand upon a storied floor,[1]
　　And flourish for an hour.

Winds out of far eternities
　　Beat on us as we go;　　　　　　　　10
Fallen are those, and risen these,
　　And that is all we know.

(n. d.)　*Copy-text: WS　Collated states: DT*, 31 July 1925, p. 6 (*A*)　*SV* (*B*)
5 And they are] They are but *A*　　fellow-men,] ~— *A*　　**6** we,] ~ *A B*　　**8** hour.]
~! *A*　　**11** those,] ~ *A*

[1] A historic place (i.e. the floor of Parliament).

143   THE GREAT NAVIGATORS

From whence do ye come, O ye rovers,
　　Who bear in your hands the gifts of the proved,
In your eyes, as in old sea-lovers,
　　The mariner's inlook, slow to be moved?
Say who ye are, ye men of eagle feature,　　　5
　　And the mien of those long brooding on a dream?
O, surely ye have made the deep your creature,
　　And it hath acknowledged you o'er it supreme!

Wayfarers we, burdened unknowing,
　　From darkness drawn to the traverse of life;　　10
We are seed of an ancient sowing,
　　Fashioned for conquest, and measured for strife.

For life hath endued us with fullness of stature,
    And the might, though we fall, to rise and redeem;
We are the passionate firstborn of nature,   15
    Time-marked, and time-held to be children of dream.

Ere we were born, lapped in a seeming,
    E'en as the dumb-lipped we heard the sea's call;
Saw in the dark a strange star gleaming,
    Stirred to the pull of the tide in its fall;   20
We felt in the cradle the sea's deep hollow,
    And we saw in a rushlight a Pharos[1] gleam;
The cry of the waters called us to follow;
    We rose and we answered it, children of dream.

They name us Columbus, Balboa,   25
    Magellan, di Gama;[2] we trod the wave
In ships little more than a proa;[3]
    Yet beaten of winds, and of storms that drave,
Like ravens of Haakon, like eagles of Rollo,[4]
    From terror of rock, and the whirlpool's scream,   30
Back from the deep we returned as the swallow,
    With the seas of the world made ours by a dream.

(n. d.)   *Copy-text: WS*   *Collated states:* None

[1] Lighthouse: from the island Pharos, near Alexandria, site of the tower lighthouse listed among the Seven Wonders of the Ancient World.
[2] Christopher Columbus (1451–1506) and Vasco Núñez de Balboa (1475–1519) explored the New World on behalf of Spain, and Ferdinand Magellan (1480–1521) and Vasco da Gama (1469–1521) on behalf of Portugal. Cf. H56, H60 and M26.
[3] Small sailing-boat of the type used in the Malay archipelago.
[4] The raven and the eagle were insignia of the Viking seafarers of Norway and Denmark. Haakon IV of Norway (1204–63) conquered Iceland and Greenland, but was defeated by Alexander III of Scotland in 1263. Rollo, ancestor of William the Conqueror, sailed his ships up the Seine as far as Rouen and later besieged Paris before becoming the first Duke of Normandy.

144   THE OLD PORT OF SYDNEY
A BALLAD

"Now who be you, my foreign man,
      Who stand so still and stare,
   Where the streets are full of busy feet,
      And the houses rise in air?

"Who be you that ye look so long,   5
      Like a man in a manner lost,
   With your skin so brown, and your eyes so bright,
      And your locks like the white, white frost?"

He turned him round, that stranger man,
      And he looked at him who spoke;   10
"I am one who wandered far," said he,
      "And my good ship was the oak;

"My good ship was the oak," said he,
      "But her sails went one by one,
   Till never a shroud was left," said he,   15
      "And her masts were all undone.

"Her masts were all undone," said he,
      "And yet did the good ship stand,
   And I steered her course by the Southern Cross,
      And I sought for my own dear land.   20

"O wanner and wanner grew the men,
      The steersman died at the wheel,
   The bo'sun flung himself to the waves,
      Where the waters spun like a reel,

"But I trimmed the ship, and I kept the course,   25
      Though the seas ran mountains high;
   Like a man in a dream I turned the spoke,
      As the days and the nights went by.

"And I sailed till I came to the narrow strait,
      And the two Heads great and bold;   30

But the very planks were all I held,
    And the hulk was naught but a hold.

"I have come to the place and the place is strange![1]
    And I ask you now," said he,
"To tell me here, as I wander lost,   35
    How my own land this can be!"

"Nay," said the other, "but this is your land!"
    And he took him and showed him where
The city went down, by step and step,
    To the sea as it were by a stair;   40

He took him and showed him the water-leap
    Where the sea-wall binds the sea,
And the iron ships of every land
    Lie in like sheep at the knee;

He showed him the tide-mark at the Fort,   45
    And the Pinchgut[2] light that shows,
Like a star in the black, black heart of night,
    When the storm in a tempest blows.

He measured the depth of the Plimsoll mark,[3]
    Where the liners bask at ease,   50
And he pointed the House-flags[4] flaunting out
    By the great and the lesser quays.

"Nay then, nay then," said the old man, then,
    "When Flinders sailed,"[5] said he,
"Never a one of these things ye show   55
    Could any man show to me.

[1] Details of the voyage recall Samuel Taylor Coleridge's 'Rime of the Ancient Mariner' (1798), but returning to find all changed is more akin to the experience in Washington Irving's 'Rip Van Winkle' (1820).
[2] Small island in Sydney Harbour, used in early times for punitive isolation of convicts. Fort Denison was erected there in 1829.
[3] Mark or line on British merchant ships, showing the depth to which they may be submerged when loaded.
[4] Flags of the commercial house or line to which a merchant ship belongs.
[5] Matthew Flinders (1774–1814) circumnavigated Van Diemen's Land in the *Norfolk* in 1798 and Australia in the *Investigator* (1801–02).

"And my heart is asking for mine own land,
    Is hungry for things I knew;
For the place where the waves ran up on the sand,
    And the green grass white with the dew;   60

"For the dip where a little stream ran down,
    And the wind was a scented breeze,
Where only the rocks stood bare and brown,
    For the land was a land of trees!"

"Nay!" said the other, "But this is your land,   65
    And none ever fairer knew! . . ."
But the old man asked for his ship of wood,
    And the coast where the tall trees grew.

(n. d.)   *Copy-text: WS   Collated states:* None

BOOK II: *OF BEAUTY THAT IS PRAISE*

145   THE SINGER

I, a poor singer, send out song
   In flights upon the air,
All homely as a sparrow throng
   In brown and hodden[1] wear.

And yet, where others stand, and round   5
   Their melodies of worth,
How oft I hear, in their full sound,
   Some song asked me for birth!

We all have, deep within us set,
   Chords that we never know,   10
Till horns, in others' hunting met,
   Winding about us blow.

(n. d.)   *Copy-text: WS   Collated states: DT*, 7 June 1926, p. 4 (*A*)   *SV* (*B*)
3 All] And *A*   throng] ~, *A*   **5** stand] sing *A*   **7** hear,] ~ *A*   **9** have,] ~ *A*
12 us] ~, *A*

[1] Coarse undyed grey woollen cloth: cf. E5 and E91.

146   I WHO NO BEAUTY HAD

I who no beauty had
   Loved it alway,
Sought it with wondering,
   Drank its allay.[1]

The wilderness showed me   5
   Beauty unshamed—
Moons at the scimitar,
   Planets that flamed;

[1] I.e. its capacity to allay my thirst for beauty.

Showed—and I lived!—where the
     Stars, at the Horn,[2]   10
Shone as though thundered, there,
     Light as first born.

Bred to one sensitive
     Gift of clay,
I, who no beauty had,   15
     Loved it alway.

(n. d.)   *Copy-text: WS   Collated states:* None

[2] Cape Horn, the notoriously stormy southernmost tip of South America.

147   OF BEAUTY THAT IS PRAISE

O Beauty that is praise,
That speaks the Eternal, and declares His name,
How shall a man, whose days are brief as flame,
Know thee, and understand?

Thou dost not end! Though man   5
Must count his fleeting hours, and pass while still
He names his tiny span, thy cisterns fill,
Thy living tree still flowers.

Ambition falls with breath,
The throne's high tapestry grows dim—defined   10
To dust; but thou, though death on all else bind
Decay, he mars not thee!

(n. d.)   *Copy-text: WS   Collated states:* None

148   BEAUTY WITHOUT A PEER

Beauty without a peer
     Hath me in thrall;
Not life, itself, more near
     Standeth, withal.

Though at the sere   5
  Its golden leaf may fall,
Yet shall be stayed the shear:
  Love keepeth all.

Who hath known beauty where
  Its look is seen,   10
A kingdom hath, whate'er
  His lot hath been!

Ah! through the air
  One cometh like a queen,
Beauty her stair,   15
  My heart and hers, between.

(n. d.)   *Copy-text: WS*   *Collated states:* None

I49   SILK OF THE SUNLIGHT

Put away beauty,
  Bury it deep,
Never to waken
  Out of its sleep!

Gold of her hair and   5
  Rose of her skin,
Silk of the sunlight,
  Find their last inn.

Where by the fountain
  Pines her lone bird,   10
What if her spirit
  Whispering stirred?

Silent forever!
  Ah, never more
Will she, impatient   15
  Tap at the door!

[cont. overleaf

(n. d.)   *Copy-text: WS*   *Collated states: SV (A)*   Mackaness1 (B)
3 waken] awaken B

Cold, cold the hand[1]
That led her away:
Housed but in memory
Laughter and play!   20

Gold of her hair and
Rose of her skin,
Out of the darkness
Come no more in.

17 Cold . . . hand] Gold of her hair, and *A*   18 away:] ~; *A*   21 hair] ~, *A*

---

[1] *A*'s variant line 17 is a nonsense attributable to compositor's eye-skip to line 21.

I50   ETERNAL BEAUTY

O, beauty of beauty,
Too long have I lost thee,
Too late have I found thee;*[1]
    In the cry of my heart
    To thee, I must depart.   5

Though thou wast forever
Around and about me,
Blind, blind were my eyes that
    Beheld thee unseeing,
    That knew not thy being.   10

Now wonder enfolds me,
Who tremblingly touch but
Thy mantle, thy sandals—
    The sills where enamber[2]
    The lamps of thy chamber.   15

---

[1] From the *Confessions* of St Augustine of Hippo (AD 354–430): 'Late have I loved you, O Beauty ever ancient, ever new, late have I loved you! You were within me, but I was outside, and it was there that I searched for you. In my unloveliness I plunged into the lovely things which you created. You were with me, but I was not with you. Created things kept me from you; yet if they had not been in you they would have not been at all.'   [2] Perfume – as if by ambergris, a scented wax-like resin.

My heart I have set at
Thy hands for an altar,
O beauty of beauty,
   Where, who hath perceived thee,
   He hath received thee.   20

O joy of perception!
O glory of knowing!
Here as a sheaf, as a
   Bowed down stem of the wheat,
   I kneel at thy feet.   25

Too long have I lost thee,
Too late have I found thee,
O beauty of beauty;
   In the cry of my heart
   To thee, I must depart.   30

* Saint Augustine.

(n. d.)   *Copy-text: WS   Collated states:* None

151   I SAW THE NEW MOON IN THE SKY

Death hath its beauty, too:
   Even though it were but
     That the pale mirror knew
   When the proud eyes lay shut.
Yet of that beauty life shall comfort take,   5
Lest of its own despair the heart should break.

But now—ere it was dawn—
   I saw the moon, a thread
Of silver sharply drawn
   In curve; and she was dead.   10
But O, the beauty of that dead world in
That place wherein all beauty dwelleth kin!

[cont. overleaf

(19 April 1928)   *Copy-text: WS   Collated states: SV (A)*
1 too:] ~, *A*   3 the pale] which the *A*   11 O,] ~ *A*

. . . I saw the new moon in the sky, and I
Was stunned alive to know that beauty could not die.

13 ^s. . . I] ~ *A*

I5₂   ON A DEAD GIRL

Beauty was here that now is gone away;
Short, short the time it made its stay!
   It was a morn in Summer,
     It was the Spring's delight;
   Death came,—O, the black comer!—   5
     And brought the night.

All we who have known beauty, how we weep
To see it perish in a sleep!
   There the dropped lids deny us,
     E'en as we seek the eyes,   10
   That now—so strange!—look by us
     In cold surprise.

Who would believe that she could go away—
Could die so soon! But yesterday
   She bloomed, in her bright gladness,   15
     A full bud on life's tree;
   Then, as we watched in sadness,
     Death named his fee.

Now, though we call to her, slipped are the bonds
That held between, for the slim hands   20
   No more reach out enfolding,
     Palm laid on palm, as though
   Life spake in that close holding,
     And would not go!

And all love's commerce ends where once the gay   25
Glad laugh made music of the day,
   For, from the inward altar
     Of the spirit, the heart

That knew not how to falter,
   Turned to depart.   30

Now none shall remember beauty and dream
To make of it love's happy theme,
   For, though the dawn came splendid,
     Calling us to its praise,
   Here is the glory ended,   35
     Muted the phrase.

Beauty was here that now is gone away;
How short the time it made its stay!

(n. d.)   *Copy-text: WS*   *Collated states:* None

153   THE LOVER OF BEAUTY

I have been drunken on beauty as a bee on a flower;
Now beauty is slipping away with each passionate hour!
How shall I stay beauty, who cannot stay time,
Though it stand at the turn of its last full prime?
   I have loved beauty . . .   5
God grant I may sing, ere fallen to rust,
The red of the rose, the glory of dust.

(n. d.)   *Copy-text: WS*   *Collated states:* None

154   WINTER IN HYDE PARK

The sun moves north;[1] too swift
   His flight away,
And coldly mourns the wind
   The shortened day!

High on a naked bough,   5
   Half comatose,

[1] I.e. towards its winter solstice at the Tropic of Cancer.

The hungry sparrows sit
　　Huddled up close.

Yet from a ruffled breast
　　There slips a thin   10
Lost note, which, lone as life
　　That finds no kin,

Dies mateless out; for there
　　The frost-chilled ear,
Unkeyed, tunes not such sounds   15
　　To hold and hear.

Bare are the distant trees;
　　No butterfly,
To tell us of Spring, comes
　　Fluttering by;   20

But the casemoth's basket
　　Swings to and fro,
Where the eucalypt leaves
　　Hang green and low.

No passionate scent now   25
　　Calls to the bees;
The sap is asleep in
　　The poplar trees;

For Winter is come with
　　His cold, cold breath;   30
Yet in golden beauty
　　The leaves meet death.

(n. d.)   *Copy-text: WS   Collated states: SV (A)*

19 Spring] spring *A*   **28** poplar trees] poplar-trees *A*   **29** Winter] winter *A*

I55   SPRING SONG

Let the air be clamorous,
  Bid all the wild to sing,
Beauty upon the earth
  Is wed to Spring.

Now will flowers breed awake,   5
  And the young leaf bud out,
And every bush echo
  The plover's shout;

The pee-wee will cry *kling-klang*,
  Klirry-klang! and again   10
Will the brolgas gather
  And dance like men;

There will be gladness abroad,
  For in every hill
The thrid[1] of the cicad's   15
  Jews-harp[2] will thrill;

The sun-worshipping crickets
  Will leap high in the grass,
And the jet of their wings
  Will shine like glass!   20

When all things a marriage song
  Make and joyfully sing
Of beauty to earth come,
  Briding the Spring,

I, too, will a marriage sing,   25
  Humbly as dust, yet proud,
For over love's down-bent
  Head I have bowed.

(n. d.)   *Copy-text: WS   Collated states:* None

---

[1] Obsolete spelling of *thread*.
[2] Musical instrument with a piercing note: see F122 n. 3.

I56   THE SONG OF THE FURROW

Who shall with joy declare the night
        As he, who, from his toil,
Stretcheth his arms of might
        Where he tilleth the soil?

Though his hours run out on their tide   5
        With as even a strain,
Where the muscles abide,
        As a team on the chain,[1]

Yet he flingeth aside the plough,
        Clear of the furrow's rough,   10
And he lifteth his brow,
        Crying, It is enough!

For the day's work proveth his best;[2]
        And at night he turneth,
A man an-hungered for rest,   15
        Where the hearth-fire burneth.

(n. d.)   *Copy-text: WS   Collated states: AinA* (March 1930), n. p. (*A*)   *SV* (*B*)
Not otherwise recorded: A's text is in italics throughout.
3 Stretcheth] Stretches *B*   might] *might, A*   *4* Where] As *B*   *4* tilleth] breaks
up *B*   *8* the] a *B*   chain,] *chain. A*   *9* Yet . . . aside] He shall fling on its side *B*
10 furrow's] *furrows A*   *11* And he lifteth] And, in lifting *B*   *12* Crying] Will
cry *B*   It] *it A*   "~ *B*   *12* enough!] ~!" *B*   *13* proveth] asks of *B*   *13* best;]
~, *B*   *14* And] Till *B*   *14* night] evening *B*   *14* turneth] turns *B*
16 burneth] burns *B*

[1] The chained team pulling a bullock wagon.
[2] Tests and demonstrates his best qualities or efforts: cf. entry for line 13.

I57   FIVE SONS SHE HAD

Old Granny on the hill,
As she sweeps with a will,

(n. d.)   *Copy-text: WS   Collated states: Wr*, 7 March 1928, p. 5 (*A*)   *SV* (*B*)
1 Granny . . . hill] Granny-on-the-hill *A*

Surely she knows,
As each year goes,
The burden laid on her still!   5

Five sons she had—all wed;
Five girls she had—all dead;
Sons and sons' wives
Lead their own lives;
Granny eats pensioner's bread.   10

Old and a pensioner . . .
As the leaves fall, and stir
When the wind blows,
Surely earth knows,
Lonely, none lonelier.   15

Yet in her sad old might,
In her hut in the height,
Like a last leaf
She cries, "Too brief,
O Life!" shrinking from flight.   20

3 knows,] ~ *A*   4 goes,] ~ *A*   5 laid] *Om. A*   6 had— *A*] ~ X   9 lives;]
~: *A*   11 Old] ~, *A*   pensioner . . .] ~. . . . *A*   ~! *B*   12 fall,] ~ *A B*
13 When] And *A*   16 might] night *A*   17 in] on *A B*   19 cries,] ~: *A*
brief,] ~ *A*   20 Life!"] life!"— *A*   life!" *B*   shrinking from] dreading the *A*

158   WHO SPRING DELIGHTED HEARS

How wonderful is man,
Who, with his eye all heights can span,
Who, with his ear distinguishing,
Finds his delight in Spring!

[cont. overleaf

(n. d.)   *Copy-text: WS   Collated states: SV (A)*

Not otherwise recorded: A sets the refrain as the second half of the preceding stanza
in each instance.

2 eye] ~, *A*   4 Spring] spring *A*

Over the rose poises a bee,   5
 And the bee is sound, and the rose an ear;
And the bee has taken a word from me,
 A word from my heart for love to hear.

  Rose unto rose
  The pollen goes;   10
  And, but for a word,
  Love perished unheard.

I have looked into eyes and seen
 Love's eyes look back again to me, and there
Was wakened in the deep all that had been   15
 Asleep; the hidden by a look laid bare.

  Rose unto rose
  The pollen goes;
  Love looks, and the spirit
  Wakes to inherit.   20

I have heard in a tree a bird,
 And the bird sang only a single note,
That, there, as it sprang to its fullness, stirred
 My heart as it stirred in the singer's throat.

  Rose unto rose   25
  The pollen goes;
  Love (starving alone)
  Grows rich on a tone.

How wonderful is man,
Who with his eyes can span   30
All space, and in his ears
The Spring delighted hears!

  Rose unto rose
  The pollen goes . . .
  Rose unto rose . . .   35

---

23 sprang] lifted *A* its] *Om. A* **24** stirred in] sprang to *A* **27** alone)] ~), *A*
30 eyes] eye *A* **32** Spring] spring *A* **34** goes . . .] ~, *A* **35** ˢrose . . .] ~ . . . . *A*

I59   THE SONG OF THE HAND

Blessed be God who gave us the need
To break the clod for the good round seed;
Who set the hand, and the fingers five,
Over the land and over the hive.

The harvest home shall reward the toil,   5
The bee-built comb shall declare the spoil;
Monarch of man are the fingers five,
He by their span must measure to thrive.

Contest is life! not war that destroys,
And breaks, in strife, as a child breaks toys;   10
But joy and pain, with honey in comb,
The good round grain and the harvest home.

He who shall sow with his fingers five,
Love he shall know, and his soul alive;
He shall abide a Winter of days,   15
Till Spring set wide the gate of its praise.

Then sap shall flood through the briary brake,
The hip shall bud, and the thorn awake;[1]
And there shall sing of its nest a bird—
The heart of Spring in a man's breast stirred.   20

Tender his eyes at the young lamb's bleat,
Where weak it lies a flake at his feet;
Yet proud he stands as he looks, abroad,
Over the lands where the plough is sword.

Monarch of man are the fingers five,   25
His soul their span shall carry alive.

[*cont. overleaf*

(n. d.)   *Copy-text: WS   Collated states: SV* (*A*)

5 harvest home] harvest-home *A*   **7** five,] ~; *A*   **10** And] That *A*   **12** grain]
~, *A*   **15** Winter] winter *A*   **16** Spring] spring *A*   **17** briary] briery *A*
20 heart] pulse *A*   Spring] spring *A*   **22** lies] ~, *A*   **23** looks, abroad,] ~ ~ *A*

---

[1] I.e. The thicket of wild rose ('hip') and hawthorn ('briary brake') will bud and
blossom.

What the reward? Sleeps deep in the womb
The child—life's hoard of honey in comb.

28 The] His *A*

160   OF PRIDE WILL I SING

Of pride will I sing, in a song
I will make to the meek and strong;
For I will sing you of dust, which,
Wakened by life, leapt from the ditch;
Dust, servant of man, who was born   5
Of a breath as sound in a horn.

Palaces, crowns, history's masque,
The broad strong back bent to the task,
The seed man willed of love and lust,
These are but shapes upraised from the dust.   10
Only the dust is mighty; man
In a dream of the dust began.

        Lo, I have sung
            Of pride; a song
        Of the dust that   15
            Is meek and strong.

(n. d.)   *Copy-text: WS   Collated states:* None

161   THE UNDELIVERED

    As the soft gloaming fell,
        And the flowers closed their eyes—

(n. d.)   *Copy-text: WS   Collated states: Des* (February 1930), p. 14 (*A*)   *Wr*, 14
May 1930, p. 5, signed Mary Gilmore (in *Desiderata*, a literary review published in
Adelaide) (*B*)   *SV* (*C*)

Not otherwise recorded: There is no stanza break in the collated states. In *A* the initial
letter of every alternate line is lower case.
2 eyes—] ~, *C*

As homeward the last late bird
   Blackened against the skies—
As the thin cloud of eve   5
   Frittered away in laces—

While yet a faint light veiled
   The woods and shadowy places,
I stood as one to whom, as a dream,
   An old memory clung;   10
And suddenly I heard the yoes[1]
   That wait for their young.

4 skies—] ~, *C*   **10** clung;] ~, *A B*

[1] Ewes.

162   THE TRESPASSER

He hath a hunger of the eyes
   For all things beautiful and fine,
And ever sees with quick surprise
   The young moon silver-pointed shine.

He loves, as though he were a child,   5
   The new-born lamb so white and still,
And bends to note how softly piled
   The velvet moss beside the rill.

And he will stand at even-time
   To catch the last note of some bird,   10
As, on the wing's uplifting climb,
   Dropped from the sky the sound is heard.

He hath a child's heart, though a man
   Counts in him long-destroying years—

(n. d.)   *Copy-text: WS   Collated states: DT*, 27 March 1926, p. 5 as HE HATH A
HUNGER OF THE EYES (*A*)

2 beautiful] beautful *A*   **3** sees] ~, *A*   surprise] ~, *A*   **6** lamb] ~, *A*   **7** bends]
leans *A*   note] feel *A*   softly piled] soft and mild *A*   **11** uplifting] uplifted *A*

To ache, as but a man's heart can,   15
    In wild remorse and tears.

163   THE ROAD

The road broke under the wheels,
And a new rut made a new road;
The mare's foal ran at her heels—
The quick when her pulse had slowed;
Seed in the furrow knew Spring,   5
And, high in the air, the wing
Of a gull soared upward going:—
And suddenly I was immortal,
Knowing the old beauty of death!

(n. d.)   *Copy-text: WS   Collated states: SV* (*A*)
4 when] where *A*   slowed;] ~. *A*   **5** Spring] spring *A*   **7** going:—] ~— *A*

164   OUT IN THE STORM

Now turned toward its doom,
Dark is the soul with gloom,
As in the sky the thunder-head,
Where soon will the lightning-thread
Cross-shuttle the loom,   5
And the torment tread.

Grey is the vale, below,
Where the slack waters flow
Like a tired pulse that would sleep;
Like eyes, that mourned to weep,   10
The vortices grow
Where the dun clouds sweep.

Yet, in this dim forlorn,
High on the winds upborne,

Like a lute in the air, there flies   15
A cage-bird's song to the skies,
In eloquent scorn
Of the faith that dies.

Shall we remember less
Than he, whom no duress   20
Can break from his tribute of song,
However his heart may long
For the fields that bless,
And the wings that throng?

Dark, dark is the soul with gloom   25
In its narrowing room,
But the Infinite Will
Covers it still.

(27 July 1923)   *Copy-text: WS*   *Collated states:* None

165   THROUGH WHAT DARK HUNGERS
           OF THE FLESH

Through what dark hungers of the flesh the soul peeps out,
    And through what clash is made its cry,
E'en as the moon looks through the cloudy rout,
    That veils it, passing by.

Only in earthquake slacks the rind of earth, to loose   5
    The hidden springs that lie within;
So with the hardened world of men, whom use
    Indures[1] lest weakness win.

Yet from man's dark enveloping cloud, his thickened crust,
    Sometimes, somehow, in moments rare,   10
An angel face looks out, and love, with trust,
    Turns back to meet it there.

(n. d.)   *Copy-text: WS*   *Collated states:* None

---

[1] Obsolete form of *indurate*, to toughen; of human beings, to render hard-hearted.

166   DUST

"I reign!" said man;
    And the dust: "Your rule is chaos!"
"We are the law,"
    Said man, "All things obey us!"
Now in the law's great halls   5
Dust falls, and falls, and falls.
Only the rhythms of the dust endure.

Mighty is man,
    Who, in his mountainy measures,
Digs like a wolf,   10
    Seeking the things he treasures;
Then on his treasure falls
Dust of his roof and walls.
Only the rhythms of the dust endure.

Softly and slow,   15
    The dust in its long, long falling
Masses in sleep;
    Tenderly shawling, shawling,
Over the crumbling walls,
Heaping it falls, and falls . . .   20
Only the rhythms of the dust endure.

(n. d.)   *Copy-text: WS   Collated states: SV* (*A*)
2 dust:] ~, *A*   **7** of the *A*] of *X*

167   SPRING SONG

Spring is not gone—not yet! not yet!
Across Gundary Plain[1] the shadows flight,
And where Monaro gleams, a snowdrift glistens white;

(10 November 1923)   *Copy-text: WS   Collated states: SMH*, 13 September 1924,
p. 13 (*A*)
1 yet! not] ~, ~ *A*   **2** flight] flit *A*   **3** gleams,] ~ *A*   **4** tawny] dark and *A*

---

[1] Places named in 167 are in the Southern Highlands, from Gundary Plain near Goulburn

Against her tawny eucalyptine hills
Tarlo still holds her willow-green,   5
Tender as when it first was seen;
While o'er the Kookbundoons, faint, fainter growing,
The Wind-Boy whistles in his going.[2]

Spring is not gone—not yet, not yet!
Still mounts the speeding cloud its airy steed,   10
And still on Goulburn hills the yellow weed
The glory of its blossom spills;
While, from his close, the wintered bee
Drops to the pollened gold he takes in fee,
As, far within the skyey vague's[3] blue showing,   15
The Wind-Boy whistles to his going.

Spring is not gone—not yet, not yet!
Barely is lost the lamb's first flickering bleat—
The little white thing, lying in the sun's new heat,
Thin as the snowflake seen on mountain sills;   20
Scarcely the unbound, budded leaf
On orchard trees forgets its sheaf,
Where winter-held it knew not Spring's bestowing—
The Wind-Boy whistling in his going.

Not yet the Spring is o'er—not yet!   25
The blood of winter in the charging vein
Leaps like a courser scornful of the rein—
Swift as the purling Pomeroy rills,[4]

6 seen;] ~. *A*   7 Kookbundoons] Cookbundoons *A*   10 airy] flying *A*
11 Goulburn hills] Eastgrove Hill *A*   12 spills;] ~, *A*   13 While,] And *A*
14 Drops to the] Fattens on *A*   fee,] ~; *A*   15 As,] While *A*   16 to] in *A*
19 thing, lying] ~ ~, *A*   in . . . heat] where the shadows fleet *A*   20 snowflake]
snowflakes *A*   22 sheaf,] ~ *A*   23 Where winter-held] ~, ~, *A*   bestowing—]
~, *A*   25 o'er] past *A*   26 winter] ~, *A*   vein] ~, *A*   27 courser] ~, *A*

(see F165, H7 and J13) to the high tablelands of the Monaro region near the Snowy
Mountains to the s. and the Kookbundoons to the n. On the latter, see F98, H94 and
cf. *A*'s spelling in line 7; cf. also I28 line 7.

[2] For comparisons of the wind to an energetic or mischievous boy, see C17 and C18
and cf. Henry Wadsworth Longfellow's refrain 'A boy's will is the wind's will' in 'My
Lost Youth' (1858).   [3] See I7 n. 2.
[4] Rivulets, small streams: the small township of Pomeroy is e. of the Great Dividing

That whisper, whisper through the leaves
Where the glad sun his wayward pattern weaves,   30
And the loud cock hears echo crowing—crowing—
The Wind-Boy whistling in his going.

Not yet the Spring is gone—not yet!
In all the radiance of the ambient height,
In loveliness of day, in loveliness of night,   35
Hovers eternal power that o'er life wills,
Waiting the movement that shall wake
When young things from their swaddlings break,
Hearing the sap within them flowing—flowing—
The Wind-Boy whistling in his going.   40

Not yet the Spring is gone—not yet!
Not while within the heart a full note sings,
And love can play upon deep, hidden springs
Till quivering life in answer thrills!
Not yet the Spring is gone—not though   45
Upon the head the years sift down their snow!
. . . Alas! how Time the Scythe-man[5] answers—mowing—
The Wind-Boy whistling in his going!

28 purling] quickened *A*   rills,] ~ *A*   29 leaves] ~, *A*   30 glad] gay *A*
wayward pattern] patterned measure *A*   32 going.] ~! *A*   34 all . . . the]
radiant splendour held in *A*   height,] ~ *A*   35 In . . . in] The . . . the *A*
36 Hovers] Hover *A*   wills] stills *A*   37 movement] moments *A*   shall wake]
awake. *A*   38 break,] ~ *A*   39 Hearing] And hear *A*   42 sings] springs *A*
43 And] Or *A*   deep,] the *A*   45 gone—] ~!— *A*   46–7 snow!/ . . . Alas!
how] ~ . . . // ~! How *A*   47 Scythe-man] Scytheman *A*   answers—mowing—]
~, ~, *A*

Range, about 50 km from Goulburn. Heffernans and Ryans Creeks are nearby.

[5] The figure of Father Time (like that of Death) often carries a scythe or sickle to indicate
that he mows down all living things; cf. J21 line 52.

168   WINTER

Who now cometh here
With his locks at the sere,[1]
And a face like a boy?
Winter full of joy,
Young heart and old head,   5
Appetite for bread,
And a laugh like a lad
Who is glad.

With wind and with rain
He knocketh on the pane;   10
He calleth to the fire,
And the heart, leap higher!
And palms on his knees,
As the long nights freeze,
He laugheth like a boy   15
Full of joy.

With ice and with frost
He wrappeth pool and post;
And, sickle-new and bright
In the cold sweet night,   20
Like a far-flung shoe
The moon peepeth through,
While the star showeth white
In the height.

With thick porridge cool,   25
Put in chair, put in stool;

(n. d.)   *Copy-text: WS*   *Collated states: SV* (*A*)

1 cometh] enters *A*   here] ~, *A*   10 knocketh on] knocks upon *A*   11 He calleth] While he calls *A*   13 And] Then *A*   15 laugheth] laughs *A*   18 wrappeth] covers *A*   post;] ~, *A*   19 sickle-new] silver-new *A*   bright] ~, *A*   20 In . . . sweet] He shows, on the *A*   21–2 Like . . . through] The moon shining through,/ Like an upflung shoe *A*   23 star showeth] stars glisten *A*

[1] See 119 n. 1.

For, with hunger sharp set,
Naught need'st now to whet
Appetite the bold,
Edged up by the cold,   30
As the eave ice drippeth,
And slippeth.

Now winter to the bird
Sayeth, "Sleep thou unstirred!
With bill under feather   35
Heed not the weather!
Though the wind bloweth,
Though the cloud snoweth,
Yet at day cometh sun,
Little one."   40

And saith he to love,
"With coverlet above,
When thou shalt hear the rain
Thou shalt turn again,
And, whispering and warm,   45
With arm under arm,
And with breast unto breast,
Thou shalt rest."

28 need'st] needs *A*   31 As] Where *A*   drippeth,] slips *A*   32 And slippeth]
As it drips *A*   34 Sayeth] Says *A*   thou] on *A*   37 wind bloweth] sharp wind
blow *A*   38 cloud snoweth] dark cloud snow *A*   39 cometh] comes the *A*
41 saith he] then he says *A*   43 thou shalt] you shall *A*   44 Thou shalt] You
will *A*   45 And,] ~ *A*   48 Thou shalt] You shall *A*

I69   THE RED-BREAST HASTETH AWAY

Now lifteth the ice its pack
    And pricketh its way on the ground,
Now slippeth the hoof on the track
    That frost with its iron hath bound;
Now rougheth the hair   5
    On the thick o' th' hide,

Where oxen and horse
　　The winter abide.

The red-breast hasteth away,
　　Hasteth away from Crookwell town,　　　10
For he heareth the winds that say
　　Soon will a whippet of snow come down.
He flee-eth the wind,
　　And flee-eth the snow,
But where he hideth　　　15
　　There's none to know.

Aloft on Roslyn heights,
　　Where the polar[1] sheddeth his fire,
As the lamp at Maryvale[2] lights,
　　There memory writeth a quire.[3]　　　20
There under the snow
　　The crocuses hide—
But who shall the winter
　　Of time abide?

So heap the wood on the hearth　　　25
　　Till the chimney roast with the flame,
Let of logs be never a dearth,
　　Lest wanderers call on us shame;
For breedeth a wind
　　(And breedeth a snow)　　　30
And who shall abide it
　　There's none may know.

(n. d.)　　*Copy-text: WS*　　*Collated states:* None

---

[1] The pole star is the nearest naked-eye star to the celestial pole – in the southern hemisphere, Sigma Octantis.
[2] MG's maternal grandparents' property, where she was born. Crookwell (line 10) and Roslyn (line 17) are nearby.
[3] I.e. enough to fill a set of twenty-four sheets of writing paper or, in printed books, a gathering (the sequential leaves that make up a folded sheet).

170   THE YELLOW DAFFODIL

Why should I ask
To follow folly's way,
For folly 'tis
Thy wilfulness to follow!
Yet I, who would   5
The careless huntsman play,
Losing thee pine my loss
By every height and hollow.

For still must I,
What way thou deign to turn,   10
Or through what hurt
Thy wayward going lead me,
Where'er thy foot
Step, my heart's candle burn,
And, lost, must cry my loss   15
In hope that thou shouldst heed me.

O, were I but
The yellow daffodil
That thou within
Thy wood bent stooping over,   20
Or were I but
Thy chambered window-sill!
But I my loss must cry,
Longing to be thy lover.

(n. d.)   *Copy-text: WS   Collated states: BPMag* (December 1929 – February 1930),
p. 47 (*A*)   *SV* (*B*)

Not otherwise recorded: A is in italics throughout.

11 Or] *And A*   ***13*** Where'er] Or where *B*   **14** Step, *B*] ~ *X   Step A*   **15** And,
lost,] *And lost A*   **17** O,] *O A*   ~ *B*   **18** yellow daffodil] *Yellow Daffodil A*

171   THE MOPOKE, MEMORY

O Memory, mopoke of the heart,
　　How often does thy hollow note,
Like the bird's cry, mournful, apart,
　　Over the spirit's twilight float!

Beneath a moon, whose pallid hue   5
　　Blackens each shadow where it lies,
That voice calls solitary through
　　The night, by range, and rill, and rise.[1]

O, lone, lone note! O Memory, thou
　　Who, too, dost wake by night to call,   10
Thou mak'st the human heart thy bough,
　　Thy grievous moonlight covering all.

(n. d.)   *Copy-text: WS   Collated states: Wr*, 29 August 1928, p. 5 (*A*)
2 hollow] echoing *A*   3 cry,] ~—*A*   mournful, apart,] hollow, remote— *A*
5–8 Beneath . . . rise.] The bird calls solitary through/ The darkling night, by range
and rise,/ Or 'neath a moon whose pallid hue/ Blackens each shadow where it lies. *A*
9 O, lone, lone] O lonely *A*   Memory,] ~!— *A*   10 dost] must *A*   11 Thou]
Who *A*   12 Thy grievous] Grievous thy *A*

[1] Cf. 18.

172   I SAW THEIR DREAMS

Young love that has no fear,
　　That, knowing nothing, understands,
Stepped up into the tram, last night,
　　And sat beside me holding hands.

Shoulder to shoulder leaned,   5
　　While thought in each knew only faith.

[cont. overleaf

(29 March 1920)   *Copy-text: WS   Collated states: Wr*, 1 September 1921, p. 9 as IN
OXFORD STREET (*A*)   *Wr*, 27 November 1929, p. 5 (*B*)
3 tram,] ~ *A B*   4 me] ~, *A*   6 thought] ~, *A*   each] ~, *A*   knew *A*] know *X*
faith.] ~; *B*

Theirs th' eternal immemorial world;
This world was but its wraith!

Love in their eyes looked forth,
    As innocent as heaven's first star: 10
I saw their dreams; they did not know
    I saw—how sweet they seemed, how far.

7 th'] the *A*   eternal] ~, *A B*   **8** its] the *A*   wraith!] ~. *A*   **9** forth,] ~ *A B*
10 star:] ~; *A B*   **12** far.] ~! *A*

I73 NEVER ADMIT THE PAIN

Never admit the pain,
    Bury it deep;
Only the weak complain,
    Complaint is cheap.

Cover thy wound, fold down   5
    Its curtained place;
Silence is still a crown,
    Courage a grace.

(n. d.) *Copy-text: WS Collated states: PPA* (*A*) Mackaness2 (*B*) *SV* (*C*) Wright2
(*D*) Mackaness3 reprints *B*
7 crown,] ~ *B*   **8** a] is *A*

I74 SOMETIMES A PETAL FALLS

Speak soft above her grave,
    Put no slight on her;
She was of love the slave,
    His blight he laid upon her.
Only she asked to give,   5
    Love's insolence obeying;

(21 March 1924) *Copy-text: WS Collated states: Wr*, 11 December 1929, p. 5 (*A*) *SV*
as SOMETIME A PETAL FALLS (*B*)

Not otherwise recorded: A divides the poem into four 4-line stanzas.
6 obeying;] ~— *B*

Love, the wild fugitive,
   Home from the straying.

Sometimes a petal falls,
   Silently, slightly;   10
Never the ear forestalls[1]
   Where it drops lightly;
So went she, wanned and white
   As a bud that uncloses;
Dropped as a petal might,   15
   Fallen from roses.

---

9 Sometimes] Sometime *B*   **12** lightly;] ~. *A*   **13** white] ~, *A*   **15** Dropped]
~, *A B*

---

[1] Anticipates, and thus prevents.

I75   LET NEVER DESPAIR

Let never despair
   Upon thy heart his name
Grave deeply down; share
   Not in his evil fame!

Yet grieve, if thou must,   5
   Lest memory should fail,
And leave but the dust
   To hold love's long entail.[1]

(n. d.)   *Copy-text: WS*   *Collated states: SV* (*A*)
2 thy] the *A*   **5** thou] you *A*

---

[1] Inherited obligation.

176   THE ROOK,
THE RAVEN, AND THE CHOUGH[1]

I have wept long enough!
   Now let me sing
The rook, the raven, and the chough,[2]
   And the bold black wing.

The rook to the raven said,   5
   "My nest is bare,
Except for a single thread
   Of a girl's gold hair."

And the chough croaked, "It is enough!"
   But the raven said,   10
"Down in the clough[3]
   A lamb lies dead."
He sleeked his shining wings:
   "I am fed," he said,
      "I am fed!"   15

(n. d.)   *Copy-text: WS*   *Collated states: SV* (no variants)

[1] Cryptic ballads, often medieval in inspiration, were a particular interest of the Pre-Raphaelite movement, e.g. of poets Dante Gabriel Rossetti (1828–82), Christina Rossetti (1830–94), William Morris (1834–96) and Algernon Charles Swinburne (1837–1909). Other examples, some faux-medieval, are: J85, J96, K93, K94, M19 and M21.
[2] In England, a bird of the crow family, a jackdaw.
[3] Steep-sided ravine or valley.

177   WHOM SHOULD LOVE PITY?

Whom should love pity if not the lover,
Mourning and mateless like a lone plover!
Nay, let him go to muse in his dreaming;
Little his loss who still has the seeming.

     What if the dust   5
     Of the long years cover?
     There shall survive,

As comb in the hive,
Beauty to dwell
In the heart of a lover!   10

Spoil of the bee the sweet of the clover,
Sweeter the spoil that falls to the lover!
Yet never the flesh brightens the ember—
Only the dreamer knows to remember.

Look in her eyes,   15
Let beauty uncover!
Held in the comb
Of the heart for home,
Beauty is born
In the eyes of a lover!   20

(n. d.)   *Copy-text: WS   Collated states:* None

178   HATH SHE NO MORE THAN MOODS

Hath she no more than moods?
   Is her love but a breath,
Which, when the whim is passed,
   Falleth to death?

Nay! had I thought her so,   5
   I had not turned again,
Fearing the parting word,
   Dreading the pain!

(n. d.)   *Copy-text: WS   Collated states: Tri* (December 1927), p. 32 as IS HER LOVE BUT A BREATH? (*A*)

Not otherwise recorded: A's text is in italics throughout.

3 passed] *past A*   **5** Nay!] *Ah, A*

179   IT WAS MY LOVE COMPLAINED

It was my love complained,
    Not I;
My love that pined thee
    When not nigh.

Hungry it waited,   5
    Hungry watched
The moments time
    Unfeeling snatched.

It was my love complained;
    My heart   10
Still knew thee constant
    As thou art.

Ah, wayward love that would
    Complain,
That old pursuit might   15
    Sound again!

(n. d.)   *Copy-text: WS   Collated states: Tri* (December 1927), p. 32 (*A*)

Not otherwise recorded: A's text is in italics throughout.

7 moments time] *moments' Time A*   **9** complained;] *complained, A*   **12** art.] *art! A*
15 That old] *So that A*   **15–16** might/ Sound again] *might sound/ Again A*

180   IN THE SPRING

Hath the bud heard of the bee,
    As it reddens and flushes,
There as it hangs on the tree,
    Like a maiden that blushes?

(n. d.)   *Copy-text: WS   Collated states: Tri* (December 1927), p. 32 as A SONG OF THE BUD (*A*)

Not otherwise recorded: A's text is in italics throughout.

1 bee,] *bee A*   **2** As] *That A*   **3** There] *There, A*

Hath the twig word of the down,
    And of two blue eggs resting
Under the feathers of brown,
    At the end of the nesting?

Ah, hath my lady, my own,
    Dreamed, as the white breasts blossom,   10
Of the bee, the bud and the down,
    Or the nest in her bosom?

6 resting] *resting*, *A*   **7** brown,] *brown A*   **8** nesting] *questing A*   **9** lady] *boy A*
11 Of the] *O' th' A*   **12** Or] *And A*

181   WHERE THE WATERS LOOPED

Tenderly she stooped,
    Then slenderly stepped
Where the waters looped
    As the current swept;
And I saw in her hand   5
    A broken flower,
Such pity God gave her
    For dower![1]

(n. d.)   *Copy-text: WS*   *Collated states:* None

[1] Natural endowment.

182   CONTEST IS ENDED IN SURRENDER

Contest is ended in surrender;
    What is there left to say,
O passionate and tender
    One at bay?

Thou hast no word? and yet, O veiling   5
    Lids, what speaks so loudly,
Here where my heart, thine quailing,
    Beats proudly?

(n. d.)   *Copy-text: WS*   *Collated states:* None

183   STRANGELY UPON THE NIGHT

Strangely upon the night,
    Strangely upon the pane,
There fell a shadow, light,
    That paused and went again.

Ah, was it death that came,   5
    With hungry eyes that sought
The firelit hearth, the flame,
    The silence love had wrought?

(n. d.)   *Copy-text: WS*   *Collated states:* None

184   THE PRAYER

Suffer no more thy anger
    To burn me with its fire,
For I have conquered longing,
    And I have quenched desire.

Only do I remember   5
    One strange, one haunting look—
When soul met soul and grappled,
    And my world shook.

(27 April 1919)   *Copy-text: WS*   *Collated states:* None

185   SPEAK LOW OF LOVE

Speak low of love;
    Hast thou not known the Spring?
Heard the young grass rise
    To it, whispering?

Speak low of love,   5
    So that thy heart may hear

Its rumour on the wind
  Against thy ear.

Speak low of love—
  Wonder that wonder wakes!   10
Hush! lest a tendril,
  Tremulous, breaks.

(7 February 1920)   *Copy-text: WS*   *Collated states:* None

186   HOT LOVE THAT COMES AND GOES

Once like an ocean ran
  Love from his heart to hers;
Now spreads a desert, wan,
  And there no memory stirs.

Slain, in a moment brief,   5
  By some word hotly said,
How like a stricken leaf
  Love from its height falls dead!

How like, how like to life
  Is love that comes and goes;   10
The edged word, like a knife,
  Stabs—and the death-feud grows.

(n. d.)   *Copy-text: WS*   *Collated states:* None

187   NURSE NO LONG GRIEF

O, could we weep,
  And weeping bring relief!
But life asks more than tears
  And falling leaf.

[*cont. overleaf*

(n. d.)   *Copy-text: WS*   *Collated states: SV* (*A*)   Pizer (*B*)   *Trib*, 10 February 1954,
p. 1 (*C*)
1 O] Oh *A*   weep,] ~ *C*

Though year by year   5
   Tears fall and leaves are shed,
Spring bids new sap arise
   And blood run red.

Nurse no long grief,
   Lest thy heart flower no more;   10
Grief builds no barns; its plough
   Rusts at the door.

6 shed,] ~ C   7 arise] ~, A   9 grief,] ~ C   10 thy] the A

188   THE GIFT

Tortured, tormented, and enslaved,
   A prisoner love made of me,
   Who, as a wild bird, once was free;
But from the heart's death me he saved.

(n. d.)   *Copy-text: WS   Collated states: SV* (no variants)

189   OF WISDOM

There is no wisdom but
   It has love for its root;
Love brought to flower the bud
   Upon the tawny shoot.

Fear watched the skies; but love   5
   Saw God beyond the cloud,
And took the hands of life,
   And left death but the shroud.

(n. d.)   *Copy-text: WS   Collated states:* None

190   THE DESERTED ORCHARD*

Rome,[1] he sleeps at my feet,
    And I pull on the silk of his ears,
Thinking how passion is fleet,
    How salt is a portion of tears.
And over by hill and by the hollow,   5
    An apple-tree, blooming alone,
Seems as one who would whisper,
        Come follow! Come follow!
    To ask for a word of his own.

For the apple tree, there,   10
    Is the only thing living is left,
Telling a tale on the air
    Of patterns half done in the weft.
So ever by hill and by hollow,
    And out of the distance, alone,   15
It seems as one who would whisper,
        Come follow! Come follow!
    To ask for a word of his own.

Rome, he sleeps at my feet,
    And I pull on his satiny ears,   20
Thinking how passion is fleet,
    How salt is a portion of tears!

* On the road to Gunning.[2]

(30 October 1922)   *Copy-text: WS*   *Collated states:* None

[1] Cf. Rome's appearance in A10 and Z3.
[2] Cf. G37.

191   FAMOUS

He sat, a leader and acclaimed by men,
　　And all his heart was with the yellow corn;
He saw the paddocks of his youth again,
　　The weathered hut where he and his were born.

And as he dreamed he heard the wind   5
　　Blow up and down upon the tawny wheat,
And marked the rustle, how it fell and thinned,
　　And died upon the wind in its retreat.

He heard the milkers lowing at the rails,
　　And saw his father rise and let them in;   10
Caught the horn's rattle on the closing bails,
　　Heard the first milking on the pail strike thin.

The firelight leaped behind his chiselled brass,
　　A bell beside his polished table rang;
He only heard a troop of horses pass,   15
　　The battered door of an old stable clang.

Upon the wall the great companioned him:
　　His heart was with a little barefoot lad,
Running to find a ferny brookside dim,
　　And chequered waters by a forest pad.[1]   20

(n. d.)   *Copy-text: WS   Collated states: BPMag* (June 1929), p. 64 as FAME (*A*)   *SV*
(*B*)

Not otherwise recorded: A's text is in italics throughout.

1 by] *of A*   **2** And] But *B*   heart was] *thoughts were A*   **9** rails,] *rails A*
11 horn's] *horns' A*   **13** leaped] *leapt A*   leapt *B*   chiselled] *burnished A*
14 A] *The A*   **17** him:] ~; *B*   **18** lad,] *lad A*   **19** brookside] ~, *B*

---

[1] Path or track, worn by animals.

192　THERE SHALL COME DREAMS UPON A MAN

There shall come dreams upon a man,
　And he shall see the sun;
He shall look upon the waters,
　And watch them as they run,
And he shall know them wonderful,　　　5
　Or ere his day is done.

There shall come dreams upon a man,
　They shall be quiet dreams,
Then he shall see with open sight
　Where once he saw in gleams;　　　10
And he shall find a friend in trees,
　And brotherhood in streams.

There shall come dreams upon a man;
　He will not count them loss,
For he shall trawl the blue serene　　　15
　Where sails the cloudy floss;
And his shall be the emerald
　Within the little moss.

He shall awaken in the night,
　And look from star to star,　　　20
Till he shall know them one with him,
　Not vague things set afar;
And he shall there forget himself
　In thinking what they are.

There shall come dreams upon a man,　　　25
　Or ere his day is done,
And he shall stand, a conqueror,
　And know all battles won;
He shall look up, though it were dark,
　And he shall see the sun.　　　30

(n. d.)　*Copy-text: WS　Collated states: SMH*, 11 October 1924, p. 13 as DREAMS SHALL
COME (*A*)　Pizer (*B*)

2 sun;] ~, *A*　　**3** waters,] ~ *A*　　**5** wonderful,] ~ *A*　　**7** man,] ~; *A*　　**9** Then]
Where *A*　　**14** loss,] ~. *A*　　**19** night,] ~ *A*　　**21** Till he shall know] Until he knows *A*

I93   THE BLANKET

What art thou whom I seek but a wind!
  Then blow to me hither,
For the branches above me are thinned,
  The scattered leaves wither;
Parching I go under pitiless skies,   5
  Who ask but the dew of thy lips,
    And thine eyes!

What art thou whom I seek but the sun!
  The wintered I perish,
Like a tree where the blossom is done,   10
  And no one to cherish.
O, would I were lying, warm at thy heart,
  One roof-tree to cover, and
    No one to part!

And to thee I am wind, and am sun,   15
  And, love, thy pursuer!
Come then to me, come, O, wistfullest one,
  Let need be the lure.
O that thou wert with me, close to my heart,
  One blanket to cover, and   20
    No one to part!

(n. d.)   *Copy-text: WS*   *Collated states:* None

I94   DOWN BY THE POLDER

Down by the polder,[1] where
  Knee deep the cattle stand
With drowsy cud and stare,
  And stilled is all the land
Beneath the Summer haze,   5
  I walk once more in dreams,

[1] Pasture land, especially river flats.

And with me one dream stays,
    And more than seems.

Was it a shadow stood,
    Half hidden and half seen,   10
Where, with its shade, the wood
    Darkened the luscious green?
Once two were there, while youth
    Spoke its adventurous will;
Would that in very truth   15
    They stood there still.

Age writes upon the face
    Its furrowing of lines,
And through its filmy trace
    Life's pattern there defines;   20
But in the polder no
    Lines show; the grass is still
As when, O, long ago,
    Love wept its will.

(n. d.)   *Copy-text:* WS   *Collated states:* None

195   IN THE WINTERING SNOW

Where alone he sits with his dreams,
As the flame of the candle gleams,
A shadow rises and falls, and seems
Like one who was there,
    O, long long ago,   5
    Ere the wintering snow
Had whitened his hair.

And it almost seemed that she stooped
Low over him, there, as he drooped,
And her white arms about him she looped   10
In the old, old way,

Of long long ago,
Ere the wintering snow
Had whitened the grey.

Dreams! dreams! dreams! and yet to what shore   15
Do they reach, that there, evermore,
We must go forth to seek—to restore—
The look that was fair,
   O, long long ago,
   Ere the wintering snow   20
Fell white on our hair?

(n. d.)   *Copy-text: WS*   *Collated states:* None

I96   REMEMBERING

When you will some day turn old letters over,
   Reading familiar phrases you will say,
"Here was no cheap love-rover,
   Changing from day to day;
But here was one to whom love meant   5
All should be given—not lent!"

And when, at evening, you will stand in lonely
   And nostalgic mood, and in the grey
Low dusk see one star only
   Lift in the sky, O say   10
"So lone was she: to whom love meant
All to be given—not lent."

(n. d.)   *Copy-text: WS*   *Collated states: WMag* (December 1927), n. p. as SPENDTHRIFT
OF LOVE (*A*)[1]

1 When] (Specially written for the Wentworth Magazine)// When *A*   2 say,] ~: *A*
3 love-rover,] ~ *A*   6 should] to *A*   lent!] ~ *A*   10 say] ~: *A*   11 she:] ~— *A*

---

[1] The *WMag* archives are incomplete. *A* occurs, with Z11 and Z12, as part of a single
page of print cuttings held in NLA 727 11/9/2. All are annotated by MG as printed
in *WMag* and display its characteristic typography.

When by the hearthside you will linger dreaming
    Of days far gone, then you will think of her
Tenderly—without seeming—   15
    And an old longing stir,
Remembering how, to her, love meant
All to be given—not lent.

13 When] ~, *A*   hearthside] hearth-side, *A*   17 meant] ~: *A*

197 THE WOOD-DOVE

O, with what passionate,
    With what upsoaring love
I heard the long-looked-for
    Call of the first wood-dove;
Wandering I followed,   5
    Peering through bush and brake,
All the wild dreams of life
    Within the heart awake!

For the whole world was there,
    Deep in a child's heart hid;   10
Books I had read, old tales
    Oft heard—the Moor, the Cid,
Aladdin, Lalla Rookh,
    The horn by Roland wound,
Mount Ida, Italy[1]—   15
    Dwelt in that moving sound.

[cont. overleaf

(n. d.) *Copy-text: WS Collated states: SMH*, 31 December 1927, p. 9 as THE WOOD DOVE (*A*) *SV* as THE WOOD DOVE (*B*)

1 O,] ~ *B* 2 love] ~, *A* 3 long-looked-for] long-looked for *A* long looked-for *B* 4 wood-dove;] wood dove. *A* wood dove; *B* 8 the] my *A* awake!] ~ *A* 14 horn] Horn *B* wound,] ~ *A*

[1] Respectively, the eponymous heroes of Shakespeare's *Othello* (*c.* 1604) and the early medieval Spanish epic *El Cid*; Aladdin of *The Arabian Nights* (translated 1885–88 by Richard Burton from the medieval Arabic); the heroine of *Lalla Rookh: An Oriental Romance* (1817) by Thomas Moore (1779–1852); the hero of the medieval French *Chanson de Roland*; and Mt Ida, the site of Troy (Ilium). Cf. I30 n. 5.

Never, through what long years
    May come to me and bring
Full harvest in, shall I,
    As then, with that swift spring   20
O' the heart entranced run,
    And stand, and run again,
In such a joy released,
    Almost it seemed like pain!

18 me] ~, *A*   19 I,] ~ *A*   21 O'] Of *B*   entranced] ~, *A*   entrancéd *B*   run,]
~ *A*   24 pain!] ~. *A*

I98 THE PLOVER

I shall not need the moon
    To find thy trysting-place;
The plovers, late and soon,
    O'er it in flight enlace;
Forward and back they fly,   5
    Hearts in eternal hover;
My cry is in their cry,
    My heart thy plover.

I shall not need the moon!
    No night too dark for me,   10
Who count thee all my boon,
    To watch where thou shalt be!
Backward and forth they fly,
    Wings of the heart at hover—
The bird's cry is my cry,   15
    My heart thy plover.

About Life's darkling field,[1]
    Moves in unending flight,

(n. d.)   *Copy-text: WS   Collated states: SMH*, 2 February 1929, p. 13 (*A*)   *SV* (*B*)
1 moon] ~, *A*   2 trysting-place] trysting place *A*   4 enlace;] ~. *A*   6 hover;]
~, *A*   12 be!] ~. *A*   13 they] must *B*   fly,] ~— *A*   ~ *B*   14 heart] ~, *B*
at] and *B*   hover—] ~; *A*   17 About Life's] Above life's *A B*   18 Moves] ~, *A*
unending] eternal *A*

Grief that may not be healed,
    To cry upon the night;   20
Therefore, as time goes by,
    Love still must call the lover:
The bird's cry is my cry,
    My heart the plover.

19 Grief] ~, *B*   **20** cry] weep *B*   night;] ~. *A*   **21** goes] runs *B*   **22** lover:]
~. *A*   ~—— *B*

---

[1] Growing dark, in darkness – common poetic usage; cf. 'Darkling I listen' in John Keats's 'Ode to a Nightingale' (1820) or 'the darkling plain' in Matthew Arnold's 'Dover Beach' (1867). See also I128 line 3.

I99   NINETTE

The marigold shuts her leaves,
    While the clover folds its hands,
And the bees creep out like thieves
    From the honeysuckle strands,
And the honeysuckle breathes   5
    Its scent on the evening air:
Are you there, Ninette, at the gate?
    Ninette, are you there?

The lamp of the evening star
    Like a glow-worm lights the sky,   10
And the poplar's slender spar
    Lifts like a finger on high;
The curlew wistfully calls
    His lonely cry on the air:
Are you there, at the gate, Ninette?   15
    Ninette, are you there?

Swallows are home to the nest;
    And under the wing, to sleep,

(n. d.) *Copy-text: WS Collated states: SMH*, 10 March 1928, p. 13 as NINETTE, ARE YOU THERE (*A*)   *SV* (*B*)

2 its] her *A*   **4** strands,] ~; *A*   **5** honeysuckle] dark carnation *A*   **6** air:]
~—— *B*   **14** air:] ~—— *B*   **15** there,] ~ *A*

Under the soft warm breast,
    The last of the nestlings creep;   20
Tenderly darkens the eve,
    The stars are a silver stair:
Are you there at the gate, Ninette?
    Ninette, are you there?

The fire-flame leaps at the hob,   25
    And the candle lifts its light—
Was it the sound of a sob
    Like a lost thing stirred the night?
Out of the distance I call,
    My heart in its pain laid bare,   30
Are you there at the gate, Ninette?
    Ninette, are you there?

19 breast,] ~ *A*   22 stair:] ~— *B*

I100   TO HAVE LIVED IS ENOUGH

Oft have I stood to see the failing
    Of the great star[1] mark the coming dawn,
And watched, upon the earth, the veiling
    Of the night move backward o'er the lawn;
And I have seen, at eve, the day   5
    Draw to an end and go,
And I have asked, as it passed away,
    Did it know? Did it know?

I have watched flowers that in the burning
    Beauty of their hour glowed like the sun,   10
And I have bent above them, yearning,
    Lovingly have touched them, one by one;

(n. d.)   *Copy-text: WS   Collated states: SMH,* 19 May 1928, p. 13 (*A*)

1 see] watch *A*   **2** great star] daystar *A*   mark the] tell of *A*   **3** watched,] marked *A*   earth,] ~ *A*   **8** know? Did] ~, did *A*   know?] ~. *A*   **9** watched] loved *A*   **12** Lovingly] Tenderly *A*

[1] Venus, which is both evening and morning star: see entry for line 2.

And I have seen their splendour fade,
   At eve their petals strown,
And I have asked of the thing betrayed,   15
   Had it known? Had it known?

I have asked my soul, with wonder:
   O brief sojourner in this clay, say
When the bonds now binding sunder,
   Whither away, O, whither away?   20
Or is it enough, in thy spark,
   To see life in the buff?[2]
And it answered me out of the dark,
   And said, It is enough.

Only the lover of beauty knows   25
How eternity dwells in the heart of a rose.

14 strown] strewn *A*   **15** asked] ~, *A*   **16** known? Had] ~, had *A*   known?]
~. *A*   **17** my] of my *A*   soul,] ~ *A*   **18** say] ~, *A*   **19** sunder] shall sunder *A*
20 O,] ~ *A*   **24** said,] ~: *A*   **25** Only] . . . ~ *A*

[2] Naked, i.e. as it is in itself.

I101   THE LAMENT

To what far shore shall I turn me,
   And in what dark shade shall I seek,
That thou may'st pause to discern me,
   Thy voice in my ears to speak!

Whitens the dawn to its breaking,   5
   And thy bird wakes, knowing the light;
But my heart, in loneliness aching,
   Pines like a child in the night.

[*cont. overleaf*

(n. d.)   *Copy-text: WS   Collated states: Wr*, 15 August 1928, p. 5 as A LAMENT (*A*)
2 shall] will *A*   **3** may'st] shalt *A*   **4** Thy] That thy *A*   to] shall *A*   **5** to its]
for the *A*   **6** wakes,] ~ *A*   knowing] glad of *A*   **7** heart,] ~ *A*   loneliness]
lonely *A*   aching,] ~ *A*   **8** Pines] Pines on *A*   the] its *A*

If thou could'st but whisper to me,
    Were it ever so small a sound!   10
The hushes of silence pursue me,
    The stillness deepens, profound.

9 could'st] couldst *A*   **10** small] low *A*   sound!] ~!— *A*

I102 THE PEAR TREE

What though thou should'st declare
    Thyself a broken thing,
Yet will the wintered, bare
    Tree blossom in the Spring,
And, in the orchard where   5
    The nests no longer cling,
In yet enambered[1] air
    Will newer nestlings sing.

Ah, not for pain shall man
    Give up his gifts to death;   10
He hath so short a span
    Wherein to sigh his breath!
Though thy flower withereth,
    Art thou beneath the ban?[2]
Summer still something saith   15
    Of harvest and its fan.[3]

(n. d.) *Copy-text: WS*   *Collated states:* None

[1] See I50 n. 2.   [2] Curse.
[3] Winnowing fan, used to separate the chaff from the grain.

I103 THE FLAIL

O! Life, beat not so heavy with thy flail—
Not all the grain is worth the pain
Where, broken, lies the straw thy strokes assail!

Ah! Could we but escape thy heavy hand,
And, wandering go, softly and slow,   5
Into the quiet of some childhood's land,

And there, at peace, forget the bruised grain,
So much defaced, so much poor waste,
Thrown where so little lies to count as gain!

Once, as a child, upon the night I heard   10
A bird cry, note by note, a rote[1]
Of song, as though some tenderness had stirred,

Deep in his sleep, his happy heart to sing
Though all else slept, and o'er me swept,
E'en then, prevision of thy flailing fling!   15

(n. d.)   *Copy-text: WS   Collated states: DT*, 13 March 1926, p. 4 (*A*)   *SV* (*B*)

1 O!] ~ *B*   **5** And,] ~ *A*   **6** childhood's *A*] chidhood's *X*   land,] ~. *A*
7 bruised] stricken *B*   grain,] ~ *A*   **8** defaced, so] ~ (~ *A*   waste,] ~), *A*
9 Thrown] And *A*   **13** sing] ~, *A*   **14** slept,] ~; *A*

[1] See I9 n. I.

BOOK III: *AS THE WAYS DESCEND*

1104   FANTASY

In a haunted wood
Lay a secret pool,
Crying there aloud,
"Wrap me, O thou cloud!
In thy shadowy hood   5
Hide me out of sight,
Lest the pointed moon
Stab me with her horn,
As I lie forlorn,
In the night—in the night!"   10

(n. d.)   *Copy-text: WS   Collated states:* None

1105   HUNGER

I have known bread hunger,
Yet have I strength;
I have known heart hunger,
Yet do I live;
I have known soul hunger,   5
And faith is not dead.

When the body cried
I lit love in my heart;
When the heart wept
I lit a lamp in my soul;   10

(8 January 1917)   *Copy-text: WS   Collated states: Wr*, 18 January 1917, p. 11 (*A*)   *SV*
(*B*)

1–2 hunger,/ Yet] ~: yet *A*   **2** strength;] ~. *A*   **3–4** heart hunger,/ Yet] heart-
hunger: yet *A*   **4** live;] ~. *A*   **5** known] *Om. A*   **5–6** hunger,/ And] ~: and *A*
6–7 dead.// When] ~./ ~ *A*   **7** cried] ~, *A*   **8** heart;] ~, *A*   **9** wept] ~, *A*
10 soul;] ~. *A*

Yet all the while I heard the cry of life
Asking its goal.
. . . I was as one looking out of a house,
Knowing the empty rooms.

11 the cry of] *Om. B*   life] each the other *A*   13 ⁵. . . I] ~ *A B*   a] the *A*

1106   THE UNCHAINED HEART

Do I mind poverty? Never!
Poverty hurt no man's heart—
Only the word of the mean
Has the power to smart!
Though I were poor as the deer,   5
Were I free
I had sung like a bird,
Though but a beggar heard,
Lifting his head to see
    Whose was the song that stirred!   10

(n. d.)   *Copy-text: WS   Collated states:* None

1107   HILARIA*¹

Lift it from the dust,
    Beauty that has stumbled,
Wake again the trust
    In the heart was humbled;

Innocence is not   5
    Bought and sold—and sundered—
From the flesh that, caught,
    Suffered and was plundered!

* In *Blind Raftery*, by Donn Byrne.

(n. d.)   *Copy-text: WS   Collated states:* None

¹ The erring wife in *Blind Raftery and his Wife Hilaria* (1924) by Irish novelist Donn Byrne.

1108   LET ME, TOO, MAKE MY PRAYER

Let me, too, make my prayer,
One with that company,
Which, in hope's last despair,
Lifting the lute e'en there,
Still played full symphony.   5

And I would make, as these
Whom the rich prime has named,
Something old Herrick's bees,[1]
Moving amid their trees,
Might hear and unashamed.   10

Something, though small it be,
One in his hour of dread
Might whisper lingeringly,
Might whisper tenderly,
Leaving all else unsaid.   15

(n. d.)   *Copy-text: WS   Collated states:* None

[1] With MG's version of the modesty trope, cf. Robert Herrick (1591–1674): 'As my small pipe best fits my little note' in 'A Ternary of Littles' from *Hesperides* (1648), the title-page of which is decorated with bees, probably in reference to the commonplace comparison of poetic activity to the gathering of honey by bees.

1109   WHEN FROM ITS SECRET PLACE

When from its secret place speaks the unconscious mind,
    Calling upon the unaccustomed flesh to hear,
Maybe it is the soul of man that seeks to find
    Some way to tell its presence to the ear.
        Maybe the spirit is thus moved   5
            As move the buds to form in Spring;
        Maybe as when the music of his heart
            Bids some bird sing.

And in that mystery that deeper lies than flesh—
    Held in the flesh as life is held within its shell—   10

As the trapped leopard thrusts from out the netted mesh,
  So this, too, turns and thrusts from out its cell.
      Maybe the soul of man is stirred
        As are the sudden thews[1] of Spring;
      Maybe as when young leaves awake;   15
        As when birds sing.

Something within us speaks, we know not how or why,
  Its language still untaught us who must live by breath:
Poor breath that lives by that first Breath[2] which cannot die,
  And Which, though in the tomb, still conquers death.   20
        Ah, Love, with man (and words) behind
          The less a greater meaning springs;
        For him who hears the flowing sap
          A spirit sings.

(25 April 1926)   *Copy-text: WS*   *Collated states:* None
11 trapped *Ed.*] tripped *X*

---

[1] Physical powers.   [2] Metonym for God, who as Creator breathed life into Adam, whose fall condemned humanity to mortality ('Poor breath'). Line 20 refers to Christ, who manifests the breath of divine life in his resurrection from the dead.

I110   O, TO SING BEAUTY

O movement of the dust above decay,
  Singest thou, Summer? Singest thou the Spring?
What is it in thee, hid away,
  That stirreth thee to sing? . . .

O, to sing beauty as it should be sung,   5
  To name it in the fullness of its measure—
Not as from some poor spirit wrung,
  Or misers yield their treasure;

(3 November 1923)   *Copy-text: WS*   *Collated states: DT*, 25 December 1924, p. 4 as O TO SING BEAUTY (*A*)

2 thou, Summer] ~ ~ *A*   4 stirreth] stirrest *A*   ⁵sing? . . .] ~? *A*   5 O,] ~ *A*
8 treasure;] ~, *A*

But in untrammelled verse to rise on wings,
  Now the swift swallow, now an eagle soaring,   10
And still in each note, as it springs,
  Beauty to be adoring!

O, for the piercing word to wound and burn,
  Till of that wounding joy itself is born;
As when, with eyes dream-filled, we turn   15
  To watch the bursting thorn!

There to look in upon the folded leaf, and find
  New worlds of beauty where new buds unroll;
And then the wond'rous thing to bind
  Upon the written scroll!   20

Could we sing beauty as it should be sung,
  Loosed from the heart's full deep, free from the portal,
From what low depths he risen sprung,
  Then were man made immortal!

12 adoring!] ~. *A*   13 O,] ~ *A*   14 born;] ~, *A*   15 when,] ~ *A*   eyes] ~, *A*
16 thorn!] ~. *A*   17 There] O, *A*   leaf,] ~ *A*   18 new] now *A*   21 Could]
Ah, could *A*   beauty] it *A*   23 he risen] ~, ~, *A*

I111   SONG IMMORTAL

    Still must I sing, though I should die
    Consumed by fire I cannot hold!
    Though in grave cold I come too soon to lie,
    Song waits not on a mounting sigh.

    Sweet song that burns us in the heart!   5
    Sweet song that rends us to the bone!
    Though all alone, with death my only chart,
    Still must I give thee all my art!

(24 June 1923)   *Copy-text: WS   Collated states: DT*, 7 July 1923, p. 13 AS THE SONG
IMMORTAL (*A*)

1 sing,] ~ *A*   die] ~, *A*   3 cold I] ~/ ~ *A*   lie,] ~ *A*   7 alone, with] ~,/
With *A*

What if by breath life makes its way?
Yet in the bud the root is held!   10
So, God-impelled, though death the body slay,
Sings on one song death cannot stay.

9 What if] Though but *A*   way?] ~, *A*   **10** held!] ~: *A*   **11** God-impelled,
though] ~,/ Though *A*

I112   O FOR THE WINGS OF A DOVE[1]

O, with the careless heart
    Of a bird to rise in the height and go,
With only the wave of the wind to part—
    Earth, and the sea below!

Never to feel the weight   5
    Of the day's long care make claim of the hour,
But only to know in the vast, elate,
    All space for a dower.[2]

Not to be bound by time,
    But, uplifted high in the silent air,   10
With a fetterless will to soar and climb,
    Naught but the wing for stair;

There, as a swift made free,
    Outsailed all else in a passion of power,
To poise where the uttermost spaces be,   15
    At rest in the nower.[3]

(n. d.)   *Copy-text: WS   Collated states: DT*, 7 March 1925, p. 10 as O, FOR THE WINGS
OF A DOVE (*A*)   *WWld* (October 1930), p. 6, signed By Mary Gilmore, in "The Wild
Swan." (*B*)

Not otherwise recorded: *B*'s text is in italics throughout.

2 height] air *A*   **4** Earth,] ~ *A*   **4** below!] ~. *A*   **6** care] ~, *A*   **6** make]
the *A*   **8** All . . . dower] The infinite power *A*   **10** But,] ~ *A*   **10** uplifted]
~, *A*   **10** silent air] silence, rare *A*   **12** wing] *wind B*   **15** poise] ~, *A*
15 be,] ~. *A*   **16** in the nower] like a rower *A*

[1] I.e. to escape an unacceptable situation – traditional.
[2] See I81 n. 1.   [3] See I4 n. 1.

I113   THE DOOR

I have come lonely to my house,
    The house of flesh,
As one who from the little hut
    Of his young, fresh
And happy years went wandering forth,   5
    And then returns once more
    To its old hospitable door.

I have come lonely to my house,
    And it is dust;
Gone is the glowing form wherein   10
    Once lay my trust,
Gone the proud splendour of its worth!
    How strange from death's dark shore
    To come and seek in vain that door!

I have come back, eager as one   15
    To his old place
Who hopes for long familiar things—
    And finds no trace;
One who has never ceased to hear

(n. d.)   *Copy-text: WS   Collated states: Spin* (October 1924), pp. 10–11 (*A*)   *Wr*, 29
October 1924, p. 5 (*B*)[1]   *NZT*, 24 December 1924, p. 30 (*C*)[2]
1 house,] ~— *A–C*   **2** flesh,] ~— *A–C*   **3** who] ~, *A C*   **4** fresh] ~, *A–C*
5 years] ~, *A C*   **8** house,] ~: *A–C*   **9** dust;] ~ . . . *A*   ~. *B*   ~. . . . *C*
12 splendour] splendor *B C*   worth!] ~. *B*   **13** death's] Death's *A C*   **14** seek in
vain] find no more *A C*   ~, ~ ~, *B*   door!] ~. *A C*   **15** back] here *A C*   **17** for
long] to find *A C*   **18** trace;] ~— *B*

[1] See entry for lines 29–35. *B* explains: 'Reprinted from "The Spinner," a small
magazine of verse and prose newly published in Melbourne – a verse accidentally
omitted before being added.' In a letter to MG of 30 September 1924 R. A. Broinowski,
editor of *Spin*, apologised that it was too late for a new verse to be included, as the
journal had already gone to press. He continued: 'I am glad that you sent "The Door".
I[t] is a very striking and poignant thing, and I often think of it. It is rather terrible in
a way . . . if, after all the suffering in this world, we should be exposed to the danger
and horror of the situation you describe' (ML Papers vol. 11).
[2] *NZT* printed the poem as part of a notice for *Spin*, which provided its copy-text (see,
e.g., entry for line 9) but included the stanza missing from *A*, presumably deriving it
from *B* or from the manuscript sent to Broinowski (see preceding note).

Cry, deep in his heart's core,   20
    Sounds he had heard round one old door.

So, far at sea, will sailors dream
    They hear a cock
Crow from a farmyard fence, and wake
    In sudden shock,   25
To feel upon the face a tear
    For things they know no more,
    Known long ago round one old door.

And in The Scattered Lands[3] a man
    Will ride all day,   30
And in and out the grass will see
    A kitten play,
Hear a child's laughter, there, and dream
    He sees himself once more
    Sit by an old familiar door.   35

And in The Scattered Lands a man,
    Sodden with drink,
Will pause and sway as one whom some
    Sharp pang made shrink
(Struck as the dim-eyed by a gleam!)   40
    When, as from youth's far shore,
    A thought hails, passing, one old door.

And in The Scattered Lands where lone
    A woman sits,
Or, risen, trims her housewife fire,   45
    A shadow flits,
Or a voice calls, and suddenly

20 Cry,] ~ *A–C*   core,] ~ *A–C*   22 So] Far *A–C*   sea,] ~ *B*   24 wake] ~, *B*
28 long ago] *Om. A–C*   one] an *A–C*   old] old familiar *A–C*   (29–35) And . . .
door.] *Om. A*   29 The] the *C*   33 laughter,] ~ *B C*   36 man,] ~ *A–C*   39 pang]
thought *A–C*   40 gleam!] ~ *B*   42 thought] sound *A–C*   46 flits,] ~ *A–C*

---

[3] Combines two elements in Celtic myths of the Otherworld paradise, sometimes called
Tir-nan-Og, the Land of Youth. After the defeat of the Irish 'old people' (inadequately
translated as fairies) by humans, some retired to Tir-nan-Og. But some were dispersed
overseas where they retained the memory of this happy and longed-for place. In other
accounts, Tir-nan-Og is a place that, once left, could not be re-entered.

She sees far Sydney's shore,
And an old, old door she knows no more.

And I, coming again to mine   50
    Own house, find but
An empty echo answer there,
    And an old door shut.
. . . Ah, with the flesh sleeps memory,
    Not to be wakened more,   55
    Save through its own familiar door!

47 and suddenly] ~, ~, *B*   52 An empty] A haunted *A C*   53 an old door] a door
long *C*   shut.] ~. . . . *A C*   54 ˢ. . . Ah] ~ *A C*   55 more,] ~ *A–C*   56 through]
by *A C*   its own] that old *A–C*   door!] ~. *A–C*

1114   MOTHER AND SON

Born of my spirit, still mine in loss or merit,
    Child of my body, and fondling of my heart,
What wilt thou render me of whom did'st inherit,
    Wide the way or narrow where life sets thy part?

From the void I brought thee, in the darkness carried,   5
    Blind mouth I nourished, and formless that I formed;
Dreamed of thee, hoped for thee through what changes tarried,
    Curtained thee with calm though tempest round me stormed.

Thou whom from night I brought to wake at morning,
    Drawn out of chaos to fullness of estate,   10
Thou for whom I suffered, all my weakness scorning,
    How wilt answer, when life trumpets at thy gate?

(n. d.) *Copy-text: WS   Collated states: Spin* (December 1924), pp. 42–4 (*A*)[1]   *SV* (*B*)
Not otherwise recorded: Lines 1 and 3 are reversed in *A*.
2 heart,] ~; *A*   3 did'st] didst *A*   4 Wide the] What wide *A*   way] ~, *A*
narrow] ~, *A B*   where] *Om. A*   sets] shall set *A*   5 carried,] ~. *X B*
7 thee] ~, *A*   8 with] in *A*   stormed.] ~— *A*   9 whom] ~, *A*   night] ~, *A*
11 scorning, *A*] ~. *X*   12 How wilt] What of thine *A*   answer,] ~ *A*   thou
answer, *B*   trumpets] beats *A*

---

[1] Broinowski (see I 113 n. 1) wrote on 22 December 1924: 'I also want to congratulate
you on the poem which I had the honour of including in the December "Spinner."'

From the first fore-fathers brought I bone to make thee,
　　Brought thee steadfast pulses, shaped thee slim and tall;
Brought thee from the fathers fire to wake and shake thee,   15
　　When toward strange horizons power within should call;

Brought thee by my suffering, brought thee by my longing,
　　Twice ten thousand rhythms tuned to life's appeal;
I, the string high-tensioned to vibrations thronging,
　　Set and marked them on thy being as my seal!   20

I, the cup that held thee, leaned above thee hearing
　　All the moaning forest crying in the night;
Heard the winds wide raging, saw the lightning, searing,
　　Smite upon the shuddering lid of hidden sight;

Heard the long roll where the valley of the thunder   25
　　Shaken moved beneath the shout of heaven's might,
Gazed upon the stars, and, trembling at their wonder,
　　Knew the sudden thought that flies beyond all sight;

Watched in ecstasy where like a child's sweet smiling
　　Gleamed the new-cut silver of the threaded moon,   30
Marked, in gentled darkness, star by star come filing—
　　Planetary verse of an eternal rune!²

Aye, and long ere thou beneath my heart cam'st moving,
　　Gathered I an unthought harvest for thy sake;
Bent my head to swift obedience in behooving³   35
　　Ere the high tide of my being turned to wake.

All my heritage—thou still unknown—I brought thee;
　　On the altar of my heart I laid it down;

13 first] farthest *A*   fore-fathers] fathers *A*   forefathers *B*   15 thee,] ~ *A*
16 toward] towards *A*   call;] ~— *A*   18 rhythms] rhymes *A*   19 high-tensioned]
high tensioned *A*   vibrations] ~, *A*   21 thee] ~, *A B*   24 sight;] ~— *A*
26 might,] ~; *A*   27 and,] ~ *A*   28 sight;] ~— *A*   29 ecstasy] ectasy *A*
where] ~, *A*   smiling] ~, *A*   30 moon,] ~; *A*   32 rune] tune *A*   33 Aye,]
Ay! *A*   and] ~, *A*   37 heritage—] garnering . . . *A*   unknown—] ~ . . . *A*

I think it is one of the finest things produced by an Australian poet – it is most moving
and rich in music' (ML Papers vol. 11).
² Song: cf. entry for line 32, and E66 n. 2.
³ Obedience to that which is proper or needful (archaic).

Inly held as thine until I rose and sought thee
 By mine ancient birthright of the woman's crown.   40

Now what yield is mine of all my beaten harvest,
 Thorns that I have watered, sheaves that I have bound?
This, that where shalt ride, or in what hunger starvest,
 Some grain saved from out my gathering shall be found.

Ah, and more is mine! for, in thy blood immortal,   45
 I being dead cease not though seeming I am gone;
Lo, my life is but the step, and thine the portal
 Thorough which to ends far set I follow on.

---

39 Inly] Only *A* I only *B* thee] ~, *B* 40 crown.] ~! *A* 42 watered]
gathered *A* 44 saved] garnered *A* out] *Om. A* 45 Ah,] Ay! *A* mine!]
~!— *A* for,] For *A* blood] ~, *A* 46 I] ~, *A* dead] ~, *A* 47 step,] ~ *A*
48 Thorough] Through *A* which] ~, *A* set] ~, *A*

I115 TO MY SON

O thou, My Son, who, when thy youth began,
Put off thy childhood to become a man,
Who, where the tropic sees each day begun,[1]
Dost watch the coursing hours how swift they run,
"Mark ye tradition," sayest thou, and lo,   5
Thou speakest of "Eve—that woman long ago,"
Around whose name still fancy weaves her spell,
Whose name men call forever out of hell.

If I have failed thee aught, or helped thee on,
Think this of me when I away am gone: 10

(19 November 1920) *Copy-text: WS* *Collated states: Bn*, 10 February 1921, p. 3 as
UNTIL IN ME (*A*) *SV* (*B*)

1 O] Oh, *A* My Son] my son *A B* when] as *A* 3 where . . . begun] while the
table of the year is spun *A* 4 watch] match *A* run,] ~. *A* 5 tradition,"]
~", *B* thou, and] ~; ~, *A* 6 ago,"] ~", *B* 8 hell.] Hell! *A* 10 away] afar *A*
gone:] ~— *A*

---

[1] Springbank, the Gilmore property e. of Cloncurry in Queensland was close to the
Tropic of Capricorn.

How that we two were friends; such friends, it seems
As though that ancient woman's power still held,
Through all the blood of womanhood impelled,
Until, in me, thou tellest her thy dreams.

11 seems] ~, *A*   14 Until,] ~ *A*   me,] ~ *A*

I116   TO A BABE

Dear messenger of Spring,
   Who hast not yet
Forgotten thy white wing
   In the world's fret,

But still dost hold of God,   5
   In innocence,
All that life's withered rod
   Clothes with pretence—

The Spring has welcomed thee,
   Tying its bows   10
Upon the orchard tree,
   In white and rose,

And where young leaves still fold
   In sarcinet,[1]
For thee, in crimson rolled,   15
   Love's name is set!

O rainbow fair! O, bud
   Of heaven! thou dew
That on our earthly mud
   Shin'st ever new,   20

Surely thou art our Spring;
   The love of God
About thee, who dost bring
   Joy where grief trod!

---

[1] *Sarsenet*, a fine and soft silk material, in various colours (obsolete form).

O thou, love's innocent!   25
  Thou whom the star
Within the firmament,
  Watching afar,

Still knoweth for his peer:
  When, from thy home   30
Down wandering to us here
  Wast newly come—

When from thy heavenly range
  Thou camest near,
And found this world so strange,   35
  Knewest thou fear?

White as a pearl that shone
  Within the dark,
No earthly stain upon
  Thee set its mark,   40

And as I look on thee
  I ask, What bough
Of the heavenly tree,
  What bud, wast thou?

Wast thou thy father's? or   45
  Wast thou all mine
In the slow hours before
  My look met thine?

Or wast thou just a leaf
  Of Paradise,   50
Blown where my heart was thief,
  Love all thy price?

Ah! like a petal from
  A flower, so sweet,
So soft, so light to come   55
  Were thy small feet!

Spring's messenger art thou?
  Thou who dost bring

Joy's presence here, and now,
　　Thou *art* the Spring.   60

(n. d.)   *Copy-text: WS*   *Collated states:* None

I117   KILLED IN THE STREET

He was so frail,
　　So small where he lay dead,
Hands at the trail,
　　And slack the little head!
They laid him in her lap,   5
　　And still she did not weep,
But with his tattered cap
　　Fanned him asleep.
And then, "O God!" she said,
　　And then, again, "O God!"   10
　　And touched him where the shod
Hard hoof had marked his head.

(n. d.)   *Copy-text: WS*   *Collated states: Wr*, 2 February 1927, p. 5 as THE DEAD CHILD
(*A*)   *SV* (*B*)
Not otherwise recorded: A divides the poem into three 4-line stanzas.
3 trail,] ~ *A*   **4** head!] ~. *A*   ~; *B*   **5** lap,] ~ *A B*   **9** then,] ~ *A*   **10** then,] ~ *A*

I118   THE LITTLE BROTHER

He went. His going made no sound,
　　No door made movement as to close;
And now no vision shows his bound,
　　And where he journeys no man knows.

Only we know he went. Only   5
　　We know that, as the long hours go,
We count the empty days, lonely
　　For that loved face we used to know.
[cont. overleaf

(25 January 1926)   *Copy-text: WS*   *Collated states: Wr*, 24 February 1926, p. 5 (*A*)
7 the] each *A*   days,] day— *A*

Beside the gate his sheep-dog lies,
　　And, waiting, watches down the road;   10
Or, restless, moves about and sighs,
　　As though his heart, too, felt a load.

Sometimes he lifts his head and looks
　　With that long look all men may read,
Or seeks in old familiar nooks   15
　　The presence once blessed all his need.

And by the fence his pony stands,
　　And wonders why no more he feels
The reins beneath a boy's young hands,
　　The urging of two eager heels.   20

Ah, if, some day, this journey done—
　　Somewhere—upon some other plane—
We could but hear his quick feet run,
　　Old Bruno at his side again!

9 sheep-dog lies] old dog sighs *A*   10 road;] ~, *A*   11 sighs,] ~ *A*   13 head]
~, *A*   14 read,] ~; *A*   15 old] long *A*   19 reins] rein *A*   21 if,] ~ *A*
22 Somewhere—] ~, *A*   24 side] heels *A*

I119   LUIKIN' AWA' DOON

Luikin'[1] awa' doon, luikin' awa',
　　The Lord saw Jeannie playin' at ba';
An' though He had heaven itself and a',
　　Wistfu' He luikit at Jeannie's ba'.

Wistfu' He luikit as though nane saw,   5
　　Leanin' doon owre the heavenly wa';
An' intil His hert cam' cryin' the ca'
　　A bairn wad mak' for hittin a ba'.

[1] Looking. Other Scots words include 'ba'' (ball, line 2), 'luikit' (looked, 4), 'owre'
(over, 6), 'intil' (into, 7), 'wad' (would, 8), 'roustin'' (shouting, clamour, 9) and 'Yin'
(One, 10).

An' He saw a roustin' o' bairnies, plain,
  Wi' the wee Yin rinnin' ahint, alane;[2]   10
The ithers had ba's an' He had nane,
  Awa' in Bethlehem fields, lang gane.

Luikin' awa' doon, luikin' awa',
  The Lord saw Jeannie playin' at ba';
An' though He had heaven itself an' a',   15
  Wistfu' He luikit at Jeannie's ba'.

(n. d.)   *Copy-text:* WS   *Collated states:* None

[2] MG wrote to Hugh McCrae on 22 September 1930: 'I am glad you liked "Luikin awa doon . . . wistfu' he luikit at Jeannie's ba'." I could hardly see for tears when I was writing that, & "The wee Yin rinnin' ahint alane". I see him still, a little fellow in a not overclean well worn and faded garment, following on after the older longer legs *and always left behind*' (ADFA G62 1/2).

I120   THE SICK CHILD

Creep thou up to my shoulder,
  Lean there thy head;
Thou wilt forget, when older,
  Love was thy bed.

Only the old remember!   5
  Youth, in its day,
Knows but its burning ember;
  Age, the decay.

Hush, then, and slumber;
  Hush, then nor ail!   10
What should thee cumber,[1]
  Small and so frail?

[cont. overleaf

(16 March 1924)   *Copy-text:* WS   *Collated states:* Bn, 4 December 1924, p. 7 (*A*)
5 remember!] ~: *A*   **6** Youth,] ~ *A*   day,] ~ *A*   **7** ember;] ~— *A*   **10** then]
~, *A*

[1] What should burden or trouble you.

Ah, with my arms for cover,
  Sleep yet awhile;
Love, that must pine thy lover,   15
  Waits but thy smile.

I121   THE CRADLE SONG

Leave me not, leave me not,
  My little love,
Thou art my nursling,
  Thou art my dove;
Thou art my comfort   5
  When blows the cold blast,
Thou art my hope
  When Summer is past.

Leave me not, leave me not,
  My little lamb!   10
Shall I not hold thee
  With all that I am?
Home is thy sheepfold,
  My arm is thy nook,
Stay with me, then,   15
  And rest in my look.

Leave me not, leave me not,
  Little white bird;
Here, at my heart,
  Let sleep be unstirred!   20
Ah, though thy wing
  Hath its ache for the sky,
Mother would fold it,
  Lest thou should'st fly.

(8 September 1924)   *Copy-text: WS   Collated states: Wr*, 15 October 1924, p. 5 as
MOTHER SONG (*A*)

2 love,] ~! *A*   **3** art] are *A*   **6** cold] cruel *A*   **8** Summer] winter *A*
13 Home] Earth *A*   **16** look.] ~! *A*   **18** bird;] ~! *A*   **20** unstirred!] ~. *A*
23 it,] ~ *A*   **24** should'st] shouldst *A*

1122 SLEEP, HUSHLING, SLEEP

Sleep, hushling, sleep;
    Peace, restless one;
Arms for a cradle,
    My little son!

Arms for a cradle—   5
    Nay, never start!
Pillow and slumber
    Close to my heart.

Sleep, then, my babe,
    Softly and deep,   10
While I sing Jesu
    Tending His sheep;

Jesu whom Mary
    Held at her breast,
Lulled as I lull thee,   15
    Hush thee to rest.

Hush to my bosom,
    Thy mother am I;
Close to me, close,
    My little one lie!   20

While Jesukin, watching,
    Sings from the sky,
"Hush, little lambkin,
    Hush thee a-bye!"

(16 March 1924)   *Copy-text: WS*   *Collated states:* None

1123 A CRADLE SONG

Husha-husha-bye!
    In a lamb's skin
I shall wrap thee warm,
    Lest the winds break in.

I shall pillow thee   5
   On the swan's breast;
Hush, then, husha-bye,
   For soft thou shalt rest.

I shall cradle thee
   Deep in my arm,   10
Where, as thou liest,
   Nothing need alarm.

Hush, Innocent,
   My heart is thy throne!
Yet, on the man's path,   15
   Thou shalt walk alone.

(n. d.)   *Copy-text: WS*   *Collated states:* None

1124   THE SLEEPING CHILD

Draw near to beauty as it sleeps
   And holds an empery[1] all its own,
Which, as ye ask what state it keeps,
   Though ye are answered, dwells alone.

Ye, too, to that far country go,   5
   Where sleep gives boundary and frame;
Yet of that realm ye nothing know,
   Save the community of name.

But, O, the beauty of the child,
   As innocent and flexed it lies;   10
Beauty man sees, so dear and mild,
   And ever with his first surprise.

(n. d.)   *Copy-text: WS*   *Collated states: BPMag* (June–August 1930), p. 44 (*A*)
Not otherwise recorded: A's text is in italics throughout.
11 sees,] *sees A*   **12** surprise.] *surprise! A*

[1] Majesty.

I125   SYDNEY

There is an isle, a city isle,
   Laced by a thousand streets;
And summer, like a woman's smile,
Lingers about it for a while,
   Turns, and returns, and then retreats.   5
      And there like butterflies
         Yachts fill the Bay,
      While the white-caps[1] leap
         Like seals at play.

Beautiful are its women, and   10
   Great the hearts of its men,
They have furrowed seas at command,
And answered the call of land,
   Were it one man alone, or ten.
      And now, like butterflies,   15
         Yachts fill the Bay,
      And the white-caps leap
         Like seals at play.

Once on its coasts the dingo howled,
   The dim grey curlew cried;   20
And there the grisly bush-cat prowled,
And, under its feathery helmet, cowled,
   The mopoke's hautbois[2] fluted wide.
      Today, like butterflies,
         Yachts fill the Bay,   25

(n. d.)   *Copy-text: WS   Collated states: Hermes* (Michaelmas 1928), pp. 160–1 (*A*)

Not otherwise recorded: A divides the poem into alternating five- and four-line stanzas.
The collation for lines 26 and 35 is identical to 17.

2 streets;] ~, *A*   **5** Turns,] ~ *A*   returns,] ~ *A*   and then] ere it *A*   **6** there]
~, *A*   butterflies] ~, *A*   **8** white-caps] white caps *A*   **11** men,] ~; *A*
12 seas] the seas *A*   **13** land] the land *A*   **17** And] As *A*   white-caps] light
waves *A*   **19** coasts] coast *A*   **21** bush-cat] bush cat *A*   **22** helmet,] ~ *A*
23 wide.] ~! *A*

---

[1] Breaking waves.   [2] Oboe. See also I8 line 1 and author's note.

And the white-caps leap
Like seals at play.

Far down, in the dusk and the cool
Of lucent watery sweeps,
The great shark made its breeding pool,   30
And the sleek porpoise, school by school,
Played tig through the hummocky deeps.
And now, like butterflies,
Yachts fill the Bay,
And the white-caps leap   35
Like seals at play.

And this is our isle, our city isle,
Laced by its thousand streets!
May Summer ever upon it smile,
And Winters strengthen it as they file   40
Where the round o' the year repeats.
O, ever more like butterflies
May her white yachts fill the Bay,
And her rising waters crest, and run,
With a leap like seals at play.   45

28 down,] ~ *A*   and the] and *A*   29 lucent] limpid *A*   32 through the]
through *A*   deeps.] ~— *A*   33 And] Where *A*   38 its] a *A*   streets!] ~; *A*
39 Summer ever] ever the summers *A*   40 Winters] the winters *A*   it] ~, *A*
41 Where] When *A*   o' the] o' th' *A*   repeats.] ~! *A*   42 O,] ~ *A*   more] ~, *A*
butterflies] ~, *A*   43 her] the *A*   44 And . . . run,] Where the crests of the
wavelets rise *A*

I126   THE CAB-HORSE

Time has devoured him—taken him away!
No more we hear his homely *klip-klop* sound
In hasty tattoo from some distant bound,
Telling a tale of revellers, late astray,

(26 December 1926)   *Copy-text: WS   Collated states: DT*, 29 December 1926, p. 6
(*A*)   *SV* (*B*)

2 homely *klip-klop*] lovely klip-klop *A*   sound] ~, *A*   3 tattoo] ~, *A*
4 Telling] To tell *A*

Who yet have hope of haven ere the day;   5
While we, awakened in the dark profound,
Half vision at his heels some shadowy hound
Of night, haunting the streets in search of prey.

And with him also went the tinkling bell
That told how urban cows came home, at eve,   10
Through city streets to some familiar stall;
Gone, too, in Paddington, the travellers' well,
And, by the Barrack Gate,[1] where use gave leave,
The fire of him who camped beside the wall.

5 day;] ~— *A*   8–9 prey.// And] ~./ ~ *A*   9 bell] ~, *A*   11 stall;] ~. *A*
13 Gate] gate *A*

---

[1] Victoria Barracks, constructed 1841–50 in Paddington, Sydney, a focal point of military activity until the mid-twentieth century.

I127   OF WONDER

Give life its full domain and feed thy soul
With wonder; find thou in a clod a world,
Or, gazing on the rounded dewdrop purled
Upon a leaf, mark how its tiny bowl
Includes the sun: that sun in whose control   5
The planets run their courses, and the furled
Comet, onward driven, resists what hurled
It downward, outward to its nether goal!

[cont. overleaf

(n. d.)   *Copy-text: WS   Collated states: SMH*, 17 December 1927, p. 13 (*A*)   *SMH*, 7
April 1928, p. 7 as OF BEAUTY (*B*)   *SV* (*C*)   Wright1 (*D*)   Wright2 (*E*)

Not otherwise recorded: No stanza break after line 8 in *A* and *B*.
1 life its full] thou they heart *B*   domain] ~, *A B*   feed] build *B*   thy] they *B*
the *C–E*   1–2 soul/ With] ~ with *B*   2 wonder; find] ~. Find *A*   ~!/ Find *B*
thou in] within *C–E*   world,] ~ *B*   3 Or, gazing on] E'en as thou seest, in *B*
rounded] *Om. B*   4 mark . . . bowl] how from each limpid Pole *B*   (5) Includes
the sun:] The sun rays out— *B*   sun:] ~— *A*   ~; *D E*   that] That *B*
7 onward driven] outward driven *A*   in its fiery fall *B*   8 outward] ~, *A C–E*
its] some *A*   goal!] ~. *D*

O, as a child, how often have I stood
And watched a turning furrow, beauty spelled!   10
That rhythm, that curve of moving earth that felled
In endless seam upon the narrowing rood,[1]
Not e'en the sea itself has me so held,
So to my heart brought full beatitude.

9 O] Oh *B*   10 beauty spelled!] beauty-spelled: *A*   11 curve] roll *A*
12 rood,] ~! *A*   road; *B*   13 held,] ~; *A*   14 So] ~, *A*   beatitude.] ~! *B*

[1] *To fell* in sewing is to stitch down the wider of the two edges left projecting by a seam so that it lies flat over the outer edge. A 'rood' is a measure of distance or of land; here, the amount of land unploughed.

I128   THE THUNDER ROLL

He whom the tempest calls shall stand,
And he shall see, unfurled upon the land,
The darkling shadow of the cloud
That wraps the heavens as in a shroud;
And he, exultant, there shall hear   5
The deep, reverberant thunder rear
Its cresting head toward some far redoubt,[1]
Ere from its height it drops in mighty scroll,
      To slowly dwindle out
      In distant roll.   10

And he, who through long years has fought,
At last made free of storm (where youth distraught
Fared on, and knew nor way nor end,
Or but the torment's wide extend)
His clash gone over, he shall stand,   15
And hear beyond his falling sand,[2]

(n. d.)   *Copy-text: WS   Collated states: SV (A)*
2 unfurled] down-flung *A*   5 he] there *A*   there] he *A*   13 and] nor *A*
nor . . . end] the way it went *A*   14 extend] extent *A*   15 gone over] being ended *A*   16 hear] ~, *A*

[1] Bastion, raised work of fortification.
[2] Declining lifetime, as in sand running out in an hourglass.

Through endless generations borne, his own
Reverberations rolling, rolling on,
   To burst in seed far sown,
    When he is gone.   20

I129   THE LOOK DOWN[1]

BUNGONIA

Vast is the chasm, and in the deep, below,
Silence has fallen asleep beneath her tree;
But we, above the stark declivity,
Hear there the hush of winds we do not know,
While, in the void that covers all, the slow   5
Trail of the air, like thick soft hair flung free,
Draws with the moving earth, that far stars see
Like some unbodied head swayed to and fro.

O pigmy man, so like a thistle seed
Blown hitherward from out of space! O mote[2]   10
In an eternal wind! O little float
On Time's scarce entered sea, art thou the crown
Of all immensity? Nay, would'st thou read
Thy finite place, o'er this dark brink look down!

(n. d.) *Copy-text: WS* *Collated states: SMH*, 4 February 1927, p. 13 (*A*)

1 deep, below,] ~ ~ *A*   **2** her] its *A*   **3** But] Yet *A*   **4** Hear there] Still hear *A*
know,] ~; *A*   **5** While] For *A*   void] vague *A*   **6** thick soft] floating *A*
7 earth,] ~; *A*   that] which *A*   **8** Like] As *A*   unbodied] titanic *A*   **9** thistle
seed] thistleseed, *A*   **10** out of] distant *A*   mote] note *A*   **12** Time's] time's *A*
13 would'st] wouldst *A*   **14** finite] *Om. A*   brink] brink look down, *A*

---

[1] Cf. F154 and *HR*, Pt II, Chapter IX 'Bungonia and the Look-down'.
[2] Speck.

1130   OF POWER

All powers recessive in the atom lie;
From dominant to dominant we spring;
And yet, as in progression on we swing,
We lift recessives we had thought passed by.[1]
For the great pendulum of change, swung high,   5
Swung low, arcs wider than its upward fling;
We climb, but, if to climb were all, a king
Unkingdomed, man went spindling to the sky.

Therefore we stoop, must ever stoop to rise,
And what recessive backward falls must bring   10
To power lest progress fail, and, failing, dies
Like the lost bud that knows no pollened wing.
Yet there are those who ask Nirvana—where
All power recessive lies, unfecund,[2] bare!

(n. d.)   *Copy-text: WS*   *Collated states: SV* (*A*)
8 Unkingdomed, *Ed.*] ~ X *A*   11 failing] fruitless *A*

[1] E58, E59 and E90 exemplify MG's early interest in eugenics, in which mental deficiencies or disorders were seen as the result of faulty inheritance due to parental vice, 'bad blood' or a mysteriously adverse fate (see volume 1, Introduction, n. 66, and N1). But I130, R36 and R45 exemplify Lionel Penrose's observation in 1940 that '[m]uch attention is paid in all books dealing with human genetics to dominant, recessive and sex-linked types of inheritance': *The Biology of Mental Defect* (London: Sidgwick & Jackson), p. 102. MG became attracted to the new idea that recessive genes were not simply 'bad', but a potential resource – cf. 'all the powers, that once were ours,/ In life's still deep recessive sleep' (R45). See also O7.   [2] Infertile, barren.

1131   TO A FAR SHIP

O thou great ocean on
   Whose breast yon ship, less than a leaf,
Hath chosen its way, how small
   To thee its course, how brief!

(n. d.)   *Copy-text: WS*   *Collated states: BPMag* (March–May 1930), p. 31 (*A*)
Not otherwise recorded: A's text is in italics throughout.
1 ocean] *ocean, A*

As a shell thou could'st bruise,   5
　　And of its ribs could'st make
A hermitage for death,
　　Deep down where no dreams wake.
　　　And yet it plougheth over thee
　　　　With its short keel its path,   10
　　　And ministers of power it
　　　　Maketh thy winds, daring thy wrath.

And thou, O distant ship,
　　That on the far horizon gleamest,
So lone 'twixt sea and sky,   15
　　What in thy lot thou seemest,
No loneliness is thine,
　　For thou hast, even as man,
More than the kingdom of
　　Thine inch of length and span!   20
　　　And whether thou dost make thy port,
　　　　Or whether goest down,
　　　Thou hadst the tides in fellowship,
　　　　And in the storm was thy renown.

Though in thee no words be,   25
Yet, where man's life
　　Ascending veereth,
All that full speech might say
　　In thy making inhereth,[1]
O thou immortal dream   30
　　Of beauty wrought by man,
Who by devisal made,
　　While yet unknown the plan!
　　　Thou'st gone? My spelled eyes follow where,
　　　　Upon th' horizon seen,   35
　　　Thy trail of smoke still treadeth air,
　　　　To show the watcher where hast been.

---

13 ship,] *ship A*　　**14** gleamest,] *gleamest A*　　**26–7** life/ Ascending] *life
ascending A*　　**33** unknown] *unknown, A*　　**36** air,] *air A*

---

[1] Inheres, i.e. is inherent, innate.

We, too, like thee on life's
　Impulsing sea in wandering go;
In solitudes not lone:　　　　　　　　　　　　40
　For, in the to and fro
Of warp and change that make
　This lot of ours, we find
All things are one in the
　Wide kingdom of the mind.　　　　　　　　45
　　And when at ending we fare on,
　　　O, be the far-flung smoke
　　We leave behind, some song we sung,
　　　Some word of love we spoke!

46 fare on] *must go* A　　**47** O,] *O* A

I132　CHANGE[1]

The Gods, grown weary, passed from earth and came
Not back—all save the witling of the heights,
Who bore a scullion's[2] part, a scullion's name.
And he, grown sick of long, laborious work,
Found him a cranny by the lone seaside,　　　　5
And there he entered in and slept.
And as he slept there came upon his peace
A dream of dreadfulness, in which he saw
All movement cease, himself stand motionless;

(n. d.)　*Copy-text: WS　Collated states: Wr*, 26 September 1928, p. 5 (A)　*SV* (B)
2 back—] ~; A　　**3** bore A] bare X　　**4** long,] ~ A B　　**5** the] a B　　seaside]
sea side A　　sea cliff B　　**6** in] in awhile A　　**9** motionless;] ~. A

[1] Cf. 'To change and to flow . . . Is law and the world', from Ralph Waldo Emerson's
'Illusions' (Part ix of *The Conduct of Life*, 1860, rev. 1876), where Momus (Greek God
of mockery – 'witling', line 2) is mentioned in the prose commentary among masters of
illusion. He was banished from Mount Olympus for disrespect to the other gods. His
association with a cave (line 5) may be due to his mother, cave-dwelling Nyx (Night),
or to conflation with another of her sons, Morpheus, god of sleep. Cf. also George
Meredith's 'Ode to the Comic Spirit' (1888), where the eviction of Momus is causally
related to the passing of the gods (Book iv, lines 95–115).
[2] Low fellow, menial worker in kitchen and scullery.

And in his fear he wept, and like a child   10
That in the dark puts out its hand toward
Its mother's face, he waked and sought the sea.
And, as his pulses hammered heart and brain,
He heard the great slow-moving tongue
Of ocean lick upon the shore;   15
And there, returning to his place,
He slept again.

10 and] ~, *A*   then, *B*   13 And,] ~ *A*   15 shore;] ~, *A*   16 And] ~, *B*
there] so *B*

I133   HORSES OF THE MIND

Beautiful are they, that, ranging on the mountains,
Crop the green pasture, and drink at the fountains;
Bunching and scattering, and quick with sudden greeting,
Touching nose and high crest in a friendly meeting.

But more wonderful than these, bred on the mountains,   5
Are the thoughts a man thinks, unseen their fountains;
Unknown their eager birth, uncontrolled their breeding,
As they rise and range and scatter, onward speeding.

Like a herd, like a host—a flight of birds winging—
Now turn they hither, and now thither, swinging;   10
Unbitted as a foal, and yet, caught and bridled,
Man upon them rides, who as dreamer idled.

Beautiful the wild horse, screaming on the mountains,
Climbing on the height, quenching at the fountains;
But, more wonderful than these, man's thoughts awaking: 15
Drawn from out the vast, Creation in the making.

(n. d.)   *Copy-text: WS   Collated states: SMH*, 28 July 1928, p. 11 (*A*)   *SV* (*B*)

3 with] in *B*   greeting] meeting *B*   4 meeting.] ~ *A*   greeting. *B*   5 on]
upon *A*   9 host—] ~, *A*   ~,— *B*   a flight of] as light as *B*   winging—] ~, *A*
10 thither,] ~ *A*   11 and] ~, *A*   12 as] as a *A*   13 mountains] mountain *A*
14 fountains] fountain *A*   15 these] this *A*   thoughts] thought *A*   awaking:] ~, *A*
~; *B*   16 Drawn . . . the] Viewless, wingless, *A*   vast,] ~: *A*   Creation] creation *B*

1134 THE OLD BOOKSELLER

My heart (he said) is hungry for
The many friends I knew of yore,
Who, like young leaves upon a tree,
In high hope lusted young with me;
Death came and gathered them, and left,   5
In his strange choosing, me bereft.

Happy who at the good prime goes;
Not his the loneliness of those
Who sit, heart-starved, 'mid empty chairs,
In houses mocked by empty stairs;   10
Not his in suddenness to come
Where once familiar speech is dumb.

I have grown old (he said) and I
Am hungry for a day gone by.

(n. d.)   *Copy-text:* WS   *Collated states:* None

1135 DANUBE OR DARLING

Less than the Tiber? Nay!
Danube or Tiber, we have rivers fine as they![1]

Time is a slate where man
Writes down in deeds for script the way his wild course ran;

Thus the old rivers wear   5
The glamour of the past, born of life's current there.

And looking back one cries,
"Behold the Tiber!" as he sees with dewy eyes

Ranks of the dead in hosts
Go marching by, clothing its movement with their ghosts.   10

[1] On this theme, cf. T5.

So, too, one day shall we
Clothe rivers here that flow majestic to the sea.

(n. d.)   *Copy-text: WS*   *Collated states:* None

1136   THE BAGS OF DEATH

O the ungathered that decay has stolen—
    Keats in his youth and Shelley in his prime![1]
The heavy bags of storeman Death are swollen
    With harvest that was ripened ere its time.

Had these no deeper root than the frail flesh,   5
    Which, senile as it came, could only fail?
That gave no floor where they might later thresh
    A riper harvest with a wider flail?

They wrote a full man's thought in terms of youth,
    They ran before their feet had learned to walk;   10
Theirs was a stripling prime; then inborn drouth
    Took them while yet the flower was on its stalk.

Keats in his youth, and Shelley ere his time!—
    And Hardy, singing like a king of men,
Chanting the vision of his richer, fuller prime,   15
    In the deep measure of three score and ten.[2]

(13 January 1929)   *Copy-text: WS*   *Collated states:* None
3 swollen *Ed.*] swolen *X*

---

[1] Poets John Keats and Percy Bysshe Shelley died young: 1795–1821 and 1792–1822 respectively.
[2] Thomas Hardy (b. 1840) died 11 January 1928. I136 marks the first anniversary of his death.

1137   WHEN IN THE DUST I LIE

When in the dust my light is hid,
Tell if you must the things I did,
But let no word betray
Truth from its narrow way.

I shall not ask to be as one
Whom death must mask when all is done;
Mine be the light, although
Ragged and patched I go.

Pity I take not of any—
Few to forsake me, or many;
Only I ask that you
Tell that my heart was true.

(n. d.)   *Copy-text: WS   Collated states: Wr*, 31 August 1927, p. 5 as WHEN IN THE
DUST (*A*)   *SV* (*B*)

2 did,] ~; *A*   4 narrow] own strait *A*   6 all] life *A*   9 any—] ~; *B*   10 to]
who *A*   many;] ~: *A*   11 ask] would *A*   12 Tell] Told *A*

1138   OF WONDERS

I have heard trumpets on the wind,
And I have seen the cloudy banners of the sun thinned
Until distance hid them out of sight!
And I have heard upon the night
The roar of ocean haunt along the shore,
And lifting up my eyes have marked afar
The gleaming whiteness of a star;

(n. d.)   *Copy-text: WS   Collated states: DT*, 28 February 1925, p. 7 (*A*)   *SV* (*B*)

1 wind,] ~! *A*   wind's wild roar, *B*   2 cloudy . . . thinned] clouds about the sun
race *B*   3 Until] Until the *B*   sight!] ~; *B*   5 roar] voice *B*   shore,] ~; *A B*
6 And lifting] Have lifted *A*   have] and *A*   marked] ~, *A B*   afar] ~, *B*
7 The gleaming] Within the deep, the shining *A*   star;] ~. *B*

And I have watched the moon slow pace
The age-long path where heaven has set her face,
And looked upon the flower—   10
Love's beauty radiant for an hour—
And then, with sudden longing turned,
Back, where the homely hearth-fire burned.

But I have been drunken on
The beauty that has shone   15
Where the Incomprehensible has deigned to write!

8 I have] *Om. A*   9 heaven] Heaven *A*   face,] ~; *A*   10 And] And I have *A*
12 And] ~, *A B*   turned,] ~ *A*

I139   THE ROCK IS THY ROCK[1]

Lord, Thou hast pitten me oot on a rock,
    Thou hast beaten me wi' thy seas;
Thy hand has smitten me, bent and bowed,
    Thy wrath has wringit my knees;
Thou hast flung the breath of the win' at me   5
    Till the darkness covered me over,
Yet to the end, to the end of a',
    Lord, I was still Thy lover.

Thou hast stricken me sore, hast broken me doon;
    Thou hast left me alone i' the nicht;   10

(27 September 1918)   *Copy-text: WS   Collated states:* Wilkinson1 as YEA! THOUGH HE
SLAY ME (*A*)   *SV* (*B*)

Not otherwise recorded: Wherever copy-text has 'Thou hast', *A* has 'Ye ha'e'.
1 Lord,] God! *A*   2 hast] has *B*   thy] Thy *A*   seas;] ~, *A*   3 hand] Han' *A*
me . . . bowed] an' broken me sore *A*   5 of the] o' th' *A*   7 of] o' it *A*
8 lover.] Lover! *A*   (9) stricken . . . broken] pierced my soul, Ye ha'e hammered *A*
hast] has *B*   doon;] ~, *A*   10 alone] alane *A*   the] th' *A*   nicht;] ~, *A*

---

[1] MG wrote to A. G. Stephens on 17 March 1907: 'I have the broad easy mind of the
free thinker with the prejudices of Calvin. I keep off the rocks of Calvin as much as
possible, yet all my altars are built there' (*Letters* 38). 'Pitten' (line 1) is Scots for put;
other Scots forms include 'nicht' (night, 10), 'frae' (from, 11), 'mune-licht' (moonlight,
12) and 'en'' (end, 15).

Thou hast ta'en frae me the stars that shone,
   Thou hast darkened the white mune-licht;
Thou hast flung the spear, Thou hast swung the sword,
   Thou hast leant like an eagle at hover,
And yet, to Thy Face, I stan' at the en',   15
   For ever and ever Thy lover!
Yea, Thou art God! but Thou madest me;
The rock is Thy rock; the sea is Thy sea.

---

11 ta'en] taken *A*   stars that shone] sun i' th' noon *A*   **12** white] fair *A*   mune-licht;] ~, *A*   **13** flung] shotten *A*   **15** And yet,] Yet— *A*   Face,] ~!— *A*   stan'] ~, *A*   stand *B*   **16** For ever] Forever *A*   **16–17** lover!/ Yea] Lover.// ~ *A*   **17** God!] ~: *A*   madest] mad'st *A*   me;] ~: *A*   **18** rock;] ~, *A*

I140   ONE READ A WORD, AND ANOTHER REMEMBERED

The lightning looped a word across the sky:
   "I am: and That I am.[1]
Jehovah, Jahveh, Buddha, Brahm[2]—
   Above, and in all Gods am I.

"I am That which perisheth not, nor dies: 5
   I am: and That I am.
I am the mountain and the gramme,
   The dust, and that which risen flies.

"I am That which hath not been made by hands:
   I am love and death; I am Life;   10
I am the maker, I am strife—
   The void still waits on my commands.

"Tides pass not over me, nor tempests shake;
   I am, O man, I am!"
And I remembered there a Lamb,[3]   15
   Which came and suffered for man's sake.

---

[1] Cf. Exodus 3. 14: 'And God said unto Moses , I AM THAT I AM: and he said, Thus shalt thou say unto the children of Israel, I AM hath sent me unto you.'
[2] 'Jahveh' and 'Brahm' are alternative forms of Jehovah and Buddha.
[3] Christ the Redeemer, represented as the sacrificial lamb.

How shall we compass Him whose lightning flies,
   And writes in words across the skies,
When even the word, which instant dies,
   Blinds as it falls upon the eyes!   20

(22 April 1923)   *Copy-text: WS*   *Collated states:* None

I141   TO MAUD R. LISTON[1]

   Ah, if to me had never come
   The adding of the sum
   Wherein the flower
   Gave bees their dower,[2]

   If I had not watched willows leaf   5
   Themselves into a sheaf,
   Where-through was wrought
   An unknown thought,

   Or if that I had never seen,
   How, from its heavy teen,[3]   10
   Life, with each sigh
   That passes by,

   Still lifts on high its prayer, its hope,
   Than the blind things that grope
   The dark and die,   15
   What more were I?

(n. d.)   *Copy-text: WS*   *Collated states:* None

---

[1] Maud Renner Liston (1875–1944), author of eleven books of verse and the illustrated children's book *Cinderella's Party*.
[2] Endowment, portion.
[3] See I36 n. 3.

I142   DAVID McKEE WRIGHT[1]

Thou hadst thy song—
  Mine was the dream
Of one who still must long,
  Fitly the theme
To shape and know it strong.   5

Yet though with grace
  Song thou did'st make,
Left me is still the chase
  Whose echoes wake
My solitary place.   10

Thine was the realm
  Of words benign
In silken fields of vellum;
  The tempest mine—
Whose burst my words o'erwhelm.   15

Thine was the throng,
  Mine but the dream:
Who ever still must long,
  Fitly the theme
To measure with thy song.   20

(n. d.)   *Copy-text: WS*   *Collated states:* None

_____

[1] (1869–1928), Arthur Adams's successor as editor of the *Bn* Red Page, editor of Henry Lawson's *Poetical Works* (1925) and a prolific writer of verse.

I143   THE DEAD SINGER

"Youth came to his face!"
  They wondering said;
But I who had known him living
  Mourned for him, dead,
With his curtained eyes, and his dark hair   5
  Dank on his head.

And grieving I thought of
  His once quick ways,
And of how he had hungered,
  Defrauded of praise,
Till the pen from his tired hand fell
  In his last sad days.

What of youth had he
  To live in his face,
In the poor dead face so cold
  In the oaken case?
Only his look of pride he kept,
  Which naught could erase.

In the stark dignity
  Of death he lay,
Austere and calm, while the griefs
  He had held at bay,
Like a summer breath that is blown,
  Were fallen away.

In the stillness of death,
  Dark pages clean,
Like a dreamer in slumber
  He lay serene:
But O, the dropped lids on the eyes
  Where the tears had been!

10

15

20

25

30

(n. d.)   *Copy-text: WS   Collated states: Wr*, 19 October 1927, p. 5 (*A*)

Not otherwise recorded: A has 'she' and 'her' wherever copy-text has 'he' and 'his'; these
are listed if combined with another variant.

4 Mourned for him,] Thought of her *A*   dead,] ~ *A*   **5** eyes,] ~ *A*   **7–8** of/
His once] of her/ Once *A*   **9** hungered,] wandered *A*   **10** praise,] ~ *A*
11–12 fell/ In his] fell in/ Her *A*   **13–14** he/ To live] she to/ Live *A*
15–16 cold/ In the] cold in/ Its *A*   **17–18** kept,/ Which naught] ~, which/
Naught *A*   **18** erase] abuse *A*   **19** In] . . . ~ *A*   **20** lay,] ~ *A*   **21** calm,] ~; *A*
while] and *A*   **21–2** griefs/ He had] griefs she/ Had *A*   **25** death,] ~ *A*
26 Dark pages clean] She lay, serene *A*   **27** dreamer in slumber] sleeper who
slumbers *A*   **28** He lay serene:] Forgetting life's teen; *A*   **29–30** eyes/ Where
the] ~ where/ The *A*

1144   FRANK MORTON[1]

Whither shall our hunger turn to be fed,
Now that he is dead?
Snapped is the silver chord that sung so sweet.

When I heard a sound as of running feet
Come fleet, and more fleet,   5
"What is this woe they bear to us?" I said.

Then the beat of the feet
To me said, "He is dead;
The singer of songs is dead. . . ."

I heard the echoes repeat,   10
"He is dead";
The rocks of the hills repeat,
"He is dead";

And the saddened heart cries,
Like a leaf in the wind,   15
When the summer-time dies,
And the branches are thinned:

"He is dead! He is dead!
The singer of songs is dead!"

(17 December 1923)   *Copy-text: WS   Collated states:* None

---

[1] (1869–1923), journalist, novelist and contributor to many of the journals in which MG published, notably *Bn, Bkfw* and *Tri.* He published three poetry collections during 1916–22.

1145   DOWELL PHILLIP O'REILLY[1]

IN MEMORY

The leaves fall,
I watch them as they fall—

---

[1] (1865–1923), poet and fiction writer, prominent member of the Sydney literary scene and close friend of MG.

A little sound upon the ear
Only a friend could hear.

The leaves fall,   5
I watch them as they fall;
For time, or long or brief,
I knew each single leaf,
And each one gave to me
Some page in memory.   10

The leaves fall,
I watch them as they fall,
Marking from year to year
How few have reached the sere;
Some fell in early prime,   15
Finding too sharp the clime,
Finding too soon the spring
Had taken wing.

The leaves fall,
I watch them as they fall;   20
Some time I, too, shall go,
And maybe none will know
How much I loved all these,
My foresting of trees!

The leaves fall.   25
I watch them as they fall.

(6 November 1923)   *Copy-text: WS   Collated states: Bn*, 22 November 1923, Red
Page as MEMORIAL (no subtitle) (*A*)

Not otherwise recorded: The collation for lines 5, 11 and 19 is identical to 1.
1 fall,] ~: *A*   **2** fall—] ~. *A*   **6** fall;] ~. *A*   **7** time,] ~ *A*   brief,] ~ *A*
8 leaf,] ~; *A*   **13** Marking] ~, *A*   to year] ~ ~, *A*   **14** sere;] ~. *A*   **16** clime,]
~; *A*   **17** spring] Spring *A*   **20** fall;] ~. *A*   **22** And maybe] ~, ~, *A*
24 trees!] ~. *A*   **25** fall.] ~: *A*

1146   THE PALMER[1]

When thou canst no more with the eyes
   Of one who has loved life gaze on
The tender little flower that lies
   Beneath thy glance, and when is gone
The old hot-foot delight that would outstrip   5
Time in a rush of comradeship,
Turn toward the world thou once did'st know,
And in that look prepare to go.

Put away longing for the old delight
   That comes not back, and yet nor take   10
Thy palmer's scrip readied for flight
   As one who, though the sun awake,
Asks still the moon upon his face;
Who cowering huddles in his place,
Knowing to waken is to go,   15
Last look on all he used to know!

But fare thou on as one who in
   The pausing unafraid can stand
And wait the call, yet through the thin
   Voice still can hear life's full command,   20
Imperative, though his no more;
One who, beside the nether shore,
Can toward the world he once did know
Turn back, and look his love; and go.

(n. d.)   *Copy-text: WS*   *Collated states:* None

---

[1] Pilgrim. The 'palmer's scrip' (line 11) was a small bag or wallet, possibly for the receipt of alms, part of the medieval pilgrim's traditional insignia.

1147   THE SONG OF BILOELA[1]

Long long ago when I was a woman,
Then was my heart as the heart of a storm;
Then a ray of light in the night awoke me,
Or even a dream, unfolded afar.

I was an arrow in flight, and a sword;   5
I was a bough in the wind and a flame;
I was a tree with a nest of nestlings,
And the nestlings all had songs of their own.

I was a harp where the wind blew over,
And I was a leaf as I was the dew;   10
I heard the sun as he journeyed singing,
And I felt earth stir as he called her name.

When life was the quest, and life the treasure,
Then I was a house with a thousand fears;
I was the quick, and all things were alive,   15
In the days gone by when I was a woman.

I who was wild now ever go gently,
Though the pulse may leap to a moment's stir;
But never it leaps as it leapt and trembled,
Long long ago when I was a woman.   20

Now is the stress all fallen to smoothness,
And I look abroad as one from a bay;
I measure the storm, my storm gone ever,
As I ride with the reins in my hand, away.

(n. d.)   *Copy-text: WS*   *Collated states: Bn,* 5 March 1930, p. 52 (*A*)   *SV* (*B*)

1 Long] ~, *A B*   **3** Then a] A *A*   **4** dream,] ~ *B*   **6** wind] ~, *B*   **10** leaf] ~, *B*
13 quest,] ~ *A*   **20** Long] ~, *A B*   **23** ever] over *A*   **24** ride] ~, *B*   hand,]
~ *A*

[1] From *biloëla*: white cockatoo (Ridley). See Preface, p. xxxiii.

I148   AS THE WAYS DESCEND

I thought of a thousand things as I sat in the place
Where of old we sat ere time had wrinkled my face;
Now I could lean my cheek on your arm, the storms gone over,
My fingers laid on your hand as a friendly lover.

For combat is ended, combat the gesture of youth;   5
Old sieges threaten no more with their pitiless ruth;[1]
Only is left the heart, by its memories holden,
The rose on the far grey cloud, and the sunset golden.

What loomed and shook in the past shakes now no more;
Quiet lies on the sea, the rocks are far from the shore;   10
The bark is nearing at last the port of ending,
The watch called down from the peak, and the sails descending.

To some is given a calm in the younger years;
A kiss is only a kiss, not theirs the clamour that fears;
They can lean over the fence, safely linger and dally;[2]   15
Not theirs the leaping of power at life's revally.[3]

The tame lie free in the paddock; the fierce are chained and
        barred,
Strained by an inward fever, restless, ever on guard:—
Then how a touch can stir, or even a look can waken,
Till the terrible tides arise, and the house is shaken!   20

Storm is the blazon[4] of youth, the old are quiet;
Strange is that blossoming time, the pulses riot;
But stranger the calm that comes as the ways descend,
When two, who would kiss, can part in peace, combat at end.

(n. d.)   *Copy-text: WS   Collated states: Bn*, 22 January 1930, p. 50 (*A*)   *SV* (*B*)
3 storms] stress *B*   **7** heart,] ~ *A*   **14** clamour] clamor *A*   **16** revally]
reveille *A*   quick rally *B*   **18** guard:—] ~— *A B*   **19** Then] These, *A*   or]
how *A*   **22** pulses] pulses' *A*   **24** two,] ~ *A*   kiss,] ~ *A*

[1] Perhaps calamity, ruin, mischief (obsolete meaning of *ruth*); otherwise, pitiless pity
– the appearance of pity.   [2] Cf. E63.
[3] Waking call, variant spelling of *reveille* (military term). Cf. E20.
[4] Coat of arms or banner bearing an identifying heraldic sign.

I149   MEHALAH[1]

I have looked on life, she said, and life has been good;
    Toil it has held, and the pain that all must suffer;
The road has been rough, but in its roughness I stood,
    With a margin left for a rougher.

Now at last am I come to the end of it all,   5
    Where the winds have softened, the tempest is quiet;
But one pause yet, and I shall pass out at the call,
    With as little care as a ryot.[2]

I have watered my field, and have gathered my grain,
    I have looked for night with a harvester's longing;   10
But I bound not all, for a sheaf I spread on the plain
    Where the handless[3] came in their thronging.

Naked I stood, and now shall I grieve for the night?
    Shall I fear the dark as it clothes me in falling?
I have dwelt alone in my tent as an Arab might,   15
    Where I heard but the cry of the wild thing calling.

I shall not be afraid for the end of the day!
    Too long have I suffered the dread of the lonely,
That I should turn from the last of the sun with dismay,
    When faces me death, and death only.   20

I have stood neighbour to fear, but I fought the fear,
    Though the pulses hammered in sudden awaking;
But now is the fear all gone as a leaf at the sere,
    As a thirst that called for the slaking.

[cont. overleaf

(n. d.)   *Copy-text: WS*   *Collated states: Bn*, 18 December 1929, p. 58 (*A*)   *SV* (*B*)

Not otherwise recorded: Lines 29–30 are in italics in *A*.

8 ryot] pyot *B*   **11** plain] ~, *B*   **21** neighbour] neighbor *A*

---

[1] The source is obscure. S. Baring-Gould's *Mehalah: A Story of the Salt Marshes* (1880) has a proud and defiant female heroine, but no other relevance.

[2] See entry for line 8: a 'pyot' is a magpie or similar bird, a 'ryot' is an Indian peasant.

[3] Inactive, but especially incompetent in or incapable of action (obsolete). Cf. I151 line 37 and J20 line 1.

There is naught left to be done, for all has been paid;   25
   I have taken my wage, and look for no guerdon;
And now from the heat I have come at last to the shade,
   Who have borne the day and its burden.

   She stood at the threshold, old and gaunt.
   The Great Unconquered met her with chaunt.   30

29 threshold,] *threshold A*   gaunt.] *gaunt; A*

I150   EL CAMPO SANTO[1]

White like an orchard in the frost,
   Each glistening tree a stone,
Deep as a forest is the place
   Where each must lie alone;
Here the loud tongue of clamour dies,   5
   Here but the winds may speak,
The far gull cry, and in the night,
   The moon come pale and meek.

How many a father of the land
   Lies here in stately sleep!   10
They watched the land, and now the land
   For them the watch will keep;
The strong, the bitter, and the proud,
   Bides each within his place,
Who still, where history turns the page,   15
   With newer runners race!

Here falls all littleness away,
   And faults decay as rust;
Only nobility withstands
   The conquest of the dust;   20

(n. d.)   *Copy-text: WS   Collated states: SV (A)*
20 dust;] ~. *A*

[1] The Sacred Field (Spanish), referring to Waverley Cemetery, Sydney (see line 43, F126 and J28). The final line calls on the less common sense of *campo* as *encampment*.

And so, the child of later years
    Brings reverence, where the sire
Cherished an ancient enmity,
    Nourished a word of ire.

Death gives us immortality,   25
    'Tis life denies the crown;
'Tis life, the old penurious,
    Is niggard of renown!
We see the man, but seldom see
    Behind the man the flame;   30
And then death comes, and, at a breath,
    Glows from the ash his name!

Far in his Elban solitude
    Wentworth broods on alone;
Great Parkes, upon his mountain height,   35
    Speaks from a graven stone;
But old Sir John, companionable,
    As drum beats o'er him rolled,
Came forth amid a people's tears
    To lie in friendly mould.[2]   40

And here, for many an age to come,
    The young will tune the string,
And in the winds of Waverley
    Find other voices sing—
Hear Kendall's flute, and Daley's harp,   45
    And Lawson's lonely horn,
Which, from his own dark tower he turned,
    In sorrow all forlorn.[3]

---

21 And so,] So here *A*   22 Brings] Will *A*   29 see] ~, *A*   30 man] ~, *A*
41 come,] ~ *A*

---

[2] Sir John See (1845–1907), long-term politician, strong supporter of Federation and Premier of NSW 1901–04, was buried in the Anglican section of Waverley Cemetery, but not two other 'founding fathers' of Australia: Henry Parkes (1815–96, line 35) was buried on his property Faulconbridge, in the NSW Blue Mountains, while William Charles Wentworth (1790–1872), who died in England where he had spent the previous ten years, was buried on his family estate at Vaucluse, a situation likened by MG to Napoleon's exile in Elba (lines 33–4).
[3] Henry Kendall (1839–82), Victor Daley (1858–1905) and Henry Lawson (1867–1922)

And others, too, abide; for, here,
    A whispering multitude   50
Seeks for the laurel in the leaf,
    Upon the Celtic Rood![4]
And many a dreamer, dream-possessed,
    Shall see a host go by,
And, at a touch invisible,   55
    Time's ancient feuds shall die.

Peace be upon this quiet place,
    Where life forgets its wrongs;
Where man's dim sight enlarges on
    The thing for which it longs;   60
Where death denies that it is dark,
    And holds on high a lamp,
To show the Army of the Dead,[5]
    Stilled for a while, in camp.

51 leaf,] ~ *A*   **55** And,] ~ *A*

are buried at Waverley. The lyrical music of Kendall's and Daley's verse is contrasted to Lawson's more sorrowful mode, seen as lacking the heroism of Robert Browning's Childe Roland's final lines as he reaches the Dark Tower he has been seeking: 'Dauntless the slughorn to my lips I set,/ And blew' (see I30 n. 5).

[4] The Waverley memorial to the Irish patriots killed in the uprising of 1798 incorporates a Celtic Cross ('Rood'), having a circle behind the four arms. See also J28.

[5] Cf. I38 for a development of this trope.

I151   THE LAST SHIFT[1]

Each year The Caller at my door
Knocks, with his last call, one knock more;
"Awake!" he cries and onward flies;
    Soon I shall cross my floor,
And face the dusk of life's last door.   5

(n. d.) *Copy-text: WS* *Collated states: Wr*, 11 February 1931, p. 5, signed Mary Gilmore, in "The Wild Swan." (*A*)

2 Knocks,] ~ *A*   call,] ~ *A*   **3** cries] ~, *A*   **4** floor,] ~ *A*

[1] Published on MG's final Women's Page in *Wr*: see textual note.

And so against the years to come,
When eyes are blind, and lips are dumb,
In leaf by leaf I write my brief—
My testament which says
Praise be to God for all my days.   10

If in the place to which I go
There be no little lamp to show,
If in the pit no spark is lit,
And no door opes again
By which to climb the ways of men,   15

If darkness there must ever fall,
Dust be the common lot of all,
Still do I say while yet I may,
Blessed be God, Whose might
Brings day forever out of night.   20

For Spring shall bloom no less that I
Deep-mouldering in the earth must lie;
So in this hour I bless the flower
Whatever flower it be,
And grass whose sheaf shall cover me.   25

I bless the bees that shall hang over
Garden and heath and bloomy clover,
And bless the laughter coming after,
Where children's voices rise
Higher than wisdom in old eyes.   30

I bless the little birds shall sing
"Comes Summer soon, for now is Spring!"
As, through the brake[2] where fledglings wake,
The dew-bright sun looks down
Where life has built its little town;   35

And blessed, too (with rest and peace,)
Be storm and stress, lest handless ease

---

11 If] ~, *A*   go] ~, *A*   15 men,] ~. *A*   18 say] ~, *A*   19 God,] ~ *A*   22 earth]
dust *A*   23 flower] ~, *A*   30 eyes.] ~... *A*   31–45 I bless ... roam.] *Om. A*

[2] See I59 n. 1.

In sloth betray, to slow decay,
All this dear race has won
Where nations must their courses run;   40

And blessed be God, that, though men die,
The heavenly hosts unchanged reply;
That, o'er the hill, the fold-star[3] will
At eventide bring home,
With every flock, the feet that roam.   45

O friends, when this day ends, and I
To the last call must make reply,
Think only this of mine amiss:
Forgiveness covers all,
Where best is naught, and strongest fall.   50

For I have loved my kind; have held
None enemy; none have compelled
Unwilled to take aught for my sake;
None have I bound—lest might,
Far set, should fail of utmost height.   55

The hour is come? The Caller knocks?
Slip out the bars, unkey the locks!
"Awake!" he cries? Now must I rise
And face, the last shift o'er,
Death's old, oft-opened, battered door.   60

46 O] ~, *A*   47 the] that *A*   56 come?] ~! *A*   knocks?] ~! *A*   58 cries?] ~. *A*

[3] Evening star: see F6 n. 1.

I152   THE TOTEM POLE

Though all should pass with careless look,
O book
That is my boomerang and spear,
It is my heart lies buried here.

(n. d.)   *Copy-text: WS   Collated states: SV* (no variants)

SECTION J

The Rue Tree (1931)

BOOK I: *ST. PHILOMENA*[1]

[1] *RT*'s dedication reads: 'This Book is inscribed to Four Saints to whom through whom and for whom it was written and three of them are named Brigid: Gabriel: and Philomena.' These are the religious names of three of the nuns of the Convent of Mercy who nursed MG during her time in Goulburn (see volume 1, Introduction, pp. li–liii). St Brigid, b. *c.* 450 of a pagan father and Christian mother, played a major role in establishing Christianity in Ireland and was a patron of learning and the arts. St Gabriel the Archangel, venerated as the messenger of God, is one of only three angels named in the Bible. St Philomena, a putative youthful Italian martyr of the early Church, was made patroness of the Children of Mary by Pius IX in 1849 but her cult was suppressed in 1961 by John XXIII.

Little is known of the three nuns, except that Sister Philomena was Mother Superior (*CG* 277). Several unpublished poems relate to her: one MS (NLA 727 2/3/11) of Pt II of the unpublished 'Behold Thy God' (alternatively titled 'In Exitu Israel') is annotated by MG: 'For Mother Philomena's Jubilee'; a poem titled 'Written for Mother Philomena' in NLA 8766 10/7/7 but entitled 'Sister Philomena' in Buf 173/5/95 is dated 20 June 1921; NLA 727 2/3/7 holds a different poem with the latter title, dated 22 December 1922 ; and in NLA 727 2/3/2 'The Plaint', dated 1 September 1919, is headed 'Verse for Mother Philomena and Goulburn Convent'. See volume 1, Appendix, for manuscript locations and descriptions.

J1   A CHRISTMAS CAROL

"Nowell!" rang the great bell,
    And "Nowell!" rang the small,
"Christmas comes a-wassailing[1]
    By house and by hall;

"Christmas comes a-wassailing,   5
    As though, with kingly air,
Someone more than mortal came
    Walking down a stair."

[cont. overleaf

(16 December 1928)   *Copy-text: RT*   *Collated states: ST*, 23 December 1928, p. 18 (*A*)

Not otherwise recorded: The collation for lines 2, 21 and 22 is identical to 1.
1 Nowell!] ~, *A*   **4** hall;] ~. *A*   **5** a-wassailing,] a-waissailing *A*

[1] Celebrating, making good cheer, especially by going from house to house to sing carols and

Then louder sang the great bell,
    And louder sang the small;   10
Yet He who came with kingly air—
    They found Him in a stall;

They found Him in a manger,
    His mother kneeled beside,
But high above that humble place   15
    Kings saw a star abide;

They saw the star and followed it,
    And then they louted[2] low,
As come the Kings of earth, to-day,
    To lout as long ago.   20

So "Nowell!" sing the great bells,
    And "Nowell!" sing the small,
That He Who came to Bethlehem
    May come to house and Hall.

10 small;] ~, *A*   11 Yet] But *A*   air—] ~ *A*   12 stall;] ~. *A*   13 manger,]
~ *A*   15 But high] And yet, *A*   that humble] His sleeping *A*   place] ~, *A*
16 abide;] ~. *A*   19 As . . . earth,] Where kings of earth bow down *A*   20 To]
And *A*   21 So] *Om. A*   24 Hall] hall *A*

___

songs of good wishes for Christmas and the coming year. For biblical accounts of Christ's
birth see Matthew 1.18 – 2.12 and Luke 2. 1–20. The annunciation of the Nativity to the
shepherds is in Luke, the arrival of the star-summoned Magi in Matthew: in popular
tradition the two accounts merge. See also M57 and M60.
[2] Bowed, made obeisance.

J2   AVE MARIA PLENA GRATIA[*][1]

Ah, as by Him man climbed to God,
So by His Mother's hand men climbed to Him!
Warring the old gods lived, vast, vague, and dim;
With dreadful faults the heavens they trod;

[1] Hail Mary Full of Grace: see J75 n. 1.

Then, on their conflict, and their verge,   5
See the frail figure of a Maid[2] emerge!

And as before He breathed she held Him close,
Who knew not any flesh save hers,
So through the Middle Centuries, dark and gross,
Mark how again she ministers.   10
Twice hath she given Him to earth;
Twice had He, of her, human birth.

[*] An Anglican clergyman, deprecating bigotry, said that it must never
be forgotten that it was to the devotion of Mary, in the Middle Ages,
that we owe to-day's belief in the humanity of Christ.

(10 January 1924)   *Copy-text: RT*   *Collated states:* None

[2] The doctrine of Mary's Immaculate Conception (conceiving and giving birth without
sexual intercourse) is based on Matthew 1. 18–23 and Luke 1. 26–38.

J3   LIKE SOME WHITE CITY FAR

There is a nun in every woman born,
Who, though beside the very gates of hell,
Still keeps within her heart a secret cell;
And, like the nightingale, which, night and morn,
Leans down its throbbing breast upon a thorn,   5
That sweeter, higher yet, her song may swell,
So stoops she, in a love no words can tell,
To lift the broken and to heal the torn.

O woman, who for all mankind still sees
In shining vision some white city, far,   10
Rise for an instant on the day's dim sight,
O soul of steadfast hope, whose tender knees
Bend in a worship where still glows the Star,[1]
How fair thou shinest in man's dreadful night!

(22 December 1921)   *Copy-text: RT*   *Collated states:* None

[1] The Star of Bethlehem, pointing the way to Christ: see J1 n. 1.

J4   THE DEVOTED

They do not break—not these! But sometimes toward
The end they faint, and flags the tireless beat
Of the intrepid heart, as though the heat
Of their long strife had brayed the silver cord,[1]
And stolen upon the margins of life's hoard.   5
They do not break; but, O, where sails their fleet,
And stormy hours in endless round repeat,
The sea of time is with their wreckage stored.

For this they gave, and that; and here they bled,
As of the heart's deep cargo naught was saved   10
When love with shrouded face went by, a wraith!
And still they kept the code where'er it led,[2]
The course, what coasts its lonely waters laved,[3]
Proud in resolve and venerable as faith!

(25 December 1921)   *Copy-text: RT   Collated states:* None

[1] In Ecclesiastes 12. 6, the silver cord is a symbol of life; to bray is to break into pieces, usually by pounding, as in a mortar.
[2] Obeyed the religious Rule. Vows of chastity taken by monastic orders, including nuns, not only required celibacy, but forbade 'special affections' within the community (cf. 'lonely', line 13).   [3] Washed.

J5   A PRAYER

Lord, when Thou lookest towards the earth,
    Wilt Thou remember them,
Who, making Thee their only worth,
    Touch life but by its hem;[1]
Whose eyes look not upon the child,   5
    Save as all men are theirs,
Who suffer, and are reconciled,
    Though all the flesh despairs?

[1] Cf. J4 and n. 2.

When to this earth Thou shalt look down,
   Remembering far-off ways,   10
Where Thine Own heart knew sorrow's crown,
   Suffered its lonely days,
Wilt Thou not turn Thine eyes where these
   Follow where Thou didst tread,
Who, though they drink life's darkest lees,   15
   Still bless for Thee Thy Bread?

What though in hungers each must bleed,
   Each on his cross must hang,
Self-sacrificed for others' need,
   Yet Thine they count each pang!   20
Ah, and in what deep love for man,
   For whom Thou death didst dare,
The long, slow death Thy cross began,
   For Thee they bear, they bear![2]

(6 December 1923)   *Copy-text: RT*   *Collated states:* None

[2] Christ's sacrificial death on the cross (see Matthew 27, Luke 23, Mark 15 and John 19) was regarded as the model for Christian sacrifice of personal desires, worldly goods, even life, in his service (see J11).

J6   THE SILENT FELLOWSHIP[1]

I

They wait, the Silent Fellowship,
Your grief and mine to hear;
They lean, whose feet must never slip,
Life's whisper at their ear.

They, for the sake of other's need,   5
By faith stand ever bound;

(7 December 1924)   *Copy-text: RT*   *Collated states: CP*, 18 December 1924, p. 24, Pt I only, as THE PRIESTHOOD (*A*)

0.1 ⁵I] *Om. A*   **5** They,] ~ *A*   need,] ~— *A*   **6** By faith] For us!— *A*

[1] The priesthood, as in the title of *A*.

I have not known so great a deed,
Save where much love was found.

II

To them the broken turn,
Where, with old longings born of pain,   10
Men, scarcely knowing, yearn
To find th' Eternal breast again.

For they are those who serve
Men's wandering souls as they were ships;
Who, though the current swerve,   15
Bring each one homing to the slips.

8 much] such *A*   8.1–16 ᵛII . . . slips.] *Om. A*

J7   THE RUE TREE[1]

The Rue Tree is the tallest tree,
    None other is so tall;
The Rue Tree is the smallest tree,
    None other is so small;
But O, where'er its dark head grows,
    One root is in the heart,
And every man its sad fruit knows,
    Or walks as one apart.

There was a Rue Tree had no leaf
    But a cross-piece set above;   10
On either hand there hung a thief,
    But at its heart was Love;[2]
And judges walked behind a Rue
    That grew a gallows-tree,

(13 July 1930)   *Copy-text: RT   Collated states: SV (A)*
9 leaf] ~, *A*

[1] Specifically the cross on which Christ was crucified; generally, a symbol of sorrow
and compassion. Rue appears in *RT* in several linked senses: the literal one of the

Where they who followed after knew   15
    Whose breath came piteously.

And many a one in prison cell
    Waters a Rue Tree there,
As down his slow tears dropping well,
    And his sighs break on air.   20
For the Rue Tree is the tallest tree,
    None other is so tall;
The Rue Tree is the smallest tree,
    O none so sad and small.

19 down . . . tears] his slow tears down *A*   **22** None] No *A*

aromatic perennial herb used for medicinal purposes, and the abstract ones of regret, grief and compassion.

[2] On the crucifixion of Christ ('Love') between two thieves, see Matthew 27. 35–8, Mark 16. 25–8, Luke 23. 32–43 (the sole account of the penitent thief) and John 19. 18, where they are not identified as thieves.

J8   SOGGARTH AROON[1]

O, there will come a day
In the full round of time,
Measure it swift or slow,
In set of sun or climb,

A day that will not know   5
One whom they loved, so much,
The very child, that fell,
Went happier for his touch.

They shall remember him,
All in some strange, sad day,   10
Crying its emptiness
For him, away, away!

[1] Literally, 'Priest dear' (Gaelic): the title of a poem by John Banim (1798–1844) in praise of the priest who 'Knelt by me, sick and poor' and 'Made the poor cabin gay': in *The Golden Treasury of Irish Songs and Lyrics*, ed. Charles Welsh (New York: Dodge, 1907).

There by the foot of the stair,
There where you see him stand,
Think of the empty air   15
Meeting the outstretched hand!

(17 April 1921)   *Copy-text: RT   Collated states:* None

J9   THE DEVOTED

Ah, through what storms, what storms
    Of flesh that sweated off the bones,
Yet which through tempest kept the key,
    And answered to the higher tones!

In this strange thing called life, we see   5
    The mass walk where the road is wide;
Nor stress nor deepening undertones
    The slackness of their common chord divide.

But they who from lone watchings meet
    The sunlight gleaming on the height,   10
Who look from alp to higher alp,
    What vigils theirs by day and night.

Stringed to a code, like some full harp,
    These must their steadfast answer make,
Though through each throbbing chord sings life,   15
    Higher, and yet higher—sometimes to break.

(24 December 1921)   *Copy-text: RT   Collated states:* None

J10   WHO SHALL BE JUDGE?

Who shall be judge? The meek who find
Never a thorn within the mind,
For whom no thistles grow
Where in their milding ways they go,

Whose lives are but a little song,   5
Unknown the full note of the strong?
Or shall they judge, in whom the thorn
In lacerating strength is born?

Ah, where life's deepening hunger waits,
Who shall be judge? Who keeps the slates   10
Where passion writes its pain,
And love's sad eyes look out, in vain,
Asking if help come o'er the plain?
Who shall be judge? No judge they need,
Who forward march, and inly bleed.   15

(7 December 1923)   *Copy-text: RT   Collated states: SV (A)*
3 grow] ~, *A*   **4** Where] ~, *A*   ways] ~, *A*   go,] ~. *A*   **10** keeps] keep *A*

J11   THE PRIEST

Like a tall pine, the winds about his head,
"Though thou dost buffet me thou art of God,
O stormy wind," he said;
"And shall not He, Who made, declare the rod?"

Ah, though the world deny,   5
Who would not find Thee, such being nigh?

For these are sight to eyes that wander blind,
And they are masts that save the beaten sail;
Are those who stand and bind
The sheaves, that else were scattered to the gale.   10

What though the world decry?
Man still shall find Thee, such being nigh!

                                        [cont. overleaf

(n. d.)   *Copy-text: RT   Collated states: NZT,* 17 December 1924, p. 32 *(A)*
1 Like] (For the *N.Z. Tablet.*)// Like *A*   head,] ~! *A*   **5** deny] decry *A*
9 stand and] still must *A*   **10** sheaves,] ~— *A*   **11** What] Ah! *A*   decry?]
~, *A*   **12** Man . . . Thee] Who would not find Him *A*   nigh!] ~? *A*

Like a tall pine! The howling winds of life
May beat and bruise, yet never bend that head,
As, steadfast in the strife,   15
"Though He should slay me, I am His," he said.

13 pine!] ~! . . . *A*   14 beat] ~, *A*   yet] but *A*   16 me,] ~ *A*

J12   JESUIT FATHERS

Amen, Amen, and they went,
Out on the trail of Thy Bugles;
The star and the lonely pine
On the mountain peak their fugles.[1]

Death beckoned them;   5
Death followed them;
Death, an[2] he could, had conquered them;
But still they followed Thy Bugle.

Lord, Thou art towering tall!
Who but the mighty could call,   10
And, strong men, take up Thy cross,
And follow Thee, careless of loss!

(6 September 1928)   *Copy-text: RT   Collated states: Adv,* 1 November 1928, p. 5 (*A*)
2 Bugles] bugles *A*   3 star] ~, *A*   4 peak] ~, *A*   fugles.] ~! *A*   7 an] an' *A*
them;] ~, *A*   8 Bugle] bugle *A*   11 cross] Cross *A*

[1] Guides; the specialised military sense here (see I3 n. 3) amplifies the metaphor of
God's bugle-call to arms (lines 2 and 8).
[2] If (archaic).

J13   GUNDARY PLAIN[1]

I have seen distance and have drunk of it,
Quenching a soul's thirst in unmeasured space;

[1] See F165 n. 1 and H7 n. 1.

Seen on the pampa's[2] edge great stars enlace
Courses eternal on the darkness lit;
Seen the still snows whose messages time writ   5
On Andean peaks, where the blue glacier's trace
Shrinks to a line upon a distant face:
On whose far heights the waiting condors sit.

And I have come once more to mine own land,
And stayed my wanderer's heart to her again.   10
Ah, with what joy unabated now to stand,
Here, in this little town where I was born,
To watch the shadows cross Gundary Plain,
And see the sun dance up on Easter Morn!*[3]

* When we were very little children our parents used to wake us on
Easter Morn to see the sun dance, rejoicing in the Resurrection. And
as he danced like a great golden dish of light we were taught to turn to
our parents and to one another and say, "The Lord is risen! Christ is
risen today!" I understand that Russia is the last country in which this   n5
custom retains, though no longer officially.

(n. d.)   *Copy-text: RT   Collated states: Spin* (March 1925), p. 91 (*A*)

3 pampa's] pampas' *A*   **4** eternal] ~— *A*   on the] upon *A*   **5** Seen] See *A*
6 peaks,] ~: *A*   **9** once more] again *A*   land,] ~ *A*   **10** to her again.] in her
pure calm! *A*   **11** Ah] Oh *A*   unabated] unbated *A*   stand,] ~ *A*   **12** Here,]
~ *A*   **13** To watch the] Where the long *A*   cross] mark *A*   Gundary Plain]
Gundary's palm *A*   **14** Morn!*] morn! *A*   n1–6 *When . . . officially.] *Om. A*

[2] Wide grassy plains of Argentina: for MG's time there, see volume 1, Introduction,
pp. xxxv–xxxix.
[3] Nettie Palmer wrote to MG on 20 May 1925: 'Although it's a little behindhand, I can't
help writing to tell you that your lovely "Spinner" sonnet inspired these Palmers to rise
before daylight and climb a fine eastern hill to "See the sun dance upon an Eastern morn".
It did, too' (ML Papers vol. 16).

J14   CATHLEEN-NI-HOULAHAN[1]

O Thou, my Lord, Who on the cross didst hang,
Thou from Whose side the wounded blood-stream sprang,
The nails, that broke Thy flesh within,
Asked of Thee, trembling, to forgive the sin;

[1] The legendary figure who sold her soul to the devil to gain food for her people in a time

The sun that might have burned Thee veiled its face,   5
And only man was fallen from his grace;
And, when entombed didst lie beneath death's spell,
E'en Satan mourned for Thee awhile in hell.

Man wounded Thee and left Thee without care,
Man took Thy robe and reft Thy body bare,   10
Man nailed Thee on the cross—the women crept
About Thy bruised feet, and o'er them wept.
And yet, I, Magdalen, would dare man's sin,
If, by that sin, man's pardon I might win.²

(19 November 1920)   *Copy-text: RT*   *Collated states:* None

of famine: her identification with Mary Magdalene in line 13 is based on the traditional
representation (involving conflation of several biblical references and narratives) of the
Magdalene as exemplary of the repented female sinner.

² In lines 1–12 the tradition (e.g. the Anglo-Saxon 'Dream of the Rood') that the
natural instruments of the Crucifixion (wood, nails) were appalled emphasises man's
sinful brutality as does the compassion of the women, including Mary Magdalene
(line 13), at the foot of the cross (John 19. 25). Cathleen's argument in lines 13–14 must
be seen as preceding the altruistic pact with the devil that will nonetheless align her
as a sinner, not only with Mary Magdalene but with all mankind ('man's sin'). The
(implicit) parallel argument is that the Original Sin of Adam and Eve had a fortunate
outcome in necessitating the manifestation of God's love in the redeeming life and
death of Christ.

J15   ACCUSING EYES¹

I saw the pale procession come, with heads
Down-bent and shadowed eyes that looked at me;
Accusing eyes that from their hollow beds
Burned with a sombre fire, dark as the sea,
When light, dimly reflected and diffused,   5
Breaks through a cloudy dun livid as though
The very heart of heaven itself were bruised,
And its tremendous pulse beat slow, beat slow!

¹ Homiletic literature often represents the soul reproaching the body for its unrepented
sins during the judgement that follows the resurrection of the dead (see Revelation 20.
12–13). Here the sins themselves lament their loss of Heaven because of humanity's
failure to fulfil Christ's injunction to teach men to seek its kingdom before all else.

I saw the pale procession come, my sins,
Thy sins, the sins of all the world: so sad   10
In their dim resurrection there! They yearned
And wept: "Alas, for us no heavenly Inns
Are held as ours! poor thwarted deeds that had
Been gifts to God, had man us Godward turned!"
I saw the pale procession come . . . my sins . . . thy sins! . . . 15

(23 April 1922)   *Copy-text: RT*   *Collated states:* None

J16   THE COMFORTER

The son shall love his mother first,
    Yet hold her woman to the end;
His heart shall call to her in thirst,
    And in its quenching none offend;
For strait[1] is kept, by each man's will,   5
    The compact that no man may scorn;
So each man holds in reverence, still,
    The nun in every woman born.

High rides man's wrath above the world,
    Like some red sun within the sky,   10
The javelins of hate are hurled,
    And faiths once sacred fail and die;
Yet to a woman's knee man turns,
    In spirit wounded, bruised, and torn,
And seeks—poor Lazarus[2] who learns—   15
    The nun in every woman born.

[cont. overleaf

(20 December 1921)   *Copy-text: RT*   *Collated states: Wr*, 1 March 1922, p. 5 (*A*)

1 first,] ~ *A*   **2** Yet] And *A*   her woman] ~, ~, *A*   end;] ~, *A*   **3** thirst,] ~ *A*
4 offend;] ~. *A*   **5** For strait] And there *A*   kept,] ~ *A*   will,] ~ *A*   **6** scorn;]
~, *A*   **7** So] For *A*   reverence, still,] ~ ~ ~ *A*   **9** above] upon *A*   world,] ~ *A*
12 die;] ~. *A*   **13** turns,] ~ *A*   **14** spirit] ~, *A*   bruised,] ~ *A*   **15** learns—]
~!— *A*

---

[1] Strictly.
[2] Lazarus of Bethany owed his resurrection from the dead by Christ to the intercession
of his sisters, Mary and Martha (John 11. 1–44). In exegetical tradition he became a

Backward through storied annals go,
  And open wide the sealing doors,
There let life's raying lantern throw
  Its beam across time's dusty floors;   20
Then ask who holds, through ages long,
  The crown by Helen[3] never worn—
And find, when sorrow needs the strong,
  The nun in every woman born.

Mother of men, who, love-impelled,   25
  Must find in all mankind her sons,
Always we find her hands out-held,
  Wherever life's thread broken runs;
And back to her, when others fail,
  The strong return—the sad forlorn—   30
And there she wraps them in her veil:
  The nun in every woman born.

O deepest gift of sacrifice!—
  O selflessness the selfish ask!—
That, giving, needs no other price   35
  Than love's fulfilment of its task!
Though man may wander (as he will),
  Though he may go the shamed, the shorn,
Yet must he worship, sacred still,
  The nun in every woman born.   40

---

17 storied] historied *A*   go,] ~ *A*   **19** life's] time's *A*   **20** time's] the *A*
21 Then . . . holds] Ask who holds, then *A*   long,] ~ *A*   **22** The] A *A*
23 And . . . needs] Ah! comforter, when breaks *A*   **25** who, love-impelled,] ~ ~ *A*
27 Always] Ever *A*   out-held,] upheld *A*   **28** Wherever] Where *A*   broken]
snarled and broken *A*   runs;] ~. *A*   **29** And back] Always *A*   **30** return—]
~, *A*   forlorn—] ~; *A*   **31** there] she, *A*   veil:] ~— *A*   **33** sacrifice!—]
~— *A*   **34** O] The *A*   the selfish] that can but *A*   ask!—] ~, *A*
35 That, giving,] ~ ~ *A*   needs] finds *A*   **37** (as] ~ *A*   will),] ~ *A*
38 Though . . . shorn] Toward the trough, by bramble thorn *A*   **39** Yet] Still *A*

---

type of the awakened sinner, living a subsequent life of virtue: see *A Dictionary of Biblical Tradition*, ed. David Lyle Jeffrey (Michigan: William B. Erdmans, 1992), p. 429.

[3] Helen of Troy, the destructive *femme fatale* as opposed to the maternal feminine, seen here as essentially nun-like: on MG's admiration for nuns, see volume 1, Introduction, pp. liii–liv.

With bowed head bending at her knee,
   He holds her hands of tenderness;
And there, whate'er his faults may be,
   She will not leave him comfortless;
For she will fling her pity wide,   45
   This comforter of souls forlorn,
Who conqueror stands, though self-denied—
   The nun in every woman born.

---

41 bowed] bent *A*   bending at] leaned upon *A*   **42** tenderness;] ~, *A*
43 whate'er his] whatever *A*   **44** comfortless;] ~. *A*   **45** For she will] There will
she *A*   wide,] ~ *A*   **46** comforter . . . forlorn] helper of poor souls that mourn *A*
47 Who] And *A*   stands] stand *A*

J17   CAHAL OF THE THORN[1]

Cahal of the long descent,
   Cahal proudly born,
Followed where His Master went,
   Night and noon and morn.

Tall he was above all men,   5
   Tall and greatly humble;
God, Who loved him, strength of ten,
   Gave lest he should stumble.

Cahal of the kingly mien[2]
   Of the high descent,   10
Following in liege and lien[3]
   Where His Master went,

Bound his hands with linen cords,
   Kneeled in holy dread,

(20 April 1923)   *Copy-text: RT*   *Collated states:* None
7 him *Ed.*] Him *X*

[1] As a Celtic name, Cahal means Strong in Battle or Great Warrior, but MG's source is unidentified.
[2] Bearing, demeanour.
[3] Loyalty and indebtedness. (A lien is a right over property in respect of which a debt has been created.)

Heard the Angels of the swords   15
    Wheeling overhead;

Felt the Wielder of the spear
    Threat toward his side,[4]
Grieved for Peter, sick with fear,
    Ere the cock had cried.[5]   20

Low he kneeled beneath the swords,
    'Neath the spear had torn,
Rose in knighthood all his Lord's—
    Cahal of the Thorn.

Tall he was above all men,   25
    Tall and strangely humble;
God, Who loved him, strength of ten
    Gave lest he should stumble.

[4] The Roman soldier who pierced Christ's side with his spear during the Crucifixion is unnamed (see John 19. 34), but early Christian legends identified him with the centurion who acknowledges Christ's divinity in Luke 23. 47. As Longinus, he appears in the definitive medieval collection of saints' lives, the *Aurea Legenda* (Golden Legend, 1275). In the various versions of the legend of the Holy Grail, his spear is part of the Grail regalia.   [5] See J23 n. 2.

J18   THE THRUSH

There sang a thrush at morn, he sang again at even;
O happy, happy born, that there set up his steven![1]
And in that gush of song was heard as in refrain,
This shall remain, and ever shall endure:
He lendeth to the Lord, who giveth to the poor.[2]   5

Grey is the thrush, but silver is his singing,
Lovely as the rush of fountains in their springing;
And while so sweet he sang, we heard as in refrain,
This shall remain, and ever shall endure:
He lendeth to the Lord, who giveth to the poor.   10

[1] Voice, or the sound of a voice, utterance (archaic).
[2] Cf. Proverbs 19.17: 'He that hath pity upon the poor lendeth unto the Lord; and that which he giveth will he pay him again'.

O, poor shall go the poorer, if, as he takes his way,
His step is not the surer for such a roundelay!³
Alms⁴ are in such singing, for speaks the old refrain,
This shall remain, and ever shall endure:
He lendeth to the Lord, who giveth to the poor.					15

O blithe and blessed bird, thy alms I gladly take;
I name them for His Word, and honour for His sake,
For, in thy happy carol, I hear, in full refrain,
This shall remain, and ever shall endure:
He lendeth to the Lord, who giveth to the poor.					20

(7 March 1923)   *Copy-text: RT   Collated states:* None

³ Short simple song with a refrain, often applied to birdsong.
⁴ Charitable gifts.

J19   THE SOUL TO THE BODY¹

Strive on, O flesh, and so refuse to die!
Thou art my bread, my voice, my pathway to the sky;
Thou art to me as is the cylinder to steam,
To me as words that clothe for man his dream;
Thou art my instrument, my foot, my hand—				5
If thou shouldst fail me, how then should I stand?

Strive on, O flesh, where I am planted tree!
For, as the sap through wood, I only bloom through thee;

(n. d.)²   *Copy-text: RT   Collated states: NZT,* 28 April 1926, p. 32 (*A*)   *SV* (*B*)
1 Strive] (For the *N.Z. Tablet.*)// Strive *A*	**2** pathway] path-/ way *A*	**3** art]
~, *A*	to] for *A*	me] ~, *A*	**4** To] For *A*	dream;] ~. *A*	**5** hand—] ~, *A*
6 should] shall *B*	**7** tree!] ~, *A*	**8** For,] ~ *A*	bloom through] bloom by *A*

¹ Discussions of the relationship between the soul or inner spirit and the body as its
outward container go back to ancient literature (e.g. Plato's *Symposium*). Dialogues between
body and soul, common in medieval literature, generally present antagonism: see J15 n.
1. Here, the body as the soul's enabler contrasts with the more traditional theme of J20.
² 28 April 1926 is annotated on one of the ML 5/2 MSS, but this is the date of *B*'s
publication, not of composition.

I, an eternal, who would blossom endlessly,
Must find my field where thou dost cover me.   10
O flesh, who art my instrument, my hand,
If thou shouldst fail me, how then should I stand?

I am a reaper, whose first seed was sown
When, out of highest heaven, man's living breath was blown!
Mine is the right of harvest, yet no harvest mine,   15
If death our paths dissever, mine and thine.
Thou who art instrument, and foot, and hand,
If thou shouldst fail me, how then should I stand?

I, given forth as man, have need of thee;
God hath no need, and yet He set the need in me: 20
Bid that through flesh shall each man speak to brother man,
And all souls blossom in that blossoming span:
O flesh, for this thou art my way, my hand;
If thou shouldst fail me, how then shall I stand!

I am the will to write, thou pencil art;   25
I am the will to pulse, and thou the beating heart!
I come with empty palms that they through thee might fill,
And I by thee declare an Heavenly will.
O flesh, who art to me both foot and hand,
Bear witness for me to Him how I stand!   30

12 should] shall *B*   13 reaper,] ~ *A*   sown] ~, *A*   14 When,] ~ *A*   highest]
Om. A   heaven,] ~ *A*   man's] man's young *A*   blown!] ~; *A*   15 mine,] ~ *A*
20 He] he *B*   me:] ~— *A*   ~; *B*   22 span:] ~. *A*   24 stand!] ~? *A*
26 pulse,] ~ *A*   heart!] ~; *A*   27 palms] hands *A*

J20   THE SOUL'S CRY[1]

Handless[2] I go, encased within the flesh,
    Whose eyes of spirit turn to Thee as goal;
A prisoner, whom the bonds of sense enmesh—
    Jesu, have pity on a poor man's soul!

[1] See J19 n. 1.   [2] See I149 n. 3.

Only the foot of flesh is mine, whereby   5
    To walk whatever way my path unroll;
Only the tongue of flesh may voice my cry—
    Jesu, have pity on a poor man's soul!

I am essential man, but I am held
    Even as flame is held within the coal;   10
I would have wings, who in the flesh am felled[3]—
    Jesu, have pity on a poor man's soul!

I, who would pour out all I am for Thee,
    Am bound like water fall'n within a bowl;
Hungry for Thee, as rivers for the sea—   15
    Jesu, have pity on a poor man's soul!

Where the foot slips I fall as it must fall;
    Where the flesh sins, unfleshed I pay the toll;
By Thine own flesh, and in Whose Name I call,
    Jesu, have pity on a poor man's soul!   20

(19 April 1925)   *Copy-text: RT*   *Collated states:* None

---

[3] Brought low.

J21   I WILL ARISE AND GO TO MY FATHER[1]

I will arise and go to my Father,
    O, I will go to Him!
I have put by the noisy feast,
    The beakers at the brim;
I have grown weary of the song,   5
    Of voices whispering low,
And the loud laugh like empty wind
    That crackles to and fro.

---

[1] After the parable of the prodigal son (Luke 15. 11–32). The story of the Creation and the Fall of Man (Genesis 2. 7 and 3. 1–19) is evoked in lines 25–32 and 49–52, the latter also reflecting Romans 6. 23 ('The wages of sin is death'). Lines 31–6 follow Exodus 20. 5 ('For I the Lord thy God am a jealous God, visiting the iniquity of the fathers upon the children unto the third and fourth generation').

I will arise and go to my Father!
   Now will I rise and go,   10
Though it should be on bleeding feet,
   In stumbling ways and slow;
And He will see me from afar,
   And I shall kneel and say:
"Out of the dust, Thy wandering child   15
   Comes home from far away!"

I will arise and go to my Father,
   My Father Who is God,
Who holds within His mighty hand
   The spirit and the clod;[2]   20
And, coming, I shall say to Him,
   "O Father of mankind,
Are we but ghosts, residual,
   Of all the years behind?

"Thy first man stood an empty cup[3]—   25
   The next man caught his tears:
What hast Thou given us, who stand
   Within these later years?
Are we but blind inheritors,
   The thousandth thousandth son?—   30
Sins of the fathers quickening back
   To that first tempted one?"

Then shall my Father say to me,
   "Has My love ever failed,
Though to the pit ye wandered down,   35
   And children's children ailed? . . ."

I will arise and go to my Father,
   With an humble and contrite heart;
And the sins I sinned shall go with me,
   My sins, of me a part;   40

---

[2] Body (as created from earth).
[3] Adam as initially created is 'empty' (a blank page) in being sinless, but is also without history.

And He will upon me lay His hand,
    And He will say, "Poor Child! . . ."
And I shall look in my Father's face,
    And kneel to the Undefiled.[4]

I will arise and go to my Father,   45
    Will lay all burdens down;
For what, at best, is man but a leaf,
    Though of the trees' high crown?
For God still keeps the Word He gave
    When clay moved at His breath,   50
Though of man's ancient sin He made
    The sickle hook of death.[5]

(23–25 August 1920)   *Copy-text:* RT   *Collated states:* None

---

[4] Christ, the lamb without stain (of sin); cf. J26 line 54 where it is the Christ-child who is 'undefiled'.   [5] See I67 n. 5.

J22   IS THE ROOM SET?

Is the room set where I must go?
The room is set and the lights are low,
The candles are lit for head and feet,
Whiter than snow is the winding sheet.

How shall I know to enter in,   5
Where the candles burn so tall and thin?
They will garment you as one at rest,
They will fold your hands upon your breast,
They will close your eyes, and bind your chin,
And there at the last will you go in.   10

Will none be with me, there in the dark,
Where the candles stand so strange and stark?
There is a Hand with print of a nail,
Take thou that Hand, for It will not fail;
There is a Side was pierced by a spear,[1]   15
Stay close to that Side and know no fear;

---

[1] See J17 n. 4.

There is a Voice—Ah! when It shall call,
O, low at the Feet wilt fall, wilt fall!

(1 August 1923)   *Copy-text: RT   Collated states:* None

J23   IN THE HOUR OF DARKNESS

". . . But my star always shines!" said the Priest.[1]

Lord, when it comes to my hour to die,
Give me the prayers of my human kind—
Saints who were sinners even as I,
One with my flesh in the ties that bind,
Rising and falling, and yet made free   5
By the ladder of self to come to Thee!

Give me the prayers of my human kind!
Trembles the world, denier of Thee,
The cock crows loud—but the sky's dark blind
Is lifted that man the sun may see.[2]   10
Sun and the Son! . . . and the Word made Flesh . . .
That life from its chaff the grain might thresh!

And yet of my kind give me, give me!
Thy heavenly heights are all so high—
And how shall these eyes dare lift to see   15
Where angels kneel in their passing by,

(12 April 1922)   *Copy-text: RT   Collated states: CP,* 14 December 1922, p. 22 (*A*)

Not otherwise recorded: A's epigraph in roman font reads '". . . But my star always shines," said the priest.'
2 kind—] ~! *A*   **4** One with] Flesh, as *A*   flesh] ~, *A*   **6** the ladder] ladders *A*
Thee!] ~. *A*   **8** Thee,] ~; *A*   **9** loud—] ~, *A*   dark] wide *A*   **10** see.]
~— *A*   **11** Sun] ~, *A*   . . . and] And *A*   Flesh . . .] ~, *A*   **12** life] man *A*
its] his *A*   thresh!] ~. *A*

---

[1] In religious symbolism, the guiding star is the Star of Bethlehem (see J3) pointing to Christ, the unfailing light of the world (e.g. John 8. 12: 'I am the light of the world: he that followeth me shall not walk in darkness, but shall have the light of life'). In secular terms, stars guide navigation; for a merging of the senses, see J68 line 7 and J71 line 5.
[2] Lines 8–10 refer to the fulfilment of Christ's prophecy to Peter ('the cock shall not

And wings of the Cherubim[3] fold and veil
The Feet once pierced by the wounding Nail?

O, at the last to fall at His feet!
Lo, He was flesh and even as I;   20
Suffered the buffeting hands that beat,
The lonely hour and the heart's deep cry,
The passion of pain, love's long, long loss,
And, end of the day, the cross, the cross!
Ah, shall I want for my human kind   25
When this Humanest Hand of all I find?

---

17 the Cherubim] cherubim *A*   18 once pierced by] that suffered *A*   wounding]
Wounding *A*   19 O] Ah *A*   feet] Feet *A*   20 flesh] ~, *A*   I;] ~ *A*
21 buffeting] buffetting *A*   24 cross . . . cross] Cross . . . Cross *A*

---

crow, till thou hast denied me thrice': John 13. 38) and to the darkness that covered
the earth during the final hours of the Crucifixion (Matthew 27. 45, Mark 15. 33 and
Luke 27. 44–5).

[3] Winged angelic beings, traditionally associated with wisdom, whose name goes back
through Hebrew to Arabic. Among the nine angelic orders classified hierarchically
by Pope Gregory the Great (AD 540–604) they occupy the highest rank, along with
thrones and seraphim.

J24   THE OLD PRESBYTERY GARDEN[*]
AT GOULBURN

"Though man's hand set the root,
 Yet His hand gave us drink,
 Opened a thousand lips
 In leaf and bud and shoot!"
 Thus spake the lilac tree,   5
 Praising God's name to me.

"Though man's hand set us here,
 Yet ere man was we stood,

(13 May 1925) *Copy-text: RT   Collated states: Adv*, 8 April 1926, p. 3 as THE OLD
PRESBYTERY GARDEN AT GOULBURN (N.S.W.) (*A*)

Not otherwise recorded: MG's note is signalled in *A*.

1 "Though] (Specially written for "The Advocate.")// "Though *A*   2 drink,]
~: *A*   6 name] Name *A*   8 Yet] ~, *A*   was] ~, *A*   stood,] ~ *A*

Planted in Paradise,
And heard God walking near."   10
So spake the laurel tree,
And praised God's name to me.

"Yea!" cried the holly tree,
"And in my heart I bore
Unknown, a spear, a thorn,   15
A sword—all three—
That in long after years
Burst from my leaves as tears."
Softly I touched each thorn
That for Christ's grief was born.[1]   20

[*] This garden, partly planted by Dr. Gallagher,[2] no longer exists. It
was one of the beautiful things of the city, and was known all over the
State. Many artists came to see it.

10 near.] ~! *A*   12 name] Name *A*   15 Unknown,] ~ *A*   16 sword—]
~, *A*   three—] ~, *A*   18 tears.] ~! *A*   n1–3 This . . . it.] *No longer in
existence. *A*

[1] The holly's evergreen leaves symbolised Christ's immortality, its thorns the crown of
thorns worn at the Crucifixion and its red berries his blood shed to redeem mankind.
[2] Dr John Gallagher, b. Ireland 1836, parish priest at Wagga Wagga 1887–*c*. 1895 (see
G35 author's note), and Bishop of Goulburn from 1900 until his death in 1923. See
J27 and author's note.

J25   VIA CRUCIS[1]

"Hush! it is Eastertide!"[2] . . . "Be still! Be still!
So short a time ago was Calvary Hill!

(23 March 1923)   *Copy-text: RT   Collated states: GEPP*, 29 March 1923, p. 4 as AT
EASTERTIDE (*A*)

Not otherwise recorded: A divides each line into two. Unless collated otherwise, the
line break follows the first six syllables, and the word commencing the new line is
capitalised.

1 Hush!] ~, *A*   Eastertide!" . . .] ~. . . ." *A*   still! Be] ~, be *A*   2 Hill!] ~. *A*

[1] Way of the Cross (Latin): see further J99 n. 1.
[2] Eastertide is a time of grief for the Crucifixion (Calvary Hill) on Good Friday, and of
rejoicing for the Resurrection on Easter Sunday (line 5).

Scarcely the blood is dry upon the stones,
Scarce ceased the double sound of breaking bones!"

"Yet it is Eastertide; come, then, rejoice . . ."   5
"Not till this heart forgets that broken Voice,
   Which in its anguish cried beneath His rod,
   'Hast Thou forgotten me, My God, My God?'

"Ah, let me wait this hour! Too soon, too soon
   It is to blot out grief and ask the boon;[3]   10
   Too soon to put away the nail, the spear,
   Forget the bloody sweat, the scourge, the tear,
   Deny, like Peter, ere the cock can crow,[4]
   And in glad garments rise and go!"

"Nay but, dear heart, it still is Eastertide!   15
   He bids thee weep no more His love denied,
   For He has put away the spear, the Cross . . ."
"Save when man nails Him there in love's long loss!
   Ah, must my heart its cry make still,
   How short the time since Calvary Hill!"   20

---

5 Eastertide;] ~ . . . *A*   **5** come,] Come *A*   rejoice . . .] ~! *A*   **6** Voice,] voice *A*
8 *'Hast . . . God?'*] 'Hast thou forgotten Me,/ My God, My God!' *A*
10–11 boon;/ Too] ~;// ~ *A*   **11** spear,] ~; *A*   **12** tear,] ~; *A*   **14** garments
rise] ~/ Rise *A*   **17–18** Cross . . ."/ "Save] cross,"// "~ *A*   *18* in love's long]
To his own *A*   loss!] ~! . . . . *A*   **19** heart its] ~/ Its *A*   **20** How] So *A*
time since] ~/ Since *A*   Hill!] ~. *A*

---

[3] Benefit.   [4] See J23 n. 2.

J26   "PRAISE GOD," SAID THE TREE

"Praise God!" said the tree,
"Praise God!" it said to me,
   But I, upon the ground,
   Sullen-brooding frowned:
"Why should I give praise,   5
   Who suffer all my days?"

Then the trees sang louder yet,
"Canst thou not awhile forget,
Look beyond the narrow bound,
See the stars at heaven's bars,   10
Though the sun is set?"

But I upon the ground,
Sullenly I frowned:
Then I heard, above,
All the angels' song of love,   15
All the planets as they sang,
Rank on rank, till heaven rang;
And the music pealing forth,
East and west and south and north,
Rolled in one harmonious whole,   20
Drawing in each passing soul.

But I upon the ground,
Sullenly I frowned:
Why should I give praise
Who suffered all my days?   25
Then a little child
Leaned on me and smiled
Touched me on the cheek,
In a touch that seemed to speak!
Broken was the frost of being,   30
Broken like a summer freeing,
Broken there was all that bound,
Me, who lay upon the ground!

Now I, beneath the sky,
Hear with wonder all the thunder   35
Of the systems passing by;
Hear the movement of the grasses
As a breath above them passes—
Surely man is but as they,
At a breath he is away!   40

Nay! It was a Breath that gave
Man dominion o'er the grave,[1]
Gave him power to measure suns
Though his course the briefest runs,
Gave him courage to endure   45
Darkness where is nothing sure—
Nothing save the hand of God,
Held above the shaken clod.

Is it I, beneath the sky,
Filled with wonder at the thunder   50
Of the seasons passing by? . . .
Ah! the child,
He sets us free!
Innocent and undefiled,
Weakest of all things that be,   55
Lo, he comes, in stress or calm,
Life and love within his palm.[2]

(25 August 1920)   *Copy-text: RT*   *Collated states:* None

---

[1] God's breathing of life into Adam (Genesis 1. 7) is re-affirmed in Christ's Redemption, which changes the sentence of death passed on Adam and Eve for their disobedience, making possible the continuing life of the soul.
[2] The human child of line 26 becomes the redemptive Christ-child in lines 52–7; on 'undefiled' (line 54), see J21 n. 4.

J27   ETERNAL REST GIVE HIM, O LORD

For him who is gone, pray one and all,*
But thanks be given for his length of days;
Though the tears may fall,
Yet give God praise,
Where, face to the Rood, he heard the Call.   5

[cont. overleaf

(22 November 1923)   *Copy-text: RT*   *Collated states: GEPP*, 29 November 1923, p. 2 (*A*)   *SV* (*B*)

1 For] (*The Right Reverend Dr John Gallagher, Bishop of Goulburn*)// For *B*
all,*] ~, *A*   2 But] Yet *A*   3 fall,] ~ *A*   4 Yet give God] Give God the *A*
praise,] ~ *A*   5 Call] call *A*

Once ere he passed, Lord John of the Sword,[1]
"I have fought to the end of the day,"
He said, "and the Lord,
He will repay,
Be it crown of praise, or scourge and cord.   10

"What He hath given me I take. No more.
What was mine own goes down to the dust.
In His wounds I bore
Life's deepest thrust,
And now to His Hands I yield my trust.   15

"I have held the faith, have kept the law:
Firm in His word I go to my rest;
And never I saw
One go unblest
Who followed His way, and His behest."   20

Toll slowly, bell, toll slowly,
   Toll for the great Lord John!
Follow him high and lowly,
   On the way he has gone.

Toll slowly, bell, toll slowly!   25
   He was a man, Lord John;
Yet, as a child, was lowly,
   Who to his rest has gone.

Toll slowly, bell, toll slowly;
   Thy tears of sound let fall!   30
Lowly he lived, and, lowly,
   Heard he that last long call.

Toll slowly, bell, toll slowly;
   Toll for the great Lord John;

---

6 Once] ~, *A*   8 and] And *A*   Lord,] ~ *A*   11 What] That which *B*   He] he *A*
hath given] gave to *B*   me] ~, *B*   12 mine] my *B*   15 And now] ~, ~, *A*
to His Hands] in His eyes *A*   yield] meet *A*   16 law:] ~; *A*   20 His way] the
way *A*   behest.] ~. . . . *B*   21 Toll] ~, *B*   toll slowly,] ~ ~; *A*   23 him] ~, *A*
27 as] like *B*   lowly,] ~ *A*   33 toll slowly;] ~ ~: *A*   34 John;] ~. *A*

---

[1] The official title of a Bishop ('Lord') is incorporated in the image of a knightly soldier

Follow him, high and lowly,   35
On the way he has gone.

* The Right Rev. Dr. John Gallagher, Bishop of Goulburn. Died
November, 1923.[2]

n1–2 *The . . . 1923.] *Om. A B*

of Christ, wielder of the 'Sword of the Spirit, which is the word of God' (Ephesians
6. 17).

[2] See J24 n. 2.

J28   THE IRISH PATRIOTS' MEMORIAL
(WAVERLEY)[*][1]

The sun shines on the tomb
    Where the Hounds of Erin couch;[2]
And, vast, O vast the room,
    Their spirits to avouch,[3]
Though scattered bones lie far,   5
They followed Erin's star;
    Be theirs the memory of prayer,
The dead who living are.

The round tower points above,
    And the cabin foots the hill;   10
Through both the harper, Love,
    Can touch our feelings still;

(n. d.) *Copy-text: RT   Collated states: FJ*, 8 December 1927, p. 40 as THE IRISH
MEMORIAL, WAVERLEY (*A*)

2 couch] Couch *A*   3 And,] O *A*   5 far,] ~ *A*   6 They] The *A*   7 prayer,]
~— *A*   9 above,] ~ *A*   10 And] By *A*   foots] and *A*   11 Through]
Though *A*   both] ~, *A*   Love] love *A*   12 feelings] spirits *A*

[1] Erected in 1898 to mark the centenary of the Irish Rebellion of 1798; see I150 n. 4
on its form. For Waverley Cemetery, see also I150 and n. 1.
[2] The magical twin hounds, Bran and Sceolan (or Skolawn) figure in several of the
legendary stories of Finn MacCumhail, notably the birth of Finn's son Oisin. They
are given to Finn by Tuiren, who gave birth to them after being transformed into a
wolfhound by a banshee (fairy woman).
[3] Acknowledge; in line 28, acknowledgement.

The shamrock, carried wide,
Floats in on every tide:
   "Pray for the souls of Michael Dwyer,   15
Mary his wife beside!"[4]

The white gulls wheel and cry
   Where the Hounds of Erin couch,
Calm in their rest they lie,
   Who knew not how to crouch;   20
One in their patriot creed,
One in their sacred need,
   Catholic, Protestant, name them, there,
One in the falling bead.

Shine, sun, upon the tomb   25
   Where the Hounds of Erin couch;
Thou of the Vaster Room,
   Give them Thine Own avouch.

[*] The Rev. R. Hamilton, whose name is on this monument, is a collateral ancestor on my mother's side.—M.G.

14 tide:] ~— *A*   16 Mary] ~, *A*   wife] ~, *A*   beside!] ~. *A*   17 wheel]
whirl *A*   cry] ~, *A*   18 couch,] ~; *A*   20 knew] know *A*   crouch;] ~! *A*
21 creed,] ~— *A*   22 need,] ~— *A*   25 sun] Sun *A*   26 couch] Couch *A*
27 Thou] ~, *A*   28 Own] own *A*   n1–2 The . . . M. G.] *Om. A*

[4] Traditional symbols of Ireland in lines 9–14 are: its ancient round towers (vertical stone vaults) built by monks as protection from Viking raiders (65 towers survive, many as ruins); its peasant cabins; the harp; and the shamrock, the clover plant associated especially with St Patrick. The shamrock's drift represents the Irish diaspora, exemplified in Michael Dwyer (1772–1825), exiled to NSW with nine other ringleaders of the 1798 Rebellion. He arrived in 1806 with his wife Mary (née Doyle), who lived until 1860. Originally buried in the Devonshire St. Cemetery, Sydney, their bodies were re-interred when the Waverley memorial was erected.

BOOK II: *ST. BRIGID*

J29　WHO WALKETH WONDER SHOD

Feed the mind, feed the mind,
　Feed the mind with wonder!
Feel the marvel of the wind,
　Th' astonishment of thunder;
Find enigmas in the grass,　　　　　　　5
　Splendours in the dew,
Till all things shall, as a glass,
　Show the glory through.

Feed the mind, feed the mind,
　Feed the mind with wonder!　　　　　10
Wonders you shall ever find
　Above the earth and under.
As through wavelets, though so small,
　All the ocean speaks,
Wonders answer, to his call,　　　　　15
　Him who wonder seeks.

Feed the mind and feed the heart,
　Fill thy life with wonder!
Wonder binds, and, though all part,
　Naught there is can sunder.　　　　　20
Wonder is the word of God
　Spoken in the soul;
He, who walketh wonder shod,
　Walketh not in dole.[1]

(16 July 1923)　*Copy-text: RT*　Collated states: *Adv*, 6 November 1924, p. 3 as WALK
IN WONDER SHOD (*A*)　*SV* (*B*)

1 Feed] (Specially written for "The Advocate.")// Feed *A*　　3 of] in *A*　　7 all
things] each thing *A*　　shall] shall show *A*　　a] *Om. A*　　in a *B*　　8 Show the
glory] All His glories *A*　　11 find] ~, *A*　　12 under.] ~; *A*　　15 answer,] ~ *A*
his] the *A*　　call,] ~ *A*　　16 Him who wonder] Of the soul that *A*　　17 mind] ~, *A*
18 wonder!] ~; *A*　　19 binds,] ~— *A*　　all part] apart *A*　　20 sunder.] ~! *A*
22 soul;] ~: *A*　　23 He,] ~ *A B*　　walketh] ~, *A*　　shod,] ~ *B*

---

[1] Sorrow, dejection (archaic).

J30   THE LANTERN OF WONDER

If thy heart never shake with wonder
    Little thy life has, loss or gain;
Thine ears are deaf where speaks the thunder,
    The lightning writes for thee in vain.

The frailest flower that, in the garden,   5
    Shines blinking skyward from the dew,
Is even as man of wonder warden,
    As from the seed the buds renew.

Never a mountain stands so stately
    But it is brother to the dust;   10
Never a river runs so straitly
    But holds some tiny stream in trust;

Never a star in burning splendour
    Declares its onward march through space,
But thou, with some small thing and tender,   15
    Shalt find a link between them lace!

(27 March 1926)   *Copy-text: RT   Collated states: Wr*, 23 June 1926, p. 5 (*A*)

1 If] Look out upon the world with wonder,/ Ask not to use a colored glass,/ Lest, where sight shortens thou see under,/ And courage fail as fancies pass.// If *A*
3 where] when *A*   6 skyward] upward *A*   7 Is] Stands *A*   man] ~, *A*   wonder]
~, *A*   8 As] When *A*   renew.] ~! *A*   11 so straitly] sedately *A*   12 tiny]
smallest *A*   13 splendour] splendor *A*   15 small] frail *A*   thing] ~, *A*   16 lace!]
lace!// All men are but as lanterns lifted,/ And walking in that light each goes—/
Ah, if the lamp lift not, though gifted,/ How narrow is the world it shows! *A*

J31   ICELAND POPPIES

Let not the sense of wonder die,
    For in its dying you die too;
Who lives with an unseeing eye
    Sails in a ship lacks half its crew.

I wandered in a gardened place,*   5
    A fragrant plot where colours glow;

A city's haven of grace,
   Where flowers blossomed row on row.

Pansies were there, with modest eyes
   Scarce lifted from the sheltering earth,   10
Yet as though some surprise
   Still questioned whence, and why, their birth.

There a great bush of lavender
   Fashioned itself a lovely veil—
A purple pavander,[1]   15
   Catching the sunlight in its trail.

There, too, a thousand stocks breathed out
   Full scents like thoughts from some rich mind;
For them no troubled doubt!
   They lived, and knew the sun was kind.   20

The primula held up its head,
   The gay ranunculus was there,
And from a shaded bed
   A lovely lily sweetened air.

But, where the sunlit poppies grew,   25
   One stilled, in sudden wonder spelled;
There self from self withdrew,
   Silently mused—amazed—dream-held.

How shall we speak of things like these,
   That waken thoughts that rise within,   30
Wave after wave, like seas
   That widen where new worlds begin?

O, if man for one moment felt
   One flower itself created, cell by cell,
He had in worship knelt,   35
   Reverent beyond what words can tell.

Too careless are we, day by day,
   Of marvels that about us lie:

[1] Perhaps a nonce word meaning mauve, created for its rhyme (not listed in *OED* or *Webster*).

"Ah, yes! it grows . . ." we say,
    And that is all as life goes by.   40

Let not the sense of wonder die,
    Lest in its dying you die, too;
Who lives with an unseeing eye,
    Sails in a ship lacks half its crew.

* The Court House Gardens at Goulburn.

(10 November 1923)   *Copy-text: RT*   *Collated states:* None

J32   FOR THESE MAKE MAN

Flowers that their sweetness give,
How much to them we owe!
Give him a world deprived,
Give but himself to know,
Take from him scents,   5
Take from him the blue sky,
The mountain peak,
The white cloud hurrying by,
And what were man
More than the moth,   10
Or vermin where it ran!

Flowers that their sweetness give,
Man lives a man through these:
These, and the sisterly
Fair things whose subtleties   15
Are nature's plough,
And nature's spade to dig
Deep into him,
And there, of his young twig
Of sense, to make   20
Branching his bough,
His powers to breed and wake.

How small were man were he
But self, and self-enclosed!
If by the thorny brake,   25
If by the briar that rosed[1]
In fragrant bloom,
If by the emmet's[2] house
He went the blind,
Nor saw the little mouse   30
Her nest line warm,
What were he more
Than the dim things that swarm?

Ah, if from what we know
All went; if then should fall   35
Upon earth's nakedness
Only one feather small:
O, with what swift
And startled sight would we
Not stoop to lift,   40
And with what wonder see!
How that slight thing
Would quicken thought,
How give to life a wing!

(6 January 1929)   *Copy-text: RT*   *Collated states:* None

---

[1] See I59 n. 1.   [2] Ant's.

J33   I HEARD A THRUSH IN A TREE TO-DAY

I heard a thrush in a tree to-day
    And Spring! he said, and, O Spring!
And my thousand cares went all away,
    As though they had taken wing.

Why should the song of a happy bird,   5
    The pipe of a little throat,

Stir like a fellowing call,[1] though heard
  In speech no more than a note?

I think at times (as the years go round,
  And I ponder o'er long ways trod)   10
The ladder by which man rose was sound,
  For in sound man first knew God.

Let there be light: and the light it came,
  Let there be life: and it spoke;[2]
Let there be love: and, swift as a flame,   15
  The music of life awoke!

A thrush sang sweet in his tree, to-day,
  O, Spring! he said, and O, Spring!
Why in my heart did a full chord play,
  As I heard the grey bird sing?   20

(17 June 1923)   *Copy-text: RT   Collated states:* None

---

[1] Call to fellowship; cf. E1.

[2] Line 13 recalls Genesis 1. 3: 'And God said, let there be light: and there was light'.
Lines 12 and 14 refer to the voice of God as Adam's first experience after his creation
(Genesis 2.16) but may also refer to John 1. 1: 'In the beginning was the Word'.

J34   NOT WHAT WE KNOW

Not what we know but what we apprehend,
  There lies man's guiding lamp!
The saint holds by it to the end,
  Adventure in its camp.

Balboa felt—and climbed the Isthmean peak,[1]   5
  Columbus set his sail;
Magellan, dreaming worlds to seek,
  In that light could not fail;

---

[1] Balboa (see I43 n. 2) is credited with being the first of the 'New World' explorers to
sight the Pacific Ocean, from a mountain peak on the Isthmus of Panama. On Columbus
and Magellan (lines 6, 7), see I43 n. 2.

The great Franciscan talking to the birds,[2]
    St. Martin with his swallow,[3]   10
They left a seed of more than words—
    They ploughed an unseen fallow.

Truly a spirit dwells unknown in man,
    A will beyond his will,
That bids him, where sense fails in span,   15
    Climb by a vision still.

(11 August 1925)   *Copy-text: RT   Collated states: SV (A)*
10 St.] Saint *A*   **11** words—] ~; *A*

[2] St Francis of Assisi (1181/82–1226), patron saint of animals and the environment and founder of the Franciscan Order of friars.
[3] No legend linking any St Martin to the swallow (also called *martin*) has been found.

J35   THINGS THAT IN LOVELINESS SPEAK HIM

Three things to me a wonder are,
Aye, three!
The quiet of the evening star,
Dawn moving in the early skies,
The Eden look in infant eyes.   5

And all these things are loveliness—
These three!
God, I adore Thee, and I bless,
That Thou hast given me to see
This loveliness, that speaketh Thee!   10

(14 November 1923)   *Copy-text: RT   Collated states:* None

J36   OF WONDERS

O, when I brood upon this frame,
    Of how it is compact of twice

Ten thousand centres, none the same
    In any blazon[1] or device:

When on the independent blood   5
    I think, how in full course it takes
Unerring constancy of flood,
    Which tiding runs, yet never breaks:

When even on this hand I look,
    This simple thing that serveth me,   10
How it is still a closèd book,
    Its covering all these eyes may see:

How that in my first hour it clenched,
    Ere unawakened will applied,
When, from the air, the hot lung blenched,   15
    And waking life found voice, and cried,

And that this hand, to-day as then,
    Knoweth no service to my will
Save as some servant among men,
    Who, called, makes answer, and is still: 20

When I observe how the frail sight
    Takes in the image of the world,
Or holds the very stars of night
    Under its covering lid unfurled,

And know no will of mine commands   25
    What the unbidden sight may do:
When I remember eyes and hands
    Are but the outer gates where-through

The interior, myriad self out-peers,
    Is served and serves: then am I filled,   30
Until my very eyes know tears,
    With wonder at the Power that willed!

(2 August 1923)   *Copy-text: RT   Collated states:* None

---

[1] See I148 n. 4.

J37   A LEVERET[1] AT THE DAWN

So timid and so still, she scarce
Seemed living as she gazed at me,
Ages in endless range behind her eyes,
That, seeming not to see,
Yet were so strangely wise.   5

Here mind moved matter toward an end,
Shaped form, and from the formless brought
The full round sight, the ear so sensitive.
Whose mind, *what* mind here wrought,
That this shy thing might live?   10

Scarcely I breathed, and yet she saw,
And drew herself to poise, until
It seemed as though even the very air
Stilled to the steady will,
That held her moveless there!   15

That watchful eye, that listening ear
Which swayed like shadow 'mid the flowers,
That padded foot, so swift, so soft it is,
That strong control of all her powers,
Did *her* mind shape? Or *His!*   20

(23 June 1923)   *Copy-text: RT   Collated states:* None

[1] Young hare (strictly, less than one year old).

J38   IN THE PARK

He was a Council man,
    Shabby and dungareed,[1]

(n. d.)   *Copy-text: RT   Collated states: Annals* (December 1926), p. 627 as OF WONDERS
(*A*)
Not otherwise recorded: A's text is in italics throughout.
1 He] 1.—*IN THE PARK.// He A*

[1] Dressed in overalls.

And, stumbling out his span,
  His life was plain to read.

What else was there to spy,   5
  All in the morning sun,
Ye dreary men who cry
  Wonders are dead and done?

The grumbling creature, there,
  Lifted a dingy hose,   10
And spangling on the air
  Ten thousand dewdrops rose.

. . . Wonder is dead? O fool,
  Wonder can never die:
Not while, within a pool,   15
  A man can see the sky!

3 stumbling . . . span] *grumbling as he walked A*   **5** spy,] *see A*   **8** done] *gone A*
9 grumbling . . . there,] *shambling Council man A*   **13** . . . Wonder] *II.—BY*
THE ROADSIDE.// Wonder A   dead?] *dead, A*   O fool,] *you say? A*   **14** die:]
die— A   **15** while,] *while A*   a] *a shining A*   pool,] *pool A*   **16** sky!] *sky. A*

J39   THE ROBIN ON THE PATH

Blue sky through lattice of pine,
  And bluer where trellising rose
Peeped through the lace of a vine!

And, out on the path, a thing
  Like a leaf that a light wind blows,   5
Dropped in the fall of a wing.

Was it chance that gathered together
That bundle of singer and feather?

(26 July 1923)   *Copy-text: RT   Collated states: TribM*, 13 March 1924, p. 6 (*A*)
1 Blue] (For "The Tribune")// Blue *A*   **3** Peeped] *Peeps A*   **4** on] *in A*
path,] ~ *A*   **6** Dropped] *Drops A*

Atom by atom it grew,
   That wonderful, beautiful thing   10
Singing its music of dew.

Ah, as it fashioned to form,
   Did it know of itself to bring
Out of the nothing the morn?

Whose was the Hand that shaped in the dark?   15
Gave us, in song, the flame of the spark?

11 Singing . . . dew.] That sang in the air it drew! *A*   13 bring] ~, *A*
14 nothing] ~, *A*   morn] norm *A*   15 *Whose*] Whose *A*   Hand] hand *A*
dark?] ~, *A*   16 Gave . . . of] That fashioned the song—and life for *A*

J40   HABAKKUK

Yea, though the vision tarry wait for it!*
Yea, though the vision tarry it will come!
Who dreams the vision, surely he has lit,
Though dimly, candles in this earthly room.

Yea, though the vision tarry wait for it! . . .   5
Nay, but the vision stands full in the way;[1]
'Tis we who fail, who hunger far from it,
In devious pathways wandering, and astray!

For, as the suns in splendour o'er us shine,
So all about us still the Eternal stands.   10
Open thy locked door, Spirit! There define,
E'en as thou openest, Thy Father's Hands.

* Habakkuk II: 3.[2]

(n. d.)   *Copy-text: RT   Collated states: Adv*, 17 January 1929, p. 5 as HABBAKUK (*A*)

1 Yea] (Original.)// Yea *A*   tarry] ~, *A*   it!*] ~! *A*   2 tarry] ~, *A*   3 vision,]
~ *A*   5 tarry] ~, *A*   6 way;] ~. *A*   8 pathways wandering,] ~, ~ *A*   astray!]
~. *A*   9 For,] ~ *A*   10 the] th' *A*   stands.] ~; *A*   11 Spirit] spirit *A*
12 Thy] thy *A*   Hands] hands *A*   n1 * . . . II: 3.] *Om. A*

[1] Like the angel who stood in the way of the erring prophet Balaam to redirect him
towards fulfilment of God's instructions (Numbers 22. 22–35).
[2] 'For the vision is yet for an appointed time . . . though it tarry, wait for it' (Habakkuk
2. 3).

J41   AND I THY FUGITIVE[1]

I am Thy fugitive, who, path to path,
   With ever hasting feet must fly,
Seeking by flight some way t' escape Thy wrath,
   Which, if it fall on me, I die.

Yet though as eagle in the height—I dove—   5
   Thou dost me circle, still I live;
For lo, not wrath, but Thy constraining love
   Seeks me: and I Thy fugitive!

Ashamed that Thou art shamed in me,
From Thy pursuing love I flee.   10

(1 October 1923)   *Copy-text: RT*   *Collated states:* None

---

[1] For God as a feared but loving hunter of the soul, cf. the opening lines of 'The Hound of Heaven' (1890) by Francis Thompson (1859–1907): 'I fled Him, down the nights and down the days;/ I fled Him, down the arches of the years', and the concluding 'Thou dravest love from thee, who dravest Me'.

J42   THE COMMONAGE OF GOD

Common of pasture* in Thy field
   Give me, that love, once naught,
May feed like sheep where pastures yield
   A herbage long, long sought.

Common of mast I ask of Thee—   5
   I, Thy poor prodigal!
My sheep these thoughts that, hungrily,
   Seek the Mast Mystical.[1]

---

* The rights of Commonage are of pasture, of mast, estovars, and turbary, *i.e.*, of grass, nuts and acorns, wood, and turf.

(20 February 1924)   *Copy-text: RT*   *Collated states:* None

---

[1] Spiritual food, available to all Christians, just as mast – the fruit of forest trees such as beech, oak and chestnut – was available for foraging, especially as animal food. It is usually included under commonage of pasture, the fourth major category being *pescary* (fishing), omitted in MG's note.

J43   IN THE CRY OF THE SPIRIT[1]

Homeless I go, who ever longed for home;
No rest I know, whose feet must onward roam;
Who still must seek one Look to hold my gaze,
One Voice to speak, one Way amid all ways.

Homeless I go, who ever longed for home,   5
Through ebb and flow like flotsam on the foam;
Yet though far driven, though beaten, bruised and sore,
Waits my replevin,[2] keeps for me, still, my shore!

Homeless and sad I go, long scourged by pain
(Yet to be glad so little served for gain!)   10
Who but for star, and moonlight in the night,
Were lonelier, far, through all my weary plight.

Up through the trees I lift my searching eyes
Toward those strange seas where heavenly lanterns rise,
And watch star-ships pass out beyond our hail,   15
Launched from their slips in farthest space to sail!

Changeless they change upon the curve of night,
Mutating range on tides that mock the sight,

(20 November 1923)   *Copy-text: RT   Collated states: Bn*, 5 June 1924, p. 47 as
HOMELESS I GO (*A*)

Not otherwise recorded: Lines 21 and 22 are reversed in *A*.

1 Homeless] (FOR THE BULLETIN.)// HOMELESS *A*   3 Look] look *A*   4 Voice]
voice *A*   Way] way *A*   6 flow] ~, *A*   on] in *A*   7 driven] driv'n *A*
8 replevin,] ~: *A*   me, still,] ~ ~ *A*   9 sad] ~, *A*   I go,] like one *A*   pain] ~, *A*
10 (Yet] ~ *A*   served for gain!)] serves the grain, *A*   11 and] for *A*   the] his *A*
12 lonelier, far,] ~ ~ *A*   my] his *A*   14 Toward those] Towards these *A*   rise,]
~; *A*   15 And] There *A*   out beyond] on, unseen *A*   16 their] what *A*
farthest space] that far deep *A*   17 night,] ~; *A*   18 sight,] ~; *A*

[1] Nettie Palmer wrote to MG on 8 June 1924: 'Your poem in [the *Bn*] this week was
perhaps the most impressive work of yours that I have ever seen. The feeling & rare
rhythm seemed so thoroughly one. The subject was treated with such depth that the
lyric had a quality of universality & permanence. We read the poem aloud & of course
are keeping it' (ML Papers vol. 16).
[2] Figuratively, restoration of her home (legal term, usually relating to goods and
chattels).

Yet through what deep, what course the compass shows,
Onward a-sweep, in certainty each goes.   20

Strange are these ships that sail the heavenly vast!
What cargo strips[3] beneath each mighty mast?
Bear they the small, sad freight of human thought,
Frailest of all frail things that God hath wrought?

Bear they within (these galleons of God)   25
Earth's ancient sin, life's sufferings of the rod?
Or hold they, each, such things as here but seem—
Beyond the reach of man, yet in his dream?

Homeless I go, who have so longed for rest,
A bended bow whose arrow never prest   30
Into far height, released the tensioned throe,[4]
So that by flight the soul itself might know.

Therefore must I a wanderer ever go,
Change with each sky, nor harvest what I sow;
Therefore do I, who so much long for home,   35
Pass lonely by in worlds I still must roam.

20 Onward] ~, *A*   a-sweep] asweep *A*   **21** Strange are these] Of these strange *A*
21 vast!] ~? *A*   **22** mast?] ~ *A*   **23** small, sad] sad small *A*   **25** within] ~, *A*
(these] ~ *A*   God)] ~, *A*   **26** ancient] cargoed *A*   **27** they, each,] ~ ~ *A*
seem—] ~, *A*   **30** prest] drest *A*   **31** Into] Swift to *A*   height,] ~— *A*
throe,] bow *A*   **32** So that by] That by that *A*   know.] ~! *A*   **33** ever]
onward *A*   **34** each] the *A*   **35** so much] ever *A*   **36** in worlds] on roads *A*

[3] Moves, passes (obsolete).   [4] Pang, anguish.

J44   THE LOBELIA

I

Thou Who didst waken from her sleep,
The blue Lobelia to creep
On barren rock and naked steep,

(30 November 1924)   *Copy-text: RT*   *Collated states: CP*, 18 December 1924, p. 24
(*A*)   *SV* (*B*)

Not otherwise recorded: A sets each section as a single stanza.
1 Who] who *A B*   sleep,] ~ *B*   **2** Lobelia] ~, *A*

And, from the height of heaven's air,
Didst bid the wind run down his stair   5
To gather of her sweetness there,

And lettest fall the gentle dew,
So that each leaf, and blossomy hue,
Shall find each day its life renew,

And who dost wash her in the rain,   10
To dry her in the sun again,
So that she stands withouten[1] stain,

Wilt Thou not, from infinity,
Lean down and also care for me?

                    II
The wind that o'er the desert flies,   15
That moves where mighty mountains rise,
And falls at last and sighing dies,

That runs the wave with wanton feet,
Yet at the mast-head sings so sweet
It makes a song, for angels meet,   20

That bears aloft the little cloud
Where no voice whispers there aloud,
And silence is the world's wide shroud,

That sifts the seed and thistledown
Over the pasture, burnt and brown,   25
To bud once more as Spring's bright crown,

He, by Whose will such things may be,
Will He not also think of me?

---

5 stair] ~, *A*   7 And] Who *B*   10 who] Who *A*   12 withouten] without *A*
stain,] ~: *A*   13 not,] ~ *A*   14 Lean] Look *A*   16 That . . . mighty] Moves
where eternal *A*   rise,] ~; *A*   17 And falls] Falls as *A*   at last] a veil, *A*   ~ ~, *B*
dies,] ~; *A*   19 sweet] ~, *A*   20 song,] ~ *B*   meet,] ~; *A*   21 cloud] ~, *A*
26 Spring's] spring's *B*   27 Whose] whose *B*

---

[1] Without: Old English form, probably used for metre.

III

He Who above both hedge and hall
Opens the cloud that rain may fall,   30
And quenches thirst of things most small,

Who threads the vast inane[2] with light,
And gives us day and gives us night,
And by the eyelid sets the sight,

Who puts the hinge within the shell,   35
And gave direction to the cell,
And to the flower its musky spell,

Who bids the colour in the rose
Its wonder to the world disclose
And yet whose secret no man knows,   40

Will not that Will which bid these be,
In its own time remember me?

---

29 Who] who *B*   hall] ~, *A*   31 small,] ~; *A*   32 Who threads] Sends
through *A*   with] the *A*   33 day] ~, *B*   34 sight,] ~; *A*   35 puts] put *A B*
37 spell,] ~; *A*   smell, *B*   38 bids] bade *A*   made *B*   39 disclose] ~, *A B*
40 knows,] ~; *A*   41 that Will] ~ ~, *A*   bid] bade *A*   42 its own] Its Own *A*
Its ~ *B*

---

[2] Formless void of infinite space.

BOOK III: *ST. GABRIEL*

J45   OF HIDDEN THINGS

Why does the finite ask
   For the infinite wing,
If it be not the mask
   Of a mightier thing?
If the Infinite Will,   5
   Which created him first,
Never knew to instil
   In him infinite thirst,
Why can man not in man,
   In his brother man, find   10
All he would ask, or can,
   Of Infinite Mind?

(6 August 1923)   *Copy-text: RT   Collated states:* None

J46   "CHRIST IN THE NEVER NEVER"

One in the Never Never[1]
Took up his swag and walked;
His head was bent, his shoulders hunched,
He hardly ever talked;
And, as he went, his downcast eyes   5
Nor this nor that way turned;
The once green root of fellowship
To dull, dead ashes burned.

[cont. overleaf

(18 November 1920)   *Copy-text: RT   Collated states: Fwp* (January 1921), p. 82 as
IN AFFIRMATION (*A*)

Not otherwise recorded: A divides the poem into four 4-line stanzas.

1 One] CHRIST *A*   4 talked;] ~. *A*   5 And,] ~ *A*   went] walked *A*   downcast]
down-pent *A*   6 this] ~, *A*

[1] On the name, see G15 n. 1 and R65 author's note, lines 27–30.

Yet when he flung his swag to earth,
And sat without a word,   10
Out of the nearest bush there dropped
A friendly little bird,
And from the grass a lizard came;
And there, with head aside,
Maybe, as each one watched, it saw   15
The Christ the man denied.

9 Yet] ~, *A*   12 bird,] ~. *A*   13 came;] crept *A*   14 there,] stood *A*   aside,]
~; *A*   15 Maybe . . . watched,] And as it looked, maybe *A*

J47   IN THE BEAUTY OF THE ROSE

This troubled dust of human kind
Is like a gardened place,
Where, in the freedom of man's mind,
Weeds with the flowers enlace.

There some shoots, cultured, grow full height;   5
There some degenerate,
Until, as waste, they break and blight
The buds of nobler state.

Yet from a weed man bred the rose,
And from a grass the wheat,   10
Showing how fixed intent o'ergrows
What hindrance it may meet.

And when of faith man made ally
To bind th' inconstant will,
Weeds might not, flaunting, rise too high,   15
Where that spade turned to till.

(6 September 1924)   *Copy-text: RT*   *Collated states: NZT*, 10 December 1924, p. 32
(*A*)

1 This] (For the *N.Z. Tablet*.)// This *A*   12 What] The *A*   13 when] ~, *A*
faith] ~, *A*   15 high,] ~ *A*   16 spade turned to] bright spade might *A*

Ah, if the beauty of the rose
   Be lifted from the briar,
And if the wheat, that richer grows,
   From low is raised to higher,   20

If even faults stand held at bay,
   Where man's will overcame,
May we not rise, in some far day,
   Willed upward on a Name?

19 And] Ah, *A*   **21** bay,] ~ *A*   **24** Name?] ~! *A*

J48   THE WITNESS OF THE STARS

Oh, let us call again!
   The very power to call,
Though it should be in pain,
   Is something after all.

Beat on the gate of heaven,   5
   E'en though thy bitter cry,
As sounds that fail at even,
   Should on the silence die;

And lift thy voice in prayer,
   Though thou shouldst only hear   10
Thy own sad calling, there,
   Return upon the ear.

Better the cry, O Soul,
   Than of the dumb to be;
The cry still shows thee whole,   15
   Though none should answer thee.

It is the look proves sight;
   Even the poor dark blind
Raise upward eyes of night,
   To lift them through the mind!   20

Is not thy spirit free?
What holds thee with its bars?
Look up, O Soul, and see
The witness of the stars!

(11 October 1921)   *Copy-text: RT*   *Collated states:* None

J49   PRAYER

If God be God, what use to pray,
    Asking of Him to give
That which we must have, day by day,
    That flesh He made may live?

Language decays in solitude: 5
    The Church has need of prayer,
Lest man forget, in silence rude,
    What set the altar there.

And though by them our wants we tell
    To Him whence we began,   10
Prayers are the means by which we spell
    God's Name from man to man.

(n. d.)   *Copy-text: RT*   *Collated states:* None

J50   THE CHILD AND THE CLOCK

"I do not hear the clock!" she said,
    Yet had the clock ticked on,
In its high place above her head,
    As round by round had gone.

She did not hear that sound which all   5
    Day long had measured time,
Marking eternity let fall
    Each hour in silver chime.

She did not hear the clock—so near
    Her hand could reach its face;   10
So near, surely upon her ear
    Its movement left some trace!

She did not hear. The constant things
    Grown intimate, which lie
About us like fair folding wings,   15
    We pass oblivious by;

So, in the Love which all men seek,
    About us, yet not found,
So may the Voice Eternal speak,
    And man not hear It sound.   20

(21 April 1923)   *Copy-text: RT   Collated states:* None

J51   THE WRITING

God wrote upon the hills with trees,
    In grass upon the plain;
And these, with every stirring breeze,
    Whisper His Name again.

He wrote, with sand within a glass,   5
    His Name upon the year;
And moon by moon, as cycles pass,
    That Name the seasons hear.

He wrote in stars upon the sky,
    The whole wide heavens His scroll;   10
Then, when He heard an infant cry,
    He turned and wrote man's soul.

(3 April 1926)   *Copy-text: RT   Collated states:* None

J52   THE "RATIONALIST"

My mind has lost its range, my thought its wing;
Never again shall I of God ask anything;
Within myself I live, more circumscribed each day,
Narrowing down, withering in, as rock contracts from clay.

There are no wonders, now, to greet the hidden sight;   5
That sight is dead; and, so, no more the morning light
Seems to my mind like some dear, loving thought from Him,
Raying earth's darkness through to shine on what was dim!

Even a rose comes, cell on cell in blindness set,
Till chance makes law! There no deep mem'ry may forget,   10
No will decide to still, or loose to action, range
On range of everlasting yet impulsive change!

Wonder no longer breeds in anything I see,
A tree is timber; never more is it to me
A miracle of growth, purposed, and held in earth   15
To cry, "I, too, I, too, had of Him heavenly birth!"

There is but that which knows not how to merge or end,
Initiate or choose, or even break and mend;
All but diffusion hath, with no inheritance
Save routine change, through which, alone, we may advance!   20

Cell neighbouring cell, as, grain to grain, the sand
That falls in trickles from the movement of the hand,
Thus I see life—with love itself no more
Than the chance-blown, that dreams nor whence nor where
        its shore.

When on the far horizon shines the golden cloud,   25
Or spreads a mackerel sky in some far wind-field, ploughed
To even furrow by the sharp, aerial share,[1]
Nothing I see but cold mechanic law laid bare.

---

[1] The cutting blade of the plough.

And when upon my young child's face I look, I see
Only the algebraic sign "Plus, minus Three,"   30
And Plus, in lonely Minus, he is man,
A tumbling atom as he first began.

I know no will in anything to master change;
I know but one fixed law, immutable in range—
Deaf, dumb, and blind as bats that o'er us flit,   35
And I as helpless, there, as it.

(13 January 1924)   *Copy-text: RT   Collated states:* None

J53   THE DEED LIVES ON

Only to know is not enough,
For us still waits the deed to do!
But what if ways be hard and rough,
Twined with the rose, the rue?[1]

Ever the path before us lies,   5
And for us made by hands long gone;
It is the man, the man, who dies,
It is the deed lives on.

Then be your every deed well done,
For, surely as night follows day,   10
The deed is your begotten son,
Your son begotten clay.

And ye must act, that, in his clay,
Your son of flesh shall stand a man.
Deeds make the race; in their decay   15
The nations meet their ban.[2]

(21 December 1928)   *Copy-text: RT   Collated states:* None

---

[1] See J7 n. 1.
[2] Curse, or possibly their denunciation as accursed, anathema.

J54   THINK HIM

There is no good in all the earth,
No sin man may deplore,
No evil wakened to rebirth,
But thinking makes it more.

Therefore think Him, Who, for our sakes,   5
Let down, from heaven above,
His hand, that, whosoever takes,
Must think His thoughts of love.

Think Him and give His thoughts release,
Your thought His thought in flower;   10
So shall His thinking never cease
To blossom every hour.

We are the words of God—His beads[1]—
And, should these words be mute,
What were we more than worthless weeds,   15
With earth for all our root?

Earth is our lot, but heaven will rise,
Full on the soul's desire,
Wherever men raise upward eyes,
Wherever hearts aspire.   20

(2 October 1921)   *Copy-text: RT*   *Collated states:* None

[1] Prayers.

J55   DUST THAT HIS HAND DEVISED

"Vile is this dust!" they said,
     And scorned it as they spoke,
Who from the world of beauty fled,
     And love's commandment broke.

Yet in this lowly thing,   5
    And in this dust of mine,
I have with these eyes seen the spring,
    I have gone forth to the Divine.

Dust that His Hand devised,
    How can it take the ban,[1]   10
When in its garment came the Christ,
    And by it showed Himself to man!

(n. d.)   *Copy-text: RT*   *Collated states:* None

---

[1] See J53 n. 2.

J56 AND YET THE MYSTERIES REMAIN

No longer now by brake and byre
    The cattle kneel on Christmas Eve,[1]
No longer now, a Christmas choir,
    Bees hum their Credo and believe;
The robin's breast is red, but none   5
Comes telling how the red was won.[2]

The world, material, lies round
    About us all so close, that we
Are dazed and deafened by its sound,
    Which surges o'er us like a sea;   10
And so we go sense-held, till all
Old wonders, like leaves falling, fall.

And yet the mysteries remain—
    That field behind the visible

---

[1] Refers to the folklore tradition that cattle knelt on Christmas Eve in memory of their presence at the birth of Christ. On 'brake' see I59 n. 1. A byre is a cowshed: the phrase suggests indoors and out.

[2] According to legend, from a drop of blood shed by the crucified Christ when the robin tried to remove from his head embedded thorns from the crown of thorns; cf. J86 lines 7–15.

Which no man's wisdom can explain, 15
   Its symbol stark upon its hill.
Lo, One is there behind our brass,[3]
   As He behind the idol was!

(23 December 1928)   *Copy-text: RT*   *Collated states:* None

[3] Age of brass, a time inferior to earlier ages of gold and silver, as in Daniel's interpretation of the dream of Nebuchadnezzar (Daniel 2. 27–45). Brass was then copper rather than the modern alloy and not all biblical references to it are negative (e.g. Exodus 27. 2), but the connection of brazen images with idols has been reinforced by New Testament references (e.g. Revelation 9. 20). The idol in line 18 is unidentified.

J57   THE LADY RELIGION

I saw a Lady with a Lamp,[1]
   And O, she wept full sore;
Yet, as she walked, she lifted high
   The silver bowl she bore.

Her eyes were dark as shadowed pools 5
   Where summer burns the light,
And which, as in the shade they glowed,
   Were luminous as night.

And, held within their lovely dark,
   Her look it drew all men, 10
And never one there turned to gaze
   But longed to look again.

(30 November 1925)   *Copy-text: RT*   *Collated states:* DT, 5 December 1925, p. 6 (*A*)   *Adv*, 20 August 1931, p. 5 (*B*)

Not otherwise recorded: A has this headnote: '"I do not think religious feeling is ever aroused except by ideas of objective truth and value. . . ." Quotation from Dean Inge, "The Daily Telegraph," 1/12/'25.'[2]

2 And O] ~, oh *A*   **3** Yet,] ~ *A*   walked,] came *A*   lifted high] turned about *A*
6 light] sight *A*   **7** And which, as in] Which, as within *A*   glowed] gleamed *A*
8 as night] with light *A*   **9** their] that *A*   **10** men,] ~; *A*   **11** And . . . gaze] For no man turned and, dreaming, gazed, *A*

[1] The association is with Florence Nightingale, 'the lady of the lamp', the 'noble type of good,/ Heroic womanhood' in Henry Wadsworth Longfellow's 'Santa Filomena'

And ever as she went she mourned:
   "Once where I passed all came;
They scattered palms beneath my feet,   15
   And named me in a Name!³

"Then was the world a place of praise,
   That ever, and around,
Rose wondering on air, or sprang
   As incense in a sound.   20

"Now all my paths are dark," she said;
   "Are empty, where, so oft,
I gathered with full hands, and held
   My gathering aloft! . . ."

O Lady of the Lamp, the world   25
   Is old as it can be—
He knows not youth, who never felt
   The need to bend the knee—

And so no more beneath a Star⁴
   All heaven about us lies;   30
Wonder is fallen from our hearts,
   Is withered in our eyes.

---

13 mourned:] ~, *A*   14 passed] walked *A*   15–16 They . . . Name!] With palms
they strewed my path about,/ And called me by my name. *A*   19 Rose] Sang *A*
wondering on] wond'ring on the *A*   20 in a sound] from the ground *A*
21 said;] ~, *A*   23 hands,] arms *A*   24 gathering] gathering there *A*
aloft! . . ."] aloft! . . ."// O Lady of the Lamp, the world/ Is lonely, wanting thee;/
Its face is desert, and its lips/ Parch by a brackish sea. *A*   26 be—] ~; *A*
27 youth,] ~ *B*   28 knee—] ~. *A*   29 And . . . Star] No more by furrow, and
by star, *A*

<hr style="width:20%" />

(1851), which links her to one of the *RT* 'Saints' (see p. 173 n. 1). At line 15 the 'Lady'
is identified with Christ and his entry to Jerusalem on Palm Sunday (see Matthew 21.
6–11). Religion also figures as a woman in B122.

² William Ralph Inge (1860–1954), Professor of Divinity at Cambridge (from 1907) and
Dean of St Paul's Cathedral, London (1911–34); author of several books on mysticism,
he was a much-quoted columnist for the London *Evening Standard* (1921–46).
³ In naming him 'Son of David' (Matthew 21. 9), the crowd effectively names Christ
as the Messiah.
⁴ See J3 n. 1 and J23 n. 1.

J58   THE BELLS OF GOULBURN[1]

The bells of the town ring out,
   Deep or shallow or high;
And ever they round about,
   A prayer, a praise, a cry.

The Presbyterian bell,   5
   Steadfast in storm and calm,
In pride, that naught could quell,
   Chants of an ancient psalm.

The Methodist children's bell,
   Like feet that rise and run,   10
In haste its message to tell
   Triples its three in one.

Over the distance St. Jude
   Sounds like a silver chime,
The ardours of youth, once crude,   15
   Softened and toned by time.

St. Saviour's bell on the air,
   Sings like a violin,
In a surpliced call to prayer,
   Of "O come in! come in!"   20

But the bell of Peter and Paul,
   With its deepened call,
   Says: *"God! God! God!"* . . .

(3 January 1924)   *Copy-text: RT   Collated states:* None

---

[1] Bells of: the old St Andrew's Presbyterian Church, opened in 1841 and replaced in 1925 by a new church of the same name on a different site; the Methodist Church, founded 1870, now the Uniting Church; St Saviour's Anglican Cathedral, built 1874–88; and the Catholic Cathedral of Sts Peter and Paul, built 1871–79. No record of a St Jude's in Goulburn has been found.

J59   THE PETITION[1]

Give us this day our daily bread,
Lord God of earth and sky and sea;
Give strength to stand when sore bestead,
And will to serve and worship Thee!
Take not Thy favour from us, lest   5
The nation break before Thy test.

Forgive us our trespasses, who, even
As little children do, forget;
And though we fail to seven times seven,
O, be Thy mercy with us yet.   10
Take not Thy favour from us, Lord,
Lest we be shamed before Thy word.

Let not temptation us assail,
To smite as kings, who servants are,
Lest when temptation come we fail,   15
And recreant stand before Thy bar.[2]
Be ours to seek and do the right,
In the humility of might.

Our Father which art in heaven, upon
Our lips be writ Thy hallowed Name;   20
Thy Kingdom come, Thy will be done,
As is in heaven, on earth the same;

(4 November 1928)   *Copy-text: RT*   *Collated states: FJ*, 20 December 1928, p. 21 as
IN MEMORIAM: ANZAC (*A*)

2 God of earth] of the mountain *A*   sky and sea;] the sea— *A*   **3** Give strength]
The faith *A*   **4** And] The *A*   **5** Take] Move *A*   favour] favor *A*   **9** And]
~, *A*   **10** O . . . mercy] Be Thy forgiveness *A*   **11** Take] Move *A*   favour]
favor *A*   **12** be] go *A*   **13** not] no *A*   assail,] ~ *A*   **14** smite] strike *A*
kings,] lords *A*   **15** Lest] ~, *A*   temptation come] power come to us, *A*
19 heaven] Heaven *A*   **22** heaven] Heaven *A*

[1] Adapts the Lord's Prayer as attributed to Christ in Matthew 6. 9–13 and Luke 11.
2–4 and incorporates other texts: e.g. at line 6, God's Old Testament threat to 'break in
pieces the nations' (Jeremiah 51. 20) and at lines 9–10 Christ's teaching on forgiveness
(Matthew 18. 21–2 and Luke 17. 4).
[2] Unfaithful one, apostate, liable to stand accused (at the bar) on Judgement Day.

Then, in this broken world of men,
Grant us Thy peace. Amen. Amen.

24 peace. Amen] ~! ~ *A*

J60 TODDLIN' HAME

Toddlin' Hame! aye, toddlin' Hame,
The slack an' the slow, the halt an' the lame;
An' there's never a fratch,[1] nor a word of blame,
    But jist the wee touch o' His Han',
      An' they're Hame.   5

An' He'll stan' at the gate an' He'll bring them a' in,
The saft an' the sad, an' the lost He would win;
An' they'll fa' in the dust rememberin' sin,
    But He'll gie the wee touch o' His Han',
      An' they're in.   10

There shall be rest for the best an' the worst,
Where the first may be last, an' last may be first,[2]
An' the judgments o' man may all be reversed;
    For the tender wee touch o' His Han'
      Makes a' hairst.[3]   15

Sae it's toddlin' Hame! aye, toddlin' Hame,
Led there by a licht that shines in a Name;
An' He'll blot oot the tears, an' wipe oot the shame,
    An', wi' jist the wee touch o' His Han',
      Make it Hame!   20

(22 December 1926) *Copy-text: RT*   *Collated states:* None

---

[1] Quarrel, disagreement.
[2] Christ's description of the reversal of earthly values in heaven, e.g. in Matthew 19. 30 and affirmed in the parable of the workers in the vineyard (20. 16).
[3] Harvest, i.e. of souls: Scandinavian-derived variant spelling.

J61   BEING HIS FRIEND

Being his friend she did not mind
The foolish world that dwelt unkind;
But turning from it went her way,
Finding in friendship strength and stay.

Being his friend she did not ask   5
Too much his love to overtask;
The dumb she stood, O many a day,
Lest to his hurt she bid him stay!

(n. d.)   *Copy-text: RT   Collated states: WMag* (June 1926), p. 43 as FRIENDS (*A*)
2 dwelt] went, *A*   **7** day,] ~! *A*   **8** stay!] ~. *A*

J62   PEACE SHALL LIE ON THE HOUSETOP

Peace shall lie on the housetop
    But not in my heart, my dear,
For all night long it wakens,
    Your voice in the deep to hear;
And all day long it questions,   5
    And cries, "Are you there, dear one?"
As though, but a hand-breadth off,
    Back to your heart I might run.

Peace shall lie on the housetop,
    Peace for the feathery nest;   10
But never a moment of peace
    Can this poor heart invest!
But all day long it is asking,
    "Dear, are you there? . . . Are you there?"
As though but a hand-breadth out   15
    You went with me everywhere.

Peace shall lie on the housetop,
    But O, if you only knew

How all day long, in my heart,
 I carry the thought of you!   20
How all day long I am feeling
 Just as though, on the air,
If I should reach to touch you,
 I would find you waiting there.

(18 May 1921) *Copy-text: RT* *Collated states:* None

J63 A SONG OF THE SPIRIT

Not till the Lord of the House
Knock on the door, though He pass,
Shall life be anything more
Than shadows flung upon glass;[1]
And not till His Voice wake echo   5
Where memory sitteth alone,
Shall spirit cease of its hunger,
In knowing, at last, its own!

From out of what infinite regions
Love, in the ultimate, comes!   10
Not with a clashing of cymbals,
Not with a tempest of drums,
Not in a flaunting of conquest,
Nor shouts where victory goes,
But, suddenly, all in a moment,   15
As life in the heart of a rose.

(11 September 1921) *Copy-text: RT* *Collated states:* None

[1] Cf. St Paul's 'For now we see through a glass, darkly' (Corinthians 13. 12).

J64 WHEN JESUS WAS A LITTLE BOY

When Jesus was a little boy
 (You know He used to be!)

His mother called Him all her joy,
   And nursed Him on her knee;
And then she'd make His supper sop,   5
   Like mother does for me.

And sometimes when it rained and rained,
   And dripped from every briar,
She'd spread His coat out on a stool,
   And feel if it were drier—   10
And, like my mother, hold His feet
   And warm them at the fire.

And just the same as mother does,
   When it is time for bed,
His mother'd lift Him in her arms   15
   And let Him lean His head;
And, as He'd lean, He'd tell her there
   The things He did and said.

And then, just like my mother, too,
   When I am all undressed,   20
She'd wrap both arms about Him close,
   And squeeze Him to her breast;
And then she'd hear Him say His prayers,
   With all the names He blest.

And, like my mother *always* does,   25
   She'd reach and get a shawl,
And tuck it well behind His neck,
   And round His feet and all;
And then, "I'll make His pillow warm!"
   To Joseph she would call.   30

And Joseph, kneeling by the fire
   Would turn the pillow over,

(11 August 1925)   *Copy-text: RT   Collated states: TribM*, 1 April 1926, p. 7 (*A*)

2 be!)] ~), *A*   **3** called Him all] said He was *A*   **5** sop,] ~ *A*   **7** rained] ~, *A*
9 stool,] ~ *A*   **10** drier—] ~; *A*   **19** mother, too] mother does *A*   **21** close,]
tight *A*   **23** prayers,] ~ *A*   **24** With all] And name *A*   **25** *always*] always *A*
28 all;] ~. *A*   **29** warm!"] ~' *A*   **31** fire] ~, *A*   **32** over,] ~. *A*

First this side up, then that side up,
Till it was warm as clover;
And, as they'd put Him in His cot,   35
How they o'er Him would hover!

34 clover;] ~. *A*   35 And,] ~ *A*   as] when *A*

J65   LOVE THAT IS NOT CHARITY
IS LESS THAN LOVE

"Me," said the Lord, "ye have denied!"
    "Nay, Lord! each night our prayers we say,
And Thy great Name, whate'er betide,
    Ends all we ask by night and day!"
"Yet," said the Lord (O accents sweet!)   5
"I saw a woman begging in your street."

"Ye have denied Me," said the Lord,
    "Nay, Lord! each night Thy Word we read,
Our souls all Thine in calm accord;
    Thy servants, we, for all Thy need!"
"Yet," said the Lord (O mournful tones!)   10
"In every beggar's body ache My bones."

"Ye have put Me away," He said!
    "Nay! but Thy cross is on our walls,
Thy Face hangs sacred overhead,
    While every hour Thy Name recalls!"   15
"Yet," said the Lord, and turned away,
"A child went hungry in your town, to-day."

(14 November 1920)   *Copy-text: RT   Collated states: SV* (*A*)
2 each] Each *A*   **7** Lord,] ~. *A*   **8** each] Each *A*   **14** but] But *A*
16 While] And *A*   **18** to-day] today *A*

J66   THE CHURCH

"Not books, but men I send," He said,
  And chose the Twelve.
And so, although the Book is read
  Wherein men delve,
And twist and turn His Words to naught,   5
  Yet what He taught
His followers still teach, as they
Who walked with Him in that far day.

He stooped to sand. No book, no leaf
  However brief,   10
Lies where His fingers made their note;[1]
  But, like the rote[2]
Of endless onward waves, we find,
  From mind to mind
Of those who keep them for His sake,   15
His Words still held as when He spake.

Not all by written words, but ear
  To ear we hear!
Not all by written words; but, man
  To man, began,   20
Continues, re-creates, is heard
  His sacred Word!
He wrote on sand . . . O human sand,
That kept the impress of His Hand!

(26 February 1924) *Copy-text: RT* *Collated states: Adv*, 20 August 1931, p. 5 (*A*)
1 books,] ~ *A*   13 find,] ~ *A*

[1] See John 8. 6–8.   [2] See I9 n. 1.

J67   TIDES

Tides in the sea, and tides within the blood;
Storms for the ship, and storms within the heart;
Rivers that rise, and passions brought to flood:
O man, are rise and fall but all thou art?
And hast thou, then, no meaning more than these—   5
Rivers and winds, and storms that lash the indifferent seas?

Tides in the sea! what bridle hath the sea
Save the insensate[1] cliff, and the high riding moon?
What the swift risen river flooding free?
What the sirocco and the wild typhoon?   10
But man, he hath a bridle in his heart—
A curb within that sets him from all else apart.

Yea, he hath storm! But he shall ride the storm;
He hath a tide—the tide shall bear him home;
For him transcendent "ought" must still inform,   15
Till from its lowest ebb his full tide comb![2]
. . . Man hath the bridle of his living will,
Where the dumb wave but lifts, is fallen, and is still.

(20 April 1924)   *Copy-text: RT*   *Collated states:* None

[1] Incapable of feeling, lacking sensation.
[2] Roll over or break at the crest, as of a wave.

J68   THE HANDS OF GOD

"I have given," He said,
"Make ye the garment;
* I have spun—make ye the cloth!"*

Ah! we would run to heaven;
We would run through flowery meads,   5
Where never would come the levin,[1]
But only the star that leads;[2]

[1] Lightning, i.e. storm.   [2] See J23 n. 1.

There we would gather of flowers,
Through sweet uncounted hours,
But that God for His needs,   10
Bid us make flowers of weeds.
We are the hands of God,
Shaping for Him the clod.

(15 December 1917)   *Copy-text: RT   Collated states:* None

J69   SWARF

Swarf * of His grindstone, scattered afar,
Will it move as man, will it wheel as star?
Will it bud in the green, green life of spring,
There to be flower and honey, or sting?
   Swarf of the grindstone,   5
    Dust that He makes,
   Scattered abroad till the
    Life awakes!

I was that dust, and you were that dust,
Flung out by the stone as it grinding thrust;   10
And the dust that was you, the dust was I,
Met here in a moment of hastening by;
   And then for ever,
    To like, like drew,
   The swarf of His grindstone,   15
    I and you!

* Dust.

(6 December 1922)   *Copy-text: RT   Collated states:* None

J70   THE PRAISING LEAF

"Ever," said the tree, "my days
   Pass for me in prayer and praise;
   Praise, the young leaves lifted up—
   Thankful hands for well-filled cup;

"Prayer, the leaves that fall a-down   5
   To the earth so kind and brown!"
   Prayers that feed both earth and tree,
   Is there lesson here for me?

(19 May 1921)   *Copy-text: RT*   *Collated states:* None

J71   PRAYER

   As light is measure of the sun,
   Is prayer the measure of the soul,
   That like the flash, where clouds hang dun,
   Leaps ever toward its pole?

   Ah, Pole-star[1] of the soul!   5
   O Mightiest!
   Prayers are the feet by which we run
   To meet Thy breast.

(1 December 1921)   *Copy-text: RT*   *Collated states:* None

[1] See I69 n. 1 and J23 n. 1.

J72   THOU AS THE LEAF

   He Who is all—Teller and Story—
   Swim in His ineffable glory!
   Stand thou no more alone,
   All thy hope gone,

But lean on His love,   5
Loosed from thy grief,
Love as a tree set over above,
Thou as the leaf.

(26 November 1917)   *Copy-text: RT*   *Collated states:* None

J73   NO ROOM AT THE INN[1]

No room at the Inn! No room at the Inn!
Yet sin by sin
Comes in at the door.

No room at the Inn! No room at the Inn!
Though shames may win   5
To traverse the floor.

No room at the Inn! No room at the Inn!
O heart, the Inn
That Christ would win!

(21 December 1923)   *Copy-text: RT*   *Collated states:* None

[1] Luke's is the only Gospel to contain this element of the Nativity story (see 2. 7).

J74   WHO ONCE WAST BOUGH

Stand, though by standing thou shouldst fall!
Best so, than like a worm to crawl,
And but the dust to know.

Call up thy tides that thou mayst know
What lies within; else, when tides flow,   5
Thine shall not know to rise.

Yet bid no power to overgrow,
Lest thou, as thou in journeyings go,
Fall waste, who once wast bough.

(8 March 1924)   *Copy-text: RT*   *Collated states:* None

J75   THE ANGELUS OF THE HEART

Bells on the air,
    Angelus[1] in the heart,
Set for a stair
    To lift the soul apart—

Slender or round,   5
    Silver or gold the notes,
How sweet their sound
    From earth toward heaven floats!

Now as they swell,
    And as Thy Name we raise,   10
O make me, too, a bell,
    Clappered to sing Thy praise!

(14 December 1923)   *Copy-text: RT*   *Collated states:* None

[1] Named for its threefold repetition of the Angelic Salutation (Hail Mary) and to be said morning, noon and sunset in response to a summoning bell, it commemorates the archangel Gabriel's Annunciation to the Virgin of the miraculous conception and birth of the Son of God in human flesh: see Luke 1. 26–35. Cf. J2.

J76   GOD GAVE ME STORM

Life is a sea of flush and veer,[1]
    And we the flotsam of its surge;
Dredged upward from its deep, we hear
    Within us its inquiet urge.

Yet there are some whom no storms rieve,[2]   5
    Whom never wild winds break and beat;
They see the sunrise, and, at eve,
    In peace lie down and know no heat.

And some in shallow waters float,
    Dreaming they know life's farthest seas,   10

[1] Sudden flowing and changing of direction.   [2] Tear, break apart (obsolete).

Startled when some small, trembling rote[3]
    Ruffles their moment, and their ease.

But some, land-locked, and yet forthright,
    Are prisonered souls of circumstance;
They hear, afar, the heaving might,   15
    And strive, who never may advance.

Never for them that greater verge
    To draw them upward, outward—far—
In swift relief of all their urge,
    In full release of all they are!   20

God gave me storm, and on the rock
    Of my resistance broken lie
My helm, my oar. Now, to His dock,
    Once more I bring the hulk was I.

(26 December 1921)   *Copy-text: RT   Collated states:* None

---

[3] Possibly the sound of the sea or surf: see I9 line 18 and n. 1, and J66 lines 12–13.

BOOK IV: *ALL SOULS AND ALL SAINTS*

J77   THE SHIPMAN'S PRAYER

God and Our Lady and St. Nicholas,[1]
Give help to us poor sailors in the dark;
The seas are falling in a broken mass,
The sky is shaken in the thunder-spark.

In the wind's whistling hear us make our prayer,   5
Who in the thrash of ocean supplicate;
Now, in the tempest, all our poles are bare,[2]
And on the deck the waters roll in spate.

We are but sinful men, but this good ship
Hath done no evil, and hath dealt none shame;   10
She hath rode gallant where the wild winds whip,
She hath not asked to bed her with the tame.

She hath gone cargoed to the Indian isles,
Her planks unstarting in the tropic heat;
And she hath sailed the sea that all beguiles,   15
Where the Sargassos burn, and no winds beat.[3]

She hath stood where the ice that binds the Pole
Gleamed on her sheets[4] until they bit like steel;
And though the trembling icefields took their toll,
Still was she faithful to the turning wheel.   20

(1924, revised 15 September 1930)   *Copy-text: RT*   *Collated states: Adv*, 20 August 1931,
p. 5, lines 27–62 only as *FROM* "THE SHIPMAN'S PRAYER" (*A*)   *SV* (*B*)

(**1–26**) God . . . pass!] *Om. A*   **1** God] I// God *B*   St.] Saint *B*
19 trembling] tumbling *B*

---

[1] Either Nicholas of Myra (d. *c.* 346) or Nicholas of Tolentino (1245–1305), both credited
with miraculously quelling a storm at sea and regarded as patron saint of sailors.
[2] The masts are stripped of sails.
[3] The Sargasso Sea, named by Christopher Columbus (see I43 n. 2): a drifting portion
of the Atlantic Ocean so heavily infested with algae that sailors feared their ships
would be entangled and becalmed there. Cf. its use in K33 and M93 n. 1 as a symbol
of psychological entrapment and inertia.
[4] Sails.

She who left port as though she were a queen,
Bowing above the waves that served her then,
On every sea her pennon has been seen,
And we have loved her and have been her men.

God and Our Lady and St. Nicholas   25
Aid now the good ship lest she pass!

    The little boat rocks
    And the great seas roll;
    While the dark fear knocks,
    And trembles the soul!   30
    Pray for us, pray for us,
    Out in the sea!
    Jesu-Maria,
    Our trust is in Thee.

    The tempest is high,   35
    And wild the winds blow;
    We dip, and we fly,
    As driven we go!
    Pray for us, pray for us,
    Out in the sea!   40
    Jesu-Maria,
    Our hope is in Thee.

    Helplessly tossing,
    The shadow draws nigh;
    Dark is the crossing,   45
    And feeble our cry!
    Pray for us, pray for us,
    Out in the sea!
    Yet ever, dear Jesu,
    Our trust is in Thee!   50

    Fierce is the lightning,
    And loud is the roar;

---

24 her and] ~, ~ *B*   **25** Lady] ~, *B*   St.] Saint *B*   Nicholas] ~, *B*   **27** The]
II// The *B*

No lamp for the bright'ning
Comes from the shore;
Only the darkness,   55
The wind and the wave,
And death in its starkness
Pointing the grave.

Pray for us, pray for us,
Out in the sea!   60
Jesu-Maria,
We come unto Thee.

62 unto] now to *B*

J78   ST. MARY'S BELLS[1]

O sweet the bells of Easter-tide
Telling their story far and wide,
O, sweet the bells St. Mary's plays
That we may turn to prayer and praise,
O, sweet they call, and sweet they chime   5
A silver stair for man to climb.

To-day they flung a lacing out,
In many a circling round about,
Now high, now low, now in the sky,
Now downward stooped on earth to fly;   10
Yet, whereso'er the flight went on,
The Easter story there had gone.

(6 April 1926)   *Copy-text: RT   Collated states: Spin* (July 1926), pp. 101–4 (*A*)   *NZT*,
18 August 1926, p. 32, lines 49–78 and 91–6 only, signed MARY GILMORE, in *The Spinner*
(*B*)   *SV* as SAINT MARY'S BELLS (*C*)

Not otherwise recorded: B indicates the omission of lines 79–90 with a row of six
dots.
(**1–48**) O . . . bereft.] *Om. B*   **1** O] ~, *A*   Easter-tide] Eastertide *C*
2 wide,] ~; *A*   **3** O,] ~ *C*   St.] St *C*   Mary's] Mary *A C*   plays] ~, *C*
4 praise,] ~; *A*   **5** O,] ~ *C*   **7** To-day] Today *C*   out,] ~ *A*   **8** In] Of *A*
11 Yet,] ~ *A*   whereso'er] wheresoe'er *A C*   on,] ~ *A*

[1] St Mary's Catholic Church (1891), Crookwell, which MG knew well: near Goulburn,

Then through the chimes there crashed a sound
That told us of the dreadful swound,[2]
The swound where drops of blood were let,   15
As though with tears a Face was wet;
And, whose the Face that looked on hell,
The holy bells of Easter tell.

Again crashed out a sound that held,
A sound as though a trumpet belled,   20
A sound as though a sword flashed out,
A sound as though a mighty shout
Through endless ages onward ran,
A message, full, to tell to man.

Then round on round, in wide resound,   25
Made storm that held within its bound
The rending of the temple veil,
The dark wherein the sun grew pale,
The earthquake, and the dreadful sigh
Of One Who gave Himself to die.   30

And yet, and yet, amid the dark,
Above the quake there gleamed a spark,
A light that burned though all was fell,[3]
Though steps were stilled awhile in hell,
Though One lay dead within the tomb,   35
As mortal held by mortal doom.

A spark, a light, a hope, a cry!
And sound again like wings went by,

---

15 let,] ~ *A*   **17** And,] ~ *A C*   hell,] ~ *A*   **19** held,] ~; *A*   **24** message,] ~ *A*
full,] still *A*   **25** wide] full *A*   resound] redound *C*   **29** earthquake,] ~ *A*
30 Who] who *A C*   **31** yet, and yet,] ~ ~ ~ *A*   **35** tomb,] ~ *A*   **37** cry!]
~!— *A*

---

it is mentioned in H9, I28, I69 and Q8. She annotated an unpublished poem (in NLA
727 2/4/3) 'Written at Crookwell 1925', and cf. *Letters* 256.

[2] Swoon, fainting fit (archaic), experienced during the Agony in the Garden of Olives
(Luke 22. 44); the final stages of Christ's Passion in lines 26–30 are from Matthew 27,
Mark 16 and Luke 23.

[3] Dreadful, deadly.

And, rising, told through earth and heaven
Of Mary and the Dolours Seven;[4]   40
Told of the Judgment and the Cross,
Where naught was saved but Love's long loss;

Told of the Pillar and the Scourge,
And how the Mockers cried their urge;
Told of the Brow beneath the Thorn,   45
And of the taunt so meekly borne;
Told of the last sad Cry that left
That saddest of sad hearts bereft.

Ah, if upon some little hill,
When falls the evening calm and still,   50
There sudden showed against the sky
Three crosses standing stark and high,
What bitter loss was his who saw,
And, seeing, felt no thrill of awe.

And if, upon some Easter morn,   55
When comes the radiant sun, newborn,
What loss were his who never found
A wonder in that dancing round—
Who never grieved his want of will
To see if it were dancing still.[5]   60

And if, on some remembered road,
Where childhood learned its early code,
He heard the homing people go,
Singing the hymns he used to know,
How deep his loss, if, there, no pain   65
Ached for the old words heard again.

---

39 And, rising,] ~ ~ *A C*   told] ~, *C*   heaven] ~, *C*   **40** Dolours] Dolorous *A*
42 loss;] ~. *C*   **44** Mockers] mockers *C*   **46** taunt] Taunt *A*   **47** last *A*] Last *X*
Cry] cry *C*   **55** And if,] ~, ~ *B*   **58** wonder] symbol *A B*   round—] ~; *C*
63 go,] ~ *A B*   **65** loss, if,] ~ ~, *A*   ~, ~ *B*

---

[4] The Seven Sorrows of the Virgin were the prophecy of Simeon (Luke 2. 35), the flight
into Egypt (Matthew 2. 13), the finding in the Temple (Luke 3. 48), the meeting on the
path to Calvary (Luke 23. 27), the Crucifixion (John 19. 25), the deposition from the
Cross (John 19. 40) and the burial (Luke 23. 55).   [5] Cf. J13 author's note.

And if his children, round his knee,
Questioned how this, or that, might be,
Or asked to hear the story told
Of one small Lamb without a fold,[6]   70
What loss, what loss were his to find
Wonder had perished from his mind.

Sweet are the bells of Easter-tide,
Telling their story far and wide;
Sweet are the bells St. Mary plays   75
That men may turn to prayer and praise;
O, sweet they call, and sweet they chime,
A silver stair for faith to climb.

Maybe the ladder Jacob found[7]
Was but a stair of sound on sound;   80
Maybe the Voice that Sinai heard[8]
Was music held within a word;
Maybe the shout that Chaos woke
Trembled to music as it broke.

It seemed when all the bells I heard,   85
As though, storm passed, sang forth a bird,
As though where grief its sorrow wept
Joy at its side a place had kept,
As though beyond a night of doubt
Love waited there to lead us out.   90

O happy bells, and happier earth,
Not death denies immortal birth!

67 And] ~, *C*   children,] ~ *B*   knee,] ~ *B*   73 Easter-tide,] ~ *A B*
Eastertide, *C*   75 St.] Saint *C*   Mary] Mary's *B*   plays] ~, *C*   77 O,] ~! *B*
~ *C*   call,] ~ *A B*   chime,] ~ *A*   78 stair] star *A B*   (79–90) Maybe . . . out.]
Om. B   83 shout] ~, *C*   woke] ~, *C*   85 seemed] ~, *C*   86 bird,] ~; *C*
87 though] ~, *C*   wept] ~, *C*   88 kept,] ~; *C*   89 though] ~, *C*
doubt] ~, *C*

---

[6] The parable of the one lost sheep in Luke 15. 4–7 is often re-told with a lamb in the role of the errant animal.

[7] On Jacob's dream of the ladder to heaven, see Genesis 28. 12.

[8] On Mount Sinai God delivered the Ten Commandments to Moses (Exodus 19. 1–24).

The tomb is rent, and rolled away
The stone that at its entrance lay;
And One is risen, was wrapt therein   95
In conquest over death and sin.

Then, O ye bells, ring loud and clear,
The world is hungry for your cheer;
Cry *Resurrection* to all men,
And lead the wandering home again!   100
Let Judas weep! His day is done,
When bells proclaim the Holy One.

Ah, what is sweeter than when bells,
Filling the void with tripling swells,
Roil[9] on the air with wings that rise,   105
And beat the gates of Paradise,
On wings that take the soul of man
Homing to where he first began.

What if the years estranged—defiled!
Again the heart that heard as child,   110
Stirred by remembrance, full and hot,
Shall yearn in tears that long were not—
As Easter bells awake, and ring,
Jesu: Redeemer: Lord: and King.

---

93 and] ~, *C*   away] ~, *C*   **95** risen,] ~ *A B*   wrapt] ~, *A*   drapt *B*   therein]
~, *A–C*   (**97–114**) Then . . . King.] *Om. B*   **99** *Resurrection*] "Resurrection" *A*
men,] ~ *A*   **101** weep! His] ~, his *A*   done,] ~ *A C*   **105** rise,] ~ *A C*
106 Paradise,] ~; *A C*   **109** estranged—] ~, *C*   **110** heart] ~, *A*
111 remembrance,] ~ *A C*   **112** were] are *A*   **114** Jesu: Redeemer: Lord:]
~—~—~ *A*

---

[9] See I5 n. 2.

J79 ONLY THE BOOK OF HER NAME FOR TROVER[1]

"Mary Gilmore, she died in the faith . . ."[2]
Never again will she fear for scaith;[3]
The wind may blow, and the rain may fall,
She will not know though she loved them all—
Mary Gilmore, who died in the faith!   5

"Mary Gilmore, she died in the faith . . ."
Here is the burden at last laid down;
Hope with a spur, or fate with a frown,
Nothing to her, so quiet her town—
Mary Gilmore, who died in the faith.   10

"Mary Gilmore, she died in the faith . . ."
Only the words her shadowy wraith;
Who was she, what was she? who can tell?
Here on the spot but her name we spell,
Mary Gilmore, who died in the faith.   15

"Mary Gilmore, she died in the faith . . ."
What was her life? Was her heart a rover?
Ah! she had faith, and faith is a lover.

[cont. overleaf

(12 October 1921)   *Copy-text: RT   Collated states: Bkfw*, 30 November 1921, p. 183
(*A*)

Not otherwise recorded: The collation for lines 6 and 11 is identical to 1. Lines 17–18
follow 20 in *A*.

1 *"Mary . . . faith . . ."*] "Mary Gilmore: She died in the faith." . . . *A*
2 scaith;] ~. *A*   **3** blow,] blow, and *A*   fall,] ~: *A*   **4** know] ~, *A*   all—]
~—, *A*   **5** Gilmore, *A*] ~ X   faith!] ~. *A*   **7** down;] ~. *A*   **12** the words]
a word *A*   wraith;] ~. *A*   **13** she, what] ~? ~ *A*   tell?] ~! *A*   **14** spell,]
~—*A*   **16** *"Mary . . . faith . . ."*] *Om. A*   **17** Was] was *A*   **18** faith, and faith]
faith. Faith *A*

---

[1] Treasure trove.
[2] See volume 1, Introduction, p. liii and Jennifer Strauss, "'Mary Gilmore, she died
in the faith'" in *'Unemployed at last!' Essays on Australian Literature to 2002 for Julian
Croft*, ed. Ken Stewart and Shirley Walker (Armidale, NSW: Centre for Australian
Studies, University of New England, 2002).
[3] Harm, injury: for her precocious use of this and other rare words as a girl, see MG's
letter to Nettie Palmer on 20 September 1922 (*Letters* 91).

. . . Turn down the page, let the leaf fall over,
Nothing to read from cover to cover,   20
Only the book of her name for trover—
Mary Gilmore, who died in the faith.

19 . . . Turn] ~ *A*   over,] ~— *A*   **20** read from] read, *A*   cover,] ~! *A*
21–2 Only . . . faith.] *Om. A*

J80   AN OLD SAYING

Long ago there was a saying used of woman-kind,
Of one gentle in her manner, noble in her mind;
"God increase her!" said the people as they named her name;
Now there's never anybody wishin' wan[1] that same.

"God increase her!" said the people, light within their eyes;   5
"God increase her!" said they, and their words were very wise;
But, now, it's not the childer[2] but passions they would raise,
Though of old 'twas mother-love that bid them to their praise.

"God increase her!" said the women, thinking Bethlehem,
Thinking of a tender maid, bud of Jesse's stem;[3]   10
"God increase her!" said the men, and never thought it shame;
Now there's never anybody wishin' wan that same.

(21 December 1923)   *Copy-text: RT*   *Collated states: NZT*, 11 August 1926, p. 32 (*A*)
Not otherwise recorded: Wherever copy-text has 'her!', *A* has 'her,'.
1 Long ago] (For the *N.Z. Tablet.*)// Once *A*   woman-kind] women-/kind *A*
2 mind;] ~: *A*   **3** name;] ~— *A*   **7** But, now,] ~ ~ *A*   it's] 'tis *A*   childer]
childher, *A*   passions] fashions *A*   **8** Though] Where, *A*   old] ~, *A*
10 maid, bud] Maid, Bud *A*   **11** shame;] ~— *A*

[1] One, anyone.
[2] Children (archaic).
[3] The Virgin Mary's descent from Jesse, father of King David, arguably showed that
Christ fulfilled the prophecy in Isaiah 11. 1: 'And there shall come forth a rod out of
the stem of Jesse, and a Branch shall grow out of his roots'.

J81 IN THE DAY OF THE RUE[1]

Of Christ, my Redeemer, I asked for a word,
   My heart for its casket to show that He heard;
But, just as I asked it, I felt the tears rise,
   For a poor beggar-child looked into my eyes.

His face was so wan, and his rags were so old,   5
   I could not but give him my coat for the cold;
And lo, as I wrapped him and happed him with care,
   I felt my Redeemer stood close to me there.

To Christ, my Redeemer, I turned me one day,
   And asked would He hearken the prayer I would pray;   10
The birds sang so sweet and the rose burned so red,
   I knew that He heard every word that I said.

I knelt in the roadway to make Him my prayer,
   But ere I could speak it a stranger stood there;
He said, "I have hungered and thirsted full sore,"   15
   And begged me to give him the half of my store.

I took the wee loaf and I broke it in two,
   I halved him the water I dipped at the dew;
He lifted his hands, and 'twas then my heart stirred,
   For Christ, my Redeemer, He spoke there the word.   20

The bread that ye give it is bread for the soul,
   The cup that ye share it shall make a man whole,
And wounds ye have washed shall be washing for you,
   When Christ at the Judgment comes bearing the rue.

(5 December 1922)   *Copy-text: RT*   *Collated states:* None

---

[1] See J7 n. 1.

J82   THE WASTED BOUGH

Once, I remember, when to some poor home,
  Shouting his first sharp breath upon the air
The newborn babe would come,
  How everywhere the word would run,
So glad the neighbours were to share   5
  The happy tidings of that little one.

To-day the wonder has died out; no more
  The miracle its mystery holds, for now
The tree destroys the bud it bore.
  Life's golden bough[1] is shaken bare;   10
The fruit lies rotting in a slough;[2]
  The maggot and the moth devour it there.

(n. d.)   *Copy-text: RT   Collated states: NZT*, 9 June 1926, p. 32 as THE TREE (*A*)   *Wr*,
28 July 1926, p. 5 as THE TREE, signed (Reprint.) MARY GILMORE (*B*)

1 Once] (For the *N.Z. Tablet*.)// Once *A*   ONCE *B*   when] ~, *B*   home,] ~ *A*
3 newborn] new-born *A B*   **4** everywhere the] everywhere/ The *A*
5 neighbours] neighbors *A B*   **6** happy] *Om. A B*   that] the *A B*   one.] ~! *B*
7 out; no] ~. No *A B*   **9** bud] buds *A B*   **10** Life's] The *A B*   bough is]
~/ Is *A*   **11** The] Its *A B*

[1] Symbol of fertility that enabled Aeneas to enter Hades, the realm of the dead (Virgil's
Aeneid, Bk VI).
[2] Muddy ground, a bog.

J83   LAUDATE DOMINUM[1]

"We are the dreams chance dreamed," he said.
  And she: "Not while we feel the red
  Blood in its current flow,
  And hear the whispering beat or slow
  Or quick o' th' heart! Ah, No!   5
  From naught came naught (she said)
  Though, when we go,
  'Tis naught that will be dead!"

[1] Praise the Lord (Latin), frequently used in church services, psalms and hymns.

Man never as a phantom grew!
Something there is loves morning dew,   10
And asks in spring to hear,
Joyous, the first thrush sing i' th' year,
And seeks the dew-web in
The grass, hung nightly new,
Where spiders spin   15
And twine the threads they clew.[2]

Something there is bends o'er the rose
And marks with what an air it blows,
And counts the folded buds
That tell how swiftly upward floods   20
The tide of rising sap
As on its course it flows,
When, from the lap
O' th' year, the winter goes!

Something there is that, half in shade,   25
Looks out upon the falling blade,
Be it of corn or weed,
And sees beyond the waiting seed
Vision on vision: dream
On dream: a world God made   30
Though all things seem—
Immortal, unafraid!

Ah, not from nothing have we come!
The woods shall testify, the dumb
Dust speak, and each new voice   35
That Spring awakens to rejoice
Declare, from field to fen,
Whence hath been all our sum
And source! *Amen!*
Laudate Dominum.   40

(6 May 1926)   *Copy-text: RT   Collated states:* None

---

[2] Follow or track as by a clue (of instinct).

J84   A CANTICLE[1] OF WORK

Praise God with work
For God in work rejoices;
Be thou not dumb,
But praise with all thy voices.

Dumb toil is naught,   5
But work with praise saves thee,
Though but in thought
Thy richest song may be!

Praise Him with trees,
And in the axes praise Him;   10
By the swift saw,
O Man, in vision raise Him;

Name Him in ships,
Declare Him on the sea,
Until thy lips   15
His Name make one with thee.

Praise as of old
The ancient fathers taught us;
Blessed be God
For all that He hath wrought us!   20

Praise Him, O tongue,
And praise Him hands and feet,
Seed ye have flung,
And furrows of the wheat!

(9 September 1928)   *Copy-text: RT   Collated states: NZT*, 14 November 1928, p.
25 as A CANTICLE OF PRAISE, signed Mary Gilmore. Sydney, 9/9/28. The day of the
Procession of the Host (*A*)

Not otherwise recorded: A divides the poem into four 8-line stanzas with a concluding
stanza of four lines.
1 Praise] (For the "N.Z. Tablet.")// Praise *A*   work] ~, *A*   **4** voices.] ~! *A*
8 be!] ~. *A*   **9** trees,] ~— *A*   **10** And] Yea, *A*   **12** Man] man *A*   Him;] ~ *A*
16 His Name make] Shall make Him *A*   thee.] ~! *A*   **23** Seed ye have] In seed
far *A*   **24** wheat!] ~!! *A*

[1] Song; strictly, a hymn, mostly taken from Scripture and used in church services. Like

Praise Him in winds,   25
And with the waters name Him,
There, with thy cry,
Let every voice proclaim Him,

Till, as sounds throng,
He singeth with thee, too,   30
As though thy song
Him nearer to thee drew.

Yea, though thy thought
Be but a child's declaring,
The miracle is wrought,   35
The wings descend upbearing.[2]

25 winds,] ~ *A*   **26** with] in *A*   name] sing *A*   Him,] ~; *A*   **27** There,] ~ *A*
with thy] as ye *A*   **28** Let . . . proclaim] Your voices toward ye bring *A*
Him,] ~; *A*   **29** Till,] There *A*   sounds throng] ye sing *A*   **30** with thee, too]
in with you *A*   **31** thy song] some wing *A*   **32** thee] you *A*   **36** wings]
wing's *A*

J84, Psalms (notably 145–50) enjoin the praise of God: cf. 'Praise ye the Lord, Sing
unto the Lord a new song' (149. 1).

[2] The Holy Ghost is traditionally figured as a dove, descending with grace to raise the
soul towards God (John 1. 32).

J85   THE KNIGHT OF THE SEPULCHRE[1]

Thine the return,
    And mine the quest:
Honour my bourne,[2]
    Thou to thy nest.

   Pray thou for me   5
   That I may be
   Faithful to God and thee!

                                              [*cont. overleaf*]

(7 November 1923)   *Copy-text: RT   Collated states:* None
5 *thou* Ed.] *Thou* X

[1] Member of the military Order of the Holy Sepulchre, initiated in the medieval
Crusades to free the Holy Land, including Christ's tomb, from Muslim rule; devoted

Here do we part,
    Face turned away,
Lest, as they start,   10
    Tears should betray.

> *Pray thou for me*
> *That I may be*
> *Faithful to God and thee!*

Nay! look not back   15
    When thou shalt go,
Lest for thy lack
    Splinters my bow.

> *But pray for me*
> *That I may be*   20
> *Faithful to God and thee!*

Where thou wilt fare thee,
    God and my fay,[3]
Jesu and Mary,
    Keep thee alway.   25

> *Pray thou for me*
> *That I may be*
> *Faithful to God and thee!*

Ah, though I go
    Losel[4] and low,   30
These shall abide:
    Earth for my stair
Sword for my bride,
    Christ for my fere.[5]

> *Pray thou for me*   35
> *That I may be*
> *Faithful to God and thee!*

---

12 *thou Ed.] Thou X*

to defending the Sepulchre during the Christian Kingdom of Jerusalem (1099–1291). The Knight will remain in the Holy Land but the one returning home (line 1) may be a loved woman rather than a fellow crusader. See further I76 n. 1.

[2] Destination, goal – but see K101 n. 1.   [3] Faith.   [4] Worthless person (archaic).
[5] Companion.

J86   O ANCIENT LOVELY LORE

Is it that life has so much aged
That none now come to trove[1]
The simple stories that of old we wove?
How that the nightingale her breast
Leaned down upon the thorn   5
That her sweet song might rise forlorn;[2]
How that the robins once so loved the dead
They heaped with fallen leaves their lonely bed;[3]
How that above the Cross
One grieving hung,   10
Until at last a thorn
The white breast stung,
Turning its hue to red,
That, evermore, proclaims to faith
That love, most lovely, heeds nor death nor scaith![4]   15

Now none, alas, believes
The lark uplifts her on her aery flight
Where high the ether drifts,
Because, earth-held, she has no song, no note
To pour us from the chalice of her throat;   20
That when she mounts beyond our sight
Her heart swells, bursting, till
In fiery founts its ecstasies out-spill!

                                          [*cont. overleaf*]

(26 September 1920)   *Copy-text: RT*   *Collated states: CP*, 24 November 1921, p.
21 as O, ANCIENT, LOVELY LORE (*A*)

5 the] a *A*   **7** dead] ~, *A*   **8** leaves their] ~/ Their *A*   **12** stung,] ~— *A*
15 love,] ~ *A*   most lovely, heeds] in loving counts, *A*   **16** believes] believe *A*
17 aery] airy *A*   **18–19** drifts,/ Because] ~, because *A*   **19** earth-held, she]
earth-/held,/ She *A*   **20** chalice] furnace *A*   throat;] ~ *A*   **21** That] ~, *A*
mounts] ~, *A*   beyond our sight] *Om. A*   **23** out-spill!] ~. *A*

[1] Seek treasure in.
[2] As in 'The Nightingale and the Rose', a short story in *The Happy Prince* (1888) by
Oscar Wilde (1854–1900).
[3] The legendary action of the robin in burying the dead; for lines 9–15, see J56 and
n. 2.   [4] See J79 n. 3.

Ah me! the nightingale
By Tereus so pursued,[5]   25
Age after age, as year by year ensued,
Has her sweet song so failed
That none now hear it echoing fleet
Through twilight deeps and ferny glades,
Throbbing as though on wings that beat   30
Eternally where memory sleeps?

O spinning lark—
Without thee in the dark!
O nightingale of dreams! O ancient lovely lore
That Tereus-Time pursues for evermore!   35
O red-breast of the Cross,
What shall redeem us for thy loss!

25 pursued,] ~ *A*   **26** age,] ~ *A*   ensued,] ~— *A*   **28** it echoing] ~, ~, *A*
31 sleeps?] ~! *A*   **33** *Without . . . dark!*] Without thee in the dark— *A*
35 evermore!] ~; *A*   **36** red-breast] red breast *A*

[5] In Greek mythology, Procne, wife of Tereus, punishes his rape of her sister Philomela by killing his son. The gods intervene and the sisters escape Tereus by being transformed into a swallow and a nightingale, but further divine intervention makes him a hawk, in which form he continues an eternal pursuit of the song-birds.

J87   THE NAVIGATOR

Now God be my shield,
For soon I must sail,
Where, over my head,
The tempest will flail;
There the wave, like a wolf,   5
Will leap at my side,
And, though deep be the dark,
No star shall abide.

Be Jesu my help,
For I must away,   10
Where naught but His hand
Can be to me stay;

For the stroke of the hail,
The whip of the snow,
Shall be my companions   15
Wherever I go.

Ave Maria!
O, look from thy place:
To Him, was thy Babe,
Thy prayer be my grace!   20
To the Three Who are One,
To her who was Maid,
I cry for protection,
And pray for their aid.

Ave Maria,   25
Thou Star of the height,
Watch as a mother
Might watch me by night!
O Jesu, Redeemer,
Thou Friend I would know,   30
Be now, through the darkness,
My help as I go.

(6 November 1924)   *Copy-text: RT   Collated states:* None

J88   WHEN CHRIST'S DAY COMES TO THE EARTH[1]

When Christ's day comes to the earth,
    In centuries one or twenty,
Then all shall be happy with mirth,
    And poverty eat in plenty.

For Christ hath said, as we know,   5
    The hungry shall all be filled,

---

[1] The Second Coming (Christ's return to inaugurate the age preceding the end of creation) is variously foretold in Old and New Testaments as the Day of the Lord, of the Lord Jesus, of Jesus Christ. The literal feeding of the poor as a prerequisite (lines 9–12) is based on Matthew 25. 34–40: 'For I was anhungered, and ye gave me meat: I was thirsty, and ye gave me drink . . . Verily I say unto you, Inasmuch as ye have done it unto one of the least of these my brethren, ye have done it unto me'.

Fallen the fardels of woe,
   And gathered the fields He tilled.[2]

Then the sooner we fill with meat
   The starven and hungry child,
The sooner to earth, His seat,
   Comes Jesus, gentle and mild.

Pity hath Jesus for all
   Poor ones who suffer and weep;
He brings them home at a call,
   He numbers them all His sheep.[3]

(2 July 1923)   *Copy-text: RT   Collated states: SV (A)*
12 Jesus,] ~ *A*   **13** all] ~, *A*   **14** Poor ones] For all *A*

---

[2] Lines 4–8 call on the Sermon on the Mount ('Blessed are they that mourn: for they shall be comforted. . . . Blessed are they that hunger and thirst after righteousness, for they shall be filled' – Matthew 5. 4, 6) and Revelation 7. 16–17; 'fardels' (line 7) are burdens.   [3] Cf. John 10. 7–16.

J89   THE PENDULUM

In flight eternally, the pendulum
Makes answer to a rhythm that no man knows,
As backward, forward, calling *Rise and Come*,
Scythe-like in movement, counting time it goes.

The tongue of ocean licks upon the shore;
The hand of man would harness up the tides;
The tide moves on, man falls and is no more;
Where once earth stood, the wave above it rides.

(30 July 1924)   *Copy-text: RT   Collated states: Wr,* 6 August 1924, p. 5 (*A*)   *GEPP,* 14 August 1924, p. 1 (*B*)   *SV* (*C*)

Not otherwise recorded: A, B and *C* add part numbering before lines 1 and 15, and *C* adds III before line 29. *A* and *B* signal this note at line 9: 'In some Indian mythology the sea is a cow, unless recollections of childhood are in error. As children we used to call the tide "the end {cud *B*} of earth."'
1 flight] ~, *A B*   **3** *Rise and*] "Rise and *A–C   Come,*] come!" *A B*   come", *C*
4 movement,] ~ *A B*   counting] over *A B*   time] ~, *C*   goes.] ~ *B*   **5** tongue] lip *C*   licks upon] moves along *C*   **6** tides;] ~: *A B*

Then dust on dust the cud of ocean[1] fills;
The mountains that were eaten conquer her;   10
She, the invader, invaded by the hills,
Slips from the silt her laving waters stir.

Earth sweetens ocean, ocean sweetens earth;
So swings the pendulum of death and birth.

So swings the pendulum!—The slayer shall   15
Be victim of the slain, the conqueror
Be beaten of the lifted manacle,
Slaves trample on thy head, Imperator;

Old Æsop[2] sitting by the road shall write
A simple tale that shall outlast a king;   20
And yet on Æsop, too, must fall the night,
Lest in some dawn no newer voice should sing!

The blade that thrust dies down before the ear,
The ear is eaten of the leaf that thrust;
Even as courage germines up from fear,   25
And fear itself is monitor to trust.

Change, change alone eternal is, which through
All else must plough, and, ploughing, life renew.

Yet is declared a greater thing than change!
For change is but a proving and a sign   30

---

8 once earth] one earth *B*   earth once *C*   stood,] ~ *A–C*   9 fills;] ~,* *A B*
10 her;] ~: *A*   12 from] on *A B*   her laving] she made her *A B*   her moving *C*
waters stir] minister *A B*   13 earth;] ~. *A–C*   15 pendulum!—] ~. *A B*   ~! *C*
16 Be *A*] Be the *X*   slain,] ~; *A B*   17 manacle,] ~— *A B*   18 Imperator;]
~! *A B*   19 Æsop] Aesop *A B*   Aesop, *C*   sitting] siting *B*   road] ~, *C*
20 king;] ~: *A B*   ~— *C*   21 And yet] ~, ~, *A B*   Æsop] Aesop *A–C*   22 Lest]
~, *A B*   in] on *A B*   dawn] ~, *A B*   newer voice] nightingales *A B*   sing!]
~. *A B*   23 blade] leaf *A B*   24 is . . . leaf] dissolves before the leaves *A B*
thrust;] ~— *A B*   25 germines up] germinates *A B*   26 fear] bear *A*   27 is,]
~! *A B*   which] That *A B*   28 All else] The dust *A B*   (29–40) Yet . . . light?]
Om. A B

---

[1] See the *Not otherwise recorded* statement for MG's gloss in *A* and *B*.
[2] Greek composer of animal fables (*fl. c.* 570 BC) who espoused a life of extreme
simplicity.

Of that which lies above the moody range
Where every broken grape must yield its wine!

Change answers more than change, else it had end,
And, ended, woke no more the shining dust,
Which, risen, turns and marks its wide extend,   35
And knows law governs all, and ever must.

The moon upon man's path sheds down her ray,
White witness of the sun beyond our sight;
And does not change, in all its changing day,
Bear equal witness with the moon's cold light?   40

Ah, if Leviathan[3] must turn to dust,
Still o'er Leviathan His Hand keeps trust!

---

35 its] life's *C*   41 Ah,] . . .Yet *A*   . . . . Yet *B*   Leviathan] leviathan *A B*   dust,]
~ *B*   42 Leviathan] leviathan *A B*   Hand] hand *A B*   trust!] ~. *A B*

[3] Follows the tradition, established by the early Christian theologian Origen (AD 185–254), in which the Old Testament monster Leviathan symbolises the fallen world and fallen humanity.

J90   WHEN I IN GARDENS WALK

When I in gardens walk,
And view the pretty flowers,
Each raised upon its stalk,
Telling the sun its hours,

When I do watch how they,   5
Fresh from the morning dew,
Spread out upon the day
The richness of their hue,

Then do I ask why man
Sits like a dog at chain,   10

(3 July 1923)   *Copy-text: RT   Collated states: MP*, 7 September 1923, p. 23 (*A*)   *SV*
(*B*)

3 stalk,] ~ *A*   4 its] his *A*

Who may such beauties scan,
And count them for his gain.

When in fair skies I see
Blue bent and cloudy wrack,[1]
Where wild winds run so free,   15
Then fall awhile, to slack,

When through the dusky pine
The sun shoots down his ray,
Gold, that no hand may mine,
Patterned upon the clay,   20

When on the perfumed air
The violet breathes its life,
Then do I ask why care
Sits with each man as wife!

When comes the mountain thrush   25
With his soft quivering note,
And fledglings of the brush
Put on Spring's Sunday coat,

When apple blossoms bud,
And wattle fills the hollow   30
With scents that waft in flood,
Where light the winds do follow,

When at the rising sun
Long shadows shield the grass,
And dewdrops, waking, run   35
To hold him in their glass,

As these I note and scan,
So near, and none aloof,

---

11 scan,] ~ *A*   12 gain.] ~! *B*   13 When] And when *A*   fair] *Om. A*
16 fall] ~, *A*   awhile,] ~ *B*   19 Gold,] ~ *A*   mine,] ~ *A*   23 care] Care *A*
24 Sits . . . as] Each man takes for his *A*   27 fledglings] fledgings *A*   fledgelings *B*
28 Spring's] spring's *A B*   29 apple blossoms] apple-blossoms *A*   31 that] ~, *A*
waft in] wafting, *A*   flood,] ~ *A*   32 Where light] ~, ~, *A*   35 dewdrops,
waking,] ~ ~ *A*   36 glass,] ~. *A*

[1] Clouds dispersed and distorted by storms or strong winds.

Then do I ask why man,
Sits prisoned by a roof!   40

Then, when I mark how mind
Moves in all things that are,
Unseen—about—behind—
In bindweed as in star,

When I observe how law   45
Garners each waste thing in,
That grain must gather straw,
And straw to grain must win,

When on time's rimless seas
I find loss feed advance,   50
How can I think that these
Measure but windy chance!

39 man,] ~ *A*   40 roof!] ~. *A*   43 Unseen—about—] ~, ~, *A*   44 star,] ~; *A*
47 grain] straw *A*   48 win,] ~; *A*   49 time's] Time's *A*   51 think that]
ask if *A*   52 Measure but] Fall from some *A*   chance!] ~? *A*

J91   IN PRAISE OF SPRING

So bright the birds do sing,
    Their little rafts of song
Do seem like buds green Spring
    Shook out in sudden throng!

And where on wing they lift   5
    Their choiring throats on high,
They fill the ear with drift
    Of sweet sound to the sky.

All day new songs fly out,
    Like floating petals strown,   10

(24 June 1923) *Copy-text:* RT   *Collated states:* Wr, 18 July 1923, p. 5 (*A*)   MP, 26
October 1923, p. 22, signed MARY GILMORE in the Worker (*B*)   SV (*C*)

1 bright] sweet *A B*   the] they *C*   sing,] ~. *A B*   2 rafts] shoots *A B*
3 Spring] spring *C*   4 Shook] Spilled *A B*   in sudden] to vocal *A B*   throng!]
~; *A B*   5 And] So *A B*   7 ear] air *A B*   8 sound] song *A B*   9 out,] ~
A–C   10 strown,] ~; *A B*

And, through the air about,
    Like blossoms they are blown.

And though on ears they dote,
    Soft-sounding like a dream,
Eyes half can see each note,   15
    So fair such songs do seem.

Sweet lust[1] of sound! Sweet Spring,
    That bids the dear birds sing!

11 And,] Till *A B*   air] ~, *A B*   12 blossoms] petals *A B*   13 dote,] ~ *A B*
14 Soft-sounding] (~ *A B*   dream] ~) *A B*   15 half can see] look to mark *A B*
16 such] their *A B*   17 Spring,] ~ *A B*   spring, *C*   18 the] they *C*   sing!] ~. *A B*

[1] Vitality, energy (archaic sense preserved in modern *lustiness*); cf. K107 n. 1.

J92   VIOLETS IN SPRING

How fair the hour of Spring
    When flowers do come to birth,
When birds in bushes sing,
    And violets breathe the earth.

The rose puts forth its leaf,   5
    The day lets out its girth,
The bind-weed twines its sheaf,
    But violets breathe the earth.

The apple-buds swell out
    Like little breasts of green,   10
And, as they lift and lout,[1]
    So plenteous are they seen;

(24 June 1923)   *Copy-text: RT   Collated states: DT*, 25 August 1923, p. 13 as SWEET
VIOLETS IN SPRING (*A*)   *SV* (*B*)

1 How fair] It is *A*   Spring] ~, *A*   spring *B*   3 sing,] ~ *A*   4 earth.] ~! *B*
7 bind-weed] bin-weed *A*   bindweed *B*   twines] seeks *A*   11 And,] ~ *A*   lout,]
~ *A*

[1] Bow down, bend (obsolete); cf. J1 n. 2.

For this is Spring, my fellow,
    The master over dearth;
Let summer be so mellow,   15
    'Tis violets breathe the earth.

So sweet the violets smell,
    They make my heart to sing,
With all the buds that tell,
    To us, the song of Spring.   20

As fair in shade they grow,
    And spill on winds their mirth,
I say, as they do blow,
    How sweet they breathe the earth.

13 Spring] spring *B*   15 summer] Summer *A*   (17–24) So . . . earth.] *Om. B*
19–20 With . . . of] Like green buds that do swell/ To tell us of the *A*
20 Spring.] ~; *A*   21 As fair] So deep *A*   22 mirth,] ~. *A*   23 say] sing *A*

J93   BEHOLD, O EARTH

Behold, O earth, the Man of Sorrow;
    Behold, ye heavens, the Holy One;
Look on Him, moon, for light to borrow,
    Your crown lay down to Him, O sun!

Tell out, O winds, how He, in pity,   5
    Took on the raiment of our earth,
That man, in an eternal city,
    Might dwell with Him in second birth.[1]

Ye fixed stars, cry aloud His glory,
    And, O ye planets, where ye roll,   10
Write out in lines of flame His story,
    Where all the heavens are made His scroll.

(26 July 1925)   *Copy-text: RT*   *Collated states: CP*, 1 April 1926, p. 8 (*A*)
3 borrow,] ~; *A*   4 Him,] ~ *A*   5 Tell] Blow *A*   6 the] a *A*   our] the *A*
earth,] ~; *A*   7 city,] ~ *A*   11 story,] ~ *A*

---

[1] On man's rebirth through Christ's death, see J26 n. 1 and cf. 'Born to raise the sons

Waters, that lave the listening earth,
    And, O ye caves of Bethlehem,
Declare abroad what mighty birth   15
    Sprang from the Maid of Jesse's stem.[2]

Ye little fish that, in the sea
    Dreamed of a light where He once trod,
Bid all remember how that He
    Bore flesh as man, and yet was God.   20

And, O ye trees, and all ye flowers,
    Ye wingèd things that in these dwell,
Tell how the Lord, Who made the hours,
    Walked for a space, for man, in hell.[3]

17 that,] ~ *A*   **22** wingèd] winged *A*   these] them *A*   dwell,] ~; *A*
23 Lord,] ~ *A*

---

of earth,/ Born to give them second birth' in the hymn 'Hark the herald angels sing'. J93 encompasses Christ as the Man of Sorrows (Isaiah 53. 3), the light of the world (John 1. 4–9), the Babe of Bethlehem (Isaiah 11. 1, Matthew 2 and Luke 2) and the miracle-worker walking on the waters (Matthew 14. 25–7, John 6. 19–20).

[2] See J80 n. 3.
[3] During the three days between the Crucifixion and the Resurrection, Christ descended into hell to wrest the souls of the righteous dead from the devil (the so-called Harrowing of Hell). This belief was developed in early Christianity through interpretations of Old Testament prophecies (e.g. in Psalms 16. 10 and 24. 7–10): see, e.g., the fifth-century apocryphal Gospel of Nicodemus.

J94   A SONG OF PRAISE

O heart, be a timbrel,[1] O lips be a lute!
O throat be a trumpet to sound at His Name!
The mountains shall speak it, the valleys repeat it,
The roll of the thunder be filled with His fame!

The heart of the earth shall stir at His footstep,   5
The wheel of the planets shall turn to His praise;
Darkness shall tell through the stars of his splendour,
The march of the season shall show us His ways!

---

[1] Tambourine. The imagery of lines 1–38 is based on the Psalms (especially 148–50) enjoining the praise of God.

Blessed be God, Who gave us His altar,
From whence cometh strength to those who would falter.   10

Praise Him, O winds that ever more fly!
What shall restrain you, mounting on high?
Praise Him, ye clouds, ye lightning, ye hail;
The delicate mist that spreadeth her veil!

Praise Him ye armies of life, one and all,   15
To whom must His name be blazon[2] and call—
The bee in her hive, the ant on his hill,
The trees and the wild, the swift and the still!

Praise Him, ye tempests prouder than ships;
Praise Him, all people, out of your lips,   20
Till, from the multitude, music is made
In passion of worships, and prayer unafraid!

Praise Him till ocean shall lift at his bars,
And the song of the infinite small
Awakened shall rise to the stars!   25
Praise Him, all souls! Bless ye His name,
Who, from His altar
Where lifteth His flame,
Broodeth o'er all who would falter,
And fall.   30

Sweeter than doves is the sound of His Voice:
Praise ye, all nations, His Name!
Deeper than death is the chord of His love:
Praise ye, all nations, His Name!
He Who is highest has bent to the low: 35
Praise ye, all nations, His Name!
Nearer than life He leaneth above:
Praise ye, all nations, His Name!

(18 July 1921)   *Copy-text: RT*   *Collated states:* None
10 falter. *Ed.*] ~, *X*   **33** love: *Ed.*] ~; *X*   **36** nations, *Ed.*] ~ *X*

---

[2] See I148 n. 4 and cf. J36 line 4.

Turn Thy Face from my sins,[3]
O Maker and Master of men;   40
Put away all my misdeeds,
And remember them never again;
Take not Thy holy Spirit from me,
And cast me not ever away,
Like a lost lamb out in the fen,   45
In darkness that knoweth not day.
But make me a clean heart, O God,
And renew a right spirit within me:
Then let me follow, forever,
The Mercy that asked but to win me.   50

---

[3] Apart from the motif of the lost lamb (see J78 n. 6), lines 39–50 are based on Psalm 50. 9–11, with similar wording to that in the Penitential Service of the Scottish Book of Common Prayer.

J95   I WENT WITH CHRIST TO THE WILDERNESS[1]

Why went I out to the wilderness?
    Why went I to walk with Christ?
What was the longing, what the distress,
    Where the old ways once sufficed?

Alone, alone in the wilderness,   5
    I heard the lion cry,
I saw the jackal his rage impress,
    The bale of his changeless eye;

I felt the dim like a dreadful thing
    That wound me round and about,   10
Like a veil from which no morn could bring
    My soul from its bondage out.

I caught the waft of a phantom flight
    That was bat-winged, foul and rank,

---

[1] See Mark 1. 13 and Luke 4. 1–13 on Christ's sojourn in the wilderness. These forty days (line 40) were a period of trial and temptation, an important aspect of Christian experience.

Where a darker dark than darkest night   15
   Discovered it, flank by flank;

I heard the cries as the flying mewed
   Their wound of sound on the air,
Where in rounds oblique they swung and slewed,
   Till the flesh grew thin with fear.   20

Yet, to Him there in the wilderness,
   I turned me about and went,
There to be His in His loneliness,
   To be spent as He was spent.

And there, with Him in the wilderness,   25
   I put away all my fears,
And knelt in the dust His Feet to dress,
   And watered Their wounds with tears.

Ah, what were lion, and shadow and dark,
   To one who might watch with Him,   30
The light of His Face the heavenly mark,
   To beckon by dark and dim;

Or what the terror that flies by night[2]
   To one who might stand, sufficed,
And measure the world, and its despite,   35
   A servant of Love and Christ.

Yet what of the dark? Never I knew.
   I only knew that I went,
One whom the wild and the desert drew,
   Where the Forty Days were spent.   40

(18 March 1924)   *Copy-text: RT   Collated states:* None

[2] Cf. Psalm 91. 5.

J96   THE BALLAD OF ELIZABETH[1]

She took her staff within her hand,
    And measuring its span,
She found it but a withy wand,[2]
    And so her grief began.

She took again within her hand   5
    A staff she thought a friend;
It had no strength at its command,
    Either to give or lend.

And so she took another staff,
    She took the staff of pride;   10
She found it but a thing of chaff,
    And threw it down aside.

All shorn she stood upon the ground,
    In nakedness of pain,
But as she wept she made no sound,   15
    For sound itself was vain;

All shorn she wept and stood forlorn
    In nakedness of woe,
As one whose feet upon a thorn
    Must ever walking go;   20

She wept, alas, as one alone
    In nakedness of grief,
As though no other made His moan
    And died beside a thief.

She wept as one who had no eyes,   25
    As one who had no ears,
Save as the foolish mock the skies,
    And wash the earth with tears.

And then she put her grief away,
    She looked not on its face,   30

---

[1] No source identified. See further I76 n. I.   [2] A small willow branch.

And yet she heard it, night and day,
    Cry in its narrow place.

She said, "The grief I laid away,
    Why should it cry to me,
As though my heart must with it stay,   35
    To bear it company?

"Why should the staff that wounded me
    Still hang upon my hand,
So that, whatever hap may be,
    Beside it I must stand?"   40

She turned toward her buried grief,
    She dug it from its grave;
She took and bound it as a sheaf,
    That measured man and stave.

And then she raised it in her hand,   45
    She offered it to Him,
Before Whose throne the Angels stand,
    And kneel the Seraphim.[3]

He dried the tears that wet its face,
    He kissed it on the eyes,   50
And now no more within its place
    That old grief wakes and cries.

Christ, Who was born in Bethlehem,
    Look down on all in grief;
By Thine Own tears remember them,   55
    And bind them in, Thy sheaf.

(2 August 1924)   *Copy-text: RT*   *Collated states:* None

[3] See C58 n. 2 and J23 n. 3.

J97   SAID LEVERET TO HARE

As Joseph was a-walking
    With Mary and the Child,[1]
The sun shone to bless Them,
    The wind it blew mild;

While the hare in its form,[2]   5
    The leveret[3] in the grass,
Lifted up their furry ears,
    To hear who should pass.

As Joseph came a-walking,
    Said leveret to hare,   10
"Who is this comes walking
    With his face shining fair?

"Who is this comes walking,
    The stars in his eyes,
So pitiful and tender,   15
    Father-like and wise?"

Said hare then to leveret,
    "The Holy Family
Is Jesus, Mary, Joseph,
    As here you do see.   20

"As Jesus slept at Mary's heart,
    So Joseph must hold
Jesus and the Mother Maid,
    As though in a fold.

"His hands they must serve them,   25
    His love it must feed,

---

[1] Joseph as a benign figure, part of a Holy Family (line 18), depends on stressing his acceptance of Mary as his wife (see Matthew 1. 18–24) and his role in the flight into Egypt (Matthew 2. 13–14). A counter-tradition stresses his initial intention to reject her (Matthew 1.19): see, e.g., the medieval 'Cherry-tree Carol' in Francis James Child, *English and Scottish Popular Ballads*, 5 vols (1882–98), no. 54.
[2] The nest or lair in the grass in which a hare crouches.
[3] See J37 n. 1.

So that little Jesus
Shall not suffer need."

Says leveret to hare,
   "Why seems the Virgin sad?   30
Her eyes they are darkling,
   As she looks upon the lad!"[4]

Then hare said to leveret,
   "She sees the thorny way
The feet she held against her heart   35
   Must walk upon some day;

"She sees where a scourge is wound,
   And where a thorn-tree grows;
She hears over feet and hands
   The sound of hammer blows;   40

"She sees high against a sky
   A hill with crosses three,
And there will little Jesus come,
   To die on the tree!"

As Jesus was a-walking   45
   With Joseph and the Maid,
The leveret and hare,
   They saw them unafraid;

And low the leveret louted,[5]
   And low kneeled the hare,   50
To see the Holy Family,
   In the field come walking there.

(25 April 1923)   *Copy-text: RT*   *Collated states:* None

---

[4] On the Sorrows of the Virgin, see J78 n. 4. Her foreknowledge of Christ's fate is not biblical but developed as part of her cult.
[5] See J1 n. 2.

J98   THE ANNUNCIATION[1]

All innocent she came,
  Like a child, like a child;
The rose it breathed her name,
  The lily undefiled;

The daisies at her feet   5
  Made her a silver crown;
The mignonette, its sweet,
  Spilled all her pathway down.

Each alabaster box[2]
  Wherein their scents did lie,   10
The gillyflower, and clocks,
  Opened as she passed by;

The rosemary its hood
  Drew back and on her smiled,
As once amazed she stood,   15
  Like a child, like a child.

The very bees hung still,
  Lest they should startle her,
As, by Almighty Will,
  Love at her heart made stir.   20

Spiders that webbed in grass
  Set free each prisoned fly,
Lest, where her foot might pass,
  Her heart should hear them cry.

Far in the field the ox   25
  Stood like a carven thing,
As though, through herds and flocks,
  All earth heard angels sing;

---

[1] See J75 n. 1.
[2] In the ancient world, boxes of alabaster – a fine translucent material of carbonate or
sulphate of lime – were used to seal up unguents and perfumes.

And then a lamb looked up,
    And ran and kneeled him down,   30
Where lay, as in a cup,
    Of heaven the Kingly Crown.

Then Mountains held their shade,
    That only might the sun
Shine on the little maid,   35
    Who bore the heavenly One.

(23 November 1924)   *Copy-text: RT*   *Collated states:* None

J99   STATIONS[1]

I. Here came the Lord, and here He laid Him down,
        A little child, helpless and lost
    As any babe who to his mother's gown
        Clings, and must ever cling at any cost.
    Here came the Lord, and here lay down.   5

II. Here came the Lord, a young boy wandering,
        Yet with strange wisdom in His speech,
    And in His eyes a look that seemed to spring
        From knowledge far beyond our human reach.
    Here came He young, and wandering.   10

III. Here came the Lord, here to a marriage feast,
        Where life eternal stooping takes
    Its lowly part with the fermenting yeast
        That bubbling sings its little while, and breaks.
    Here came the Lord, and blessed the feast.   15

(26 December 1928)   *Copy-text: RT*   *Collated states: SV* (*A*)
Not otherwise recorded: A has no stanza numbering.
3 who] ~, *A*   gown] ~, *A*   **4** Clings,] ~ *A*   **7** His *A*] his *X*

---

[1] The Stations of the Cross (also the Way of the Cross, Via Dolorosa or Via Crucis;
cf. J25) – fourteen episodes from the Passion of Christ from his condemnation to the
entombment – allow Catholics (mainly) to meditate on the successive scenes of Christ's
suffering and death. J99 draws broadly on Christ's life and ministry.

IV. Here came the Lord, and standing by the lake
          Had pity on the multitude;
     And for their hunger took, and blessed, and brake
          Five little foundling loaves, and made them food.
     Here stood the Lord beside the lake.   20

 V. Here came the Lord upon the fishers' sea,
          And being weary slept; as man
     He slept, until awaked: then "Peace!" said He
          To storm, and there peace fell, and ravin² ran.
     Here walked the Lord upon the sea.   25

VI. Here came the Lord, and heard the lepers cry,
          "Unclean! Unclean!" that all might know
     Them the untouchable; but He drew nigh
          And, touching, healed them there and bid them go.
     Here came the Lord Who heard man cry.   30

VII. Here came the Lord to Lazarus, three days dead,
          And stopped the bier, and "Lazarus! Rise,
     And stand thou up alive!" to him He said;
          And Lazarus came forth with living eyes.
     Here stood the Lord with man long dead.   35

VIII. Here came the Lord, and brake the holy bread,
          And supped, then supped no more on earth;
     Upon His breast the loved John laid his head,
          Nor ever dreamed that death must crown His Birth.
     Here brake the Lord the holy bread.   40

IX. Here came the Lord, alone, and all alone;
          Here drops of blood His body wept;
     While they, who deemed themselves to be His own,
          Unconscious of His anguish by Him slept.
     Here came the Lord alone, alone.   45

---

17 multitude;] ~, *A*   19 loaves *A*] leaves *X*   27 "Unclean! Unclean!"] *Unclean!*
Unclean! A   know] ~, *A*   28 Them] ~, *A*   30 Who] who *A*   31 Lazarus,]
~ *A*   three] four *A*   32 stopped] touched *A*   and] ~, *A*   39 His] that *A*

---

² Apparently, a violent rush of water, a rare sense of *ravine*: cf. 'ravening' in K58 line
54 and K115 line 5.

   X.   Here came the Lord, and here the soldiers came;
        Here Judas kissed Him on the cheek;
    And, though in Heaven was cried the mighty Name,
        Yet He went captive as a lamb most meek.
    Here came the Lord, and soldiers came.   50

  XI.   Here came the Lord where troubled Pilate sat,
        Christ the betrayed, of men the scorn;
    Peter denied Him here, the rabble spat,
        Scourged Him and mocked, and crowned Him with
           a thorn.
    Here came the Lord, where Pilate sat.   55

 XII.   Here came the Lord, and stumbling, to this hill,
        Here died He on the Cross man's death;
    Here was He pierced, here did His blood outspill,
        Who cried His Father's Name with His last breath.
    Here came the Lord: here comes He still.   60

56 and] ~, *A*   hill,] ~; *A*

SECTION K

Under the Wilgas (1932)

K I   LAND OF MIRRABOOKA

Land of Mirrabooka,*
Land of Kollarendi,*
Lo, we have wakened thee,
We of the Northland.

Put by the throwing stick   5
(The ancient womerah),
Break ye the boomerang,
Lay down tharunka.*

Thou shalt no more, at dusk,
Hear the lone complaining,   10
Where wanders Willaroo*
Calling Meewidgee;*

For we have wakened thee,
Land of Koonewarra,*
We who, as conquerors,   15
Came from the Northland.

Thou shalt not again, by night,
Hear in the forest
The whirling woman-drawer*
Crying the voice of love;   20

Nor ever more, at morn,
Watch, mountain to mountain,
Kallimatta* flinging
Smoke signals upward.

Land of Minnathunka,*   25
Land of the Churingas,*
Lo, we have conquered thee,
Made thee our own.

* The Southern Cross.[1]   *[l. 2] Coolibah blossom.[2]
*[l. 8] The message stick.[3]   *[l. 11] The curlew, whose shriller cry
foretold rain.   *[l. 12] The rain.   *[l. 14] The black swan.[4]
*[l. 19] The small bull-roarer, caller, or serenader of women; the
nurmi.[5]   *[l. 23] A native message-bringer.   *[l. 25] The dawn.   n5
*[l. 26] Sacred tribal emblems; each tribe had its own, and no two tribes
had the same markings.[6]

(10 December 1930)   *Copy-text: UW   Collated states: SV (A)*

Not otherwise recorded: In K1, K2 and K4, MG's notes are glosses of Aboriginal words;
SV does not signal them – repeating instead, at foot of page, the word with a colon.
The gloss starts with a lower-case letter, except for proper nouns.
n1 Coolibah] Coolabah *A*   **n4** caller,] ~ *A*   **n5** message-bringer] message
bringer *A*   The] *Om. A*   **n6–7** emblems . . . markings.] emblems. *A*

---

[1] See Preface for MG's use and glossing of Aboriginal words.
[2] On 'Kollarendi', cf. *kolorin*: flowers of the kuluba tree (Ridley) and *collarene*: Coolabah
blossom (Parker 1905); on 'Coolibah', cf. Ridley and Parker and note spelling in *A* (see
entry for line n1).
[3] Apparently from Eora (Sydney region) language, but not in Thiesinger who otherwise
lists Eora words; author's notes to lines 11, 12, 23 and 25 are uncorroborated.
[4] From Wembawemba *kunawarr*: black swan (Thieberger).
[5] See I26 n. 2.   [6] See I23 n. 4.

K2   WARIAPENDI: A DIRGE

Land of the Churingas,[1]
Mark in the dim darkness
How Arunta[2] passes,
Lone Arunta crying,
Wariapendi, to Biami,*   5
Wariapendi,* to the past.

(n. d.)   *Copy-text: UW   Collated states:* Ingamells (*A*)   *SV* (*B*)   Wannan (*C*)

Not otherwise recorded: The collation for line 5 is identical at lines 6, 12 and 13. Glosses
are unsignalled in *A–C*. *A* includes poems by several authors; it provides a general
glossary of all Aboriginal words used. In its editorial note, *C* cites *A* as its source
in glossing 'Churinga', 'Arunta', 'Wariapendi' and 'Biami'. There is no substantive
difference between these glosses and those provided by MG. *B* reverses the order of its
two notes; for their presentation see the *Not otherwise recorded* statement for K1.
5 *Wariapendi*] Wariapendi *A C*

---

[1] See I23 author's note and n. 4.   [2] See I19 n. 3.

Mark, O Churinga-land,
Where in the dusk stands a dim shadow!
Soon thou shalt seek and not find it—
Thou who hast driven Arunta outward,   10
Sent Arunta crying
Wariapendi, to Biami,
Wariapendi, for the lost.

* God the All-Father.[3]
*[l. 6] *"We go seeking."*[4]

---

10 hast] has *B C*   **11** crying] ~, *A C*   **13** for the lost] to the last *A C*   *n2* *"We go seeking."*] "we go seeking". *B*

---

[3] See I4 n. 2.   [4] Uncorroborated.

K3   THE CHILDREN OF MIRRABOOKA[1]

I

Only the children of Mirrabooka
Knew the secret things
The Lord of the earth
Bid men write on the Churingas;[2]

Only the children of Mirrabooka   5
Knew the voice of the forest,
And all the separate sounds
That, in the dark, whispered together;

Only the children of Mirrabooka
Read, in the flight   10
Of a bird by night,
The meaning of movements unseen, and afar.

[cont. overleaf

(14 December 1930)   *Copy-text: UW   Collated states: SV (A)*
Not otherwise recorded: For *A*, see the corresponding statement for K4.
0.1–12 *§I . . . afar.] Om. A*

---

[1] See Preface, p. xxxiii.   [2] See I23 author's note and n. 4.

II

Once, long ago, the children of Mirrabooka
Conserved in the forest the tree,
That there the koala might breed,   15
And the possum should bring forth her young.

Long, long ago, the children of Mirrabooka
Forbade the beating of waters out of due season,
Lest the fishing should fail,
And hunger should stalk through the land.   20

And long, long ago, the children of Mirrabooka
Made servant of fire,
That the seedling might sprout from the flame-loosed
        shell,
And the bees find blossom and honey.

III

Children of Mirrabooka,   25
Pause in your going;
Stay for a moment,
And tell us your story!

Name for us the stars,
Recount to us their meanings,   30
Even as your fathers told them,
In the days that are no more.

Tell to us that long relating,
Spoken round the fire:
Names the fathers of the fathers   35
Counted from the far beginnings;

Tell us of the great law-givers,
Tell us of the ancient heroes,
Tell of him, the long enduring,
Dying for his people.   40

12.1 ^sII] I *A*   **15** koala] koalo *A*   **17** Long] And long *A*   **21** the . . .
Mirrabooka] *Om. A*   **22** Made] Her children made *A*   **24.1–40** ^sIII . . . people.]
Om. A

K4   WEENYAH! WEENYAH! WEENYAH![1]

I

Vales of Mirrabooka,*
Where are the children?
We call, but none answer,
Though we call weeping.

Still is the forest   5
Where once they walked,
Empty are the mountains,
Lone are the rivers;

Cold is the firestick,
Dust fills the wurleys,*   10
Never one but Moolpa*
Walks by the cowal.*

II

Only the moon
Peers through the shadows,
Calling *Weenyah, Weenyah,**   15
Weenyah, to the dark.

Only the wind
Runs through the valleys,
Weenyah, Weenyah, crying,
Very lonely.   20

Only the rain,
The rain in the night-time,

(6 April 1931)   *Copy-text: UW*   *Collated states: SV (A)*

Not otherwise recorded: K4 is set in *A* as Pts II and III of THE CHILDREN OF MIRRABOOKA (see K3 entries for 0.1–12 and 24.1–40). On the presentation of glosses in *A*, see the *Not otherwise recorded* statement for K1.

0.1 ᔆI] II *A*   **1** Mirrabooka,*] ~ *A*   **12.1** ᔆII] III *A*

---

[1] MG to Nettie Palmer on 20 September 1922: 'The Labor Daily and also another paper said the Aboriginal verse was not poetry and then quoted "Weenyah weenyah" in proof of the statement. My innermost soul said "Gosh!" ' (*Letters* 91).

Fingers at its eyes,
Weeps for Arunta.*

* The Southern Cross.[2]   *[l. 10] Gunyahs, or shelter-places.[3]
*[l. 11] The spoon-bill.[4]   *[l. 12] A coolamon-hole or small lake.[5]
*[l. 15] A word meaning "*Whither.*"
*[l. 24] A tribe of Central Australia, the name being used here as a
general designation for reasons of the drama and poetry.[6]   n5

---

n1 *The Southern Cross.] *Om. A*   shelter-places] shelter places *A*
n2 spoon-bill] spoonbill *A*   n3 *A word meaning "*Whither.*"] "whither". *A*

---

[2] See Preface, p. xxxiii.
[3] On gunyah, see I19 n. 2; *wurley* is from Kaurna *wa(d)li* (Thieberger).
[4] Uncorroborated, as is author's note for line 15.
[5] From Kamilaroi *guwal*: gully, but used early as a swampy depression, a lake (Dixon);
on 'coolamon-hole', see I30 n. 6.
[6] See I19 n. 3.

K5   A SONG OF KOONEWARRA

Land of Koonewarra,*
    Hail! Hail! Ho!
Warm on thee shine the sun,
    Soft fall the snow!
(*Blow scented o'er her,*   5
    *Winds of Attunga!**)

Currawarna* brings thee
    Flowers for thy brow,
Koonabulla,* dusting,
    Lies in the shade,   10
Kurrawurra* hails thee,
    Far in the sky.

Land of Koonewarra,
    Hail! Hail! Ho!
Warm on thee shine the sun,   15
    Soft fall the snow.
(*Winds of Attunga,*
    Blow scented o'er her!)

* The black swan.[1]   *[l. 6] The height (or place) of the gods, equivalent to Olympus.[2]   *[l. 7] The currajong tree.
*[l. 9] The kangaroo. The bush animals and birds are very clean in a natural state. They all have their dusting holes. My own impression is that, apart from ants, small native flies, etc., there was no vermin in Australia till brought here in ships.   *[l. 11] The eagle hawk.

n5

(7 December 1930)   *Copy-text: UW   Collated states:* None

[1] See K1 n 4.
[2] Uncorroborated, as are author's notes for lines 7, 9 and 11.

k6   AUSTRALIA

I

There was great beauty in the names her people called her,
Shaping to patterns of sound the form of their words;
They wove to measure of speech the cry of the bird,
And the voices that rose from the reeds of the cowal.[1]

There, when the trumpeting frog boomed forth in the night,   5
Gobbagumbalin! he said, *Gobbagumbalin!*
And even as Aristophanes heard in the far-off deeps
Of his Grecian marshes, the frogs,[2] so we in that word.
"*Gobbagumbalin! . . . Gobbagumbalin! . . . Gobbagumbalin! . . .*"
Hearken, and measure the sound!   10

II

Mark where, fallen, the tribes move in the shadow;
Dark are the silent places where Arunta[3] walks—
Dark as the dim valleys of Hades, where stalk,
Grey-shaped, the heroes and the gods of the Greeks.
These were the young, for even then Arunta was old.   15

[cont. overleaf

(15 December 1930)   *Copy-text: UW   Collated states: SV* (A)

7 heard] ~, A   **9** *Gobbagumbalin! . . .*] *Om.* A   **10** Hearken] Harken A
13 Hades,] ~ A   **14** heroes and the gods] Gods and heroes A   **15** young,] ~; A

[1] Waterhole; see K4 n. 5.
[2] *The Frogs* (405 BC), a comedy by Aristophanes (c. 448–385 BC). The sound of his Grecian frogs translates as 'Brekekekex, ko-ax, ko-ax', unlike MG's Aboriginal mimetic presentation.   [3] See I19 n. 3.

Very old was Arunta when Alexander wept;[4]
Old, old was Arunta when over Bethlehem
Was seen the star that told the birth of Christ;
Old, old was Arunta when upward from the deep
Was swung the hammer-symbol of Poseidon.[5]   20
Troy rose and fell, but Arunta lived on.
Then was Arunta put out in a night.

15–16 old.// Very] ~./ ~ *A*

---

[4] I.e. Alexander the Great (356–323 BC), for the death of his closest friend and campaign companion, Macedonian nobleman Hephaestion (*c.* 357–324 BC).
[5] The sea-god Poseidon's trident is hammerlike in its power to smash rocks, causing earthquakes and releasing fountains. In Homer's *Iliad* Poseidon helps build the walls of Troy but, when the Trojans default on due payment, he assists the Greeks to destroy the city (line 21).

K7   THE WILGA TREE

What have I heard in the wilga,*
    The wilga tree on the plain?
Was it Willeroo* that I heard,
    Willeroo crying in pain?

White, white is the face of the moon,   5
    But black the shadow that cries,
Where, at the foot of the wilga tree,
    Something was Willeroo lies.

---

* The wilga (which also was called woolga) used to be an excellent tree for shade and feed for cattle in drought time.[1] I remember two very fine examples that were long a landmark out toward Ben Hall's old place. As the aboriginal did not destroy living trees, they grew to greater size than is possible now-a-days, and died of old age only.   n5
*[l. 3] The stone-curlew, and among the tribes a man's name. The name Willeroo is also Willaura, Williaru, Willara, and probably Woollahra.[2] The words are onomatopoeic, as they represent the different variations in the curlew's call.

(8 April 1931)   *Copy-text: UW   Collated states:* None

[1] From Wiradjuri *wilgarr*: small tree of the genus *Geijera*, having a spreading crown, much used for fodder in early farming (Thieberger).   [2] I.e. the Sydney suburb (derivation uncorroborated); cf. K12 author's note lines n58–60.

к8   THE WOMAN-DRAWER[1] IS MADE

In the night there came a sound,
A little sound like the wind
When it whispers in the Spring,
And the reeds are young.

And, above the sound, the moon   5
Looked down from the sky and saw
The face of one wandering there,
Song-haunting the night.

And softly she[2] called to him,
"Say who art thou who singest   10
Thy heart as sing the dream-held?"
And he said, "I am Youth."

Then he said, "When thus I sing,
I make for myself a world
Wherein for ever I reign   15
A king, but my realm

Is a dream." Then said the moon,
"Take thou the heart of thy song,
And, shaping, make thou from it
The woman-drawer!"   20

Now, when with her woman's face
The moon looks down in the night,
She hears the woman-drawer
Call the awakening.

Now, when with her woman's face   25
The moon looks down on the earth,
She hears a whirl on the wind:
And the whirl is life.[*]

[*] It was at the full moon, and at the time of the year decreed, that the

---

[1] On this type of bull-roarer, see K9 author's note and I26 n. 2.
[2] On the moon's gender, see author's notes to K16 and M62.

three days' tribal feasting occurred, and the young were chosen and
given in marriage.

(3 June 1931)   *Copy-text: UW   Collated states:* None

K9   THE SONG OF THE WOMAN-DRAWER[*]

> I am the woman-drawer,
>   I am the cry;
> I am the secret voice;
>   I am the sigh;
>
> I am that which is heard   5
>   Low in the dusk;
> Birds by a note reply,
>   The flowers in musk;
>
> I am that dol'rous plaint,
>   Uttered where calls   10
> A lone bird wand'ring by
>   Dim waterfalls;
>
> I am the woman-drawer,
>   Pass me not by;
> I am the secret voice;   15
>   Hear ye my cry;
>
> I am that power which night
>   Looses abroad;
> I am the root of life;
>   I am the chord.   20

[*] The small bull-roarer (the nurmi or nama) is called the woman-
drawer.[1] It is only whirled to attract women, and its sound is equivalent
to the serenade. It is made very small and has special decorations, so
that in its note is a thin, but special, singing sound, not heard in the

(9 May 1931)   *Copy-text: UW   Collated states: SV* (*A*)

9 dol'rous] dolorous *A*   **13** woman-drawer, *Ed.*] woman drawer, *X*   ~; *A*
15 voice;] ~, *A*

whirl of the great bull-roarers. The latter are the voice of the vortex and   n5
the void; in great ceremonials the spirits hear them and answer, and the
demons fear them and keep away.[1]

n6 ceremonials *A*] ceremonial *X*

[1] Cf. K8 and see I26 n. 2 and R69 entry for n17–24.

K10   BOOLEE, THE BRINGER OF LIFE[*]

Breast to breast in the whirling,
    Palm to palm in the strife,
Boolee spins over the plain,
    Boolee the bringer of life.

Head to the sky up-towering,   5
    Swift-treading foot on the earth,
Held in his loins the tempest,
    Boolee comes, giver of birth.

O Boolee, woman and man!
    O Boolee, terror and flame!   10
Yea against *Nay* in the night,
    Out of the whirlwind I came.

[*] The aboriginals described the conflict of sex and the coming of life by
the symbol of the whirlwind (boolee).[1] Two separated winds or beings
crossed space and met; in conflict they formed a whirlwind. Out of their
whirlwind came life. Where we said the baby came in a cabbage, they
said it came in a whirlwind.   n5

(7 June 1931)   *Copy-text: UW   Collated states: SV (A)*   Wright1 (*B*)
4 Boolee] ~, *A B*   **5** up-towering] uptowering *B*   (**n1–5**) The . . . whirlwind.]
Om. B   **n3** met;] ~, *A*

[1] Cf. Parker: *Boolee*: whirlwind.

K11   THE BURRAGORANG VALLEY

Out of the pomp of the mountains,
Up from the dusk of the vales,
Murmur the winds that are thine—
O bold Burragorang.

Marked where the first tribes wandered,   5
Ancientry clings to thy ribs;
Sleeps in thy heart its totem—
Lost, O Burragorang.[1]

(2 December 1930)   *Copy-text: UW   Collated states:* None

[1] Situated n.e. of Goulburn (see K12 author's note for line 1), the valley's fertile grazing lands attracted white settlers who displaced the original Tharawal people. Their fierce resistance during 1812–16 led to a massacre (hence 'lost') at Cataract Gorge. Name possibly from *burru*: kangaroo (or *booroon*, small animal) and *gang*: hunting – a meaning consistent with K12 line 2 and author's note; cf. also *bohrah*: kangaroo (Parker 1905).

K12   BURRAGORANG

Blow winds through Burragorang,*
    Bring back the hunting![1]
. . . *There was a dream I had;*
The dream was lost
    In a dark confronting.   5

Blow winds of Burragorang,
    Wake the old glamour,
As when at night glowed red
Yeringa's* eyes,
    And Braak* made clamour!   10

But that, O Burragorang,
    Was ere the falling—
Ere lost Arunta[2] went,

[1] See K11 n. 1.
[2] See I19 n. 3.

Like the last flight
Of the swans, far calling!   15

* Burragorang, according to what was told my father, both by "old
hands" and by aboriginal elder men whom he knew, was set apart by
the tribes as an animal sanctuary, in which, because of its fertility and
its seclusion, the creatures could breed in safety, and with a plentiful
food supply. This setting apart was done in order to provide a stock   n5
(and its sustenance), when drought, disease or floods reduced the food
sources in other places, so that natural increase was destroyed. Stock
(possums, kangaroos, reptiles and birds, plants or seed) was taken from
the sanctuary to the devastated area. This spot also was closed to hunting
till it was again replenished with life. To the preserved of Burragorang,   n10
from time to time, was added the best of kangaroos or possums taken
in chase outside the valley, so that there would be no deterioration or
diminution, by in-breeding, among the animals in conservation. The
marriage laws of the tribes so remarkably maintained strain without
in-breeding, that the same knowledge and thought was applied here. I   n15
have heard my father speak of three coastal sanctuaries known to him,
but that none could so easily be closed to access as Burragorang. As far
as I recollect, the second was the Kangaroo Valley, thus named because
when found it was so full of unusually fine kangaroos. The blacks' name
for it I have forgotten. The third was somewhere towards Wollongong.   n20
Then, near Tumut or Gundagai, there was Willie Ploma ("The place
of the big possums"), which, when I was a girl, was still a sanctuary.
And long after the blacks were killed there, the size and plentifulness
of the animals in this place still proved it. In relation to the sanctuaries,
death was the penalty for anyone without authority being found in   n25
them; no one was allowed to hunt or disturb the animals, especially
when the females were with young. Except for dire necessity, no entry
at all was allowed at that time. There were similar known sanctuaries
in Queensland and in Victoria. Cape Otway was one in Victoria. And
I can recollect the amazed wonder of some of my own relatives who   n30
had been to Cape Otway, at the density of the animal population there,
and how it was of so much better quality than that found elsewhere. It
may also be recalled that when the Cape Otway forest was explored for
purposes of settlement, trappers from New South Wales, as well as from
all parts of Victoria, flocked there, the skins taken being thought of then   n35
as the Tasmanian black possum is thought of to-day. Many articles were
written in the papers on the subject. My father spoke of it as the last of
the aboriginal animal sanctuaries, and said that the others had all been
broken down and lost by settlement.
    Of places in Queensland, I have heard the same thing said. This   n40
accounts for some localities being found literally swarming with life,
while other places, seemingly as good, had no more than ordinary.

Indeed, the large number of aboriginal words, which mean breeding
place of whatever it may be, is itself evidence of sanctuary. Had these
places not been protected, there would have been no return to them   n45
in following years, and no permanency in the names, yet these were
permanent everywhere. My father was told that the first white men to
find these closed places were killed as a precaution against their invasion,
and, in order to keep secret and safe the emergency food-supply of
the already harried tribes; news of the preserves would be spread if   n50
strangers, having found them, were allowed to live. But the white man
had guns and the law with him, and against these the natives could make
no stand. The sanctuaries, one after another, were taken possession of
by the invading new-comers, and the only witness to them now lies in
the names—Maneroo, the breeding sanctuary of the black duck; Taralga   n55
(Baralga), the breeding place of baralga (the brolga); Willie Ploma, "the
place of the big possums."[3] Other similar names lie dormant in memory.
Willaura, the breeding place of the curlew, is one just now recalled.
And Woollahra was probably this bird's sanctuary for the coast district
of the Cammeray tribes.[4] Another law of animal preservation lay in the   n60
totem. The tribe only ate the animal, bird, or reptile of the totem, as
a last resort. Hence the Iguana tribe might not eat the iguana, which
meant that their territory was an iguana sanctuary, from which could be
replenished a territory eaten out by those who were not Iguanas. This
went on throughout all the totems and territories. The lesser sanctuaries   n65
were under the law of the local tribe; but the larger sanctuaries were
under what was known as "the Great Law." A tribe could not hunt
in these without an inter-tribal permission, and this was limited by
"the Great Law," i.e., the inter-tribal regulations made, confirmed, or
amended, in the inter-tribal Conferences.   n70
*[l. 9] Yeringa, Yeranga, Yeringi (with probably Yerong and Yurong as
corruptions), are forms of tribal names for the possum.
*[l. 10] Braak, one of the onomatopoeic names of the cockatoo.

(n. d.)   *Copy-text: UW   Collated states:* None

[3] Of the names mentioned here and in author's notes to lines 9 and 10, only that for the
brolga has been confirmed (see I26 n. 4). 'Maneroo' (meaning *plain*) is the name of a
tribe in, and an old spelling of, the Monaro district of NSW: as in Henry Kingsley, *The
Recollections of Geoffry Hamlyn* (1859), ed. Stanton Mellick, Patrick Morgan and Paul
Eggert (St Lucia: University of Queensland Press, 1996), pp. 203 and 622.
[4] Possibly the Kamilaroi people; see Preface, p. xxxv.

K13   THE SONG OF HUNTAWANG[1]

Come with me, my delight,
   The blossom on the goom*
Tree breaks upon the night
   Its honey heart of bloom;
Dusky the shadows lie   5
   Like furry deeps beneath;
The moon is in the sky,
   And every cloud a wreath.

Come with me, O my mate!
   There is no hour my heart   10
Speaks not to thee elate—
   Its wurley* where thou art.
O, as when death-wounds part
   Whom one nest binds and ties,
Cleft is baralga's* heart,   15
   So, wanting thee, mine dies!

Come, then! the goom tree breaks
   Its heart of honey on
The night, and sweetness aches—
   Too soon love's hour is gone;   20
Wook-wook,* within his tree,
   Moves in a shadow-flight,
But my eyes, wanting thee,
   Are fire-flies in the night.

* Goombah, or goom tree, is the gum tree. The word was common when I was a child, whites and aboriginals alike using it. To the latter our debt for the name has never been acknowledged as far as I know, at least not in print, for we spell the word "gum" instead of according to the native sound, "goom."[2]   n5
*[l. 12] A wurley (gunyah or mia mia) is a shelter or home.[3]
*[l. 15] Baralga, after whom (mispronounced) Taralga is called, is the brolga or native companion.[4] The brolga (baralga) was called "native

---

[1] Name unidentified; see Preface, n. 15.   [2] Uncorroborated.   [3] See I19
n. 2.   [4] See I26 n. 4.

companion" (by an awkward inverted translation of the aboriginal word) because, when his mate died or was killed, he became "an old man" or "an old bachelor," and, as the blacks pointed out, was always alone. I saw many such when the guns increased with settlement. Female brolgas "made better eating," so, to the dismay of the blacks, who used to come and tell my father about it, they were the ones shot. No native under natural tribal law ever killed any mothering bird or animal. And even when the young were grown, and out of the nest, or weaned, laws still regulated the amount of the killing. n10

n15

*[l. 21] Wook-wook is the mopoke.[5]

(14 March 1931) *Copy-text: UW* *Collated states:* None

[5] One of a number of onomatopoeic Aboriginal words, such as Dharuk *bugbug/bubug*, for the boobook owl and the mopoke.

K14 THE CAPTIVE

The housed man says, *My pretty lamb!*
    The wild man says, *My deer!*
One dwells like water in a dam,
    One where the stream runs clear.

And I, the captive and the schooled,
    Beat on my prison wall,
Asking the sleep by tree-tops cooled,
    The star-shine over all.

5

The housed man dwells with flocks and herds;
    He makes the woods a park;
We had the forest and the birds,
    We had the firelit dark.

10

And all my heart remembers how,
    In dusk of even-fall,
The night-jar dropped from bough to bough,
    And the owlet would call.

15

And I remember, there, the sweet
    Of water to the mouth,

(17 November 1928) *Copy-text: UW* *Collated states: SV (A)*
9 herds;] ~, *A*   **13** remembers] is telling *A*

Whose taste the flat town-waters cheat;
   Who, drinking, suffer drouth.   20

Here are no whispers of the woods,
   No scent of quarry near;
Here is the housed smell; here obtrudes
   The locked door and the fear.

And my teeth crave the olden meat,   25
   Rich-tasting from the fire;
Who the long-killed and soft must eat,
   Hungry with old desire.

The housed man says, *"My pretty lamb!"*
   The wild man says, *"My deer!"*   30
One dwells like water in a dam,
   One where the stream runs clear.

29 *"My*] ~ *A*   *lamb!"*] ~*! A*   **30** *"My deer!"*] ~ ~*! A*   **32** stream] streams *A*

    K15   THE MYALL IN PRISON*

Lone, lone, and lone I stand,
   With none to hear my cry,
As the black feet of the night
   Go walking down the sky.

The stars they seem but dust   5
   Under those passing feet,
As they, for an instant's space,
   Flicker and flame, and fleet.

So, on my heart, my grief
   Hangs with the weight of doom,   10

(2 December 1931)   *Copy-text: UW   Collated states: Bn*, 30 March 1932, p. 20
(*A*)   *SV* (*B*)   Wright1 (*C*)

Not otherwise recorded: MG's note, omitted in *A* and *C*, is not signalled in *B*.
1 Lone] (FOR THE BULLETIN.)// Lone *A*   lone,] ~ *C*   **2** cry,] ~. *C*   **8** flame,]
~ *A C*

And the black feet of its night
Go walking through my room.

* The myalls were aboriginals.[1]

n1 myalls] Myalls *B*   *n1* aboriginals.] aboriginals. The name is also that of a tree
like the wilga, the yarran, and the boree. In some localities the boree used to be
called the weeping myall. *B*

[1] See I25 n. 1.

K16   THE WILLI-WA MAN*

I

As I came down from the mountain tops,
I heard a voice behind me
Crying, "Stay, O stay!"

But, though I would have stayed, there was that
Which drove me ever onward,   5
Outward to the plains—

The plains where trees stand scattered like
The stars that, faint and weak, run
Lost behind the moon.*

II

Yet as I came down the mountain tops,   10
I heard the woman-drawer[1]
Cry out to me, the wanderer,
"O Man, hast thou no will to life through me?"

But deep within me there was that which called
Louder than any woman-drawer,   15
So that I turned me from the mountain tops,
To pass for ever outward with the sun.

(n. d.) *Copy-text: UW   Collated states: SV (A)*

Not otherwise recorded: MG's first note is not signalled in *A*, and the second is
omitted.

8 stars] ~, *A*   **17** for ever] forever *A*

[1] See K8, and K9 and author's note.

* The Willi-wa is a Patagonian Indian wind. The word willi-wa and the wind it represents, are really the same as our willy-willy.[2] It is one of the examples I sent to Sir Baldwin Spencer, when I wrote to him urging him to go to Patagonia (where I had once lived) and compare Indian and aboriginal roots, words, and lore, before Indian and aboriginal alike were dead, and it was too late to do anything. He went about eight months after I wrote, and I am told that his findings justified all that I had said. Unfortunately the rigour of the climate was too much for his years, and he died there.

*[l. 9] There was an aboriginal folk-story, most of the words of which I have forgotten, but which showed in full the feeling for tragedy and wistfulness which characterised the aboriginal's natural love of the dramatic. Also, it may possibly measure, in some degree, lost astronomical beliefs, or theories, in that it made the moon the child of earth and the younger daughter of the sky. The story was to the effect that the moon, the youngest and last of the sky maidens, was sent by the earth (flung from the earth?) to take the stars out for a walk. She was given strict injunctions not to let them out of her sight (lose their orbits?), because if she did they would get lost, would never be able to come home again, and would wander farther and farther away. As she walked with them, there seemed nothing that could hurt them, and nowhere that they could not be seen; so she began gathering flowers, and, by and by, feeling tired, she fell asleep. (This represented the dark phase of the moon). When she woke it was already late. Frantic, she looked for the children, but she could neither hear them nor see them. Then she began to run, thinking they might be ahead of her, and on their way home. But the faster she ran the farther behind she left them, yet they, from the distance, were running after her and fruitlessly calling. They ran and ran, but could not catch up to her, and she, in terror and agony at their loss, forgot to look behind. Now if you watch the moon you will see, when she is new, how like a slender slip of a girl she is, and so young is she in looks that the stars seem bright and large beside her. Then after she has fallen asleep and waked up, you see her, shock-white, running through the sky, and the stars like little pale lost faces running behind her.[3]

It is my father's translation of the story that I recollect best. I remember how he used the expression "a slender slip of a girl." I have used "pale lost faces" myself, in order to convey the remembered impression of the words that I have, too, lost.

n5

n10

n15

n20

n25

n30

n35

---

n1 willi-wa] *Om. A*   **n8** Unfortunately] ~, *A*   **n18** orbits *Ed.*] obits x

[2] On 'willy-willy', cf. Wembawemba *wilang-wilang*; Yindjibarndi (Western Australia) *wili-wili* (Dixon).

[3] See MG's correction to the authenticity of this story in her note to M62. Parker has the moon (*bahloo*) as masculine.

K17   THE WOLLUNDRY LAGOON
WAGGA WAGGA[1]

There came a cry from far away,
　　And then a shadow crossed the moon;
There was a movement scarcely seen,
　　Swift turning toward the dark lagoon.

And like a kite that sloping fell,   5
　　And like a bolt in swift release,
The black duck, with his whistling wing,
　　Dropped by a trail of midget geese.*

Once nested there the pelican,
　　And there the swan sailed stately by;   10
By day the ibis stalked, and night
　　Was startled by the curlew's cry.

There slashed the whipping plover's wing,
　　And there the mopoke haunted low,
At dawn the sauntering emu stooped,   15
　　And drank unhindered long ago.

And when the river floods were out,
　　And when within the waters leapt
The great fish shining in the moon,
　　There came the tribes, and Bora[2] kept.   20

And once again I see the fires
　　Flicker and flame upon the night,

(3 December 1930)   *Copy-text: UW   Collated states: PPA (A)*

Not otherwise recorded: A is in eight-line stanzas throughout, and MG's notes are
omitted.

2 moon;] ~, *A*   **3** movement] ~, *A*   **4** toward] to *A*   lagoon.] ~, *A*   **9** there]
here *A*   **10** there] here *A*   stately] slowly *A*   **13** There] Here *A*   **14** there]
here *A*   **20** There] Then *A*   tribes,] ~ *A*   **21** And] So *A*   the] their *A*

[1] From *wahgunyah – wah*: crow and *gunyah*: home, shelter, with intensifying repetition
(Reed); cf. H63 and R65 author's note, line 43. For 'wah', cf. *waun* (Ridley) and *wahn*
(Parker 1905).   [2] See I21 n. 1.

The shadows darkling on the trees,
    The bodies gleaming in the light!

And I remember how, a child,   25
    I trembling caught my father's hand,
Hearing the massed bull-roarers roll
    Traditioned runes across the land.*

Mighty the rote,[3] now swift, now slow;
    Now high, now deep; now with a sound   30
Like all the winds upon the earth,
    Drawn in and held in one great round.

And there each day the hunters came,
    Home with the chase upon the back;
Youths whom the elders sent abroad,   35
    To prove their skill by craft and track.

And oft I stood while swimmers slipt
    Beneath the lines of duck and teal,
Or noosed the swan, or slid beneath
    The pelican's slow paddling heel!   40

And there I saw the spearman stand
    Where sprang the fish toward the fly;
So still his shadow, that the deep
    The stiller seemed where it would lie!*

Where, long ago, the kangaroo   45
    Loped to the water's edge to drink,
A wall of willows later stood,
    Root-fasted on the townward brink.

Yet there I heard the lubra's hail
    (So wide, so still the aery space)   50

23 The] Their *A*   24 The] Their *A*   light!] ~. *A*   31 earth,] ~ *A*   33 there
each] every *A*   34 back;] ~— *A*   40 heel!] ~. *A*   41 And there] Sometimes
A   saw the] watched a *A*   42 fly;] ~, *A*   44 lie!] ~. *A*   45–8 Where . . .
brink.] *Om. A*   49 Yet there] And *A*   heard] would hear *A*   hail] ~, *A*
50 (So . . . so] Across the *A*   the] and *A*   space)] ~, *A*

[3] See I9 n. 1.

Float like a petal dropped from sound,
  Me-ward soft falling from its place.

And there I saw the stars within
  The waters lace like golden bees,
Or watched, enchanted, as the moon   55
  Rose like a shield amid the trees.

And I remember how, a child,
  I felt a glamour there enfold
Even the huge black logs the floods
  Swung out, where swift the currents rolled.   60

O lovely, lovely were the curves
  Wherever bird arched neck and drank,
And lovely was the arrowy track,
  Where swan and duck sailed, rank on rank;

And lovely, lovely as he stood,   65
  And lovely as he stooping bent,
The kangaroo, that, dainty-lipped,
  Sipped of the waters ere he went.

But memory dies with those who go,
  And I am lonely in a vast,[4]   70
Where, in their myriads, went the slain,
  Spoke in full panoply the past;

Yet it may be, the old lagoon
  Remembers those who came; and keeps,
Within its deeper depths, the watch,   75
  Where their lost history buried sleeps.

* The teal is the midget goose.
*[l. 28] There were many kinds of bull-roarers, each kind having its own
_____

52 soft falling] soft-falling *A*   53 And there] At night *A*   55 watched,
enchanted,] ~ ~ *A*   56 amid] above *A*   trees.] ~; *A*   58 a] the *A*
60 currents] current *A*   63 track,] ~ *A*   69 But] What *A*   go,] ~! *A*
70 And I am] Now am I *A*   71 Where,] ~ *A*   myriads,] ~ *A*   72 past;] ~. *A*
73 Yet] But *A*   be,] ~ *A*   lagoon] ~, *A*   74 Remembers] Remembering *A*
came;] ~, *A*   and] still *A*   keeps,] ~ *A*   75 depths,] ~ *A*   76 their] our *A*

[4] See I7 n. 3.

note and special use. Every kind of note and every different roll, and
there were hundreds of them, had its own meaning. The ambassadors
from other tribes, as when the great assemblies met, were always heralded   n5
by a bull-roarer as they approached the visited people. Pitcheri, Bora,
messages, war, great news, all had their own special roll or note.
*[l. 44] As to the fishing mentioned in this verse, at night I have seen
the Murrumbidgee like a sky full of stars, it was so lit by fishing flares.
The waders stood in the shallow curves of the stream, the canoes stood   n10
out in the deeper waters. Only small twigs were used for flares, each
being lit just for the moment of spearing. The firestick from which the
flare was ignited was kept on a wad of earth laid in the bottom of the
canoe or dug-out. Dug-outs were permanent boats, and were kept in
use from year to year. They were not carried about. The canoes were, as   n15
when billabongs and lagoons dried and other water had to be sought, or
when rivers had to be crossed. A seasoned canoe was more trustworthy in
crossing a stream than newly cut sappy bark would be. When travelling,
the men usually carried the canoes; they were borne Indian fashion on
the back. A very small coracle-shaped one might be carried by a woman,   n20
but only once do I remember seeing this. As fishing was a universal right,
there was no need to remove the dug-out, canoes or boats. Ownership
of common necessities not being personal, they originally lay turned
over so that rain would not rot them, and where anyone needing them
could see them. When the white man came, predatory and cruel, they   n25
were rolled away into the bush and hidden, the directions for finding
them being marked in aboriginal script, or signs, on two trees near the
river bank. Triangulation from these two marks brought the point to the
dug-out, so that hunted blacks, needing to escape by crossing a river,
could always find one. When the white man discovered this it became   n30
his aim to find the dug-outs, and either split them in two or burn a hole
in the bottom. I have seen numbers of such burnt holes, ranging in size
from the palm of the hand to that of a small dish. The holes were such
that no black could caulk or close them.

K18   THE SONG OF KITTAGORAH[1]

Lean down, O breast of love,
    And call, from out the deep,
That which but thou canst move
    To wake from sleep;

---

[1] Name unidentified; see Preface, n. 15.

Then in the ocean of thy look   5
  Let these eyes drown,
As palms reach up to love,
  To draw love down.

Lean down, O breast of love,
  And touch my timid heart,   10
Hidden like some shy dove
  In shades apart;
I have been fearful of all things
  Save only thee;
Then lean, O breast of love,   15
  And comfort me.

Lean down, O breast of love,
  And teach my heart to wake;
Move it as low winds move
  The sleeping lake;   20
Then, by the full power of thy look
  Bid mine to lift,
The falcon thou above,
  My heart thy swift.[2]

(4 November 1926)   *Copy-text: UW*   *Collated states:* None

[2] On the bird, see I12; 'thy swift [one]' – prompt in response – may also be implied.

K19   COOLOOLA, FLOWER OF THE PINE[1]

I have been happy oft (she said,)
  And have forgotten grief,
Hearing some joyous bird that sang
  Beneath his covering leaf.

And I have run, as feather-light   5
  As the blown thistle-seed,
To stand a little while and watch
  The water-beetle speed.

[1] From Gabi-Gabi *gululay*: cypress pine (Dixon).

And, then, back to be drudge and butt,
   Like some wing-fallen bird,   10
Back to the house fear-driven I sped,
   If but my name I heard.

(6 April 1929)   *Copy-text: UW*   *Collated states:* None

K20   THE WARADGERY TRIBE[1]

Harried we were, and spent,
   Broken and falling,
Ere as the cranes we went,
   Crying and calling.

Summer shall see the bird   5
   Backward returning;
Never shall there be heard,
   Us, who went yearning.

Emptied of us the land;
   Ghostly our going;   10
Fallen, like spears the hand
   Dropped in the throwing.

We are the lost who went,
   Like the cranes, crying;
Hunted, lonely, and spent;   15
   Broken and dying.*

* The Waradgery tribe was one whose domain, and law of domain,
extended from Scone to the Murray and the Darling. It was the last great

(28 October 1931)   *Copy-text: UW*   *Collated states:* SV (*A*)   Wright1 (*B*)
Wright2 (*c*)

Not otherwise recorded: MG's note is not signalled in *A* and is omitted in *B* and *c*.

7 heard,] ~ *B C*   **8** Us] Those *A–C*   **9** land;] ~, *B*   **10** going;] ~, *B*
13 went,] ~ *B*   **14** cranes *A*] birds *X*   **15** lonely,] ~ *C*   spent;] ~, *B C*
n1 domain,] ~ *A*   ***n1*** of domain,] *Om. A*

[1] Alternative form of *Wiradjuri* (Parker 1905) from *Wirraayjuurraay* (Dixon); see
Preface, pp. xxxiii–xxxiv. ML 3/M holds a musical setting (*c.* 1932) of K20 by J. Ploog:
see volume 1, Appendix for manuscript locations and descriptions.

chief of this tribe (or collection of septs as one tribe) whom my father
compared, as a law-giver and chief ruler of a scattered people, to Solon.[2]
The two men became such friends that my father was made a full blood-   n5
brother by the intermingling of a drop of blood from one arm to the
other. By whose instance this was done I do not know, but I do know that
it was done. I, too, was made a child of the tribe and a "sister." Apart
from my father, I was the only one of the family given relationship. The
result was that wherever the blacks were I was protected. Once when   n10
poisoned by arsenic intended for them, I was with them on the banks
of the Murrumbidgee, alone, for six weeks. I grieved to leave them and
they "wept" me as I left.[3] Being a "sister," all the men and boys had to
be away when this occurred—a rare ceremony, and given to very few
white people indeed. But as we rode away, my father carrying me on   n15
the front of the saddle, the chief waited by a tree to see us pass, cried a
few words of friendship, and waved us farewell. I never saw any of that
kind, friendly body of people again. They were raided, and all that were
not in hiding were killed. It was because of word that this was to happen
that my father had to come for *me*. What warning he *could* give he had   n20
given the chief, knowing he took his own life in his hand by even hinting
a warning, should it leak out that he had given one. "Better we should
all die," said the chief, sadly, "than that my clean young men should
become like the white men's sons." I remember, too, that the men of
this group, knowing how few could escape, themselves killed the young   n25
women of the tribe so that they might avoid capture and pollution. A
feast was ordered by the chief, and when the girls, replete with food,
were asleep—they slept on.

---

n4 compared *A*] campared *X*   *n8* sister."] ~". *A*   *n13* sister,"] ~", *A*
n16 cried] spoke *A*

[2] (*c.* 638–558 BC), renowned Athenian poet and lawmaker.
[3] Cf. M62 Pts V, VI and author's note, lines 27–33.

K21   THE WANDERER

When you shall come again,
    Like a drift on waters moving,
In the old high disdain
    Of the ways that ask no proving,[1]
Will you remember, still,   5
    In the hour of dusk, slow falling,

---

[1] Questioning, testing.

Out by the darkling hill,
   The cry of the plover calling?

Though, in insolent pride,
   You come like the spear-winged swallow,   10
Though with the outward tide
   You turn, and the light waves follow,
Yet, when the shadows mask
   The white of the moonbeams falling,
Will you not sometimes ask   15
   Whose was the heart that was calling?

She was of those who live
   For joy of the world, and laughter;
She was of those who give—
   The giving her roof and rafter.   20
Yet when the giving ends,
   From the dust of the years, slow falling,
Comes, and the high head bends,
   The cry of the plover calling.

(9 March 1932)   *Copy-text:* UW   *Collated states:* None

K22   TARALGA[*]

He came not back who fled,
   Thinking in flight to leave
Behind him, as though dead,
   The memory of an eve,
When, in the twilight low,   5
   As lord of love he walked
The hills where, long ago,
   Baralga stalked.

Now if his heart afford
   One memory of that night,   10
Where love itself outpoured,
   And of its own delight

Took the full chalice and
Drank deep, how there would wake
To longing, passion-fanned,   15
Love's golden ache!

[*] Taralga is a corruption of Baralga, the brolga.[1] My father often told
how there was a certain place, or sanctuary, "where the birds were thick
like sheep," and where there were "nests every few yards." Settlement
ate the birds, forgot the place, and changed its very name.

(15 April 1931)   *Copy-text: UW   Collated states:* None

[1] See I26 n. 4 and K13 author's note for line 15.

K23   THE YARRAN TREE[1]

Under the Yarran Tree I have sat down,
    And there, as those who hanged their harps upon
    The willow trees of Babylon
And wept for far Jerusalem their town,[2]
So for the lost who once here proudly stept,   5
Lo, even as Israel, I, too, have wept.

By the Yarran Tree I have sat me down,
    And I have turned and hanged upon each leaf
    A passion and a cry of grief;
And I have pleaded with the rains that drown   10
Upon the earth, that they shall be as tears
To fall upon the Wounding of The Spears.[3]

Under the Yarran Tree The Spears once moved
    As armies in their pride, and there was heard
    (As though in some wild bush a bird   15
Sang to its mate,) the singing of the grooved

[1] Name for both the small inland *Acacia homalophylla* and the coastal *Acacia glaucescens*,
also called 'bastard myall' (*Macquarie*), but here may be Kamilaroi for a river gum;
Parker lists *yaräan* as 'large white eucalyptus'.
[2] Lines 1–6 and 19–24 adapt the Jewish exiles' lament in Psalm 137. 1: 'By the rivers
of Babylon, there we sat down, yea, we wept, when we remembered Zion'. After the
conquest of Jerusalem in 586 BC, the Assyrians carried off the Israelites into their
'Babylonian Captivity': 2 Kings 24–5, Ezekiel 17.20 and Jeremiah 20–50. See also K73
and M9.   [3] I.e. the destruction of the Aborigines.

Plane of the woman-drawer whirled upon
The air; now bird and myall both are gone.*

Under the Yarran Tree I have sat down,
   And there, as those who hanged their harps upon   20
   The willow trees of Babylon
And wept for far Jerusalem their town,
So, for the lost who once here proudly stept,
O, even as Israel, I, too, have wept.

* The blacks were called myalls as a general name.[4]

(21 January 1932)   *Copy-text: UW*   *Collated states:* None

[4] See I25 n. 1.

K24   MIGRANT SWANS[1]

O swan, cry out in the night—
   Let us hear, as of old,
The beat, beat, beat of the flight,
   As fold by fold,
Feather on feather, the wing   5
Moves rhythmic out in its swing!

Call out in the night, O swan!
   We, too, with thee would fly;
Would sail, sail, sail in the wan
   White light of the sky,   10
   Where fold by fold,
Feather on feather, the wing
Beats, beats on the air, in swing.

Lean on the breast of the wind,
   O swan! Lean till the flight   15

(7 August 1931)   *Copy-text: UW*   *Collated states: SV (A)*
8 thee] you *A*   14 wind] air *A*

[1] Cf. the similar theme in I3–I7.

Shows black, black, black on the thinned
       White cirrus of night,
       While fold by fold,
Feather on feather, the wing,
Untiring, pleats for the swing.   20

Forging thy way in the height,
       None so lonely as thou,
O swan, swan, swan, in thy flight,
       First: point: of the plough—
       As fold by fold,   25
Feather on feather, the wing,
Furrowing, sharps to the swing.

O white moon measure the night,
       And eve follow the noon,
Till weave, weave, weave on the sight,   30
       Dim: shines: the lagoon,
       While fold by fold,
Feather on feather, the wing
Moves on in untiring swing.

Now mark in the height the frogs   35
       That call, sombre and slow,
Their boom, boom, boom, from the logs
       In shadow below,
       As fold by fold,
Feather on feather, the wing   40
Beats, beats on the air in swing.

Then, in the journeying done,
       There, at end of the quest,
Down, down, down, with the sun:
       Drop: to thy rest.   45

16 thinned] fair *A*   **20** for] on *A*   **21** thy] your *A*   **22** thou] you *A*
23 thy] your *A*   **24** First] Spear *A*   of] in *A*   plough—] blue, *A*   **25** As]
Where *A*   **27** Furrowing] Narrowing *A*   sharps] shapes *A*   **31** Dim: shines:]
~ ~ *A*   lagoon,] ~; *A*   **34** on in untiring] with unfaltering *A*   **35** in] from *A*
44 sun:] ~, *A*   **45** Drop:] ~ *A*   to thy] down to *A*

K25   THE MOUNTAIN THRUSH

Thou loved grey bird,
  Round whom shall yet grow many a story,
Dream not that all alone is heard
  The nightingale in glory;

For, as she sings,   5
  Full-choired tradition sings with her,
Until we hear its thousand wings,
  Its thousand echoes stir.

But thou, shy friend,
  Wast robbed of all that native lore   10
Of which we wantonly made end—[1]
  And naught can now restore!

So no one sings
  With thee: thy song is set alone;
No chords ancestral tune their strings   15
  To add to thine their tone!

Only the air
  Is thine to wake to thy resound;
No historied corridors of time declare
  For thee in myths profound;   20

No memories
  For thee their undertones set free:

(30 January 1924)   *Copy-text: UW*   *Collated states: DT*, 31 October 1924, p. 5 (*A*)

1 Thou] O, *A*   **2** Round . . . grow] Who yet shall gather *A*   story] glory *A*
3 that all] *Om. A*   **4** glory;] story! *A*   **5** For,] ~ *A*   **9** shy] O, *A*   **10** that]
the *A*   **11** Of . . . made] They gave of whom we made an *A*   end—] ~ *A*
12 And] (~ *A*   naught can now] time may not *A*   restore!] ~). *A*   **13** no one]
that none *A*   **14** thee:] ~. *A*   thy . . . set] Thou sing'st *A*   alone;] ~, *A*
16 add to thine] deep with thee *A*   **19** historied] *Om. A*   **20** thee] ~, *A*   in]
no *A*   **22** For thee] Give up *A*   set free:] for thee— *A*

_____
[1] Lines 9–11 instance MG's conviction that Aboriginal mythological traditions, destroyed
during white settlement, could have invested Australian flora, fauna and geographical
features with the resonance necessary to literature (and enjoyed by the classical cultures

Who art but as a sound on seas
    Where no sounds be.

We hear not through   25
    Thy song the fathers' fathers sing,
No Thracian fragrance brings, anew,
    Stories of thy young spring;[2]

No Roman score[3]
    Lends thee its splendour, as the strain   30
Thou flutest for us, o'er and o'er,
    Issues in full refrain!

Yet with thee dwells
    A note of perfect sound, so pure,
We thirst upon it as it wells,   35
    Held by its lovely lure;

And melody,
    Full as from some old violin,
Beats on our hearts, until its key
    Opens all doors within.   40

23 Who . . . on] Flung as upon unhistoried *A*   **24** be.] ~! *A*   **25** through] in *A*
26 sing,] ~; *A*   **27** brings, anew,] urns within *A*   **28** young spring;] wild wing. *A*
29 score] lore *A*   **30** Lends . . . splendour,] Leaps from its confines *A*
32 Issues . . . refrain] Seeks of our memory fane *A*   **34** A] A rhythm, a *A*
perfect] *Om. A*   sound,] ~ *A*   pure,] ~; *A*   **35** thirst upon] lean toward *A*
it] ~, *A*   **36** lure;] ~. *A*   **37** And] Till *A*   **39** Beats . . . until] Floods through
the heart as though *A*   **40** Opens] Opened *A*

referred to at lines 25–30). Cf. volume 1, Introduction, pp. lv–lvi, and author's notes,
e.g. for F105.

[2] With Thrace are associated Philomela, the nightingale, traditionally celebrated for
its song (see J86 n. 5), and Orpheus, father of music. Before meeting his death at the
hands of Thracian maenads, he wandered its woods and mountains lamenting the loss
of his wife, Eurydice.

[3] Greek myths were transmitted into Western culture largely though the works of the
Roman poet Ovid (43 BC – AD 17), although Virgil (70–19 BC) may also be implied.

K26   A SONG OF SPRING

O, in what loveliness
The spring is raimented!
Even the little grass
Wears jewels on its head,
While, in the dells, the moss   5
Velvets each rill[1] to bed.
Now darts the kingfisher,
A blue flash to the lake,
And my heart goes with him,
Down where the waters make,   10
For the blue sky, a glass,
Its loveliness to take.
Above the lake slow sails
An eagle, height his veils.

Ever in comeliness   15
Earth decks herself to greet
The swift-returning Spring!
Then every bush blows sweet,
And in and out the wild
Rude[2] briar the blue wrens fleet!   20
Deep in its heart, the round
Cup of a tiny nest
Huddles two eggs of blue
Against the robin's breast;
How seemly, in that breast   25
So warm, the earth is dressed!

The trees are mighty, and
The forest lifts its cry

(30 April 1931)   *Copy-text: UW   Collated states: SV (A)*

1 O] Oh *A*   **13** lake] ~, *A*   **17** swift-returning] swift returning *A*   Spring]
spring *A*   **20** briar] brier *A*   **22** Cup] ~, *A*   nest] ~, *A*   **24** breast;] ~: *A*

[1] Rivulet, small stream.
[2] Uncultivated.

Of thunder through the hills;
Yet, where the sunbeams lie,   30
Sparkles a gem—the blue
Steel of the dragonfly.
And where the yarran[3] stands
With tawny head, the gay
Blue of the parrot weaves   35
Amid the leaves its way,
And blue-white butterflies,
Darting the air, make play.
Down by the cowal's[4] edge,
A blue crane eyes the sedge.   40

[3] See K23 n. 1.   [4] See K4 n. 5.

K27   THE VIXEN

We found it as the hunt went by,
    The secret rocky stair,
Where lengthened down leaf-patterns lie,
    That hide the vixen's lair.

Within her den, so dim and cool,   5
    We saw her pointed eyes
Gleam like the sunspots in a pool,
    Where black the shadow lies.

We saw the gleam, we saw no more,
    For, in that velvet shade,   10
She of its ebon was the core,
    Its deeper dark she made.

We left her there, whose beating heart,
    Above her helpless young,
Throbbed, though she stilled her sudden start,   15
    As fear of danger wrung.

We left her there, a mother wild,
    Who, as we stepped back, turned,

And licked, with gestures fierce and mild,
    The babes o'er whom she yearned.   20

(31 August 1929)   *Copy-text: UW*   *Collated states:* None

K28   THE CRY OF A LITTLE POSSUM[*]

Leave us a little longer in the wild,
    We do not hurt the trees;
Here our poor lives refresh the earth to strength,
    As fish renew the seas.

Leave us a little longer still to run—   5
    Not in this bush is need;
Not here the hungry streets whose mounting tides
    Ask bread on which to feed!

Here is the wild where no man dwells, save as
    A wanderer passing by;   10
That lone sojourner of a night we serve,
    So not as waste we die.

Then leave us yet our little while to live;
    Too soon we pass away!
There is a better destiny for man,   15
    Than that he maim and slay.

[*] An open season for killing possums and other wild animals is periodically allowed. One such open season almost destroyed the native bear, making "Koala Park" a necessity if the few left were not to die out and the koala become totally extinct. When an open season is declared in the bush, rare specimens of every kind of bird or animal go; the best   n5
are killed and the worst left to breed from. The old law of the aboriginal was that the best should always be spared to breed from, in order to fitly replace what was taken. It was a tribal offence to kill the best of anything unless hunger could not be satisfied in any other way.

(21 May 1931)   *Copy-text: UW*   *Collated states:* None

K29   THE LITTLE LAMB

"Aa-k! Aa-k!" said the crow;
   And I asked of him, "What do you know
   That you cry 'Aa-k! Aa-k!' as you go?"
"Aa-k! Aa-k!" he said,
   As he flew overhead,   5
"In the paddock, below,
   A ewe lies dead!"

   . . . And I heard the bleat,
   And the running feet,
   Of a little lamb.   10

(8 March 1922) *Copy-text: UW* *Collated states: Wr*, 20 September 1922, p. 5
(*A*) *Wr*, 12 September 1923, p. 5 (*B*) *NZT*, 4 August 1926, p. 32 (*C*)
Not otherwise recorded: A sets lines 4–7 as a separate stanza. No stanza break in *C*.
1 "Aa-k! Aa-k] Aᴜʀᴋ! Aurk *A*   "Aurk! Aurk *B*   *"Aurk! Aurk C*   crow;] ~. *A–C*
2 asked of] said to *A–C*   know] ~, *A*   **3** cry] ~, *A C*   Aa-k! Aa-k] Aurk!
Aurk *A B*   *Aurk! Aurk C*   **4** Aa-k! Aa-k] Aurk! Aurk *A B*   *Aurk! Aurk C*   said,]
~ *A C*   **6** paddock, below,] ~ ~ *A B*   ~ ~, *C*   **7** dead!] ~— *A*   **8** . . . And]
~ *A–C*   bleat,] ~ *A B*   **9** feet,] ~ *A B*   **10** lamb.] lamb.// {lamb./ *B*} "Aurk!
Aurk!"/ Said the crow. *A B*

K30   THE WARATAH[1]

Mark where the waratah*
Lifts high his kingly head,
And shall we shame him there,
His native honour shed?

(5 October 1926) *Copy-text: UW* *Collated states: DT*, 23 October 1926, p. 21 as ᴀ
ᴘʟᴇᴀ ꜰᴏʀ ᴛʜᴇ ᴡᴀʀᴀᴛᴀʜ (*A*)
Not otherwise recorded: A has two notes (see entry for n1–44) signalled from lines 42
and 62 by an asterisk and double asterisk respectively; these signals are followed by
quotations from the relevant lines.
1 Mark] See *A*   waratah*] ~ *A*   **2** head,] ~! *A*   **3** shame] leave *A*   **4** His
. . . shed] Robbed of pre-eminence and bare *A*

---

[1] MG's last poem (after F61, F95, G30 and H38) to argue that the waratah become the
national flower of Australia. Native only to the e. coast, it was proclaimed the official

Ah, though we have erased
His charter, long high placed,
Not yet is fallen down
The full height of his first renown.

How comradely at morn
The sun upon him shines,
And how, as evening slopes,
Each ray about him twines!
Even the moon, swan-white,
Attends him with her light,
And weaves from him, night through,
Her silver filigree of dew.

The very winds draw near
To greet him as they go,
Who hail defies, and sleet,
As these about him blow;
E'en when the tempests tread,
He bends not down his head;
He has a king's pride there;
He stands: and yet we stript him bare!

His is no feeble stem,
The unbruised leaf he bears,
Which, as the thistle-thorn,²
His country's pride declares.

5 have erased] should erase *A*   6 charter,] name *A*   long] from its *A*   placed] place *A*   7 Not . . . fallen] Earth hath not written *A*   down] ~, *A*   8 The . . . first] Than his, one name of more *A*   renown.] ~! *A*   9 comradely] brightly *A* at] at the *A*   10 shines,] ~; *A*   11 And . . . slopes] How, when the course is low *A*   12 Each . . . twines] The lingering last rays on him glow *A*   15 weaves from] pleats for *A*   16 filigree] coronet *A*   18 To . . . go] In homage where he stands *A*   20 As . . . blow;] That in their season on him beat! *A*   21 when] where *A*   tread,] ~ *A*   23 has] hath *A*   24 stands:] ~! *A*   yet] shall *A* stript] strip *A*   bare!] ~? *A*   25 His] Here *A*   stem,] ~; *A*   26 he bears,] is his; *A*   27 Which] That *A*   thistle-thorn] thistle dares *A*   28 pride] name and fame *A*

floral emblem of NSW on 24 October 1962. (MG died 2 December.)
² The thistle is the emblematic flower of Scotland, as the rose (line 30) is of England.

Ah! in his lordly red,
The rose lifts up her head,　　　　　30
And sees a greater rose
Blossom in splendour where he glows.

Where the lone Anzac stood,
And met the foeman's sword,
In dreams he saw that crest,　　　　35
Whatever fate was to'ard;
Above the worn and spent,
A spirit clear, he went;
And where he led none turned,
However fierce the battle burned.　　40

Where sailed our early ships,
He blazed upon the mast;
There was no tide too high
For him, no sea too vast;
The inland caravan　　　　　　45
Talked of him, child and man,
And every camp-fire told
The tale of that high head and bold.

When up the Lapstone Hill[3]
Our first teams climbed—spellbound　　50
Men asked what marvel this,
Their wondering eyes had found.

<hr>

32 splendour] splendor *A*　　glows] grows *A*　　34 And . . . sword] His young blood
ebbing fast *A*　　35 In dreams] He dreamed *A*　　crest,] ~ *A*　　36 Whatever . . .
to'ard] Lifted where thickest tumult pressed *A*　　37–8 Above . . . went] There in
men's thoughts he went/ Above the battle-spent *A*　　39 And . . . none] He led;
and no man *A*　　40 However . . . battle] For all the terror where he *A*
41 Where . . . ships] Our first ships bore him forth *A*　　42 mast;] ~;* *A*
43 high] great, *A*　　44 For . . . vast] No sea too vast, for his estate *A*　　46 child
and] man to *A*　　man,] ~; *A*　　47 every] by the *A*　　48 tale] child *A*　　head] ~, *A*
49–52 When . . . found.] Where the first teamsters climbed/ Up Lapstone Hill, they
asked:/ What flower was this they found/ That rose so royal from the ground! *A*
53 when] as *A*　　came,] ~ *A*　　54 flaunted there] strode beneath *A*　　55 Laced to
the] Borne high on *A*　　yokes—] ~, *A*

<hr>

[3] Lapstone Hill, on the eastern edge of the Blue Mountains, was the first obstacle to be
encountered in the westward movement of settlement from Sydney.

And when they homeward came,
They flaunted there his flame,
Laced to the hames and yokes—[4]   55
When young were Parramatta oaks.[5]

Penrith and Castlereagh,
Windsor and Richmond, too,
Long ere the roads were made,
His kingly splendour knew;   60
Doorstep and lintel, then,
Glowed in the eyes of men,
As to each wall was bound
The proudest flower man ever found.

* In regard to the waratah, my grandmother, Mary Beatty, often told
me that when she first came to the country, the flower was thought so

---

56 When . . . Parramatta] Ere Parramatta grew her *A*   59–60 Long . . . knew]
Saw him, in triumph brought,/ As one long-wondering had sought *A*
61 Doorstep] Hearth-stone *A*   lintel] doorway *A*   62 Glowed . . . men,] Saw
him stand up again,** *A*   63 to] at *A*   wall was] side they *A*   64 man] men *A*
n1–44 * In regard . . . place.] * I have often heard my grandparents, Hugh and Mary
Beattie, talk of the astonishment and wonder of the early colonists at the discovery
of the waratah. Shipmasters leaving port when it was in season used to tie it as a
splendor to the masthead, and sometimes fasten it all over the ship. People would
bring it specially down from the mountains to give it to friends who were leaving,
in the hope that it would retain some semblance of itself at the end of the voyage.
Often the expedition for it had to go on foot. (In those days a bullock often had to do
the work of a horse, and even bullocks were few in number!) I doubt if any flower in
the world created such an impress of wonder and admiration as the waratah—"the
native tulip" of the first settlers. For one thing, Botanic Gardens were not what
they are to-day; and this new and uniquely splendid creation of a new and strange
world struck on people's imagination a sense of beauty as no other flower has ever
done. To them it was Australia; to their friends it represented Australia. And in
many an old letter kept long in kitchen dressers and stair cupboards, if they could
now be found, would be read descriptions of it. *P* ** It was a fashion of this early
period of Australian settlement to fasten the waratah on each side of the house door.
Sometimes the house was fenced, sometimes it was not, but the front yard was of
bare earth, swept and kept clean whatever the condition of the dwelling, for here
the family sat as an out-of-doors parlor in the shade of evening, or after supper
(it was "supper" then) on hot nights. The decoration of the doorposts by flowers
or branches was probably a relic of the old Eastern, and subsequently European,
custom of the use of the vine and fig leaf. *A*

---

[4] Parts of the team harness; on 'hames', see F81 n. 2.
[5] Parramatta, w. of Sydney, was the second NSW settlement: its oak trees, emblematic
in England of tradition and age, were imported.

wonderful that ships leaving "the Port" (and it was still "the Port"
when I was a child), if it were in bloom, had great bunches of it tied to
mast and rigging. Sometimes a ship had them fastened like rosettes all   n5
round the rail, so that the vessel was outlined in waratahs. In those days
people so little realised time and distance and the perishable nature of
plants, that some couples picked great bunches and took them to the
outward-bound vessels to send them home to the countries they had
left. A whole literature might be written on the first amazement of the   n10
early settlers in this new land, which was so different from everything
they had seen; but so far, no one has ever troubled to gather the stories
told of it, or to use them as a subject. I can recollect my grandfather
and grandmother saying that nothing stirred them like the scent of the
wild flowers, especially of the box-trees. They used to go outside the   n15
house together and stand, night after night, just to smell it. They also
told me it was still a general custom (come down from the Druids, or
perhaps from the early Christians who sought a symbol) to bind flowers
to the door-posts and lintels, and the house-gate, especially on a Sunday.
When the waratahs were out they were used on every house. In similar   n20
fashion I have seen all the gates, doors and even windows of home
decorated with flowers and greenery for parties, birthdays, Easter and
Christmas; and also at certain church festivals on a Sunday. The bushes
we sometimes see tied to verandah-posts at Christmas time are the only
survival now left us of this beautiful custom. The Harvest Festival, kept   n25
up by the Methodists more than by anyone else, is another instance of
this. Harvest Home was still a living usage when I was a child. Once
when I was about seven years old I was chosen Queen. I had a new
book-muslin frock with a watchet-blue[6] ribbon-sash and sleeve-bows
especially made for the occasion and I wore a wreath of wheatears round   n30
my head. Though I had ribboned pantalettes down to my ankles, I do
not know which prickled me the most, the stiff edges of the muslin or
the wheat-sheaves amongst which I rode. I had to sit on the last sheaf
tossed up on the load, as I was too small to carry it in my left arm; and I
had a sceptre of some sort in my right hand. The position had so many   n35
difficulties and discomforts, I never wanted to be Queen again. In regard
to the waratah, it should be our flower. The wattle was a South African
emblem before it was taken as ours. In England our wattle is called the
Rivièra Mimosa. It is not regarded as Australian at all. But no one can
deny, at least as yet, that the waratah is ours, that it was considered our   n40
national flower for long enough before we had a regular Coat of Arms,
and that the people in Australia, as well as in other countries, looked
upon it as such for at least a century. It should be given back its natural
and its national place.

------

[6] Light-blue.

K31   THE MEN OF EUREKA[*][1]
A RECOLLECTION

They have gone out, the men of Eureka,
One by one they have passed. Now there is none
Of them left to sit by the fire and talk;
For them, life's journey is over and done.
   Digger by digger they marched,   5
      Each man in his order;
   As digger by digger they went,
      Over the border.

I was a child while still we talked of them,
And, when there came one walking lame, I ran   10
To my father, and, my hand in his, cried,
Eager for stories, "Here comes a Eureka man!"
   Digger by digger they marched,
      All named in their order,
   As digger by digger they went,   15
      Over the border.

And the men who had been at Eureka
Made me a flag of stars,[2] and gave me
A name, and the name they gave was *Eureka*:
"For the child," they said, "is one of our kin."   20
   Digger by digger they marched,
      Each numbered in order,

(13 November 1931)   *Copy-text: UW*   *Collated states: Bn*, 23 March 1932, p. 50
(*A*)   Ingamells (*B*)   *SV* (*C*)   *Trib*, 3 December 1952, p. 5 (*D*)

Not otherwise recorded: D prefaces its version of the note with 'Dame Mary adds a footnote:'.

1 out,] ~ *A*   **4** them,] ~ *A*   **6** order;] ~, *D*   **7** went,] ~ *D*   **10** And,] ~ *A*
lame,] ~ *A*   **12** man!] ~. *A*   **18** Made] They made *A*   stars,] ~ *D*   **19** gave]
gave me *D*   *Eureka*:] ~: *A*   **Eureka:** *D*   **20** child,"] ~", *D*   kin."] ~"! *D*
22 numbered] number *A*

---

[1] The Eureka Stockade, site of the 1854 rebellion of miners (diggers) on the Ballarat goldfields, became a symbol of Australian national independence.
[2] The Eureka flag bore the stars of the Southern Cross without the (British) Union Jack.

Who digger by digger are gone,
   Over the border.

And many a time, with a wooden sword,   25
I stood, my father's kinsman, *Ross*,[3] and laced
Upon the air with glancing strokes, while cried
They there, "Well placed! Well struck, *Eureka!*"
   Digger by digger they marched,
      Each man in his order,   30
   Who, digger by digger, are gone,
      Over the border.

Now shall I weep them, even as the tribes
Wept those they deemed illustrious,[4] who passed
From them forever, or, far-journeying,   35
Moved outward from their ken, the seen no more.

[*] It is said that the last lone survivor of the Eureka Stockade died in
1931. His name, I believe, was Potter, and his grave is in New Zealand.
Surely that grave should be in Australia, and with an Australian
monument over it.

---

26 stood,] stood, with *A*   kinsman,] ~ *A*   *Ross*] Ross *A C D*   **28** there,] ~ *D*
"Well . . . struck,] *"Well placed—well struck—A*   *"Well placed! Well struck,* c
"Well placed! Well struck, *D   Eureka!"*] ~." *A   ~!" B   ~!" c   **Eureka!"** *D*
29 marched,] ~ *A C*   **31** Who,] ~ *A C D*   digger,] ~ *A C D*   gone,] ~ *D*
34 passed] went *A*   **35** forever] for ever *A*   **36** Moved] Passed *A*   ken] kin *B*
the] then *D*   (*n1–4*) It . . . it.] *Om. A B*   **n2** Potter,] ~ *D*   **n3** Surely that]
That *C D*   Australia,] ~ *D*

---

[3] Canadian Henry (also known as Charles) Ross (1829–54), credited with designing
the Eureka flag and one of the rebel leaders, died in the government assault on the
stockade. His grandfather, John Ross, stayed on in Canada after a term of duty there
with the 26th Cameronian Light Infantry Regiment – evidently to MG a sufficient
claim to (Cameron) kinship.
[4] Cf. K20 author's note, line 13, and M62 Pts v, vi and author's note, lines 27–33.

K32   CREATION

What loveliness lies shaped in stone—
   The Samothrace, the Belvedere—[1]
Yet, though the sculptor be unknown,
   He of the work says, "I am there!"

But though all perfect be the form,   5
     Cold, cold the marble where it stands,
Save when creation, in a storm,
     Adds, to the rock, the maker's hands.

(6 December 1931)   *Copy-text: UW*   *Collated states:* None

---

[1] Two Hellenistic marble statues regarded as the noblest representations of the human form. The winged statue of the goddess Nike (Victory, 220–190 BC) found on the island of Samothrace in 1863 is now in the Louvre in Paris. The Roman copy of a fifth century BC Greek statue of Apollo is named for the Belvedere gallery of the Vatican palace in Rome, where it now stands.

K33   THE SHIP THAT IS A WORD

O dusty words we find
In ancient book and script,
What of the lips that used,
Now of all using stript?

New-born as any babe   5
Just come to this our earth,
You, the forgotten dead,
Risen again, have birth.

Out of the tomb of loss,
Into the world of use,   10
Beauty will utter you,
Science will let you loose.

There young discoverers,
Bold Hakluyts[1] in word-seas,
Shall find in you a chart,   15
And measure time's decrees.

---

[1] Richard Hakluyt (1551/52–1616), geographer and historian, espoused the cause of English imperialism in *The Principall Navigations, Voiages and Discoveries of the English Nation Made by Sea or Over Land, in the Most Remote and Farthest Distant Quarters of the Earth at Any Time within the Compasse of these 1500 Yeares* (1589). The better known 1599 version (short title, *Voyages*) was reprinted in 12 vols, 1903–05.

O words but newly made,
O lost words that we lift,
You come to us as sails,
Lest minds Sargassos[2] drift.   20

You are both mast and crew,
You are both keel and oar;
Thoughts are your passengers,
And every man your shore!

And though thought is a wind   25
That blows where'er it lists,
Or, like a flame that springs,
Burns for a while—desists—

Yet words give frame to thought,
They make it hearth and home;   30
Build it their argosies;[3]
Are London, Athens, Rome.

(7 May 1931)   *Copy-text: UW*   *Collated states: SV (A)*
27 Or,] ~ *A*   **28** for] up *A*

[2] See J77 n. 3.   [3] See I2 n. 1.

K34   THE MAKER

O that I too might make
One thing, that, for its sake,
Beauty, if but an hour,
Would dwell within and dower—[1]

Something, when I am gone,   5
Some one might look upon,
And, through this longing will,
Find beauty living still.

(15 November 1931)   *Copy-text: UW*   *Collated states:* None

[1] Endow, make valuable.

K35   HENRY KENDALL[1]

Whence was thy song? How hither borne?
Of what far deep? From what clear dream,
O Singer of our early morn?

O voice, whose melody unworn
Still lives where Austral waters gleam,   5
Whence was thy song? How hither borne?

For *Her* thou hadst no notes forlorn,
Nostalgic as the moon's pale beam,
O Singer of our early morn.

But inland, through the scented corn,   10
Roundelled thy fresh, immortal theme—
Whence was thy song? How hither borne?

And, dear as ever elf-land horn,[2]
We heard thee lute by hill and stream,
O Singer of our early morn!   15

Was it thy heart that felt the thorn,
That sweetness might old pain redeem?
Whence was thy song? How hither borne,
O Singer of our early morn?

(2 August 1920)   *Copy-text: UW   Collated states: MP*, 22 July 1921, p. 13 as AUSTRALIA'S
HENRY KENDALL (*A*)   *Wr*, 5 November 1924, p. 5 as HENRY KENDALL, SINGER OF AUSTRALIA,
signed MARY GILMORE (Reprinted from 1920.) (*B*)

1 Whence] (For The Pioneer.)// Whence *A*   WHENCE *B*   2 dream] stream *B*
3 Singer] singer *B*   our] Her *A*   her *B*   4 voice] Voice *A*   7 *Her*] Her *A*
HER *B*   9 Singer] singer *A B*   our] Her *A*   her *B*   morn.] ~! *A B*
10 inland,] ~ *A B*   corn,] ~ *A B*   11 fresh] sweet *A*   13 And,] ~ *A*   elf-land]
elfland *B*   horn,] ~ *A*   14 thee] thy *A*   15 Singer] singer *A B*   our] Her *A*
her *B*   16 thorn,] ~ *A B*   19 Singer] singer *A B*   our] Her *A*   her *B*

---

[1] (1839–82), commonly regarded as Australia's first major lyric poet; he had a life
troubled by financial difficulties and domestic tragedy. See also F91, and K44 lines
33–40.
[2] Cf. 'The horns of elf-land faintly blowing' in 'The Splendour Falls on Castle Walls'
by Alfred, Lord Tennyson (1809–92), added to the third edition (1850) of *The Princess;
A Medley*.

K36   THE ARTIST

N. L.[1]

He is a forest, not a gentle wood,
A forest where a fire in evil mood
Left all the trees unshaped; and yet what fair
Green leaves on blackened branches burgeon there!

He is a tempest of tormented clouds,   5
And his the dun that thick eruption shrouds;
Seen through his dusk the stars are falling clods,
But O, where'er he walks, there walk the Gods!

(8 September 1930)   *Copy-text: UW*   *Collated states: SV* as THE ARTIST/ (NORMAN
LINDSAY) (*A*)
8 O] oh *A*

[1] Norman Lindsay (1879–1969), a vociferous and influential figure in Australian cultural
life, especially *c.* 1919–39. His vitalist philosophy, reflecting his admiration for Plato,
Rabelais and Nietzsche and his rejection of modernism, was expressed in satirical and
libidinous fiction and polemical essays; but he is best known for the comic verve of *The
Magic Pudding* (1918), ostensibly a work for children.

K37   SHAW NEILSON[1]

How he has sung
    That thou, too, might'st have part—
Hear, in the wind's low sigh,
    The music of his heart!

Still must he sing,   5
    The spring of life, the green!
On every hidden path
    This dreamer's soul hath been.

[1] On poet John Shaw Neilson (1872–1942), see F36 and n. 1, and F166. K37, written
on 19 February 1920, is a tribute to his *Heart of Spring* (1919).

Hast thou the lover's heart?
    Thou, too, must sing;   10
Must hear, as he,
    The whispering.

(19 February 1920)   *Copy-text: UW*   *Collated states:* None

K38   WRITTEN FOR MRS. ZABEL[1]

When at last I shall stand
    Where judgment of all is spoken,
And if there I shall stand
    As one who may stand unbroken,
I shall give thanks to God,   5
    As a man may to his Maker,
For the stroke of His rod,
    The shaping rough of the breaker.

(13 March 1929)   *Copy-text: UW*   *Collated states:* None

[1] 'A Woman's Letter', *Bn* 1 November 1923 recorded: 'Mrs. Frances ZABEL, has come to anchor in Sydney after 26 voyages in Europe, Asia and Africa. Westralians need no introduction to her; she was an early goldfielder, and was later connected for years with the Perth Daily News. It was she who founded the Book Lovers' Library in the western capital, that oasis of art and literature which all young aspirants to fame looked upon as a high altar. She has now taken over the Roycroft Library in City House, Pitt-street.' Of American extraction, she died by 1933.

K39   SIR HENRY PARKES[1]

The pedestalled upon their country's need,
    Men stand like giants in the public eye;
Yet 'tis the people's movement shapes the deed—
    The man is but its symbol raised on high.

Still there are giants—who, like some great rock   5
    Set in the middle of a rising stream,

(19 August 1929)   *Copy-text: UW*   *Collated states: SV* (*A*)

5 giants—] ~, *A*

[1] (1815–96), five times Premier of NSW and author of *Fifty Years in the Making of*

Divide the currents, and deflect the shock,
 And nurture peace although the eddies cream.

When Parkes stepped forth in our young nationhood,
 Then in this land of ours one such man stood.   10

Australian History (1892); he was a major figure in the movement for Federation. See
also M5.

K40   TO LESLIE HAYLEN: WRITER OF PLAYS[1]

What are we but the vision of a thought?
 What are we but the striving of a dream?
What are we but the hope of that which wrought,
 And hope itself but of the things that seem?

Nay! though all were a seeming, something joyed—   5
 That singing went, though all at ending fell;
It holds the vision, never quite destroyed,
 The fountain living, though a dream, in hell.

(6 May 1931)   *Copy-text: UW   Collated states:* None

[1] (1898–1977), Labor member for Parkes 1943–63, playwright, novelist and a foundation
member of the FAW (see volume 1, Introduction, p. li). See composition date: MG may
have seen unpublished scripts, e.g. of *Two Minutes' Silence* (1933), his first-published,
anti-war drama.

K41   TO LIONEL LE GAY BRERETON[1]

Blow, winds of strife,
Upon the candle of the heart,
Blow, lest too straight the flame—
Too like a dart
Its pattern on the wall where life   5
Is man's white canvas and his frame!

[1] One of the four sons of John le Gay Brereton (1871–1933), poet and Professor of
English at the University of Sydney from 1921 (see H79 lines 11–12 and n. 2).

Blow that the flame may leap,
And, leaping, widen sweep!

(24 October 1931)   *Copy-text: UW*   *Collated states:* None

K42   HENRY LAWSON[1]

As weeds grow out of graves and vaults,
So from his broken heart his faults;
And yet, so marvellous is power,
His very faults brought forth in flower.

(28 September 1924)   *Copy-text: UW*   *Collated states: SV* (no variants)

[1] On Lawson (1867–1922), see volume 1, Introduction p. xxxv, C7, F91, F100, F115, H15, K43 n. 1, K52 n. 1, K53 and K54.

K43   ISABEL BYERS[1]

She had an innocence no time effaced;
And, as from heaven a star looks down,
So shined she out for him whose life lay waste,
Till sacrifice made her renown.

(1 October 1924)   *Copy-text: UW*   *Collated states: SV* (no variants)

[1] From 1904 the widowed Isabel Byers provided food and shelter for Henry Lawson, who was often virtually destitute in the final years of his life. MG admired her devotion and wrote to George Robertson on 26 September 1932: 'I could not [lie] in my grave if I had not done something worth while in tribute to her. It is only worth while because it really does cover her, in her sacrifice: which never counted its loss or its pains: and I put it where juxtaposition would deepen its value as a tribute' (*Letters* 92).

K44   "FATHER BULLETIN"

Though newer lights may rise,
    The old love holds!
You cannot speak a name
    But thought unfolds,
Reaching remembering out   5
    To far-off times,
When none asked reason, and
    We laughed in rhymes.

Writes life with careless hand
    His easy scrawl,   10
And nature sends her breeds
    To creep and crawl,
And neither minds the end:
    Nor we, yon times,
When youth spurned reason, and   15
    We laughed in rhymes.

George Street was George Street, then,[1]
    A road of dreams;
Now it's a place of trade
    Where traffic screams,   20
Save when some wanderer seeks
    That stair, which climbs
Where hope jibed reason, and
    We laughed in rhymes.

What shades from *Bulletins*   25
    Long dead arise,
And ghost familiar ways
    With shadowed eyes,
Who looked on gathered gold
    As half a crime,   30
And scoffed at reason, while
    They laughed in rhyme!

[1] Refers to 214 George St. Nth, original address of the *Bn* (its move to 252 George
St. came in 1932).

There Kendall singing came,[2]
  His darkling eyes
Like tarns within whose dusk   35
  A sunbeam lies—
That bright flower of our young
  Australian prime,
When none asked reason, and
  We laughed in rhyme!   40

Daley walked splendid there,[3]
  And Farrell quipped,[4]
While Archibald and Haynes[5]
  The arrow tipped;
And there the bold Phil May[6]   45
  Lashed all with mime;
Fancy his reason, as
  We laughed in rhyme.

Though gone the early group,
  Still comes the late,   50
With Quinn and Hugh McCrae,[7]
  And "Lawson's mate";[8]
While Nora wields the pen
  Of Sappho's prime,
And laughs with reason as   55
  She mocks in rhyme![9]

[2] See K35 n. 1.
[3] Victor Daley (1858–1905) published his first collection of poems *At Dawn and Dusk* in 1898 and *Wine and Roses* posthumously in 1911.
[4] John Farrell (1851–1904), best known for the radical verse satires and narratives published in the *Bn*. For his influence on MG, see volume 1, Introduction, p. xxxv.
[5] The *Bn* was co-founded in 1880 by J. F. Archibald (1856–1919: see F44) and the lesser known John Haynes (1850–1917), whose connection with the journal ended in 1885.
[6] (1864–1903), a prolific and admired cartoonist for the *Bn* for three years from 1885.
[7] Roderic Quinn (1867–1949), a writer of fiction and poetry, some of which first appeared on MG's Women's Page in the *Wr*. McCrae (1876–1958) was highly regarded as a poet and otherwise active in the Australian literary scene; he was one of MG's closest literary friends.
[8] Probably J. W. Gordon ('Jim Grahame'): see H79 line 42.
[9] Nora Kelly, editor of the *Bn* Women's Page for many years, published extensively as Nora McAuliffe. Her poems appeared in the *Bn* from 1916; volumes included *The Song-Maker and Other Verse* (1937) and the war-narrative *1940–42* (1944).

And O, how bright there shine
  The golden years,
When A. G. Stephens skelpt
  Us with his shears,[10]   60
And Brennan stalked in Greek,[11]
  And clashed a chime—
A bay leaf reason, as
  We laughed in rhyme.

Ah, well, good luck the new,   65
  But old love holds!
You cannot ink a line
  But thought unfolds,
Reaching in memory back
  To far-off times—   70
When youth was reason, and
  We laughed in rhymes!

(28 February 1920)   *Copy-text: UW*   *Other state: Wr*, 2 December 1920, p. 9 as THE
OLD BRIGADE (*A*)[12]

---

[10] Literary editor of the *Bn* 1894–1906 and controller of its publishing division from 1897, he earned a reputation as a highly interventionist editor: 'skelpt' merges *skelp*, to scold or drive on with blows, with *scalped*, literally to remove a scalp, metaphorically to make cuts in a poem or story. For his relationship with MG, see volume 1, Introduction, pp. xxxv, xxxix–xli, xliv–xlv, and F161 and n. 1.

[11] C. J. Brennan (1870–1932), a graduate in classics and philosophy from Sydney University, with an uncompleted doctorate in Berlin, brought a new intellectual dimension to Australian poetry. His arguments ('reason') were spiced with wit (as a 'bay leaf' flavours culinary dishes), but his poetry was sometimes regarded as discordant ('clashed a chime').

[12] *A*'s differences in content and ordering of material are so substantial that it is given below in its entirety:

THE OLD BRIGADE

Though newer lights may rise
  The old love holds;
You cannot lift a line
  But thought unfolds,
Reaching, with wandering hands,
  To other times,
Where none asked reasons, and
  We laughed in rhymes.

Writes Time with easy hand
  His wavering scrawl,

And Nature sends her breeds
  To creep and crawl;
And neither minds the end—
  Like us yon times
When none asked reasons, and
  We laughed in rhymes.

George-street was George-street then,
  A road of dreams,
But now 'tis filled with touts
  And shady schemes,

Save when one finds an old
  Dark stairs, and climbs
Where none asked reasons, and
  We laughed in rhymes.

Daley walked there. He's gone.
  There Farrell quipped,
And there the young Phil May
  His arrow tipped,
Where Archibald no more
  The quick thought limes—
And none asked reasons, and
  We laughed in rhymes.

There broken-hearted Kendall
  Wept his bitter tears,
And A. G. Stephens skelpt
  Us with his shears;
There Dowell sang
  And Brereton clashed his chimes:
Where none asked reasons, and
  We laughed in rhymes.

The bushman's friendly foot
  Stepped shyly on

The moulded stairs, but aye
  'Twas swift! . . . ALL GONE!
THE EAGERNESS IS OUT,
  And life sweats mimes
Where none asked reasons, and
  We laughed in rhymes.

The shades of "Bulletins"
  Long dead rise up,
And ghost the long-dead ways
  Of bite and sup,
Where we rang happy gold
  As it were dimes,
And none asked reasons, and
  We laughed in rhymes.

To-day life greets the new,
  But old love holds;
At each remembered line
  Long thought unfolds,
Turning in memory back
  To yon old times
Where none asked reasons, and
  We laughed in rhymes.

K45   TO THOSE WHO REMAIN

The old years toss their banners to the new,
Their dust flies, scattered by time's passing hoof—
A golden dust that gilds our partial view,
Till what is half, and what is wholly true,
Blend like a silken pattern on a woof;   5
And we, who now but ask a solid roof,
Tell youth of days that loosed the heart like wine,
When danger charmed, and age stood far aloof,
And A. G. Stephens wrote of Doodlekine.[1]

[cont. overleaf

(1 December 1926)   *Copy-text: UW*   *Collated states: Wr*, 8 December 1926, p. 5 (*A*)
Not otherwise recorded: MG's note is asterisked to line 9 in *A*.
1 The] (With all due apologies.)// THE *A*   years] days *A*   new,] ~; *A*   **2** flies,]
~ *A*   **3** our partial] youth's later *A*   view,] ~ *A*   **4** wholly] truly *A*   **5** on]
in *A*   woof;] ~. *A*   **6** we,] ~— *A*   who now but] we only *A*   **7** Tell youth]
And dreams *A*   **8** age stood] death seemed *A*

---

[1] On Stephens, see K44 n. 10. His 'Paid to Doodlekine, W. A.' is a comic poem about

Then life was just a case of "beans to spill,"   10
And hope backed hazard as though hope could pay;
Then every mountain peak seemed but a hill,
And feet had wings, and wings were in the will,
And time went like an hour that could not stay;
Now it is twenty-four hours to the day,   15
For us who watched the stars of morning shine,
When danger charmed, and loss seemed far away,
And A. G. Stephens wrote of Doodlekine!

Maybe regrets are only joys reversed—
The shades that mark the passage of the sun;   20
But life's a play that opens unrehearsed,
Where lonely last looks back on lucky first,
As years thin out the players, one by one!
And yet the teeth of time we hold at bay,
When olden friends remember what was fine,   25
When danger drew, and death seemed far away,
And A. G. Stephens wrote of Doodlekine.*

* In "The Pearl and the Octopus."

11 backed] tipped *A*   12 peak seemed] steep was *A*   13 in] on *A*   14 went . . . that] itself flew by and *A*   stay;] ~. *A*   15 day,] ~; *A*   16 For . . . shine,] And once we rose while stars were still ashine!— *A*   17 loss] age *A*
18 Doodlekine!] ~. *A*   20 passage] pathway *A*   sun;] ~— *A*   21 But life's] And life *A*   22 on] to *A*   first,] ~ *A*   23 players,] ~ *A*   one!] ~; *A*
24 And yet] ~, ~, *A*   bay,] ~ *A*   25 olden] still old *A*   fine,] ~ *A*
n1 Octopus."] Octopus." A book: where few others are more than print and paper.—M.G. *A*

the name of a Western Australian town; *The Pearl and the Octopus and Other Exercises in Prose and Verse* (see author's note) appeared *c.* 1911.

k46   OUR AUSTRAL SEA

Emerald are they, beloved of sailors,*
　　These waves that ever landward roll;
They bring us tales of ancient whalers,
　　They sing the chanteys[1] of the Pole.

They tell us of the bold Ben Boyd　　　　　　　　　　　5
　　Who built beside the sea his tower;[2]
He chased the whales where they deployed,
　　He drove upon the winds in power.

They tell to us of Portland Town,
　　Of sails long white upon the Bay;　　　　　　　　　10
And there the stories still came down
　　Of how the Hentys, anchored, lay.[3]

For there they loosed their tattered sail,
　　And there above the oars they bent,
And there is told again the tale　　　　　　　　　　　15
　　Of how to chase the whales they went.

[cont. overleaf

(9 January 1931)   *Copy-text:* UW   *Collated states:* BPMag (September 1931), p. 89
as OUR AUSTRAL SEAS (*A*)

Not otherwise recorded: Except for MG's note, *A*'s text is in italics throughout; the
swung dash means the repeated word is in italics.

3 whalers, *Ed.*] sailors, *X*   whalers— *A*   **4** They . . . of the] *The seaman's saga,*
Pole to A   **5** They . . . bold] *There was a man went forth*— *A*   **5** Boyd] ~— *A*
6 beside the sea] *by Bega Head A*   **7** chased] *sought A*   **8** He . . . in] *The*
harpoon in his hand his A   **9** They . . . of*] *And there were two in A*   Town]
town A   **10** Of . . . Bay] *The little hamlet of the bay A*   **11** And . . . came] *The*
stories still are handed A   **12** Of . . . Hentys,] *Where Henty Brothers A*
12 anchored,] ~ *A*   **13** their tattered] *the flowing A*   **15–16** is . . . they] *they*
fought and flensed the whale/ Who followed where he, sounding, A

---

[1] Variant spelling of *shanties*, sailors' songs usually sung while working.
[2] In 1843 Benjamin Boyd (1797?–1851) established a whaling station and port for coastal
shipping at Boydtown on Twofold Bay, NSW. The monolithic Tower on the southern
headland, intended as a landmark as well as a whaling lookout and lighthouse, was left
unfinished when his enterprise failed in 1849.
[3] The Hentys, who came to Portland from Van Diemen's Land in 1834, are regarded
as Victoria's first settlers, although William Dutton had already established a whaling
station at Portland Bay: cf. E94 line 12 and n. 1.

And they were ours—Henty, Ben Boyd!
   O build remembrance on their names,
Lest, by forgetfulness destroyed,
   The fire of dream no longer flames!   20

Emerald are they, beloved of sailors,
   These waves that ever landward roll,
They bring us tales of ancient whalers,
   The South, and its immortal toll.

* An English form of a French line.

17 Boyd!] ~— *A*   *19* Lest,] ~ *A*   *19* destroyed,] ~ *A*   *20* flames!] ~. *A*
22 roll,] ~; *A*   23 bring] *tell A*   24 South,] *south A*   n1 line.] line, whose
author's name has escaped me.—M.G. *A*

K47   A MEMORY[*]

I saw the man who rode the Barb,[1]
   I held him by the hand,
I looked into his eager eyes,
   His weathered face I scanned.

And, talking once, I heard him say,   5
   "No whip man ever made,
Upon that sleek and satin skin,
   By any hand was laid!"

I saw the man who rode the Barb,
   And I the taller stand,   10

(31 August 1930)   *Copy-text: UW*   *Collated states: Wr*, 10 December 1930, p. 5 as
A RECOLLECTION (*A*)

Not otherwise recorded: For line 1, *A* has a note: 'The famous racehorse.'
1 the Barb] The ~ *A*   2 the] his *A*   3 into] and saw *A*   5 say,] ~: *A*
6 made,] ~ *A*   7 skin,] ~ *A*   8 By any] My *A*   was] has ever *A*   laid!] ~. *A*
9 the Barb,] The ~; *A*

[1] Mentioned several times in Adam Lindsay Gordon's poems of horse-racing, especially
in '*Credat Judæus Apella*', otherwise known as 'A Short Rhyme at Random' (*Sea Spray
and Smoke Drift*, 1867). See also M1 line 81. The Barb was an ancient breed of horse
from Barbary or Morocco, related to the modern Arabian and noted for its speed and
endurance.

That once I looked into his eyes,
That once I touched his hand.

[*] This was about the same time that Henry Kendall first came to our place—in the early or middle Eighties. It was at our house that he wrote "The Last of His Tribe,"[2] following upon a talk on the cruelties inflicted upon the disappearing blacks. He had the same pity for the aborigines that we had.   n5

11 into] within *A*   12 touched] held *A*   n1–5 This . . . had.] *Om. A*

[2] Published in *Leaves from Australian Forests* (1869) and a popular expression of the idea that the Aborigines were a disappearing race. On Kendall, see K35 and n. 1.

K48   SHAKESPEARE[1]

Thou whose compelling word
In this our day is heard,
As when in thy first prime
'Twas spoken for all time;
And who, where'er thought breed,   5
Or in what book men read,
Still hast for us the Spring
Of thy first blossoming;

Thou who life's wintry deeps
Touchest until there weeps   10
In swift and sudden heats
Tears that no time defeats;
Who hast all depth, all height,
And takest in thy flight

(n. d.)   *Copy-text: UW   Collated states: SV (A)*
8 blossoming;] ~, *A*   10 Touchest] Dost touch, *A*   11 heats] ~, *A*   14 And]
Who *A*

[1] MG urged George Mackaness on 20 May 1940 to select this poem rather than K30 for his revised edition (1948) of *The Wide Brown Land* (correspondence in ADFA G137 6/47). On 30 August 1940 she wrote: '[T]hank God you have chosen that! I think it is my high water mark as literature, and also no one else here has done it as I have' (*Letters* 171); but in the event, Mackaness used neither poem, retaining the selection of the 1934 anthology.

(E'en as the eagles take   15
The edgeless void,) the ache,
The pain of life, the joy—
As thine in thy deploy;

Hear us, O thou great Mind!
Thou in whose script we find   20
More than the phrases hold—
That something in the fold
Of word on word, of sound
On sound, too scantly found
Save where thy genius primed,   25
Thy thought ascending climbed.

Naught limits thee, for thou
Art leaf, and trunk, and bough
To that great tree whose flower
Is to our people dower,[2]   30
To kings their pride, to youth,
In its romantic truth,
The measure of the young
Love trembling at its tongue.

Even the rags thy poor   35
Put on as gold endure;
No silk outlasts thy words;
No proud insignia, girds
A king, outlives the sigh
Of Juliet[3] come to die;   40

---

15 E'en as the] Boldly as *A*   **16** void,] ~ *A*   **17** joy—] ~, *A*   **18** deploy;]
~, *A*   **21** hold—] ~; *A*   **24** found] ~, *A*   **28** bough] ~, *A*   **38** insignia,]
investment *A*   **39** king,] ~ *A*

---

[2] See I141 n. 2.

[3] Heroine of *Romeo and Juliet*. Other characters in K48 are drawn from *King Lear* (line
44), *Hamlet* (lines 51 and 72), *As You Like It* (lines 54–5 and 73), *Othello* (lines 62–4 and
72), *Richard II* (line 73), *Henry VIII* (line 81), *Henry V* (line 83) and *The Tempest* (line 89).
Falstaff appears in *1* and *2 Henry IV* and in *The Merry Wives of Windsor*; 'camlet' (line 52,
meaning a garment) is nowhere used in relation to him, but appears only in *Henry VIII*,
v. 4. 93. The lines on Falstaff's death (83–8) are adapted from *Henry V*, II. 3. 9–26.

No Autumn-fallen leaf
Is greyer than the grief
That darkness turned to fear
In that gaunt shadow, Lear:
The wintry tear of age   45
Is frozen on thy page.

O, we have ripened on
Thee, where, pretences gone,
The pageantry of time
Thou show'st in pantomime!   50
For we have grieved with Hamlet,
And in the heavy camlet
Of Falstaff we have lurched;
In Arden we have searched,
Seeking fair Rosalind—   55
Her name still on the wind.

And men are one in thee!
In race, in bond or free,
No man is less than man
Where thy quick fancy ran;   60
Therefore the sad allure
Of that dark man, the Moor,
Falls on us, too, as on
The gentle Desdemon,
Till in us pity weeps,   65
And sorrow sorrow keeps.

There was naught mean to thee;
And none too fine to be
In added splendour dressed
Where thy great thumb-print pressed;   70
So on what shadowy coast
Wanders Ophelia's ghost,

41 Autumn-fallen] autumn-fallen *A*   50 show'st] showest *A*

Motly[4] and John o' Gaunt,
Scullion[5] and Cæsar haunt.

And in thee no repine—   75
No conquest brought decline
To man's inhering pride:
That worth from which his tide
Of action floods, what state
Life choose him for his fate.   80
So Wolsey mourns; how grown
In stature overthrown!

And Falstaff dies, and yields
A babble o' green fields,
In that last plucking hour,   85
Has never lost the power
To wring the sigh, and to
The eyes draw tears anew:
And thy dread Caliban
Weeps at the heart, a man.   90

Shakespeare! the world had need
Of thee, for in thy brede,
If life its braid would lift,
The old and kingly wift
Of pride still strands to bind   95
Its sheaf upon the mind,
E'en though, in slackness, men
Lie soft as pigs in pen.[6]

O, if thou couldst have stood
With us to-day, we would   100

---

74 Cæsar] Caesar *A*   **85** plucking] pinching *A*   **87** wring] bring *A*   **99** O,]
~ *A*   couldst] could'st *A*   **100** to-day] today *A*

[4] Probably not a generic reference to clowns and jesters, but to Touchstone in *As You Like It*, who is regularly addressed by this name by Jaques.
[5] Generic reference to servants and lowlife characters, as against kings and rulers.
[6] If the world is to improve (literally, 'lift' its 'braid', i.e. fabric, line 93), it needs Shakespeare's breadth ('brede'), within which a venerable ('old and kingly') trace ('wift', a breath of wind, possibly echoing *whiff*) of pride is threaded ('strands') so as to impress its value ('bind its sheaf') upon the minds of slothful men (lines 97–8).

Not now lie low, and sup
From out a weakling's cup!
We would have shook the world,
Though we went from it hurled
To darkness—ripped from hope—   105
On some harsh gallows' rope.

Thou wast not born to sing
The sonnet of one string!
Thou wast the wind-blown ship
Whose pennon flew as whip,   110
Till every foreign boom[7]
Fled where thy mast cried "Room"!
And thine the bold romaunt
That made the rose our vaunt.[8]

Yet sweet thy flowering buds!   115
How on yon bank still floods
The violet her scent
Toward the moonlit bent
Of heaven, whose comely clouds
Are drawn to silver shrouds;[9]   120
How clear thy lute beneath
The moon's last silken wreath!

The jays of time once mocked
At thee, who later flocked
To crow abroad thy name,   125
And strut upon thy fame.

---

105 darkness—] ~, *A*   hope—] ~, *A*   **110** flew] ~, *A*   **112** mast] sail *A*
cried] ~, *A*   "Room"!] *"Room!" A*

---

[7] Nautical term for a long spar run out to extend (*boom out*) the foot of a particular sail: i.e. of less importance than the main mast – see next line.
[8] MG compares Shakespeare's plays of the Wars of the Roses to the achievement of the famous medieval poem *Le Roman de la Rose* (left unfinished by Guillaume de Lorris 1237, completed by Jean de Meun *c.* 1277), partially translated by Geoffrey Chaucer as *The Romaunt of the Rose* (pre-1372).
[9] Lines 115–20 allude to the moonlit bank of *The Merchant of Venice*, V. 1. 54 and the sweet-smelling bank of *A Midsummer Night's Dream*, II. 1. 249.

They passed; as dust they passed,
O eagle of the vast,
Whom Time, in Time's despite,
Shows widening still thy flight.   130

Thou who our speech didst take,
And who of it didst make
Thy stage, whereon, to-day,
Is shown in full display
Life's light and shade, the fire   135
And dusk of its desire,
Thou hast filled many a paunch
That on the narrow haunch
Of famine else had fed,
Hadst thou not been their bread;   140
And thou hast been the wine
Made drunken men divine.

I, too, have drunk of thee;
Have drowned me in thy sea.

131 who] whom *A*   didst] did'st *A*   **132** didst] did'st *A*   **133** to-day] today *A*
140 Hadst] Had'st *A*

K49   ROSALIND IN ARDEN[1]

Leave, Rosalind, leave
Thy name upon the wind,
Lest there be echoes none,
To wake and run,
Where whispering leaves   5
Make forest eaves!

Leave, Rosalind, leave
Thy name upon the wind;
Let Arden answer still
To thy sweet will,   10
Else to the cold
Of life we mould!

O, Rosalind, leave
Thy name upon the wind!
Lay it upon our lips   15
To lie, lest slips
The sceptre of
The world from love!

(n. d.)   *Copy-text: UW*   *Collated states:* None

[1] Heroine of Shakespeare's *As You Like It,* who takes refuge with her exiled father in
the Forest of Arden.

K50   MYRTLE BRADSTREET[1]

They have put Myrtle away where none may find her,
    Myrtle, whose spirit never knew to lie down;
Now all the world is the poorer for her going—
    Myrtle of the high heart, and the eyes of brown.

We shall not see her again, no matter how   5
    We look as we walk through the streets of the town;
She will come no more to our doors in passing—
    Myrtle of the gay heart, and the eyes of brown.

Myrtle would take a flower, and, pinning it
    On shoulder or breast of her smart little gown,   10
Make us all think of sunshine and gardens—
    Myrtle of the brave heart, and the eyes of brown.

Now we who knew her best have seen her go out,
    Over the top like a soldier, courage her crown;
But something is lost, and we never shall find it—   15
    Myrtle of the true heart, and the eyes so brown.

(20 October 1930)   *Copy-text: UW*   *Collated states: Wr,* 29 October 1930, p. 17 (*A*)

2 Myrtle,] ~ *A*   **3** is the] is *A*   **6** We] We may *A*   **7** She] And she *A*
come] knock *A*   to our doors] on the door *A*   **9–10** it/ On shoulder] ~ on/
Shoulder *A*   **12** brave] glad *A*   **13** knew] have known *A*

[1] Unidentified.

K51   LAURA BOGUE-LUFFMAN[1]

She went on, who once was here.
Is she lost who stood so near?
Nay! what bright
    Far field she tread,
Still her light   5
    Is round us shed.

She loved beauty all her days;
Beauty moved her to her praise;
Now, in what
    Far field she sow,   10
She will not
    An-hungered go.

Things grown lovely still abide;
Death can not the spirit hide;
Though her dust   15
    To dust return,
Only rust
    Is in the urn.

(20 September 1929)   *Copy-text: UW*   *Collated states:* None

---

[1] Laura Bogue Luffman (1846–1929), feminist, children's writer and prolific journalist, active in the Women's Branch of the Liberal League (advocates of Free Trade), president of the Women's Reform League during the campaign for preferential voting and a strong supporter of the League of Nations.

K52   RUTH[1]

He laid her hand in mine
    In the young, young years;
He brought me again her name—
    A man broken in tears—

---

[1] Based on Henry Lawson's account of his relationship, from *c.* 1898, with Hannah Thornburn (d. June 1902, possibly as the result of an abortion), his turbulent marriage (e.g. lines 66–7, 74–5 and 88) and his early friendship with MG

Saying, "Let not the story of Ruth   5
    Die out in the land;
Leave not her name
    To perish for ever!"

        "She walked with me where *we* once walked," he said;
And then he bowed his head   10
And dreamed upon her lovely name.
How could I think it shame
That he should speak of her? or loss that he
Thought of her tenderly,
When all our own young years had had their day,   15
And in his heart they lay
Like some sweet child asleep—
Which memory kept, and could not weep?
Nay! as above a babe, I leaned and kissed
That old love on the face,   20
And touched his greying hair, and blessed
That other for her grace.

        "She used to talk like you," he said. And then:
"Strange that the two who meant so much
    Should be so like!" His mind reached out to touch   25
The hem of love's dear garment once again,
And with his eyes I saw—I swear I saw!—
Her spirit standing there,
And on its face her look of love
Mourned still her last farewell, like some sad dove.   30
O, how my heart went out to her
(And ever yet!)
As there upon me fell his debt,
That, undischarged, it lay
Upon me still to pay: 35

(e.g. lines 9–18, 22–5 and 41–3); see volume 1, Introduction, p. xxxv and n. 17. MG
could not have met Hannah (despite lines 1–2 and 126–7), being in Paraguay at the time
of the affair, but MG's (unpublished) MS 'Personal History, Henry Lawson and I' (1923)
and an accompanying letter to George Robertson claim she was in his confidence: see
'Hannah Thornburn' (1905?) in Henry Lawson's *Collected Verse*, ed. Colin Roderick,
vol. 2 (Sydney: Angus & Robertson, 1968), pp. 149–52 and editor's note, pp. 376–82.
For 'Ruth' and rue, see J7 n. 1 and cf. M52.

As though the spur
Of some deep urgency, from other-where,
Was bound upon me as its law.
That debt I pay in words, in tears,
Here in these after years.   40

    "Easily as I talked with you I talked
With her," he said. "And she, she seemed to know
As you, without the full words' flow . . ."
(In misered speech, slow-drooped like gold,
In this sad manner was the story told.)   45
    And then: "Through the old ways we walked;
Her voice sounding like yours upon my ear!
So strange it seemed—
One never could have dreamed
Two voices, not the same—each different—   50
Should in their likeness lighten strained intent,
So that speech, softened, and yet clear,
My dullness heard as others hear!"
He paused. And, there as memory backward yearned,
Grief for his grief my spirit burned.   55

    "She loved me! . . . O, in my dark life,
She was, if ever woman was, my wife.
So patient, she! So sweet; so kind!
From her dear lips I heard no scorn
Of folly out of suffering born;   60
She had no bitterness of mind
That, morning, noon and night,
Clacked out its petty spite;
No egotism bit; no morbid taint,
Touched where her lovely soul stood saint!   65
So from the torture of my daily hell,
Storm-driven, I ran to her, and like a spell
Peace stilled me even ere my head
Against her gentle breast I laid . . ."
He sighed as one broken with pain;   70
Still slower came his words; and grew the strain

On that bruised heart, remembering how upon
The torment of his life her light had shone.
" . . . She was so different from her at home,
Who hated, hated that the child should come!   75
But she, '*O, that* (she said) *in motherhood*
My heart might brood
Above a child that was your blood:
Your child and mine! . . .
Your look, your gift, to live   80
In all the undiminished power that love could give—
And half divine! . . .' "

    Again he paused. Again he dreamed upon
The shadow of a day long gone.
"Then came our parting hour," he said. "No word,   85
No written line from then between us passed;
Only I held a name, to which, should I return . . .
    "O God, those years—those dreadful years!
Yet through their length, their grief and tears,
Three little words—a name, a town, a street—   90
Lay on my heart and heard it beat;
Lay on my heart as dew on thirsty grass,
As hope through hopeless hours that slowly pass,
As that far love of God which seems
Last harbourage of desolate dreams,   95
When on the famished bread of shipwreck men
Must eat or starve, and starve to eat again! . . .
    "Time brought release, and in my heart there sprung
Once more the founts of life, and I again grew young.
And then, too slow my ship returned to her, however fast,   100
Too slow the painted smoke behind the mast,
Too slow the long hours, linked like wave to wave,
For my wild heart so long a slave;
My heart that could but crave
For her, for him who should be hers and mine,   105
And in whose eyes her look of love would shine!"
    He held and showed me there that written line,

Kept through the famine years,
Wet with his tears,
And sad to see as his sad face.   110
"Thither I went," he said. "I found the place . . .
And she was dead."

>   They told him that, when anguish ceased, she smiled
>   and said,
> *"Tell him I never knew regret:*
> *Bid him not grieve, and yet not quite forget;*   115
> *Say I was happy in his love."* She sighed;
> Then said, *"Dear love!"* and, saying, died.

This is the story of Ruth,
    And I, the bidden, speak it;
Here is hidden the truth   120
    That all may find who seek it;
But thou, O wounded soul, in thy grave[2]
    No longer fret,
Let peace flow over thee there, and lave:
    Paid is thy debt.   125

He laid her hand in mine
    In the young, young years;
He brought me again her name,
    In a passion of tears.

(18 November 1923)   *Copy-text: UW*   *Collated states:* None

---

[2] Lawson died in 1922. K53 and K54 continue the depiction of him as a 'wounded soul'; see also K42 n. 1.

K53   A SHADE UPON THE STREET[1]

They laughed to see him go,
    A shade upon the street,
So little did they know
    The grief that was his meat;

---

[1] The subtitle 'H. L. (Henry Lawson)' added in MG's hand to a manuscript in ML 5/3 confirms that he is the poem's subject; cf. C7 and F115.

And what he wrote they read,　　　5
　　Nor knew (so it appears,)
Until the man was dead,
　　That there he wrote his tears.

(5 September 1924)　*Copy-text: UW*　*Collated states: Wr*, 8 October 1924, p. 5 as
IN MEMORIAM (*A*)

4–5 meat;/ And] ~.// ~ *A*　　6 appears,)] ~), *A*　　7 dead,] ~ *A*

K54　THE BALLAD OF THE LENDING

*"He lent me a pound to get married. . . .
It was the worst day's work I ever did."*[1]

The Judas Pound[2] upon the earth
　　Went walking round and round—
An evil thing that no man touched
　　But grief and shame he found;
Where'er it went it left a trail　　　5
　　Of sad and bitter tears,
The Judas Pound that, round and round,
　　Went round the world for years.

A shipwrecked man, he told to me
　　The story of the Pound　　　10
That led him by a shoreless sea,
　　And there his heart was drowned;
He looked at me with eyes that mourned,
　　He spake a grief profound:
"Was never man did me such wrong　　　15
　　As he who lent that Pound."

The friend of one who was sorrowful grieveth for him.

He telleth the story of grief.

[1] The only MS in ML 5/3 to contain the side-note summaries of the narrative is annotated: 'Written about February, 1923'. Of the six MSS in NLA 727 1/H, two consist only of the three stanzas describing the death-bed scene of lines 113–36. One is dated 13 November 1922 and attributes K54's (untraced) epigraph to 'H. L.' (Lawson died 2 September 1922). For other poems about Lawson, see K42 n. 1.

[2] A gift that betrays, like the kiss with which Judas Iscariot betrayed Christ (Matthew 26. 47–50). In K54 it betrays into an unhappy marriage (cf. K52), which becomes analogous to the albatross in 'The Rime of the Ancient Mariner' (see I4 n. 3): lines

His heart it was a golden vase
    That bled in drops of red,
But no one knew that heart of gold
    Until the man was dead;   20
And then upon his breast they laid
    The children of the Pound,
The Judas Pound that round and round,
    That through the world went round.

All uncompanioned day by day   25
    A lonely man he went,
And still went with him, all the way,
    The Judas Pound, unspent;
It drained like leeches on his heart,
    It sucked the drops blood red,   30
And still it clung and still it hung
    When that poor man was dead.

Here he telleth of the loneliness of the sorrowful.

The Judas Pound, the Judas Pound,
    That through the world went round,
It heard the silver bugles cry   35
    That day his grief was drowned:
It followed him slow journeying
    To hollow trumpet sound,
And when at last they heaped the sod
    It crawled upon his mound.   40

The Pound, the Pound, the Judas Pound,
    That all love withereth,
It leeched upon the living man,
    It leeched on him in death.

          *   *   *   *

"I would," said the sorrowful man to his friend, "that I might lay my

Alas! alas, that this should be!   45
    Alas, that men should cry
The wares that never have been theirs,
    And want them till they die;

108–18 of Coleridge's poem are alluded to in lines 70–3 of K54, which also imitates its use of side notes.

And, O, alas, that men should go
   Companionless alway,   50
While can be found a Judas Pound
   To mark them for its prey!

I saw the sad, the lonely man,
   I saw his lonely grave:
(The winds of summer o'er it blow,   55
   The winds of winter rave);
And out by his dark and empty house
   And the room wherein he died,
The sinister sound of the Judas Pound
   Clocked at the pane outside.   60

I knew the man the Pound had bound,
   The stars had looked in his eyes,
The ancient wisdom given him words,
   And grief had made him wise;
And when he spoke the deeps were drawn,   65
   Like tides through a mighty Keep,
But under the tide a greater tide
   Hung like a thing asleep.

For the Judas Pound it held him fast
   Like one in a swounded³ sea,   70
Where never a wind might serve the mast,
   And never a current free;
And deep in the man a deeper deep
   Than ever he knew lay locked,
Held down and bound by the Judas Pound,   75
   That fleered in his face and mocked.

His life it swung like a drowned man
   Whom never a compass steered,
A frustrate log in a broken sea,
   Its lack-land course it veered;   80
He drifted as one who knew no port,
   And yet, he was port to many,

head in the lap of one I loved, and there tell all my grief."

The friend telleth what manner of man was the sorrowful one.

Of his life the friend speaketh a word.

---

³ In a swoon, inert.

The many who wept at his passing out,
   And tossed, for his luck, a penny.

At night, at night, in the wind and rain,   85
   Where the howling tempest spreads,
Where the storm comes buffetting up to the pane,

He
speaketh
it with
tears.
   And the water spouts from the leads;
When streets are rivers and rivers are seas,
   And the lights burn dim and blind,   90
I see the wraith of a broken man
   Out in the night unkind.

Wind at his ears, rain at his neck,
   His shoulders hunched to the blast,
The squish-squish waters out of his boots   95
   That never were made to last;
Patient, enduring, suffering, sad,
   With a proud reserve, unbroken,
Alone he goes like a ship on a sea
   Where never a ship is spoken.[4]   100

A shipwrecked man he told to me
   The tale of the Judas Pound
That led him away to a shoreless sea,
   And there was his poor heart drowned;
He looked in my face with eyes that mourned,   105
   And he spoke with a grief profound:
"There never was one such wrong did me
   As the man who lent that Pound."

The Pound, the Pound, the Judas Pound,
   That all love withereth,   110
It leeched on the living heart of the man,
   And it leeched on him in death.

       *   *   *   *

They showed to me a naked room
   Where alone and alone he lay;

---

[4] I.e. spoken to; *to speak a ship* is to communicate at sea with a passing vessel.

There was no candle in the gloom   115
    To keep the night at bay;
There was no hearth-fire broke the loom
    Where darkness made its stay:
Only the silence of the tomb,
    And a little mouse at play.   120

The friend telleth of the house of death.

Still, O, still was that darkened room,
    But stiller yet was the man,
So still, the mouse, all unafraid,
    About and about him ran;
So still it crossed the hollow palm,   125
    And, turning there, began
To pull a thread from the fallen band
    That covered the arm's thin span.

He telleth of the darkened room.

Still, O, still as in a sleep,
    Still, O, still he lay;   130
Slowly did the night hours creep,
    Slowly came the day;
Slowly, where the thread was spun
    One late spider twined,
Slowly came the morning sun,   135
    And peered through the blind.

Christ Jesu, sold and on the Cross,
Pity the wanderer sold to loss.

He speaketh of the hope that is Christ.

Christ of the dark and bloody sweat,
Thine eyes of love shall find him yet.   140

Oh, Jesu sweet, the wronged and bound,
Pity all men of the Judas Pound.

(*c.* February 1923)   *Copy-text: UW   Collated states:* None

K55   YUAN KANG SU*1

Lo, on a day appointed,
   I shall go to a silent place,
And the winds, as His anointed,
   Shall blow upon my face;
And there I shall gaze abroad,   5
   Over the world below,
And with me shall be the sword,
   And the message I shall know.

There I shall look on the trees,
   Those lovers of the earth,   10
Whose song is as the seas
   Where ancient time had birth;
And I shall follow the sun,
   At morning and at eve,
And measure a day is done,   15
   Or ever I take my leave.

There I shall dream again
   Of an old and shadowy road,
The road of living men,
   Who held them to the code;   20
And I shall feel their hands,
   And hear their voices speak,
There, where the sword commands,
   As the sun lies on the peak.

Behind me the winding path,   25
   Before me the curtained way:
Yet what it held still hath
   The soul that loved its day;
For it hath drawn the green,
   And the sun, within its ken,   30
And followed a dream unseen,
   And held by the hands of men.

Out of the living earth
   The living thought it drew;

Laughter it brought from dearth,   35
 Drank passion from the dew;
For life it held in fief,
 By conquest over death,
Asking his moment brief
 On the last thin stream of breath!   40

Then I shall say, "It is well!"
 For the cup I asked was filled,
Upon it no shadow fell,
 And never a drop was spilled!
And there, at the last, shall I   45
 Stand by the falling sword:
One with the earth and the sky,
 In the knot of the silver cord.

* *The Bridge of Living Men*, by Will Levington Comfort.

(27 September 1920)   *Copy-text: UW   Collated states:* None

[1] In the theosophical novel *The Road of Living Men* (Philadelphia: Lippincott, 1913), by Will Levington Comfort (1878–1932) set during 1900–01, Yuan Kang Su is given a mission to study the world in order to bring modernism to China. He rejects love of a woman for his country (cf. line 43), but his ultimate advice, that China must 'liberate her women to raise men' (p. 269), is not accepted. He is given the symbolic 'silver cord' (line 48, and cf. J4 n. 1), ordaining his suicide – where K55 opens.

K56   RENUNCIATION[1]

I

To say farewell, and then to go,
 Knowing that never more in any street,
Or house or road, be time or swift or slow,
 We two may meet:

(Pt I: 26 February 1921; Pt II: 5 November 1920)   *Copy-text: UW   Collated states:* Bn, 8 December 1923, p. 16 (*A*)
Not otherwise recorded: Wherever copy-text has 'But O', *A* has 'But, oh'.
1 farewell,] ~ *A*   2 street,] ~ *A*   4 meet:] ~; *A*

[1] On this (conventional) theme, cf. C34 and J85.

To yearn alone, across the years,   5
   Toward the path that once so glad we trod,
And count each well-loved turn through mists of tears,
   And kiss the rod:

To forward look, and still to know
   That not again through all the time to be   10
Shall ever I behold your face, your low
   Voice comfort me:

To count each bygone word, each hoarded look
   From those dear eyes, each turn of that dear head,
And then to close for evermore the book,   15
   And no word said!

O tears to shed!
   O dear, dear love whom never once within
These arms I took, how can I let
   You go, save that if Christ His Word must win,   20
Love pays the debt.

II

To-morrow thou shalt go
   Where glory calls thee on,
Adventure thou shalt know,
   This day for ever gone!   25
Hunger, and wounds, and thirst,
   The fiery hail and shot—
Thy comrades call, Follow on!
   But O, forget me not.

Follow on! Follow on! Follow on!   30
   But O, forget me not—
The night for thy pavilion,
   And danger for thy lot;

5 alone,] ~ *A*   years,] ~ *A*   7 well-loved] well loved *A*   8 rod:] ~; *A*
10 again] ~, *A*   be] ~, *A*   12 me:] ~; *A*   16 said!] ~— *A*   18 dear, dear
love] dearly loved *A*   20 Word] word *A*   win,] ~ *A*   21 debt.] ~! *A*   25 for
ever] forever *A*   gone!] ~; *A*   27 shot—] ~. *A*   28 call,] ~. *A*   31 not—]
~!— *A*   33 lot;] ~. *A*

With me love's anguish dwells,
    Since death rides forth with thee,   35
Yet must I say, Follow on!
    But O, forget not me.

The rain shall drench thee through,
    The cold shall pierce thy reins;
And fear, whose damps bedew,   40
    Shall, shuddering, chill thy veins;
Thou shalt be gorged with filth,
    Where dead men oozing rot;
And, yet, Follow on! Follow on!
    But O, forget me not.   45

Thy head, this hour so high,
    To-morrow may be low,
This clear and candid eye
    In darkness ever go,
These strong triumphant limbs   50
    Waste in the falling lot—
Yet must I say, Follow on!
    But O, forget me not.

I shall sit in the dark
    What sun shall shine o'erhead,   55
Thy name my only mark
    In ways my feet must tread;
No light save in the spark
    Where thy sad camp must be—
But still, Follow on! Follow on!   60
    And O, forget not me.

Thy name upon my lips
    Shall lie by night and day,
Where love its own self strips,
    And feels the whips that flay;   65

34–5 With . . . thee,] Though death will ride with thee, / Love's anguish dwells with me; *A*   **36** say,] ~ *A*   **37** not me] me not *A*   **42** filth,] ~ *A*   **43** rot;] ~: *A*
46 head,] ~ *A*   **47** To-morrow] To morrow *A*   **50** strong] ~, *A*   **51** lot—] ~; *A*
52 say,] ~ *A*   on!] ~!— *A*   **55** shall] may *A*   **59** be—] ~; *A*   **61** And] ~, *A*
O] oh *A*   **64** its . . . strips,] itself unstrips *A*

Where fear, and dread, and doubt,
   Each after each creep out,
There, in the nights to be,
Must I still say, Follow on! Follow on!
But O, remember me!   70

67 out,] ~— *A*   **69** say,] ~ *A*

κ57   "T. B."[1]

Come soon, Summer, come soon! For cloud
Lies like a winding sheet—a shroud—
Upon the wintry sky, and all
Day long, all night, I hear the rain's slow fall;
The vines are bare, the trees are stark, and no   5
Birds sing the day aloud,
But silently with drooping wings they go.
O, Summer, come soon, come soon,
For if thou come not soon I die!

Come soon, Summer, come soon!   10
Take down the darkling curtains from the moon,
And from the drowning stars of night draw back
The weeping folds of dripping wrack[2]
That trail in heavy veils across the sky;
O Summer, come! Summer, come soon!   15
For if thou come not soon I die.

Once, on a happy day of long ago,
I heard like feet the rustling wheat
Beat on the pavements of the wind;
Then, with a whispering low,   20
In sudden waves they rolled, down, down, and down,
Crown after crown of bearded grain,
Like seas in flow,

---

[1] At age twelve, MG was diagnosed with incipient tuberculosis (TB), a disease prevalent in Australia until the advent of antibiotics after World War II. Damp conditions were considered to aggravate all forms of chest infection.
[2] See J90 n. 1.

Until the stems were rippling gems,
That flashed the sun, and rose again,   25
Till, as the soft air thinned,
They stood and shone upon the sight
Like an army ribboned in light!

And once the wind blew over
A field of trefoil as deep as the clover,   30
And I saw the thousand blossoming eyes of gold
(That twinkled like stars in the sky grown bold)
Dance, and flicker, and glance
To the wind in the swing of the stover,[3]
As it swayed and billowed and bent,   35
Where the leap and the run of the swift gusts went,
Fleeter and fleeter, over and over!

And once I stood where the stately corn
Clashed with its sabres morn by morn,
And the aisles of shadow ran down between   40
The tall straight stalks in their marshal of green,
Where the tassel of silk was mother, and nurse,
To the milky grain in its slender purse!
Green, green were the blades of the corn,
And green the spathes[4] where the cobs were born,   45
And green, green was the gossamer dusk between
The furrow of earth and the leafy sheen.

And high in the air a peewee sang,
Like a small church-bell that hastily rang,
And the darting wing of the soldier-bird   50
Slept in its hour of noon, unstirred,
While the scrolled dry bark of the goom-tree[5] swayed
With a wooden sound like a tune half-played,
And white as the linen beneath the Rood,[6]
Still, in a cowal,[7] a spoonbill stood.   55

[3] Uncut grass or crop providing fodder; cf. K59 line 54.
[4] See I10 n. 2.   [5] See K13 author's note for line 2.
[6] Christ's robe at the foot of the Cross (Rood).
[7] See K4 n. 5.

And climbing a hill a red road ran
Through a mat of grass like a silver fleece,
And the dust hung low in the wind's light fan,
Warm in the web of the sun's increase;
While, under the curve of the sky's arched hood,　　60
Like a velvet plume a pine-tree stood,
And the ripples of air broke sharp, like glass,
Where only the eagle's wing might pass.

And once, O Summer! Summer! there was a day
When the great round bulk of the thunderheads,[8]　　65
Heaped in their feathering high in the blue,
Massed like the fleet that treads
Upon the ocean in a flowering May
Of shining sails! And there, as on they drew
To stations in the deepening arch　　70
Of heaven, they hung at poise betwixt
Two worlds of space, and each one fixed
Within its own and separate march.
And I, O Summer, I stood there,
And watched them ride upon the sight,　　75
Until upon my head I felt my hair
Tingle as though in hackles it would rise,
Because of all that beauty, and that might,
Held by the chambers of mine eyes! . . .

And now, remembering all that past, I cry,　　80
As one may cry a boon,
O Summer, come! Come soon!
Lest ere thou come again I die!

(10 September 1924)　*Copy-text: UW*　*Collated states:* None

[8] MG wrote to Nettie Palmer on 20 September 1932 that K57 was written 'practically at one sitting' but that 'there is an addition (and one can feel it!) to the original stanza of reshaped and extended lines, and that is in the first ten lines of the stanza about the "thunderheads" – the ten were originally six. The first three and the last six had a paunch stuck in the middle of them, and I do not know that it adds to their dignity' (*Letters* 91).

κ58   ETERNAL CHAOS AND ETERNAL LAW

Life, the All-Mother, widowed of her youth,
But yet in fullness of her ripened years,
Stood with sad eyes wherein no softening tears
Might break for her their dreadful drouth,
And saw her elder children stand,   5
And gnash each other in the face—
Hate facing hate—as though no tie of blood
Had made them, long ago, one kindred race,
Or bred and bound them children of one brood!

And, as she anguished watched, she turned and caught   10
Our Land—her youngest—in her arms as though
She of herself would make a shield, that no
Defaming gesture, evil-wrought,
Should blot that innocent young face, and which—
Child-like, and O, how unaware!—   15
The look of infant amplitude still bore.
But not her all-enveloping arms could spare
That tender one the dreadful tide of war.

Yet though love's sharded[1] bones enrich far fields,
And though the wheat grows high where dead men fell,   20
Grief stills itself, and shuts the gates of hell.
So the torn tree new blossom yields,
And we, to-day, like the house-mother, who,
Tears on her face, dusts to restore
What death and time have wasted and undone,   25
Arise to wind the clock of hope once more,
And lift again our little candles to the sun.

*   *   *   *

(n. d.)   *Copy-text: UW   Collated states: SV* (A)

1 All-Mother] All-mother A   **6** face—] ~, A   **7** hate—] ~ A   **11** Land]
land A   **15** Child-like] Childlike A   O,] ~ A   **19** sharded] mouldered A
23 we,] ~ A   to-day] today A   **27.1** *. . . *] Om. A

---

[1] Shattered, broken into pieces.

Toward the stars of heaven I looked, and saw
How calmly unimpeded law
Moved without hasting on;   30
And, seeing, felt how small this febrile span
Where men mingle awhile like ants, and then are gone.
And as I stood the wind went by, the thunder of
Unnumbered ages in its wings sounding above
The fretful cry of time-tormented man.   35

Then slowly up the shadowy base of heaven
The moon's fore-running aura came,
Paler than Milky Way or Sisters Seven,
Softer than candle flame;
And followed there the moon, from out the cloud,   40
Wan and white as a spirit from its shroud.
And once again, 'mid tearing wrack,[2] I saw
Eternal chaos mock eternal law.

Who has not marked the noon-day cloud,
    Or watched one turret lonely stand,   45
Or seen mass, eminent and proud,
    As mountains lift on either hand!

Remote in poise, serene and cool,
    By summery blue horizons sashed,
Snow is not whiter, nor the wool   50
    That is the lamb's fleece, newly washed.

Yet, if one stood beneath their height,
    No peace is theirs; for, there, in wrath,
Storm moves on ravening[3] wings of might,
    And tears and rends all in its path.   55

And when is fallen the night, the flare
    The sheeted lightning upward sends

31 span] ~, *A*   32 awhile] ~, *A*   37 fore-running] forerunning *A*   40 moon,]
~ *A*   the] a *A*   44 noon-day] noonday *A*   47 on either hand!] above the
land. *A*   53 for, there,] ~ ~ *A*   wrath,] ~ *A*   57 sends *A*] ~, *X*

[2] See J90 n. 1.
[3] Violently rushing; cf. J99 n. 2.

Shows these tremendous freights of air
  Know but the calm that distance lends.

So it may be, though move the stars   60
In seeming peace, dark tumult mars.

к59   THE BULL[1]

Bellow, bull, bellow!
Low thy dark sound
Like a moan!
Call out to the herd,
Call to thine own!   5
Bellow, bull, bellow!
Stand with thy head on the fence,
And bellow, bull, bellow!
What if thy girth be immense,
O thou, the begetter of flesh for the block,   10
That, sleek as a cat, in thy fat
Must lie on a sheltering mat,
Lest thy sensitive skin suffer shock
From the touch of the unstrawed earth—
Thy satin-smooth skin, that shrinks in the bleak   15
Of the wind like an unfledged bird, or the weak
Small thing of the flock that shudders at birth!
Bellow, bull, bellow!

Thou wast not bred for thy strength,
But for depth of the flank,   20
And for thickness of shoulder;
Not for the charge of a heart grown prouder and bolder,
Not for the hoof that scattered the dust,
Not for the wrath that, swift to the thrust,

(17 May 1924)   *Copy-text: UW   Collated states: SV (A)*
3 moan!] ~, *A*   4 Call . . . herd,] *Om. A*   6 Bellow . . . bellow!] *Om. A*
18 Bellow . . . bellow!] *Om. A*

---

[1] MG wrote to J. K. Ewers on 17 December 1932: 'I saw that bull stand at his fence, it must be thirty years ago, and then suddenly, in 1924 it just flew into being, almost without

Came down to thy sire   25
And rose in his blood like fire!
But thou art the thrall
Of a fence, and a stall!
Bellow, bull, bellow!

Speed once lay in thy feet,   30
That still have the grace of the fleet
Small feet of thy sister the deer:
She who would leap from the smutch
Of a hand, that, venturing near,
Asked but to fondle and touch!   35
But thou, thou art a craver of hands;
Of comfort and ease; of the things that enmesh,
And are soothing and soft to the flesh.
Yet, bellow, bull, bellow;
Might still in thy frame lies hid.   40

    Ah, if thou wouldst but in fullness of wrath
Trample thyself from thy bonds, and, rid
Of the softness and sloth,
Forth as a leader in pride,
Then who had denied thee? Who had defied?   45
Thou hadst then fed with the herd,
Thou hadst then ruled undeterred,
Who now art the slave of a fence,
The led of a ring in the nose,
And no man taketh thee hence,   50
Save as his will and his own wish goes.
Bellow, bull, bellow!

Esau of beasts![2] Might that, once bold,
All for a measure of stover,[3] basks and is sold!

---

41 Ah, if] If *A*   wouldst but] would'st only *A*   **54** stover,] ~ *A*

---

additions, almost without corrections. Practically one sitting wrote it. But I do not know
how many the few corrections took! They came years after and had to be few lest tonal
quality altered. Many corrections would have meant re-writing and that would have meant
a complete change' (*Letters* 95).

[2] Esau, the older of the twin sons of Isaac, symbolises those who choose carnal pleasure

What to thee if the mountain should call,   55
What to thee if the valley resound
To the multiple rush, the rout, and the fall
And the click of the hooves as onward they bound,
Till afar in the distance they sound
Like a tide on the run?   60
What to thee of the pattering, one after one,
Of the hooves of the calves, that tap like the falling of leaves,
And trip like a trickle of water at eaves,
While still thou dost stand
Like a wave that rose on the land—   65
That rose and is done?

   Ah, when the moon shines out in the sky,
Riding up like a hunter over the hills,
When the moon-glades sway to her whitening beam,
And the swirling core of the river spills   70
Where the break of the current is turned at the sedge
With a ripple like jewels of light at the edge,
Do there never awaken within
Thy luxurious flesh, and thy too soft skin,
Longings that breed (as of some great dream,   75
Mighty in sleep, held when awake,)
For the mountain height, and the sunlit lake,
For the cool green turf and the mottle of rills,
Till thy shortened breath and thy sleek sides ache,
There to plunge forth and be free,   80
As a swimmer aches for the sea?

Is there never a craving of feet
To climb to some far retreat,
High and yet higher, and conquer and keep?
   Nay! thou art only the skin of a seed,   85

58 hooves] hoofs *A*   59 Till] ~, *A*   distance] ~, *A*   67 Ah] Now *A*
71 sedge] ~, *A*   76 awake,] ~ *A*   78 turf] ~, *A*

over higher values, in that he sold his birthright to his brother Jacob 'for a mess of red
pottage' (Genesis 25. 30–5).
[3] See K57 n. 3.

Ease-loving, and asking no more than to sleep
And to breed; to wake and to feed . . .
Bellow, bull, bellow!

87 feed . . .] ~. . . . *A*   88 Bellow . . . bellow!] *Om. A*

K60   A SAILOR'S EAR-RING*

A scuttering wind
    Sprang overhead,
A sudden wave
    Flung up and fled;
I loosed the sail,   5
    I took the wheel,
The sheets they twanged
    As they were steel,
And "Home!" I said—
    But said the sea,   10
"What home, O man,
    Hast thou but me?"

About, about,
    The ship, her course,
Took from my hand   15
    As though a horse;
I reined her in,
    I drove her on,
Until the fear
    Of storm was gone;   20
Then "Home!" I said—
    But spake the sea,
"What home hast thou,
    O man, but me?"

I trimmed the ship,   25
    I set the jib—[1]

---

[1] A triangular stay-sail; 'shrouds' (line 41) are the set of ropes leading from the head of
a mast in order to relieve it of lateral strain.

The sea ran sweet
   Upon her rib;
And then across
   The waters came   30
The lovely reek
   Of heath in flame.
Then "Home!" I cried—
   But cried the sea,
"O sailor man,   35
   Thou hast but me!"

I swung the barque
   Adown the bay,
I slipped the chain
   With length to play;   40
I strapped the shrouds,
   I furled the sail,
Alight for house,
   And fire and ale;
"'Tis home!" I cried—   45
   Then laughed the sea,
"How canst thou home,
   And not with me?"

I sit beside
   The fire and hear   50
All day the sea
   Upon my ear;
And all day long
   I feel the tide,
And watch the wind   55
   A javelin wide;
And dreamed it home!—
   To whom the sea
Cried, "What of home
   Hast thou but me?"   60

I tread the wharf
   With hungry feet;

Upon my lips
       The salt is sweet,
The salt that lies   65
       Within the sea,
The friendly salt
       That talks to me;
And all my heart
       Cries, "O the sea,   70
And O the ship
       Was home to me!"

* I remember the sailors in ear-rings. I even remember men who wore
queues,[2] and who sometimes begged ribbons of me to tie them. I also
have recollections of men with their hair in plaits worn piled up under
their hats, but slipped down inside their smocks as they worked. Some
of these came from Yarmouth in the north of England. They carried   n5
snuff-boxes and were either dry-salters[3] or net-fishers. The others, the
ones with queues, chewed nail-rod tobacco and were deep-sea men. They
sailed wide oceans and told strange stories of far-off countries. I have a
bunch of tiny charms one such, who wore long flittering "drops," gave
me. I remember many men with Spanish and Indian filigree ear-rings,   n10
as well as with "sleepers" and jewelled "drops."[4]
   "What is filigree?" I asked, and was told. To this day I never hear
the word without seeing a stiff little queue, a dark, sea-tanned face, and
beyond these the shadowy form of a Spanish West Indian woman who
had worn the "filigrees" she had given with love to a man, who, even in n15
Australia, wore them for her sake.

(24 April 1931)   *Copy-text:* UW   *Collated states:* None

[2] Single pigtails.
[3] Fishermen whose catch was to be dry-cured with salt, e.g. herrings.
[4] Types of ear-rings: long dangling drops or small plain sleepers inserted to maintain
piercing; filigree ones were made of fine twisted silver thread.

K61   WAR[*][1]

Out in the dust he lies;
    Flies in his mouth,
    Ants in his eyes . . .

[1] See volume 1, Introduction, p. xlvi and n. 37.

I stood at the door
  Where he went out;   5
Full-grown man,
  Ruddy and stout;

I heard the march
  Of the trampling feet,
Slow and steady   10
  Come down the street;

The beat of the drum
  Was clods on the heart,
For all that the regiment
  Looked so smart!   15

I heard the crackle
  Of hasty cheers
Run like the breaking
  Of unshed tears,

And just for a moment,   20
  As he went by,
I had sight of his face,
  And the flash of his eye.

He died a hero's death,
  They said,   25
When they came to tell me
  My boy was dead;

But out in the street
  A dead dog lies;

(2 April 1916)   *Copy-text:* UW   *Collated states:* Bn, 5 April 1917, p. 3 as THE MOTHER (*A*)
Wr, 26 April 1917, p. 11 as THE MOTHER, signed Mary Gilmore (in "The Bulletin") (*B*)
Not otherwise recorded: The first and penultimate stanzas in *A* are followed by a line
of four dots.
1 dust] street *A*   lies;] ~— *A*   **2** Flies] Blood *A B*   **3** Ants] Dust *A B*   **3** eyes
. . .] ~. *A B*   **5** out;] ~, *A*   ~: *B*   **7** stout;] ~. *A B*   **8** march] sound *A*
9 trampling] marching *A*   **10** steady] ~, *A B*   **11** street;] ~. *A B*   **13** heart,]
~; *B*   **15** smart!] ~. *B*   **17** cheers] ~, *A*   **18** Run] As they rose *A B*
19 unshed] crushed *A*   tears,] ~. *A*   ~; *B*   **20** moment,] second *B*   **22** face,]
~ *B*   **27** dead;] ~. *A B*

Flies in his mouth,   30
Ants in his eyes.

[*] On the afternoon of the day on which this was written I passed a
little dog lying dead and swollen in Pitt Street. And on the same date,
two years later, when the verse appeared in *The Bulletin*, just such
another little dog lay dead in Hunter Street, "flies in his mouth, ants
in his eyes."   n5

---

30 Flies] Blood *A B*   in] on *A*   **31** Ants] Dust *A B*   **n1–5** On . . . eyes."]
Om. A B

к62   A SONG OF YOUTH

O ye wild dreams, wild dreams of youth that rise
Like smoke unseen above a sunlit fire,
How with the flame of living ye aspire!
And though through passing years young heads grow wise,
Time takes, and gives not back, not even in mime,   5
The golden glamour of the early prime.

Then was the moon a silver bell, the sun
A shield, the starry heavens a bannered camp,
And every lumbering horse, that trudged in tramp,
Became a steed in gay caparison,   10
E'en though the clanking chain betrayed his race,
As heavy-hoofed he clumped the market-place.

How sweet is woodland singing when the song
The heart once raised is mute! . . . Silent within,
We note th' external choristers begin;   15
So, when the hours of night grow strange and long,
How dear the cloudy alps of dawn to sight.
But youth lies deep in dream, nor asks the light.

Dreams are the leap of life; the old forget,
And seek no more the golden path whereon   20
Space loses bound, and time, in hurrying gone,

(n. d.)   *Copy-text: UW*   *Collated states:* None
10 caparison *Ed.*] comparison *X*

Knows not the slow-clocked hours the hard years set,
To tell the slack pulse, lagging down life's stair,
How far behind it fancies once thought fair.

O, if the flame could last! Could keenness live,   25
And lift the flagging powers that still must bear
The burden of long travail as they wear
To end! If but that love's imperative
Still in its fresh young errantry might go,
Dreams in its eyes, its burning heart at glow!   30

O dreams of youth—so like the bird of air—
The fowler, life, pursues to net you down! . . .
For age, the groves it walked are sere and brown,
The trees that filled its woods are ringed and bare;
It turns and looks toward another dawn,   35
Where cypress shadows lengthen on the lawn.

But thou, O youth, so gay, so debonair!
Thou gift and glory of the prime the gods
Gave man that he might better bear the rods
Of adverse fate, the dew is on thy hair,   40
And at thy breast, a silver bell, the moon
Calls *Wake! . . . Awake! . . .* O youth, wake not too soon!

к63   POOR TOM O' BEDLAM[1]

He came, caught up in the fold of a lost mind's veil,
    And now he sits beside the little door of dream;
He hears no sound but the sound of the suns in trail,
    And the ripple of stars in stream.

"I have held the universe in my hand (he said,)   5
    And I have looked into space and have kept my sight;

(31 January 1931)   *Copy-text: UW   Collated states: SMH*, 16 May 1931, p. 9 (*A*)
5 said,)] ~), *A*

---

[1] Crazy beggar: from London's Bethlehem (Bedlam) Hospital for the insane, founded 1247, and Edgar's role in *King Lear* (II. 3. 5–21 and III. 4 from line 35). K63 owes more to Romantic ideas of the madman as visionary.

And I have seen might fall like a leaf that is shed,
   Or a strickle² of grass in flight.

"I have gone forth on the winds of the world, wing-spread,
   Till I have heard the challenge of conquering time;   10
Then I have turned and watched the atom called man (he said,)
   By the stem of a wheat-straw climb.

"I have been where the small frail hand of man took hold,
   Though the buffet of th' Eternal shook all things great;
And I have seen man shrink like a worm in the cold,   15
   Though he shattered the rocks like slate . . ."

He goes, caught up in the folds of a dreamer's veil,
   Poor Tom o' Bedlam, the salt in all wistful eyes;
He hears the sound of the suns as they sweep in trail,
   And the ripple of stars that rise.   20

---

7 might] night *A*   **10** heard] met *A*   **11** said,)] ~), *A*   **13** small frail]
human *A*   of man] *Om. A*   took] has taken *A*   **17** folds] fold *A*

---

² Bundle; more commonly *strick*: see I39 n. 2.

K64   A POET SANG

What is this magic men have praised,
   Crying it round the world,
Like gaberlunzie's¹ chanting, crazed,
   Old rants the Gael skirled?²

What is this beauty Helen had?—   5
   Made Cleopatra wine?—

(6 December 1927)   *Copy-text: UW*   *Collated states: Wr,* 14 December 1927, p. 5
as SOMEWHERE A POET SANG (*A*)

1 magic] beauty *A*   praised,] ~ *A*   **2** world,] ~ *A*   **3** gaberlunzie's chanting]
singing gaberlunzies *A*   **4** Old . . . Gael] Where some mad piper *A*   **5** had?—]
~, *A*   **6** wine?—] ~? *A*

---

¹ Strolling beggar or mendicant.
² The Celts (Irish and Scots) played on the bagpipes ('skirled').

Somewhere a poet sang, half-mad,
And made the flesh divine.[3]

7 half-mad] half sad *A*

---

[3] Lines 5–8 argue that poets turn mere women into the legendary, intoxicating beauties Helen of Troy (see J16 n. 3 and H65 lines 45–6) and Cleopatra, destroyer of the Roman virtues of Mark Antony.

K65   THE PITILESS

Strange with what worship
    Men will kneel,
To a hank of hair,
    And a will of steel!

No storms betray her shallow calm,   5
    No tempests break;
And yet she held, within her palm,
    Love who went hungry for her sake.

(28 September 1924)   *Copy-text: UW*   *Collated states:* None

K66   COURAGE

Grave were her eyes,
    I knew none graver;
Brave was her heart,
    I knew none braver;
For she forsook one love had proved,   5
Lest from his height, him, love had moved.

(12 June 1930)   *Copy-text: UW*   *Collated states:* None

κ67   THE SUICIDE

I am that man, who, in an hour of grief,
Tore from his book of life its one blank leaf;
Now am I left without the page, whereon
The one thing, that I fain would write, had gone.

(10 June 1930)   *Copy-text: UW*   *Collated states:* None

κ68   EPITAPH ON AN INFANT

Weep not for me that I soon went,
Like to a water-brook soon spent;
But say that in this world I could not stay,
Lest I should fear to haste from it away.

(10 June 1930)   *Copy-text: UW*   *Collated states:* None

κ69   THE ADOLESCENT

All that he was behind him lies,
    A lad who stands upon life's brink;
Lost in the glens that are her eyes,
    Only he knows that thirst would drink.

(12 May 1931)   *Copy-text: UW*   *Collated states:* None

κ70   LIFE AND DEATH

I

When death poor love devours,
    How brazenly they moan,
And lay the bed with flowers,
    Who let love die alone!

II

How death across the earth   5
    Sweeps on as though his wave
Were all! And then comes birth,
    And digs for him a grave.

III

Naked as any worm,
    Man from the womb comes forth;   10
Who only in storm
    Can measure his worth.

IV

Death as a conqueror came—
    Whom, life, like a flame
From an ash in the dark,   15
    Struck with his spark.

V

O life, how I have loved
    Thy ravaged face!
Now am I moved
    By death's cold grace.   20

(25 January 1931)   *Copy-text: UW*   *Collated states:* None

K71   THE DEAD HARLOT

O men, tread softly as you pass,
    For here one lies
Whose heart was but a shadowed glass,
    To hold your eyes.

She with her secret look called man,   5
    As his dark need called her;
She had her dream; now no dream can
    Her dust, low-fallen, stir.

All that she was she gave, till naught
　　Of her was left to give;　　　　　　　　　10
She flung herself to those who sought;
　　She died that they might live.

O men, tread softly as you pass,
　　Where low she lies;
Bruise not above her head the grass;　　　15
　　She had love's eyes.

(17 February 1926)　*Copy-text: UW*　*Collated states:* None

K72   BURNT OUT

Staid in her ways, to-day;
　　Hair, middle part;
Done in an old-fashioned way
　　Once thought so smart.

Waist still "a span of three";[1]　　　　　5
　　Figure, "the Queen's"—
Braced as it used to be,
　　Back in her teens.

Mild in her manner, as
　　Mild in her speech,　　　　　　　　　10
Who would have thought she was
　　Once a town leech?[2]

So one asks, wondering,
　　If, from dead fires,
Wake with a sudden spring　　　　　　　15
　　Ancient desires;

What she remembers, and
　　What she forgets;

[1] Three handspans in circumference.
[2] Harpy who leeches the vitality out of men.

> If, for an old demand,
>   Sometimes she frets.   20

(19 December 1925)   *Copy-text: UW*   *Collated states:* None

K73   A CHANT FOR ANZAC DAY[1]

By the waters of Babylon we sat down and wept,
    And we hanged our harps upon the willow trees;[2]
For there we grieved for thee, O Zion, and them that slept
    Where no hand in the darkened doors may turn the keys.

But though awhile they lay alone as dust, wind-drifted,   5
    Who went to death like forest leaves that fall and flake,
Yet to thy gates, O Zion, have their names been lifted,
    And in thy courts shall they, the sleepers, all awake.

Now, therefore, though by strange waters we have sat down
        and wept,
    From the willow trees we have taken again the harp,   10
That we may sing the song of them that are one Sept,[3]
    In the Five Great Wounds,[4] the trench, and the broken scarp.

(12 November 1928)   *Copy-text: UW*   *Collated states: SMH*, 23 April 1932, p. 9 (*A*)
3 For] And *A*   **4** Where no hand in] Behind *A*   may turn] wherein none lifts
A   **5** dust,] ~ *A*   wind-drifted] wind drifted *A*   **9** have] *Om. A*   **11** that]
who *A*   one] One *A*

[1] MS in NLA 727 2/4/19 has been misfiled among war poems from 1940.
[2] See K23 n. 2.   [3] A division of a nation or tribe, a clan.
[4] Those suffered by Christ in the Crucifixion; for his sacrifice compared to that of fallen
soldiers in World War I, see E99 n. 1.

K74   A CHILD'S GRIEF

"She was so strong," they said;
"She did not feel the pang,
 Nor suffered she as they!"—
She who, so sensitive,

Felt for the trodden grass,   5
And wept a robbed bird's grief;
She, the derided, whose one strength
Was fear, whose only hope
Lay in her power to hide, withdrawn,
From all their bitter jibes and scorn.   10

"She was so strong," they said,
"Nor suffered she as they . . ."
Yet her bruised heart,
Broken with childhood's wrongs,
Ached till her head was grey.   15

(3 February 1929)   *Copy-text: UW*   *Collated states:* None

K75   SHE DWELT SERENE AS THOUGH APART[1]

She dwelt serene, as though apart,
In the warm garden of her heart;
There all the flowers were flowers of love,
And every bird a dove.

There the loud clamour of our lives   5
Came not, for ev'n as bees in hives
Was she, or as the house-built bird,
Nest-holden and unstirred.

Kind hands she ever had, whose palms
Were those where fear its own fear calms;   10
And whom they held went comforted,
Although no word was said.

Judgment she had, as ever such
Deep women have, but at a touch
The doors of pity in her heart   15
Flew open wide apart.

No creaking charity was hers;
No grudging help, that slowly stirs

And brings the suppliant to shame,
Ever from her hand came;   20

So, comforted a child might run
In haste to her, a man undone
Lay on her knee his head, his tear
All that her heart would hear.

And all day long she did her tasks   25
With that dear diligence that asks
Not to be great, but to fulfil
In love and life one will.

I could not wish for her, how great,
A wider world than this estate—   30
Who fanned, as eve by evening came,
Hearth-fire and love's deep flame.

(10 May 1932)   *Copy-text: UW*   *Collated states:* None
22 In *Ed.*] Its *x*

---

[1] MG wrote to Nettie Palmer on 20 September 1932 : ' "She dwelt Serene" was written at
top speed to get another thing taken out of the galley proofs. Its date is 10.5.32. Most of the
book was written '30 and '31 and '32' (*Letters* 90). It recalls one of William Wordsworth's
'Lucy' poems, the (untitled) 'She dwelt among the untrodden ways' (1800).

к76   BLACK BREAD OF NIGHT[1]

Black bread of night,
The bread of black despair;
Black bread of night
What foulness do ye wear!
The evil that men do   5
Rises like yeast within,

(25 January 1924)   *Copy-text: UW*   *Collated states: Wr*, 6 February 1924, p. 5 (*A*)
Not otherwise recorded: A adds the note: 'If I remember rightly, at the inquiry held some
years ago into the claims for night-baking, it was stated that 28 loaves more could be got
out of a bag of flour by night-baking than by day-baking. These represented water!!'
3 night] ~, *A*

---

[1] MG wrote to Nettie Palmer on 20 September 1932: 'That "Black Bread of Night" ran

So that, who eats of you,
He eats that death may win.

Black bread of night,
Denier of the sun;   10
Black bread of night
Where dreadful evils run,
Shall we not cry of you,
Unclean! Unclean! Unclean![2]
And lay the sweetening rue   15
Where your dark lot has been?

Black bread of night! . . .
Give unto us, alway,
The kind bread of the light,
The clean face of the day!   20
Above night's baking floor
What evil things have been;
Behind its bolted door
The darkness breeds obscene.

---

7 that,] ~ *A*   you,] ~ *A*   **11** night] ~, *A*   **12** dreadful evils] evils oozing *A*
13 you,] ~ *A*   **14** *Unclean! . . . Unclean!*] **Unclean! Unclean! Unclean!** *A*
15 sweetening] shaming *A*   **16** lot] way *A*   **17** night! . . .] ~! — *A*   **18** us,
alway,] ~ ~ *A*   **22** What] Creep *A*   have been] unseen *A*   **24** obscene]
unclean *A*

---

away from me, and became, before the middle of it, the black bread of the night of the
street. Themes do that with one sometimes' (*Letters* 90).

[2] Traditional warning cry of lepers.

K77   THE DECOY[*]

How shall their longing tell itself aloud,
     Their love declare its pain?
For they are broken, who were proud,
     And all their poor pretences vain.

The opening bud, moved by a passing air,   5
     Pours outward on it odours sweet;

The haunting bee discerns it there,
    And circles toward it ere it fleet.

In the dark forests where they roam,
    Lions lift tawny heads upon   10
The wind their quivering nostrils comb—
    And each finds there what draws him on.

Within the marches where the swans deploy,
    Or turning seek a wider waste,
Nature still sets her old decoy,   15
    And calls on laggard life to haste.

So in the streets the scented courtesan
    Declares herself, and what she is;
And, through the nostrils of the man,
    Makes him her prey, as she is his.   20

But the high-conscious may not turn again
    To loose the wiles of beast and bird;
For they have made a crown of pain,
    And fenced a hunger with a word.

They have stepped out from olden ways, and taught   25
    Young lips to long, young thoughts to yearn,
Yet ordered eyes to hide, besought,
    And perfume but in secret burn.

So must their fortress ever find defence,
    And watch and keep a thousand gates;   30
They make an ambush of pretence,
    And flee what all their being waits.

---

[*] Anyone accustomed to the bush, in the earlier days when it teemed
with life could tell at once what fur or feather smell came on the air.
Musk-duck, wood-duck, teal, widgeon, or swan, all were different, just
as 'possum, kangaroo, iguana, koala or emu were different. I have often
caught the smell of a 'possum or an iguana, and pointed him out in his   n5
tree, when I was a child. It is the same with all fur and feather. If you go
to the Botanical Gardens of Sydney and stand near either swan or emu
enclosure, you will catch the different feather smell at once.

(21 October 1926)   *Copy-text:* UW   *Collated states:* None

K78   MY LITTLE ONE WHO WAS MY SON

I

Whom have I here? This man
　　With strong and hasty tread,
　　Whose eyes, above my head
Look on another span
Than where his life began,   5
Is this my son, my little one?

O time, how ye have robbed
　　This heart, these empty arms
That o'er his smallness throbbed,
　　When, sick for love's alarms,   10
Love's fearful anguish sobbed
Its grief o'er him, my little son!

Now comes this man, to whom
　　I am but one beside
The road—a hostel-room   15
　　My heart—who would have died
To shield from evil doom
The little one who was my son!

His step outpaces mine,
　　Which, could I run, were still   20
Too slow for me to twine
　　My arm with his uphill!
(*How cold life's wintry chill*
As years creep on, my little son!)

This man's thought passes me,   25
　　And ranges out, alone,
Fields where his young eyes see,
　　'Midst seed that I have sown,
Seed, never mine to free—
O, little one, who was my son!   30

Yet whence this man? Not this
   The child I bore, which day
By day found all his bliss
   Where in my arms he lay,
And only asked my kiss—   35
My little son, my tender one!

Then were my arms his fold!
   Then was my heart his haven!
Now fears he neither cold
   Nor storm, nor wind's wild raven—   40
Whom these hands once could hold,
My son, my son, my little one!

II

Not mine, grown old in tears,
   Not mine to bind on him
The burden of my years,   45
   Who on th' horizon's rim
Sees clear where my eye peers!

Not mine to call to earth
   This searcher of the sky,
Whose wing to gather worth   50
   Full-stretched must lift and fly;
Not mine, by mine own dearth,[1]
   To strain him to a tie.

O, if love could but know
   It must not hold to hurt;   55
Free what must onward go,
   And its own self desert;
And, when its pulse falls slow,
   Gird, though it go ungirt!

Therefore, not mine to chain—   60
   To weight these urgent feet
That will so soon find pain
   Where freedom seems so sweet;

[1] Lack, poverty.

Which, when he most would gain,
Must still find stress to meet.   65

Only I ask that he,
When he in fullness grow,
Sometimes remember me;
Sometimes look back as though
His heart my heart would know.   70

(20 December 1924)   *Copy-text: UW   Collated states:* None

K79   DIED IN HOSPITAL

She died—she died before her child was born,
And at the morn
The grumbling undertaker's men came out,
And stood about
That poor dead body in its scanty shift,   5
And with a drift
Of idle talk mocked the dead woman, there,
That she was bare.

She died before her child was born; and, so,
Her poor head low,   10
Her outline showed, as stark she lay, the round
Form of a mound;
Showed how the tender frozen breasts stood up,
Each like a cup
Some hasty hand had overturned, and left,   15
Ah, how bereft!

But, O, her knees! her poor thin fallen knees!
The cold white breeze

(2 April 1926)   *Copy-text: UW   Collated states: Tri* (September 1926), p. 31 (*A*)
Not otherwise recorded: A is in italics throughout.
1 born,] *born; A*   11 stark she lay] *she lay there A*   12 a] *Om. A*
15 overturned,] *overturned A*   17 O] *Oh A*

That o'er them swept was not more chill than they—
Her wasted clay—   20
Left there exposed for strange men's hands and eyes
To vulgarise.

What grief to think that one of woman born
Lay so forlorn!

19 o'er] *o've A*   than] *then A*   **22–3** vulgarise.// What] *vulgarise./ What A*
23 born] *born: A*

к80   JOY ALL HER NAME

Softly, as though one still might hear
On the retreating wind love's last
Low accents calling to the ear
Of memory from an old past,
So softly came to earth,   5
Joy, in an infant's birth.

And like the petal of a flower
Slow falling down, and like the brush
Of dove's wings in the aery nower,[1]
And like the silky, silken hush   10
Of winds upon the wheat,
So light were the small feet
Of her who to earth came,
And Joy we named her name.

And whiter than the snow upon   15
Far mountain sills, and whiter than
The moonlit cloud that floating on
The ether spreads in silver fan,
And white as meerschaum[2] sea,
So wonder-white is she—   20

[1] See I4 n.1.
[2] Foaming (from German *Meerschaum*, meaning *sea-foam*).

She who to find earth came,
And Joy we named her name.

And like the cool shade where the vine
Throws on the clod its patterned shape
Like hands, and soft as moss where twine   25
The woodbines o'er the streams their crape,[3]
So cool the tender lips,
So soft the finger-tips,
Of her who to earth came,
And Joy we named her name.   30

(23 March 1930)   *Copy-text: UW*   *Collated states:* None

---

[3] Anglicised spelling of French *crêpe*, a fine fabric of twisted silk, used as material in mourning veils.

K81   LOVE HAS A STRENGTH

Hush, hush, little babe, O hush thee!
    Wild is the storm without!
I dare not hear with it thy cry,
    As it raves with windy rout!
    So hush then! Sleep then!   5
        As lullaby
        Sing I.

Sleep, little love! Soon dawn will bring
    The swallow to the eave;
The tempest shall have passed away,   10
    And the winds no longer grieve.
    O hush then! Sleep then!
        While lullaby
        Sing I.

Love has a strength beyond the flaw,   15
    Love has a lamp to trim,
It shall bring father home, although
    In the storm seas leapt at him.

So hush then! Sleep then!
While lullaby   20
Sing I.

(29 June 1930)   *Copy-text: UW   Collated states:* None

κ82   OUT ON THE HILLSIDE[1]

Summer will come with its warm, clear light,
    And the long grasses wave;
But O, may the rain fall soft, to–night,
    On that little last grave.

Nay! he is wrapped and warm in his nest,   5
    He would not hear the rain;
It is only I would know no rest,
    If it beat on the pane.

But, rain, if thou fall, O softly fall,
    Wet not too soon the mould,   10
Lest I should listen to hear him call,
    Crying out in the cold.

(15 June 1930)   *Copy-text: UW   Collated states: SV (A)*
3 soft,] ~ *A*   to–night,] tonight *A*   **5** he] He *A*

[1] R. D. FitzGerald wrote to MG on 11 February 1940: 'It is obviously right in the fore-front of your best work – and yet, as you say, easy for men to pass over. A man might feel like that and yet never write like that, or appreciate a piece like that unless brought right under his nose. I don't know. Please Heaven I never will know: the youngest of my three kiddies is 7 months old. It is a very moving lyric, flawlessly executed' (ML Papers vol. 12).

κ83   IN HEAVEN

There is a lonely place in heaven,
    A garden fair,
More beautiful than words can tell,
    Yet empty air.

There no birds sing, although   5
  A wind goes by;
No wandering bee hums there,
  No light winds sigh.

Still as an ice-floe in a dream,
  Still as the dead;   10
Still as the silence of a tomb,
  Where naught is said,

Still as the Frozen Lands,
  The sun gone out,
Still as the level cloud,   15
  Aloof in drought,

Still as the thin look of the blind,
  Asking lost light,
Empty as poor dumb, seeking hands,
  Dark in the night—   20

There is a lonely place,
  It has no name,
Kept like a cradle bed,
  Where no babe came;

And there come women seeking: *"Heard*   25
  You not a cry? . . ."
"Came not a little foot
  Pattering by? . . ."

"Did not a baby's hand
  Touch as it went? . . ."   30
"Hush! Hush! for a crying,
  Feeble and spent! . . ."

There is a lonely place in heaven,
  Like white robes kept unworn;
Empty as hoarded garments held,   35
  Where babes were never born;

And there come women walking,
  Seeking in heaven the stir

(O memory the most forlorn!)
   Of babes that never were.   40

(17 January 1920)   *Copy-text: UW*   *Collated states:* None

κ84 THE HEART'S CRY

Give me, she said, my earthen floor,
   The sun on its rough slab walls;
Keep you the splendour your poets score,
   Your tessellated[1] halls.

I ask, she said, my hut on the rise,   5
   My kindly cows to milk,
With their creamy breath, their friendly eyes,
   Their skins that shine like silk.

Give me the rustling corn at night,
   As the light winds play, and over;   10
Give me by day the kestrel's flight,
   His poise to an instant hover;

Give me, she said, the kind old place,
   The eaves where the winds blow under,
And stars that gleam where the leaves enlace   15
   In lattices of wonder;

Give me, she said, my simple cot,[2]
   I do not ask some towering height;
Only I ask my own familiar lot,
   My man come home at night.   20

(1 October 1921)   *Copy-text: UW*   *Collated states:* None

---

[1] Expensive flooring, patterned with small blocks of variously coloured material, as in Roman villas.   [2] Cottage.

K85   THE CRY OF THE PROUD

Will there come peace at last,
   And a quiet mind,
With the storms all past,
   And the road defined?
And shall I be there   5
   As one curtained in,
With nothing to share,
   And nothing to win?

Shall I be as a house
   With the lights put out,   10
Where scarcely a mouse
   Comes moving about—
I, whose heart was full
   As a school of noise,
Shall I sit as the null,   15
   In endless poise?

Ah! if the calm ape death,
   Let the end come soon;
Not merely in breath
   Life counts as a boon;   20
But in combat fierce,
   And in hard things done,
In the thorns that pierce—
   And the conflict won!

(16 December 1926)   *Copy-text: UW*   *Collated states:* None

к86   PENELOPE[1]

Twice I waked in the night,
    Feeling if you were there—
Softly touched your cheek,
    Softly kissed your hair;
Then turned to sleep again,   5
    Lying against your arm,
Just as a child might do,
    Fearing nor hurt, nor harm.

No fastened windows, now,
    No bolting down the door,   10
Shaking at every sound
    Of creaking chair and floor;
No watchful, wistful sleep,
    Anxious, ever on guard,
Waked if only a dog   15
    Moved in a neighbour's yard!

No start at a rattling blind,
    No holding back the breath,
Fearful of some menace
    Crueller far than death!   20
All of it gone! and why?
    Somebody's home at last!
. . . Strange how real the fear;
    Stranger still that it passed.

(5 March 1919)   *Copy-text: UW*   *Collated states: Tri* (April 1919), p. 48 (*A*)
1 Twice] (For the TRIAD.)// Twice *A*   night,] ~ *A*   **2** there—] ~, *A*
4 kissed] touched *A*   hair;] ~— *A*   **6** arm,] ~ *A*   **8** Fearing] Knowing *A*
nor . . . nor] no *A*   **9** windows,] ~ *A*   **11** Shaking] Quaking *A*   **20** Crueller
far] ~, ~, *A*   death!] ~; *A*   **21** All of it] But all that *A*   and] And *A*
23 . . . Strange] ~ *A*   **24** Stranger still] ~, ~, *A*

[1] The wife whose anxious waiting is relieved by her husband's return, typified by
Penelope, long-suffering wife of Ulysses in Homer's *Odyssey*.

κ87   LONE

I had come home,
Home to my house;
Only was heard the beetle's hum,
The scud of a mouse.

I had come home,   5
Home as of yore;
Nor knew, till I entered in, how lone
The familiar floor.

(20 February 1930)   *Copy-text: UW*   *Collated states:* None

κ88   DREAMS WERE HER PORTION

Dreams were her portion, O Death
   Be kind to her now,
Here where, alone, she awaits
   Thy touch on her brow!

There will come never again   5
   One with so full a heart,
In whom loving and giving
   So much were a part.

Yet dreams were her portion;
   Tears salted her breath: 10
O thou, in thy coming,
   Be kind to her, Death.

(25 September 1929)   *Copy-text: UW*   *Collated states:* None

κ89   OF WOMEN

You who wrought me ill,
You who brought me grief,

You I remember with anger like flame,
Do I hate you? How can I tell.
Only I know that at sound of your name
I tremble like a leaf;
Only I know, when I hear your voice on the air,
My heart like a wound
Is broken there!

(25 September 1917)   *Copy-text: UW   Collated states:* None

K90   ANDREAS

Though to your heart I came not home,
Yet, at the last, I knew it home.
Now in the twilight hour I dream,
Seeing your look, that never was born,
In the eyes of children
Yours and mine.

(16 March 1917)   *Copy-text: UW   Collated states: Wr,* 16 May 1923, p. 5 AS ANDREA
(*A*)

2 knew] know *A*   **3** twilight] ~, *A*   hour] still, *A*   dream,] ~ *A*   **4** look,] ~ *A*
5 children] ~, *A*

K91   MINE ENEMY

In my prayer I have kept mine enemy,
To God I have spoken him fair;
For I could not leave him naked and bare,
Alone with my hate, like a frightened hare!

For my own soul's sake I have set him free;
I could not have him lost, because of me:
I have covered him up with a robe of prayer,
Lest the hounds of my hate go hunting there.

(22 November 1927)   *Copy-text: UW   Collated states:* None

K92   THE RETURN

I shall come back, some day,
    And I shall sit in the pew,
Where they, who are now away,
    Sat when the church was new.

I shall see, as of old   5
    The sunlight stream through the pane,
With the great saints aureoled,[1]
    And the Lamb without stain.

And I shall whisper, when
    The Commandments shall be read,   10
The plea as of old—Amen!—
    At the solemn words said.

I shall come back again!
    Though strangers sit in their places,
I shall see, unchanged, and plain,   15
    The old familiar faces.

Many a well-thumbed book
    Will speak of a hand long gone,
And many a stranger's look
    Seem one love pondered on.   20

There will my mother come,
    My father stand as of old,
Young whisp'rers fallen dumb,
    Still by his look controlled.

And there will kneel, unchanged,   25
    Lost love, whatever else changed be,
Forgiving and unestranged,
    Though the strange fetter me.

(30 August 1926)   *Copy-text: UW*   *Collated states:* None
―――――――
[1] Haloed in gold; 'the Lamb' (next line) is Christ: see J21 n. 4.

K93   AN OLD SONG[1]

"Long, long ago, in this old town,
My dear love walked in her white gown."— (Old Song).

Long, long ago,
In this old town,
My dear love walked
In her white gown;
Long is she gone,   5
Lone am I left,
Like a tall tree
Storm hath bereft.

Long, long ago,
In this old town,   10
My dear love walked
In her white gown;
Into my eyes
She looked her love;
Warm in the heart   15
Of my dear dove!

Under the tall
Green leaves we went,
She like a lily
Slenderly bent;   20
Under the tall
Green leaves we stood,
Lint-white[2] her face,
Under her hood.

She was so sweet,   25
In her white gown,
Who walked with me
In this old town;
Moonlight, starlight . . .
. . . Now, she is gone;   30
Quenched the light where
Her dear eyes shone.

> *Long, long ago,*
> *In this old town,*
> *My dear love walked*   35
> *In her white gown.*

(8 November 1923)   *Copy-text: UW*   *Collated states:* None

[1] See I76 n. 1.   [2] White as lint (a soft fabric made from flax); rare adjective (*OED*).

K94   THE JEWEL[1]

They came to woo the King's daughter
With heralds full a score,
The men-at-arms they came behind,
The knights they went before.

The suitors bent to make their pleas,   5
They poured out gems like water;
All except one, who silent stood,
Looking at the King's daughter.

Noble and knight, and chieftain bold,
Harpers to sing their fame,   10
They came with banners like the sun,
They fell away like flame.

All except one who silent stood,
Looking at the King's daughter;
He made no move, he spoke no word,   15
Though all the others sought her.

Suitor by suitor came and went,
Each passed before the throne,
All except him—and, in the end,
He stood in the hall alone.   20

He stood so straight, he stood so tall,
And a strong right arm he brought her;

[1] See I76 n. 1.

But still he said not any word,
Looking at the King's daughter.

I think she trembled where she sat,   25
As he stepped by the floor;
I think, when he bent and took her hand,
I think she trembled more.

"What gift," said the King, "what gift ha' ye,
That ye bring to the King's daughter?"   30
"I bring the jewel of my heart," he said,
And with that jewel he bought her.

(7 March 1920)   *Copy-text: UW*   *Collated states:* None

K95   I SHALL GIVE FOR THY SAKE

Though all should turn from thee
Whom the world wounded,
Thy wounds shall draw from me,
Of love, depths yet unsounded.

And when thou feel'st the pain   5
Of pride itself forsaking,
I shall there lift again,
Up from its fall, the breaking.

For know, so true is love,
So faithful in its daring,   10
Whispers no plea above,
So fond in its declaring.

Ah, when my prayer I make,
Like a child kneeling,
I shall give, for thy sake,   15
My heart's unsealing.

(2 September 1927)   *Copy-text: UW*   *Collated states:* None

K96   WHEN AS WITH CHARITY YE DWELL

Some day, when I shall be dead, they will write
And say, "We, too, once knew her!" And will tell
Of things remembered still, though comes the night
That brings forgetfulness to strike their knell.
When on such words in charity ye dwell,   5
Let one with greater charity recite,
Among the things admitted I did well,
Or sung with pride as greater singers might,
How in some little human way I fell—
Lest winter on my memory light.   10

(16 September 1928)   *Copy-text: UW*   *Collated states: Wr*, 3 October 1928, p. 5 as
EXPERIMENTS IN VERSE (*A*)

1 they] you *A*   **2** And will] and will *A*   **3** still] long *A*   though comes] or
ere *A*   **4–5** to . . . knell./ When] declares its spell.// And *A*   **5** on . . . in] yet,
as there with *A*   **6** Let one] One let *A*   **7** admitted I did] that I have most
done *A*   **8** singers] poets *A*   **10** on] all *A*   light.] smite./ . . . The knell/
Would be less dead were love warm on the swell/ Where the dull toll of death
defines in flight./ But O, when spades shall mound me in my cell,/ Who so have
loved my kind, may earth fall light! *A*

K97   LANGUAGE

I

Say now, Horatio, has language hours?[1]
Sleeps it awhile, to wake again renewed,
As chrysalids pupate the many-hued?[2]
Or does it, man-like, mellow ageing powers?

(10 May 1919)   *Copy-text: UW*   *Collated states: Bn*, 20 November 1919, Red Page
as OF LANGUAGE (*A*)   Lavater, Pt II only, as WORDS (*B*)   *SV* (*c*)

(**0.1–14.1**) I . . . II] *Om. B*   **0.1** I] (FOR THE BULLETIN.)// I. *A*   **1** Say] How *A*
Horatio,] Horatius! *A*   has] Hath *A*   **4** does it] aging *A*   mellow ageing] hath
it mellowed *A*

---

[1] Draws on Shakespeare's Horatio, the man of ordinary good sense confronted with
difficult questions: 'There are more things in Heaven and Earth, Horatio/ Than are
dream't of in your Philosophy' (*Hamlet*, I. 5. 166–7). Cf. MG's use of Penelope in
K86.   [2] Insect larvae ('chrysalids') produce out of the dormancy of their encasing

Sometime, I think, language like time devours   5
The end to which it moved in early mood,
Or wills to utterance a stranger brood,
As flowers are changed to seed, and seed to flowers.
So this raw speech of ours, in use to-day,
Crude as new Must,[3] time-ripened may seem fine   10
As anything we heard great Sidney[4] say,
Or Shakespeare plunder from the Muses nine.
Some future yet may find within this pack
All that these few poor words, so halting, lack.

II

Flower turns to seed, and seed becomes a flower;   15
One seed makes many flowers, one flower much seed!
Thus from a word does mighty thinking breed,
And simple thoughts, to great, increase the dower.
Are not all words old thought new-set to power—
Late-visible where we, late-come, may read,   20
To lose by them the low place of the weed,
And climb, where, if unlearned, our hearts would cower?
Speak not of history in stone! For I
Can show you history written deeper yet:

5 Sometime,] Sometimes *A*   I think,] (I dream) *A*   language] ~, *A*   time]
Time, *A*   6 to which] that earliest *A*   moved . . . mood] urgent wooed *A*
7 Or . . . utterance a] Changing its dandling to still *A*   brood,] ~ *A*   8 are
changed] will change *A*   8–9 flowers./ So] flowers!// And *A*   9 raw] crude *A*
ours,] ~ *A C*   in] we *A*   to-day] today *C*   10 Must] must *A C*   time-ripened]
Time-ripened *A*   12 Shakespeare] Shakspeare *A*   Muses] muses *A*   nine.]
Nine; *A*   ~, *C*   13 Some] While *A*   And some far *C*   yet] times *A*   *Om. C*
may] ~, *A*   *Om. C*   find . . . pack] even here, unpack *A*   14 lack.] ~! *A*
15 becomes] returns— *A*   flower;] ~. *A*   16 seed!] ~. *A*   17 does] shall *A*
18 simple] single *A*   thoughts,] ~ *A B*   great,] words *A*   ~ *B*   dower.] ~, *B*
19 thought] ~, *B*   power—] ~, *A B*   20 Late-visible *A*] Late visible *X C*
21 To lose by] Losing in *A*   low place] habit *A*   weed,] ~ *B*   22 climb,]
climbing *A*   ~ *B*   if] *Om. A*   our hearts would] we still must *A C*
22–3 cower?/ Speak] ~?// ~ *A*   24 yet:] ~— *A*   ~; *C*

---

pupa ('pupate') butterflies and moths ('the many-hued').

[3] New wine or the grape of the juice before fermentation is complete.

[4] Sir Philip Sidney (1554–86), poet, soldier and diplomat, wrote *Arcadia* (1590), *Astrophel and Stella* (1591) and *Defence of Poetry* (1595).

The simple words nor youth nor age forget,   25
Passed lip to lip, as centuries go by;
The caravans of time these leave behind—
Shards[5] from which man makes ladders for the mind.

26 lip,] ~ *A B*   go] went *A*   **27** time] years *A*   behind—] ~, *A*   ~; *B*
28 makes] made *A*

[5] See I2 n. 3.

K98   THE SWAN IN CENTENNIAL PARK (SYDNEY)

How calmly on her floating nest she sits,
And faithful, keeps the entail[1] of a dream,
As, there, the ducks sail idly out in stream,
Or some lone sparrow o'er her island flits!
These she heeds not, but all day long she knits   5
Reed into reed, as though some need supreme,
Lit by love's scarcely comprehended gleam,
Issued life's mandate through unchanging writs.
Though storm about her rage, and thunder tread,
Though traffic loud as battle shout its quest,   10
Yet with each shuttling movement of her head,
Mark how her lovely neck still stoops to thread
Some loosened strand more closely in the nest,
Where broods, o'er life's eternal theme, her breast.

(1 September 1926)   *Copy-text:* UW   *Collated states:* None

[1] See I75 n. 1.

K99   OF BEAUTY[*]

AZALEAS AT WAHROONGA[1]

I have seen beauty where a creviced slat
Gave me the freedom of its fenced abode,

[1] A Sydney suburb.

Mine all the loveliness where blossom glowed,
And light and shadow wove their checkered mat.
And he who master of the garden sat,   5
Who plucked and pruned, and ordered all its mode,
What had he more than I, save that a code
Gave frame to ownership—and only that.
I through the shuttered place looked in and saw—
And beauty dwelt with me, O many a day!   10
I needed not the title-deeds of law
That I might have and hold,[2] and take away!
Give him his fence, give me the eye that sees;
Then, though the skep[3] be his, I have the bees.

[*] Written for Lady Poynter, who wrote *"With the Seasons,"* *"Along the Winding Road,"* *"When Turkey was Turkey,"* and *"Around the Shores of Asia."*[4]

(7 October 1929)   *Copy-text: UW   Collated states: Verse* (May–June 1930), p. 38 as THE GARDEN (no subtitle) (*A*)

2 abode,] ~; *A*   3 where] as *A*   4 wove] made *A*   checkered mat] moving plait *A*   8 that.] ~! *A*   9 shuttered place] slotted fence *A*   11 title-deeds] title deeds *A*   13 fence,] ~; *A*   14 Then . . . the] He but the skep has, I the honey *A*   n1–3 Written . . . *Asia.*] *Om. A*

[2] From *habendum et tenendum* (law Latin), indicating continuance of possession.
[3] A beehive, especially one made of wicker or straw.
[4] Mary Dickenson (1868–1930) married Sir Hugh Poynter (1888–1968) of Sydney in Constantinople in 1905. *When Turkey Was Turkey* (1921) and *Around the Shores of Asia* (1921) are listed under her married name in the British Library catalogue but the other two are unidentified.

K100   LIFE[1]

What part has cruelty in God's good plan,
That it should flaunt itself in fellowship
With power—this black hound in the selfsame slip[2]
Where justice faithful moves, and shapes for man

[1] Buf 170/13 is annotated as arising from 'A discussion as to cruelty which I had with Julian Ashton and Monty Grovers at the [George] Lambert Loan Exhibition' – in 1930 at the NSW State Gallery.
[2] Construction for the building, repairing and launching of ships (more usually *slips*).

His dream of God? What strangely-shaking span   5
'Twixt changing good and ill, what sudden flip
Of time, flings life's progression to a grip
As evil now as when it first began?
Within the sea the waves that onward bear
In fruitful course, the ship, are those that bring   10
It down again to wreck; and why the wreck,
And whose the value none can tell. The air
That upward rears the wing, shatters the wing.
So chaos lays on law its dreadful check.

(26 November 1930)   *Copy-text: UW*   *Collated states:* None

κ101   THE BABE

Why wakens life? And from what bourne[1] was it
Here bidden come—this swallow that in flight
From one world to another, in alight
On man as bough, drops for a while to sit?
The gull's wing measures seas, and the god-wit,   5
Stirred from within, makes conquest of the night,
And marks at dawn his Asian coast in sight;[2]
But who knows how the course of life is writ?
O, in what innocence awakes that which
None yet may call at will, and in what fair   10
And lovely tissue comes it to enrich
With beauty all the world! The bird of air,
Hued to a thousand dyes, pales when compared
Where any babe in loveliness lies bared!

(27 February 1929)   *Copy-text: UW*   *Collated states:* None

---

[1] Territory or domain – properly, boundary or limit – a common misunderstanding of its use in *Hamlet*, III. 1.79–80: 'The undiscover'd country from whose bourn/ No traveller returns'. Cf. J85 line 3 and n. 2.
[2] Cf. I11 author's note.

K102   THE LIVING GRIST[1] OF BREATH

O life, thou battle-ground! O blood, of tides
The summit and the crown! O flesh, thou thorn
Whose woundings ever by thyself are borne,
Say what is man when death from him divides
The deep unsensual self that in him hides?   5
And what to man the immortal, if, forlorn,
Unhoused—as of the flesh he wanders shorn—
Naught that his own frame held in him abides?
Only the lover can forgive; only
The strung chord[2] answers, trembling to a touch;   10
So from life's full moments come the lonely,
And starved is he who never felt too much.
Then what of man if unrelenting death
Take from him all the living grist of breath?

(25 February 1929)   *Copy-text: UW*   *Collated states: SV* (no variants)

[1] Figuratively, a substance that provides benefit in being processed or used – here, the
body.   [2] I.e. a tensed string.

K103   TWO WORLDS WE LIVE IN

Two worlds we live in, one of dreams, and one
Wherein we daily toil. Here the slow plod
Of spade to spade, of step by step, of clod
To clod, moves by a mole's eye,[1] though the sun
Flashes in splendour as the seasons run,   5
And time, who hails him passing golden-shod,

(7 April 1930)   *Copy-text: UW*   *Collated states: Wr*, 21 May 1930, p. 5 (*A*)

1 in,] ~; *A*   **2** Wherein . . . toil] Less than the dreamer's world *A*   Here]
There *A*   **4** though *A*] through *X*   **5** splendour] splendor *A*   as the] down
his *A*   seasons *Ed.*] season's *X*   daily *A*   **6** who . . . passing] watching the swift
feet, *A*   golden-shod] golden shod *A*

[1] Underground creatures, moles are half-blind in daylight.

Mocks the poor hind[2] who bounds by share and sod
His universe, its measure labour done.
And yet the furrow clothes desire, and man
Is winged, not by the vision in escape,   10
But by the patient weaver's homely beam,
The chains that knit the ploughman's horse in span,
And by the calloused hand that yearns to shape,
Yet knows not how, life's deep, unuttered dream.

7 hind *A*] ~: X   8 universe,] ~— *A*   8–9 its . . . done./ And] and dreams of
conquests won.// And *A*   9 desire, and] the dream. And *A*   13 that yearns]
long trained *A*   14 Yet . . . unuttered] From stock and stone, a vision and a *A*

---

[2] Peasant, lowly person.

K104   THE FOX TEMPTATION KNOWETH

How strangely life, forever asked to eat
The bitter rind of pain, the seed of death,
Whose engine is a thought, whose strength is breath,
How strangely is it furnished forth to meet
The long enduring feuds that on it beat!   5
And man, who lifts a harvest from a heath,
Who bids the briary thorn in roses wreath,
Who from the grass has bred the all-conquering wheat,
What powers are his! And yet the ant has store,
The bee has honey in the cell, the fox   10
Temptation knoweth, and an older lore than
These the tree in its ascent unlocks.
And yet, though these have tongues, man's ears hear but
His own; where all these speak, his mind is shut.

(1 March 1929)   *Copy-text: UW*   *Collated states:* None

K105   ABIDES

Adown the centuries still sounds the cry
Of Priam grieving o'er his son, who in
The dust of fatal Ilium lay:[1] the din
Of battle, in a ghostly passing by,
Linking the years where'er a boy's quick sigh   5
Breaks from his burdened heart, as, leaning chin
On hand above his books, for him begin
The glories of a tale that cannot die.
Strange how still aches the heart for Hector's fall,
How each one feels within his own sad bones   10
Love's long-drawn agony, as round the wall
Of Troy slipt that young body o'er the stones!
Abides, while'er life bends that page above,
Eternal pity and immortal love.

(27 August 1929)   *Copy-text: UW*   *Collated states:* None

[1] In the *Iliad*, the Greek Achilles slays the Trojan Hector, oldest son of King Priam, and circles the walls of Troy, dragging the corpse behind his chariot (lines 11–12).

K106   THE ROAD

Bare-armed, strong-thewed,[1] and hardened out by toil,
The road-men as an army stoop and swing,
Their weapons picks and spades that clouting fling
The clay in sudden conquest from the soil.
And as in rhythms of energy they moil,[2]   5
And out of chaos constant order bring,
So too from contest peace itself may spring,
As life is nursed by movements of recoil.

[*cont. overleaf*

(27 February 1929)   *Copy-text: UW*   *Collated states: SV* (*A*)   Pizer (*B*)

4 clay] ~, *A*   conquest] ~, *A*

[1] Strongly muscled.   [2] Labour, work hard.

Yet life no peace ensues, no treaty makes,
Not e'en before that door which shuts away   10
Th' incessant urge where force lifts last—and breaks.
Creation asks no peace, no sheltering bay
Wherein to quiet lie; but hour by hour
It bends, the slave of ever-changing power.

K107   THE CRY OF THE VITAL

Leave me not Life, who from a shallow dust
Raised man, and set him where the rolling spheres
Chant the unchanging circle of the years!
O leave me not! too soon will come the thrust
That puts an end to all the soul's high lust,[1]   5
Too soon will silence fill the hollow ears,
And darkness weight the brow where no eye peers;
The sheet above the bones a mouldered must.[2]

O Life, I have so loved my human kind,
Have loved the day's march tent to tent,   10
And must these go? The grave is dark and blind;
The spender still would spend though all be spent!
O friends, the empty dead have little range—
Remember how I loved this world of change!

(11 May 1919)   *Copy-text: UW   Collated states:* None

[1] Desire (in the earlier, non-pejorative sense).
[2] Mustiness.

K108   THE DREAMER

So careless he of impress left behind,
As time, un-noted, passed him in its flight,
That in but lightest script life seemed to write
Upon the page of his unconscious mind.

And as he dreamed he saw as see the blind,   5
Marking the far untransomed[1] years, whose light
Was the dark splendour of that olden might,
Where boundless pride in unchained power defined.
As hour by hour, spell-drowned he held his place,
He saw the chaptered ruins of the world   10
Rise where the milling wheel of time had hurled;
Unfelt the sun's change on his dreamer's face,
He heard the thunder of the ancient years,
Rolling unbroken on his chambered ears.

(8 November 1923)   *Copy-text: UW*   *Collated states:* None

[1] Unlit: a transom is a fanlight window above a door.

K109   NOT TILL THE HANDS ARE SLACK

Not till the hands are slack, and all the hot
High hopes of life are fallen to the sere,
Do we look back and mark, how, year by year,
The drifts of power rose, ripened, yet were not
Employed or gathered in, but died forgot—   5
Gifts that were once as rich as wheat in ear
Left all to wither, even as in the drear
Of winter fall the leaves to mould and rot.
And when upon life's scantly-written page
We see dark Dissolution lean his hand,   10
And with the pen of Death write, *Make an end!*
With what a sense of anxious dread we wage[1]
Upon our strength, in longing to withstand
Awhile, and out of loss to make—and mend!

(15 November 1931)   *Copy-text: UW*   *Collated states:* None

[1] I.e. make a bet.

K110   MOTHER TO SON

Thou shalt find travail where thou wouldst find rest,
And hunger be thy good to make thee strong;
Thou shalt in weeping shape thy fullest song,
And know in nakedness thy spirit dressed.
Thou shalt be servant where thou camest guest,   5
O little child made man beneath life's thong:[1]
Who, when he standeth least amid the throng,
Is more the surely by himself possessed.
And thou shalt look into thy fellows' eyes,
And read thine own by what therein is writ;   10
And though thou walk where mortal darkness lies,
And though thou stumble where the strong have gone,
Life still hath gifts, for there shall fall upon
Thy soul a dream, and thou shalt answer it.

(26 September 1929)   *Copy-text: UW   Collated states: SV (A)*
1 wouldst] would'st *A*

[1] Strip of leather forming the lash of a whip.

K111   THE SPADE

Though some may reap at last of leisure come
To later years, how many are there left
Whose genius stifles in a narrow cleft,
Dying in darkness, and forever dumb![1]
Thought in a sparrow cage may grow, being fed;   5
But all too oft it pines, slow-starved, and none

(28 May 1919)   *Copy-text: UW   Collated states: Wr, 20 February 1929, p. 5 as
THE SONG (A)*
1 Though some may] HERE do I *A*   of] in *A*   2 years,] ~! *A*   how ... there]
But, O, the many *A*   3 genius stifles] thought must stifle *A*   cleft,] ~— *A*
5 Thought] Song *A*   sparrow] narrow *A*   6 it ... slow-starved] is song unfed *A*

[1] On the general theme cf. F111; lines 9–14 probably refer to John Shaw Neilson (see
F36 and n. 1, F166 and K37).

Comes by to give it aid, so that undone,
Unknown, it lies with the unfruitful dead.
Once there was one, who, in creative mood,
Sang words like jewels on a silver air;   10
Entranced my whole heart listened as I stood;
Then died the sound, and there was nothing there.
Instead, I heard a slow spade strike the earth,
In hungry toil that slew the song at birth.

7 give it aid,] ope the bars; *A*   so that] and, so, *A*   8 Unknown] Unwaked *A*
it lies] song passes *A*   unfruitful] unborn *A*   8–9 dead./ Once] ~.// ~ *A*
9 there was] I heard *A*   one, who,] ~ ~ *A*   mood,] ~ *A*   10 Sang . . . jewels]
Flung notes of silver *A*   silver] golden *A*   air;] ~! *A*   11 my . . . as] I paused to
listen where *A*   12 Then . . . sound,] And then sound died *A*   13 Instead,]
~ *A*   earth,] ~ *A*

K112   THE HALLELUJAH OF WAR[1]

Last year I saw him pass—proud heart—proud head—
Laughter upon his lips and in his eyes;
The new-born colour of the warm sunrise
Flushed all his boy's young face to rosy red.
Firm came the marching feet in steady tread!   5
Who asked on this glad morning to be wise,
When all youth's egotism laughed surprise,
At any anxious look, or word half-said?

Fiercely the savage hail upon him fell,
As, senses reeling, soul upon the rack,   10

(10 May 1919)   *Copy-text: UW   Collated states: Wr*, 5 June 1919, p. 11 as SONGS OF
THE PEOPLE. VII (*A*)[2]

1 pass—] ~, *A*   heart—] ~, *A*   head—] ~! *A*   3 colour] color *A*   4 all . . .
young] on each passing *A*   4–5 red./ Firm] ~.// ~ *A*   5 came . . . steady] feet
of men, came by the passing *A*   tread!] ~— *A*   6 glad] bright *A*   wise,] ~ *A*
7 all youth's] this young *A*   surprise,] ~ *A*   8 any] *Om. A*   look,] ~ *A*
or word] and broken words *A*   half-said?] ~! *A*   9 Fiercely] . . . ~ *A*
10 As,] ~ *A*   upon the rack] that would not slack *A*

[1] Cf. the 'Glory! Glory! Hallelujah!' of 'The Battle Hymn of the Republic' (words by
Julia Ward Howe, 1861).   [2] For the series of which *A* was part, see F28 n. 1.

Outward he charged through War's low-muzzling hell—
On, and yet on—and knew no turning back.

To-day a blind man faltered in the Park,
Shocked in a sudden terror of the dark.

11 Outward] Onward *A*   War's] that *A*   12 On,] ~ *A*   on—] ~! *A*   back.] ~!
. . . *A*   13 Park,] ~ *A*

K113   OF FELLOWSHIP

Who hath not musing walked abroad, and heard,
Deep in the shaded wood, some singing bird,
Or turned and listened, silent, till it seemed
He felt the earth slow-breathing as it dreamed;
Who hath not found, new-webbed upon the green,   5
The spider's silken knot, and touched the thread
With reverent fingers, and low-bending head,
Feeling that One with this frail thing had been;
Who hath not wondered, in some quiet hour,
How near His footstep where the wistful tree   10
Answers the wandering winds in melody,
Nor marked the midgeling[1] utter forth His power:
When He comes gathering in His scattered host,[2]
How strange will such one feel, how lone, how lost.

(3 May 1919)   *Copy-text: UW   Collated states: Bn*, 24 July 1919, p. 3 as FELLOWSHIP
(*A*)
1 musing] *Om. A*   abroad,] ~ *A*   and] and, musing, *A*   2 wood,] ~ *A*
some singing] the piping *A*   4 as] where *A*   5 found,] seen *A*   green,] ~ *A*
7 fingers,] ~ *A*   8 One] He *A*   9 Who] And *A*   wondered,] felt Him *A*
some] the *A*   10 How near] Nor heard *A*   12 midgeling] midgling *A*
power:] ~? *A*   13 His] this *A*   14 lost.] ~! *A*

[1] Very small flying insect (a miniature midge).
[2] In the Second Coming (see J88 n. 1), Christ is expected to gather all believers ('His
scattered host') under his protection (e.g. 2 Thessalonians 2. 1).

K114 AUSTRALIA

For Father Eris O'Brien[1]

Fair is my Land, there is none other fairer!
Let others make to other lands their vow,
I still shall see her stand, as she stands now,
Youth's happiest, most gallant standard bearer.
She with the summer sun has been the sharer   5
Of many a joyous hour beneath the bough,
While time, who felled the nations with his plough,
Turned a slow furrow, hoping still to spare her.
So, though the Dutchman swept her chartless seas,[2]
And though the Portugee beached dark galloons,[3]   10
And though the dreaded Dampier roamed at ease,[4]
She slept unwakened on through drowsy noons.
The dim Antarctic seemed no more remote
Than she, when all of these her young name wrote.

(18 November 1930)   *Copy-text: UW   Collated states:* None

---

[1] Eris O'Brien (1895–1974), priest and author of the play *The Hostage* and *The Dawn of Catholicism in Australia* (both 1928). In 1953 he became Archbishop of Canberra and Goulburn and in 1965 contributed memorabilia to the launch of *Mary Gilmore: A Tribute*: see Chronology, p. xxi.
[2] Abel Tasman (*c.* 1603–59), one of the first to chart parts of the Australian coastline. Sailing from the Dutch East Indies, he reached the coast of what he named Van Diemen's Land (Tasmania) in 1642. In 1644 he sailed along the n. coast of the continent from Cape York to North West Cape.
[3] Probably refers to the purportedly Portuguese Mahogany Ship, a wreck reported, but since unlocatable, on the s.w. coast of Victoria near Port Fairy.
[4] William Dampier (1652–1715), an English privateer who visited the n.w. coast of Australia in 1688 and again, in command of an official English naval expedition, in 1699 – described in *A Voyage to New Holland in the Year 1699* (1703, 1709).

KII5   EPHEMERA OF TIME

Upon the earth vast empires rise and die[1]
Even as man. Each after each, like grass
They go, or as the wandering airs that pass
And dissipate beneath th' unheeding sky.
And on the sea are winds that ravening fly,   5
To fret and ruffle there the watery mass,
Till storm, like murder, breaks upon its glass,
And all its silences awake and cry.

But in the deep there is no stir, no sound;
Only the stillness of a great profound.   10

(22 August 1920)   *Copy-text: UW*   *Collated states: Wr*, 27 February 1929, p. 5 as
EVEN AS MAN (*A*)

2 man.] ~! *A*   each,] ~ *A*   **3** go] fall *A*   as the] fail like *A*   **4–5** sky./ And]
~,// ~ *A*   **5** fly,] ~ *A*   **6** mass,] ~ *A*   **7** storm,] ~ *A*   murder,] ~ *A*
8–9 cry.// But] ~./ ~ *A*   **9** deep] depths *A*   sound;] ~, *A*

---

[1] On this theme, cf. H86, M39 and M73.

SECTION L

Uncollected Poems 1930–1938

L1   IMMORTALITY

A piper at the door
   Played me a calling air,
But when I went to the door
   No piper was there.

Starlight or sunlight, flowers   5
   Upon the orchard tree,
Never there, though long I sought,
   The pipes played to me.

But when the eve had come,
   In the dusk and the dim,   10
There shone a yellow star,
   Above the earth's rim;

And there beneath the star,
   Beneath its yellow sheen,
I heard the piper play—   15
   And a grave lay between.

(n. d.)   *Copy-text: Wr*, 5 March 1930, p. 5   *Collated states:* None

L2   AGNUS DEI[1]

Weary He came, and in His mother's lap
   Weary He laid His head;
And she, so tenderly stroking His hair,
   Waited, and no word said.

She, as though He were still the little lad   5
   Who, running, asked for bread,

[1] Lamb of God, i.e. Christ (late Latin).

Leaned to gather Him up in her arms;
  And still no word was said.

There was no need of words for these two there.
  They felt the looming cross,   10
And the long Calvary that knows no end,
  Of loss, of bitter loss.

He Who in love for man that cross saw lifted up,
Who took on flesh and held irrevocable the cup,
Who drank the draught in fulness, dregs and brim,   15
How we should worship Him!

(16 November 1923)   *Copy-text: Annals* (April 1930), p. 195   *Collated states:* None

L3   ROBERT BRIDGES[1]

Though in thy clay
Thy might has fallen low,
  As when, full play,
A wind might cease and go,
  Praise God, O friend,   5
That, ere thou didst lie down,
  Thou'dst brought to end
The work made thy renown.

(24 April 1930)   *Copy-text: Wr*, 7 May 1930, p. 5   *Collated states:* None

---

[1] (1844–1930), poet laureate 1913–30. He enjoyed an extremely high reputation during his lifetime; in her foreword to L3, MG calls him 'a Titan amongst moderns'.

L4   TO A SEA-BIRD

O thou bright bird! I watch thee to and fro
  Pass ever fearless through the storm,
And mark thee, like a falling snow,
  Turn on the gust thy wing and change thy form,

And in thy flight I go with thee, and strain   5
Upon the air my breast, as though
   With thee I, too, went out above the main.

Love gloweth like a flame, but O, with thee,
   Liveth a joy love could not hold!
For, where thy light course flingeth free,   10
   Dwelleth the dream love held when love was bold,
   Or ere he put adventure by, nor knew
His old unrest: in whose decree
   Thy wings still conquer air, thy days pursue!

And thou above the sea dost float, and sail,   15
   With the same rise and fall as moves
The waves that whiten to the gale,
   Where ocean lifts from out his hollow grooves,
   And, listening to the torment, waits to leap
Into its heart, and, in its flail,   20
   Find all his hidden currents waked from sleep.

The soft palm of thy foot above the sea
   Nests in thy down, and from the height
Thy shadow falleth over me.
   How soft that foot which never knew to light   25
   Upon a tree! Beneath whose gentle curve
Only the winds turn endlessly,
   Only the waters wreathe in upward curve!

Long have I watched thee in thy tireless flight,
   Who madest of the winds a glide   30
To bear thee upward to the height,
   Where on the ether thou didst soaring ride,
   And in thy fall didst rest upon the gale,
To rise refreshed against its might.
   . . . O breast that was thy keel! O wing thy sail!   35

(n. d.)   *Copy-text: Wr*, 25 June 1930, p. 5   *Collated states:* None

L5   THE VEIL

With what deep reverence have I lifted up
   Even this hand of mine,
And seen within the curvèd palm's hollow cup
   Mark of the power Divine.

These fingers flexible and wise, where each   5
   In free dominion stands,
And yet, combined, make almost moving speech—
   So wonderful are hands:

This thumb, this wrist, the round protecting nail,
   The tingling nerve, the skin,   10
In fine integument,[1] which like a veil
   Holds everything within!

So doth His Spirit hide beneath its veil,
To answer as all these, and never fail.

(25 March 1923)   *Copy-text: Annals* (July 1930), p. 387   *Collated states:* None

[1] Bodily covering, skin.

L6   THE BLACK SOUTHERLY

Now comes this Falcon of the South,
Flame in his eyes, and storm about his mouth!
Mark how he darts and dives, then flings his might,
As though passion-impelled, against the height!
Then, when anear[1] each leaf and bud is still,   5
   A moving shadow-swift afar,
The dapple of a cloud upon a hill
   Show where he tramples over cliff and scaur.[2]

[1] Almost (archaic).   [2] The ridge of a hill.

Who has not heard this King of Winds?
Who has not seen him where his wrath rescinds   10
The sun's tremendous word, as with his wings
He fans the face of heaven, and coolness brings?
He comes like armies—roaring, ranting, raving,
    Trumpets aloft, earth-shaking, bold;
He comes with cohorts, all his banners waving,   15
    His cloud fore-runner black before him rolled.

(1 January 1931) *Copy-text: Wr*, 21 January 1931, p. 5 *Collated states:* None
9 has not *Ed.*] has *x*

L7   BROOKLYN ROAD[1]

What years since last I heard the trotting hoof
Beat Brooklyn road in tuckettings[2] of sound,
Which, thrown from matted hedge and jutted roof
Followed each rider in a quick rebound!
There love was wont to speak its own gay proof,   5
When, ambling two by two, the young were found,
And there, in sweet contentedness aloof,
Good comradeship by solitude was crowned.

There, too, the friendly neighbours, homeward turned,
Sang through star-dusted twilights all the way,   10
As summer whitened where the planets burned,
Or silver in a mane of frost earth lay.
Now, where an eager child I used to wait,
Mine is the stranger's hand upon the gate.

(7 September 1929) *Copy-text: Verse* (July–August 1931), p. 45 *Collated states:*
None

---

[1] In 1866 MG's Beattie grandparents moved from Goulburn to Wagga Wagga and rented
Brooklyn, a property on the Brucedale Road (now the Olympic Way). Though there is
no systematic record of MG's family's movements, during her childhood in 1874 MG
attended Wagga Wagga Public School while the family lived opposite. See volume 1,
Introduction, p. xxxiii, F152 and n. 1, G33 and G35 author's notes.
[2] Onomatopoeic word suggesting the beat of hooves, possibly influenced by *tucket*, a
short trumpet fanfare.

L8   BROKEN

I have a roof tree,
    And I have a bed,
Him whom I hate
    Has naught overhead.

I have a fine chair,   5
    But, him whom I hate,
Sits like a dog
    Hunched up at a gate.

My plate has a fork,
    But, him I hate, eats   10
Rough as a whelp
    That savages meats.

I pick the rich marrow.
    Him whom I hate,
Licks like a dog   15
    The edge of his plate.

But him I hate walks
    On his two sound feet,
While I, on a gong,
    My hand must beat.   20

(8 April 1931)   *Copy-text: Ink* (1932), p. 18   *Collated states:* None

L9   [MY ARMY! O, MY ARMY!]

"My Army! O, My Army!"—Henry Lawson.[1]

My Army, O My Army!
    Of never-ending quest;

---

[1] Focused on women's experience, L9 is a companion piece to the title poem of Henry Lawson's collection, *My Army, O, My Army! and Other Songs* (1915). In both, the working poor are conscripts in a bitter battle for survival.

Whose boots are always handy,
   As it lies down to rest;
Whose empty frock still keeps its shape,   5
   So long it has been worn—
Flat, where the child is off the milk,
   Round for the newly-born!

My Army, O My Army!
   My Army without end,   10
Day after day enlisted,
   On life to wait and tend;
Beyond the bush, the little town,
   And from the city street,
Out to the utmost ends of earth,   15
   You hear its marching feet.

Tramp-tramp! Tramp-tramp, my Army,
   Of burdened back, and bowed,
That never dreams of leisure,
   Save when it wears a shroud!   20
Though men talk honors of the sword
   Praise self in other men,
Let be whatever pride he boast,
   Here stands the strength of ten!

My Army, O My Army!   25
   So young at morn and fair,
Sweet as the rosebud waking
   Upon the dewy air;
How fades the damask of your cheek,
   The satin of your skin,   30
As, tramp-tramp-tramp, you keep the step
   Of those enlisted in.

My ever-marching Army,
   The target of man's mirth,
You bear upon your bosom   35
   The burden of our birth;

Yours to walk all the ways of pain,
    And yours to stoop and lift
From death's dark floor the fallen chaff,
    And make of it life's thrift.   40

O Woman, ever gleaner,
    Where others waste the seed,
O Constant and unbeaten,
    Whatever hopes may bleed,
Yours still it is to sacrifice—   45
    Known wrecked upon unknown—
To keep the faith, and fight the fight,
    Though nameless on a stone!

(8 March 1926)   *Copy-text: LD*, 2 May 1932, p. 4   *Collated states:* None

                L10   THE HORN

The roar of constant traffic flies
    Like wings that, round and round,
Through endless effort to arise,
    In vortices[1] are bound.

The ceaseless wheels devour the day,   5
    The streets are hoof-forlorn;
Yet memory holds, amid the bray,
    The far sound of a horn.

Mailman and horse, huntsman and hound,
    How long since ye were known?   10
Yet am I haunted by that sound—
    A horn in distance blown!

(23 January 1932)   *Copy-text: Bn*, 25 May 1932, p. 40   *Collated states:* None

---

[1] Whirling or eddying movements.

LII   O LAUGHING STAR

O Durramela,* hear,
O hear me as I speak!
Euroka,* in the west,
Glows red upon the peak;
Soon will Jiemba* burn   5
Her fire-stick in the sky,
But thou, *my* Laughing Star,
Far from my side must lie.

O Durramela, hear,
O hear me! Thou dost go   10
Through the long valley where
Life's swiftest foot is slow;
Where in the mould'ring dust
Pride cumbers¹ with the low.
Lost in the darkling west   15
Euroka passed away,
As thou, O Durramela,
Passed from me away.

O Durramela, hear!
Wait as of old my call!   20
Ah, wilt thou nevermore
Hear, like the wistful fall
Of grey Burimba's* cry,
My whisper, quick and small?
It was my heart, Durramela,   25
Crying for thee;
Thou who away hast gone
Like a gull to the sea.

Now, O Durramela,
My boomerang is laid   30
Low by the tented tree
Will knit for thee its shade,

¹ I.e. encumbers itself.

Though through the leaves all night
The moon her light will braid;
And I my womerah   35
And spear have buried deep
There where I come no more
My watch o'er thee to keep.

The night, O Durramela,
Falls upon my heart,   40
The night that falls on thee
In what strange world thou art—
O Durramela, flung
From me apart!

* An aboriginal name.   *[l. 3] The sun.
*[l. 5] The Laughing Star, otherwise Venus.
*[l. 23] The grey-winged plover—with a red bill.

(23 June 1932)   *Copy-text: AJSU* (Michaelmas Term 1932), p. 10   *Collated states:*
None

L12   BALKIS OF SHEBA CAME[1]

Balkis of Sheba came,
To the king's eyes a flame.
To her, slow pacing there,
The king, from out his chair,
Turned as his pulses leapt,   5
Downward toward her stept.

The palace jackals played
About the balustrade
No more that day; the lute
Against the wall was mute;   10

[1] In 1 Kings 10. 1–13 and 2 Chronicles 9. 1–12, the (unnamed) Queen of Sheba visits
Solomon, but there is no sexual relationship – that originates in rabbinical texts.
Aspendus (modern Belkis Kalé in Antalya, Turkey) has a legendary connection with
the Queen of Sheba: in the ruins of its fine second-century Roman theatre is a relief
of Bacchus supposed to be a female called the Bal-kis, or Honey Girl. 'Balkis' is the
Queen's Islamic name.

Only the peacock's scream
Broke on that day of dream.

Balkis of Sheba came,
To the king's eyes a flame.

(2 April 1932) *Copy-text: Verse* (March–April 1933), p. 29 *Collated states:* None

L13 G. R.[1]

Mourn not the dead,
  But take him to his rest;
The great heart beats no more,
  Ended at last the quest.
His was the warrior soul;   5
  His, pride that fronted life—
The unseen shield, to hope,
  All faint in strife.

(n. d.) *Copy-text: SMH*, 29 August 1933, p. 102[2] *Collated states:* None

[1] Publisher George Robertson, of Angus & Robertson, an important figure in MG's career (see volume 1, Introduction, pp. xlvi–xlviii and lvii, and *Letters* 92–3 and 229); he died on 27 August 1933.
[2] MG's poem follows prose items by Thomas Courtney and C. E. W. Bean in a column headed 'GEORGE ROBERTSON. APPRECIATIONS'.

L14 IN THE FLICKER-LIGHT

Night-night! . . . Candlelight . . .
  Time to go to bed!
See, the shepherd's star is bright,[1]
  Little sleepy head.

Just one little while   5
  Feet and hands to warm,
While the flame, with flicker-smile,
  Kisses face and arm.

[1] Evening or 'fold-star' (F6 line 1), signal for bringing sheep into the fold for the night.

But no time to watch
   Shadow-islands grow,   10
Where the firelight leaves a patch
   In its leaping flow.

No more time to count
   Capes upon the wall,
For, although the shadows mount,   15
   Heavy eyelids fall.

So to bed we run—
   (Kiss me feather-light!)
Now, with prayers all said and done,
   Little child, good night!   20

(5 October 1931)   *Copy-text: WB*, 28 February 1934, p. 11   *Collated states:* None

L15   THE IBIS

(WRITTEN FOR "THE WINGHAM CHRONICLE.")

Where feedest thou to-day,
   O migrant of the marsh,[1]
Since now no echoes bray
   Thy cry so loud and harsh?

Thy sentinels are seen   5
   In silhouette no more
On barren trees, and green,
   Above a reedy shore!

Then where hast flown? In what
   Far fields of waters wade   10
Thy marsh-broad feet, whose slot
   Sinks ever unbetrayed?

[1] Seventeen genera of ibises occur throughout the swamps and marshes of the tropical and warm temperate regions of the world. MG mistakes this, and the trailing flight of groups of ibis (line 38), for evidence of migration; see also M29 and n. 1.

Hast found the Congo? or
   Art thou where Nilus[2] spreads
Until his watery shore   15
   The ancient desert treads?

When Egypt holds thee not,
   Nor Amazon, nor black
Hoang-ho, nor yet the hot
   Euphrates, falling slack,   20

The lone Danubian hears
   Thee come, the tundras note
Thy going forth; Algiers
   Awaits thy flattened note.

What passion moves in thee—   25
   What driving urges wake—
That thou each perilous sea
   Must seek to overtake?

What calls thee till the waste
   Declares thee in the height?   30
What draws thee on, in haste,
   Where lifts thy wing in flight?

The winds deter thee not,
   Nor yet the storm's dark mail,
Who thine appointed lot   35
   Dost take, to what strange pale.

So thou to us wilt come
   In long trails through the sky,
For here thou makest home,
   And here thy sentinels cry.   40

(24 July 1932)   *Copy-text: WmC*, 31 September 1934, p. 6   *Collated states:* None
14 Nilus *Ed.*] Nilcis *x*

---

[2] Latin for the Nile, home of the sacred ibis (*Threskionis ethiopicus*).

L16   JAEL[1]

I was one born to love,
  And mine was love to give;
My heart set hope above,
  Hope died that grief might live.

But though hope's clear light set   5
  That should have shined so fair,
Yet I denied regret,
  And manacled despair.

Still was I chained—who looked
  With longing eyes afar;   10
I knew my range: no stooked[2]
  Field mine, but mine a star.

The star shines on; but I
  Held by life's long entwine,
Though to what heights I fly,   15
  Never my star make mine.

(1934)   *Copy-text: AWA* (1936), p. 85   *Collated states:* None

---

[1] Elusive references: the biblical Jael offers refuge to Sisera, the defeated Canaanite general, but slays him while he sleeps (Judges 4. 17–22); later (5. 28) his mother 'looked out at a window' (cf. lines 9-10) for his return.
[2] As when the harvested grain is gathered into stooks (stacks of sheaves).

L17   DEATH COMES[1]

Death comes to serfs and kings—
  Nor pomp nor power
Can hold at bay
  That last dread hour.

---

[1] In Fryer 2/2975 and NLA 727 2/4/15, this is the first of a three-part sequence, the second part being L18. The third, 'There is no Death', is unpublished. See volume 1, Appendix for manuscript locations and descriptions.

And yet 'tis who remain   5
Who grieve. The dead
Lie half a-smile,
The last word said.

(18 January 1936)   *Copy-text: SMH*, 25 January 1936, p. 13   *Collated states:* None[2]

---

[2] A print clipping with no variants, held in ML 6/3, is attributed in a hand other than that of MG to the New Zealand *Marlborough Express* of 1 February 1936: not verified.

L18   NOT ALL OF ME SHALL DIE[1]

"Not all of me shall die"—
    'Twas Horace said it long ago;[2]
And I, later two thousand years,
    The same thing say, the same thing know.

Out of the painted clay   5
    Life's formless thought is breathed and heard;
The clay resolves itself to dust,
    Immortal rises still the word.

"Not all of me shall die"—
    And Horace said it long ago.   10
Man is a city, thoughts are winds,
    That where the cities stood still blow.

(18 January 1936)   *Copy-text: SMH*, 8 February 1936, p. 13   *Collated states:* None

---

[1] See L17 n. 1.
[2] Quintus Horatius Flaccus (65–8 BC), one of the most successful Roman poets. His *Ars Poetica* was extremely influential in later neo-classical literary theory, but MG probably refers to *non omnis moriar* in line 6 of 'The Immortality of Poetry' (*Carmina* III. xxx); she may have seen the engraving of the phrase on a bust in the vestibule of the ML.

L19   FATHER PIQUET[1]

He died? Not so: he lived!
There was no moment of
His life he grieved;
But his the open hand,
And his to understand,   5
And his to love.

All day about his door
There came the lonely poor;
Now, too, are we the lonely poor,
Seeing his face no more.   10

With this most generous soul
There was no chill of dole;[2]
Where his heart went!
Himself he spent,
And all men were his poor.   15
Now he is gone afar; his feet upon the street
He walked are heard no more;
But, yet, where beats a grateful heart,
In some dim twilight will
His shadow seem to pass,   20
And some lone passer-by will start,
Deeming him with us still.

(n. d.)   *Copy-text: FJ*, 13 August 1936, p. 28   *Collated states: Adv*, 20 August 1936,
p. 5 (*A*)[3]

1 so:] ~; *A*

---

[1] An account of the life of Marist priest Jean Pierre Piquet was published near L19 in
FJ. He gave 56 years' service at St Patrick's, Church Hill, Sydney, and was active in
the St Vincent de Paul Society, which has a special mission to the poor.

[2] As a sustenance allowance to the unemployed, 'dole' (something dealt out) was often
associated by the more fortunate with undeserving poverty.

[3] An editorial note to *A* reads: 'This poetic tribute to a saintly priest by a well-known
Australian poet is republished from the "Catholic Freeman's Journal."'

L20   FROM THE BATTLEFIELD

IN MEMORY

We have come at last from the gentile's land,
For the gentile's land was a land of hate;[1]
Though beggared and broken, lofty or banned,
We have quenched the flames that of old we fanned,
    And the mercy of God is upon us.   5

We have risen up and the sword put by,
We have laid down wrath in its bitter bed;
To hate we have sworn that love shall not die,
And the oath we have made, it shall not lie,
    That the mercy of God be upon us.   10

We have asked of them whom we fought as foe
That they shall forgive us the thing we did,
Since the seeding of death we no longer sow,
We have given the hand where we gave the blow,
    And the mercy of God is upon us.   15

We have gathered the bones that once were men,
And with humbled hearts have lifted them up,
From the shot-stormed trench and the drowned-out fen;
In the Maker's hands they are whole again,
    And the mercy of God is upon us.   20

He shall forgive us as we forgave them;
He shall forgive them as they forgave us;
Thus shall the branches be one with the stem,
And justice shall shine as a King's diadem,
    And the mercy of God be upon us.   25

    In the name of the Christ Who died for us all,
Bid them wound no more as His wounds bled;

[1] The 'gentile's land' of the Jews was the Babylonian captivity (see K23 n. 2) which they never forgave; for Christians, the hate-filled period of World War I can now, through the mercy of God (line 5), be put behind them.

Let the grey guns rust on the crumbling wall,
And the tears of the nations no longer fall,
That God in His mercy be with us.   30

(16 April 1932)   *Copy-text: QD* (April 1937), p. 9, signed By DAME MARY GILMORE   *Collated states:* None

L21   AN AUSTRALIAN TOAST

Blow the man down[1] who will not laud
   Australia's lovely name;
For him the frown; for her the crown,
   The Anzac and his fame!

   Then up! Up! Up!   5
   Come lift it up
In glass or pannikin or cup.

   Blow the man down—
   Blow the man down—
   Blow the man down!   10

TOAST

   The glass is up,
   The man is down—
   Aus—tra—lia!

(22 January 1934)   *Copy-text: QD* (June 1937), p. 27, signed By Dame Mary Gilmore   *Collated states:* None

[1] Opening phrase and chorus adapted from sea-shanty, 'Blow the Man Down, Boys'.

L22   THE WOLD[1]

"Call me in, call me in,
   Call me in from the cold!

[1] Here, the wilderness, in a dialogue based on the parable of the strayed sheep and the good shepherd (see J78 n. 6).

I have been out in the waste so long,
    I have come to the fold."

"You would not stay in the warmth   5
    Of the fold, my child;
Too long you have sat with the fire-lit dark
    In a lease of the wild."

"Nay, but I crave for the fold—
    Home and children to keep,   10
The hearth to tend as the evening comes,
    The friendly floor to sweep."

"You would not rest with home
    And child; not yours the floor
To sweep; yours are the mountain peaks to climb,   15
    And yours the wide-set door."

"Yet call me in, call me in,
    Call me in from the wold!
I have been out in its wastes so long,
    I am fain for the fold."   20

(5 November 1938)   *Copy-text: SMH*, 26 November 1938, p. 23   *Collated states:*
None

L23   BLACKFOOT AND BALL

They were the kings,
    The kings of the road,
Mighty as ships
    As they hauled the load;
Then a new power rose—   5
    A day and a day,
And the teams were gone,
    The bullocks away.[1]

[1] Cf. G41, G42 and their author's notes.

But out on the rim,
　　At the uttermost bound,   10
Cropping the grass
　　With a rich, warm sound,
In the fields of heaven,
　　Gold-tipped of horn,
Feed Blackfoot and Ball   15
　　In a golden morn.

And the Lord Himself
　　Comes walking there
Where the brave heads lift
　　In a friendly stare;   20
"Get over!" He says,
　　And, sober and slow,
Just as on earth
　　They turn and go.

He says, "Pincher—stand up!"   25
　　And "Ball—get under!"
And "Whoa there, Blazer!"
　　And "Back there, Thunder!"
And then, as He turns
　　To His great gold throne,   30
He hears the bullocks—
　　The bells' far tone.

(13 October 1938)   *Copy-text: Bn*, 7 December 1938, p. 24   *Collated states:* None

SECTION M
Battlefields (1939)

BATTLEFIELDS[1]

[1] *Battlefields* is divided into three: BATTLEFIELDS (M1–M39), THE BAYING HOUNDS (M40–M69) and LEAVES IN THE WIND (M70–M121).

M1   THE RINGER[*][1]

EL CAMPEADOR[2]

Never allow the thoughtless to declare
That we have no tradition here!
They have not heard the strong tread of the feet
That, as first-footers,[3] crossed our inland plains—
Vast as Sahara and silent as Siberia;   5
Nor have they seen the solitary wing
That climbed the very heavens for purchase o'er
The nether world that is the sea;[4]

(25 July 1936)   *Copy-text:* Bat   *Collated states:* *ANR* (September 1938), pp. 49–51 (no subtitle) (*A*)   *SV* (*B*)

Not otherwise recorded: Apparently owing to space constraints *A* begins a new section at lines 34, 56, 82 and 104, with lines 13, 24, 34, 56, 74 and 82 indented. In *B* lines 13, 24, 34, 56, 82 and 104 begin a new section; indenting is absent. The note in *A* consists of a single paragraph.

4 That,] ~ *A*   first-footers,] ~ *A*   plains—] ~, *B*   **8** world] void *A*

---

[1] The champion shearer in a team, able to despatch his quota of sheep most skilfully and quickly. MG extends the sense to cover a diversity of Australian heroes; see especially lines 29–30, 82–102 and her author's note.

[2] In the medieval Spanish epic *Poema del Cid* (*c.* 1140), 'Campeador', meaning both champion and country, is the honorific of the eponymous hero. See also I97 line 12 and n. 1.   [3] Cf. I41.

[4] See lines 92–8 and, on aviators Hawker and Parer, see F43 and H36.

Nor have they watched, as though a star,
The fitful beam of some small fire   10
Shooting the dark, and by remoteness marking where
Some Ringer of the land had made his camp!

    Tradition lies with deeds, not time. One man,
One deed, one hour, as he of Marathon,
Or as Leonidas,   15
Or as Gallipoli and Villers Bret—[5]
A thousand years are thistledown to these,
A thousand thousand years can nothing add to them.

For Marathon was once as new as Suvla Bay,[6]
Leonidas as young as our Monash;[7]   20
But what tradition these in all their newness made!
So once more be it said:
Tradition lies in deeds, not time.

    Australia's wells are deep and full,
But every shallow thinker looks afar,   25
And says, "There is no water here;
The windlasses are new."
And yet tradition ranges through our land!
For here the Ringer strode in seven-leagued boots,[8]
Or shears, or pride, or courage, moving eager on,   30
Till he out-swam the seas, out-climbed the mountain tops,
Made servant of the air—and dared—and dared—
And, daring, out-paced time.

---

11 and by] by its *A*   marking] proving *A*   12 had] has *A*   22 more] again *A*
22–3 be it said:/ Tradition] I say tradition *A*   25 afar,] ~ *A*   26 here;] ~. *A*
27 new."] ~ . . ." *A* ~". *B*   28 land!] ~. *A*   29 seven-leagued] seven-league *A B*
33 And, daring,] ~ ~ *A*

---

[5] Parallels the Australian troops at Gallipoli and Villers Bretonneux (in 1918) with the heroism of Pheippides who died, exhausted, after carrying news to the Athenians of their victory over the Persians at Marathon in 490/491 BC and the Spartan Leonidas who died defending the pass at Thermopylae against an overwhelming force of invading Persians in 480 BC.   [6] See I38 n. 7.
[7] General (later Sir John) Monash (1865–1931), commander of the 4th Infantry Brigade at Gallipoli and the 3rd Division in France, regarded as the finest Australian commander in World War I.
[8] Worn by the giant in the fairy tale *The Seven-leagued Boots*, they enabled the wearer to cover that distance (*c.* 33 km) in one pace.

. . . I sought the Ringer as a clansman seeks his chief,
And missing him I turned to where   35
The great sea-cows,[9] full laden, bellowed through
The morning fogs toward their milking yards,
Thinking to find him there. Wharf, pier, and quay
Gave up their hosts in tumbling stream, to where
In waiting fleets the trams and trains filled up,   40
And like great buckets bore the freight
To its appointed place—the milk of earth
That flows as human kind,
And in its little dishes set,
Yields up its cream to give the world romance,   45
And re-create creation to its will.
The Ringer was not there. And then one said,
"The last I saw of him was on the Thompson,
Booked for shearing at Barcaldine Downs;"[10]
But hearing it another said, "That wasn't him,   50
For when I came to Midgeon Lake, they told me
I'd just missed him . . . He'd gone the day before;"
And still another, "Don't make no mistake!
The Ringer's out at Ivanhoe. I heard
It at Desailly's camp as I came through."   55

    O was it Ivanhoe, Barcaldine Downs,
Or Hungerford, or was it east or west,

---

34 ˢ. . . I] ~ *A B*   chief,] ~! *A*   **36** laden] uddered *A*   **44** And] ~, *B*
45 romance] romance and pride *A*   **49** Downs;"] ~." *A*   ~"; *B*   **50** him,] ~. *A*
52 He'd] he'd *B*   before;"] ~." *A*   ~", *B*   **56** O] ~, *B*   **57** west,] ~; *B*

---

[9] I.e. ships.

[10] Both are in outback w. Queensland: the Thompson R. is associated with the bushranger Capt. Starlight, while Barcaldine was the site of the largest camp of the striking shearers in 1891 (see F81 and n. 1). Lake Midgeon (line 51) is a lake near Narrandera in the NSW Riverina and a pioneering local property; Ivanhoe (54) is in w. NSW, between Hay and Wilcannia; Hungerford (57) is in outback Queensland on the NSW border. On the Jardines (58), see *Narrative of the Overland Expedition of the Messrs. Jardine, from Rockhampton to Cape York, Northern Queensland* (1867), ed. Frederick J. Byerley. 'Hay, Hell, and Booligal' (60), on the Riverina plains of NSW, are notorious through 'Banjo' Paterson's poem of that title (1896). 'Hell' is One Tree Plain, on the stock route 40 km n. of Hay.

Or was it where upon Cape York the Jardines set their mark
And Somerset still holds their name,
Or was it where Hay, Hell, and Booligal　　　　　　　　　60
In that dark order ran as farthest out
And worst—no matter where!—
The Ringer's cry was heard—*is* heard—
That, in whatever hour men stand the vision-held,
Calls the out-venturing from the quiet hearth,　　　　　65
Calls to the spirit that inheres in force to break for liberty,
For right to set power free and conquer worlds.
For in it each one hears the leader's voice,
The fledgling's thrust on embryo wings for flight,
The shout of life to prove combatively its will to live;　　70
And in it ever cries the need of man as man
To leave the clocked hour and the street,
And know himself, as God, master of time and space.
　　No Scholar Gipsy this, not even Lob,[11]
But one who flamed with lightning speed　　　　　　　75
From need to need, endlessly on
Through our Australian history,
To grow at last so tall, men leaning on a fence
Will speak of him as churchmen speak of kings,
Or as forgotten stable-lads among the straw　　　　　80
Talked once of Carbine and the Barb.[12]

　　O many names the Ringer had![13]
You'll find him in McKinley's Pound—

---

58 York] Yorke *A*　　60 Hell,] hell *A*　　63 cry] blade *A*　　heard—*is* heard—]
~, ~ ~, *B*　　69 fledgling's] fledgeling's *B*　　71 man as man] ~, ~ ~, *B*
75 speed] shears *A*　　76 From] From shed to shed, from *A*　　80 stable-lads]
~, *B*　　straw] ~, *B*　　83 Pound—] ~, *A*

[11] The Scholar-Gipsy of Matthew Arnold's poem of that name (1853) has withdrawn from the world of action, while the rustic activities of the folktale Lob Lie-by-the-Fire in Milton's *L'Allegro* (?1631) are utilitarian not heroic. The Lob in the poem of that name by Edward Thomas (1878–1917) is a figure of folk memory, a type of English countryman manifest in multiple identities (cf. line 82); Thomas's *Collected Poems* appeared in 1920 and 1928. See MG's author's note n5–6.
[12] Carbine won the 1890 Melbourne Cup carrying a record weight of 67 kg. On the Barb, see K47 and n. 1.
[13] Places named in lines 83–8 are early pastoral sites (Wave Hill, Northern Territory

Oanagin the native name in old S.A.—
In Sturt's Lookout, Lake Eyre, and Leichhardt's Tree;   85
Then there's Fort Bourke (from which they dropped the Fort,
I don't know why), the Flinders, Tennant's Creek, Wave Hill,
The Kimberleys, and even in poor lost Lasseter's Last Ride.
Again you'll find him known as Hawdon, Kennedy, or Hume,
Sometimes as Gilbert or Ben Hall,   90
But mostly in the sheds he wrote his name Jack Howe.
Later we find him as that Parer, who, with MacIntosh,
Crossed seas on wire-held mats for wings,
And then we heard of him as Kingsford Smith, the man
Who rode the air as other men would ride a horse,   95
And sometimes, too, I think he must have been the one
They called Jack Hides; Hawker of course he was,
And gallant young Ross Smith.

84 Oanagin] (*Oanagin*, *A*   ~— *B*   name] ~, *B*   in old S.A.—] ~ ~ ~) *A*
as South Australia knew— *B*   85 Lookout] Look-Out *A*   87 why),] ~) *A B*
Wave Hill,] *Om. A*   88 The Kimberleys,] *Om. A*   and] And *A*   Lasseter's]
Lassetter's *A*   92 who,] ~ *A*   MacIntosh,] ~ *A*   95 horse,] ~; *A*

and the Kimberleys, n. Western Australia) or commemorate (except for Sir Richard
Bourke, Governor of NSW 1831–37), early explorers. John McKinlay (1819–72) led
the expedition (1861) in search of Burke and Wills. ('Pound' signifies a large rock basin
inside a hollowed-out mountain – the Aboriginal place name (line 84) has been restored.)
Charles Sturt (1795–1869) explored the s.e. river system 1827–30. Edward John Eyre
(1815–1901) and Ludwig Leichhardt (1813–?48) between them explored inland Australia
from e. to w. and s. to n.; on navigator Matthew Flinders (1774–1814), see I44 n. 5.
Tennant's Creek, Northern Territory, was named by explorer John McDouall Stuart
(1815–66) for South Australian pastoralist John Tennant, a financial supporter of Stuart's
expedition. Further explorers (line 89) are Edmund Kennedy (1818–48), killed while
on an expedition from Rockhampton to Cape York, and Hamilton Hume (1797–1873),
who (with William Hovell) led an expedition s. from near Yass, NSW to the Victorian
coastline (1824). Claims by adventurer Harold Lasseter (1880–1931) to have discovered
and lost a fabulously rich gold reef in central Australia inspired Ion Idriess's popular
novel *Lasseter's Last Ride* (1931).
    Further exemplars of the 'Ringer' (lines 89–103) include pioneers (Joseph Hawdon),
bushrangers (Ben Hall), shearers (Jack Howe), aviators (Parer and Hawker – see n.
4 above), Charles Kingsford Smith and Ross Smith, both World War I pilots and
respectively the first to fly from USA to Australia (1928) and winner of the 1919
England–Australia air race, activists Peter Lalor, Eureka rebel later turned politician,
and William Lane, and politicians John Dunmore Lang (1799–1878) and William Morris
Hughes (see M5 n. 2, Q12, R9 and R31). Jack Hides is probably John Gordon Hides
(1906–38) who, as a patrol officer and magistrate in Papua, led exploratory expeditions
in 1931 and 1937 (see his *Through Wildest Papua*, 1935).

For years as Peter Lalor he was known;
And once they called him William Lane,   100
And once John Dunmore Lang, whose very name
Was thunder in a narrow sky;
And once they called him William Morris Hughes.

Still in the well the water lies, although
None draw it forth: the well a well because of it.   105
Here is my parable; let each man read it as he may.

[*] "The Ringer," which first appeared in *The Australian National Review*
(September, 1938), is little more than an unfinished fragment, but
because it may give others a lead, and because it uses nationally an
Australian word originally applied to a section only, I have included it
here. What it owes to Matthew Arnold in his "Scholar Gipsy," and to   n5
Edward Thomas in "Lob," is plain to see. But I make no plea for mercy,
for the terrain is ours—a neglected ours—and for which I would use
any match to light it, and any spade to dig it.

I have only touched with wide leaps on Ringers of the out-of-doors
and in other directions. But there is a wider field in which there are   n10
sheaves of others—Marcus Clarke, Julian Ashton, and the Lindsays
(Lionel Lindsay not so fully recognized as a track-breaker because of the
immediateness of his spectacular brother). Then there are those like Dr
Badham, Sir Mungo MacCallum, Sir Robert Garran, J. F. Archibald, and
"G.R." (George Robertson), who gave Australia scholarship, editorship,   n15
and, for its time, a fully printed literature, while in Unionism no name
stands like that of W. G. Spence.[14] So far, Australian writers have only

99 known;] ~. *A*   105 forth:] ~; *A*   106 parable;] ~. *B*   let] Let *B*
n1 Ringer,"] ~" *A*   ~", *B*   (n1–2) which . . . 1938),] *Om. A*   n2 September,]
~ *B*   fragment,] ~. *A*   n2–5 but . . . here.] *Om. A*   n5 in his] and his *A*
Gipsy,"] ~", *B*   n6 Lob,"] ~" *A*   ~", *B*   n7 neglected ours] ~ ~! *A*
use] take *A*   n9–10 wide . . . directions.] kangaroo hops what has been done by
the Ringers of Australia, the hops, of course, being names and nothing else; the
spheres are chiefly out-of-doors, and, in a small way, politics. *A*   n10 field] side *A*
n11 sheaves of] so many *A*   others] others to be recalled *A*   and] *Om. A*   n12–
13 (Lionel . . . brother)] (whose real value to Australia is not yet properly grasped) *A*
Om. B   n13–14 Dr Badham,] *Om. A*   n14 Archibald,] ~ *A*   n15 George]
Mr. *A*   Robertson)] Robertson), Dr. Badham, William MacLeay (to give him his
original spelling) *A*   who] all of whom *A*   Australia] us *A*   Australian *B*
editorship] a national editorship *A*   n16 and,] ~ *A*   for . . . time,] *Om. A*
fully] *Om. A*   literature, while] literature, as well as other things. And *A*
(n17–24) So far . . . drama.] All these names, along with others, should recall what
those who bore them did; and what they did, and the times in which they made

[14] Additional 'Ringers' include Marcus Clarke (1846–81), author of the classic *His
Natural Life* (1874); Julian Ashton (1851–1942), landscape painter and founder of the

established these, and others like them, by newspaper recognition. But a reporter's routine record is not enough to feed imagination, nor is it sufficient to produce the creative feeling needed for the nationally   n20 historical. Yet whoever comes later will only have what we have done, and what the papers have given, by which to know the Ringers. In this I refer chiefly to verse and poetry. For prose there is a still wider field, including the drama.

As to verse, I think we are due for a return to the simple and direct.   n25 We have had a long period of the inverted, the contorted, and even the pretentious, but in that time we have not improved on any of the older forms of verse, nor, as America has done, have we developed from the hackneyed something fresh, and at times even new. Moreover Australia has been neglected for the sectional, the individually personal, and the   n30 emotional. But this land is not contained in these. Something greater is required. If it is simple, so much to the good, since folk-song, psalm, and balladry are, of all forms of literature, the most lasting. Indeed it is perhaps in these that nationality is most truly expressed; and it may be that publishers have ceased to foster verse, and readers to buy it, because   n35 the simple and the direct have not been written, at least not sufficiently by those whose writing is the most worth while. Here I except Hugh McCrae[15] and one or two others.

------

their names, should feed the imagination and the historical mind of this country. No matter who comes in the future, they can only build on what these (and their kind) did and left as a foundation. But, if we do not begin to give them a place in our literature as well as in our ordinary newspaper annals, they will never be the stimulus to action and to pride that they should be. "The Ringer" is in verse as that seems to be the proper medium for such a recording. *A*   **n17** far,] ~ *B*   **n25** As to verse] Actually *A*   and] and the *A*   direct] direct in verse *A*   **n26** period] spell *A*   **n27–9** but . . . new] which is perhaps why verse has ceased to be bought and read *A*   **n29** Moreover] In any case *A*   ~, *B*   **n30** sectional] personal *A* individually personal] individual *A*   **n31** But this land] She *A*   these] these— not even when blasphemously expressed *A*   **n32** required. If] required, and if *A* simple,] ~ *A*   folk-song,] ~ *A*   psalm,] psalms *A*   **n33** most] most national and the most *A*   Indeed] ~, *A*   **n34** perhaps] perhaps only *A*   most truly] really *A*   expressed;] ~.—M. G. *A*   **(n34–8)** and it . . . others.] *Om. A* **n38** and . . . others] and, now in 1948, some of the younger ones *B*

Sydney Art School; Norman and Lionel Lindsay (see K36 n. 1 and M6 n. 1); publisher George Robertson (see L13 n. 1); scholars Charles Badham (1813–84), professor of classics and logic, University of Sydney 1867–84, and Mungo William MacCallum, knighted in 1926 for services to education; lawyer and public servant Sir Robert Garran (1867–1957) and union leader William Guthrie Spence (1846–1926).

[15] See K44 n. 7.

M2   CORONATION ANTHEM (1937)[*]¹

The air shall hearken and the earth give ear,
The air shall hearken and the earth give ear,
When, as the trumpets sound in Westminster,
The King, in might, is crowned.
The people of the wilderness shall know this hour,   5
The powers that ride above the sea shall homage make,
Army and Navy wait upon his word—
Sceptred: and crowned: and King.

Now, where he stands in sovereign power,
The burden of our yoke is laid on him;   10
Within his hand our unity abides,
Nations his word obey.
Son of his people and King, great and yet humble,
The air shall hearken and the earth give ear,
The air shall hearken and the earth give ear,   15
When, as the trumpets sound in Westminster,
The King, in might, is crowned.

The ancient Kingdoms of his realm declare his royal line:
India bends down to touch his robe:
Canada, New Zealand, and Australia obeisance make: 20
Anzac and Africa before him kneel:
For all men know that only in the King are we made one,
Only in the King His Majesty are all these peoples one;
In him are we crowned and he in us.

But, in this day of splendour, let us remember those who
          went before,   25
Who did greatly for the moulding of this people;

(13 March 1936)   *Copy-text: Bat   Collated states: SV* as CORONATION ANTHEM, 1937
(*A*)

9 sovereign power] sovereignty *A*   **21** kneel:] ~; *A*

¹ Originally written in an earlier version (M61) for Edward VIII (1894–1972; reigned and
abdicated 1936), but sung in 1937 in the revised form of M2 for the Sydney Coronation
Concert of his brother George VI (1895–1952; reigned 1936–52); cf. author's notes for
M2 and M61, and see M61 nn. 2 and 3.

For in a young face there shall be seen their look again,
And in a son's voice shall be heard counsels of wisdom deep
    and true sincerity.
So from this hour his name shall stand forever,
Renowned as any king before him.   30
Pride dwells with kings, and the King's name is a great name.

INVOCATION

Lord God of Hosts, Maker of heaven and earth and all
    that in them is,
We pray Thee, we implore, bless Thou George the King
    upon his throne;
Lord of Compassion, grant him Thy hand,
And peace be Thy gift to this realm,   35
Peace in Thy name evermore.

[*] This, I understand, is the first coronation anthem wholly written, composed, and produced in Australia. The music is by Mr. Howard Carr, an Englishman who conducted his own works at the Queen's Hall, London, before coming to Sydney. Here he conducted the singing of this anthem by massed choirs at the Official Coronation Concert in the   n5 Sydney Town Hall on the 15th of May, 1937. Two earlier performances were given, the first by the Royal Philharmonic Society on the 21st of April, and the second at the Anglican Church Concert on the 11th of May. These also were held in the Sydney Town Hall, with Mr Carr as conductor. These details are given as a matter of historical reference.   n10

---

35 realm,] ~. *A*   **n2** Mr.] ~ *A*   **n5** in] at *A*   **n6** the 15th of] 15 *A*   May,] ~ *A*
n7 the 21st of] 21 *A*   **n8** the 11th of] 11 *A*

M3   ODE TO THE PIONEER WOMEN[*]

    O braiding thought move out—move on!
    Twine, Memory, your golden thread!
    Marble, be monument to them,
    Our homage here their diadem,

(1937)   *Copy-text:* Bat   *Collated states:* Eldershaw (*A*)   *SV* (*B*)

Not otherwise recorded: Lines 57–62 are not italicised in *A*. Line 45 is not indented in *B*.

  1 thought] ~, *A*   out—] ~, *B*   **3** them,] ~— *A*   ~! *B*   **4** diadem,] ~— *A*

Lest, as with nations long since gone,   5
We lose the names should be our bread.

Call them, Australia! Call them once again,
For they are those who on these silent shores first stood,
And on whose long endurings rest
The might and majesty acclaimed by us to-day.   10

   They are the women who by lonely doorsteps sat,
And heard with inward ears the throstle[1] and
The nightingale that they would never hear again;
Who saw as in a dream the little corncrake in dim distant fields,
Or talked of moons of silver as they watched   15
The torrid rising of our orb of gold.

   And though with wistful longing they looked back,
And knew so oft the sudden tear of memory,
They bore the burden of the strange—they who had never
      known
But homely things: the dovecot by the barn,   20
The skep[2] beside the door, the kindly thatch
That covered them, the woodbine and the rose,
The singing lark, that, all day long,
Thrilled out above the gorse his jewelled song.

         O firmaments of time,   25
            Whose planets ages are,
         Ye shall the past sublime,
            And make each name a star!

         For these were they who came—
            A cockleshell for ship—   30
         Daring the sun's red flame,
            And the wind's wild whip.

---

7 again,] ~! *B*   8 silent] *Om. A*   stood,] ~; *A*   9 And on] Women upon *A*
endurings] enduring *B*   10 to-day] today *A B*   13 again;] ~, *A*   14 dream
the] ~/ The *A*   16–17 gold.// And] ~./ ~ *A*   18 so oft] (~ ~!) *A*   20 barn,]
~; *A*   21 door,] ~; *A*   22 them,] ~; *A*   rose,] ~; *A*   23 singing] singing of
the *A*   lark,] ~ *B*   26 Whose] Where *A*   27 Ye] You *B*   sublime,] ~ *A*   ~. *B*
28 make] set *A*   star!] ~. *A*   30 cockleshell] cockle shell *A*

---

[1] Thrush.   [2] See K99 n. 3.

The vast about them lay,
   The unknown walled them round;
Through alien night and day,   35
   Loneliness was their bound!

Theirs but a grain of wheat,
   Theirs but the small frail hand,
But they gave the race to eat,
   And they made the land.   40

  The handless dreamer wasteful sits among his dreams
While worlds about him fall. These, too, had dreams;
But theirs were dreams of home, of hope, and pride,
And these they braced with deeds!
  They were the sainted ones, haloed by courage,   45
As by endurance they were crowned;
For they were women who at need took up
And plied the axe, or bent above the clodded spade;
Who herded sheep, who rode the hills, and brought
The half-wild cattle home—helpmates of man,   50
Whose children lay within their arms,
Or at the rider's saddle-pommel hung,
And at whose knees, by night, were said familiar prayers.
Ah! though the towers of Ilium topped the skies,[3]
Yet here were women rising higher still.   55
Of such as these was born the Anzac and his pride. . . .

   If ever in the dark embrace
   Of fear it is our lot to stand,
   Vouchsafe, O God, to us this grace:

---

34 round;] ~, *A*   **35** Through . . . day] Like doors, that knew no way *A*
36 bound!] ~. *A*   **42** dreams;] ~. *A*   **43** home] homes *A*   hope,] ~ *A B*
pride,] ~: *A*   ~; *B*   **45** ones,] ~— *A*   **46** crowned;] ~. *A*   **49** sheep,] ~; *A*
50 home—] ~; *B*   man] men *A*   **51** arms,] ~ *B*   **54** though] Though *A*
56 pride. . . .] ~. *A B*

[3] Troy (Ilium) was celebrated for its magnificent buildings; cf. Faustus's well-known greeting to the simulacrum of Helen of Troy in Christopher Marlowe's *Doctor Faustus* (1604): 'Was this the face that launcht a thousand shippes?/ And burnt the toplesse Towres of Ilium?' (V. 1. 1770): *The Complete Works*, ed. Fredson Bowers, vol. II (Cambridge: Cambridge University Press, 1973), p. 220.

That we may be as those who stood,   60
Lone on the threshold of this land,
In their enduring womanhood.

[*] This was specially written for the Sesqui-centenary, and appeared in the women's publication, *The Peaceful Army*.[4]

n1–2 This . . . *Army*.] *Om. A*

[4] Prepared by the FAW to celebrate the NSW sesquicentenary (1938); the editorial committee consisted of Flora Eldershaw, Marjorie Barnard, Dora Wilcox, Miles Franklin and MG.

M4   THE WOMAN OF SIX FIELDS

I met the woman of Six Fields,
    And a fine woman was she;
A better one, as people go,
    You'd be hard put to see.

She had five children, all her own,   5
    And one, a little stray;
She found it left beside her gate,
    And brought it in to stay.

The whole young six were hard to keep,
    And bitter work she had   10
Filling the hunger-set young mouths
    Of each young lass and lad!

Somehow she managed it, and kept
    The old selection too;
I thought it very fine of her,   15
    And a stout thing to do.

I called there once—she'd lost some stock,
    Loss she could ill afford;
For, though she was a woman, she
    Was taxed through bed and board.   20

I saw the children; four fine lads,
  But urchins bold and free;
And two wee girls—I took both up,
  And nursed them on my knee.

Old fashioned little girls they were,   25
  With pig-tails hanging down;
And one was fair with ribboned plaits,
  And one was golden brown.

I asked their names: *"Vic-toria!"*
  Up-spoke the smallest maid,   30
And when I asked the other's name,
  She whispered, *"Adelaide!"*

As for the boys: well, boys are boys;
  Maybe that's half their worth;
And so young *Hobart* beats his drum   35
  With *Sydney—Brisbane—Perth*.

And what a noise the six do make
  When they all get together!
You'd think the world was bursting out,
  When they make rowdy weather.   40

Yet once they stood, grim-faced and stern,
  In fierce and bloody wealds,[1]
Lest some unsanctioned hand should touch
  Their Woman of Six Fields![2]

(22 April 1927)   *Copy-text: Bat*   *Collated states:* None

---

[1] Archaic form for wooded or open country, used here to avoid repetition in a rhyme pair.
[2] I.e. the six Australian states; the 'little stray' (line 6) is presumably Tasmania. Except for Victoria (line 29), each is identified by its capital city.

M5   OLD HENRY PARKES[1]

Coming down the street
In his out-of-date carriage,
The trot of the hoofs
In a rat-a-tat barrage,
Old Henry Parkes,   5
In his big top hat,
His lion-like head,
Eyes like a sword,
Blazing in a thought,
Blazing at affront,   10
Blazing for a word—
But, in-drawn, still, and cold as the ice,
As vision-held he sat, and saw (as William Morris Hughes)[2]
Commonwealth and Empire, brotherly and brother,
This State and that State, all linked together.   15
For Parkes had a vision,
And the vision came true;
And Pitt Street, Macquarie Street,
Never shall forget
That great old man coming down the way,   20
Coming into Sydney like a king!

(9 March 1938)   *Copy-text: Bat   Collated states: ANR* (November 1938), pp. 36–7
as "OLD HENRY PARKES" (*A*)   *SV* (*B*)

1–2 street/ In] ~ in *A*   2 out-of-date] old-time *A*   3–4 hoofs/ In] hoofs like *A*
4 rat-a-tat] small-shot *A*   8 Eyes] His eyes *A*   9 in] on *A*   12 But, in-
drawn,] ~ ~ *A*   13 (as William Morris Hughes)] *Om. B*   14 Empire, brotherly]
~,/ Brotherly *A*   15 State, all] ~/ All *A*   20 That . . . man] Old Henry
Parkes *A*   21 Sydney] town *A*   king!] ~. *A*

---

[1] See K39 n. 1.
[2] 'Billy' Hughes (1862–1952), seen as implementing the 'vision', was a founding member
of the Labor Party and Prime Minister 1915–23. After his failure to gain endorsement
of conscription in the referendum of 1916, he left the Labor Party and, with Opposition
members, formed a governing Nationalist Party; but in 1929 he co-operated with Labor
to overthrow the Nationalist government of Stanley Bruce on the issue of the federal
arbitration system and would be expelled from the right-wing United Australia Party
in 1944 for supporting wartime measures of John Curtin's Labor government (see O11
n. 1). MG consistently admired Hughes. See also M1 (line 103), Q12, R9 and R31.

And Parkes was a king,
A king among men;
Men were his stubble,
Where he bound the best in sheaf,   25
And men were his sheep, that, line after line,
Orderly as sheep, followed after him—
Old Man Parkes,
The leader of them all,
Who, drawing out his fan,   30
Blew the chaff from the wheat—
Blew the chaff from the wheat
And gave the land the grain,
The grain that was unity,
Nationhood, and pride—   35
Old Henry Parkes,
Driving into town,
Driving down the streets,
With the rattle of the hoofs
Rat-tat-tat, rat-a-tat, like a barrage.   40
    Did you say that Parkes was dead?
Parkes couldn't die!
Parkes couldn't go like a cloud in the sky,
Like a flurry in the snow, like a leaf that was shed,
Not while the land   45
Had need of his hand—
His hand on the rein,
His foot on the thill,³
His eyes like a spark,
His tongue like a whip,   50
His leonine head,
His hair like a mat,
And his big top hat,
Coming down the hill,

24 stubble,] ~ *A*   25 sheaf,] ~; *B*   28 Man] man *A*   29 The leader] Leader *A*
35 Nationhood,] ~ *A B*   pride—] ~: *A*   40 Rat-tat-tat,] Like a *A*   Rat-a-tat, *B*
rat-a-tat,] ~ *A*   like a] *Om. A*   40–1 barrage./ Did] ~.// ~ *B*   42 Parkes]
Parkes A   50 whip,] whip,/ His great folded arms, *A*

³ One of a pair of shafts between which a single animal drawing a vehicle is placed.

Coming down the street,   55
Coming into Sydney
In his old borrowed carriage!

57 old borrowed] ~——~— *A*   carriage!] ~. *A*

м6   FOR ANZAC (1939)

I saw the bird arise!
His mighty wings were golden beams,
His head was gold, and his breast;
His eyes were golden fire—
I could not look in his eyes   5
For the flame of their golden fire.

I saw the bird arise,
The pride-renewing and ever immortal Austral bird!
Over the edge of the sea he came,
Over the edge of the world;   10
Nothing could stay his path!
He had the feet that Lionel Lindsay[1] drew,*
The dancer's stately and unhindered feet;
The pinions of his shouldered wings
Were flared for freedom, verge to verge.   15
Higher and higher he rose;
I saw him rise! He was a bird—A bird?
He was a man who bore the sun,
Our own effulgent and unchanging Austral sun![2]

I saw him rise . . .   20
Anzac eternally shall see him rise,

---

[1] (1874–1961), artist, art critic and brother of Norman Lindsay, with whom he worked
closely in the early stages of their careers: see K36 n. 1. His 1924 wood-engraving
(author's note) depicts a brolga, the dancing Australian native bird: cf. I27 lines 25–7.
[2] 'Rising Sun' emblem, the only identifying badge worn by the first Australian Imperial
Force (AIF) when it left for the Middle East in 1914 and still the emblem of the
Australian Army, the title that replaced AIF in 1948.

Unconquered in his bright
Ascending flame.

* "The Dancer"; a wood-cut.

(16 December 1938)   *Copy-text: Bat*   *Collated states:* None

M7   THE OLD BRIGADE[*]

Now they are gone, and I am come
To the waterless ford where none
Drink, but where, with a heart grown numb,
Each mourns for those whose race is run.

Where now shall we turn, we ask, when   5
Out of the years we greet again
Friends we have missed like the lost men
Held in the ebb of war's dark plain?

And in meetings to come, on whom
Shall we call to tell of the things   10
That, sitting round, as in a room
Of memory, each full heart brings?

One day I found after long years
A lost old comrade, whom I left
With the aching of unshed tears,   15
Having learned how life was bereft.

For of this that we told, and that—
Of what we remembered and said—
Remained, from all who might have sat
With us there, not one. They were dead.   20

Now *he* is gone. I am the last.
And of those who once were a host,

(28 July 1936)   *Copy-text: Bat*   *Collated states: QD* (October 1936), p. 6 (*A*)

6 greet] meet, *A*   again] ~, *A*   **7** missed] ~, *A*   **9** meetings to come] meeting anew *A*   on] to *A*   **10** call . . . the] re-tell the talked-of *A*   things] ~, *A*   **11** round,] close *A*   **12** full heart] to the other *A*   **15** the] an *A*   **16** Having learned] As I felt *A*   **18** what] all *A*   **19** from all] of those *A*   **20** one. They] ~; they *A*   **21** *he*] he *A*   gone.] ~, *A*

Since on to the shades they have passed,
Lone in the dusk, I am the ghost.

[*] This relates to a Digger, the last of his group. He was in the Sudan campaign as a youth, then with my brothers at the Boer War,[1] and last in 1914–18. He sat on the same bench with us at school. Now he, too, is gone.

23 Since on] Although *A*   24 am the] am a *A*   n1 This relates to a] These lines were inspired after a visit to an old *A*   Sudan] Soudan *A*   n2 youth] lad *A* then] ~, *A*   at] in *A*   n2–3 last in] later in the Great War of *A*   n3 18] 1918 *A* He . . . school.] Greatly be-medalled, he was the last of his school of war friends. *A* n4 gone.] gone.—M.G., Sydney, 28th July, 1936. *A*

[1] A contingent of Australian colonial soldiers joined the British Sudan campaign in 1885 but saw little active service, unlike in the Boer War, 1899–1902.

M8   BATTLEFIELDS

"Art lonely, lad, now the earth covers thee?"
Nay; them I fought talk friendly here with me.

"Hast thou no patriot grief? No sense of loss?"
Not now! 'Twas flags hung Christ again on Cross;

For, Nineteen-fourteen to the end, as died   5
Each man, in him was Christ re-crucified.

Now He is weary; now He rests with us,
In quiet of the grave, all piteous.

Jewry Him crucified but once, with leave
To lay His body where no rat might thieve,   10

No beaked bird tear upon His flesh, no fly
Light down upon His mouth to putrefy;

But here, His sworn Church men, as armies died,
Gave to the rat, and fly, men crucified.

So we forget about them and their ways—   15
They who slew peace to chant a killer's praise—

And we, who once were young and loved the sun,
Talk in the dark with Christ: as Him undone.

Christ or Barabbas, Judah's choosing ran;[1]
For us no choice; we had but war's red fan.   20

Now in the grave meet all the sacrificed:
We and the foe, and Church's outcast Christ.

(23 April 1932) *Copy-text: Bat*   *Collated states:* None
19 Barabbas *Ed.*] Barrabas *X*

---

[1] All four gospels record that the Jewish crowd, offered a choice between Christ and Barabbas the thief as the one prisoner to be freed by Pilate, chose the latter (e.g. Matthew 27. 15–23).

M9   THE JEWS[*]

We are the Jews!
We are they who in all lands
Have wandered and have wept,
But who, through tribulation, still have held
The law; and our hands   5
Are a Jew's hands yet.
    We are they, who, destitute and driven,
From the depths have raised our eyes,
And with an upward look have sung the Lord's song
In a stranger land. O, even as our fathers,   10
We have kept the law; our priests still bless
The bread that marked deliverance,[1]
As when two doves were sacrificed,
And the old scape-goat was loosed
In the far-off years of splendour and the kings.   15
And though we have lived an-hungered,
And though we have wandered homeless in all lands,

---

[1] Eating unleavened bread in memory of the deliverance of the Israelites from Egypt is enjoined in Exodus 12. 14–20, and the sacrifice of doves and goats (lines 13–14) as ritual atonement and purification in Leviticus 14. 22 and 16. 7–10.

We held the covenant with God,
And still through loss—yea, even in death!—
Unchanged we stand with Abraham for our father.   20

We are the Jews!
London grew rich upon the Jew![2]
In London's market place,
For a Jew's ransom, one by one
Our living teeth were drawn, and a Jew's marred face   25
Was record of the persecutor's hand.[3]
The lash, the cell, the rack, the stake,
Slit ears, and the sad, bent back were ours;
And yet we stood—and we emerged—
And are the Jews.   30
    We are they who to that England brought
The goldsmith's art, and on the raw
Mass of her nation's being wrought,
Until by her Jew-widened power she queened the seas,
Or saw her libbards creep   35
Where the dark cliffs of Ireland caught
The sound of battle from far France and Spain.[4]
Now as a Jew's tooth still see London stand,
Mighty among the mighty, and the mightier through us.

    We are they who gave to Spain   40
That proud pre-eminence that never since was hers;

[2] Many Sephardic Jews expelled from Spain by Ferdinand and Isabella in 1492 migrated to England, where they contributed substantially to its increasing economic power during the sixteenth century and its subsequent maritime predominance (line 34).

[3] According to *Brewer's Dictionary of Phrase and Fable*, this tradition is based on reports that Jews were tortured to extort money. When a rich Jew of Bristol resisted King John's demand for 10,000 marks, the King ordered that one of his teeth should be pulled every day till he paid. When the tortured man capitulated after seven days, John reportedly quipped: 'A Jew's eye may be a quick ransom, but a Jew's teeth give the richer harvest' (14th edn by Ivor H. Evans; London: Cassell, 1990), p. 605. Lines 38–9 appear to mean that in the twentieth century the Jews keep their teeth and London its power.

[4] Protestant England's conquest of Catholic Ireland, begun under Elizabeth I (reigned 1558–1603) and pursued in Oliver Cromwell's campaigns (1649–52), was always under threat from local rebellion and real or feared intervention from the Catholic powers of Spain (in 1588) and France (in 1690, and during the Napoleonic Wars). On the 'libbards' of England's royal crest (line 35), see H75 n. 3.

And on the Tiber once we stood mighty in pride;
The Adriatic knew our ships; and our brave pennon
Floated out on every breeze, and wheresoe'er we trading went
The wealth of nations grew.   45

We are the Jews—
The hunted Lazarus[5] of all the world!
And yet the world was Lazarus to us,
When safe beneath our table, on the crumbs that fell,
It lived. War had destroyed it   50
Had the Jew not been its stay;
Famine had eaten it, had not the Jew,
With open coffers, fed it from his hand;
And pest had swept its people to the grave,
Had not a Jew's eyes looked with pity   55
On its grief. Invention—science—art—
A Jew's tooth still is ransom for the world.
But O, Jerusalem, how we have wept for thee![6]

[*] No people have been so persecuted as the Jews. With the exception
of America and Australia, no nation is free of the charge. Every land
has dispersed them, every country has robbed them. Time has made no
difference to this mistreatment. Yet, to wherever the Jew has gone, he has
returned good for evil. He has brought trade, given trade, and, no matter   n5
out of what poverty, has created wealth. If "to love your enemies, bless
them that curse you, do good to them that hate you and pray for them
which despitefully use you and persecute you," is an essential root of
Christianity, then, judged by his conduct, the Jew is the most Christian
of peoples. Australia has been kind to the Jews, but with an exceeding   n10
niggardliness of written tribute—General Monash excepted.[7]

(6 January 1933)   *Copy-text: Bat   Collated states:* None

5 The leprous beggar of Luke 16. 20, not the resurrected brother of Mary and
Martha.
6 Links the diaspora to the Babylonian captivity (see K23 and n. 2 and cf. K73).
7 On Monash, see M1 n. 7. The biblical quotation (n6–8) is Matthew 5. 44–5.

M10   THE YARRAN TREE[1]

The Lady of the Yarran tree,
  She built herself a house,
And, happy in it, there she lived
  As tidy as a mouse;
She set a stool against the fire,   5
  And hung the broom beside,
And yet, although she sat alone,
  The door was open wide.

And she beside the Yarran tree
  Was busy as could be;   10
She kept her sheep, she carded wool,
  Her bleach[2] was white to see;
She baked her bread from wheat she grew,
  She tanned the good ox-hide;
And still, for all she sat alone,   15
  Her door was open wide.

The Lady of the Yarran tree
  Looked out, one night, and saw
The dark hand of a stranger reach
  To lay on her his law;   20
She rose and drew the curtain close,
  Her little lamp to hide—
And yet, for all she was alone,
  The door stood open wide.

I asked her if she didn't know   25
  The fears of woman-kind,

(21 April 1927) Copy-text: Bat Collated states: ANR (January 1938), pp. 61–2
(A)   Mackaness2 (B)   SV as THE YARRAN-TREE (C)   Mackaness3 reprints B

Not otherwise recorded: Wherever copy-text has 'Yarran tree', A has 'Yarran Tree' and
C has 'Yarran-tree'.

1 Lady] Woman A   1 tree,] Tree A   3 And,] ~ A   it, there] its space A
7 yet] there A   9 And she beside] The Woman of A   17 Lady] Woman A
18 out,] ~ A   night,] ~ A   19 dark hand] Dark Hand A   26 woman-kind]
womankind A

[1] See K23 n. 1.   [2] Linen (bleached in laundering).

That, though by day they come and go,
  Are still within the mind.
She looked at me and slowly said,
  "Such fears in me abide!"   30
And yet I knew she sat alone,
  The door left open wide.

The Yarran tree against the spring
  Put out its amber green,
Like golden berries, on each twig,   35
  Its blossoms all were seen;
I saw the stranger watch the tree,
  The woman there inside—
And still, although she sat alone,
  The door was open wide.   40

To her beside the Yarran tree,
  I said, "Go buy a ring,
A ring of silver laced with steel,
  From which a shot may sing;
Then, when the stranger hears its song,   45
  As winds shall bear it wide,
It will be safe to sit alone,
  The house-door open wide."

Then she beside the Yarran tree,
  She turned and looked at me,   50
She laid the spinning from her hand,
  And spake as still could be;
"Go you," she said, "and make the ring,
  And make of it your pride;
That I may safely sit alone,   55
  The door set open wide."

29 slowly said] answered there *A*   30 abide!"] ~"; *A*   35 berries,] ~ *A*   twig,]
~ *A*   38 inside] beside *A*   39 still] yet *A*   40 The] Her *A*   was] stood *A*
43 steel,] ~ *A*   44 From] Through *C*   45 its] the *C*   song,] ~ *A*   46 As]
The *A*   shall] *Om. A*   it] far and *A*   48 house-door] house door *A*   49 Then
she beside] The Woman of *A*   52 And] Then *A*   53 ring,] ~ *C*   55 That]
Then *A*

I took the woman at her word,
    And straitly³ there I made
A ring of silver laced with steel,
    That sang as trumpets played;   60
I set it down against the step,
    And, though the door is wide,
The Lady of the Yarran tree
    Dwells ever safe inside.

57 woman] Woman *A*   58 straitly] straightly *A*   59 steel,] ~ *A*   61 against
the step] beside her door *A*   62 And,] ~ *C*   the door is] it still stands *A*
63 Lady] Woman *A*

³ Strictly to requirements (archaic), but cf. *A*'s reading (entry for line 58), meaning
urgently.

M11   TO MY BROTHER HUGH¹

Now comes the hour in which I say farewell and go;
Yet I shall return, who go I know not whither,
And when I have come again I shall talk with you,
And we will remember we were children once.

For though we are but as shadows of a long-gone day,   5
Though with eyes darkened with years we backward look,
Yet are we two one when memory awakes,
And in an old thought, with mine, your heart will leap.

(15 July 1933)   *Copy-text: Bat   Collated states: SMH*, 19 August 1933, p. 9 as TO MY
BROTHER (*A*)   *SV* (*B*)

1 ⁸Now] Soon *A*   farewell] ~, *A*   2 whither,] ~: *A*   5 as shadows] the
shades *A*   6 years] our tears *B*   7 awakes] goes by *A*   8 thought,] ~ *A*
mine,] ~ *A*   leap] break *A*

¹ Hugh Cameron, oldest of MG's younger brothers (1866–1935). See textual note: in
1933 MG was in her late sixties and Hugh already in ill-health; cf. entries for lines 1 and
22. They had become estranged after his marriage broke down, despite his earlier help
in financing the *Bkfw*: see further, volume 1, Introduction, p. xlv and *CG* 177–81.

Twice have I stood by the once familiar door,
Where as children we entered in and knew it home;   10
It was the stranger's face looked out at me there;
When my hand went up to the latch a strange voice spoke.

Yet there were ghosts at the forge, and down by the well
I heard the windlass creak, and the oil-drum bucket drip;
And Chessie stamped for her feed in the high thatched stall,   15
While the peaches were all in bloom, and the vines in leaf.

In the grey stackyard[2] the house-dog pulled on his chain,
And there, full-voiced, he barked me his glad surprise;
Neptune! I called—I?—Nay, 'twas a child long gone,
With the stack, and the dog, and our yesterdays.   20

We were a long time children, O my brother,
It will be longer, yet, ere we two shall forget;
For we held by a dream, and the dream still stands,
Though the stranger walks in the ways that once were ours.

---

11 It was the] But only a *A*   there;] ~: *A*   **14** creak,] ~ *A*   oil-drum] *Om. A*
16 While the peaches] The peach trees *A*   all] out *A*   vines] vines were *A*
17 In] And up by *A*   grey stackyard] stack *A*   grey stock-yard *B*   the house-dog]
an old dog *A*   **18** And] As *A*   there, full-voiced,] ~ ~ *A*   surprise;] ~. *A*
19 *Neptune!*] "Neptune!" *A*   ~! *B*   called—I?—] ~. ~? *A*   **20** stack,] ~ *A B*
22 It . . . forget] Who turn in these last still hours and backward look *A*
23 For] But *A*   stands] lives *A*

---

[2] Farmyard or enclosure containing the 'stack' (line 20), presumably of firewood or hay;
B's emendation to 'stock-yard' is unwarranted (see entry for line 17).

M12   EL BARCALDINO[1]

I

The time you came you sat awhile and talked,
Just the small simple talk of every day;
But I heard a wind from memory's distant hills,
And from its valleys far away.

You had no knowledge of those hills;   5
You had not seen the dawn come linking over them,
Nor had you seen the twilight of the valleys
Shadow the sun's high diadem.

And yet you called the past who never knew the past—
Some trick of speech, some movement of the head—   10
Maybe not even these! But when you went
My heart was withered for a day long dead.

II

So many times I think of you,
    Yet, ever as I think,
I see the running feet of a child,   15
    At the world's high brink.

Why should I think of you as a child,
    Who think not of others so?
Only God, Who has made all things,
    And the ancestors know.   20

(Pt I: 3 July 1938; Pt II: 4 September 1938)[2]   *Copy-text: Bat   Collated states: SMH*, 24
September 1938, p. 21, Pt II only, as WITH A CHILD'S SMALL FEET (*A*)

0.1–12.1 ˢI . . . II] *Om. A*   **15** child,] ~ *A*   **17** should] do *A*   think of] see *A*
18 think not of] see not *A*   **19** has] hath *A*

---

[1] Spanish-sounding nonce word: cf. the (authentic) titles of B50 and I150. M12's may
refer to someone connected with Barcaldine Downs, a site of the shearers' strike of
1891; see F81 n. 1 and M1 line 49.
[2] In ML 6/2 and 6/3, the parts occur as separate poems; the NLA MSS in 727 1/M
and 727 2/4/17 are of Pt II only: see volume 1, Appendix for manuscript locations and
descriptions.

MI3   THE OLD SCHOOLFELLOWS[1]

THE GIRLS' SCHOOL

Ah, whither are ye gone, who, from the old school door,
Came forth tumultuous as a mountain stream?
Now but in memory do we behold you,
Save when one, down-bent and old, is seen
Reading lost names upon a stone.   5
Then, like the tide the moon draws up,
Rises the eagre[2] of the mind.

Whither, the heart cries, are they gone,
Who, when the clattering slates were passed
And in the olden cedar presses piled-up lay,   10
Rushed eddying out like leaves the wind
In drifts uplifted from the playground sand—
To whirl awhile and hold, and then let fall again!

The Murrumbidgee (*Mother-of-Great-Waters*)[3]
Flows as then; the rain makes runnels as it did   15
When we, in buttoned coats, from out the porch
Thrust headlong forth to meet the storm,
Or at its going stood and watched
The cumulus ride on like kings.

[cont. overleaf

(n. d.)   *Copy-text: Bat   Collated states: WDA*, 22 March 1935, p. 4, signed MARY
GILMORE. The Lyceum Club, Sydney (*A*)[4]   *SV* (*B*)

0.1 THE] (i) THE *B*   **1** Ah, whither] Whither *A*   old] *Om. A*   door,] ~ *A*
2 Came] Issued *A*   tumultuous] tempestuous *A*   **4** one,] ~ *A*   **5** stone.] ~; *A*
~, *B*   **9** passed] ~, *A*   **10** piled-up] piled up *A*   **11** Rushed] Ran *A*
12 sand—] ~ *A*   **13** To . . . hold,] And spun—and spun again— *A*   fall again!]
fall. *A*   **14** Murrumbidgee] ~, *A B*   (*Mother-of-Great-Waters*)] Mother of great
Waters, *A*   ~, *B*   **17** Thrust] Rushed *A*   storm,] ~; *A*   **18** Or] ~, *B*   going]
~, *B*

---

[1] At Wagga Wagga Public School: see L7 n. 1 and n. 4 below. Separation of girls and
boys within school areas was standard practice.
[2] Dangerous wave in front of a flood-tide, especially in a river.
[3] See I3 n. 5.
[4] *A* has this note: 'This fragment is part of what I intended as tribute to my old school
and its town [Wagga Wagga], but which now will probably never be written.—M.G.'

How many and many a time we heard   20
The thunder rolling down the sky,
Or shook beneath a crash, or marked
The distant rumble in the hills
As tempest rose, then slowly dwindled out,
And left the sweet of rain-wet air!   25

And always there was one who led.
. . . Now is that golden head grown white
As snow with years, the dancing feet
Are heavy with the lead of time.

THE BOYS' SCHOOL

And there were others—boys who in the lower   30
Playground took the bat, or pulled the jangling bell;
Who leapt and raced, or swung upon the grey
Trapeze and thought they spanned the world!
Now but as shades they come to me and say:
"We were as wanderers who might not stay,   35
And though hands clung, and though loved voices called,
Always we must away. For in us stirred
A forward will that would not rest,
Though, at the end, the desert lag was ours,
And all the dreadfulness of hope   40
In the long sea-death of thirst.
But only they know, who have heard
The sea call, and the land beckon,
How forever it was with us."
So one would tell of things that he,   45
In his far-off journeyings, had seen;
Or of how, dwelling again in peace at home,
The moving plough would seem a ship,

23 hills] ~, *A*   24 then] or *A*   28 As snow with] With *B*   29 time.] ~ *A*
29.1 THE] (ii) THE *B*   30 lower] other *A*   31 bell;] ~, *A*   32 Who] And *A*
33 Trapeze] ~, *A*   35 stay,] ~— *A*   36 And though] Though the *A*   though]
though the *A*   36–7 voices called,/ Always] voices/ Of children called, *A*
37 away.] ~; *A*   37–8 For . . . stirred/ A] for in/ Us stirred a *A*   39 Though,]
~ *A*   end,] ~ *A*   the desert lag] shipwreck *A*   40 And] With *A*   hope] ~, *A*
41 In] And *A*   sea-death] sea death *A*   thirst.] ~: *A*   42 But] And *A*   know,]
~ *B*   45 So one would] And then would one *A*   46 journeyings,] ~ *A*

The share a prow, and in his hand
The plough-tail seem a tillered wheel.   50
Then was he rent in twain to go.
And some would sing the drovers' song
In wraiths of sound that had been song long gone.
And as these sang, and as those talked, arose,
Like some deep ferment of the earth,   55
The old proud lusts[5] of life from sleep,
Until it seemed the unbodied will,
And hosted longings of the heart
Of man, still moved about the world,
And in that moving conquered death.   60

50 plough-tail] plough-shaft *A*   **51** go.] ~ *A*   **52** song] ~, *A B*   **53** gone.] ~; *A*
~, *B*   **57** will,] ~ *A*   **59** man,] ~ *A*

[5] See K107 n. 1.

M14   THE CLANSMAN'S CALL

Now you are gone
Remember me to the dead,
Who, living, knew me as one with them.
They fought, nor thought of reward;
I, too, have fought,   5
And all I won was that I fought:
Even as you: even as it was with them.
They lost, and you and I lost,
As the world counts loss;
But something there was   10
That was more than the winning,
More than the well-filled hand and the loud acclaim;
And that was dominion—
Dominion in ultimate power at its height.
Rustless they went.   15
As you. Now you are gone.
Give them my love, and say
I shall go rustless as they.

Clansmen before we were born,
Unknown and unknowing,   20
They, you, and I, were one.

(27 November 1930)   *Copy-text: Bat   Collated states:* None

MI5   THE SNIPE

For D. H. Drummond[1]

Out of the mist of the marsh—
Out of the dusk—came the deep dark cry
That the bitterns make, with the harsh
Flat note of the crane, and the rough
Wild call as the ibises broke   5
To descend, while the slash of the plover's wing
Cut through the echoes that woke
As the curlews wept on a note.
Then, thin as the small pale stars in the sky,
I heard on the night the voice of the snipe—   10
The bird with a reed in its throat.

   And I thought of an hour when I stood by the sea,
And ever its passionate music rose
Where the thrash of its beating waters struck
On the rock and the sand; and I heard   15
The cry of the wheeling sea-gulls close on the wind,
And, small as the voice of the snipe in the marsh,
The distant shrill of a bo'sun's pipe;
While, afar at the slips, the shout of a man,
And the roll of a winch, scarce seemed to be more   20
Than the ghost of a sound as they came
Where I stood inshore.

(16 December 1936)   *Copy-text: Bat   Collated states: SV* (*A*)
1 marsh—] ~, *A*   **2** dusk—] ~, *A*   **13** rose] ~, *A*

---

[1] Perhaps David Henry Drummond (1890–1965), long-serving Country Party member
for Armidale in the NSW Legislative Assembly and Minister for Education 1927–30
and 1932–41.

Then my thought went back to the snipe,
That, swift as an arrow,
Will flicker and dart, and harrow   25
A-high and a-low the mist of the marsh,
And I saw the far Siberian wastes,
And a small hot-hearted thing
That nor slackens nor hastes
As it furrows its way on the air,   30
But into the core of the wind
Breasts on, higher and higher,
Till the void and the cloud and the bird
Are alone in the universe.
 And my heart was shaken to think of its small frail form, 35
And the way it had fared—and must fare—
Since the first weak flight, with naught but a wing,
Thrust forth from the *tundra* ice, and the north,
To rest on a wind like the edge of a share.

 O flake, where a man asks engines of power   40
To bear him aloft, in thy small proud head
Thou hast all that his gathering might
Has charted, and written, and read,
Through the span of his centuried years!

 . . . Out of the mist of the marsh,   45
Afar and remote,
I heard the cry of the snipe—
The bird with a reed in its throat.

26–7 marsh,/ And] ~.// ~ *A* 29 hastes] ~, *A* 34–5 universe./ And] ~.// ~ *A*
39 of a] of a furrowing *A* 46 Afar] Small *A*

  M16 THIS MANY A DAY

  When he is old,
  Old in his feet and grey,
  Hearing the songs they sing of her,
  Then he will say,

"In the years gone by, when a babe I was,   5
  In her arms she held me,
  On her lap I lay,
  In her eyes I looked and her face was kind;
  Now she is gone this many a day!"

  Then he will say,   10
  As he leans on his stick,
"Quick was her step,
  And her heart was quick!"
  And, as there he stoops in the sun's high noon
  Like a candle bent over its wick,   15
  Like a spurt of flame, in a moment's trick,
  Mem'ries will wake, old dreams come thick.

  And again, as they speak of her there,
  Like a flash of light,
  Like a sudden flare,   20
  Like a beam in a forest too dense for air,
  There will fall a ray on the dim lost mind,
  And the tangles of memory out will draw,
  Ordered and orderly, flaw by flaw,
  Each after each like steps in a stair,   25
  And a tear will fall from an old man's eye,
  For a sudden loss, and an old man there.

  Yet when they ask him again,
  The old man there in the sun,
"What colour her eyes? . . . what colour her hair?"   30
"She lived as a nun!" he will say,
  As though there was nothing to find
  In his poor old mind
  Of her gone this many a day!

  As they sing their songs of her long, long gone,   35
  Why should an old man tremble to tears
  For a woman who kissed him in baby years?
  Age is the mirror of all men's years.
  When a face looks out where memory peers,
  Whose was the face? What matter.   40

Out of the fallen, the empty years,
Find in an old man's weeping all men's tears.

(5 November 1923)   *Copy-text: Bat*   *Collated states:* None

MI7   THE RIDER[1]

I draw a-near you in your sleeping city,
    Who, in mine ancient freedom,
Knew neither loss nor scant;
    Who hunted even as he who hunted Edom,[2]
And hungered not before   5
What bidding look love bore.
Now as one immigrant,
Now as one supplicant,
I draw a-near you in your sleeping city.

I draw a-near you in your sleeping city;   10
    And, on the darkness falling,
My voice to you is heard
    As lone upon the night as that far calling,
When, as his hidden word,
The lion, passion-stirred,   15

(9 July 1932)   *Copy-text: Bat*   *Collated states: Bn*, 8 November 1933, p. 41 as I DRAW
ANEAR YOU IN YOUR SLEEPING CITY (*A*)   *SV* (*B*)

Not otherwise recorded: A has 'anear' wherever copy-text has 'a-near'.
1–9 I draw . . . city.] *Om. A*   **10** city;] ~, *A B*   **11** And,] ~ *A*   on the darkness]
like far waters *A*   falling,] ~ *A*   **12** heard] ~, *A*   **13** far] lost *A*

---

[1] After reviewing *Bat*, R. D. FitzGerald wrote on 17 January 1940: 'I know exactly
what you mean when you suggest that movement is "enclosed" in this . . . The poem
moves progressively forward and you feel, as you read, the continuous approach. You
are the approaching person as you read; just as you are the *approached* person as you
read Thompson's Hound of Heaven . . . the same sense of approach – as well as mere
movement – is in both pieces. Strangely, although I admire "The Rider" greatly (as you
can see), I found it difficult to quote from: individual passages were robbed of their value
as contributing factors towards a splendidly *unified* piece of work' (ML Papers vol. 12).
[2] Another name for Esau, the hunter in contrast to his younger brother Jacob, the
cultivator, to whom Esau sold his birthright (see K59 n. 2). Esau eventually founded a
kingdom, named Edom after him (Genesis 36. 1–8).

Looses against the sky
The languors of his cry.
I draw a-near you in your sleeping city.

I draw a-near you in your sleeping city,
   Where, with its lanterns burning,   20
It seems to veil apart
   In misted light your sleep, toward which, with yearning,
Even as o'er the waste
The mourning plovers haste,
Leaps my impatient heart   25
To be to yours a dart.
I draw a-near you in your sleeping city.

I draw a-near you in your sleeping city,
   Moving as one imprisoned,
And yet as one in whom   30
   The captured as the conqueror is visioned;
For in my hollow hand
Your feet will one day stand—
Yea, even to the tomb
Love webbed us in one loom!   35
I draw a-near you in your sleeping city.

I draw a-near you in your sleeping city,
   All night toward you riding,
Who watched Orion[3] lift
   On high his sword, and marked the deep abiding   40
Of Arcturus in flame,
As though it brought to shame
The Galaxy's pale drift,

17 languors *A*] langours *X*   30 And yet] ~, ~, *A*   34 even] for love *A*
35 Love] Has *A*   42 it] he *A*

[3] Constellation known as the Hunter. Lines 40–4 contrast the consistent brilliance of Arcturus (the Bear Watcher), brightest star in the constellation of Bootes (the Herdsman), with the pallor of the Milky Way and the 'dark unthrift' of 'the Twain-Star' – a binary star, described by William Herschel (1728–1822) in 1802: see F139 n. 1. One of the binary pair may eclipse the other, or in X-Ray binaries, a black hole or neutron star devours material from its companion star, which may eventually disappear altogether.

The Twain-Star's dark unthrift.
I draw a-near you in your sleeping city.   45

I draw a-near you in your sleeping city,
    All night toward you moving;
And as I rode there broke
    The long, long cry of all my life's behoving,
That rose against what cost   50
Of living hours—and lost—
Since there was none bespoke
My heart till you it woke.
I draw a-near you in your sleeping city.

I draw a-near you in your sleeping city   55
As shipwreck draws toward its shore.
The night-wind faints upon the distant hills,
    And house-made shadows ebon lie as though
There never dawn upon the silver sills
    Of heaven waked with amber glow.   60
I draw a-near you in your sleeping city.
Now am I at your gate, my hand upon your door.

47 toward] towards *A*   moving;] ~: *A*   51 and] so *A*   lost] ~! *A*   57 hills,]
~; *A*   58 And] Ebon the *A*   ebon] *Om. A*   lie] ~, *A*   59 There] Came *A*
60 waked] *Om. A*   61 city.] ~; *A*

M18   THE MOTHER

I shall go to him, but he will not return to me.
I shall follow, follow, follow after, though the stars fade
And the sun itself die out; though earth pass,
And the waters of the firmament run dry for ever;
Though there be nothing left but the void, and still the void! 5
O even as a bird with beating wings that at the evening flies,
On—on—and ever on—
So shall I follow, follow, follow after.
He will not return to me, but I shall go to him.

(25 September 1937)   *Copy-text: Bat*   *Collated states: SMH*, 21 May 1938, p. 21 (*A*)
4 run] are *A*   6 O] ~, *A*   flies,] ~ *A*

M19   ALISON OF THE MARGE[1]

Oh, when you touch me, sweeps
To music every chord that sleeps,
And when you kiss, my blood
Leaps like the sea-tides in their flood,
And all the emptiness of years   5
Clamours in crying at my ears,
And I am caught as in a wind
That takes my breath, and I am blind—am blind!
For I have hungered for you so,
Starved like a lost bird in the snow.   10

I have known winds in desert places,
And seen the stars as frozen faces,
And watched the large relenting sun
Shield-widen as the day was done,
And marked the late bird turn to his own,   15
But I was alone, alone—
I was alone in the heat, in the cold,
Like a lamb that is strayed from her fold.

I have heard life like a voice in the night,
Lost like a light—a wandering light—   20
In the fen, in the mist,
And never a hand was there,
And no one to care—
Have hungered and striven,
And suffered unshriven;   25

(n. d.)   *Copy-text:* Bat   *Collated states:* Wilkinson2 (*A*)   *SV* (*B*)

Not otherwise recorded: Lines 11–45 are in italics in *A*.

1 Oh] Ah *A*   O *B*   **2** sleeps,] ~; *A*   **9** For] Oh, *A*   so,] ~; *A*   **10** snow.]
~! *A*   **13** large] *large*, *A*   **15** marked] *seen A*   *16* alone—] ~. *B*   **18** Like]
As A   **21** mist,] *mist; A*   **23** care—] ~; *B*

[1] See I76 n. 1. *Alisoun* was a popular medieval name, e.g. the Wife of Bath and the
heroine of 'The Miller's Tale' in *The Canterbury Tales* of Geoffrey Chaucer and the
lyric 'Betweene Merch and Averil'. 'Marge', related to *margin*, is commonly a river's
edge or bank.

Have hungered for you
As the burned up earth for the dew,
As the withering grass for the rain,
As the parching herb for the end of pain—
Have misered in anguish to spend,   30
And followed the dream, that was you, to the end!

O, I have hungered for you
As the strength in the thew
For the quoit, the axe, and the spear;
As the sap at the spring of the year   35
For the pathway of life in the tree;
As, captive, the wing of the gull for the fetterless sea—
Have hungered, and dreamed, and held to the dream,
As a light, as a gleam;
And out of the darkness I came at the end—   40
At the end—unbroken to you.

But cloud in a wan wet sky
Has wept not more than I,
And never the darkness of night has seen
A dark like the dark where my soul has been.   45

---

26 Have hungered] *Hungered A*   **27** burned up] *burned-up A*   **29** pain—] ~; *B*
31 dream,] *dream A*   you,] *you A*   **32** O,] *Oh, A*   *Om. B*   **34** quoit,] *quoit,*
and A   spear;] *spear, A*   **35** spring] *Spring A*   **36** tree;] *tree, A*   **37** wing]
wings *B*   **37** sea—] ~; *B*   **38** dream,] *dream A*   **42** wan] *wan, A*   **43** not]
no A   I,] *I; A*

M20   THE ROAD[*][1]

Friends! And the sky without a cloud.
Friends! And from the heart

(11 July 1921)   *Copy-text: Bat*   *Collated states: HR* (n. t.) (*A*)   *SV* (*B*)

Not otherwise recorded: A lacks a title, has no stanza breaks and, being in italic font
throughout, lacks the change of font at lines 52 and 64 of the copy-text.
1 Friends] *"Friends A*

---

[1] See author's note: M20 had appeared in *HR* in II. VIII: 'On the Track to Braidwood'

Fallen the day's low care!
. . . Hark! In the trees a thrush—
With only his voice to break on the hush   5
Of the sweet and the scented air!
Hush of the heart, hush of the soul,
With beauty itself for the part and the whole.

Ah! As came the even,
Wistfully at even,   10
All in the sunset steven,[2]
Wistfully turned we then,
Wistfully turned we home,
Facing the road of men,
Skirting a mottle of loam,[3]   15
Skirting the planted field
Rich in its mellowing yield,
Riding on where orchard keeps[4]
Clung about their rocky steeps,
And down the river of sedges   20
Where clear the water dredges,
And on where upland and lowland lay,
Gold at the end of a golden day!

Sister, sister, sister mine,
Hold once more my hand!   25
Was that the sky I saw? Hush!
Comes once again the song of the thrush,
And the road winds on, and on, and on . . .
. . . Nay! It is gone!

3 low] long B   4 ˢ. . . Hark] *Hark A*   thrush—] *thrush, A* ~, B   6 air!]
air— A   8 whole.] *whole! A*   9 Ah!] *"Ah! A* *Om. B*   *9–11* As . . . steven,]
Once as came the dusk, / All in the flowery musk, B   12 then,] *then; A*   18 on]
up A   20 down] *down by A*   22 lay,] *lay A*   24 Sister] . . . . *"Sister A*   28
on . . .] *on. . . . . A*   29 ˢ. . . Nay] . . . . *Nay! A* ~ B   It] *it A*

(e. of Canberra), embedded without title in a sequence of chapters from 'The House of
Memory'; it is presented as a fantasy built on a group of domestic objects found in an
abandoned settler's hut. M20 has affinities to the motif of the loved one lost to a lonely
grave (cf. A11 and G15) and tales of love lost to a friend, as in 'Loraine' in *Loraine and
Other Verses* (1898) by George Essex Evans (1863–1909).   [2] See J18 n. 1.
[3] Patch of ground patterned with a dappled surface; an unreliable footing for a horse.
[4] Enclosures.

And I am alone, in the dark,   30
Like a lost boat out in the sea,
With never a light nor a mark
To salvage me.

Yet I remember!
What was it that I remember?   35
. . . Was it the lonely grave
On the little round hill,
So quiet and still?
Ah! Could I think of it, quiet and still,
Where no bolt[5] falls and no winds rave,   40
Where only the young spring grasses wave,
And buttercups bend and hover
As ever the wind runs over and over—
Was it yesterday? . . .
Would that I might remember!   45

Are the candles lit, sister, my sister?
Light them, then, and sit with me here.
This was her ribbon . . . My dear! My dear!
And this was the rose whose scented breath
Lives in my heart and knows not death;   50
And this was the glove she wore;
And this . . . *Put them away!*
Never for me her tenderness,
Never for me her love;
Never for me her eyes' caress,   55
Never for me, my dove!

Something there was that held between:
What was it, O my sister?
Hands as it were that held unseen,
A voice that called ere love could speak,   60

---

30 alone,] *alone A*   **31** sea,] *~ A*   **34** Yet] *"Yet A*   **39** Could] *could A*
42 hover] *~, B*   **43** As ever] *As, ever, A*   over—] *over! A*   *~! B*   **44** Was] *Ah!*
was A   **46** Are] *"Are A*   **48** dear! My] *dear! my A*   **53** Never] *"Never A*
57 between:] *between— A*   **59** Hands] *Hands, A*   were] *were, A*

---

[5] Thunderbolt.

Love too sad to follow and seek.
Ah! Had I spoken!
. . . Never a word and never a token
(*Are the candles lit?*)
But only the dark, and the night,   65
To sit in alone and remember it! . . .

[*] From *Hound of the Road*, published by Angus and Robertson.

61 seek.] *seek— A*   **62** Had] *had A*   **65** dark,] *dark A*   night,] *night A*
66 ˢit! . . .] *it!" A*   **n1** From . . . Robertson.] *Om. A*

M21   THE HOUSE OF HOURNE[1]

When first she heard the cock
   She started in her bed;
"The moon is still abroad,
   The night is young," she said.

She pillowed down for sleep,   5
   And happed her[2] foot to crown;
The coverlet against her cheek
   Was soft as feather down.

She lay a lily in her shift,
   She lay like roses warm,   10
Yet in her side she shivered once,
   As though she touched an arm.

Again crowed out the bristling cock;
   His clarion went so far
It seemed as though he called the moon,   15
   Or cried upon a star.

O thrice he crowed with might and main;
   The lady turned about,

[1] See I76 n. 1.
[2] Covered herself – from Scots *hap* – to cover or tuck up (in bed).

She turned as one who would not heed,
　For all the cock did shout.   20

And then there crept upon a pane
　A sound as though a mouse,
Within a distant wainscot, broke
　The silence of a house.

And then there clicked a sound as though,   25
　When all the hours were still,
A wandering beetle of the night
　Lit down upon a sill.

And then there something moved
　As though a ghost did creep;   30
The lady in her silken shift,
　She shuddered in her sleep.

O Christ Who pardoned sin that wept,
　Lest it should go forlorn,[3]
If Thou again the flesh shouldst wear,   35
　Pass by the House of Hourne.

O Christ Who pardoned one ashamed
　Before Thy wistful eye,
If Thou again to earth shouldst come,
　The House of Hourne pass by.   40

O Christ Who through the brimstone went
　That hell might drink Thy tear,[4]
The house, where one in down once lay,
　O come Thou never near.

(2 July 1932)   *Copy-text: Bat   Collated states: SV (A)*

25 though,] ~ *A*　　**41** went] ~, *A*

---

[3] Probably refers, with lines 37–8, to Christ's forgiveness of the woman taken in adultery (John 8. 3–11). Later iconography identifies her with Mary Magdalene, frequently represented as weeping over her sins.
[4] See J93 n. 3.

M22   THEY PRAY

I

Lord, if there should a reckoning come,
And Thou with Thy great captains sit
Within Thy heaven, each on his throne
Sceptred and in the midst of it;
And if within the Book of Life   5
Thy mercy shall have set my name,
O let it still abide with me
To see the earth from whence I came.

II

MAN:

Thou of the dread and infinite things,
When through Thy last dim realms I pass,   10
Leave me, lest heaven itself be loss,
To be what on earth I was.

WOMAN:

Give me, O Lord (of all things the end)
That when I shall come to the ultimate stairs,
My heart shall keep, as it kept in the world,   15
The names that I named in my prayers.

III

When from the light I must go out,
And the great door moves in behind me,
When the music I have heard I shall hear no more,
And the wars I have waged are emptied of passion,   20

(Pt I: 1 January 1937; Pts II, III: 11 February 1937)   *Copy-text: Bat   Collated states:*
ANR (February 1937), p. 24, Pt I only, as WHO ONCE WALKED THERE (*A*)   *SV*, Pts I, II
only (*B*)

Not otherwise recorded: Lines 8.1–24 are omitted in *A. B* omits lines 16.1–24 and sets
lines 12.1–16 as Pt III.

0.1 ᵉ1] *Om. A*   I *B*   **3** Within Thy] In Thy high *A*   throne] ~, *A*   **4** Sceptred]
Centred, *A*   **4–5** it;/ And] ~,// ~ *A*   **5** the] Thy *A*   **6** shall] should *A*

Grant that, e'er the door quite closes,
I shall remember him who fathered me;
Then shall my foot be firm upon the step,
My heart not falter at the passage.

M23   REMEMBERING

Donal, my father,
  Over the years
Still wakes my sorrow,
  Still fall my tears.

Man, like the red deer   5
  On the high mountains,
Thine was a heart
  Deeper than fountains.

High was thy look,
  Son of the heather.   10
Light was thy foot,
  Lofty thy feather!

Man like a chieftain,
  To the dusk falling,
Over the seas   15
  I heard thy last calling.[1]

As thou to me,
  Now the shades gather,
So I call thee,
  Donal, my father.   20

(19 August 1929)   *Copy-text: Bat   Collated states: SV* (A)   Murdoch2 (B)
10 heather.] ~, A   **13** Man . . . chieftain] Chief of the clan A   **18** the] where A

[1] MG's father, Donald Cameron, d. 1896 while she was at Cosme (see volume 1, Introduction, p. xxxvii) . I1 is another eulogy, and in the notes to later poems she names him as her source of Aboriginal and ecological lore.

M24   MEMORIAL (HELEN HUGHES)[1]

Here once she came in beauty like a flower!
The very winds her curtains were, falling
Like silver shifts about her feet, when from
His height the Austral sun looked down
To mark which way her young proud feet had gone,   5
Lest, as she went, too soon a shadow fell
To dim the happy hours companioned her—
Who here once came in beauty like a flower.

O beauty is a lovely thing! The heavens
Declare it night and day to man, who from   10
His toil is lifted upward by its power,
Watching it stately move across the sky
In starry drift, or as the early cloud
Of dawn scatter the roses of the sun
Abroad, as we strew roses now for her—   15
Who here once came in beauty like a flower.

Ever by night the lacing planets move
Like golden bees about an heavenly hive,
And as each in its course weaves on, and in
Exactness keeps the moment of its time,   20
Beauty is shawled about us from the height,
Until it seems that we with it are one,
Its unities all ours: as she too was,
Who here once came in beauty like a flower.

The "little summer" which the black man named,   25
(That lightly in September comes, then runs

(24 August 1937)   *Copy-text: Bat   Collated states: SMH*, 25 September 1937, p. 13 as
IN MEMORIAM: HELEN HUGHES (*A*)

5 young] ~, *A*   proud] glad *A*   **7** To dim] Upon *A*   companioned her] that
were her lot *A*   **14** scatter] scattered *A*   roses] ~, *A*   **14-15** sun/ Abroad, as]
~ abroad,/ As *A*   **15** strew roses now] now scatter roses, and *A*   her—] ~, *A*
22 one,] ~— *A*   **23** ours:] ~, *A*   she too] ~, ~, *A*   **25** little] fleeting *A*
which] that *A*   **26** (That] Which *A*

[1] (1915–1927), only daughter of W. M. Hughes (see M5 n. 2) and his second wife, Dame
Mary Hughes (see R32 and n. 1).

Away again with myall² speed) upon
The winter of the year pours out its warmth
To nurture earth, and sun the frost-bound root
And seed till they abide and live. And as   30
This little summer darling wrought, so she—
Who once here came, in beauty like a flower.

27 speed)] ~, *A*   29 sun] suns *A*   30 abide] endure *A*   31 she—] ~ *A*

² Early and transient: cf. H87 n. 1.

M25   JAPAN[*]

"Oh hush!" she says, "Do you not hear
    Voices of children on the ear?
    Is not the wind a messenger?
    What is that strange insistent stir?"

In her heart is a void, and in   5
    The void it seems as though a thin
    Cry starts, while yet another lifts,
    Until, in dreadful waves and drifts
    She hears her buried children's cries. . . .

"Oh, hush!" she says. Then the world hears   10
    The long slow falling of her tears.

[*] Typhoon in Japan. It is now estimated that 1067 persons were killed
in Osaka, including 532 school children.—*Sydney Morning Herald*
cable, 24/9/34.

(24 September 1934)   *Copy-text: Bat   Collated states: SMH*, 29 September 1934, p.
11 (*A*)

1 Oh] ~, *A*   8 Until,] ~ *A*   9 cries. . . .] ~ . . . *A*   n1 Typhoon] Typoon *A*
n2 school children] school-/ children *A*   *Sydney Morning Herald*] "Sydney
Morning Herald" *A*   n3 34.] '34) *A*

M26   SPAIN

ISABELLA TO COLUMBUS[1]

Go, she said, and may God go with you;
 Go, she said, and the saints attend;
Go, she said, and my word is with you,
 The goal or failure, on to the end.

Then she took the rings from off her hands,   5
 Her crown she laid down from her head,
The chain of pearls she took from her breast,
 That she might honour the word she said.

You shall sail in your own good ship, she said,
 And measure the might of the seas again,   10
For I am Queen Isabella, she said,
 I am Isabella, of Spain.

(19 December 1927)   *Copy-text: Bat*   *Collated states:* None

[1] The foundations of a united Spain were laid in the marriage of Ferdinand of Aragon to Isabella of Castile (1451–1504). Her funding of Columbus's expedition to the New World aimed at securing riches and souls.

M27   BARCELONA[1]

How could I tell how much you meant—
That dear, that eager head,
The look that carried life's intent,
The words that broke half-said!

The world has moved since then; the dust   5
Is deep on many a face;
Yet once again war's dreadful thrust
Mocks each familiar place.

[1] From early 1938 until its fall in January 1939, Barcelona, the centre of Catalonian resistance to Franco in the Spanish Civil War (1936–39) was under attack, suffering heavy bombardment and high casualties: inspiring recall of an earlier death, presumably in World War I.

You had no fear of death, and so,
In one far, bloodied street,　　　　　　10
I see your darling head laid low,
I see your shattered feet.

Shot-torn and still, the pulse grown thick
That once leapt fountain high,
Life's candle out, only the wick　　　　15
To show how you could die!

(19 March 1938)　*Copy-text: Bat*　*Collated states: SMH*, 26 March 1938, p. 7 (*A*)
14 high,] ~; *A*　　**15** out,] ~: *A*

M28　WRITTEN FOR NEVILLE CAYLEY[1]

I

Be light, O footstep, light as you pass,
Press not too heavily down on the grass,
For here one lies who sang of the spring,
As only a bird, a bird, can sing.

Step lightly, O foot! But yet not quite　　5
Indifferent brush this mouse-broad height;
But here, where the leaf-blade bends to hover,
Whisper and say, "Here lies a lover!"

He was no more than a bird, a bird—
A pleat of feathers—and yet he heard,　　10
Through his tiny song, his wings' flit-flit,
The call of a dream, and answered it.

Then lightly, lightly O footstep pass,
Tread not too heavily down the grass,
Since here one lies who sang of the spring,　　15
As only a bird, a bird, can sing.

[1] M28 was written for Neville William Cayley (1886–1950), author of the popular ornithological study *What Bird is That?* (1931); his father, Neville H. P. Cayley (1850–1903), whose grave is referred to in Pt I, illustrated Australian birds for numerous books and journals. See *Letters* 131.

II

Always I hear them,
The Neville Cayley birds—
His art the fowler, and their friend!
Though the springs go, and winter come,   20
Though death blot out the frail
And lightsome things that are so gay,
Yet on his faithful canvas they are still alive,
And in our hearts we hear them sing.

They loved the birds—the Neville Cayley men,   25
Father and son, and son again,—
And in the bird they loved the land,
Serving Australia in that love;
The land abides through men like these.

(Pt I: n. d.; Pt II: 29 January 1937)   *Copy-text: Bat   Collated states:* None

M29   THE BIRDS

They came—
    As though by some commanding impulse led
    That gave direction and declared their way,
    As though within them something deep was set,
    Stronger than they; a constant inward urge   5
    That drove them ever onward through the void,
    Who backward would by their own will have turned,
    As from the lonely height, and from the vast,
    They drooped, wrung-eyed, towards lands where green
    Trees stood, though in the sky the eagles sailed   10
    Like dark stars wheeling endlessly within the blue.

(16 July 1932)   *Copy-text: Bat   Collated states: SV* (*A*)
Not otherwise recorded: Wherever copy-text has 'came—' *A* has 'came!—'.
2 led] ~, *A*

They came—
    The little birds with wings no wider than
    The span of children's hands! The ibis,[1] from
    His far Egyptian feeding ground, in trails,   15
    And, singly in its flight, the godwit from
    The bitter Asian coast, or from the bleak
    Siberian wastes where the grey *tundras* spread,
    Secret and strange beneath the moon, and, through
    The winter of the year, stare at the skies   20
    Like frozen eyes of ice, that lifeless look
    Toward a heaven they know not, from a world as strange.

They came—
    The darting snipe that cries upon the night,
    Angling its instant flight, in unchecked speed,   25
    As though it pivotted and swung upon
    A globe of air—the bird that knows to flit
    Before the gun and 'neath the fowler's eye
    Escape, and, thence to shoot so swiftly forth,
    But by its cry pursuit may know it still   30
    Its zig-zag way makes on with tireless wing:
    That wing the mother-bird, as though a shot
    Had broken it, so often drags to lure
    The hawking huntsman from the nest where lie her young.

They came!—   35
    What musterings of the dark wood-swallow, which,
    Enclustered like the hiving bees upon
    A tree, will hang so close men have declared
    It hibernated there, as hibernate
    The bear, the dormouse, or the squirrel curled   40
    Within his bushy tail; or even as,

---

26 pivotted] pivoted *A*   **27** air—] ~; *A*   **29** shoot] thrust *A*   **31** zig-zag]
zigzag *A*   **35–45** They . . . eat.] *Om. A*

---

[1] On the ibis, see I16 and L15 n. 1. Birds named here appear elsewhere: see, e.g., I11 for the godwit (line 16), M15 for the snipe (line 24), I10 for the green-leek (line 63), I15 for the spoonbill (line 75), I98 and R55 for the plover (line 76), and I14 and I16 for the peewee (line 83).

In this our own land, sleep the python and
The tortoise, till the spring, full with the sound
Of bird-song and the scent of mounting sap,
Calls them, lean, savage, and an-hungered, forth to eat.   45

They came!—
The dark wood-swallow is a gentle thing,
And, in its busy settling down for night,
Chatters and twitters till its lovely din
Of tiny voices, in subsiding, falls   50
Like wavelets that have lapsed and ceased upon
A quiet shore. Then from the silence, one,
And then another stirs, breaks out, and seeks
More comfort in its place, till, like a smoke
Of wings, all rise and swirl, then cling again, and sleep.   55

They came!—
Through long unmeasured years of spaciousness
This land was joyous in the sound of wings,
Of chirp and trill, whistle and rolling note,
When flocked the quarrion and gay galah,   60
And on his tree the lordly cockatoo
His sentinel set. The very grasses moved
As though alive where shawls of green-leeks crept,
Or where the waves of budgerigah flowed out,
That still in our untrammelled North sweep on   65
In flights leagues wide, that like a land-surf rise and fall.

They came—
But who knows how!—throughout the rich
Unwritten ages ere the white man wrecked
The rhythms that nature set, and ripped and broke   70
The surface of the earth with ploughs, or burnt
The forests, and with dams the creeks locked up,
Or chained the streams that made a paradise
Of marsh and swamp, within whose verges stalked
Spoonbill and heron; and which heard the sharp   75

63 alive] ~, *A*   64 waves] wave *A*   budgerigah] budgerigahs *A*   65 North]
north *A*   66 flights] ~, *A*

Cry of the plover, in the night, strike on
The new-chum settler's ear, till, though in sleep, he wept.

They came—
  Pigeons on every bush; while in the trees
  Beside deep pools, or where the gullied creeks   80
  Of our stark inland cupped the waters spring
  Had left, were colonied the nests of mud
  The peewees built. Then were the runs of clay
  Cool to the dainty feet of her whose clean
  And lovely lines so parallel, 'mong birds,   85
  Some slender yacht—each margent[2] plaited o'er
  By her close tracks, while, threading these, there ran
  The quaint goanna's mark, the snake's slow gliding curve.

They came! . . .
  They come no more. The cities have laid waste   90
  The land where once the hosted wings flocked home.
  The trees are felled—or ash. Seed-time of grass
  And blossoming of flower wake not again
  As harvest of the wild. And we? Are we
  More permanent than these that we displaced?   95
  The wilderness returns; the dust of time
  On Tyre[3] and us alike heaps up; the thing
  Man slays, slays him . . . To us the desert creeps:
  And, as it creeps, what debts, what debts it makes us pay!

86 yacht—] ~; *A*   **89** came! . . .] ~!— *A*   **98** ˢhim . . .] ~. . . . *A*

---

[2] See M19 n. 1.
[3] Flourishing Phoenician seaport (from 10th century BC), it survived Babylonian attacks (6th century BC) and destruction by Alexander the Great (332 BC) to become a Crusader stronghold in 1124, but was destroyed as an ancient city by Muslim forces in 1291.

M30   I SAW THE BEAUTY GO

I saw the beauty go,
The beauty that, in a stream,
Flowed through the breadth of the land
Like the fenceless foot of a dream.

There went the kangaroos, that, in hosts,   5
For their bedding-down grouped at even,[*]
Only the sound of the nibbling lips
Making the sunset steven.[1]

Then as they stilled, and the moon
With her white cloths mantled the trees,   10
From the shadows beneath the mopoke called,
And the curlew made her pleas.

I saw the beauty go,
The beauty that could not be tamed;
But before it went it looked at me   15
With the eyes of the maimed.

[*] The kangaroos were patriarchal. They lived in family groups, though
they fed in hundreds (and at times in thousands) on the plains and among
the trees of the forests. I do not remember them ever bedding-down in
the open, but always under or near trees, the "Old Man," as the blacks
named him, standing sentinel to the last. I have never seen an Old Man   n5
kangaroo remove sticks before lying down; perhaps his weight made it
unnecessary; or perhaps, like a man, he slept heavily and did not feel
them, while the does, like women, slept lightly because of the young. But
the does invariably lifted with their delicate "hands" even small twigs,
and tossed them away before lying down. If they felt one left under them,   n10
they would get up and look for it, throwing it away when it was found.

(18 December 1937) *Copy-text: Bat   Collated states: SMH*, 1 January 1938, p. 9
(*A*)   Mackaness2 (*B*)   *SV* (*C*)   Wright2[2] (*D*)   Mackaness3 reprints *B*

5 There went] They were *A*   kangaroos] kangaroo *B*   that,] ~ *A*   **6** bedding-
down] ~, *A*   even,] ~; *A*   **7** nibbling] cropping *A*   **9** Then] There, *A*   ~, *D*
11 From] From out of *A*   beneath] *Om. A*   (**n1–11**) The . . . found.] *Om. A B D*
n3 bedding-down] bedding down *C*   **n4** Man,"] ~", *C*

[1] See J18 n. 1.
[2] F. R. Niemann's musical setting of the text from Wright2 is held in NLA 1695/7.

M31 IDENTITY

No leaf
Has knowledge of another leaf,
Though on the self-same tree . . .

The right hand clasps the left,
A brother meeting brother,   5
But, though they cling together,
Yet neither knows the other.

Then, through life's flying weft,[1]
Two eyes, in one glance, fleeting,
Come wind, come storm, come weather,   10
Are one in that swift meeting.

Who shall construe to me
How these strange things may be!

(n. d.)   *Copy-text: Bat   Collated states: SMH*, 18 December 1937, p. 13 (*A*)
5 brother,] ~; *A*   **8** Then,] ~ *A*   **9** eyes,] ~ *A*   glance, fleeting,] look
meeting— *A*   **10** wind,] ~— *A*   storm,] ~— *A*   weather,] ~— *A*
11 meeting] greeting *A*

[1] In weaving, the flying shuttle shoots the weft threads across the web, interlacing them
with ('meeting', line 11) the warp threads at right angles to them. See also M44 line 8
and N1 lines 309–10, but cf. 'weft' and its synonym 'woof' as the completed fabric in
O1 line 9 and M46 line 15.

M32   STORM

I

Seeming as though the storm
Touched not its spirit lone,
High on a cliff, a form
Stood like a thing of stone.

[cont. overleaf

(Pt I: n. d.; Pt II: 9 December 1934)[1]   *Copy-text: Bat   Collated states: SMH*, 2 February
1935, p. 11, Pt II only, as SOMETIMES IT COMES (*A*)   *SV*, Pt II only (*B*)
0.1–8.1 ⁵I . . . II] *Om. A B*

[1] Of the three dated MSS of Pt II, those in ML 6/2 and 6/4 give 9 December as the

Yet in his heart, in surge,   5
Fierce as the lightning's fire,
Grappled, in savage urge,
Insatiable desire.

II

Sometimes it comes, and it comes to each,
  In the heart's ebb, and alone,   10
To hear, like waves on a distant beach,
  The life submerged and unknown.

Over the crest of the wave the sail,
  But, under the keel beneath,
Where quiver the deep-sea twilights pale,   15
  Grim Etnas[2] shudder and seethe.

9 comes,] ~— *A*   each,] ~ *A*   10 ebb,] ~ *A*   alone,] ~— *A*   11 hear,] ~ *A*
beach,] ~ *A*   15 pale,] ~ *A*

composition date, but Fryer MS is dated 29 December.

[2] I.e. volcanoes – Etna in Sicily is one of the best-known active ones.

M33   WAKE NOT THE SLEEPER

" . . . And then," said John MacPherson, "there comes a time
when one no longer wishes for the things one most longed for in
the young years. One has learned to do without them."[1]

Wake not the sleeper, lest
  Life come and wound his peace;
Too soon the vision ends,
  Too soon dreams cease.

Then pass with silent tread,   5
  Lest furrow that clear brow

(16 February 1934)   *Copy-text: Bat   Collated states: SMH*, 24 February 1934,
p. 11 (*A*)

0.1–0.3 ⁵" . . . *And* . . . *them.*"] " . . . And then there comes an age when one no
longer wishes for the things one most longed for in youth. . ." *A*   6 furrow] ~, *A*

[1] Unidentified.

Life's dark reality,
   Pain with its plough.

Leave the young look upon
   The fair and sleeping face;   10
None knows to dream but youth—
   The dream its grace!

Too soon the waking comes,
   Too soon life, bending down,
Puts in the hand a sword,   15
   Where dreams were crown.

brow] ~, *A*   **7** reality,] ~; *A*   **12** grace!] ~; *A*

M34   AT EVENTIDE

When life was adventure,
Reading great words of beauty
I have been almost blind
In the wonder of what they held.
And now I read them   5
With a quiet mind.

When in the night
I saw the stars shine out
In fulgor[1] from the sky,
Then was I as one whom splendour stunned.   10
And now I see them
With a quiet mind.

And when as a child
I heard the wind come bloring[2] round

(n. d.)   *Copy-text: Bat   Collated states: SMH*, 6 November 1937, p. 13 (*A*)   *SV* (*B*)
4 the] *Om. A*   **9** In fulgor] In splendour *A*   Refulgent *B*   **10** Then was I]
I was *A*   whom . . . stunned] the light had stabbed *A*   **11** And] But *A*   them]
it *A*

---

[1] Effulgence, brilliance (archaic: cf. entry for line 9).
[2] Combines senses (both archaic) of blowing violently and bellowing; cf. N1 line 325
and R15 line 13.

The chimney-corner of the house,   15
Tensioned with terror I heard it, even though
As the roaring went I longed for its return.
And now I hear it
With a quiet mind.

So strange it is   20
That terror has departed—
Terror and wonder,
Once the garmenting of life!

15 chimney-corner] chimney corner *A*   **16** with] by *A*   though] ~, *B*
17 went] ~, *B*   **23** life!] ~. *A*

M35   AN OLD MAN SPEAKS

Bride weather it is, my lad,
And old bones feel it to-day;
The wind's a tooth as sharp as a gad,
The frost is thick on the clay;
But heap the logs,   5
And shake up the fire,
And watch the flame
Sing all of a choir.

Bride weather, and no mistake!
The birds are too cold to sing;   10
But warm on its feet, in bush and brake,
Each sits with a folded wing.
So poke the fire,
And heap up the logs,
And toast your toes   15
On the iron dogs.

(21 February 1927)   *Copy-text: Bat   Collated states: HA* (October 1936), pp. 27–8
(*A*)[1]   Mackaness2 (*B*)   *SV* (*c*)   Mackaness3 reprints *B*

2 to-day] today *C*   **7** watch] hear *A*   **9** weather,] ~ *A*   **11** warm on]
warming *A*   in] on *A*

[1] Of *A*, MG wrote to Hugh McCrae on 28 September 1936: "'and hear the flame sing

Bride weather! And yonder field
  A frozen furrowy spread,
Wanting the warmth to bring to yield
  The taters and corn for bread.   20
    But dances the light
      On hearth and floor,
    So pile up the logs,
      And snib the door.

Now's the time o' the year, lamp lit,   25
  To smoke by the fire and dream,
While close to your hand the bride will sit,
  With her skin as soft as cream;
    And half asleep
      On the white hearth-stone,   30
    The cat will sing
      In a drowsy tone.

The old mare's snug in the shed,
  The cow is strawed in the byre,
And you yourself will soon be to bed,   35
  Soaked through and through by the fire.
    But bed's cold,
      And a man grows old,
    When under his arm
      No bride lies warm.   40

---

17 And] and *A*   **20** taters] tater *A*   **21** light] flame *A*   **30** On] By *A*   white]
wide *A*   **32** a] his *A*

all of a choir", the "hear" is too soft, it should have been "bid". I notice the "s" is off
[taters]; perhaps I did it. Also "the cat will sing in his drowsy tone" should have been
"*a* drowsy tone". Mea Culpa' (*Letters* 126 reads 'tables' for 'taters'); cf. entries for lines
7, 20 and 32.

M36   THE ARCHIBALD FOUNTAIN[1]

There was a man—a man once lived in this our town:
He had a dream, the city wears it as her crown.

Fall with the loveliness of rain the fountain's tears,
    As the black moonlight of the Huntress[2] with her bow
Darkles amid the shattered silver that uprears   5
    Its jetted waters from the turtle beaks below.

The dying Minotaur looks his last look on life,
    As sinks the monstrous tumult of his flesh to naught;
The dumb ox in his hands and feet no more at strife
    Against the greater beast the Gods within him wrought.   10

And there sits Pan the shepherd's friend, and keeps among
    The eternal hills of youth his flock; while, on the height,
Apollo looks beyond the morning star, low hung,
    To where dawn breaks forever on the dark of night.

There was a man—a man once lived in this our town: 15
He had a dream, the city wears it as her crown.

(24 March 1932)   *Copy-text: Bat   Collated states: SMH*, 2 July 1932, p. 9 (*A*)   *SV*
(*B*)

(1–2) There . . . crown.] *Om. A*   1 man—] ~, *B*   once] who *B*   town:] ~. *B*
4 Huntress] ~, *A B*   bow] ~, *A B*   5 amid] among *A*   8 sinks] ends *A*
monstrous] montrous *A*   of] was *A*   10 Gods] gods *A*   11 there sits] there, *A*
Pan] ~, *A*   the . . . keeps] god of field and herd, still guards *A*   12 The] Th' *A*
flock;] ~, *A*   13 morning star] Morning Star *A*   15 man—] ~, *B*   once] who *B*
town:] ~. *A B*   16 dream,] ~: *A*   the] The *A*

---

[1] Art Deco fountain in Hyde Park North, erected in 1932 from a bequest of J. F.
Archibald (1856–1919), who also founded the annual Archibald Portrait Prize as part
of his 'dream' (line 2) for Sydney to rival Paris as an artistic centre. Designed by French
sculptor François Sicard, the fountain commemorates the association between Australia
and France in World War I. MG regarded Archibald, a co-founder and editor of the *Bn*,
as a mentor: see volume 1, Introduction, n. 14, F44 and M1 author's note.
[2] Diana (Artemis), virgin goddess of the hunt and of the moon is twin sister to Apollo,
god of the sun (line 13). Lines 7–10 refer to Theseus's slaying of the Minotaur, the
mythical monster who was half-human, half-bull, and lines 11–12 to Pan, divinity of
woods and pastures.

M37   THE SEA

O Sea! Mighty: Majestic: Wonderful:
We find thy movement (earth's eternal cud)[1]
Still held as when thy first tide turned to pull
Upward and outward from the oozy mud;
And, in these waves that beat their low refrain   5
Upon the shore where Bronte[2] lies asleep,
Is heard the voice the first stars heard complain,
The first tide moving mourned from out the deep.

Man sets his tiny lamps along thy rocks,
And cuts his ant-like tracks thy cliffs upon,   10
Then, as a passing breath, away is gone;
And all that he has made thy menace mocks,
Thy sand as heaping dust lies over him,
Thy cud chews on forever, strange and grim.

(21 November 1920)   *Copy-text: Bat   Collated states:* None

[1] See the *Not otherwise recorded* statement for J89.   [2] See E73 n. 1.

M38   THE QUESTION

If into dust the mountains broken are,
If the compacted rocks erupt and fray,
To heap upon the earth as shapeless clay;
If, in the stellar space, star after star
Is shattered to a meteor rain afar;   5
If the great suns beyond the Milky Way
Must turn by turn from governed circles stray,
To waste at last in planetary war;

(27 July 1922)   *Copy-text: Bat   Collated states: Wr*, 25 October 1922, p. 5 as IF INTO
DUST (*A*)

2 If] ~, *A*   the] in the hard *A*   rocks] rock, *A*   erupt and fray,] decay *A*   **3** To
. . . clay;] Reaches with miser's fingers day by day. *A*   **4** If,] ~ *A*   stellar space,]
sky *A*   star after] the high contending *A*   **5** shattered to] scattered in *A*   afar;]
~, *A*   **6** If the great] And those proud *A*   Milky Way] milky way, *A*   **7** Must
. . . stray] Piercing the void with half-emerging ray *A*   **8** To waste] Must break *A*

If all these great must perish as the small—
These worlds innumerable, which make and fresh   10
Strange tides, as unknown oceans rise and spread
Till they too pass—if all this might must fall
To loss, and lie at last among things dead,
Why should I weep decay for this poor flesh!

war;] ~, *A*   **10** innumerable,] ~ *A*   which . . . fresh] as the sands that spread *A*
11 Strange . . . spread] Where the wild tides of ocean roll and thresh *A*
12 pass] fail *A*   **13** loss,] dust *A*   at last] *Om. A*   things] the dusty *A*
14 flesh!] ~? *A*

M39   SIC TRANSIT[1]

Raised on a pinnacle of pomp and power
See London stand. Yet Rome was great, and fell;
And that old Babylon[2] of whom men tell,
Halting for richer words, who, in her hour,
Above the very world rose up in tower;   5
And Tyre—and dark Damascus of the Well—
Time tolled the slow stroke of his passing bell,
And all these perished like a summer flower.

(15 October 1922)   *Copy-text: Bat   Collated states: Bn*, 5 April 1923, p. 13 as SIC
TRANSIT GLORIA MUNDI (*A*)

Not otherwise recorded: A has this heading: "'London.—The authorities are gravely
perturbed at the industrial situation. The problem of 1,300,000 unemployed is
accentuated by strikes among agriculturists. The trouble is widely spreading."—
Cable.'

1 Raised] (FOR THE BULLETIN.)// Raised *A*   **2** London] England *A*   great,]
~— *A*   **4** who,] ~ *A*   hour,] ~ *A*   **5** rose up in] itself did *A*   **6** Tyre—]
~; *A*   Well—] ~. *A*   **8** all these perished] each one withered *A*   summer]
grass in *A*

[1] Thus passes [worldly glory]: Latin.
[2] On Babylon, see F79 and H86 n. 1. On the ephemerality of empires, cf. K115; and
for Tyre (in modern Lebanon, line 6) see M29 n. 3. In modern Syria, Damascus claims
to be the oldest continuously inhabited capital city in the world. It had two periods
of wealth and prestige: from 661 under the Umayyads, the first dynasty of caliphs of
the Prophet Muhammad, until 750 when the victorious Abassids moved the capital to
Baghdad; and from 1174 when Saladin, conqueror of the Crusader States and founder
of the Ayyubid Dynasty, made it the capital of an empire that included Egypt, Syria

What pride uprears becomes its funeral urn,
When, frustrate, in its very vitals lurk
Great starved communities to ravage there;
So London's might will vanish in its turn,
If, at its base, like tunnelling termites work,
In massed battalions, armies of despair.

9 urn,] ~ *A*   **11** Great] The *A*   to] that *A*   there;] ~! *A*   **12** London's]
England's *A*   will] shall *A*   turn,] ~. *A*   **13** If, at] Within *A*   base,] ~ *A*
work,] ~ *A*   **14** battalions,] ~ *A*

and Northern Iraq. In 1260 the city was taken by the Mamelukes of Egypt during their
overthrow of the Ayyubids.

THE BAYING HOUNDS

M40   THE BAYING HOUNDS

There was no hunted one
With whom I did not run,
There was no fainting heart
With which I had not part;
The baying hounds bayed me,   5
Though it was I was free.

Where'er the hard-prest ran,
Was it or beast or man,
As step by step they went,
My breath with them was spent;   10
The very ant I bruised,
My heart held interfused.

(23 April 1927)   *Copy-text: Bat   Collated states: SV* (*A*)   Wright1 (*B*)
4 part;] ~, *B*   **7** Where'er *A*] Whe'er *X*   **9** went,] ~ *B*   **11** bruised,] ~ *B*

M41   UNSKILLED

I

Lunch cut and packed,
    And breakfast o'er,
The baby kissed,
    He's out the door.

His old grey coat,   5
    Threadbare and thin,
He draws up close
    To throat and chin.

With hunted speed
    He takes the road,   10

The thought of wife
  And child his goad.

II

A soldier, in
  An army which
Destroys the poor,   15
  Yet serves the rich,

For the world's market place
  Too old,
He stammers lest his plea
  Seem bold.   20

As sad and bent
  He waiting stands,
Through tears I see
  His knotted hands!

III

"I have got work!" he cried,   25
  And in his voice was heard
How his denied
  Man's heart was stirred.

She felt his thin hands shake
  With eagerness, the fears   30
Had bred life's ache,
  Wept in her tears.

(Pts I, II: 3 October 1927; Pt III: 21 November 1936)   *Copy-text: Bat   Collated states:*
None

M42   TALL BUILDINGS

I

High in the sweet
Air day by day, mounting,
Men climb to meet
Death in the way; counting
  The half-inch where,   5
  In perilous heights, they dare.

Life's wounds, long given,
Still bleed. Wrong stalks abroad
Where men are driven
And narrow balks[1] are trod,   10
  Since, should they trip,
  The strongest hold must slip.

II

He turned his head
And at the door looked back.
"Farewell!" he said,   15
As one who had no knack
  Of easy speech
  To aid affection's reach.

"Farewell!" . . . She heard,
And running came and kissed   20
  Him, strangely stirred.

(3 October 1927)   *Copy-text: Bat   Collated states: Wr*, 12 October 1927, p. 5 (*A*)   *SV*,
Pt II only (*B*)

(0.1–12.1) *S*I . . . II] *Om. B*   0.1 *S*I] *Om. A*   4 in the way;] face to face, *A*
5 where,] ~ *A*   6 In . . . heights,] Its narrow way *A*   7 wounds] wound *A*
8 bleed. Wrong] bleeds: wrong *A*   9 Where] While *A*   driven] ~, *A*
10 narrow balks] parapets *A*   11 Since] Where *A*   should they] at a *A*
12 hold] hands *A*   12.1 *S*II] *Om. A*   13 He] . . . ~ *A*   14 back.] ~, *A*   18 To
aid affection's] Toward which his heart could *A*   19 She] she *A*   21 Him,] ~ *A*
strangely stirred] at the word *A*

[1] Timber crossbeams.

Death caught the foot that missed.
    He came no more
    To his familiar door.

22 caught . . . missed] met him at his tryst *A*

M43   WIDOWS' PENSIONS[1]

The stars of night
    Were not more clear,
Than, in her eyes,
    The sudden tear.

With widowed hands,   5
    Alone and sad,
Little life held
    To make her glad.

But, now, the dread
    Of hungry years   10
Passed with the falling
    Of her tears.

She wept because
    Law gave relief—
The pinching measure   15
    Of long grief.

(3 October 1927)   *Copy-text: Bat   Collated states: Wr*, 18 January 1928, p. 5 as THE
WIDOW'S PENSION (*A*)

2 clear,] ~ *A*   3 Than,] ~ *A*   eyes,] ~ *A*   4 sudden] risen *A*   7 Little]
What could *A*   held] hold *A*   8 glad.] ~? *A*   9 But . . . dread] She felt the
weight *A*   10 hungry] starveling *A*   11 Passed] Pass *A*   falling] passing *A*
12 tears] years *A*   13 She] And *A*   15 The pinching] Her tears the *A*
16 long] old *A*

[1] The NSW Widows' Pension Scheme (for which MG campaigned on the Women's
Page) began operation in 1926 after 1925 legislation. Widows received £1 per week
plus 10s. per child.

M44 RAIN

I THE LITTLE WET FEET

"Rain!" they said as they met, "How nice to hear the rain!"
Then they smiled from their furs, and went on their way again.
But I thought of the women of the narrow street,
The children crying with the cold, and the little wet feet,
The drip at the eaves, and the wind blowing in at the door,   5
And the mud of the foot-marks thick on the floor.

I love the rain, so dear, and so fresh,
The long lines running like the warp of a mesh,[1]
Straight out of heaven, down to the earth,
That the flower may bud, and the root have birth.   10
But O, as I hear it, my heart grows thick with pain,
For I think of the women in the narrow street,
The children crying with the cold, and the little wet feet.[2]

II UNDER THE ROCKS[3]

O storms, be gentle as you come!
    Beat not too hard upon the place   15
Where lie life's shelterless,
    Uncovered each poor face,

But touch as though with fingers that
    Would comfort all their grief—
Softly as from its tree   20
    Drops the slow falling leaf.

(Pt I: 20 August 1938; Pt II: 26 January 1935)   *Copy-text: Bat   Collated states: SMH,*
27 August 1939, p. 21, Pt I only (*A*)   *SV*, Pt I only (*B*)

0.1 ˢI . . . FEET] *Om. A B*   **1** said] ~, *A*   **2** they] *Om. B*   from] in *B*
9 Straight out] Straight-out *B*   heaven,] ~ *A B*   **10** bud,] ~ *B*   **11** But] ~, *A*
13.1–21 ˢII . . . leaf.] *Om. A B*

---

[1] See M31 n. 1.
[2] Cf. Q9.
[3] Inner city suburb on the w. shore of Sydney Cove: Sydney's oldest preserved colonial
district, but a slum area until the 1950s.

M45   HE HAS NOT OLDER GROWN

He has not older grown,
    But I have added years to years,
    Until these swift remembering tears
        Are drawn from eyes he has not seen—
Lie on a face he has not known—   5
        So long, so long the years between!

Still, but the flesh declines;
    The inward spirit knows no change,
    No passages of time estrange
        In the eternal *Now*, whose past   10
Unbarriered again defines:
        The first things living as the last.

So he will know me when
    I come, hasting with eager feet
    As though the winged, to meet   15
        Him where he stands, just as of old
He stood, when, in this world of men,
        My breast, my arms, were all his fold.

(3 November 1937)   *Copy-text: Bat   Collated states:* None

M46   THE SEMPSTRESS

Starved! And they tell you she was fed,
Who walked among the living one half sped!
Her needle-pricked poor fingers could have told
How faint she was, how often cold.

The moonlight look of death upon   5
Her face, bleak witness how her life had gone,

(24 April 1937)   *Copy-text: Bat   Collated states: ANR* (July 1937), p. 26 as THE SNAPPED
THREAD (*A*)   *SV* (*B*)

1 *Starved!*] ~!— *A*   And] and *A*   2 sped!] ~; *A*   3 needle-pricked] ~, *A*

Told even less than did her fallen hand,
Trailed on the floor made all her land.

In her once dwelt life's hungers, which,
Building great nations strong, make small ones rich;   10
But not for her the home that she might crave;
Now she has earth, but earth as grave.

One daily driven to work that brought
Her starveling bread, through weeks and years she wrought
Unceasingly upon her life's thin woof[1]   15
To keep the shelter of a roof.

And then this day she did not come.
"She might have 'phoned!" they said. The poor flat thumb,
That seam by seam had pressed its form away,
Answered, "Not now; not any day."   20

7 Told] Says *A*   did] does *A*   8 Trailed on] Touching *A*   10 Building]
Making *A*   11 crave;] ~. *A B*   12 earth,] ~; *A*   14 weeks] ~, *A*   years] ~, *A*
15 woof] ~, *A B*   16 roof.] ~; *A*   18 'phoned!] ~, *A*   phoned! *B*   poor] ~, *A*
20 now;] ~: *A*

[1] Fabric: see M31 n. 1.

M47   THE DEAD BABY

Cold in thy little bed,
    Low thou dost lie,
All thou didst ask was bread—
    Never to die.

Life gave in scant to thee,   5
    Thin was thy blood,
There was but want for thee—
    Ebb-tide thy flood.

Too frail were thy small hands,
    Too frail to hold;   10

(1936)   *Copy-text: Bat   Collated states: SV (A)*
1 Cold] Low *A*   2 Low] Now *A*

Spilled were the scattered sands
   Life to thee doled.

I had no strength to give;
   My lack was thine;
Toil, that had life to sieve,   15
   Ground us too fine.

Cold in thy little bed
   Now thou dost lie;
Thou didst but ask for bread—
   Never to die.   20

O child, from me apart,
   Lest my heart hears,
Against me, where thou art,
   Loose not thy tears.

12 thee *A*] the *X*   17 Cold] Low *A*   19 bread—] ~; *A*

M48   WINTERED LIFE

I walked abroad one summer's day,
   By the unburdened sea,
And there I met three women grey,
   Dulled by adversity.

Two daughters, and a mother lone,   5
   So much alike it seemed
As though together they had grown,
   Till one they might be deemed.

Helpless and crippled, gaunt and old,
   The mother kept her chair;   10
White-faced the girls, and dead the gold
   That youth once gave their hair.

                                     [*cont. overleaf*

(21 May 1936)   *Copy-text: Bat   Collated states: SV* (*A*)
1 abroad] ~, *A*

Thinly, as in a prison-vyce,[1]
   They lived on counted bread,
The need to cut an extra slice   15
   An ever present dread.

Withered their power with life to cope;
   Privation bit too near!
What terror lies in narrowed hope,
   What cruelty in fear!   20

16 ever present] ever-present *A*   **18** near!] ~. *A*

---

[1] I.e. a vice, a tool used to maintain a tight hold on (imprison) an object while it is being worked.

M49   THE BONNET SHOP

The milliner's strained and hungry eyes,
   They haunt me as they peer
From out the dusk behind the pane,
   Where fashion's fancies veer.

Slimmed to a pose become a need,   5
   The slender outlines sway,
Obsequious, compelled to please,
   As custom comes their way.

Thin fingers ply on silk and straw,
   Young bodies bend and ache: 10
Is it a step upon the street?
   The eager hopes awake!

Where'er these shadowy shops are set
   In fashionable guise,
I see forever in the dusk,   15
   Young, haunted, anxious eyes.

(17 December 1932)   *Copy-text: Bat   Collated states:* None

M50 THE CROW

When on the sunny air there falls
   Like a black flake
His voice, the new-born lambs
   Hear it and quake.

No skyward look have they, but, where   5
   Upon the grass
His shadow runs, what fear
   Lest it not pass!

(2 September 1938) *Copy-text: Bat* *Collated states:* None

M51 THE WAIF

I saw him sitting on a fence,
   Little Ragged Britches;
Knew he hadn't any pence,
   Destitute of riches;
Maybe hadn't any sense,   5
   As the world would reckon,
   Yet he saw the great world beckon—
Little Ragged Britches!

He had a nose tip-turned to sky,
   Little Ragged Britches;   10
Somewhat bold about the eye,
   Humorous in twitches;
Seemed the sort says *Never die!*
   Laughed at wind and weather,
   When he went, went hell-for-leather—   15
Little Ragged Britches!

[*cont. overleaf*

(10 September 1924) *Copy-text: Bat* *Collated states: Wr*, 24 September 1924, p. 5
as BOARDED OUT (*A*)

4 Destitute of] Hadn't any *A*   **5** sense,] ~ *A*   **6** world] wise *A*   reckon,] ~: *A*
12 twitches;] ~. *A*   **13** *Never die!*] Never Die, *A*   **14** weather,] ~— *A*
16 Britches! *A*] ~. *X*

He had a rough and ready tongue,
    Little Ragged Britches;
Liked to fling out words that stung,
    Memory gave them niches!   20
Ah, my heart, but he was young,
    Young to face life's battle,
    Life that held as but a chattel
Little Ragged Britches!

18 Britches; *A*] ~, *X*   **19** stung,] ~ *A*   **20** Memory] (~ *A*   niches!] ~!) *A*
22 battle,] ~— *A*

M52   RUTH

I

"Let the child be called Ruth,"
    She said—
Then closed the eyes,
    And fell the head.

Within that silent room   5
    None spoke;
Yet it was there
    A man's heart broke.

II

The child so much was flower
    No other flower might bloom;   10
That spring might have its hour
    Life gave her to the tomb.

But O, had she but drawn
    Full life for her short years,
Night had not darkened dawn,   15
    Nor sorrow known these tears.

(Pt I: 21 November 1936; Pt II: 14 December 1932)   *Copy-text: Bat*   *Collated states:*
None

M53   RECORDING MAN

Ascending on the written word
    Man rises from the clod,
Till his command afar is heard,
    O'er sea and air and sod.

Barbarian by stream and lake,   5
    And lord of spear and sling,
He carves a symbol in a brake[1]
    And there begins a wing.

Letter by letter he ascends,
    Until we find, at last,   10
A phrase upon a stone subtends[2]
    The present and the past.

In proof take up life's latest man,
    The helpless new-born child,
And mark in him, as he began,   15
    The savage of the wild.

Blank is the infant's page; its mind,
    By its unwritten range,
Links with the primitive in kind,
    And no one thinks it strange.   20

Then from where mighty engines go,
    To totems on the tree,
Let us look back in thought, and know
    How script has made us free.

For there, be stone or steel his stair,   25
    We see recording man,
A bird within his upper air,
    Look down where he began.

[*cont. overleaf*

(12 December 1936)   *Copy-text: Bat*   *Collated states: SV* (*A*)
21 Then] ~, *A*

---

[1] I.e. on a tree: see further I59 n. 1.   [2] Stretches or extends under.

Man ranges upward as he will;
    His spiral is a word;   30
The ox, that writes not, bellows, still,
    The first note of the herd.

31 bellows, still,] ~ ~ *A*

M54 TO THE WAR-MONGERS

How that old Satan, who,
In the ghost time of the world,
Rebellion raised in heaven,
And out of heaven was hurled[1]—
How must his old proud heart,   5
When he walks battle-fields,
To the healing of his smart
Gloat o'er their blood-red yields!

When he the pulpit hears
Bless cannon, shot, and shell,   10
Surely he mocking jeers,
"We go less far in hell!
For there, though flames leap up,
Only the guilty roast;
But innocence is slain   15
Where the church-blessed cannon host."

(26 February 1933) *Copy-text: Bat* *Collated states:* None

---

[1] Although developed from hints in the Authorised Version, the story of the angel Lucifer, who rebels against God and is cast into Hell as Satan, belongs to the Apocrypha. The events precede Genesis: hence line 2, which may also suggest that mankind's history is haunted by Satan's sin.

M55   LOS HERIDOS[1]

I

I asked of winter what would he bring me,
    And he said,
Freedom to climb, though the hands be weary,
Freedom to sing, though the heart be broken,
Freedom to laugh, as one who has wept.   5

I asked of spring what was his gift,
    And he said,
Wings, and the pain that they bring;
Flight, and its burden;
Youth, and its ache to be loved.   10

II

Life's instant urge is in my blood!
    It cries its need, until upon
My heart the tides that in it flood
    By their own weight released must run.

Deep, deep, and ever deeper yet,   15
    Within the sick bone-marrow of
My frame, all unappeased is set
    The ache that living men call love.

But in my flesh I bear
The thing that shames love there.   20

[cont. overleaf

(Pts I, II, V: 10 December 1936; Pt III: n. d.; Pt IV: 6 May 1932)   *Copy-text: Bat   Collated states:* WB, 21 September 1932, p. 12, Pt IV only, as THE DREAM (*A*)   *SV*, Pts II, III, V only (*B*)

Not otherwise recorded: A's text is in italics throughout.

(**0.1–30.1**) [S]I . . . IV] *Om. A*   **0.1–10** [S]I . . . loved.] *Om. B*   **10.1** [S]II] I *B*
12 need,] ~ *B*   until] ~, *B*   **13** heart] ~, *B*

---

[1] 'The Wounded Ones' (Spanish).

III

She, too, could have written had she gone away
From life, but life held her.
Yet, when she grew sad for the small things she had done,
She remembered that one grain of wheat
Was better than a diamond,   25
And a whirling grass-seed more wonderful
Than a battle-ship.

Then was she comforted;
For the smallness of the things she had done
Seemed not to matter.   30

IV

There are those, who, giving all to love, lose
      Love because they should have taken;
She was of those, and often would she use
      To straik[2] the bed
      Where love lay dead,   35
Lest an old dream should go forsaken.

And when they came, who asked of her why swept
      She there a lonely floor, why guarded
She a starved and empty room, she kept
      Her steadfast will,   40
      Lest from its sill
Life's one last dream should fall the sharded.[3]

V

I have not written mad things,
      For mad things do not enchant me;
But I have written the small and simple,   45
      Lest the mad things haunt me.

20.1 ^{S}III] II *B*   (30.1–42) ^{S}IV . . . sharded.] *Om. B*   32 they] *they gave who A*
34 bed] *bed, A*   37 came,] *came A*   38 a lonely] *an empty A*   40 steadfast]
steadfast, A   will] *still A*   41 Lest] *Lest, A*   sill] *sill, A*   42 Life's one last]
One old fair A   (42.1–46) ^{S}V . . . me.] *Om. A*   42.1 ^{S}V] III *B*

---

[2] Smooth, stroke (Scots, archaic).   [3] See K58 n. 1.

M56   THEY HANGED A MAN ON GALLOWS HILL

GOULBURN[1]

They hanged a man on Gallows Hill,
   They hanged him at the morn;
Ye might have thought he had been a dog,
   Yet he was of woman born;
Ye might have thought he had been a dog,   5
   So little they seemed to care,
As they twitched the rope on his twisted neck,
   And left him hanging there.

They hanged a man on Gallows Hill.
   A man? They hanged in threes!   10
While the men who set them swinging there,
   They wined and dined at ease;
And the birds they came and picked the flesh,
   And the sun burned on the bones,
But the men who left them rotting there,   15
   Their hearts were hard as stones.

[cont. overleaf

(2 April 1921)   *Copy-text: Bat   Collated states: SnMH* (no subtitle) (*A*)[2]   *Wr*, 12 May 1921, p. 9 (no subtitle), signed MARY GILMORE, in "The Southern Morning Herald." (*B*)

Not otherwise recorded: B has a stanza break incorrectly placed between lines 15 and 16; and in the passage after line 24 (present only in *A* and *B*) *A* reverses the lines correctly printed in *B* as 'And see, again, far Calvary Hill,/ And the souls of men who die!' *A* lacks a stanza break before the final two lines, probably due to lack of space on the page.
1 Hill,] ~ *B*   **7** neck,] ~ *A B*   **8** there.] ~! *A B*   **9** Hill.] ~— *B*   **10** man?] ~?— *A B*   **11** set] left *A B*   swinging] rotting *A B*   there,] ~ *A B*   **12** dined] diced *A B*   ease;] eas[. . .] *A*   ~, *B*   **14** bones,] ~; *A B*   **15** left] sent *A B*   **16** stones.] stones.// {/ *B*} O, hard as stones were the hearts of those/ Whose hands held life and death,/ And as little cared they for the Son of God/ As they cared for the parting breath! *A B*

---

[1] Two convicted murderers were hanged at Goulburn in 1830 and their corpses left to rot (cf. line 15); an (official) gallows and flogging pole followed in 1832, and in 1866 ten bushrangers were hanged. Other multiple hangings also took place: though in 1921 they were well in the past, the link in an Easter poem (see composition date) to Calvary and the Crucifixion is direct (cf. entries for lines 16 and 24).
[2] No relevant issue of the *SnMH* has been located. Collation is based on the print clipping held in NLA 727 11/9/2; it carries the *SnMH* 's running header (but no date

High on the crest of Gallows Hill,
    In the dusk three men were strung,
As the hymns rose up from the churches all,
    And the holy psalms were sung;   20
And black as the Pit, when the moon came up,
    The dread things swung and swayed,
Where only the hearth-smoke, high on the air,
    And the stars rose unafraid.

They hanged a man on Gallows Hill?   25
They hanged not one, but Three.

---

17 Hill,] ~ *A B*   **18** In . . . strung] I see the corpses swing *A B*   **19** As . . . rose]
While song comes *A B*   churches] ~, *A B*   all,] f[. . .] *A*   far, *B*   **20** And . . .
sung] Where the little children sing *A B*   **21** And . . . up,] High on the crest of
Gallows Hill *A B*   **22** The . . . swayed] I see three corpses sway *A B*   **23** Where
. . . air,] Black in the light of the sinking sun *A B*   **24** And . . . rose] Setting at
close of *A B*   *24–5* unafraid.// They] day.// Christ of the Nations, lift Thy
hands,/ Hands where the nails were driven,/ And look on a **world** is Gallows
Hill—/ The hearts of the people riven:/ Look on the Nations!—O, Thou Who/
Hung once in the westering sky,/ And see, again, far Calvary Hill,/ And the souls
of men who die!// They hanged a man on Gallows Hill. . . {. . . . *B*}/ The balcony is
wide/ Where I sit and watch the slanting sun/ Go down where men have died;/ As
I sit and think, and dream of spires/ Where the people speak his name, {nam[. . .]
A}/ Yet the sunken fires of ancient hate/ Rise to a bigot flame!// {/ *A*}   They *A B*
25 Hill?] ~. . . *A*   ~. . . . *B*   **26** hanged] ~, *A B*   but Three.] but **Three!** *A B*

---

or page number) and gives a composition date of 11 April 1921, later than the date given
on MSS in ML 6/2 and NLA 727 3/6/1.

M57   CHRISTMAS CAROL[1]

One shall come walking,
    Walking into town,
Dust upon His sandals,
    Dust upon His gown.

Who is this comes walking,   5
    Walking into town,

---

[1] Musical setting by Gertrude Concannon is held in ML 3/M. On the Nativity, see
J1 and n. 1.

Dust upon His sandals,
   Dust upon His gown?

He is the King of Glory,
   He is the Father's Son;   10
Christ of Whom the story
   Never shall be done.

Sing then all ye nations,
   Sing of the Child was born
Unto Mary, the Virgin,   15
   That first Christmas morn.

Tell out how the shepherds
   Heard in the winter sky,
Songs that the holy angels
   Sang from heaven on high.   20

Tell out how in splendour
   Shone the burning star,
Naught in heaven might hinder,
   Naught on earth might mar.

Tell how the three kings,   25
   Wise men of the East,
Bowed before the Infant
   Knowing that they were least.

Tell how the oxen
   And the ass kneeled down,   30
Where the Lord from heaven
   Had but straw for crown.

Now comes He walking,
   Walking into town,

(27 December 1926)   *Copy-text: Bat   Collated states:* Murdoch2 (*A*)   *AWW*, 26 December 1956, p. 21 (*B*)

Not otherwise recorded: B is in italics throughout.

13 nations,] ~ *A*   *18* sky,] *sky B*   *21* splendour] *splendor B*   **25–40** Tell . . . down.] *Om. A B*

Dust upon His sandals,   35
    Dust upon His gown.

So comes He always,
    Sung and yet unknown,
Who once came, from heaven,
    As a white feather down.   40

M58   THE FISHERMAN

Jesu, the wind that softened as it neared Thee,
Cuts like a knife upon my little sail and me,
Yet I have babes at home to feed—
Dear Lord, wilt Thou not help me in my need?

Soon but the mast will stand with me,   5
Stripped down before the gale like some bare tree;
My breath is strained, my fingers bleed—
Jesu, wilt Thou not stay me in my need?

The mounting waves (once stilled before Thy feet)[1]
Against my helpless boat incessant beat;   10
My helm swings like a broken reed—
Jesu have pity on me in my need!

On shore my children and their mother wait for me,
In every tear that falls a prayer to Thee;
On their sad lips the salt waves bead—   15
Jesu, have pity on them in their need!

(28 November 1933)   *Copy-text: Bat   Collated states:* None

---

[1] On Christ walking on the stormy waves, see Matthew 14. 22–32.

M59   PREVISIONED

Mother, all night I heard a sound,
Murmur, murmur, under the ground,
Of bursting seed, and trembling root,
Of leafing bud and folded shoot,
To be, to be, and not yet born—   5
Mother, I woke, and 'twas the morn.
(Pray! Pray! Little One, pray!)

Mother, I heard a trailing thorn
Praising the day that I was born—
"I was despised, despised," it said,   10
"Yet I shall touch the Sacred Head;
The outcast of the foxes' den,[1]
The thorn shall pierce the hearts of men!"
(Pray! Pray! Little One, pray!)

Mother, I heard a tiny seed   15
Singing aloud, with none to heed:
"I am the seed from which will come
The tree to take the Saviour home—
I am the seed, and His the cup,
By which shall man be lifted up—"   20
(Pray! Pray! Little One, pray!)

Mother, I heard, as one who saw,
One who suffered under the law;

(21 July 1910)   *Copy-text:* Bat   *Collated states:* Wr, 7 December 1911, p. 7 as
PRE-VISIONED (*A*)   *MP*, 19 December 1913, p. 8 as PRE-VISIONED (*B*)

Not otherwise recorded: The collation for lines 8 and 15 is identical to line 1, and that
for lines 14, 21 and 28 is identical to line 7.

1 Mother,] ~! *A B*   3 seed,] ~ *A B*   4 shoot,] ~ *B*   6 morn.] ~— *A B*
7 One] one *A B*   9 born—] ~: *A B*   11 I shall] shall I *A B*   Sacred Head;]
sacred head:— *A B*   13 men!"] ~"— *A B*   16 heed:] ~; *A B*   18 home—]
~:— *A B*   19 seed,] ~ *A B*   cup,] ~ *A B*   20 shall man] all men shall *A B*
lifted] lift *A*   up—"] ~"— *A B*   22 Mother,] ~! *A B*   heard,] ~ *A B*

[1] Cf. Luke 9. 58: 'Foxes have holes, and the birds of the air have nests; but the Son of
man hath not where to lay his head.'

I saw a Mount where olives grew,[2]
I saw a cock, and thrice it crew;[3]   25
Mother, I woke me, thick with fears,
Mother, my face was wet with tears—
(Pray! Pray! Little One, pray!)

25 crew;] ~:— *A B*   26 me,] ~ *A B*   fears,] ~; *A B*

---

[2] The Mount of Olives is the site of the Agony in the Garden and Judas's betrayal of Christ (Luke 22. 39–48).   [3] See J23 n. 2.

M60   RING BELLS SO LIGHTLY

Dark was the night, but bright the star:
  Ring bells so lightly!
Jesu! Jesu! Cry it afar:
  Burn star so brightly!

Three Wise Men came out of the East: 5
  Ring bells so lightly!
Each one came as though to a feast:
  Burn star so brightly!

The Three Wise Men bore frankincense:
  Ring bells so lightly!   10
Gold and gems for His innocence:
  Burn star so brightly!

Rich the robes of the Three Wise Men:
  Ring bells so lightly!
Rich they were with the weight of ten: 15
  Burn star so brightly!

Rich the robes—and His bed was straw:
  Ring bells so lightly!

(26 October 1920) *Copy-text: Bat   Collated states: Wr,* 23 December 1920, p. 9 (*A*) *MP,* 11 February 1921, p. 8, signed MARY GILMORE in The Worker (*B*)

Not otherwise recorded: The refrain lines in *A* and *B* are in roman font and within parentheses and the end-of-line colons are omitted.

5 Wise Men] men *B*   9 Three *A B*] three *X*   frankincense:] frank incense *A* ~ *B*   15 with] to *A B*

They were Kings—but He was the Law:
Burn star so brightly!   20

Three Wise Men came out of the East:
Ring bells so lightly!
He was a babe, but they were least:
Burn star so brightly!

---

20 *brightly!*] brightly!) {brightly.) *B*}// His was the Star as His was {were *B*} the kine,/ The lowly birth, the Kingly line;/ And His the crown, the Cross, the rod,/ The wounding way that led to God. *A B*   **24** *brightly!*] brightly!)// Jesu! Jesu! Cry it afar/ (Ring bells so lightly!)/ Till all men come to follow the Star/ (Burn star so brightly!)// Jesu! Jesu! Cry it abroad/ (Ring bells so lightly!)/ Till man for Him drop down the sword/ (Burn star so brightly!)// Three Wise Men came out of the East/ (Ring bells so lightly!)/ He was a babe. But who was least?/ (Burn star so brightly!) *A B*

M61   EDWARDIAN CORONATION ANTHEM[*][1]

The air shall hearken and the earth shall hear,
The air shall hearken and the earth shall hear,
When, as the trumpets sound in Westminster,
Edward, the king, is crowned.

The people of the wilderness shall know the hour,   5
The powers that ride upon the sea shall homage make;

(1936)   *Copy-text: Bat   Collated states: QD* (April 1937), p. 26 as CORONATION ODE OR ANTHEM BY DAME MARY GILMORE (*A*)[2]   *SV* (*B*)[3]

Not otherwise recorded: A repeats its version of the first stanza after line 41, replacing commas with colons in the last line.

1 shall hear] give ear *A*   **2** shall hear] give ear *A*   **3** sound in] ~/ In *A*
4 Edward] The King *A*   the king] in Majesty *A*   **6** make] yield *A*

---

[1] See M2 n. 1: M61 is an earlier version of M2.
[2] *A* represents a transitional version between M61 and M2: cf. M61 author's note and the editorial note to *A*: 'This anthem, written by Australia's foremost poet, will be sung by the Philharmonic Society in Sydney. It was set to music by Howard Carr, the composer. Originally written for the Coronation of ex-King Edward, both words and music were altered to suit the coming Coronation of King George the Sixth'; see also the textual entry for n1–5. *A* deletes lines 13–17 (see entry) but retains 32–41 (later deleted for M2); lines 25–31 have been changed (see entry) and would be further adapted for M2.
[3] See *CG* 406 for Edward's letter of thanks after MG sent him a copy of *SV* in 1948.

Army and navy wait upon his word—
Sceptred: and crowned: and king.

Where he now stands in sovereign might,
The burden of our yoke is on him laid;   10
Within his hand our unity abides;
Nations his word obey.

Son of his people and king, great and yet humble,
The air shall hearken and the earth give ear,
The air shall hearken and the earth give ear,   15
When, as the trumpets sound in Westminster,
Edward shall stand the crowned.

The ancient kingdoms of his realm declare his royal line;
India bends down to touch his robe:
Canada and Australia obeisance make: 20
Anzac and Africa before him kneel:
For all men know that only in the king are we made one,
Only in the king's high majesty are all these peoples one;
In him are we crowned, and he in us.

Yet though he is our ruler and in his hand is held the sword, 25
This is he who in the young years came among us,
And in his manhood went brotherly among the poor,
And now, to us, says, "Though I am the king,
Yet am I still that man—that man who walked with you."
And in these words his name shall stand forever,   30
As never any king's before him.[4]

---

7 Army] Armies *A*   navy] navies *A*   8 king] King *A*   9 might,] power *A*
(13–17) Son . . . crowned.] *Om. A*   13 humble,] ~; *B*   18 kingdoms] kingdom *A*
realm declare] realm/ Declare *A*   19 bends] bows *A*   robe:] ~, *A*   ~; *B*
20 make:] ~, *A*   ~; *B*   21 kneel:] ~; *A*   22 king are] ~/ Are *A*   one,] ~: *A*
~; *B*   23 king's high majesty] King, His Majesty, *A*   all these] we his *A*   one;]
~: *A*   24 crowned,] ~ *A*   (25–31) Yet . . . before him.] Yet shall be remembered
those who went before/ Who did greatly for this people, till, from the vanished
past/ In a child's face shall be seen their look again,/ And in a son's voice shall a
father's voice be heard:/ The homage for their deeds our time shall waken,/ And in
our hearts they shall be kept. *A*   28 the] *Om. B*

---

[4] An undated AMS of M61 in NLA 727 is annotated with a message to Howard Carr
that begins: 'Unless I have an unexpected impulse to another form than this, I think this
is about complete. Later for the sake of euphony or for a wider swung cadential rhythm,

Pride dwells with kings; the king's name is a great name;
In the secret places it is heard,
And in the councils of the mighty it is spoken;
Princes because of it companion him;   35
The church throughout the world its supplication makes,
Praying no evil thing may threat his way.

Therefore for the sake of this great name must we make clean
        our hearts,
And in the paths of wisdom walk, and take justice to be our
        guide.
Then shall the king's name be raised above the world,   40
And nations rejoice because of him.

INVOCATION

Lord God of Hosts, Maker of heaven and earth and all that in
        them is,
We pray Thee, we implore, bless Thou Edward the king upon
        his throne;
Lord of Compassion grant him Thy hand;
And peace be Thy gift to this realm,   45
Peace in Thy Name, evermore.

[*] This anthem was originally written for Edward VIII, and was com-
pleted before the abdication. In order that the music composed for it
might not be lost, a part had to be re-written to suit the condition and
coronation subsequent to the abdication. The amended form as sung at
the official Coronation Concert is at the beginning of the book.   n5

32 kings;] ~: *A*   name;] ~: *A*   33–4 heard,/ And] ~, and *A*   34 the councils]
~/ Councils *A*   mighty] rulers *A*   36 church throughout] churches of *A*   its
supplication makes] their supplications make *A*   37 no] that never any *A*
39 guide.] sign; *A*   40 king's] King's *A*   raised above] heard throughout *A*
43 Thou Edward the king] Thou/ His Majesty *A*   his throne] the Throne *A*
45 be] by *A*   46 Name,] ~ *A*   evermore] ever more *A*   (n1–5) This
anthem . . . book.] Slightly revised to adapt to the music of Mr. Howard Carr, the
composer *A*   n3 re-written] rewritten *B*   n4–5 The . . . book.] "Coronation
Anthem" is the amended form. *B*

there may need a slight alteration or addition. If the thing suits, whatever you may think
should be omitted, one part must not, that in the stanza beginning "Yet though he is our
ruler . . ." I think no man ever made a greater monument to himself than the King in
these words.' Carr had worked initially on M61 and evidently again on M2: see n. 2 above
and M2 author's note.

M62   ABORIGINAL THEMES[*]

I   THE CALL

We dwell not among the women as the white men do.
We are the hunters; we follow the call
Of the forest and the tracks therein;
Ours is the way of the bird and the kangaroo.
But the women dwell apart; they have a world   5
Into which we do not enter, save
When the life call speaks.
Then we answer it.

II   AT DAWN

At dawn I stood to see the sun come up;
He came like the face of a man   10
Proud from the hunting;
Like a man who says, "There is food!"
And the food feeds his people.

III   IN THE NIGHT

In the night I saw the stars,
And the stars were like   15
The eyes of women
Seen through the leaves.
In the night I saw flash forth
The moon-beams from a possum's eyes;
Bright in the dark   20
They were the eyes of my woman.

(Pts I–IV, VI, VII: n. d.; Pt V: 17 October 1936; Pt VIII: 11 June 1933)   *Copy-text:*
Bat   Collated states: AWA (1936), p. 27, Pts I, III, II, IV only, as FOUR ABORIGINAL SONGS
(*A*)   *SV* (*B*)

Not otherwise recorded: A's text is in italics throughout, and II and III are reversed; part
numbers are present but not part headings. In *B*, Pt VI is divided into three stanzas of
two, three and four lines respectively, and lines 31, 38, 39 and 49 are not in italics.

1 do.] *do; A*   **2** follow] *answer A*   **6** Into] *In A*   enter,] *enter A*   **7** life call]
life-call A   speaks.] *speaks; A*   **9** up;] *up. A*   **12** says,] *says A*   **19** moon-
beams] *moonlight A*   moonbeams *B*   **20** dark] *dark, A*

IV   FALLING FEATHERS

Once, when the world was young, we were a people;
Then came the white man to this our land.
Now we are like falling feathers,
The feathers of a wounded bird.   25

V   CIVILIZED

I was a singer in a tree,
I was an eagle in the height,
From my shoulders shot the spear-heads of the sun—
Who now am but a caged bird with a broken wing.

VI   A LAMENT

Beat the breast and cry,   30
   Ai! . . . *Ai!* . . . *Ai!* . . .
Our friend is dead![1]
Our bitter bread
With us he shared;
Now he is dead   35
Who with us fared—
Beat the breast and cry,
   Ai! . . . *Ai!* . . . *Ai!* . . .

VII   WHEN THE BLACKS WEPT ME[2]

A-ee! . . . *A-ee!* . . . *A-ee!* . . .
She was a child,   40
But we loved her,
And she loved us.
She was with us
And was happy;
Now she goes away,   45
And we shall see her no more.
Heavy are our hearts at her going.
In her departure we weep.
A-eee! . . . *A-eee!* . . . *A-eee!* . . .

---

22 people;] *people,* A   (**25.1–65**) [5]V . . . stars.] *Om.* A   **36** fared—] ~; B

[1] Cf. K31 lines 33–6.   [2] Cf. K20 author's note, lines 10–13.

VIII NIGHT

The sun sinks slowly down;   50
Darkens the forest;
The shadows lengthen and run on the grass,
Or like great birds they fall.
In the trees naught moves but a leaf,
Twisting and turning;   55
Naught sounds but the click of a beetle,
Upward slow creeping.

Swift through the twilight
Like a grey phantom,
Silent the wallaroo³   60
Glides in his going.

Now, like a bird on the nest
Night feathers the earth;
In the far heavens
Sharpen the stars.   65

[*] These are expressions on themes and recollected impressions, and
are of general meaning. They are not to be taken as verbal translations,
though in a way they approach nearer to the real thing than so many of
the half translations of aboriginal song that I have come across. Even
the Rev. William Ridley,⁴ sympathetic as he was, has translated without   n5
regard to the many inflections which cover whole phrases in English,
and without which the genius or real meaning of the language is left
out. Another thing, because they lived among the birds and animals, the
forests and the insects, the winds and the stars, the daily speech of the
natives was as full of similes and references to these as the Bible itself.   n10
But no translator has ever turned them into equivalent English except by
accident, if done at all. But one can realize, say, from Keith McKeown's

---

62 nest] ~, *B*   **(n1–56)** These . . . realize it.] *Om. A*   **n12–15** But . . . writer has]
Most writers have *B*

---

³ Kangaroo-like animal (genus *Macropus*), between the size of a wallaby and a kangaroo
– from Dharuk *walaru* (Thieberger), Wiradjuri *walaroo* (Dixon).
⁴ (1819–78), Presbyterian minister. His writings include: *Aborigines of Australia: A Lecture*
(1864), *Gurre Kamilaroi: or Kamilaroi Sayings* (1856) and *Kamilaroi, Dippil and Turrubul
Languages Spoken by Australian Aborigines* (1866; revised 1875 as *Kamilaroi and Other
Australian Languages*). Kamilaroi (also Gamilaraay and Yaamilaraay) is from the Darling
R. region.

book, *The Land of Byamee*, with its collection of folk tales and legends,[5] what in this way has been lost. These tales have been carefully told, but the writer has been dependent for the most part on translators, n15 and these did not carry over into English any of the atmosphere of the generations of telling—literally the patina—that they must have drawn about them in the centuries of telling and retelling by those of whose lives they were a part. Actually all this lore has been collected by people with small knowledge of the native language, from natives with an equally n20 small knowledge of English. Further it has been gathered by the less educated, and, till lately, almost none of it for literary uses. In other words, a smattering of either tongue has been considered sufficient to cover and carry into English, the intricacy, and the intensity and time-values of both tongues. Shakespeare under such circumstances would n25 have become an infant's primer.

In connexion with the occasion when as a child I was "wept," I have told about this in *Under the Wilgas*. But here I may add that I recall that, child-like, I made some laughing remark. "Hush!" my father said, as carrying me in front of him he rode away, "You must not laugh. They n30 are very sad. They are crying because they will never see us again." It was that night they were killed. They wept him who had been their protector and their friend, as well as me.

And here it is necessary that I should correct again a mistake I made in *Under the Wilgas*, where I relate, in the notes, a story I heard father n35 tell of the moon and the stars.[6] In this I either mixed a story of some other nationality with one of Australia, or I misapplied the sexes in the aboriginal one, for I made the moon a female instead of leaving it male. (In the "Song of the Woman Drawer" I did the same thing, but I recollect, there, that in writing that I was thinking of the moon wholly n40 from our own standpoint, and applied it to the subject, forgetting to alter it before it went to print.) It is interesting to note that the natives of

---

n15 for the most part] *Om. B*   translators,] ~ *B*   n16 and these] who *B* n17 they] the legends and stories *B*   n24 intricacy,] ~ *B*   n26 primer.] primer. Here, however, I would except Mr W. E. Harney, whose work in "Brimming Billabongs", and elsewhere, is authentic. *B*   n27 wept,"] ~", *B*   n28 *Under the Wilgas*] the note to "The Waradgery Tribe" *B*   here] *Om. B*   n29 child-like] child-/ like *B*   n30 away,] ~. *B*   n34 And here] Also *B*   n39 Woman Drawer] Woman-Drawer *B*   n40 recollect,] ~ *B*   there,] *Om. B*   n41 own] *Om. B*

---

[5] *The Land of Byamee: Australian Wild Life in Legend and Fact* (Sydney: Angus & Robertson, 1938), with MG's Foreword: see Preface. McKeown (1892–1952) was a naturalist, not a linguist.
[6] In *B* (see entry for n28), MG cites her *UW* note as being to K20; it is in fact to K16. *B* adds a reference (see entry for n26) to W. E. Harney's *Brimming Billabongs: The Life Story of an Australian Aboriginal* (Sydney: Angus & Robertson, 1947); on Harney (1895–1962), see Preface, p. xxxv and R55 author's note for line 27.

Australia, certain tribes in South America, and the ancient Scandinavians all made the moon male and the sun female. Of the *Elder Edda* we are told that it is the storehouse of Germanic mythology, as well as of the allied races. From the "Voluspo," regarded as "one of the vastest conceptions of the creation and ultimate destruction of the world ever crystallized in literary form," I quote the following:— n45

> "The sun, the sister of the moon, from the south
> Her right hand cast over heaven's rim: n50
> No knowledge had she where her home should be,
> The moon knew not what might be his,
> The stars knew not where their stations were."

It will be seen that the despised native of Australia is, in this, in the company of the world's great—and someone may some day make Australia realize it. n55

n43 America,] ~ *B*   n46 Voluspo,"] ~", *B*   n48 following:—] ~: *B*
n49 south] ~, *B*   n56 it.] ~! *B*

M63   CORROBOREE[1]

A SCOUT SONG

Let us remember the people who gave us this word,
    Let us remember them day by day,
When on the air the columns of blue smoke stand unstirred,
    Or the puff of their silent speech makes play.

And let us remember this people too in the night,   5
    When our bivouac fires shine out like stars,
How under our trees they camped, and the rivers knew their
        might,
    While their torch-lights flared on the sandy bars.

And let us forever hold for our heart's long keeping,
    That they, whom this land saw shadowy pass,   10

(n. d.)   *Copy-text: Bat   Collated states: SMH*, 15 September 1934, p. 11 as
"COROBBOREE"/ (A SCOUT CHANT) (*A*)

2 day by] in the *A*   day,] ~ *A*   3 When] ~, *A*   air] ~, *A*   5 And] And
again *A*   this people too] them when, *A*   6 When our] Our *A*   7 camped,]
~ *A*   8 While] As *A*   torch-lights] torchlights *A*   9 forever] for ever *A*
10 That] How *A*

[1] Probably from Dharuk *garabari*: a style of dancing (Dixon); *corroboree* (Parker).

Taught our white forefathers the meaning of wings far-sweeping,
    The print of a footmark left in the grass.

Our fathers heard in the past what we shall never hear,
    They heard the chant and the signal drums;
They saw the heilaman[2] lift for the flight of the spear,   15
    Where now nor spear nor heilaman comes.

We are the young, and, at night, when the scout-fires are lit,
    There in the circle let us remember,
And of those who gave us the word let us talk as we sit,
    For we kindled our flame from their ember.   20

---

11 far-sweeping] far sweeping *A*   13 fathers] forefathers *A*   hear,] ~; *A*
14 drums;] ~, *A*   17 and,] ~ *A*   night,] ~ *A*   scout-fires] scout fires *A*
18 There . . . circle] By the firelight *A*   remember,] ~; *A*   19 And of] Of *A*
gave] left *A*   the] our *A*

---

[2] Shield; from Dharuk *(y)ilimay*: bark shield (Dixon).

M64   THE SONG OF KOORALINGA[1]

When you think of Kooralinga,
You will see like a shadow
A little figure come and go,
And you will say, "Once she was here,
And now she comes no more!"   5
Then you will think, "How long it is
Since she, who was so gay,
Is gone!" And maybe you will hear
A bird sing, and dream that it is she.

When you remember Kooralinga,   10
As you sit by the fire,
The fire of little sticks,

(1 February 1927)   *Copy-text: Bat   Collated states: SV (A)*
9 dream] think *A*

---

[1] See Preface, p. xxxiii.

You will dream that two dark eyes
Look shining at you from the smoke,
And when your own would hold them,   15
No longer are they there. Then you will say,
"The little bird that sang is gone;
    The eyes that looked for my coming look no more."
And you will cry,
"Where are the rushing, hurrying feet   20
    That out of hiding came to meet me?
Where are the faithful hands that served me?
Where now is my little Kooralinga?
Who has taken her away from me!"

M65   THE QUANDONG TREE[1]

The sun still lights the quandong leaves,
And on the ground a pattern weaves
        In a black lace
        Of slender trace,
As in the years gone by;   5

And spring will bring the burning red
Of the vermilion fruit, and shed
        On earth the spilth[2]
        Of nature's tilth,[3]
As in the years gone by;   10

But never now, the moon at full,
The riders come, and in the cool
        The fiddles sing,
        The dancers swing,
As in the years gone by!   15

---

[1] The Desert Quandong (*Santalum acuminatum*) or native peach, a small tree or shrub native to arid zones; its edible fruits are shiny red (cf. lines 6–7) or sometimes yellow when ripe: from Wiradjuri *guwandhaang* (Dixon).
[2] Spillage, waste.
[3] Toil, husbandry.

On quandong ridges bright beneath
The sun, in dreams alone the wreath
    Is round the vair[4]
    Of youth's bright hair.
Alas, the years gone by!   20

(4 September 1938)   *Copy-text: Bat*   *Collated states:* None

---

[4] A type of fur, variegated in colour.

M66   THE ROGERY BIRDS[*]

A SCHOOL SONG

I heard the wind blow over the hill,
    Bolderogery-rogery-O!
And it beat and bounced and banged with a will,
    Bolderogery-rogery-O!
But I didn't care how hard it blew,   5
Or if it went under the hill or through,
For I was safe and sound in the house,
Cosy and warm and snug as a mouse,
    Bolderogery! Bolderogery! Bolderogery-O!

The fire was bright, for the night was cold,   10
    Bolderogery-rogery-O!
The flame flew up, and the sparks were gold,
    Bolderogery-rogery-O!
But out in the marsh I heard the bleat
Of the little grey snipe, so swift and fleet,   15
And I heard the plover, that brings the rain,
Cry out in the dark again and again,
    Bolderogery! Bolderogery! Bolderogery-O!

Louder and louder the wind it blew,
    Bolderogery-rogery-O!   20

[*cont. overleaf*

(15 November 1932)   *Copy-text: Bat*   *Collated states: SV* (*A*)
17 again,] ~— *A*

It gathered in sound as on it flew,
    Bolderogery-rogery-O!
And the Rogery-birds cried in between
The gusts that gathered so swift and keen,
While the little black children out on the plain,   25
Cried, "Bird of the waters bring us the rain!"
    Bolderogery! Bolderogery! Bolderogery-O!

[*] The Waradgery and adjacent tribes called the plover "Bolderogery."
The word meant "the rain-bird," or "the rain-bringer." White people
contracted the word to Roger, or the Rogery birds if used in the
plural.[1]

23 Rogery-birds] rogery birds *A*   **26** Cried] Called *A*   waters] ~, *A*
n1 Bolderogery."] ~". *A*   **n2** rain-bird,"] ~", *A*   rain-bringer."] ~". *A*

[1] *Cf. Bougoodoogahdah*, Parker's version of the name in her legend of the Rain Bird:
Australian Legendary Tales (Melbourne: Melville, Mullen & Slade, 1896), pp. 90–3;
see also Q13.

M67   TRUGANINI[*][1]

Alone in her own lost land,
As at death she turned to the past,
She prayed that the white man's hand
Might give her life's wish at the last.

But they sheared her flesh from her bones,   5
Till they skeletoned one by one,
For their hearts were harder than stones,
And her plea was a plea undone.

Now, far from the rivers and fountains
Where her children once were a host,   10
Crying "Bury me over the mountains,"
Weeps Truganini-the-queen's lost ghost.

[1] Truganini or Trukanini (1812–76), 'the most famous Aborigine in white Australian
history' (*OCAH*). Instrumental in leading her people in Tasmania to accept the offer
of sanctuary on Flinders Island in Bass Strait, she later became fiercely critical of the
administration of Aboriginal affairs. After her death her body was exhumed and her

Yet it may be, through mountain and valley,
As the fountains look for their queen,
As shadow-forms wait for the rally,   15
And the unseen bides with seen,

That far from the church and the city,
In the place where the dim shadows fare,
It may be that God, in His pity,
Will listen and look for her there.   20

[*] Truganini, queen of the last of the Tasmanian blacks, when she was dying in the Hobart-town Hospital, begged of the nurses, saying, "Don't let them cut me up! . . . Bury me over the mountains." Over the mountains was the spirit home of her tribe, to which the body must be returned if (as is parallelled by us in the churches, with the unbaptized   n5 child) the soul is not to wander in another place, and alien from its own. I was only a child when Truganini died, but her pitiful cry has haunted me all my life, for it went unheeded.

(18 July 1932; revised 13 March 1936)[2] *Copy-text: Bat*   *Collated states:* None

bones exhibited until 1947 in the Tasmanian Museum. In 1976 her remains were cremated and the ashes scattered over the D'Entrecasteaux Channel.

[2] The MSS carry different composition dates – a rare case. One MS at NLA 727 2/4/12, dated 18 July 1932, is annotated: 'Written later in another form', and two others, dated 10 November and 22 December 1933, are revised states but incomplete.

M68   WIDOWED

Wheesht! Wheesht, my bairn![1] not yet for you
Thy mither weeps,
Nor for the flame that on the hearth
No longer leaps;
Nor for the cold and darkened lamp,   5
Nor yet for bread;
But for an ache that winna doon,[2]
Since love lies dead.

(23 April 1937) *Copy-text: Bat*   *Collated states:* None

[1] Child (Scottish).   [2] Will not be subdued: literally, will not down.

M69   THE RESCUER

He was uncouth, he had no manners,
His hands were rough as iron spanners;
His hob-nailed boots had twine for laces,
He had no coat, he knew no braces.

Yet, when earth trembled to the sound   5
Of blasting terror underground,
His was the first hand on the rope,
Where none might go—and hope.

(12 November 1919) *Copy-text: Bat   Collated states: Wr,* 27 November 1919, p. 11
as SONGS OF THE PEOPLE (*A*)[1]

1 uncouth, he] "~,"/ He *A*   had] "~ *A*   manners,] ~." *A*   2 rough as] ~/ As *A*
3 hob-nailed] hobnail *A*   boots had] ~/ Had *A*   laces,] ~; *A*   4 had] wore *A*
coat, he] ~,/ He *A*   4–5 braces.// Yet,] ~./ ~ *A*   5 when] when the *A*
trembled] shook *A*   6 blasting] some grim *A*   underground,] ~ *A*   7 rope,]
~ *A*   8 none . . . and] only the dead men dreamed of *A*

---

[1] On the ambiguous status of this as a title for a series and individual poems, see F28
n. 1.

LEAVES IN THE WIND

M70   OF CERTAIN CRITICS

They say, as though they sorrowed,
I have borrowed;
Yet, for all their grieving pains,
One proud certainty remains—
Never from these little gifted   5
Critics have I lifted!

(n. d.)   *Copy-text: Bat*   *Collated states:* None

M71   SHALL MAN SAY BEAUTY PASSES

Shall man say beauty passes?
Not while the sea-tide glasses
   Back the moonbeams, or the pearly
   Dewdrops in the fair and early
      Light of dawn   5
      Lie sparkling on the lawn;
         Not while in sunlit deeps
         An ocean coral sleeps.

Not while upon the mountains
Leaps the crystal of the fountains   10
   To take the sun as jewels;
   Nor while the starry newels[1]

(11 June 1932)   *Copy-text: Bat*   *Collated states: AWM,* 18 October 1932, p. 14 as SHALL
MAN SAY BEAUTY PASSES? (*A*)

Not otherwise recorded: A's text is in italics throughout.
1 Shall] (FOR THE MIRROR.)// *Shall A*   **2** the] *a A*   **3** Back] *In A*
moonbeams] *moon A*   **4** Dewdrops] *Dew-drops, A*   **5** dawn] *dawn, A*
12 Nor] *Not A*

---

[1] The supports: literally, the central pillar from which the treads of a winding staircase
radiate, or the posts at the head and foot of a stair.

Of the sky,
Piercing the void on high
With their translucent light,   15
Illume our sight.

Not while in all their tender
Loveliness shall come the slender
Striplings, who bring in fairness,
Even as spring, awareness   20
Of the prime;
Not while two longings chime,
And wakes in happy eyes
Love's young surprise.

14 Piercing] *Shafting A*   15 With their translucent] *In enfilading A*   16 Illume our sight] *Declare the night A*   18 shall] *Om. A*   20 spring] *Spring A*
23 And wakes] *Till dawns, A*   eyes] *eyes, A*

M72   THE MUSHROOM

Have ever you seen on a hillside
The mushroom white and small,
Thrusting her head through the grass,
And the dewdrops over all?

Clear and fresh in her coming,   5
And fair as the newly born,
She has seen the stars move on with the night,
And the sun rise up at morn.

A top like a baby's head,
And a hood like a baby's skin,   10
With the pink of a shell-like palm
Curtained and curled within,

She comes as the spring's evangel,[1]
The dew on her shining crown,

[1] Proclaimer, herald.

A little round thing on a hillside,   15
    White, with the white of down.

She is the meekest of all meek things,
    But her mansion is earth and sky;
Her jewels are dewdrops hung on the grass
    In a sun like a peacock's eye;   20

And yet as the day and its heat draws on,
    She opens her mantle wide,
As ever the mothering ones have done,
    That the brood might shelter and hide.

O Man, with your claims to be greater   25
    Than even the mightiest things,
Whose realm is wider than earth and sky,
    Whose servants are prelates and kings,

If you never have seen, on a hillside,
    The mushroom white and small,   30
Then whatever your state, and whatever your pride,
    You never have lived at all.

(11 October 1936) *Copy-text: Bat* *Collated states: ANR* (September 1937), p. 20 (*A*)
21 and] at *A*   on,] ~ *A*   **22** wide,] ~ *A*   **23** As] (~ *A*   ever . . . ones] mothers
all over the world *A*   done,] ~) *A*   **24** That . . . hide] To shelter the spores
inside *A*   **29** seen,] ~ *A*   hillside,] ~ *A*

     M73   THISTLEDOWN

    Troy went, and Babylon the great is low;
    Carthage is like a withered tamarind;
    To Baalbeck no more the camels go—[1]
    But thistledown still floats upon the wind.

                                     [cont. overleaf

(2 July 1932) *Copy-text: Bat* *Collated states: AWM*, 15 November 1932, p. 14 as THE
THISTLEDOWN (*A*)
Not otherwise recorded: A's text is in italics throughout.
1 Troy] (FOR THE MIRROR.)// *Troy A*   great] *Great A*   **3** Baalbeck] *Baalbec A*
4 But . . . floats] *Yet floats their thistledown A*

----

[1] On the general theme cf. H86, K115 and M39. Troy (Ilium), the ancient city in Asia

The long, long pedigree of race decays,   5
The pride and pomp of kings is disciplined,
Might sinks to dust, and lost are crowns and bays,[2]
But thistledown still floats upon the wind.

5 long] *long, A*   decays,] *decays; A*   **6** disciplined,] *disciplined; A*   **7** lost]
dead A   crowns and bays,] *olden ways— A*

Minor made famous as the adversary of the Greeks in Homer's *Iliad*, figures in several of
MG's poems, but sometimes as a symbol of romance rather than as an example of fallen
glory (see H52, H65, I97 and K105). For Babylon, see H86 n. 1. The Phoenicians of Tyre
(see M29 n. 3) founded Carthage (in modern Tunisia). From the eighth century BC it
dominated the western Mediterranean, but was challenged by Rome in three campaigns,
defeated and devastated in 146 BC. Baalbeck (in modern Lebanon) is famous for the
ruins of its magnificent temples to the sun god, begun by the Greeks in the Hellenistic
period and completed by the Romans but partially destroyed when Christianity became
the official religion of the Roman Empire. Baalbeck fell to successive Arab dynasties
after 636 AD and was sacked by the Mongols in 1260.

[2] Laurel wreaths, signifying victory.

M74   THE WANDERER

My house is all the world,
    My lamps are stars;
My bed no curtain has,
    My door no bars;

But, with the sun to wake,   5
    Unbid as he,
Mine is the night to sleep,
    As sleep the free.

Tempest I fear not, nor
    The heaped rain's fall;   10
Mine is the solitude,
    Space for my wall.

Swift foot or slow, my watch
    None measures out;

(7 April 1935)   *Copy-text: Bat   Collated states: SMH*, 11 May 1935, p. 11 (*A*)   *SV*
(*B*)

4 bars;] *~. A*   **5** But,] *~ A*   **7** is] in *A*   **12** my] its *A*

Sun, moon, and stars, for me,   15
    Pace my redoubt.[1]

[1] Stronghold, defended site.

M75   THE TENANCY

I shall go as my father went,
    A thousand plans in his mind,
With something still held unspent,
    When death let fall the blind.

I shall go as my mother went,   5
    The ink still wet on the line;
I shall pay no rust as rent,
    For the house that is mine.

(15 February 1927)   *Copy-text: Bat   Collated states: Bn*, 2 June 1927, p. 6 (*A*)   *SV*
(*B*)   Wright1 (*C*)

2 mind,] ~—*A*   **3** still held] in hand *A*   unspent,] ~ *C*   **4** let] lets *A C*
5 went,] ~. *A*   **6** line;] ~: *C*   **7** rent,] ~ *A C*

M76   VIGNETTES

I   THE HARVESTERS

In from the fields they come
To stand about the well, and, drinking, say,
"The tin gives taste!" taking in turn
The dipper from each other's hands,
The dregs out-flung as each one finishes;   5
Then as the water in the oil-drum bucket lowers,
They tip that out, to draw a fresher, cooler draught.
    And as the windlass slowly turns they talk of other days,
Of quaighs[1] and noggins[2] made of oak, old oak
Grown black with age, and on through generations   10

[*collation overleaf*

And old houses handed down to children's children,
Till at last, in scattered families, they are lost to ken.
"Yet even so the dipper tastes the best!" they say.
Then having drunk, and sluiced their hands and faces,
Talk veers to fields and folk in childhood known,   15
And names are heard of men and women long since dead,
Or gone because the spirit of adventure
Lured them from familiar scenes to strange and far.
Of these old names, some will have been so long unheard
Not all remember them; and then a word its vision brings,   20
And memory, wakened and eager, lifts anew
The fallen thread, until it seems the past is all about them
Where they group, and in two worlds they stand—
A world that was, a world in making now.
   Then in a sudden hush the voices cease,   25
The supper horn blows clear, and, from community
Where all were one, each man withdraws his mind
As men will drop a rope in haulage held,
And, individuals in a sea of time,
In separateness they turn, and to the cook-house go.   30

II   RAIN IN AUTUMN AT GOULBURN

Wet gold of the elm and russet of turning oaks in the rain,
And the sombre pines freshed-out in the clean washed air;
While softly, as one who comes slowly down on an olden stair,
The drip at the brown eave falls, and lingeringly falls again.

In the river reaches the willows fan out like a veil,   35
Grey as a grey sky swept by a feathering mist;
Yet like splinters of gold, like a butterfly's wing on a wrist,
Shine ambering leaves on boughs that hang like a hand at trail.

(Pt ɪ: 26 January 1937; Pt ɪɪ: April 1925; Pt ɪɪɪ: 22 December 1924; Pt ɪᴠ: 30 August
1936)   *Copy-text: Bat   Collated states: SV (A)*

Not otherwise recorded: A substitutes a line break for the indenting of lines in Pt ɪ of
the copy-text.

9 quaighs] quaichs *A*   oak,] ~; *A*   old] of *A*   **20** them;] ~. *A*   and then] And
yet *A*   **32** clean washed] clean-washed *A*

---

[1] Shallow two-handled drinking cups common in Scotland, of small wooden staves
hooped together.   [2] Small drinking vessels.

Over the hills above Eastgrove wind the long wreaths of the
       cloud,
And the dark river croons in a slant of the rain;   40
In burdens of dun the shroud of the vast looms over the plain,
As over a child will a mother sit brooding and bowed.

III   ON SUCH A NIGHT

Black as the blackness of a sombre thought
The shadows lie where the long street runs on;
Within the height above, the silver moon   45
Moves in the heavens, so fair to look upon
Life's thirst for beauty quenches there;
And far beyond the moon, darker than Dis,[3]
Where star-points thrust like sharpened thorn,
Hangs the deep velvet of the sky.   50

On such a night as this,[4]
The loves of half the world are born.

IV   THE VINEYARD

Scented and old was the vineyard, and there, when the vines
Were in leaf and the moon rode full in the height,
If a wandering puff of the wind came running over,   55
Like the lifting of fingers the leaves were up-flung,
And the light rays shot from their points in spears.
And always under the vines were the aisles of shadow
That darkling reached through the lines of stakes,
Where row after row they stood, while, etched on the clods
       between,   60
The leaves lay patterned in black, and shaped like our human
       hands—

---

49 star-points *A*] star-point *X*   **54** leaf] ~, *A*   **56** Like the] Like a *A*
57 points] tips *A*   **58** shadow] ~, *A*   **60** Where] ~, *A*   after row] ~ ~, *A*
stood,] ~; *A*   **61** hands—] ~, *A*

---

[3] Alternative name for Hades, both the underworld and its presiding divinity.
[4] Echoes the repeated phrase introducing a series of references to famous lovers in *The
Merchant of Venice*, V. 1. 1 and *passim*.

Hands that made movement in every wind as it passed,
Then clung to the earth, so still, they seemed to be part of it.

God made a garden, O, long long ago;
Out of the garden came toil,[5]   65
But out of the toil came beauty.

62 every] each little *A*   **64** O,] ~ *A*   **65** toil,] ~; *A*

---

[5] After eating the forbidden fruit of the Garden of Eden, Adam is sentenced to a life of toil to gain earthly sustenance (Genesis 3. 17–19).

M77   THE WILD PLUM

Race counts! The beauty of the wild
Plum lives not less because
The gardened more profusioned grows!

The winds of ages sweeping down
The terraces of time   5
Still mark it, where it stands unchanged
Upon its ancient mountain steeps,
As when it blossomed first
Upon a changing world.

Race counts. Enduring and resistant still,   10
The beauty of the wild plum lives.
The grafted and the gardened goes.

(2 September 1938)   *Copy-text: Bat   Collated states: SV* (*A*)
4 ages] ~, *A*   **5** time] ~, *A*

M78   THE WHITE HERON

The heron stands beside the pool.
Not yet the twilight dim,

(n. d.)   *Copy-text: Bat   Collated states:* Unidentified print clipping from NLA 727 11/9/2, signed Mary Gilmore From "Battlefields." (*A*)
2 dim,] ~ *A*

To seek his nest
Has driven him.

But, O, that beauty in the dusk! 5
Not any noon or night
Has ever seen
A thing so white.

5 O,] ~ *A*   **6** noon] moon *A*

M79   THE LOVING HEART

She had the loving heart,
All hurt things cried in her,
And yet she lived apart,
As though no storm might stir.

But one long dead could tell, 5
If but the grave might speak,
Why in the night, so still,
The tear lay on her cheek.

(5 September 1938)   *Copy-text: Bat   Collated states:* None

M80   HONING UP THE HILL

Blue were the waters,
And bluer was the sky,
Warm was the clover
Where the lambs loved to lie;
Not a sound I heard, 5
In the morning so still,
But an old woman honing,[1]
Honing up the hill.

[*cont. overleaf*

(10 May 1937)   *Copy-text: Bat   Collated states: Bn*, 15 September 1927, p. 14 (*A*)   *SV* (*B*)

1 Blue] (FOR THE BULLETIN.)// Blue *A*   **3** clover] ~, *B*   **5** heard,] ~ *A*

[1] Grumbling (dialect).

"Ochone!"² she cried,
   "Ochone-a-rie!   10
Bitter were the years
   That got the best of me;
Once I had beauty,
   And love that came at will,
Now I'm but an old woman,   15
   Honing up the hill."

"Glory be," says I
   To the old woman there,
"Can't you see the lark
   With his wings on the air?"   20
Says she to me, then,
   "You've got youth to your fill,
But I'm an old bent woman,
   Honing up the hill.

"Honing up the hill,   25
   And my back to the sun,
Honing up the hill
   Where the long shadows run;
Once I had beauty,
   And lovers asked my will,   30
Now I'm but an old grey woman,
   Honing up the hill."

---

10 Ochone-a-rie] Ochone-a-ree *A*   **12** me;] ~! *A*   **14** will,] ~; *A*
15 woman,] ~ *A*   **18** there,] ~. *A*   **21** me, then,] ~ ~: *A*   **26** sun,] ~; *A*
27 up] down *A*   **30** will,] ~. *A*

---

² Scots and Irish lamentation; line 10 is a melodic extension, cf. English lack-a-day-dee.

M81   SPRING

I

'Tis the time of the year
   When the buds do break,
And fledglings away
   From the nest do take;
When the thorn-bush flags   5
   In purple and yellow,
And, soft i' the sun,
   The winds do mellow.

'Tis the time of the year
   When the young hot blood   10
Is swept in a life-tide
   Up to a flood;
When lasses to lads
   Are lightning and thunder,
And lads to lasses   15
   Wonder on wonder.

II

   Beside her caravan one jesting said,
 "What of my fate, fair gipsy maid?"
   And found it, in a sudden swift surprise,
   In the black crystal of her eyes.   20

(Pt I: n. d.; Pt II: 20 May 1932)   *Copy-text: Bat*   *Collated states: SV* (*A*)
3 fledglings] fledgelings *A*   **10** young] ~, *A*

M82   RITTLE-RATTLE-RITTLE

Rittle-rattle-rittle went the wheels on the road,
The old man jolly, as he sagged upon his load;
He talked to himself, and he sang a song or two,
Then he had a little chat with a man that he knew.

[collation overleaf

Said the man that he knew, as he sat upon the shaft,   5
"My raiment is scanty, but I never feel the draught!"
He hung down his bones, and their phosphorescence glowed,
While rittle-rattle-rittle went the wheels on the road.

Said the man that he knew, as the wind blew through his vest,
His vest but a bone that was all he had of chest,   10
"It's nice to be out, for it's close in my abode!"
And rittle-rattle-rittle went the wheels on the road.

Then the old man chuckled, though the joke was rather tough,
While the Bones rubbed his chin with the end of his cuff;
Then he laughed till the joints of his backbone showed,   15
As rittle-rattle-rittle went the wheels on the road.

His cuff, I must tell you, was just a knuckle bone,
As bare as a board, and as naked as a stone;
Yet habit clothes the bones, be it man or be it code,
As rittle-rattle-rittle go the wheels on the road.   20

Away in a farmyard, a cock, he heard the sound,
He stood upon his toes and he challenged all around;
Then the Bones faded out till not a skerrick showed,
While rittle-rattle-rittle went the wheels on the road.

(5 September 1925) *Copy-text: Bat   Collated states: Wr*, 7 October 1925, p. 5 as
"BONES" (*A*)   *SV* (*B*)

Not otherwise recorded: Wherever the copy-text has 'Rittle-rattle-rittle', *A* has 'Rittle,
rattle, rittle,' and likewise for the lower-case form.
3 himself,] ~ *A*   **6** draught] draft *A*   **8** While] As *A*   **9** vest,] ~— *A*
10 chest,] ~— *A*   **13** though] for *A*   rather tough] deep enough *A*   **14** While
the] But The *A*   end] edge *A*   **15** joints] sockets *A*   backbone] vertebrae *A*
17 His] (~ *A*   must tell] may inform *A*   **18** board,] ~ *A*   **19** man] ~, *A*   or]
Om. A   code] toad *A*   **20** road.] ~.) *A*   **21** Away] But away *A*   sound,] ~; *A*
22 around;] ~. *A*   **23** the] The *A*   out] ~, *A*   **24** While] As *A*   road.]
road.// Rittle, rattle, rittle, went the wheels on the road,/ The old man jolly,
though he hiccoughed on his load;/ Says he to himself, in a sober drunken tone,/ "
'S evolushun's nuthin' but the trimmin' on a bone!" *A*

M83   THE COMPLAINT

"Though for its height I crave,
  Life does not think of me! . . .
  As breath within a fife,
  Blown the round body through,
  I sound; and soon, like smoke   5
  That falls I cease to be."
        Then from the grave
        The charnel[1] spoke:
"Life does not think of you?
  O fool, are you not life!"   10

(15 November 1938)   *Copy-text: Bat*   *Collated states:* None

[1] Skeleton.

M84   SIBYLLA

All is a cry! When the cry is o'er,
Nothing is left to answer the door.

    Life touched her not,
        So how could she know
    The gripple[1] of storm,   5
        Of the heart, the throe?

    The fling of the heart
        In a sudden leap,
    It never was hers
        For she lived asleep!   10

Life is a cry. When we cry no more,
Nothing is left to open the door.

(11 December 1938)   *Copy-text: Bat*   *Collated states:* None

[1] Grip (as in wrestling); rare and obscure, related to *grip* and *grapple*.

M85   SAID THE ELIZABETH BAY FIG-TREE

Written for Mr. W. B. Dalley, who roused public
feeling on behalf of the poisoned tree, which was
one of the veterans of these shores.[1]

For centuries I stood, as stands the Parthenon
Upon that ancient rood a world's lore builded on;
    Now am I but a ghost
    Who once was Sydney's boast.

There I an offering made the Gods, whose messengers   5
Were birds that sought for shade, my leaves their ministers.
    The dust my leaves now feed,
    Dead of an evil deed.

When I was older than his high immortal name,
I saw the first white man who to these waters came;   10
    Yet his most traitorous son
    Has left me all undone.

I was life's memory, whose root, set in the earth,
Measured by me, a tree, foundations of man's birth;
    But entered theft; the script   15
    Years wrote in me was stript.

I was man's haven once; then came the vandal, who,
Against me, none knew whence, the shaft of murder drew.
    For evermore let time
    Mark on this spot his crime.   20

(n. d.)   *Copy-text: Bat   Collated states: SMH*, 11 December 1933, p. 9, stanza 5 only,
as THE ITHACA FIG TREE (*A*)

0.1–16 Written . . . stript.] *Om. A*   **17** man's haven] a fig tree *A*   once; then] ~—/
Then *A*   **18** me . . . whence, the] mine ancient head/ The *A*   **19** For] Now *A*
evermore] ever more *A*   **20** crime.] ~! *A*

---

[1] Since M85, especially in its earlier state in *A* (see textual note), appears to relate to a
contemporary (unidentified) incident, it seems that MG is confusing John Bede Dalley
(1876–1935), a frequent contributor on social issues to the *Bn* (where he worked from
1907), *SMH* and other periodicals, with his well-known politician father W. B. Dalley
(d. 1888). *A*'s title may be a confusion of the Ischia fig with the Greek island Ithaca in
Homer's *Odyssey*; Attic figs were famous throughout the East.

M86   THE SHEPHERD[1]

Old Sam Smith
    Lived by himself so long,
He thought three people
    A "turruble throng."

But he loved "Old Shep,"   5
    Who could open and shut
The hide-hinged door
    Of his old bark hut;

And he loved the trees,
    The sun and the sky,   10
And the sound of the wind,
    Though he couldn't tell why.

But besides all these,
    He loved, to the full,
The smell of the sheep,   15
    And the greasy wool.

So they buried him out
    (For at last he died)
Out, all alone,
    On a bleak hill side,   20

And there's never a sound
    But the bleat of the sheep,
As they nibble the mound
    That marks his sleep.

(3 September 1938)   *Copy-text: Bat   Collated states: SV* (A)
4 throng."] ~". *A*   **5** Shep,"] ~", *A*

[1] Cf. G34.

M87 UNRESTING

Once, to this venturer,
    All beds were soft, and sleep
Was a thing without stir
    When the pulse was at leap!

Now sleep as a small white   5
    Doe of the forest flies,
To be hunted all night
    In a hounding of sighs.

(2 January 1939)   *Copy-text: Bat   Collated states:* None

M88   LOSS

We dared not say farewell,
    Lest farewell bring an ending;
Now is the ending come,
    Bitter, and without mending.

Only an empty place   5
    Is left us for our keeping;
And you, for loss of us,
    To the shades go weeping.

(2 January 1939)   *Copy-text: Bat   Collated states:* None

M89   THE STOIC

He has known grief, but he
    Has hidden it. Ill keeps
The mind that sits beside
    Its grief and weeps.

He has known shame, but out   5
    Of shame new strength he made,

That he might walk abroad
  The unafraid.

Where wound the onward way
  As though it had no end,   10
He looked not back: the past
  Has naught to lend—

Its lamp is out, and but
  The empty lantern swings;
He put no candle there   15
  To light dead springs.

Some day, and soon, he will
  Lie down, his journey done;
There on his virtues, friend,
  Let shine the sun.   20

(23 April 1927)   *Copy-text: Bat*   *Collated states:* None

M90   CONTEST I ASK

Bite deep, O life, bite deep!
  I do not fear thy teeth!
But, as the waves that leap
  Against the rocks in seeth,
    Smite with thy hardened palm   5
    My soul, lest it becalm.

I do not fear thee, life!
  Nor shall my spirit shrink
Though thou shouldst engine strife
  Where hope in peace should drink;   10
    Better to wounded lie,
    Than undeclared to die.

[*cont. overleaf*

(24 February 1927)   *Copy-text: Bat*   *Collated states:* Murdoch2 (*A*)
11 lie,] ~ *A*

And I, O life, I would
   Be stirred to the heart's core
As a man is stirred, my good   15
   The blows I met and bore.
      So with thee I would strive,
      That I may stand alive.

Pride must have range; the weak
   May ask their gentle meads,[1]   20
Wherein they dwell all meek
   And soft as sappy weeds;
      But ever I must cry,
      "Give tempest, lest I die!"

[1] Meadows, fields.

M91   HORN MAD I' THE MOON[1]

Horn mad i' the moon
   I dancing go,
Over the mountains
   To and fro.

Beside the brook,   5
   Tu-whit, tu-who,
A barn-yard owl
   Is dancing too,

While in the shade
   A beetle goes,   10
And dances there
   Upon his toes.

Tu-whit, tu-who,
   The howlet sings!

(29 December 1918)   *Copy-text: Bat   Collated states: SV (A)*
Not otherwise recorded: A divides the poem into five 8-line stanzas.
1 moon] ~, *A*   **14** sings!] ~, *A*

[1] Raving mad in the moonlight: in popular tradition, the full moon induces madness, cf. *lunacy.*

The lake is dancing   15
   Dancing rings,

And on the shore,
   In silver shoon,
Dances a jig
   The lady moon.   20

Tu-whit, tu-who,
   Horn mad I go,
Over the mountains
   To and fro.

And once I saw   25
   A shroudy² oak
Dance till the twelve
   Beat out the stroke,

And once I saw
   A pine tree tall   30
Dance to its shadow
   Over a wall,

And once I saw
   A snouted hog
Dancing the highway,   35
   Jiggetty-jog.

Now over the mountains,
   To and fro,
Horn mad i' the moon
   I dancing go.   40

---

32 wall,] ~. *A*   **36** Jiggetty-jog] Jiggety-jog *A*

² Dark and enveloping, like a shroud.

M92   MARIQUITA DE SAPUCAAY[1]

There was a child I knew in years gone by,
A timid, wistful, hunted, lonely child,
Whose heart was broken, though she smiled
To hide the rising tear-drop in her eye.

The sad companion of a stifled sigh,   5
In innocence of self she dwelt enisled,[2]
Or watched, in desolate hours, the stars that filed
Through solitary deeps within the sky.

And all the earth she loved, even the dried
And withered herbage summer suns had burned;   10
While, as her heart the pain of life discerned,
She grieved for all poor wounded things . . . She died. . . .

Sometimes in lonely hours I hear her tears,
The child who walked with me in dreadful years.

(29 April 1923)   *Copy-text: Bat   Collated states:* None

[1] Paraguayan town; the Gilmore family stayed there in 1900 while on their way from Cosme
to Buenos Aires and Patagonia.   [2] Socially isolated, as if on an island.

M93   INSURGENT

I

"From temptation, O Lord,
  Deliver us," men cry;
But I have prayed, "Give me
The power to feel temptation,
Lest I go empty to the grave."   5

II

Not life to sit at ease,
  Feet to the fire,
No storm that asks release,
  And no unsatisfied desire;

But life to long, to reach 10
   With hungry heart
And hands that ever more beseech
   Something still held apart.

Not life to sit released,
   Feet to the fire; 15
Life is the unappeased,
   Is passion, is desire.

(Pt I: 20 November 1937; Pt II: 17 February 1936)   *Copy-text: Bat   Collated states:*
SMH, 29 February 1936, p. 13, Pt II only, as LIFE (*A*)   *SV* (*B*)   *Other state: ANR* (May
1938), p. 29[1]

Not otherwise recorded: A sets Pt II as a single stanza.

0.1–5.1 ˢI . . . II] *Om. A*   **8** storm] storm within *A*   release,] ~ *B*   **11** heart]
~, *A B*   **12** ever more] evermore *A*   beseech] ~, *B*   **13** Something] Some
thing *A*   still held] unknown— *A*   apart.] ~! *A*   **14** Not] . . . ~ *A*

---

[1] *ANR* combines a version of Pt I with a different continuation:

SARGASSO

"From temptation, O Lord,
   Deliver us," they prayed;
But I have cried, "Give me
   The power to feel temptation,
Lest I go empty to the grave."

There are the dark Sargasso seas
   Where come nor rain nor hail;
Which, in themselves contained,
   Unchallenged and unwrung,
Rot of their own decay.
No storm upon their quiet breaks;
   But them the passing ship
Shuns as on it goes,
   Saying, "Rather the rocks than these
Least pitying things that the ocean knows."

M94   WINTER SONG

Blow out, O wind, blow full and loud,
Since hearts are hot and life is proud;
    Blood is at heat,
      And, though it sting,
    Love thinks it meet   5
      His dart to fling.

No one should want for nip and charm,
When in the cheek the pulse is warm;
    Then blow, wind blow,
      And sharpen sleet,   10
    Lest the foot slow,
      And love retreat.

From bush to bush the robin flits,
Then on the fence awhile he sits;
    And there, day long,   15
      Aloud he sings,
    As though the song
      Itself had wings!

So strong is love when blood is up,
So hot is blood when love would sup,   20
    That swift it runs
      A full-tide sweep,
    Lest all undone
      It fall asleep.

Then blow, wind, blow! Crack on the sail!   25
Let none be slack lest love should pale!
    Be thou life's whip
      From out the sky,
    That lip to lip
      Young love may lie.   30

(21 January 1934)   *Copy-text: Bat*   *Collated states:* None

M95   SHE PRAISES HIM

Whom shall I praise
    If not this dear,
Whose face is sun
    To me all year!

Stars in his eyes,   5
    For me, at night,
Candle the dark
    And make it light,

And his dear mouth
    My garden is;   10
There he is mine
    And I am his.

Him no fears mock
    As fears mock me,
Who am but leaf   15
    Where he is tree;

So in his strength
    Safe stand do I,
And ever shall,
    Until I die.   20

(9 April 1932)   *Copy-text: Bat   Collated states: AWM*, 4 October 1932, p. 14 as *SHE*
PRAISES HIM (*A*)   *SV* (*B*)

Not otherwise recorded: A's text is in italics throughout.
1 Whom] (FOR THE MIRROR.)// *Whom A*   **4** year!] *year; A*   **5** Stars] *While A*
eyes,] *eyes A*   **6** For me, at] *Stars candle A*   **7** Candle the dark] *Until for me A*
8 And make it] *The dark is A*   light,] *light!// As with strong tread/ He seeks my*
door,/ My feet are wings/ To cross the floor; A   ~. *B*   **9** And] *Then A*   **12** And]
As A   **16** tree;] ~. *B*   **19** shall,] *shall A*

M96   ONCE E'ER SHE SLEPT

Once e'er she slept
She turned, and her hand crept
    Across the coverlet
        And leaned on mine.
Upon my cheek   5
        The tear lay wet,
As I heard her weak
        Low breath decline.

And then it seemed
As though awhile she dreamed;   10
        And once a small smile ran,
            As when on shore
A ripple runs;
        Then stilled the wan
Lost lips as pale as nuns,   15
        And smiled no more.

I bowed my head
Above the dead,
And wept.

(*c.* 1935)   *Copy-text: Bat   Collated states:* None

M97   ALL YESTERDAY

All yesterday she sat with her lost youth,
    And she nor kissed its lips nor touched its hand,
Nor even guessed, till night had come, what drouth
    Had stolen the young years' promised land.

(13 May 1927)   *Copy-text: Bat   Collated states: AWM*, 5 July 1927, p. 14 as THE AFTER-
SHADOW (*A*)

Not otherwise recorded: A's text is in italics throughout, with no change of font at lines
5 and 6.

1 All] (FOR THE MIRROR.)// *All A*   **2** kissed] *pressed A*   **3** Nor even guessed]
And never knew A   night] *it A*   come] *gone A*

For all day talk had been of *"Have you seen?..."*   5
    "Do you remember?..." "Did you recollect?..."
And not till night had shown what might have been,
    She knew what cargoes had been wrecked.

He was a man grown white beneath the years,
    Who in dead days had bent and kissed her hand;   10
She was a woman whose long hindered tears
    Bruised in her eyes life's deep demand.

5 For all day] *All day the A*   seen?..."] ~?"...A   **6** *remember?..."*] ~?"
...A   Did] *Do A*   recollect?..."] ~?"...A   **7** And] *And, A*   night] *she A*
shown...have] *traced where youth had A*   **8** what cargoes] *its cargo A*
9 white] *stout A*   **11** long hindered] *long-hindered A*   **12** life's deep] *an old A*

M98   EYES OF THE HEART[1]

It is a long time that I have loved you,
    It will be longer yet e'er I forget;
By day I walk as one unbroken,
    But night sees with tears my pillow wet.

Quiet broods the eagle in his eyrey,   5
    The wallaroo[2] in shelter lies apart,
The small birds of the air are nesting—
    I have no nest save the nest of my heart.

Heavy are the years of our farewelling,
    The open wounds of life still gape, the green;   10
But though no word of love was spoken,
    The long look unforgettable passed between.

(29 November 1932)   *Copy-text: Bat*   *Collated states:* None

---

[1] See H14 n. 1.   [2] See M62 n. 3.

M99 SAY TO HIM

Say to him: "She is sad!" and leave
Him not until compassion weave
His thoughts with hers, and they
One pattern lay.

And say: "When in the night her hair   5
She loosens down, her lips touch there,
Since once upon the strands
He laid his hands."

(28 October 1936) *Copy-text:* Bat *Collated states:* None

M100 THE PRODIGAL

O prodigal of self,
   From whom the weak,
Brittle as delf,[1]
   Their meat must seek,

No back look give, though thou,   5
   Left for thine own
Heart-hunger now,
   Hast but picked bone!

(20 August 1938) *Copy-text:* Bat *Collated states:* None

[1] Pottery (see C59 n. 1), but usually regarded as sturdy.

M101 VILANELLE[1] OF PARTING

Naught is to say to make amend
For love's long loss, and love's long grief.
You have forgotten; let us end.

[1] I.e. villanelle, the rhymed form having 19 lines (5 stanzas of 3 lines and 1 of 4), with 2 rhymes and 2 refrains established by lines 1 and 3; the refrains alternate as the last lines of stanzas 2, 3, and 4 and compose the final couplet; cf. M112.

There is no hoarding now to spend,
No snares to set—and love the thief.   5
You have forgotten; let us end.

Never for us one fire to tend—
Summer is ended, all too brief—
Naught is to say to make amend.

No more will time his sickle lend   10
That I may reap and bind my sheaf;
You have forgotten; let us end.

No more for us the stars ascend;
The cruise is done, our port a reef—
Naught is to say to make amend.   15

Now, at the last, shall we pretend?
Is there a word? Though we were lief,[2]
Naught is to say to make amend.
You have forgotten; let us end.

(24 November 1920)   *Copy-text: Bat   Collated states: Wr*, 25 July 1923, p. 5 AS PARTING:
A VILANELLE (*A*)

2 loss,] ~ *A*   grief. *Ed.*] grie[. . .] *X*   ~: *A*   **5** love] ~, *A*   thief.] ~: *A*
7 for . . . tend—] again the bow will bend; *A*   **8** brief—] ~: *A*   **10** time] Love *A*
11 sheaf;] ~: *A*   **13** for . . . ascend] shall I love's altar tend *A*   **14** reef—] ~: *A*
16 Now,] ~ *A*   last,] ~ *A*   **17** lief,] ~ *A*   **18** amend.] ~: *A*

[2] Glad to do something (i.e. to say 'a word').

M102   THE ARRAS[1]

I have thrown dice, and counted cards;
    I have drained cups to mark the lees;[2]
And I have prayed to dreams, who know
    Not any answer lies in these.

I would have torn the heavens down,   5
    Have rent the curtain of the skies,

[1] Hanging curtain, able to conceal what lies behind it.
[2] As in fortune-telling by reading tea leaves.

Have made demand upon the stars,
  Had they within them held replies.

Life's arras ever holds between
  This soul and that—what fate align!   10
The earth is dumb, no fountain makes
  Response lest man become divine.

Only the lips may speak, the hands,
  The eyes; and yet, somewhere, somehow,
Something awakes—calls—understands—   15
  And sense is ripped as by a plough.

(28 October 1936)   *Copy-text: Bat   Collated states:* None

M103   THE PROMISE

Worn, as by famine, I shall come,
  A beggar at your gate;
I shall not speak, I shall be dumb,
  Yet shall I stand elate.

I shall not speak, nor you, though all   5
  Is waiting to be said;
Yet you will answer to my call,
  Your hands give me my bread.

(5 May 1927)   *Copy-text: Bat   Collated states: AWM,* 21 June 1927, p. 14 (*A*)
Not otherwise recorded: A's text is in italics throughout.
1 Worn,] (FOR THE MIRROR.)// *Worn A*   famine,] *famine A*   3 speak,] *speak; A*
dumb,] *dumb; A*   8 bread.] *bread.// I have been one who for so long/ Has famished*
on a dream, / Avid with hunger for the strong/ Sun, perished on a gleam.// Yet there
shall fall away from me/ Pain and its old, old ache;/ I shall be as one home from
sea—/ One from the dead awake. A

M104   FROM THE SPANISH[1]

In hell once met four ghosts,
    Who, for a little space,
Stood while each asked of each
    What brought them to that place.

"I from a high bridge sprang—   5
    Sped like a stone to hell."
"I from a tower." "So I."
    Then she, "I only fell."

(13 August 1933)   *Copy-text: Bat   Collated states: SV* (no variants)

---

[1] NLA 8766 10/8/12 is annotated with an unattributed Spanish source of the second
stanza: 'Yo me cai de una torre./ Yo me he caido de un puente./ Pues yo me cai de primo/
Y todavia me duele.'

M105   THE ROSE

Farewell, farewell the strife,
    Closed is the combat now;
No more to ask of life
    What foes I fought, and how!

We have known many a spring   5
    Together, you and I,
O kind warm covering
    Of flesh, so soon to die.

Yet though to dust you go,
    In some far year apart,   10
Maybe a rose will grow
    From what was once my heart.

(19 August 1938)   *Copy-text: Bat   Collated states:* None

M106　THIS HAVE I SEEN

This have I seen with joy—
A bird whose breast was burnished for the spring,
A white rose and a red,
And on the heath, in flower, the ling.[1]

And this too have I seen—　　　　　　　　　5
The love-light burning in a young lad's eyes,
And an old man, at the sere,
Measure by that lost ecstasies.

And once, years gone, I saw
Life shocked to sudden pause although its noon　　10
Still crowned the height, lest age,
The subjugator, come too soon.

(15 December 1934)　*Copy-text: Bat*　*Collated states:* None

[1] Scots name for plants of the genus *Erica*, especially heather.

M107　RANDWICK MILITARY HOSPITAL[1]

I

Lord, ere the quite forgotten
Because within the rotten
Mould of earth we lie,
Let pity come remembering
Something of love's old embering,　　　　　5
Lest even as ghosts we die.

II

The wounded snake
That o'er the grass

[1] Popular name for the 4th Australian Repatriation Hospital, est. 1915 by converting the Destitute Children's Asylum (1858) at High Cross, Randwick, to deal with wounded soldiers returning from the Gallipoli campaign.

Drags its slow length
To slowly pass,[2]   10
Aches less than I,
Who can but know
Both love and life
As feud and foe.

III

"Vengeance is Mine," saith the Lord,   15
    "And if I have stayed My hand,
If I have withheld the sword,
    Shall a man's wrath stand?"

Life in implacable need
    Asks for its own full yield,   20
As the root and the seed
    Ask for their field.

Vengeance, O Lord, is Thine?
    Where the dead men lie
Life's loss must cry,   25
"And vengeance is mine!"

(Pt I: 23 July 1932; Pt II: 7 May 1932; Pt III: 21 December 1927)   *Copy-text:*
Bat   Collated states: None

[2] Cf. 'An Essay on Criticism' (1709) by Alexander Pope (1688–1744): 'That like a
wounded snake, drags its slow length along' (line 359).

M108   VAE VICTIS[1]

I   TOO SOFT ARE THEIR HANDS

I shall go out again to the plains,
And leave behind me the roil[2] of the streets
And the chatter of men
Who read slack books, and talk always of women.

[1] Alas for the vanquished (Latin).
[2] Agitation, disorder.

I shall go out where a man is alone without fear,   5
And a woman is safe
Though but a tent is her wall.

Too soft are the hands of the men in the street,
Too hard are their hearts!
But I shall go where a man's work   10
Shows in his hands, and his sleep
Is not festered by dreams.

II   THE TIGER SLEEPS

Clasp hands and go while yet 'tis time;
    The tiger sleeps
That knows nor reason and nor rhyme.   15
The stars in their courses fought
    Against Sisera, that ancient king,[3]
But here are powers that bring to naught
    A greater thing.
    The tiger sleeps;   20
Clasp hands and go while yet 'tis time.

III   GENIUS SPEAKS

Only through sex are some men made free;
I have known many men, and many men have known me,
Yet as a bird I have kept my tree.

The weakling sits in the dust and bites on his nails,   25
Bitter his heart, and bitter his tongue as it rails,
But compassed and helmed the strong ship sails.

Pain is the spur of the world.
Only through sex are some men made free,
None but the strong-parturient[4] conquer its gale,   30
The rest are but spawn of its sea.

(Pt I: 18 August 1938; Pt II: 26 June 1926; Pt III: 30 October 1935)   *Copy-text:*
Bat   Collated states: None

---

[3] From Judges 5. 20. On Sisera, see L16 n. 1.
[4] Strong in travail (of childbirth), i.e. fruitful, productive.

M109   "POOR NELLY"

Here lies a lady,
   Low her degree;
Though she were shady,
   Still let her be.

Christ on the throne,   5
   And she on the pave,
Each lay alone,
   Alone in the grave.

So, should one whisper
   She was no good,   10
Show the dark lisper
   Death's solitude.

(12 August 1938)   *Copy-text: Bat*   *Collated states:* None

M110   THE CONSTANT HEART

If I an exile must set forth and go,
Naked where there no garment is but love—
If, uncompanioned as the widowed dove
Mourning her grief on every wind may blow,
I wander on by darkling heavens and low,   5
Where no kind star from out its far remove
Beacons like thy regard bent me above—
Enduring still shall my heart's altar glow.

O, as some jewel in the deep of night
Rays out in brilliance from itself abroad,   10
In unconsuméd fire forever burning,
So shall my spirit lift for thee its light,
And I shall dream this outward foot is to'ard,
Unto thy heart's far hermitage returning.

(10 May 1919)   *Copy-text: Bat*   *Collated states:* None

MI11   FORGIVEN

After the hard and bitter years,
    Here, where the last farewells are said,
Lift thy sad face, all wet with tears;
    Forget the faults, forgive the dead.

Thou shalt from life still take thy sheaf;   5
    In spite of loss, not all is sped;
Then, by the measure of thy grief,
    Forget the faults, forgive the dead.

Thou who hadst never will to hate
    Thine enemy who to thee pled,   10
Let thine own loss be advocate—
    Forget the faults, forgive the dead.

Though thou wast wounded sore, and none
    Might aid thee where the dark way led,
Yet at this last, where standest lone,   15
    Forget the faults, forgive the dead.

What though through long and anguished years
    Thy lips knew silence as their bread,
Now, in the falling of thy tears,
    Forget the faults, forgive the dead.   20

(8 February 1927)   *Copy-text: Bat   Collated states: SMH*, 16 October 1937, p. 13 as
FORGIVENESS (*A*)

3 tears;] ~— *A*   5 sheaf;] ~, *A*   13 sore] so *A*   19 thy] these *A*

M112   VILANELLE TO BEAUTY[1]

O Columbine, my Columbine[2]
The lights are out, thy tent away,
Yet must I follow, ever thine.

Thou art my bread and all my wine,
And thou the glamour of the play,   5
O Columbine, my Columbine.

Far in the night the fixed stars shine,
And thou the one that will not stay—
Yet must I follow, ever thine.

Sometimes I dream thy lips kiss mine,   10
Who would kiss thee, but never may,
O Columbine, my Columbine.

I who have hungered still must pine,
My heart is broken every day,
Yet must I follow, ever thine.   15

Ah, though I feed among the swine
Who may not at love's altar pray,
O Columbine, my Columbine,
Yet must I follow, ever thine.

(20 November 1920)   *Copy-text:* Bat   *Collated states:* Bn, 23 June 1921, p. 3 as IN
NOSTALGIA FOR BEAUTY (*A*)

Not otherwise recorded: Wherever the copy-text has 'Columbine', *A* has 'Colombine'.
The collation for lines 6 and 12 is identical to 1.

1 my Columbine,] ~ Colombine! *A*   2 away,] ~. *A*   5 And thou] Thou art *A*
glamour] glamor *A*   play,] ~. *A*   7 shine,] ~—*A*   8 one] light *A*   stay—]
~! *A*   10 kiss] touch *A*   mine,] ~ *A*   11 may,] ~. *A*   13 I] ~, *A*
hungered] ~, *A*   14 day,] ~: *A*   16 Ah,] ~! *A*   though] Though *A*
19 thine.] ~! *A*

---

[1] NLA 727 2/2/12 is annotated: 'In heartache – nostalgia for beauty – such as is
expressed by Hugh McCrae and in one picture to the full, by Norman Lindsay, in
McCrae's new Book Columbine. There is in it something of the wistfulness that goes
with the perception of ineffable beauty always just beyond the line of the attainable by
effort, yet sometimes achieved apparently by its own coming in fulness of time to birth.
M.G.' On the *villanelle* form, see M101 n. 1.
[2] Columbine is the beautiful but unattainable beloved of Pierrot in Italian *commedia
dell'arte.*

MI13   1936[1]

Kings to their tombs
    In majesty and pride,
The thundering of drums,
    The marching of the serried;
Banners and purple pass,   5
    News flashing far and wide:
How different it was
    When Christ was buried!

(29 February 1936)   *Copy-text: Bat*   *Collated states:* None

[1] King George V died on 20 January 1936.

MI14   THE LITTLE SHOES THAT DIED

These are the little shoes that died.
    We could not keep her still,
But all day long her busy feet
    Danced to her eager will.

Leaving the body's living warmth,   5
    The spirit ran outside;
Then from the shoes they slipped her feet,
    And the little shoes died.

(31 October 1938)   *Copy-text: Bat*   *Collated states: SMH*, 5 November 1938, p. 21 as
HER LITTLE SHOES (*A*)   *PPA* (*B*)   *SV (C)*
5 living] loving *C*   warmth,] ~ *B*

MI15   IN MEMORIAM

JESSIE MACKAY OF NEW ZEALAND[1]

What was it, in thy heart, that made
    Thee choose the sterner way,
When, at thy will, the easy path
    Had donned for thee array?[2]

Was there an iron in thy mould,   5
    That, though it slew, bade thee,
From the sophisticate and slack,
    First in the battle be?

The powers that shaped in thee thy mood,
    That bred thee as the sea   10
In depth and as the rock in will,
    Full passion gave to thee!

Thine was the eagle-feathered word,
    Thine was the clansman's cry;
Heard it the ancient Maori hosts,   15
    Heard it the land of Iye.*

Thou wast in courage ever chief;
    Thou wast Excalibur;[3]
The sharp thrust of thy vision-stroke
    No lesser thing could blur.   20

No littleness in thee had part,
    Thy palm held foe and friend;

(18 October 1931)   *Copy-text: Bat*   *Collated states: SMH*, 22 October 1938, p. 21 as IN
MEMORIAM: JESSIE MACKAY OF NEW ZEALAND (*A*)

5 mould,] ~ *A*   **16** Iye.*] ~*. *A*   **21–8** No . . . bleed!] *Om. A*

---

[1] On the Highland tradition shared by MG and Mackay (1846–1938), see B115 n. 2; and
B115 n. 1 for their other links. Mackay wrote enthusiastic reviews of *PH* and *UW*; MG
reviewed Mackay's collection *Vigil* (1935) in an article in the *Sydney Mail*, 6 November
1935. See *CG* 328 for Mackay's final letter to MG.
[2] Had put on its apparel for you, i.e. was prepared for you.
[3] The enchanted sword of King Arthur.

Never couldst thou, though combat stung,
   To pointed hurt descend;

Nor nursed thou weeping yesterdays,   25
   To rob to-morrow's need;
The scars life graved upon thy heart
   No eye but thine saw bleed!

Therefore high heart, high head, and pride
   That naught could break or shame,   30
The flame that from thy steel leapt forth
   Writes in the sky thy name.

And when at last came rest, and thou
   In peace didst lay thee down,
Death brought to thee a coronet,   35
   As life a crown.

* The ancient clan-land of the exiles—the Mackays dispossessed by the Duke of Sutherland, that sheep might breed and men decay.

29 Therefore] ~, *A*   30 naught could] could not *A*   31 flame] ~, *A*   forth]
~, *A*   36 a] its *A*   n2 Sutherland,] ~ *A*

M116 THE PILGRIM

Rain dark as pain, and wind as wild as grief,
   And in my heart the salt of unshed tears—
Scattered in sodden showers the once green leaf,
   Ended the chapter of the golden years.
The grain I sowed is sprouting in the sheaf,   5
   The stook is slack to every wind that veers;
Time, that was once my friend, is now the thief,
   And flings me to a course where no hand steers.

(n. d.) *Copy-text: Bat* *Collated states: Aus* (June 1923), p. 34 (*A*)
1 pain] tears *A*   2 tears—] ~! *A*   3 Scattered] Scatters *A*   once green]
falling *A*   leaf,] ~. *A*   4 Ended] And ends *A*   5 sprouting] growing *A*
6 stook] band *A*   to] in *A*   8 course] sea *A*

And still against the adverse winds of fate
    I hold my way toward the utmost goal,   10
Taking what punishment may still await
    As part of that which shapes the steadfast soul;
Longing, in what sad hours and desolate,
    That you may one day read this blotted scroll.

10 way] course *A*   12 shapes] makes *A*   13 Longing,] ~ *A*   and] or *A*
desolate,] ~ *A*

M117 THE NIGHT IS LONG

O that thy heart confederate were with mine!
Or that it, o'er the bounds of time and space,
Leapt in one fervent pulse to this my place,
And fuelling mine with its own fire divine,
Beat in the throb where these sad lips drink brine: 5
Then, in my desert wide, one fair oase
Burgeoned for me, whom no fond hopes enlace,
Yet who the touch invisible must pine.

The night is long. I watch the slow stars trace
The winding paths of heaven, and turn my face   10
Toward a wind that once perhaps touched thine.
The night is long. The earth is my embrace.
Yet God has given to me this one last grace:
To see in dreams thy love-look on me shine.

(11 October 1923)   *Copy-text: Bat*   *Collated states:* None

M118 FIRST IS OF MEN

First is of men, in high and stately pride,
He who hath called me from my close as his;
Me he hath made his pilgrim by a kiss,
To walk with scrip and scallop[1] at his side.

Now I securely go whate'er betide,   5
For as a child I am, where'er he is;
Where his hand stays me I can never miss
The will, once mine, that I for love denied.

In him the might I have not ever dwells,
My dower[2] is all the light within his eyes;   10
In him life's rising tide insurgent wells,
I am the dew that calls the sun and flies;
His blood the wave of instant power impels,
But in my bondage my contentment lies.

(26 November 1920)   *Copy-text: Bat   Collated states: SV* (no variants)

[1] For 'scrip', see I146 n. 1. Medieval English pilgrims wore a scallop shell to signify a
completed journey to St James of Compostela in Spain.
[2] See I141 n. 2.

M119   THE EMBER FLAME

Though we no more may mark the self-same chart,
Yet would I ask, though this last word be all,
Have we two voyaged then so far apart
The whole course ends—the pennon is at fall?
Was it so little that I gave? So small   5
A thing the deep affection of this heart,
That only knew, in turning to your call,
The swifting[1] of its answer for its art?

Ah, there will come a day when there will rise
Behind the curtain of the inner eyes   10
An ember flame, and old affection glow—
So cold to-day! But I, I shall not know,
In the deep quiet of the grave unstirred.
Then will you grieve because you spoke no word.

(23 October 1921)   *Copy-text: Bat   Collated states:* None

[1] Swift sending.

M120   AFFINITY

This shall remain unchanged though years withstand,
Nor will it pass away, what else abate!
While human hearts shall cry, *Come soon! Come late!*
Even as shipwreck for the saving land,
We ache to feel the clasp of some one hand   5
Which needs on no interpreter to wait,
Which stands, no lackey at convention's gate,
But takes the heart's full riches at command.

When fallen the fire of youth's high mounting flame,
Breathe on the embers, and find there the glow   10
That warms unchanged the pulse, grown old and slow,
Yet kindles as young love once on a name—
Young love that was so swift to praise or blame,
Itself the fire that leapt, it would or no.

(11 May 1923)   *Copy-text: Bat   Collated states: Wr*, 11 July 1923, p. 5 as FELLOWSHIP
(*A*)

1 unchanged] *Om. A*   though] though all the *A*   **2** will] shall *A*   pass . . . else]
fail, whatever tides *A*   **3** *Come . . . late!*] Come soon! Come late! *A*   **4** the
saving] remembered *A*   land,] ~ *A*   **6** wait,] ~; *A*   **8** takes] knows *A*   at]
its *A*   **9** When fallen] Burned-out *A*   high mounting] high-leaping *A*
10 Breathe] Blow *A*   embers,] ~ *A*   **11** the] the fallen *A*   pulse] pulses *A*
grown old and] *Om. A*   **12** Yet] Which *A*   **14** fire] flame *A*

M121   IN LIFE'S SAD SCHOOL

She grew, but he remained where he began.
And so, as eager fancy hungry ran,
She turned to dreams, imagining a mind
That burned to vision where the less are blind,
That held firm hands whose strong reserves lay still,   5
Or leaned upon indomitable will,

(1 November 1922)   *Copy-text: Bat   Collated states: SV* (*A*)
1 began.] ~, *A*

Which, self-contained, could haste, or pause, or wait,
Nor lose the fullness of its high estate.

Yet ever on the background of her thought
Waited the narrow forehead of the fool   10
Who called her his. I saw her tear-marked face,
I saw her deep eyes' baffled look, which sought
To know what was it that, in life's sad school,
Matched the swift-footed to the dullard's race.

8–9 estate.// Yet] ~./ ~ *A*

SECTION N

The Disinherited (1941)

N1 THE DISINHERITED[1]

I

The dice were loaded full and well
  The dreadful night that I was born,
The devils danced a tarantelle,
  The whimpering plovers fled the corn.

A fox that hunted hungry food   5
  Lifted his head in ravaged cry;
A shadow ran from out the wood,
  In after years that shade was I.

I trod the dark mile all alone,
  I trod it lone through all the years;   10
And but the midnight heard my moan,
  And but the bitter earth my tears.

I make no plaint, I make no cry,
  No back look give to yesterday;
For, where I saw the hazard lie,   15
  I played the game they bid me play.

And now I hang upon a tree,
  My lovely body all forlorn;

The textual note for N1 appears on p. 589

(0.1–306.1) I . . . XVII] *Om. B*   **0.1** I] *Om. A C E* I *D*

---

[1] Based on the life of Richard Talbot, in whose unhappy career in the Australian Infantry Force and the Royal Australian Air Force MG took an interest during 1940–42. (For a fuller account see volume 1, Introduction, p. lxv, and *CG* 340–1 and 355–6; for her related interest in eugenics see I130 n. 1.) Only NLA 2/5/1 contains all parts of the sequence. This MS shows that MG considered a variety of names for the title, the most frequent being Richard Tolby, and it contains multiple versions of many of the parts, some having variant or no numbers. See volume 1, Appendix for manuscript locations and descriptions.

The loaded dice were thrown for me,
    Upon the night that I was born.   20

II

A bird was preening overhead,
    The sunlight warmed the fern,
There was no sound might startle one,
    Or anxious ear discern.

Only the little stream went by,   25
    Kissing the reedy edge;
Only a heron silent stood,
    And watched the dewy sedge.

Space ranged, a benison[2] on life;
    Sweet was the morning air;   30
A hunted man, I looked abroad,
    And I was happy there.

III

I came where old Strathdownie heath[3]
    Ran blue as bluest seas,
I saw the smoky wind-roll wreath,   35
    And feather through the trees;

I heard the charcoal-burner's axe
    Bite on the lovely wood,
I watched men stoop with bended backs,
    Claying the ovens rude.[4]   40

The sun went down the western slip,
    The dusk became the dark;
I saw men sit in fellowship,
    The log-fire leap and spark.

---

19 me,] ~ E   (20.1–508) II . . . years.] Om. A C E   20.1–32 II . . . there.] Om. D
32.1 III] II D   33 old] Old D

[2] Blessing.
[3] See I29 n. 4.
[4] Making rough ovens sealed with clay (for burning timber to make charcoal).

Careless of life, careless of fears,   45
    Though death were on the tree,
The hunger of a thousand years
    Leapt like a wolf in me.

IV

(I never loved his father
    As I loved the wayward boy,   50
Who came and went about the house,
    Singing his heart of joy.

If he only followed the plough-tail
    He whistled[5] the live-long day;
My heart it hears him whistling still,   55
    Although he is long away.

O, he was wild, was Donald,
    Wild as a mad March hare![6]
And yet, if I were weary,
    He was the one to care.   60

My capable girls, my elder sons,
    They were too busy for me;
Their meals they had to be sharp on the clock,
    Their evenings had to be free.

But Don—O, I know the boy was mad—   65
    'A waster!' the others said;
Yet, if he were the only one home to tea,
    He'd send me off to bed.

Foolish he was, of course he was,
    But under the folly lay   70
Something so good, so sweet and clean,
    His folly seemed only play.

48.1–88 IV . . . school.] *Om.* D

[5] On whistling, see B49, Q6 and R27.
[6] Proverbial saying: hares were considered particularly wild during their rutting season in March (Spring in the northern hemisphere).

I never loved his father
    As I loved the wayward lad,
Who sang all day about the house,   75
    Till the very doors were glad!

If he only swept me the kitchen,
    He whistled as though for joy—
The prodigal son came home at last,[7]
    But not my boy.)   80

V

Joy was my name e'er I was born,[8]
But I was robbed before my birth;
So when I laughed I laughed in scorn,
For all my mirth was bitter mirth.

Laughter I made a coverlet   85
To hide my pain; fools called me fool;
But those whose eyes had seen the set[9]
Of hope, knew the old tie, and school.

VI

In what dark nights of solitude,
    Craving for human kind,   90
Against the candle light I watched
    A child's head on a blind.

And as I watched I was a child,
    Suppered, and still, and small,
Sitting in peace beside the fire,   95
    Where comfort lapped us all.

Home gave its fellowship to us;
    But, even then, there stirred,
Deep in my heart, a restless wing,
    Like that of some wild bird.   100

88.1 VI] III *D*

---

[7] As in Luke 15. 11–32; cf. J21.
[8] Adapts 'Joy is my name' ('Infant Joy') from William Blake's *Songs of Innocence* (1789).
[9] Fixed attitude.

And I in thought would drift, for dreams
    Called as the o'er-mastering sea
Calls man—and men have run to it,
    Bondsmen who thought them free.

I was the child nostalgic—Jekyll   105
    And Hyde[10]—frustrate, fear-shocked,
Disintegrate: who sought release
    In dreams; and whom dreams mocked.

VII

What nameless dread
Awaked with me at morn,   110
Supped with my spoon,
And left me spirit-worn,
And there was none to ask
Why was the babe forlorn!

Yet it was I   115
Who saw the dragonfly,
And wondering marked
The swallow mount on high;
But, in the stock-dove's note, [11]
I heard my heart's lone cry.   120

Cradled and small,
Even too small to sit,
Wistful I watched
The sparrows flock, and flit;
And then the stock-dove wept,   125
And I, I wept with it.

Too soon, too soon
I bore life's burdening weight;

---

103 man—] ~; D   **108** dreams;] ~, D   **108.1–135** VII . . . cried.] *Om.* D

[10] The protagonist of R. L. Stevenson's novel *The Strange Case of Dr Jekyll and Mr Hyde* (1886) became a type of the man divided between his good (Jekyll) and evil (Hyde) natures. See also line 160.
[11] The cry of *Columba oenas* (pigeon), often associated with grief and melancholy.

Too soon, too soon
Life called me to the gate,   130
Drew back the latch,
And drove me to my fate.

Sometimes—in darkling hours—
Sometimes I think I died
That day the stock-dove cried.   135

VIII

They who are rich know nothing of
     The slow starvation of
The poor, who ache for pence,
     And break for things they love.

Law hurts not those who have. Not theirs   140
     In life's bewildered need,
To beat against that hard,
     Unpitying face and bleed.

Blood is not always red. We bleed
     Of unconsoled desire,   145
Which burns within, as burns
     The charcoal-burner's fire.

I have seen pence and trembled but
     To hold, and I have watched
The fall of silver in   150
     A purse, till longing snatched.

IX

There was a friend who loved me well,
     Lent me a hand, and, when
Life seemed most desolate, gave me
     Again my place with other men.   155

And that dear hand that helped me up,
     So that I stood once more
Statured and sane, and living man,
     That hand I struck, nor once forebore.

135.1 VIII] IV *D*   **140** theirs] ~, *D*   **151.1–163** IX . . . fall.] *Om. D*

The darkness called, and Hyde once more   160
   Ascendant rose, till all
Was proud in me, and all my heart
   Held by as strong, went to its fall.

          X

Camped-out beside the bleak Mount Gambier road,
The moon was ice upon a field of ice,   165
The pools were ice, and every hoof-print
In the mud was shod with ice; the very breath
Was ice upon the beard.

It was so cold a night a wanted man
Might think it safe to be abroad,   170
And yet, upon that frost-bound solitude,
The rhythmic movement of a ridden horse
Was heard.

Startled I rose, and, though the fire
Was but a spark amid the icy sparks,   175
In haste I covered it,
Fearing it might be seen.

As near, and yet more near the hoof-beats came,
I bent my head to hide my face;
And then I heard the loosened shoe—   180
The sudden catch—the fall!—

I ran; all things forgotten in that human need.

          XI

So long the driven on, so long
Prepared to give a name
Not mine! And yet each camp-fire called   185
Me to its friendly flame.

And thus I met that strangest one,
The wild, wild man I found,

163.1 X] V *D*   181 fall!—] ~! *D*   182.1–226 XI . . . boy!] *Om. D*

Who carried neither scrip[12] nor purse,
Who drudged no toiler's round.   190

His thews[13] were cord, satin his skin,
This borel[14] man who drowsed,
Koala-like, upon a tree,
And whom no roof-tree housed.

Yet was he friendly to each thing   195
That in the forest stirred;
The quaint opossum feared him not,
Uncurious was the bird.

'Have you no thought of home?' I asked.
'What need of home have I?   200
My bed is where I choose,' he said,
'And time—until I die.'

With lizard grace he climbed a tree,
The slightest thing a hold;
And then, where two thick branches forked,   205
He slept; and knew no cold.

Cold is the dread of homeless man.
'A tree is warm,' he said.
I watched the wild man go at dawn.
Scarcely I heard his tread.   210

XII

Had I an angel's wings
What man would ask to tear
Them from my shouldered arms,
And leave me broken, there?

But by my lonely fire,   215
But in my prison cell,
Wings of the mind I have,
That lift me, though in hell.

[12] Wallet: cf. I146 n. 1.   [13] Sinews.
[14] Rough, wild (archaic; variant of *borrel*, *burel*).

For I can watch a bird,
And go with it in flight,   220
Then, as it turns for rest,
Home with it at the night.

No bars can prison life—
Life is a thing of joy!
Think how a bird will sing   225
Its mate—think of the boy!

XIII

I found, one day, a fox asleep,
   He too a hunted one,
Who even as I to hiding crept,
   Who even as I had run.   230

Scarcely I breathed, so full my heart
   Toward that sleeping thing,
Curved like a cat with nose to tail,
   And nested in the ling.[15]

What beauty dwells where life abounds!   235
   Death takes it all away—
The lovely sheen, the limber line,
   The muscle's silken play!

I lingered as the morning sun
   Fell kind upon his fleece,   240
Flecked it with glinting, diamond points,
   Warmed it to fullest peace.

Then, as I stood the still,[16] I saw
   The rib of breathing pause;
He flicked an ear, flicked it again,   245
   And twice he flexed his claws.

Backward I stepped; I could not drive
   Into that heart the stake

226.1 XIII] VI *D*

---

[15] See M106 n. 1.   [16] I.e. the still one, motionless.

Of fear, knowing how oft I, too,
    In dread had sprung awake.   250

Yet, though so light I moved, he heard.
    He went in one swift leap.
I stooped and touched the round, warm place,
    Where he had lain asleep.

XIV

Whenever rose a frosty moon   255
    It seemed impossible
That it should downward slope the sky,
    And earth in darkness fell.

So clear the brightness rayed, the blue
    Was powdered by its sheen;   260
The night was jewelled in the dew,
    Was silver on the green.

And once I heard a fowler's gun
    Fling its dark sound through space,
Then sink in dying round upon   265
    The void, and leave no trace.

But from the marsh the duck's wild cry
    Rang out above the land,
And, sudden castanets on high,
    The wings beat air, and fanned.   270

A possum churred,[17] and tree to tree,
    Soft as a snowflake's fall,
A mopoke flew, careless of me,
    Settled, and made his call.

Lovely the night, lovely the things   275
    Of night! I stood until
It seemed the very air had wings,
    And all things winged were still.

254.1 XIV] VII *D*

---

[17] Made a deep, hoarse whirring sound.

XV

There was a pine tree stood,
Like a king on a far hillside,   280
At dawn the sun was its crown,
And at night the moon was its bride.

I remember the pine,
And think how I, too, like it stood,
And canker seemed far away,   285
In the pride of life's young, high mood.

XVI

At rest beneath a quiet shade,
I watched the busy ants among
The leaves—road-makers long ere man
His first road-making pick had swung!   290

Year after year the leaves renewed—
Decayed—renewed again—decayed—
And still these tiny feet went on,
Till their unending tracks were made.

Rains runnelled them; they held the dew;   295
Flumes[18] by the emmet engined out
To save the world: that world where man,
With plough and axe, made roads for drought.

And these ephemera[19] we scarce
Observe, whose moment is an age   300
To them, they will be here when we
Are gone, and all our equipage.

I let them run upon my hand,
These servants of earth's pyramid,
And all the world grew wide for me,   305
Although, a hunted man, I hid.

278.1–286 XV . . . mood.] *Om.* D   **286.1** XVI] VIII D   **289** leaves—] ~; D

---

[18] Channels to carry water; 'emmet' is ant.
[19] Transient (and insignificant) things; also the technical name for insects that in their winged form live for a single day.

XVII

Sweeter than music falls
Rain on an old bark roof;
Rain as the warp of sound,
Velvet the woof.[20]   310

Rain on an old bark roof,
And the crackle of fire—
Only to dream of it
Stabs with desire.

XVIII

(*O did she know,*   315
As she heard the slow rain
Fall with a sopping sound
Outside the pane,

How, where he crouched
Like a dog in its lair,   320
The rain, as it fell,
Soaked through him there!)

XIX

The sudden autumn winds, like hounds
    That bell upon a scent,
Came bloring[21] through the forest lanes,   325
    To burst above the bent.[22]

But I lay snug within my bed,
    Although the bellied fly
Cracked like a shot-gun in the blast,
    That caught it, hurrying by.   330

Storm is the root of man,[23] or man
    Were but a flower that drank

(**306.1–322**) XVII . . . *there!*)] *Om.* D   **307** music] ~, *B*   **311** roof,] ~ *B*
(**314.1–508**) XVIII . . . years.] *Om.* B   **322.1** XIX] IX *D*

[20] On 'warp' and 'woof', see M31 n. 1.   [21] See M34 n. 2.
[22] Heath, open land.   [23] Cf. M90 and M93.

Its hour of sun and rain, and then
    To dust forgotten sank.

Dust is the womb of peace. . . . And yet,   335
    Born of the dust, began
All love, all power, all hate; and law,
    That, governing, made man.

As slowly fell the formless wind,
    There came the rounded rain;   340
I thought how it, dimensioned, lived,
    But no storm lives again.

Brooding I lay, and brooding heard
    Force cry upon the wind;
Force that, unshaped, must die, because   345
    By law undisciplined.

And I was like the wind, to life
    I gave no gift of form,
To raise, by its compelling power,
    My heritage of storm.   350

XX

Home came I, home at the even. None knew
Me as I knocked upon my father's door,
With strange, unseeing eyes my sister stood,
While I heard my mother's step on the floor.

What was it written on my face that hid   355
The child had grown to manhood there? I turned
And went away; a beggar who had knocked
Because his aching heart had homeward yearned.

XXI

O, that I might go back, and entering
The room that once was mine, turn down the bed,   360
And bathed, and fresh pyjama clad, creep in
And sleep, and there forget this ruined head!

335 peace. . . . And] ~ . . . and *D*   **350.1–430** XX . . . paid.] *Om. D*

But now my brother has the room was mine;
His clothes hang where my clothes were hung; the old
Red cedar press is his, and in the drawers   365
I loved, his linen lies in fold on fold.

XXII

I have been cold so long,
Heart cold, love cold;
Starved for that other self
Would meet me and enfold.   370

The bought are ash; the weak,
That are as drift
Before a wind, lack even
The semblance of a gift.[24]

And, so, falls from the lip   375
The empty cup,
Too shallow for a draught,
Though dredged for but a sup.

Only within the core
Of self homes love;   380
There one is hearth, and one
The ember flame above.

XXIII

Of all the kisses given and taken,
There are but two that I remember;
Neither had known the scorch of need,   385
Neither the lure of passion's ember.

One was the snow-flake of her mouth,
That was a kiss and not a kiss;
The white submissive innocence
That knows not love's dark avarice.   390

---

[24] I.e. in the search for the 'gift' of love (lines 368–70), the 'bought' (prostitutes) and the 'weak' (those incapable of strong feelings and fidelity) are as ashes and dust (lines 371–3), incapable of even appearing to give (line 374) warmth to cure the 'heart cold' of line 368.

One was a young girl's tender gift,
When, as I slept—a boy—she bent
And laid her lips to mine; then, as
I woke, swift through the darkness went.

The dreadful open-mouthed that ape   395
A passion that they hope to stir,
The loosely given, all, all are gone,
Save that I know such kisses were.

But that first adolescent kiss
Of love—love that is beautiful—   400
And *hers*: these have remained unchanged,
And shall, though time all else annul.

XXIV

Not as a beast might slake
In momentary lust
His appetite, seeking   405
No more than physical adjust,

But, as the tides elapse,
The wonder-held to lie,
Silent and still awhile;
And, then, to sleep upon a sigh.   410

XXV

Man craves his mate as woman craves
Man's child; so, in long night by night,
I dreamed that she, so dear and warm,
Beside me lay: who never might.

Sometimes in sleep I thought of fire,   415
Fire that, like God, rejects no man;
And we were there, quiet and still,
Needing no words our thoughts to span.

And once, one hunger-driven only
To look upon her face, I came   420
Out of the dusk, and standing there
I called, who scarce might speak her name.

She turned to me with mother-eyes,
And all the world was home again;
Forgotten were the dreadful years,   425
The blasting shame, the endless pain.

And in me something more than man
Shook with a sudden throe. . . . She laid
Her head against my breast, and in
That touch life's debt to me was paid.   430

                    XXVI

Sometimes the city called, the lights,
    The turmoil, and the sense
Of an unending consciousness
    Strained outward and intense.

Its tides roared chambering in my ears,   435
    Till even in sleep I moved
One with that envelope of force
    That death itself disproved.

Then on a sudden there would sweep,
    Out of the inner coasts   440
Of self, a longing for the still,
    A hatred of all hosts.

And I would go, leaving the noise,
    To sit beside the sea,
And hear the waters leap and lap,   445
    And set their music free.

And I was Saul, leaning again
    On David's harp, till fell
The torment of the mind away,
    Under that moving spell.[25]   450

But I have longed to hear her voice,
    To feel her hands' warm fire,

430.1 XXVI] X _D_   **434** outward] ~, _D_

[25] See C1 n. 1.

Until the very sinews of the heart
   Cracked with desire.

XXVII

Once on her lips, once only—   455
Then death may swing
The hinges of his door!
Though to the dark
I go the lonely,
I shall not ask for more.   460

I had not meant to hurt—
Nor she—
And yet, before we knew,
The hurt was there.
And now, for us who so much care,   465
There is not anything,
Not anything that we can do.

But if, upon her lips, once only—
Then death may swing the hinges of his door.
Though to the dark   470
I go the lonely,
I shall not ask for more.

XXVIII

All night the frost needled the air,
Or netted on the grass
Its silver points   475
Of shining glass.

And all night long the moon moved like
A white thought in the mind,
By memory held,
Yet undefined.   480

All night I heard the bittern beat
Abroad his lonely cry,

Asking his mate,
And lone as I.

All night I sat and held my hands   485
Clasped like a child in prayer,
Dreaming of her;
Dreaming her there.

XXIX

Under the tree I raised my tent,
Under the shining leaves;   490
The winds of life came there the spent,
Under those shining leaves.

Under the tree I set my tent,
And when at last the night was come,
Under the tree I laid me down,   495
Knowing that I was home.

Birds came and nested in that tree,
The ant climbed upward from the sod;
There, even as I, all things came home,
For the tree was God.   500

L'ENVOI

I, who have written this,
    Know how a spirit, rare,
Met life the broken,
    By a gest[26] unfair.

I who have written this,   505
    I who wrote it with tears,
Know how a man died
    In a child's young years.

488.1 XXIX] XII *D*   **500.1–508** L'ENVOI . . . years.] *Om. D*

[26] Story or tale, implying a predetermined outcome; or, for a journey, the route planned and followed (obsolete meaning).

(August 1940 – August 1941)[27]   *Copy-text: Dis*   *Collated states: AP 1942*, Pt I only, as *FROM THE DISINHERITED* (*A*)   *PPA*, Pt XVII only, as RAIN ON THE ROOF (*B*)   Green, Pt I only, as THE DICE WERE LOADED (*C*)   *SV*, Pts I, III, VI, VIII, X, XIII, XIV, XVI, XIX, XXVI, XXVIII and XXIX only (*D*)   Wright I, Pt I only, as THE DICE WERE LOADED (*E*)

Not otherwise recorded: D has author's notes: *For Pt I:* The "dark mile" was originally that taken by Bonnie Prince Charlie when, after Culloden Moor, my father's ancestor, Cameron of Lochiel, brought him to the Castle (Achnacarry) and hid him. Some of the trees of that dark passage still stand.[28]

For D's Pt II [reading text, Pt III]: Strathdownie was the name given to the first cattle and sheep station in what Mitchell called *Australia Felix*, that is, Western Victoria. It was taken up by the MacEacharns, who left Goulburn, New South Wales, travelling by the sun and stars. The Camerons took up Argyle, still in part owned by their descendants. Both families were related to us.[29]

Adam Lindsay Gordon,[30] when droving from Mount Gambier, asked the Mac-Eacharns to let him put his cattle in their house paddock for the night. Refused, and having to watch the stock all night, he wrote a piece of verse on the gatepost cursing the MacEacharns. I understand that the third generation still has a copy of the lines.

For D's Pt III [Pt VI]: This was in 1872. I was the child. This man worked for father.

For D's Pt VIII [Pt XVI]: If we had followed the teaching of the aboriginals, we would have had no silted rivers and no erosion; the rivers would still have been full of water and fish, and Wentworth, as in the Eighties, would still be the third largest tonnage port of New South Wales.[31]

The blacks taught us, as children, not to destroy either the ants or their roads. Through millions of years the ants' tiny feet beat the surfaces of their tracks through the grass and made them able to hold tiny drops of water, after rain. This nourished the roots of the grass, and the little tussocks or tufts were always larger and kept green longer than those away from the tracks. This applies to the small black ant. Father taught us and his men (when new-chums) to look for these drops of water, if lost. The blacks had taught him. Such drops, of course, could only be found after a shower had passed, and many a time I have seen the birds run, beaking them.

---

[27] Composition was spread over twelve months: Pt I: 18 August 1940; Pts II, III: 18 February 1941; Pt IV: 10 September 1940; Pt V: 8 May 1941; Pts VI, VII: 2 May 1941; Pt VIII: 8 June 1941; Pt IX: 29 May 1941; Pt X: 16 June 1941; Pt XI: 18 May 1941; Pt XII: 15 July 1941; Pt XIII: 9 August 1941; Pt XIV: 26 April 1941; Pts XV, XVII and L'ENVOI: 24 May 1941; Pt XVI: 20 May 1941; Pt XVIII: 26 May 1941; Pt XIX: 20 July 1941; Pt XX: 20 August 1941; Pts XXI, XXIV: 28 June 1941; Pt XXII: 6 June 1941; Pt XXIII: 14 June 1941; Pt XXV: 9 May 1941; Pt XXVI: 4 June 1941; Pt XXVII: 5 July 1941; Pt XXVIII: 15 May 1941; Pt XXIX: 14 April 1941.

[28] On Bonnie Prince Charlie, see E13 n. 3 and, on the Camerons of Lochiel, *CG* 12–14.

[29] On Strathdownie, see I29 n. 4 and R62 n. 1; and cf. *"Echoes of the Past": From the Casterton News, 1884: Together with Articles on the McEachern Family of Strathdownie*, facsimile ed. H. G. Ross (n.p., 1992); held by Marie Ross:

In the year 1855, East Strathdownie as well as West Strathdownie and Heathfield, was held by the McEachern Brothers, in conjunction with their father and their brothers-in-law – Mr James Cameron and the late Mr Hugh McPherson. The Argyle station was held by another brother-in-law – Mr John McIntyre . . . [At] the

> Kilbride station, better known as Nangwarry, Mr Allan Cameron [was] manager, his brother, Mr Donald Cameron, now of Lake Mundi, being also resident at the station in 1855.   (pp. 23–4)

Thomas Livingstone Mitchell (1792–1855), surveyor-general of NSW from 1827, gave the title *Australia Felix* (Fortunate/Happy) to the fertile lands from the Murray R. to the coast of w. Victoria that he explored in 1836.

[30] On Gordon, see I29 n. 3, and I31 and nn. 1 and 2.

[31] Wentworth, NSW, officially named in 1859 after explorer and politician William Charles Wentworth (1790–1872), was ideally placed at the junction of the Darling and Murray Rivers to profit from the river steamer trade introduced in 1853 and at its peak in the 1880s. It thereafter declined as a result of competition from railways and deteriorating river quality.

SECTION O
Uncollected Poems 1939–1943

O1   YET AM I WORSHIPPER

I write not flowering words;
   Mine are the briar, the thorn.
I am no William Yeats[1]
   Whose touch is to adorn.
Yet am I worshipper   5
   Where beauty lifts in plume
Words like a spray of doves,
   A pear-tree white with bloom.

And I have known a weft[2]
   Of beauty like a robe   10
Spun by the hand of God.
   I have read Job.[3]

(n. d.)   *Copy-text: Bn*, 12 July 1939, p. 8   *Collated states:* None

---

[1] William Butler Yeats (1865–1939): lines 1 and 4 suggest the more romantic style of his earlier poetry (up to *The Wild Swans at Coole*, 1917), but it is not known which, if any, of his many collections MG had read.
[2] Fabric: see M31 n. 1.
[3] Old Testament Book, a great depiction of the mystery of faith in God's justice despite human suffering.

O2   THE REBEL

I was not sufficiently rebel,
I bent and bowed, for I was a woman;
And yet rebellion lived in me
Like a child unborn asking for life,
And beating the bars, beating the bars.   5

Maybe, in years to come, in centuries hence,
A child remotely mine will rise,

Will proudly rise,
And, rebel, will do the things I would have done.

Childless the rebel dare not die,   10
Lest to the grave he go—
Lest in the grave he lie
The unfulfilled.

(n. d.)   *Copy-text: Boh* (March 1940), p. 7   *Collated states:* None

O3   THE FIGHTING TALBOTS[1]

When the Fighting Talbots came into the town,
Gloves on the hand, or stony broke,
Although he was Earl of Hell and all,
The devil went off into smoke;
Yet the Lord God help the foolish man   5
Who laid on a cobber[2] his hand,
Unless he wanted to wear on his hide
The mark of the Talbot Brand!

When "Whacko—Whack-o-o!" the Talbots yelled,
The walls of the earth were shook,   10
And the great town clock by the Cenotaph
Forgot it ever had strook;
For the Talbot lads were the fighting lads,
And hand, or heart, or head,
They'd scrap while ever a one of them stood,   15
Or blood in the eye was red.

"Hit!" says Jim, and "I will!" says Dick,
With Jack and Bob in the van,
While Frank, who had done his bit in France,
Looked on as a sorrowful man;   20

[1] Accompanied in *QD* by a cartoon, signed 'Cecil L. Hartt 18 Batt[alion] A.I.F', depicting two soldiers casually informing the local police sergeant: 'We're having a night out to-night, and we want to deposit the bail.'   [2] Mate, friend: cf. R65 author's note.

"Hit!" says Jack, and "I will!" says Bob,
  And at it they went like mad,
  For they were the turbulent Talbot boys,
  Where every man was a lad!

I knew them down to the youngest one,   25
I knew them, father and mother,
I nearly nursed them all on my knees
At some time or another;
But I loved them all, and I laughed at all,
Though I wept for the soldier boots,   30
As they tramp—tramp—tramped away in the mud,
With the rest of the khaki "coots."[3]

"Come back!" I cried, as they turned to go,
  But you might as well shout the wind,
  For they all went into it up to the neck,   35
  Till the Sarge had them disciplined—
They all went into it up to the neck
(But hush as to nurses and suppers),
For the Talbot lads were the men who would fight
Till their boots wore down to the uppers.   40

(3 January 1940)   *Copy-text: QD* (April 1940), p. 32   *Collated states:* None

[3] Persons (colloquial), usually mildly derogatory as in *mad coot.*

O4 VIGNETTES

I

I have come,
By what dark ways, and long,
To this my resting place;
The apples in the sun
Are ripe, but I am ripe no more.   5

[*cont. overleaf*

(2 December 1939)   *Copy-text: Boh* (May 1940), p. 6   *Collated states:* None
Not otherwise recorded: The copy-text is in italics throughout.

0.1 I *Ed.*] *Om.* X

Upon the distant hills
The hot breath of the day still burns,
My bones are cold, the once quick pulse
Has withered down to slow.

Here in the great grey eucalyptine forest   10
The aisles of shadow deepen,
In veils of darkness falls the night,
There are no stars.
I have come,
By what dark ways and long,   15
To this my resting place.

II

Yonder a brown day-spider saves her thread,
Drawing it backward through her spinnerets
To tidy up for night. When she is gone
The evening spider will come out,   20
And, anchoring her skein,
Will spin in beauty her Euclidean[1] web;
Backward and forward she will run,
Shaping the angles, perfecting the arc—
No line superfluous.   25
And all night she will watch for night's ephemera,
Then, when at dawn dew-spangled is each thread,
Under some brooding leaf she will withdraw,
And fold her slender knees, and sleep.

22 Euclidean *Ed.*] *Eucildean* X

---

[1] Euclid of Alexandria (*c.* 325 – *c.* 265 BC) whose treatise *The Elements* made him the best-known mathematician of antiquity. MG's interest went back to her childhood: see T19 n. 1 and T2.

O5   FLEDGLINGS

A handful of sticks in a tree,
A lining of hair;

A fledgling's hungry mouth,
   And a wing on the air;
Here is the courage of life,   5
   Here of its heart the core,
Ask of the pride that is man
   Has he more!

(1940)   *Copy-text: Boh* (May 1940), p. 12   *Collated states:* None
Not otherwise recorded: The copy-text is in italics throughout.
6 core, *Ed.*] *core* X

O6 NORWAY[1]

Here we made home,
Here two-winged war
Flew over us;
The hopes that soared
Lie shattered in the dust.   5

Primeval man
Made war as man,
And man is merciful
As man to man.
But this to-day of ours   10
No mercy knows.

Stricken we stand.
The woven silver of the sea
Patterns in blood,
The smoke of guns   15
Blackens the snow-white air;
The mountain peaks look down
On Norway's grief.

Here were our homes
But two-winged war   20
Flew over us.

(n. d.)   *Copy-text: SMH*, 11 May 1940, p. 11   *Collated states:* None

[1] The World War II German invasion of an unprepared Norway began on 8 April 1940.
Massive sea and air attacks forced a surrender within two months.

O7   REDEMPTION

I was the prodigal,[1]
   You were the faithful one,
Yet there had been no tale
   Had I not wandering gone.

My life the story made,   5
   You but the background were;
There, in both light and shade,
   Man's pulse I still can stir.

You were the tide at height,
   Rearward fated to go;   10
But I, though in the night,
   Held tides that still must flow.

Back from the prodigal,
   The waster and the drone,
Swings life's recessive swell,   15
   Sprung from the overthrown![2]

(26 October 1935)   *Copy-text: SMH*, 7 September 1940, p. 9   *Collated states:* None

[1] See N1 n. 7.   [2] See I130 and n. 1, and R36.

O8   SEND FORTH THE BATTLE CRY[*]

Land of the Starry Cross! Land of our Fathers!
The storm-clouds are gathering, the war-birds appear,
The lightning's wild flash marks the path of the tempest,
The cannon's loud thunder shows combat is near!
Land of our living hope! Land of our deepest love!   5
No conqueror shall stand in triumph over thee,
For we who are thy children, we thy defenders,
Shall forever hold thee, inviolate and free.

Ours is a name and a pride that is dauntless,
We bow not to tyrants, we yield not to threats!   10

The grey ships that guard us, the bright flag above us,
Are ours in an empire whose sun never sets.
Send forth the battle cry! Beat out ye rolling drums!
Boldly we gather as the silver bugles play!
Death shall not stay us, nor danger deter us,   15
The army is marching, and we must away.

We hear from Gallipoli the voice of comrades,
Of men who remembered that honour was all;
These we shall follow whatever the ending,
These shall command, as we rise to the call.   20
Adsum![1] We answer them, they answer back again,
In all the glory of that ever mighty hour,
When by their sacrifice, when by their valour,
Australia stood before the world in splendour and power.

The sands of Gallipoli,[2] the stark cliffs record her,   25
The winds bear her story away to the stars;
And proudly we swear, in this dread hour of danger,
The dark hand of conquest shall not sully hers.
Roll out upon the drums! Play up, ye Highland pipes!
Now swoop the bombers with their blasting, flaming breath—30
But through the bruit of war, fierce as tornadoes,
Come the SONS of ANZAC,[3] shouting victory or death!

---

[*] This poem can be sung to the air of "Burke's Dream"[4]

(20 June 1940) *Copy-text: QD* (March 1941), p. 31, signed BY DAME MARY GILMORE[5]
Collated states: None

21 again, *Ed.*] ~. X

---

[1] Present! (Latin).
[2] In the undated MS in ML 6/6 MG changed 'The sands of Gallipoli' to 'Tobruk and Gallipoli', reflecting participation of Australian troops in the siege of Tobruk (1941). See volume 1, Appendix for manuscript locations and descriptions.
[3] See C38 n. 1.
[4] Traditional Irish song commemorating the unsuccessful attempt to free Richard Burke from Clerkenwell Prison (London), where he was awaiting trial for participating in the failed 1876 Fenian rebellion against British rule in Ireland.
[5] A second signature at the foot of the poem reads: 'Specially written for "The Queensland Digger" by Mary Gilmore'.

O9   AND WE ALL JOINED UP

Kangaroo and Wallaroo, Wallaby, Bandicoot,
They all came hurrying into camp
To give the Hun the boot;
The Platypus brought a regular bunch,
The little Koala cut out his lunch,   5
And they all joined up!
They all joined up!
They all joined up,
To Boomerang the Hun!

Chorus:

Boomerang! . . . Boomerang! . . .   10
Boomerang! . . . Boomerang! . . .
No road was ever too long for us,
Who padded the hoof or caught the bus;
Though the guns might roar and the shells might fall,
Nothing to us it mattered at all,   15
For we all joined up!
We all joined up!
We all joined up,
To Boomerang the Hun!

Pozieres and Palestine, Gallipoli, Armentieres,[1]   20
Our fathers diggered the way for us
In far-off dusty years!
And now we are out on the same old jag,
With Nazi and Fascist to put in the bag,
For we all joined up!   25
We all joined up!
We all joined up,
To Boomerang the Hun!

Chorus.

(*c.* 1940)   *Copy-text: QD* (July 1941), p. 24   *Collated states:* None

---

[1] Sites in France, the Middle East and Turkey of campaigns involving Australian soldiers (colloquially, *diggers*, line 21). See C38 n. 1 and C49 n. 1.

O10   EDMONDSON, V.C.[1]

Let the kings pass, and shallow pomp retreat,
    This is the day of men greater than kings!
For them the drums of time shall ever beat,
    And at their tomb death stands with fallen wings.

They shall not know decay, for down the years   5
    The bugles shall declare their full renown;
Though in the eyes of grief may brim the tears,
    Above grief stands a pride tears cannot drown.

And this Australia's son! The desert watched
    Him thrusting through the flames of war, as, there,   10
From out the very jaws of death, he snatched
    A comrade from the foe he might not spare.

Twice was he wounded—yet, when asked for aid,
    Swift as the eagles of his native land
He swung, and fighting there, and unafraid,   15
    He flung defeat upon the blood-stained sand.

        (*But sometimes, waking in the night,*
            His mother will remember only
        The little lad she nursed; and then
            How empty all the house; how lonely!)   20

Hail and farewell, O gallant young V.C.—
    The Anzac echoes answer bound to bound!
Then, for all loved and lost, O memory,
    Let your reveille never cease to sound.

        (*All night he lay waiting the end maybe*   25
        Remembering Parramatta oaks,

(n. d.)   *Copy-text: AWW*, 19 July 1941, p. 15, signed By DAME MARY GILMORE   *Collated states:* None

---

[1] Corporal John Hurst Edmondson (b. Wagga Wagga, 1914) died of wounds received on 13 April 1941 during a successful action against a German infantry position at Tobruk. Although twice wounded, he rescued an officer under attack from a German soldier and received the highest military award for bravery, the Victoria Cross. On Tobruk, see O8 n. 2 and R30 n. 4.

> *Where as a boy he played, or heard the sea*
> *Of Sydney beat with silken strokes.*
>
> *Maybe he thought of home, dreaming he saw*
> *His mother stand beside the door,*   30
> *Watching his father rake the windlestraw—*[2]
> *And then he saw no more.*)

[2] Stalks withered and dried after flowering or seeding.

O11   AUSTRALIA TO ABRAHAM LINCOLN

John Curtin[1] stood at the door,
    John Curtin looked at the sky,
"It's a pretty rough night, my lads," said he,
    "But keep your powder dry!"
Then he turned his face away to the sea,   5
    And he gave our cooee-halloo,
"We're short of a hand in the fight," he called;
    "Abe Lincoln! Where are you?"

Abe Lincoln turned in his sleep,
    He lifted his great old head,   10
For, whatever the books may say,
    Abe Lincoln couldn't be dead.
He got himself into his clothes,
    His hand reached out for his gun,
And then, as he answered John Curtin's shout,   15
    Abe Lincoln came at a run.

John Curtin he opened the door,
    "How's things?" said Abe to John;
"There's a bit of a fight," John said,
    As he buckled a Sam Brown[2] on;   20

[1] John Curtin (1885–1945), Labor Prime Minister of Australia 1941–45, broke with Australia's traditional dependence on Britain for defence purposes by appealing to USA: thus the figure of Abraham Lincoln, President during the American Civil War (1861–65). Contrast O16.
[2] Belt combining a pistol belt, shoulder strap and D-rings, named after General Sir Samuel J. Browne (1824–1901) of the British Army in India, but now associated with the American army.

"There's a bit of a fight," he said,
   The lads have come in from the farms,
But the pick of the men were sent overseas,
   And, with them, the bulk of our arms.

"But the boys who are left are fighting mad   25
   In spite of the shortage of guns,
And, for all that our army's a little one,
   The men are Australia's sons!"
"I know it!" great Lincoln said,
   "I know it;" He said it again—   30
Then foot to foot, they turned to the foe,
   The Anzac and Lincoln men.

(17 March 1942)   *Copy-text: CT*, 19 March 1942, p. 1   *Collated states:* None

O12 H.M.A.S. SYDNEY[1]

Measure the plating,
   Fashion the keel,
Burnish the spindles,
   Lathe to the steel;
Up with the smoke-stacks,   5
   Engines drive on—
No one shall say
   The Sydney is gone!

She was our pride,
   They were our sons,   10
They who in flame
   Went out with the guns!
Into the dusk,
   On, and still on—
Let no one say   15
   The Sydney is gone!

[1] The cruiser HMAS *Sydney*, with her crew of 645 men, was lost at sea in the Indian Ocean on 19 November 1941, after suffering severe damage from the German raider *Kormoran*.

Out with the pennies!
    Down with the pounds!
Turned to the hunt,
    These are our hounds!   20
Hounds of the deep,
    The hunt is still on!
No one shall say
    The Sydney is gone!

Called from the dark,   25
    Called from the deep,
Mast-head and turret
    Wake from their sleep,
Hear ye not proudly
    Men marching on?   30
Dare the foe say
    The Sydney is gone?

(4 December 1941)   *Copy-text: Reveille* (April 1942), p. 20   *Collated states:* None

O13   THE LEADER

KNAP! . . . Knap! . . . Knap! . . .
A stone among stones
I sit, Knap . . . Knap . . . Knap—
Who is the leader? Not he
On the galloping horse,   5
Though he fly like the wind
In its course;
Not the wheel like a web
In the sun,
Not even the church   10
And the steeple—
But I, the roadmaker.

A stone among stones
I sit . . . Knap . . . Knap . . . Knap—
I am the people.   15

(25 January 1941)   *Copy-text: Mjn* [1].9 (1942), p. 4[1]   *Collated states:* None

---

[1] *Meanjin Papers* (from 1940; *Meanjin* from 1947) appeared in a numbered series at
first, then quarterly from 1943, identified by season and by volume and number; the
1943 issues comprised vol. 2.

O14   THE TWIN

I buried a child I loved, to-day,
    I made his grave in a forest deep;
The leaves swirl up on the place he lies,
    As the winds about it sweep.

On him the autumn drift will fall,   5
    A drift of memory soft and kind;
And ever the grass of spring will come,
    Like a thought kept warm in mind.

O child I loved I buried you deep!
    But, somewhere, unknown, a dreadful twin,   10
Evil, ragged, through filthy streets,
    Prowls like a spectre, out and in.

(17 February 1942)   *Copy-text: SMH*, 13 February 1943, p. 7   *Collated states:* None

O15   WINGS

They were over the town, flying, flying,
The last of the swans; I heard them crying, crying,
Too far for sight in the misty height,
Too far for the hand of man to blight,
Or stay their wings in their onward flight,   5
But I found in their cry a sighing, sighing,
For the hosting dead, and the dying, dying.

I saw far over the battlefields, flying, flying,
The ghosts of the planes, with the crying, crying,
Of wind in the wings, as they dipped and turned   10
In an endless search that mourned, and mourned,
What never was found, and yet was yearned.
Shadows of shadows, circling and sighing,
The pilotless planes of the dead and dying.

(8 November 1942)   *Copy-text: SMH*, 10 April 1943, p. 7   *Collated states:* None

O16   AUSTRALIA SPEAKS[*]

No parasite am I![1]
I feed my own, I clothe my own,
My Soldiers fight in every land,
My Navy fights on every hand,
My Airmen fight a world command—   5
For blood and flesh and bone.
No parasite am I.

Seven million souls, all told, are mine;
Seven million souls, all told!
No world control by usury,   10
No debtor people held in fee
Are mine—I leave the nations free.
I feed my own, I clothe my own,
And blood and flesh and bone
No parasite can be!   15

Though mine but seven million souls,
My Soldiers fight in every land,
My Navy fights in every strand,
My Airmen range a sky's command,

(n. d.)   *Copy-text: StW*, 6 May 1943, p. 4   *Collated states:* None
19 Airmen *Ed.*] airmen *x*

[1] Contrast O11 and O17.

And my bread fed a world that wept   20
As near, and near the foeman crept.
But blood and flesh and bone,
I feed my own, I clothe my own,
Because no parasite am I!

[*] On a population basis, Australia's casualties in this war exceed those
of any other Allied country. In the last war, only the Scots had a higher
percentage.

O17   THE THREE GUNNERS

To two great Australian Gunners, and one great American:
  John Curtin, Herbert Evatt, and General Macarthur.[1]

Send the call across the sea,
Send the call across the land;
Comes the hour when we must fight,
Comes the hour when we must stand.

Stripped we wait, and man by man,   5
Stripped we turn to serve the guns;
Death we deal, and death we meet,
Where the might of battle runs.

High above us flies the plane,
From the Forts the cannon roar,   10
On the sea our battle-fleet
Keeps the foeman from the shore.

Steady, lads, the hour is come!
Vast the field and sharp the call!
We must fight as one to ten,   15
Lest invasion on us fall.

[1] For Curtin, see O11 n. 1; in 1943 Herbert Vere Evatt (1894–1965) was Attorney-
General and Minister for External Affairs. As commanding general of the American
Far East Command, General Douglas MacArthur (1890–1964) frequently consulted
the Australian government and army leaders over the management of the war in the
Pacific.

Swift to move, and quick to act,
Now we drive upon the foe;
Now the battle-front is joined,
Hand to hand, and blow for blow.   20

Sound the trumpets, roll the drums!
Fling the proud flags to the sky!
Though we fought as one to ten,
Victor's honours with us lie.

(n. d.)   *Copy-text: StW*, 5 August 1943, p. 4   *Collated states:* None

O18   HUNGER

I heard the children's hungry cry
To orchards where the rich fruits rotting lie,
I heard their plea to wheat and corn,
Almost as soon as they were born.
The peach, the plum, the pear,   5
The corn and wheat in all their golden wear,
Answering said, "For you God has bid us yield,
But man has fenced us in a field."

(13 April 1943)   *Copy-text:* Sunnybrook Press 194?[1]   *Collated states:* None

---

[1] NLA 8766 10/7/9 holds multiple copies of O18 as a small single sheet printed in
two colours by E. A. Shea of Sunnybrook Press, no date. Walter Stone dates it as 194?
and records MG's statement that it was intended for private distribution to friends:
Mary Gilmore: A Tribute, ed. Dymphna Cusack, T. Inglis Moore and Barrie Ovenden
(Sydney: Australasian Book Society, 1965), p. 221.

SECTION P
Pro Patria Australia (1944)[1]

[1] Only P1 in the booklet *Pro Patria Australia and Other Poems* was not already published in a collection; the others, in their *PPA* ordering, are E1, G40, M114, K17, N1 (Pt XVII), G11, I73 and B60. *PPA* carries no publication date. Library catalogues give 1945, but MG's Diaries confirm Wilde's date of 1944 (*CG* 372 and Bibliography). On 24 August 1944 she wrote: 'Mr Honey paid me cheque for £25.1.7 Royalty for the 5016 copies of the Booklet of my verse "Pro Patria and other verses." He says every copy has been sold' (ML Papers vol. 5: Diaries 1944–45): see volume 1, Appendix for manuscript locations and descriptions.

P1   PRO PATRIA[1] AUSTRALIA

Strong be thy walls, and mighty be thy gates,
Deep be thy loves, and terrible thy hates!
Where challenge threats, and sounds the battle cry,
Where onset thrusts, and runs the conflict high,
No alien foot shall tread the sacred rand,[2]   5
Ours, in thy Totem, O Churinga-Land![3]

Fierce though the wolf, he shall not deeper bite
Than thy great sword uplifted for the right!
O Freedom-loved, as ever from the first,
Thy destiny in liberty was nursed;   10

(29 December 1918; revised 19 February 1933, 11 April 1940)   *Copy-text: PPA   Collated states: SMH*, 25 December 1943, p. 5 as PRO PATRIA AUSTRALIA/ (SUGGESTED LINES FOR A NATIONAL ANTHEM) BY DAME MARY GILMORE (*A*)[4] Mackaness2 (*B*) Mackaness3 (*C*)

Not otherwise recorded: Except for line 24.1, *A*'s text is in italics throughout. There is no line space between lines 24.1 and 25 or lines 27 and 28 in *A*, *B* or *C*.

6 thy] Thy *C*   **7** deeper] *fiercer A*   fiercer *B C*   bite] *bite, A*   ~, *B C*   8 sword] *sword, A*   ~, *B C*   **9** O Freedom-loved] *Free flies the flag A*   Free flies the flag *B C*   first,] *first; A*   ~; *B C*   **10** nursed;] *nursed! A*   ~! *B C*

---

[1] For our country or native land (Latin).
[2] Land, territory; generalised for rhyme from the sense of a rocky ridge (South African).
[3] See I23 n. 4.
[4] *A*'s subtitle shows MG thought of P1 primarily as a song. Frank Hutchens's setting of it was sung by a choir of 60 children at the Sydney Conservatorium of Music in August

And in thy flag, which sings on every air,
Thee we salute; in thee the foeman dare.[5]

Where like a snow thy silver beaches shine,
Where spreads the fallow, and the grape is wine,
Where thou art veiled in the green silk of trees,   15
Fail not for sorrow, falter not for ease!
Suns be thy light, and moons their lanterns show,
So that the world may all thy glory know.

When in the prime, the stars together sang,
God, stooping, shaped a golden boomerang,   20
God, stooping, shaped (while knelt the seraphim)
Thee whom we serve, and serving, worship Him.
Still as a maid, and greater than a king,
Winds out of heaven shall thy anthems sing.

(Drums Crescendo)

Strong be thy walls, and mighty be thy gates!   25
Strong be thy walls, and mighty be thy gates!
Strong be thy walls, and mighty be thy gates!

Australia! . . . Australia! . . .

11–12 And . . . dare] *Years, acolyte, shall censer-swinging go, / So that the world may all thy glory know A*   Years, acolyte, shall censer-swinging go, / So that the world may all thy glory know *B C*   17 be thy light] *on thee shine A*   on thee shine *B C*   their lanterns show] *thy lantern be A*   thy lantern be *B C*   18 world may all] *nations may A*   nations may *B C*   know] *see A*   see *B C*   19 prime,] *prime A*   ~ *B C*   21 shaped (while] *shaped, while A*   ~, ~ *B C*   seraphim)] *seraphim, A*   ~, *B C*   22 Thee] *Thee, A*   ~, *B C*   and] *and, A*   ~, *B C*   22 Him] him *B C*   24.1 Crescendo] crescendo. *A*   crescendo *B C*   28 Australia! . . . Australia! . . .] *Australia! . . . . . . Australia! . . . . . . A*   ~ . . . ~ . . . *B C*

1962 (see *CG* 465). MG's letter of 3 January 1962 thanking Hutchens for his setting is in NLA 1695/2. Another setting by R. Sutherland Smith is in ML Papers vol. 43, and the Rare Books collection of Monash University's Matheson Library holds a printed sheet-music setting by Alfred Hill. If its attributed date '[193–]' is correct, Hill must have worked from MG's revised but unpublished version of 1933.

[5] I.e. trusting in thee or, in thy name, we confront the foe.

SECTION Q
Uncollected Poems 1946–1953

Q1   JOSEPH O'BRIEN

O'Brien was an Irishman,
   And, when he played the fiddle,
He played the map of Ireland
   From north to south and middle.

He played St. Patrick, gentleman,   5
   Who came from dacint[1] people,
Who built a church in Dublin Town,
   And on it put a steeple;

He played the Cliffs of Donegal,
   And, as the strings he tore,   10
You'd hear, across the Ulster hills
   The loud Atlantic roar.

His bow he'd make Cuchulain's sword;[2]
   It swung with Brian Boru—[3]
He whacked it down upon the Danes,   15
   And every Dane he slew;

He mourned with Barney Brannigan,[4]
   Who pined on wather gruel,

(23 November 1943)   *Copy-text:* Bn, 6 March 1946, p. 13   *Collated states:* None

---

[1] Decent.
[2] Of the legendary warrior of the Conchubar Cuchulinn heroic cycle.
[3] Brian Boru, or Boráma, High King of Ireland 1002–14, successfully led resistance to the Danes in several battles during the second Viking Age. He died leading his troops to victory at the battle of Clondarf and is celebrated in the Icelandic *Brjanssaga*.
[4] Unidentified, but in catalogues of Irish music the name appears as the title of a number of instrumental recordings, where the tune is variously described as a slip jig or a drinking song. Gruel (line 18) was a light soup of water ('wather') or milk based on oatmeal, recommended for invalids.

He danced with Judy Callaghan,[5]
Who stepped it like a jewel;   20

But when he played Tom Finnegan's wake[6]
A whirlwind struck the fiddle;
Ye'd think it was the divvle himself
Was dancing on a griddle!

[5] 'Judy Callaghan' is in *O'Neill's Music of Ireland: Eighteen Hundred and Fifty Melodies*,
ed. Francis O'Neill, arr. James O'Neill (Chicago: Lyon and Healy, 1903).
[6] The popular Irish song, 'Finnegan's Wake': 'One morning Tom Finnegan was rather
full;/ His head felt heavy which made him shake,/ He fell off the ladder and broke his
skull;/ So they carried him home a corpse to wake': at http://www.thebards.net/music,
accessed 8 March 2006.

Q2   COMPLIMENT TO THE YOUNG

Left on the rail
By leaping Time,
We watch new minds
Chase rhythm and rhyme;

And there we see   5
Youth fling, afar,
Its seines[1] of thought,
And net a star.

But we still plait
The rhythms were ours,   10
When we, then young,
Wrote "swains" and "bowers."

(n. d.)   *Copy-text: Bn*, 25 June 1947, p. 29   *Collated states:* None

[1] Fishing nets.

Q3   CONQUEST

I

When I have watched the grass
   Master of distance prove,
And on its tiny feet
   With unseen footsteps move,
I have asked, wondering,   5
   Can man, for all his pride,
Against this marathon,
   Win, though on wings he ride!

2

There came a little voice,
   It made so small a sound,   10
It scarcely seemed as though
   It rose above the ground;

And when Life looked about
   To see where it could be,
"I am the wheat," it said,   15
   "The people all bless me!"

Then came a battleship,
   And blasted down the wheat,
Till human beings died,
   For want of food to eat;   20

And as the great guns rose,
   And slaughtered endlessly,
Each roared to highest heaven,
   "The churches all blessed me!"

(13 October 1947)   *Copy-text: SMH*, 1 November 1947, p. 10   *Collated states:* None

Q4   PRAYER OF THE
BREAD AND CHEESE CLUB[1]

Bless the bread
And bless the cheese,
Bless the ale
That goes with these.

Bless the wit   5
And bless the troll
Circles round
The friendly bowl.

Bless the pipe
And bless the smoke   10
Gently hides
The naughty folk.

Bless the board
And bless the chair
Bless the head   15
That rises bare
(Also bless
The one with hair
But that by the way).

Next, if these   20
We may exalt,
Bless the pepper
And the salt

(n. d.)   *Copy-text: Boh* (April 1949), p. 39, signed *From the one whose name is for the moment.—ANON*[2]   *Collated states:* None

Not otherwise recorded: Except for the title, the copy-text is in italics throughout.
4 these. *Ed.*] *these* x   **18** with *Ed.*] *smooth* x

[1] Founded in Melbourne in 1938 to foster Australian literature, music and the arts. Although an all-male society, it published work by women writers, including MG.
[2] Attribution to MG is based on the initialled print clipping held in NLA 727 11/9/2, the source of the emendation to line 18 (see entry). See volume 1, Appendix for manuscript locations and descriptions.

(Salty speech
And salty food   25
Bless the banquet
And the mood).

For the last
With Thee O! Lord
Be the great   30
Grand Cheese adored.

Q5   VIATOR[1] AUSTRALIS

Give me the world!
But give me leave to come again
To my own land.

Though space abide,
I ask to find, once more,   5
One old fire side.

There rests my heart;
There is my native earth—of which
I am a part.

The banners of   10
The sky are wide, but like a bird
I shall come home!

(19 April 1950)   *Copy-text: Argus*, 13 May 1950, p. 10   *Collated states:* None

[1] Traveller or wayfarer.

Q6   A WHISTLING MAN[1]

O but my heart was sad
O, but I longed to weep,

[1] Cf. N1 lines 49–80 and n. 1, and R27 and n. 1.

As though the fountains of
My tears would burst their keep!

Nothing was glad! Even   5
The very sky was dark!
Yet, in the height, the sun
Winked earth in spark by spark.

And then, above my grief,
Upward the shutters ran,   10
As down the empty street
There came a whistling man.

Somehow I think that God,
When He this world began,
Whistled, as down He bent,   15
Just like a whistling man.

(4 January 1950)   *Copy-text: SMH*, 10 June 1950, p. 9   *Collated states:* None

Q7   THE PITILESS[*]

Sharp wind and sleety rain,
And in her eyes
The mother-look of pain
Because her cold and hungry children
Cried for bread!   5
Would you be shocked to know she stole
To fill the children's empty bowl?

To war,
Well fed, well clothed
Armies we send   10
To loot and rend!
No soldier steals! He merely loots,
But mother-women, like this one,

(2 May 1952)   *Copy-text: Trib*, 21 May 1952, p. 7   *Collated states:* None
2 And *Ed.*] and x

Who for their children steal,
We send to jail.   15

[*] A news item in the press told us that an ordinary USA soldier in Korea sent his mother a national treasure. I think a skin rug, worth £26,000. Was he sent to jail? A woman stole to feed her children—and was.

Q8   PADDY LYNCH

When I was young, who now am old,
    I mind me of a man
Who never stopped to ask at all
    What way the dial ran.

"Sure I'm alive," he used to say,   5
    "It's all I want of time.
The Queen herself could ask no more
    For all she's clocks to chime.

"But I've a cow and hens, I have,
    With land to plough and sow   10
And all them put the word on me
    And I've to rise and go.

"The cow she bawls me out of bed
    The cock he crows me up
And I must out and tend the lot   15
    Since they're my bite and sup!

"But many's the time myself I wished
    That I was a tinker man
To daunder down the Crookwell Road
    And then to Queenbeyan.[1]   20

"To jog along to Tuggeranong
    And, when I lay my head,

[1] Standard spelling is *Queanbeyan*; 'daunder' (line 19) means saunter, dawdle: cf. G33 line 2.

To know that neither cock nor cow
Could bawl me out of bed."

(29 December 1947) *Copy-text: Trib*, 4 June 1952, p. 6² *Collated states:* None

---

² An editorial note in *Trib* reads: 'In a note to the Editor Dame Mary quotes from Butler's Hudibras: "A little nonsense now and then is relished by the best of men."' *Hudibras* (1663) by Samuel Butler (1613–80) is a mock-heroic poem in octosyllabic couplets satirising the Cromwellian army and the Presbyterian Church, but MG's quotation is untraced.

Q9   I HAVE WRITTEN OF THE POOR

Surely, I said,
I have written of the poor,
Have paid tribute to their need
And the hardness of their lives;
And now it may be   5
I can write just as the wind blows
And the thought would go.
But nothing came to the page,
    The ink dried
On the pen. For the poor   10
Tugged at my heart,
And to-day, in the rain,
As I have written before,¹
I see only the little cold, bare feet,
The mud on the mother's floor   15
And the pain,
The endless uncomplaining pain of the poor.

(n. d.) *Copy-text: Trib*, 6 August 1952, p. 7 *Collated states:* None
5 be *Ed.*] ~. *x*

---

¹ An editorial note reads: 'In a note to the Tribune, Dame Mary says: "This really refers to something ('Rain') I had written years ago. It [i.e. M44 Pt 1] is on page 196 in Selected Verse, if you are ever at the Mitchell to see it." Due to their great popularity, most of Dame Mary's books are now out of print.'

Q10   [NO MORE THE GROUNDLARKS COME][1]

No more the groundlarks come
To nest again,
Where once they rose in hosts
From every plain.

The pointed hoofs of stock   5
We loosed upon
The land trod nests and young
'Till all were gone.

Just there the soft foot of
The Black stepped wide,   10
Lest, in his passing by,
Some nestling died.

But we, the "noble white"
Who conquering came,
On things most innocent   15
We swept like flame.

The swan, the pelican,
Heron and lark,
Never to-day in flight
The sun make dark—   20

For we, the killers, slew
For love of gold,
'Till even our very sons
In war we sold.

(19 August 1952)   *Copy-text: Trib*, 27 August 1952, p. 7[2]   *Collated states:* None

[1] Cf. R53 author's note.
[2] Under the headline 'Mary Gilmore is loved by the people', *Trib* printed Q10 along with greetings from individuals and organisations to MG on her recent 87th birthday.

Q11   THE SAILOR MAN

A sailor man, I loved the sea
  And yet I took a job
At peeling spuds at Gunn's hotel
  A hundred for a bob.[1]

But all the time I washed and scrubbed   5
  And cut the spuds for chips
All day I saw across the pane
  A line of sailing ships.

It's I who hated to be tied
  To city, clock and street   10
To hear instead of wind and wave,
  The rattles-round of feet.

But in this stokey[2] Sydney town
  Remembrance lived in me
How once I saw the Cutty Sark[3]   15
  A snow-flake on the sea.

God surely gave two hands to man
  That he might hoist a sail
And gave him ears to hear the flutes
  That sing in every gale.   20

And maybe, too, he shaped the lip
  That when the sails are slack
The bosun,[4] whistling up the wind
  Would bring the breezes back.

(8 January 1948)   *Copy-text: Trib*, 1 October 1952, p. 5   *Collated states:* None

[1] Colloquial for a shilling.
[2] Close or sultry (provincial English, *Webster*).
[3] Famous clipper sailing ship, servicing the China tea trade till transferred to the Australian wool trade in 1879, and now berthed at Greenwich, London.
[4] Contraction of *boatswain*, the officer originally in charge of sails and rigging, whose whistle summoned crew members to their duties.

Q12 WILLIAM MORRIS HUGHES[1]

Now let all meanness die,
  And envy hide its head;
This is the hour of loss,
  In which we mourn the dead.

Although, with whiplash tongue,   5
  He turned, an asp irate,
He stood above the ruck,
  Where small men breed their hate.

Let the slow tread of feet
  March where the deep drums beat,   10
Let the sad hearts of all
  That saddest sound repeat!

He was a beacon light,
  He dared the leader's path;
His were the storms—and ours,   15
  The peaceful aftermath.

(16 September 1947)[2]   *Copy-text: Sun*, 28 October 1952, p. 19   *Collated states:*
None

---

[1] See M5 n. 2.
[2] Published on Hughes's death in 1952, Q12 was 'Written about 10 or 10.30 a.m. feeling in dread that W. M. Hughes was very ill & in danger. M. G.' (annotation to AMS, dated 16 September 1947, in NLA 727 2/5/7).

Q13 THE RAINBIRD[1]

Whenever the winding waterspouts
  Go legging across the sky
You can hear the frog in the reeds, croak-croak
  And the rainbird's quivering cry.

---

[1] See M66 and n. 1: Q13 appears to be an extension of it, not an earlier version, since Q13's two stanzas do not appear in any of M66's manuscripts, and the composition dates differ.

And though the frogs utter their high and low   5
    From coolamon, cowal and soak[2]
Yet the rainbirds cry as they rise and fly
    Bol–de–rogery! Bol–de–rogery!
        Bol–de–rogery-O!

When the lightning rips its way through the sky   10
    With a flickering flash or chain
Again in the air the rainbird's cry
    Calls to the cloud for rain!
And though the frogs croak in their high and low
    From coolamon, cowal and soak   15
The rainbirds cry as they rise and fly
    Bol–de–rogery! Bol–de–rogery!
        Bol–de–rogery-O!

(2 February 1943)   *Copy-text: Trib*, 12 November 1952, p. 8   *Collated states:* None

[2] An editorial note reads: 'MARY GILMORE hopes this poem will specially interest Tribune's boy and girl readers. P It is one of a series which reflects her love for, and knowledge of, the Australian Aborigines, whose word (so far as our letters can represent their sounds) for the rainbirds' cry was "Bol-de-rogery!" P Dame Mary was shocked to learn that the Tribune representative to whom she handed the poem did not know that coolamons and cowals were waterholes.'

Q14   [THIS BE YOUR AIM][1]

This be your aim,
That, in your race,
Nor fame nor blame
May you displace.

With purpose strong   5
And steadfast heart
Though the world wrong,
Still play your part.

(n. d.)   *Copy-text: Trib*, 17 December 1952, p. 8   *Collated states:* None

[1] Part of MG's regular Arrows column in *Trib*; on Arrows, see volume 1, Introduction, p. liv. Poems embedded among the prose items were often untitled.

Q15   [WARM IN HIS BLANKET]

Warm in his blanket
Lies one who would roam;
Though clothes make the man
The blanket makes home.

Filled in his blanket,   5
Once more is a man,
Furred, unencumbered,
As when he began.

(11 May 1944)   *Copy-text: Boh* (May 1953), p. 1[1]   *Collated states:* None

[1] *Boh* heads the untitled poem 'THE LATEST MORSEL FROM DAME MARY GILMORE'.

Q16   [WE ONLY SAW THE ROAD]

We only saw the road
In the young years—
Life's hard demanding path
So watered by our tears.

But age a difference makes;   5
As years descend,
The back look shows the tears
As dew, the road a friend.

(29 November 1952)   *Copy-text: Trib*, 16 September 1953, p. 8[1]   *Collated states:* None

[1] MG's Arrows column (see Q14 n. 1) with introductory note: 'THIS Arrow has no barb—'.

Q17   [I HAVE WEPT TEARS OF BLOOD (HE SAID)][*]

I have wept tears of blood (he said)
   For this distorted frame,
For all the quickened need
   That rose and seared like flame.

I have wept tears of blood (he said)   5
   Then laid him down and died,
Whose every hour of life
   Was death: in power denied.

[*] THIS barb is for the heart, to remind you of the spastic and their kind. Why should any child be deformed? The man of whom I write was so physically contorted that his chin was never lifted from his breast; yet he was a full-grown man in natural mind and powers. He died last week.

(19 September 1953)   *Copy-text: Trib*, 30 September 1953, p. 8[1]   *Collated states:* None

1 have wept *Ed.*] have *x*   2 frame, *Ed.*] ~ *x*   3 need *Ed.*] mud *x*   6 Then *Ed.*] They *x*   died, *Ed.*] ~ *x*

[1] In MG's Arrows column (see Q14 n. 1), where typographical errors, or misreadings of MG's handwritten material, are not infrequent. Emendations are based on her corrections to the print clipping held in NLA Series 11 and the AMSS in NLA 2/5/13 and 3/6/7.

Q18   THE FLASH

As when some blundering one,
   Lost in the dark,
Finds, in a lighted match,
   Sight from a spark,

What widened vision to   5
   Man's mind is brought,
When the intuitive
   Explodes in thought!

(6 October 1953)   *Copy-text: Mjn* 12.4 (1953), p. 420   *Collated states:* None

SECTION R

Fourteen Men (1954)

R1 INSCRIPTION

Here at this last I can come home,
 And lay me down with a quiet mind;
For the work is done that I had to do—
 A sheaf that my hand must bind.

Yours was the field that you might not till,   5
 But now I have winnowed it through;
For all I have done, and all that I am,
 Was but a house for you.

(26 January 1948)   *Copy-text: FM*   *Collated states:* None

R2 FOURTEEN MEN[*]

Fourteen men,
And each hung down
Straight as a log
From his toes to his crown.

Fourteen men,   5
Chinamen they were,
Hanging on the trees
In their pig-tailed hair.

Honest poor men,
But the diggers said "Nay!"   10

[cont. overleaf

(10 November 1938)   *Copy-text: FM*   *Collated states:* Mackaness2 as FOURTEEN POOR
MEN (*A*)

1 men] poor men *A*   2 down] ~, *A*   5 men,] ~— *A*   8 In] By *A*
pig-tailed] pigtailed *A*   hair. *A*] ~ X   10 said] ~, *A*   "Nay!"] ~! *A*

So they strung them all up
On a fine summer's day.

There they were hanging
As we drove by,
Grown-ups on the front seat,　　　　　　　15
On the back seat I.

That was Lambing Flat,[1]
And still I can see
The straight up and down
Of each on his tree.　　　　　　　　　　20

[*] Very foolishly, we have pretended that Australia had no lynchings
in her primitive years. It was only by lynchings that human safety and
order were maintained among the lawless and mixed peoples of the early
goldfields and the first far-out settlements. There the constantly armed
law-breaker would have ruled supreme but for the fact of his neighbour's　　n5
gun or a collective noose on a tree. As a rule, however, execution was by
shooting. So each goldfield and every settlement had to govern itself
and maintain its own unwritten but generally accepted laws. And one of
these was the right of execution. A father whose daughter was wronged
went out with his gun; there is today a well-known grave in the Northern　　n10
Territory that is an example of this.

Actually there was a difference between ordinary shootings and formal
lynchings. Lynching meant a trial. Shooting did not. It was instant, and
its reasons were obvious.

In regard to the fourteen Chinamen I saw hanging on the trees, raking　　n15
memory for exactness I find it was twelve we passed when going out,
but there were two more on our return a day or two later.

I remember three times when father came running for the Bible, as
someone was being tried. Prisoners always asked for him to be on the
panel, as he had the name of having a sense of law and justice, and a　　n20
mind that was above the fury of the occasion.

Either at Lambing Flat or at The Bushman (now Parkes) the trial
being over, because everyone had liked the offender, he was given a
revolver and put down an empty shaft. There was another case where a
man asked for a revolver. It was given him. He went into his tent, and　　n25
that was the end. "He was a man of honour" was his epitaph.

11 up] ~, *A*　　14 drove] came *A*　　17 Flat,] ~. *A*　　(n1–52) ⁵Very . . . article.)]
Om. A　　n14 its *Ed.*] it *X*

[1] The goldfields riots there (now Young, NSW) occurred in 1861, four years before
MG's birth: on the discrepancy, see volume 1, Introduction, pp. lxviii–lxix.

In proportion to our population, I should say we had as much lynching as North America or South Africa. In some periods we had more.

I remember the tales of a digger named Ross, once well known on Bendigo and Ballarat. In his old age he wrote a brochure on the times   n30
and his experiences on those fields. He mentioned a lynching and glossed it over by saying the police came before the man was hanged, and that everyone ran away. But when years before I heard him tell that story he said, "The bucket was kicked from under the man's feet, and his toes only just cleared the ground." The digger's bucket was long, often it   n35
was an oil drum. The goldfield's phrase, "He kicked the bucket", was a testimony to the times and of how offenders died.

To return to the Fourteen Men. It was grey dawn when we had gone out past them. It was bright moonlight a day or two later when we returned. Most of the bodies had fallen, each one a little heap under   n40
its tree. As we drove on father suddenly pulled up with a jerk. There were two more hanging beside us, one in shadow, one in the clear white light of the moon. My mother said of the latter, "This one must have been dead before being hanged, as the face is so peaceful and calm!" There was no distortion. All the others had been dressed in coarse blue   n45
nankeen[2] trousers and no shirts. This one wore a heavily embroidered, quilted, pale yellow silk coat, and long, wide, ivory-white trousers. The little head with the smooth hair was slightly on one side; the face was enamelled; and the toes of the tiny blue slippers on the "golden lily" feet just showed as they pointed straight down to the ground. It was a   n50
woman, and she was very young. (See *Pocket Book* 18/2/1950 for my complete article.)[3]

---

[2] Pale yellowish cloth, originally made at Nanking (Nanjing, s.e. China).

[3] 'When Australia Had Lynchings', *Pocket Book: Storyteller Weekly*, 18 February 1950, 20–3, 25.

R3   THE SWORD

Hear this, our prayer to Thee, O Lord!
To peace give love,
Lest, for a dove,
A vulture cleave the sky.

[cont. overleaf

(23 November 1942)   *Copy-text: FM*   *Collated states: SMH*, 2 January 1943, p. 7 as
NEW YEAR PRAYER (*A*)

Not otherwise recorded: A's text is in italics throughout.

1 Hear this,] *This is A*   prayer to Thee] *prayer A*   3 Lest,] *Lest A*   dove,]
dove A   4 sky.] *sky; A*

But, oh, give peace a sword,   5
Lest of a sword it die.

5 oh] *O A*

R4   NATIONALITY[1]

I have grown past hate and bitterness,
I see the world as one;
But though I can no longer hate,
My son is still my son.

All men at God's round table sit,   5
And all men must be fed;
But this loaf in my hand,
This loaf is my son's bread.

(12 May 1942)   *Copy-text: FM   Collated states: AP 1942* (*A*)   Mackaness2 (*B*)
Murdoch2 (*C*)   Mackaness3 (*D*)   Wright1 (*E*)   Thompson (*F*)   Wright2 reprints *E*
Not otherwise recorded: In order to fit on the page, *F* indicates the stanza break after
line 4 by indenting the following four lines.
2 one;] ~: *E*   **3** But] Yet, *A–F*   hate,] ~ *B*   **5** sit,] ~ *A B D E*

[1] As editor of *AP 1942*, R. D. FitzGerald wrote on 21 June 1942: 'I am returning them
[the set of poems sent by MG] *BUT* not before I have taken a copy of "Nationality" which
I intend to use, and that quite definitely. I wish some of the other contributors would see
how necessary it is for verses to have a *point* and could take a lesson from this admirably
pointed little piece' (ML Papers vol. 12).

R5   LOS ENCERRADOS[1]

Ghosts, hungry for the flesh of action,
Becalmed against the land they lay,
Longing again to catch the wind,
Longing to be away.

So have I seen men paralysed;   5
But, where the ships had hope,

(15 June 1948)   *Copy-text: FM   Collated states: AP 1948* (*A*)
5 paralysed;] ~, *A*

These were men slowly hanged,
With life itself as rope.

7–8 hanged,/ With] ~, with *A*   8 life itself] ~/ Itself *A*   as] the *A*

[1] The Imprisoned Ones. *Encerrar* is literally to enclose, confine (Spanish).

R6   THE SCREAM[*]

"There is a plague of fleas. I suppose the cry of a flea
is just as clear to God as the cry of a man."
Letter from M.G. to C.R.[1]

Thunder the guns of battle,
The bombs explode, the blood
Of the fallen spouts on the ground . . .
But here the scream of the flea
Goes up to God.   5

[*] If the harpooned whale had a voice in proportion to its size, its dying
scream would be heard round the world.

(14 April 1942)   *Copy-text: FM   Collated states:* None

[1] Connie Robertson, a frequent correspondent of MG's and daughter of A. G. Stephens:
on Stephens see K44 n. 10.

R7   ON THE WIRE

It was a long time going;
    It cried and cried;
Weaker and weaker growing,
    At last it died.

In war I saw men hang   5
    And die like that!
Somehow I felt a pang
    For that poor rat.

(21 February 1948)   *Copy-text: FM   Collated states:* None

R8   THESE?

Are these our people's leaders? These
Whose babbling voices
Sound in familiar keys,
Like farm-yard noises?
The world churns like a maggot-pit,   5
Turmoiled in strife,
While the mice-minded sit,
Nibbling at life.

(18 May 1940)   *Copy-text: FM   Collated states:* None

R9   THE MASTER*

William Morris Hughes[1]
Stood on the floor of the House and said,
"Tell them fellers to stop their noise;
Only wise men talk here!"
Then he spoke for an hour.   5

But even a pin couldn't drop,
Lest a word be lost.

*"At this stage there was some muttering among Government
members. Mr Hughes turned toward them and exclaimed, 'Shut up!'
(Laughter.)
    "The Speaker, Mr Rosevear, said Mr Hughes was entitled to be heard
in silence." *Sydney Morning Herald*, October 1947.   n5

(n. d.)   *Copy-text: FM   Collated states:* None

[1] On Hughes, see M5 n. 2, Q12 and R31.

R10   THE SOURCE

"In the beginning was the Word"[1]

I

I am the Maker;
I made man,
Who in the ooze
His life began.

On me, as stair,   5
Upward he climbed;
Word after word
Mated and primed.

Uttered by man,
By reason stirred,   10
I, the beginning,
I am the word.

Earth, air and sky,
Deep of the sea,[2]
All human might   15
Lives but by me.

Take from the world
Its robe of words:

(Pt 1: 21 May 1949; Pt 2: 15 July 1949; Pt 3: 16 July 1949)   *Copy-text: FM   Collated states: Jindy* (1949), Pt 1 only, as THE WORD (*A*)   *SMH*, 3 December 1949, p. 7, Pt 2 and stanza 1 of Pt 3 only, as THE MAKER (*B*)

Not otherwise recorded: A and *B* are in italics throughout, except for the final line of *B* (line 30). The epigraph, omitted in *B*, is presented without quotation marks in *A*.
(**0.2–20.1**) 1 . . . 2] *Om. B*   **0.2** 1] *Om. A*   **1** Maker;] *maker, A*   **3** Who]
Who, A   ooze] *ooze, A*   **6** climbed;] *climbed, A*   **8** Mated] *Meted A*
8–9 primed.// Uttered] *primed—/ Uttered A*   **10** stirred] *heard A*   **12** word]
Word A   **15** All human might] *The might of man A*   **18** words:] *words, A*

[1] John 1. 1. For the primacy of the word, see also K33, K97, L18, M53, R58, R61 (Pts 8 and 9), T17 and T23 (Pt 4).
[2] I.e. the created world (lines 13–14), alluding to Genesis 1. 1–10.

Man lived, again,
As beasts and birds.   20

2

Not words (said Memory) made man, but I;
For needing me a word was but a cry.

The world had nought but Now for Yea and Nay,
Till I arose and gave it Yesterday!

It was my Yesterday dimensioned time,   25
Extended Now, and gave man power to climb.

3

Nor Memory nor words
Made man, said Force;
They but his ladders are.
I am the Source.   30

Yet even I,
Inert, unnormed,
Lay powerless
Till matter formed.

---

19 lived,] *lives A*   again,] *again A*   20 As] *With A*   (20.1–34) 2 . . . formed.]
Om. A   21 Memory) made] *Memory)/ Made B*   22 For] *For, B*   needing me
a] *wanting me,/ A B*   23 nought] *naught B*   Now for Yea] *Now,/ As yea B*
Nay] *nay B*   24 Till] *Until B*   arose and] *spoke,/ And B*   25 Yesterday
dimensioned time] *Yesterday/ Extended Time B*   26 Extended Now, and]
Dimensioned Now,/ And B   gave] *bid B*   power to] *rise and B*   26.1 3] *Om. B*
27 Memory] *memory B*   30 *I . . . Source.*] **I am the source.** *B*   31–4 Yet . . .
formed.] *Om. B*

RII   NATURE

I

Nothing to me is man
(Though what made life in me began).

Man, to me, is but dust,
That lifts and falls, as fall it must;

And though his needs I stay,   5
Heedless of him I go my way.

Nothing to me man is,
And yet I made the whole world his.

2

Said man: I make,
And love the things   10
I make; great joy
The making brings.

Therefore I keep
My yesterdays,
Till time itself   15
My will obeys.

Nature is blind.
She knows nor How
Nor Why. She knows
Not even *Now*!   20

(3 March 1950)   *Copy-text: FM   Collated states:* None

R12   THE BARWON¹ FORD

The Barwon Ford was deep and wide,
    The stream was foaming mad;
I upped my petticoat over my knees,
    And followed my handsome lad.

My handsome lad, he strode ahead,   5
    He held me by the hand,
And I went after him, step by step,
    Till at last we reached the land.

We climbed the bank on the other side,
    We made a fire, we made a bed,   10

¹ Barwon R., NSW, a tributary of the Darling.

And there we lay in each other's arms,
　　Though never a word we said.

O sweet is sleep when love is near!
　　We slept as the night went by;
The round of the world turned on and on,　　15
　　Till the sun came up the sky.

The birds were preening in every tree,
　　The grass was laced with dew,
And all so sweet was the morning air
　　It seemed the world was new.　　20

Tomorrow my babe will come to me,
　　With no one to say him nay—
The morrow she spoke but one lone word,
　　And then was cold as clay.

She who had never known fear,　　25
　　We dressed her grave for a bride,
We drew her petticoat down to her feet,
　　And laid her babe beside.

(10 November 1944)　*Copy-text: FM*　*Collated states:* None

R13　OLD FORTHRIGHT

Old Forthright lived in a dell they called for his name,
He kept his gun loaded behind the front door,
His two great dogs roamed free of the leash all night,
His fences were high, his gate had a padlock and chain,
And the roses climbed over the door.　　5

Nobody came to the house in the day,
But at night the windows were lit, and the blinds
(White calico blinds washed whiter than milk)
Were drawn so that no one could see

(1940)　*Copy-text: FM*　*Collated states:* Sy 6.4 (1945), pp. 26–7 (*A*)
7 blinds] ~— *A*　**8** (White] ~ *A*　milk)] ~— *A*　**9** see] ~, *A*

Was it gentleman, tramp, policeman or lad   10
Was seated within.
Then the corks were pulled and the glasses clinked,
And a woman sang clear and high.

Stories were told of how Forthright was known as a Henry
The Eighth for wives; of how one wife died   15
Of a fire-stick stuck in her throat, and one
From a tomahawk blow in the ribs,
And one with a baby had come too soon.
As for the others, one was hanged from a beam,
And one, they said, was buried alive,   20
And one was "poisoned in gruel".[1]
Such were the stories they told of Forthright of Forthright's dell,
When as children we passed his house on our way to school—
His white-washed house with the bunches of thyme
Each side of the clean-swept path,   25
The plum-trees sweet in the spring,
The apple-trees thick with their green and gold,
The moss-rose[2] scenting the air by the locked front gate,
Where the glass of the window shone clear as the dew,
And the blinds were white in the bleach;   30
While the Cluster-rose and the Cloth of Gold
Climbed over the blue front door;
And, down in the paddock, the fat, sleek cows and the heavy
        draught-mares
Stood feeding, flank deep, in the billowing trefoil
That rolled in the wind like waves of the sea.   35

10 Was] Were *A*   tramp,] tramp, or *A*   or lad] *Om. A*   12 pulled] ~, *A*
13–14 high.// Stories] ~./ ~ *A*   18 had come] that came *A*   19 As] And as *A*
22 dell] Dell *A*   23 When] ~, *A*   children] ~, *A*   our] the *A*   school—]
~, *A*   26–7 spring,/ The] ~,// ~ *A*   29 window] windows *A*   31 While]
Where *A*   Cluster-rose] cluster-rose, *A*   32 door;] ~, *A*   33 And] While *A*

[1] See Q1 n. 4.
[2] *Rosa centifolia*, small rose with a sweet scent and partial mosslike covering; the 'Cluster-rose' (line 31) may be *Rosa pisocarpa*, a pink-flowering wild rose or any of the *floribunda* roses; 'Cloth of Gold' (line 31) is a *Jonquilla* hybrid with up to six yellow starlike flowers per stem; and 'trefoil' (line 34) is clover.

Old Forthright had teeth as clean as a hound,
And shoulders as strong as a bull;
He had eyes as blue as a midsummer sky,
And a voice like a trumpet, when shouted afar,
But soft and kind as a nesting bird's   40
When he spoke to his frail girl-child.
His fist was a hammer of iron,
And his back was marked by the convict's lash,
Old Forthright of Forthright's dell,
Ticket-of-leave man,[3] lover of flowers,   45
And father of hare-lipped sons.

Years went by, and the once trim gate
Sagged loose on its hinges, the thistle stood high
Where the wheat was reaped,
The plums ran wild, the apples lay sour in the grass,   50
The thyme died down by the weed-held path,
And the white-washed walls were white no more,
For Forthright at last was old.

Then the Parson came, and the old man's eyes
Wept crocodile tears, and his crocodile knees   55
Were bent in crocodile prayers,
As to church on Sundays he went,
And the preacher thanked God for a soul that was saved.
Then the church people[4] made him a match
With one of two sisters, gentle and sweet,   60
Whose delicate fingers stitched delicate lace,
Or on the piano played elegant airs;[5]

36 hound,] hound's *A*   38 midsummer] mid-summer *A*   39 when] when he *A*
43 convict's] convict *A*   lash,] ~—*A*   44 dell] Dell *A*   48 hinges] hinge *A*
54 Then] When *A*   56 prayers,] ~ *A*   58 And] While *A*   60 gentle] old *A*
62 elegant] ~, *A*   airs;] tinkling old airs. *A*

[3] Convict licensed to live independently and earn an income, but under surveillance until the period of his sentence expired.

[4] General term for the religiously observant, not distinguishing between Anglican church and Wesleyan chapel. Cf. 'Now the "chapel" is "church"' (G36 line 85) and 'They were church, where we were chapel' in 'Neighbours', dated 6 April 1924, unpublished, in ML 6/5 and other locations: see volume 1, Appendix for manuscript locations and descriptions.

Innocent women they were, who never once dreamed
How Henry the Eighth in Old Forthright lived,
And was only discreetly hidden away   65
Lest the bird to be snared should be startled and fly!
And the end? The end was disaster.
Back to the Highlands the shocked sisters fled,
And Forthright returned to his old bad ways,
But a thousand times worse than before.   70
(See Matthew, twelfth chapter, and verses you'll find.[6]
But this by the way.)

Then the old man died, and his sons died too—
Alike the sons of the wed and the unwed mothers;
When a lifetime later came into the port a ship,   75
And down from the gangway there stepped a girl.
A girl? Nay! It was Forthright himself, with his ice-blue eyes,
His strong square shoulders, his hard, set mouth,
And the lurch in his walk. And there, as his grandchild tripped
          to the quay,
With a start of remembrance time lifted a screen,   80
And a pane with a calico blind stood clear, a corkscrew squeaked,
And a woman sang; while away in a cottage, where lonely it lay,
A hare-lipped baby was crying.

---

64 Old] old *A*   **73** too—] ~, *A*   **74** mothers;] ~, *A*   **75** When] ~, *A*   later]
~, *A*   **78** strong] great *A*   hard,] ~ *A*

---

[5] MG wrote: 'Of the two sisters in the verse the one taught me music when I was about
16, the other was married to Old Forthright (not his name, of course) by the Wesleyan
parson' (*Letters* 215).
[6] Matthew 12. 43–5 describes the triumphant and re-enforced return of a cast-out
'unclean spirit'.

R14   THE ATOMIC BOMB[*]

I

Nothing endures but change;
Moth, are fame and renown;
The cliffs mock at the sea,
But the sea grinds them down.
The sea mothers the land   5
(No land mothers the sea),
It takes the sun for mate,
The breeding rain sets free.
The cold eye of the moon,
That flat and frozen eye,   10
Under its dead, still light,
Nothing can fructify.
But, from its driving pulse,
Out of the deep life came;
Up, from that mighty heart,   15
Jetted aloft like flame.
No ocean feeds the moon,
No atmosphere is there!
The hydrant of the wave,
For us unburned keeps air.   20
If, as St John has said,
There shall be no more sea,[1]

(Pt 1: 27 May 1948; Pts 2, 3: 29 May 1948)   *Copy-text: FM   Collated states: SMH,*
16 October 1948, p. 5, Pt 1 only, as HYDRANT OF THE SEA (*A*)   *AP 1949/50,* Pt 1 only, as
HYDRANT OF THE SEA (*B*)

Not otherwise recorded: Both *A* and *B* give the following 'News item' as an epigraph:
'Meteorological warfare is still highly secret, but it is likely to be the most destructive of
all. By chemical means the air can, if necessary, be dried up, so that people are unable
to breathe.' *A* and *B* divide Part 1 into four-line stanzas. *A*'s text is in italics throughout,
as is the epigraph in *B*.

0.1 1] *Om. A B*   1 change;] *change, A*   ~, *B*   2 Moth,] *Moth A*   ~ *B*   3 cliffs]
rocks A   rocks *B*   4 down. *B*] ~ X   *down. A*   5 land] *land, A*   ~, *B*   6 (No]
No A   ~ *B*   sea),] *sea; A*   ~; *B*   13 But,] *But A*   ~ *B*   its driving] *the sea's*
great A   the seas's great *B*   15 heart,] ~ *B*   18 there!] *there; A*   ~; *B*
19 wave] *sea A*   sea *B*   21 St] *St. A*   22 There] *"There A*   "~ *B*   sea,] *sea," A*
~," *B*

Tinder will air become,
The globe a mound of scree.[2]
If dries the ocean bed   25
Earth unfecund will lie,
In thick, mud-boltered[3] ooze,
The last of life will die.
Then comet, meteor, ash,
Compressed fire at her heart,   30
Rending earth's rock-set bonds,
Etnas[4] will fling her apart.

2

It is the sea, not land,
That is our shield of might!
The deep controls all things,   35
Is nurse to depth and height.
Leave land and take the sea,
Nothing alive remains;
The sap, ere it can form,
Is dead within the veins.   40
Leave earth and waters take,
Earth is a barren tomb!
As woman is to man,
The wave, to life, is loom.
For where the floes are locked,   45
Where, slant, the Poles are whirled,
The ice-cap serves the deep,
The ice-cap saves the world.
Unlike the ravaged soil,
No fences shame the tide,   50

---

25 If] *As* A   As B   bed] *bed,* A   ~, B   **26** lie,] *lie;* A   ~; B   **27** thick,]
thick A   ~ B   **29** Then . . . ash] *Prisoned by rock-set bonds* A   Prisoned by
rock-set bonds B   **31** Rending . . . bonds] *Meteors, comet or ash* A   Meteors,
comet or ash B   **32.1–88** 2 . . . climb.] *Om.* A B

---

[1] I.e. John of Patmos in Revelation 21. 1: 'for the first heaven and the first earth were
passed away; and there was no more sea.'   [2] Detritus of loose soil and broken rocks.
[3] Clotted or clogged: a neologism adapting *blood-boltered* as in *Macbeth,* IV. 1. 123.
[4] See M32 n. 2.

But, where it balanced rolls,
The migrant hosts abide.
There, as sweet currents move
In freshness through the main,
The over-saline blends   55
Its ratios again.
By this the finned survive,
And all the growths marine,
As flocks and herds, by rain,
In lands where drought has been.   60

                    3
As with the brimming can
A boy swings round his head,
The globe's rotation keeps
The ocean in its bed.
But if, on banked-up fires   65
Where the volcanoes sleep,
Man, with his atom bomb,
Shatters our Polar keep,
Then in explosive might
New craters will have birth,   70
Eruption shake the skies,
And lava flood the earth.
Then as the ice-fields melt,
And, loosed, their waters flow,
Too fresh will be the sea,   75
Too high its flood-tides grow.
No ark will then save man!⁵
Our "Babel",⁶ built on air,

---

⁵ Noah's ark, which saved mankind and creation from the deluge sent by an angry God (Genesis 6–8). Similar flood narratives (see author's note, line 46) are found in the Babylonian Gilgamesh epic, the Greek myth of Jove's sparing of Deucalion and his wife recounted in the *Metamorphoses* of Ovid (43 BC – AD 17) and the Indian *Mahabharata*.
⁶ Probably post-World War II civilisation, threatened by its own scientific aspirations. (In Genesis 11. 1–9, God prevents human beings from completing a projected heaven-reaching tower at Babel by depriving them of the communicative power of their shared language.) MG was active in the movement against nuclear weapons that followed the

Will from the ether crash,
And man's "one speech"[7] end there.   80
And yet, as ages pass,
If, from the altitudes,
The steam, condensed, should fall
And fill our amplitudes,
Earth will again renew,   85
And life, from out the slime,
Clutching its lowest stair,
Once more will upward climb.

[*] This verse sequence, in part published in the *Sydney Morning Herald*
in 1948, was based on a theory I put forward earlier. It originated in the
search for a reason why atomic bomb tests were made far from and not
on the uninhabited and deserted Polar ice-fields.

However, before proceeding, I would mention that scientists tell us   n5
that the atomic bomb cannot affect climate. They have never said it
cannot affect weather. Even a typhoon can do that.

Man, in general, regards the *status quo* of the world as fixed and
eternal. Yet it is possible that earth's stability depends to a great extent
on that most frangible thing, ice. There is no cohesion in ice. It has no   n10
intermediate state between solidity and liquefaction. If field-ice is deeply
fractured no man can prevent extension of fracture, and if extensive
melting takes place, that, too, man cannot stop.

Fish die in millions in a sudden change of temperature under water,
and also because of changed ratios of salt or some other constituent.   n15
In 1951 the New South Wales oyster-fishery was partly ruined by fresh
water, the result of too much rain. In the *Murray Pioneer* 22nd January
1953 we were told that the Murray cod were dying in large numbers at
Lake Bonney. The writer continued, "In 1851 the salt content of Lake
Bonney was 160 grains to the gallon. . . . Today it is 74. . . ."   n20

Rain, wind and storms will follow changed temperatures over wide
land spaces, so that it could be that, if broken into, ice-cold Polar waters
flowing to warm seas would cause slow evaporation. This need not
descend locally, but, carried by high winds or perhaps even by the
spiral of the earth's own movement, could fall in sleet and snow in   n25
distant places. So it might be that in the too high ascension of moisture,

---

n1–50 *This . . . water?] *Om. A B*

---

use of the first atomic bomb in World War II. In 1948 (see composition date) the USA
was conducting tests on Bikini Atoll and preparations were being made for testing at
desert sites such as Nevada (USA, 1951) and Woomera (Australia, 1953).

[7] Cf. Genesis 11. 1: in 1948 the United Nations was the contemporary embodiment of
projects for giving mankind a shared voice and ambition (cf. R4 line 2).

through the need of moderately tempered seas, lies the secret of drought. As perhaps related to this, though in another way, we are told (*Sydney Morning Herald*, 14th June 1949) that "by chemical means the air can, if necessary, be dried up, so that people are unable to breathe".   n30

In regard to earth-rotation and the place-stability of oceans, tidal-waves occur in equatorial and adjacent regions but not in Polar seas, and it may be that the rotation of the earth is a factor in keeping the oceans from even a slow ungoverned flowing. In this connection we may remember that at the equator the earth's rotating speed is 1000 miles   n35
an hour. Under the drawing power of 1000 miles an hour, what would happen to the water at the Poles (and to the balance of the world) if the ice-cap were not there to keep the water solid and stable?

Investigating scientists have told us that, if atomic bombs with sufficient heat and explosive power to rend and melt the Polar ice were   n40
dropped, Europe would be covered with water to a depth of thirty feet (some have said more). Because ice, as a solid, supports its own weight in the atmosphere and water does not, if Polar ice were melted, not only volume but weight would be added to the world's balanced (and balancing?) water-masses. Consequently it may be that somewhere in   n45
all this is the reason why the story of the Deluge is the most widely known world-myth.

Finally, I ask again: Why are experiments made in deserts, not in the vast, uninhabited Polar regions? Is it because they are ice, that ice has no cohesion, and if melted is water?   n50

R15   THE LESSER GRAIL[1]

I

I have no thunder in my words,
Thunder is much too high;
But I can see as far as birds,
And feel the wind go by.

(Pt 1: n. d.; Pt 2: 9 November 1944; Pt 3: 8 October 1944)   *Copy-text: FM   Collated states: SMH*, 14 November 1942, p. 7, Pt 1 only, as I HAVE NO THUNDER (*A*)   *SMH*, 23 December 1944, p. 8, Pt 2 only, as THE WILLOW BY THE FOUNTAIN (*B*)   *AP 1945*, Pt 3 only, as THE MOTHERING QUAIL (*C*)   Murdoch2, Pt 2 only, as THE WILLOW BY THE FOUNTAIN (*D*)

Not otherwise recorded: A and *B* are in italics throughout.
(0.1–28) 1 . . . woman.] *Om. C*   (0.1–16) 1 . . . quail.] *Om. B D*   0.1 1] *Om. A*
3 far] *high A*

[1] In medieval literature, especially the Arthuriad, the mystical Holy Grail can only be

And I can follow through the grass   5
    The darling-breasted quail;
For, though things great in splendour mass,
    I choose the lesser grail.

Age changes no one's heart; the field
    Is wider, that is all.   10
Childhood is never lost; concealed,
    It answers every call.

So when the wind goes bloring[2] by,
    And in the driving hail,
Or when the tempest shakes the sky,   15
    I run beside the quail.

2

The willow by the fountain
    Is just a willow-tree,
But I have seen it billow
    As though it were the sea.   20

And sometimes, in the spring,
    It seemed a woman's hair,
Tossed, and wanton-minded,
    As it played on the air.

Wintered I have seen it,   25
    And oh, it was human,
Crying on the wind
    Like an old grey woman.

---

6 quail;] *quail, A*   **7** For . . . splendour] *And so, although the thunder A*   mass,
Ed.] ~ *X   mass, A*   **9** heart;] *heart, A*   **10** wider,] *wider— A*   **11** concealed,]
concealed A   **15** when the] *when some A*   (**16.1–36**) **2** . . . bed.] *Om. A*
16.1 2] *Om. B D*   **18** willow-tree,] *willow tree, B*   willow tree; *D*   **20** though]
if B   if *D*   **21** sometimes,] ~ *D*   spring,] *Spring, B*   ~ *D*   **23** Tossed,]
Tossed B   Tost *D*   **25** it,] *it B*   ~ *D*   **26** And] *(And B*   (~ *D*   **26** oh,] ~ *D*
human,] *human!) B*   ~!) *D*   **27** wind] *wind, B*   **28** old] *old, B*

---

seen by someone who has achieved spiritual perfection, and, like Galahad in the *Morte Darthur*, will then abandon the lower order of the secular, physical world – here, the 'Lesser Grail'.

[2] See M34 n. 2.

3

The butterfly went lightly over,
Flower by flower, as though a lover;   30
And yet it had no thought of love
For any flower it poised above.

The quail upon her little feet,
Ran in and out amid the wheat,
Entreating me lest I should tread   35
Where love had made its breast a bed.

(28.1–36) 3 . . . bed.] *Om.* B D   **28.1** 3] *Om.* C   **29** lightly] flying C   over,] ~ C
30 lover;] ~, C   **31** it] he C   **32** it] he C   **33** quail] ~, C   **35** me] ~, C

R16   THE GILMORE CHIEF

He hated the town, he said,
    The scraping of boots on the street;
He asked for the sky overhead,
    And the sun on the wheat.

His was a love of the land;   5
    Pride in the furrow he knew,
The team that swung to his hand,
    And the clink of a shoe.

He held no brief for a school,
    His was a natural lore;   10
The wild mare drank at his pool,
    The wild bird came to his door.

(n. d.)   *Copy-text: FM   Collated states:* None

R17   THE DUST-BOWL

The full-fed cattle chewed the cud,
    The very earth was kind,
The grass a velvet carpet spread,
    Scented, and blossom-lined;
And in that fertile world no man   5
    Had need to delve and grind.

And then blind pillage came. For (like
    His father's fathers in their wet
And misty Isles,[1] which no sun baked)
    A dreadful plough man set   10
To tear the spartan soil, and rend
    This dry land's coverlet.[2]

Now where the drowsy cattle lay,
    And pollened bees took toll,
What served the mist defeated us,   15
    And made a vast dust-bowl!
The thieving winds lift up the dust,
    And ever seaward roll.

(7 November 1944)   *Copy-text: FM   Collated states: SMH*, 18 November 1944,
p. 8 as THE DUST BOWL (*A*)

Not otherwise recorded: A is in italics throughout.

1 cud,] *cud— A*   **3** a] *in A*   carpet] *verdure A*   **5** And] *And, A*   fertile
world no] *warm benevolence,/ No A*   **5–6** man/ Had] *man had A*   **6** delve and]
Om. A   **7** like] *as A*   **8** father's] *Om. A*   **9** Isles, which] *isles A*   sun] *sun
had A*   baked)] *baked), A*   **10** dreadful] *constant A*   set] *set, A*   **11** spartan]
Spartan A   soil,] *soil A*   **14** pollened] *pollen A*   **16** dust-bowl!] *dust bowl; A*
17 dust,] *dust A*

---

[1] I.e. the British Isles.
[2] In fact, the erosion of Australia's thin layer of topsoil was caused by both grazing
and cultivation.

R18 THE PEAR-TREE[*]

1

"What be you a-lookin' at, Emily Ann,
    Starin' with your eyes all set?"
"I bin seein' a ghost, Amanda,
    And I be a-seein' it yet."

"Where was it you seen it, Emily Ann?"   5
    "It was hung on the big pear-tree;
I seen a ghost, Amanda,
    And the ghost it said it was me.

"Put your hand on my heart, Amanda,
    Feel of the life of it there;   10
For the ghost was hung on the big pear-tree,
    It had my eyes, and my hair."

2

"O moon that blanches the grass,
    Why is the tree so white?"
There is a bird in the tree,   15
    Was never a bird so white!

Was never a bird so white,
    But its head bends over,
There, where it hangs in the tree,
    Dead for a lover.   20

"O moonlight sheeting the grass,
    What will cover her there?"
There will be frost on the tree,
    And frost on her hair.

(28 April 1940)   *Copy-text: FM*   *Collated states: Sy* 1.4 (1940), p. 29, Pt 1 only, as THE
PEAR TREE (*A*)   *AP 1941*, Pt 1 only (*B*)

0.1 1] *Om. A B*   **1** a-lookin'] a-lookin *A*   Ann,] ~? *B*   **2** Starin'] Starin *A*
3 bin] been *A B*   seein'] a-seein *A*   **4** a-seein'] a-seein *A*   **6** pear-tree;] pear
tree . . . *A*   ~. *B*   **7** a] the *A B*   **8** ghost] ~, *B*   **10** there;] ~, *B*   **11** big]
Om. A B   pear-tree,] pear tree, *A*   ~ *B*   **12** eyes,] ~ *A B*   **12.1–28** 2 . . . die!"]
Om. A B

"O white moon turn from that tree,   25
    Shine not so clear and high,
She was too young for frost on her hair,
    She was too young to die!"

[*] When I was a child there was a young girl employed as kitchen help at
Tenandra Park, then a station belonging to Edward Beveridge. Everyone
liked this girl. She was about sixteen and was courted by a young man
on the place. Suddenly the man disappeared, and though the girl said
nothing she was seen to droop. One night, to the surprise of the two elder   n5
women in the kitchen, it being the middle of the week and not Saturday,
she took a bath "all over", and put on everything clean, even to a white
frock and flounced petticoat she had saved for special occasions. In the
morning, out in the frost, they found her hanged on the big pear-tree
in the orchard. Then they knew why she had taken a bath, and why she   n10
had dressed in white. "She wanted to go clean and all in white to her
Maker", said the elder women.
    When the moon was full, the story was that her ghost could sometimes
be seen between the trees, or where she had hanged herself. As a child,
when staying at Tenandra, I used to peer out the window at night,   n15
looking for the ghost. I never saw the ghost, but the moonlight was so
white it was terrifying.

n1–17 ⁵When . . . terrifying.] *Om. A B*

R19   THE COMING

Once I came as a ghost,
I came lighter than air
From my shadowy coast,
And none saw me there.

But somebody said,   5
"It is cold, and the fire
Has gone low, poke the bed
Of the log; send the flame higher!"

[cont. overleaf

(24 September 1942)   *Copy-text: FM   Collated states: Argus*, 31 May 1950, p. 10 as
THE UNSEEN (*A*)

Not otherwise recorded: A's text is in italics throughout.

5 But somebody] *Yet one of them A*   **7** low, poke] *low! Poke A*   **7–8** bed/ Of]
bed of A   **8** log; send] *log;/ Send A*

Why did I come? I knew
Not of whence or of where,   10
Nor the door I came through,
Or why I was there.
Only I knew
That I came.

12–13 there./ Only] *there.// Only A*

R20   OUTCAST

Something came walking, last night,
    Round the house and round;
It had no face that one could see,
    And its voice had no sound.

Pity reached out to it there,   5
    But, however pity tried,
It was too lost for pity,
    The thing outside.

(4 January 1945)   *Copy-text: FM   Collated states:* None

R21   ALL SOULS*[1]

For Walter Stone[2]

Unlatch the door
And let them in;
Evil is done,
No more they sin.

(29 December 1951)   *Copy-text: FM   Collated states: AP 1953 (A)*   Stone (*B*)
Not otherwise recorded: A's dedication reads: '(*Written for Walter Stone*)'. MG's note
is omitted in *A* and *B*.
1 ˢUnlatch] Open *B*

---

[1] On All Souls Night, see F82 n. 1.
[2] (1910–81), book-collector, bibliographer, editor, printer and publisher. Stone printed
a limited edition of 100 leaflet copies of R21 at his Talkarra Press in 1954: this is *B* in the

They are the lost, 5
Even as Christ,
When, desert-held,
He kept a tryst.[3]

Pull down the blind,
Lay out the food, 10
Where, by the hearth,
Of old they stood.

Set wide the door,
Then come not near;
God is their Awe, 15
But man their fear.

* Based on an old Gaelic story, and told by my father.

5–8 They . . . tryst.] *Om. B*   9 Pull . . . blind] Open the door *B*   10 Lay] Put *B*
11 Where,] There *B*   hearth,] ~ *B*   12 Of old they] Where once one *B*
13–16 Set . . . fear.] God is their awe/ And man their fear?/ Open the door,/ Then come not near. *B*

textual note. Four of these are in NLA 727 2/5/14, one at ADFA Special Collections 295800, and a corrected proof copy has been inserted, along with two AMSS, into the Fryer copy of *FM*.

[3] I.e. with Satan during the 40 days in the wilderness (Matthew 4. 1–11, Mark 1.13 and Luke 4. 1–13).

R22   THE FOREST PRAYED

The forest prayed,
All night it prayed for rain;
By day it bowed its head;
Its prayer was vain.

The sun went down, 5
And, as up-spanned[1] the moon,

(23 October 1938)   *Copy-text: FM   Collated states: SMH*, 24 December 1938, p. 9 (*A*)
2 rain;] ~, *A*   3 head;] ~— *A*   4 Its] For *A*   6 And,] ~ *A*   moon,] ~ *A*

[1] Rose in its arch.

Again was heard that sad
And broken rune.[2]

Night-long it pled
In murmurous refrain;   10
The sun rose up red-eyed;
There came no rain.

Through the long days,
The leaves, where nothing stirred,
Hung like the feathers of   15
A wounded bird.

7 that] the *A*   8 And broken] Gregorian *A*   9 pled] fled *A*   11 red-eyed;]
~: *A*   13 days,] day *A*   14 The] Its *A*   16 wounded] drooping *A*

[2] Song; see E66 n. 2.

R23   I AM THE IDLE

I am the idle, bone-idle I lie,
Under the lift[1] where the white clouds fly.

A rose nid-nods, and the grass bows low,
Each kissed by the winds that vagrant blow.

Cicadas are scraping a riddle of song,   5
A path-finder ant goes hasting along;

Through tussock and fern the brown beetles creep—
I turn me about like a dog, and sleep.

(8 January 1940)   *Copy-text: FM   Collated states:* None

[1] Sky (archaic).

R24   THE FLOWER-STALL[1]

I really never knew, till now,
    How lovely flowers could be,
Though I had seen in Paraguay
    Lianas clothe the tree,
Though I had found in Sydney Town   5
    Her Gardens by the Sea.[2]

But yesterday, here in King's Cross,
    I passed an open stall,
Where blooms like living torches hung
    Along a slatted wall,   10
With sprays that seemed as though a hand
    Had spread a floral shawl.

And as amazed I stood, I saw,
    All unafraid and free,
A cloud of bees about the flowers,   15
    And asked how this could be.
"They follow from Wahroonga down,"
    The florist answered me.

Now, though it sat in each cut stem,
    I could not think that, there,   20
Death was triumphant over all
    That sweet and scented air,
Where life exploded, colour mad,
    With pollened hope to spare!

(29 January 1948)   *Copy-text: FM   Collated states: SMH*, 8 May 1948, p. 5 (*A*)
Not otherwise recorded: A's text is in italics throughout.
1 really never] *never really A*   **3** seen] *seen, A*   Paraguay] *Paraguay, A*
5 found] *found, A*   Town] *Town, A*   **7** here in] *in this A*   **18** florist answered]
staller said to A   **19** it] *death A*   **23** colour mad] *colour-mad A*   **24** spare!]
spare. A

[1] NLA 727 2/5/8 is annotated: 'Dear Mr Bancks [creator of the Ginger Meggs comic
strip], I wish you wd. send Ginge wide-eyed & knowledge seeking, up to this stall some
day. Ginge has never been to King's Cross. Sent "S. M. H." so still private. M. G.' See
Z13 and n. 1.   [2] The Botanical Gardens, Sydney.

R25   THE SINGING CHILD[*]

In Spring
The frosty earth
Felt the first pang
Of birth—

A shoot   5
That, spearing up
Became
A crocus cup.

The cold
Wall of the frost   10
Held fast
That little ghost

Of life,
Lest it should rise
Too soon,   15
And death surprise.

[*] Written for the little girl singer, Betty Fisher, who sang our modern
songs in the pure aboriginal voice I had not heard since I was a child.

(1 March 1946)   *Copy-text: FM   Collated states:* None

R26   OLD JANE

I

All talk is good talk,
Sittin' by the fire,
Hillin' up the spuds together,
Milkin' cows in the byre;[1]

But, of all the good talk,   5
The best talk's said

[1] See J56 n. 1.

In the comfortable fellowship
Of a double bed.

2

I didn't have no daughter,
But, when my son was wed,   10
I thought I had a daughter,
Though I didn't have her in bed.

It ain't no use of askin' why,
But them there girls our sons has wed,
However bad our husbands is   15
They ain't such bitter bread.

(1944)   *Copy-text: FM*   *Collated states:* None

R27   THE WHISTLING MAN

There came an old man down the road,
    And, oh, he whistled fine!
He brought a tune from out the wind,
    A wind as sharp as brine;
He took the pain from out the world,   5
    And from this heart of mine.[1]

And, down the stair beside my door,
    Two days ago I heard
A whistling boy come hopping by,
    As if he were a bird;   10
I felt as though I were a leaf
    A happy air had stirred.

[cont. overleaf

(28 December 1947)   *Copy-text: FM*   *Collated states: SMH*, 17 January 1948, p. 5 as
WHISTLING MEN (*A*)

Not otherwise recorded: A's text is in italics throughout.

2 oh] *O A*   fine!] *fine, A*   **3** wind,] *wind— A*   **4** sharp] *cold A*   **6** from]
saved A   **7** And,] *And A*   stair beside] *stairway by A*   **9** by,] *by A*

---

[1] See Q6 and n. 1 and cf. *HR*, Pt I, chap. v, 'THE WHISTLING MEN', p. 29: 'And, indeed,
when one thinks of it had Ned Kelly whistled more he might never have been hanged!'

God gave the whistling mouth to man,
   That he old griefs might drive
Back to the dens from which they came,   15
   And keep his soul alive!
A whistling man makes life as sweet
   As honey in a hive.

13 man,] *man A*   16 alive!] *alive. A*

R28   THE EYE OF THE WIFT[1]

1

What loveliness in leaves!
   And what are words
But leaves upon a tree
   Where we are birds.

2

The pine-tree is a king,   5
   He lifts high his steeple;
But greater is the wheat—
   The wheat is a people.

3

Where all the stars of heaven are thoughts,
   God's shining thoughts in light,   10
I saw a lonely little star
   Run in a sudden fright!

4

Though all may ask for ranging wings,
Yet all men love the simple things;
Fire on the hearth by which to settle,   15
A cat that purrs, the lazy boil of a kettle,
And on the roof the falling rain.

[1] Variant of the obsolete *whift*, a breath of wind, or a snatch of song.

There is no lovelier sound
In all the world,
Than, cosy a-bed,   20
That soak, soak, soak on the ground!

(Pt 1: 14 June 1946; Pt 2: 11 January 1947; Pt 3: 13 February 1945; Pt 4: 1 November 1948)   *Copy-text:* FM   *Collated states:* None

R29   NO FOE SHALL GATHER OUR HARVEST[*]1

Sons of the mountains of Scotland,
Welshmen of coomb[2] and defile,[3]
Breed of the moors of England,
Children of Erin's green isle,
We stand four square to the tempest,   5
Whatever the battering hail—
No foe shall gather our harvest,
Or sit on our stockyard rail.

[cont. overleaf

(16 June 1940)   *Copy-text:* FM   *Collated states:* AWW, 29 June 1940, p. 5 (*A*)[4]   AWW single sheet 1942 (*B*)[5]   *Trib,* 21 January 1953, p. 8 (*C*)

Not otherwise recorded: In *A* the refrain is in italics throughout.

2 Welshmen] *Clansmen A B*   of coomb] from corrie *A B*   from crag *C*   defile] kyle *A B*   3 Breed] Bred *A B*   4 green isle] Isle *C*   5 four square] four-square *A B*   foursquare *C*   tempest,] ~ *B*   6 hail—] ~, *C*   7 harvest,] ~ *C*

---

[1] Musical setting by Phyllis Abbott is in ML Papers vol. 43; later ones by Allan Richardson and Jennifer Mann are in the Correspondence files of ML MS 123 at 2 August 1953 and 3 November 1956. On a setting by Percy Jones, see n. 4.
[2] Deep hollow or valley; but cf. entry for line 2: *A* and *B*'s 'corrie' is Scottish for a hollow on a mountainside, surrounded with steep slopes or precipices.
[3] Narrow pass between mountains.
[4] An editorial note in *AWW* reads: 'At 75, Australian poet and writer Mary Gilmore, Dame of the British Empire, has written one of the finest Australian songs of the war. It appears above. "I'm too old to do many of the things I would like to do to win the war," she said, "but I can still write. Here is a song for the men and women of Australia." The inspiring note in the song is so vividly Australian that the Australian Women's Weekly is proud to present it to readers.' The editorial note in *Trib* reads: 'This fine poem, which many think should be Australia's national anthem, has been set to a rousing tune by Mr. Percy Jones and will be sung during this year's Eucharistic Congress. *P* Its sentiments are appropriate to Australia Day, 1953, which sees hungry Wall Street hands reaching out for Australia's harvest of manpower, uranium and other precious assets which must and shall remain Australian.'
[5] Copies of this separately sold single-sheet printing are held in NLA 727 3/6/2.2.

Our women shall walk in honour,
Our children shall know no chain,   10
This land, that is ours forever,
The invader shall strike at in vain.
Anzac! . . . Tobruk! . . . and Kokoda! . . .[6]
Could ever the old blood fail?
No foe shall gather our harvest,   15
Or sit on our stockyard rail.

So hail-fellow-met we muster,
And hail-fellow-met fall in,
Wherever the guns may thunder,
Or the rocketing air-mail spin![7]   20
Born of the soil and the whirlwind,
Though death itself be the gale—
No foe shall gather our harvest,
Or sit on our stockyard rail.

We are the sons of Australia,   25
Of the men who fashioned the land;
We are the sons of the women
Who walked with them hand in hand;
And we swear by the dead who bore us,
By the heroes who blazed the trail,   30
No foe shall gather our harvest,
Or sit on our stockyard rail.

[*] In the great old cattle days of Australia, the stranger (no one knowing who he might be) was entertained in the parlour, the friend was taken down to the stockyard. No gentleman ever saw hide, hoof or brand that he shouldn't. And that no matter what was seen or how long he sat yarning on the top rail of the fence.   n5

9 honour] honor *A–C*   10 chain,] ~. *C*   11 land,] ~ *A–C*   forever,] ~ *A–C*
13 Anzac! . . .] ~, *C*   Tobruk! . . .] Bapaume! . . . *A B*   ~ *C*   Kokoda! . . .] the
Marne! . . . *A*   the Marne! . *B*   ~, *C*   *15* harvest,] ~ *C*   (**17–24**) So . . . rail.]
Om. C   17 muster,] ~ *B*   20 air-mail] "air mail" *A B*   26 the men] forebears *C*
land;] ~, *A B*   27 of the] of *C*   28 them] ~, *A B*   hand;] ~, *C*   29 us,] ~ *C*
30 blazed] blazoned *C*   *31* harvest,] ~ *C*   n1–21 [8]In . . . them."] *Om. A–C*

[6] World War II battles defining the Anzac tradition: in 1942 (see *A* and *B*'s variants) World War I examples were required (as in O9).
[7] Anti-aircraft fire: cf. *A* and *B*'s variant.

My father had the reputation of being a man who would die rather than tell a lie. But there were emergencies when loyalty to friends came first. I recollect as we were once sitting with the owner on the top rail of a station mustering-yard near Wagga Wagga that a mounted trooper suddenly stood beside us. The only thing in the yard was a white n10 unbranded calf. An unbranded calf without its mother could put a man in jail. (That is why so many cows in those years had to have "twins".) Without seeming to see the trooper, father casually said, "The sooner you get that calf's mother back from the mob and get it branded the better." The white-faced squatter (I'll never forget his white face!) took n15 up the cue. "I will," he said, and turning to the trooper added, "Come on up to the house and have a cup of tea." The trooper, never questioning father's word, went with us.

Talking of it afterwards to my mother, father half-ruefully said, "I had to do it for the sake of the family . . . I could not let disgrace come n20 to them."

R30   SONG OF THE BREED[1]

There were three old divils set out one day
    With a bit of a rag for a sail,
And the sea, as it looked at them breezing by,
    Exclaimed, "If it isn't a whale!"
But it wasn't a whale, and it wasn't a ship,   5
    It was only a scrap of a boat;
But they belted the seven seas, they did,
    And everything else afloat.

        And now wherever a man may go,
        Whether by-guess-and-by-God and back,   10

(14 September 1942)   *Copy-text:* FM   *Collated states:* Sun (Sydney), 2 January 1943, p. 5 (*A*)

Not otherwise recorded: A is in italics throughout; emphasis at line 26 is therefore lost. The collation for lines 10 and 12 is identical at lines 22, 24 and 34, 36.

1 day] *day, A*   **2** sail,] *sail. A*   **3** as] *Om. A*   **4** Exclaimed] *And it said A*
If it isn't] *Begob! it's A*   **6** boat;] *boat, A*   **9** now] *now, A*   **10** by-guess-and-
by-God] *by-guess-and-by-God, A*

---

[1] AMS in ADFA 20 8.2/63, sent to H. M. Green, is annotated: 'Private: I like this almost best – among the best-liked – of all I wrote. This is *me*. Not just intellect looking abroad or in, & memory crying to be heard – M. G. King's Cross 28.5.51'.

He'll come on the sons of these three old divils,
Andrew: Patrick: and Jack.[2]

The Anzac lads were a branch of the stirp,[3]
  And the fighting "Rats of Tobruk",[4]
Who, whenever they lifted the lid and swore,   15
  The round of the firmament shook.
And always in war came the brood like a gale,
  They waited no call to the draft,
But hell-for-leather they went for the foe,
  And salted him fore and aft.   20

    So now, wherever a man may go,
    Whether by-guess-and-by-God and back,
    He'll come on the breed of these three old divils,
    Andrew: Patrick: and Jack.

With hymn-book in hand the three once went,   25
  On what (*they said*) was a sacred quest,
And they burgled the half of the world, they did,
  And they hog-tied half of the rest;
But they rigged their tent where the desert whined,
  On the ice-floe they grounded their mark,   30
And far, on the peak of the highest range,
  Their camp fire showed as a spark.

    Now man to man, wherever we go,
    Whether by-guess-and-by-God and back,
    We march as the sons of the great old men   35
    Andrew: Patrick: and Jack.

---

12 Andrew: Patrick:] *Andrew, Patrick, A*   13 stirp,] *tree A*   14 Tobruk",]
Tobruk," A   16 shook.] *shook; A*   17 came] *come A*   21 So] *And A*
25 went,] *went A*   31 highest] *wildest A*   32 camp fire] *camp-fire A*   33 Now]
Now, A   35 men] *men— A*

---

[2] Names respectively representative of Scotland, Ireland and England (i.e. Great Britain).
[3] Stock, or stem, of a family or clan; a lineage.
[4] Phrase coined by Lord Haw Haw (William Joyce) in 'Germany Calling', his English-language pro-Hitler broadcasts. Intended to disparage the Australian troops who resisted a long siege of Tobruk by heavily armed German and Italian forces in 1941, it was enthusiastically counter-adopted: e.g. in the feature films *The Rats of Tobruk* (1944) and *Desert Rats* (1952), the novel *We Were the Rats* (by Lawence Glassop, 1944) and the Rats of Tobruk Association formed by returned ex-servicemen. On Tobruk, see also O10.

R31 OUR ELDER STATESMAN

THE RIGHT HONOURABLE W. M. HUGHES, C. H.[*][1]

In Memory

His was the victor's pride,
   His the unbroken will,
Which, though the body died,
   Made him the conqueror still.

Fate was but circumstance   5
   To him who could not fail,
Who, as he raised the lance,
   Made even defeat his mail.[2]

Fear, that shook other men,
   Set him no craven bound,   10
Who raked the fox's den,
   And fought the eagle round!

All weapons met his hand,
   All ways were to his mind,
Who forged for this, our land,   15
   The steel to hold and bind!

He fronted King and horde,
   Nor feared to stand alone;

(18 March 1940)[3] *Copy-text: FM Collated states: DT*, 12 September 1953, p. 17 as
OUR ELDER STATESMAN/ (THE RT. HON. W. M. HUGHES) (*A*)

Not otherwise recorded: The dedication is omitted in *A*. *A*'s text is in italics through-
out.

5 circumstance] *circumstance,* A   **15** forged] *forged,* A   this,] *this* A

[1] See M5 n. 2.   [2] Armour.
[3] MSS indicate that R31 is a modified version of a poem originally written for Hughes's
76th birthday in March 1940: e.g. NLA 727 3/6/2.1 is annotated: 'Written and sent to
W. M. H. 18 March 40'.

His was Caradoc's sword,[4]
And his young David's stone.[5]   20

[*] After the 1914 war, on his return from Europe I asked Mr Hughes
what had moved him most when abroad. He thought for a moment, then
said, "When I stood with Lloyd George on the spot where Caradoc had
made his last stand for the freedom of Wales."

Even in telling this his voice was full of his moved feeling. Mr Hughes   n5
was so proud of being a Welshman that whenever he met a man who
knew the language he greeted him with "Wales forever!" in Cymric.

Had he been Irish the salutation would certainly have been "Up the
rebels!"

n1–9 ⁵After . . . rebels!"] *Om. A*

[4] *A* is preceded by a more expansive note on the circumstances of the poem and adds this
footnote: 'Caradoc (or Caractacus), Celtic chief who led British resistance against the
Roman invaders 1900 years ago. He was defeated on the border of Wales and captured
in A.D. 50. Caradoc and his family were taken to Rome, where the Emperor Claudius
granted them their lives.'
[5] David wins victory for the Israelites by slaying the giant Philistine warrior, Goliath,
with a stone from a slingshot (1 Samuel 18. 32–52).

R32   THE DEBT[1]

Not hers the noisy world,
And yet
Its constant eddies whirled
About the path
Whereon her feet were set.   5
And, there with steadfastness,
Each onset as it came
She met.

Hers was the willing hand,
The palm whose gentle touch was balm;   10
And hers the selflessness made calm
A man's tempestuous force,
Till, by the impact of its urge,
Uprose this land's triumphant surge!

[1] In the Fryer and present editor's copies of *FM* the title is annotated: 'Dame Mary
Hughes. M. G.'

Give palms to him,   15
But for her patient feet
Lay down the Cloth of Gold.

(10 January 1953)   *Copy-text: FM*   *Collated states:* None

R33   SINGAPORE[*]

They grouped together about the chief,
    And each one looked at his mate,
Ashamed to think that Australian men
    Should meet such a bitter fate;
And deep was the wrath in each man's heart,   5
    And savage the oaths they swore,
As they thought of how they had all been ditched,
    By *impregnable* Singapore![1]

Flat on her base she squatted the sea,
    And, bare as an old bald head,   10
Her idiot face looked up to the skies,
    To show she was profiteer-bred;
And there under heaven she naked lay,
    By the enemy planes confined,
While her master-builders sat back at home,   15
    Unctuous, cushioned, and wined!

                                    [*cont. overleaf*

(1 March 1942)   *Copy-text: FM*   *Collated states: AWW*, 14 March 1942, p. 9 (*A*)
2 mate,] ~ *A*   4 fate;] ~! *A*   5 deep] black *A*   man's] hot *A*   6 the] *Om. A*
7 ditched,] ~ *A*   8 *impregnable*] "Impregnable" *A*   Singapore!] ~. *A*   9 Flat
. . . base] In her vaunted place *A*   sea,] ~ *A*   10 And . . . head] On a base that was
Maginot bred *A*   11 idiot] startled *A*   to] at *A*   skies,] ~ *A*   12 show
. . . profiteer-bred;] the enemy planes o'erhead. *A*   13–16 And . . . wined!] Enemy
planes; while ours were—where?/ That cry we had heard before./ Our hearts were
wrung as it rose this time/ From beleaguered Singapore. *A*

---

[1] This failed military theory is linked in *A* (see entry for line 10) to the belief that the anti-
German fortifications of the Maginot line would make France invincible. *A*'s lines 13–16
echo complaints made by the Allied armed forces about inadequate protective air cover
during the Dunkirk evacuation and the failed campaigns in Greece and Crete. MG's 'Our
Men in Greece' (at ML 7/3 and NLA 8766 10/6/1 and other locations) refers to this:
annotations claiming publication in *QD* are unconfirmed.

> She brought forth death as her eldest child,
>   With defeat as her second son,
> Then she hung a white flag out on a staff,
>   To show that her day was done.   20
> But black with rage the Australians stood,
>   And God, how our soldiers swore—
> Bennett and all his men, alike—
>   At the old ——— Singapore!
>
> Was it her fault she betrayed our men?   25
>   Was it her fault she failed?
> Ask it of those who slaughtered the flag
>   That once to the mast was nailed!
> Ask it of those who pandered to power,
>   Traitors, whatever their rank,   30
> Who flung to the dogs the nation's pride,
>   Till the very name ——— stank!

[*] This verse is modified from the hotly written original, of which only three copies were made. Of these Mr Leslie Haylen has one.[2]

The British Army in Singapore, we were told, numbered 80,000 and the Japanese only 20,000. Also, it was said that the guns which were to be for the defence of Singapore (and Australia) were all emplaced to point   n5 in one direction only, and could not be swung for use as required.[3]

---

19 staff,] ~ *A*   20 day] task *A*   done.] ~; *A*   21 But black] And sick *A*
22 God,] ~! *A*   our soldiers] those Anzacs *A*   23 men,] ~ *A*   24 old ———] fall
of *A*   25 Was it her] Whose was the *A*   men] troops *A*   26 Was it her] Whose
was the *A*   27 slaughtered] lowered *A*   29–32 Ask . . . stank!] Tell them we'll
raise it on Anzac soil/ With hearts that are steeled to the core,/ We swear by our
dead and captive sons,/ REVENGE FOR SINGAPORE! *A*
n1–6 ⁵This . . . required.] *Om. A*

---

[2] On Haylen, see K40 n. 1. MG's retrospective annotations on MSS of R33 (in ML 4/9 and 7/3, and NLA 6/3/2.3) name, variously, four recipients: Haylen, Major-General Gordon Bennett (1887–1962), John Curtin (see O11 n. 1) and Mrs Jackson, co-editor of *AWW*.
[3] The fall of Singapore was announced on 16 February 1942, but it was some days before the extent of the military debacle became public. On 16 February MG recorded in her Diary a poem (never published) based on the assumption that heroic resistance had been offered to the Japanese. More accurate information led to the 'hotly written original' (see author's note), recorded in her Diary for 1 March as 'Major-General Bennett and his True Men':

> They grouped together about the chief,
>   And each man looked on his fate,
> Should ever the sound of a restless foot
>   Reach out to the foe in wait,

And bitter the wrath in each man's heart,
    And savage the oaths they swore,
As they thought of how they had all been ditched
    By "Impregnable" Singapore!

Flat on her base she squatted the sea,
    But, bare as an old bald head,
Her idiot face looked up the skies,
    To show she was profiteer bred;
And there under heaven she naked lay,
    By the enemy planes confined,
While the craven xxxxxxx sat safe at home,
    Till their pants wore out behind.

She brought forth death as her eldest child,
    With defeat as her second son,
Then she hung a white flag on a staff,
    To show that her task was done;
But black with rage the Australians stood,
    And God! how those Anzacs swore—
Bennett and all his men alike—
    At the old xxxxx Singapore!

Was it her fault she betrayed our troops?
    Was it her fault she failed?
Ask of those who slaughtered the flag
    That once to the mast was nailed!
Ask it of those who pandered for power,
    Traitors whatever their rank,
Who flung to the dogs the nation's pride,
    Till the very name, xxxxxxx, stank.

AWW judged, correctly, that this text would be unacceptable to the Censor and negotiation over re-wording preceded its publication on 14 March. An intermediate version, with changes suggested by the *AWW*, is printed in W. H. Wilde's 'Mary Gilmore and 1942' (*Bn*, 22 July 1980, p. 80). This is not, as claimed, 'the poem as published': that text is recorded in the collation as *A*. The *FM* text (R33) was separately developed from the second Diary version; it restores some of the indignation, but its blanks of uniform length at lines 24 and 32 obscure the probability that the number of its crosses (respectively 7, 5 and 7) in the Diary MS represent 'British', 'bitch' and 'Britain'.

R34   TEN DEAD LEAVES[*]

I saw the leaves fall.
Stripped and bare by my window
The tree stood head up against the sky,
And it was beautiful,
Its winter bareness only that of life.   5

                 [collation overleaf

I saw the leaves fall:
Men in the jungle,
Men before the guns,
Men hurtling from the height,
Men shark-eaten in the sea;   10
But when they fell
Nothing was left of loveliness,
For these leaves were the tree,
And when they died
The tree died too.   15

And then I heard pealing of organs,
And voices from great pulpits cry,
"Behold the glory! Behold the true
Fulfilment of God's holy Will!"
Then God cried out to man,   20
"*What of my Ten Commandments?*"
And no man answered God.

I saw the leaves fall.
Ten Mighty Leaves.
They rotted on the ground.   25

[*] *Sydney Morning Herald*, 15th April 1948. "New York: The Mayor of
Hiroshima this week will ask the people of the world for contributions
to a memorial which the city hopes to erect at the spot believed to be
the centre of the atomic bomb explosion. We and the world learned
through the searing radio-active blast, and the fires that followed, what   n5
atomic war might mean for mankind. Surely it would help the cause of
peace if here in Hiroshima we could build a memorial subscribed by
the people of the world to the peace of the world."

Daily Telegraph, 26th March 1948. "Sydney: The U.S.A. dropped
the first atom-bomb at Hiroshima on August 6, 1945. A U.S.A. survey,   n10
made after the end of the war, lists the killed and missing, as a result of
the Hiroshima bombing, at between 70,000 and 80,000."

———

(10 September 1945)   *Copy-text: FM   Collated states: Trib*, 30 April 1952, p. 5 as THE
DEAD LEAVES (*A*)

3 stood] ~, *A*   **4–5** And . . . life] Its winter bareness that of life;/ And it was
beautiful *A*   **6** fall:] ~; *A*   **10–11** sea;/ But] ~.// ~ *A*   **11** they] these *A*
13 tree,] ~; *A*   **16** organs,] ~ *A*   **17** cry,] ~ *A*   **19** Will] will *A*   **20** Then]
And *A*   man,] ~ *A*   **21** "*What . . . Commandments?*"] **"What of my Ten
Commandments?"** *A*   **n1–12** *Sydney* . . . 80,000."] *Om. A*

R35   INHERITANCE

I

Her heart leapt to the wind,
    That kissed, indifferent;
Then she returned to him
    Who never knew she went!

2

Greece gave that Sappho[1] who,   5
    So long ago,
Made words her violin,
    Herself the bow.
Her words, the centuries down,
    Creative throe.   10

3

A woman fled, fearing she knew not what
    Abominable thing of sex pursued.
But it was not man who frightened her,
    It was heredity.

4

This frame a man begot,   15
    And woman brought to be,
This moving self that speaks,
    This living thing is me,
It is a word which says,
    "On such and such a night   20

(Pt 1: 21 January 1949; Pt 2: n. d.; Pts 3, 4: 14 December 1944; Pt 5: 6 June 1946; Pt 6: 10 January 1947; Pt 7: 3 June 1939; Pt 8: 6 January 1945)   *Copy-text: FM   Collated states: Boh* (August 1939), p. 3, Pt 7 only, as SIMPLICITY (*A*)

Not otherwise recorded: Lines 37 and 38 are in reverse order in *A*; *A*'s text is in italics throughout.

0.1–36.1 1 . . . 7] *Om. A*

_____

[1] One of the canonical lyric poets of ancient Greece, though only fragments of her highly erotic poetry survive. Sappho (*fl. c.* 600 BC) lived on the island of Lesbos; see also E48 n. 1.

Eros and Psyche met,[2]
In full creative might."

5

They, of the past
Who fathered me,
Made me a part   25
Of Life's great tree.

But, as a leaf
Knows not its stem,
They knew not me,
Nor knew I them.   30

6

Proud and untameable
As one who rode the wind,
He raised the child who fell,
Helped the undisciplined;
And though he held all power,   35
Wondered at some small flower.

7

He was a waster, they said,
He never tried to make money;
But he knew the way of a bird,
And the tree with the honey.   40

8

Up from the ocean of ancestry
    Wave upon wave uprose and ran,
Then lapsed on the shores of time.
    I was a drop of the spray
That scattering fell,   45
    But held in the drop was the sea,
And the sea rose, living, in me.

---

38 tried] knew how *A*   **40.1–47** 8 . . . me.] *Om. A*

---

[2] The romance between Eros, the winged god of Love, and the mortal Psyche had to be conducted in darkness, under a taboo that forbade Psyche from seeing her divine lover.

R36 THE RECESSIVE*

Only the ruined know
The agony of loneliness
Where the recessive cries
Unsatisfied in its excess!

Conditioned man changes   5
With changed condition. So are born
New powers, and with new powers
There come new woes,
Until the sad recessive weeps
Its grief of unrelief.   10

They said that I was bad.
Maybe.
They said that I was mad.
Maybe.
But through eternity a Hand   15
Will write
How the recessive stormed
My citadel in might,
And never came one there
To salvage me.   20

Blind as a worm is blind,
Man with a needle meets disease;
Piles drug on drug; but where
Upon his dual self his high degrees
Are set, and the imprisoned wars   25
Against the very bars
Of life, there
As a mute sits science, cold and still,
While the unleashed recessive lifts itself,
And on its victim works its soul-destroying will.   30

* The recessive sex.[1]

(18 July 1944) *Copy-text: FM* *Collated states:* None

[1] Because of the chromosome structure of their DNA, males are much more likely to be affected by recessive genes: see also I130 n. 1 and O7 lines 13–16.

R37   1940[1]

They were my boys!
Not mine because I bore them in my bed,
Nursed them, and cradled them, and bought them toys,
Dressed them, and saw that they were fed;
But mine because they used to come   5
To me and say, "It's nice here . . . just like home!"
There I would make them tea, while they would tell
Me of the camp and what each day befell;
How their damned leader didn't know a thing,
But had to ask them how to lay a gun,[2]   10
How even the youngest man belonging to the crew
Could captain *him*, so little all he knew!
Then with that subject tossed aside and done,
They'd say how such-and-such-a-one drank far too much,
But somehow, though he drank, he had the touch   15
That made men men, no matter what!
But always they would talk of home, and what their mother
        said,
And how the girls were knitting socks,
With all the little things whereby the heart unlocks
A tension that has grown too high.   20

Now on the wire and in the mud they lie;
And I am here, and all the chairs are empty where
They used to sit; the lonely air

(10 November 1940) *Copy-text: FM   Collated states: SMH,* 17 October 1942,
p. 7 (*A*)

Not otherwise recorded: A's text is in italics throughout; emphasis in line 12 is therefore
lost.

4 fed;] *fed, A*   **5** come] *come, A*   **6** To me and] *And A*   **7** There] *Then A*
8 camp] *camp, A*   befell] *befel A*   **12** captain] *Captain A*   **16** men,] *men, so
that/ They'd stick to him, A*   **20** has] *had A*   **21** wire] *wire, A*   mud] *dust A*
lie;] *lie, A*

---

[1] MG responded to W. D. Mitchell, a soldier correspondent: 'I think I felt your letter
more than any other that came about "1940" . . . It was itself my heart's tears – for this
war & last. For the last still aches in us' (letter in NLA 1695/1).
[2] To set a gun in the correct position for hitting a mark.

Echoes their voices; almost I turn
To answer them. And I have but my tears that burn   25
For them . . . my boys! . . . my boys!

26 boys! . . .] *boys . . . A*

R38   CASUALTY LISTS

Though grief lies like a burden on the heart,
And every hour cries out, "Alas!"
Burdens must still be borne;
And this will pass.

Only by seconds at a time we bear,   5
As step by step some mountain mass
Of alpine height we climb.
Seconds will pass.

Wash not the dead with tears, for, should they know,
They too will grieve! But, while they sleep,   10
Gather the fallen sheaf
Was theirs to reap.

(n. d.)   *Copy-text: FM   Collated states: SMH*, 1 March 1941, p. 9 (*A*)[1]
1 lies] lie *A*   on the] [. . .] *A*   2 And] Any *A*   out,] ~ *A*   Alas!"]
~[. . .] *A*   3 borne;] ~— *A*   5 bear,] be[. . .] *A*   6 step by] by the single *A*
some mountain mass] (though m[. . .] *A*   7 Of alpine height] The mountain
peak) *A*   climb.] ~— *A*   9 should] [. . .] *A*   10 while] as *A*   sleep,] [. . .] *A*
11 Gather . . . sheaf] Bind up the sheaf that once *A*

---

[1] The text in *SMH* is lacking or indecipherable in places.

R39   THE LITTLE FEET

The little running feet
Sit side by side,
As death has bidden them—
Life, the denied.

All day they are so still,   5
    Almost they seem
Something the moon had kissed,
    And sent to dream.

But no moon, now, though it
    Whiten to snow,   10
Can touch them to a dream
    Where they must go.

Lightly as air, about
    My heart all day
They ran; and now they do   15
    Not even play.

(1 January 1948)   *Copy-text: FM   Collated states:* None

R40   OUT ON THE FARM

His once thick hair is thin;
At times I think his sight
Flickers, a little,
In the light.

His teeth are long, long gone,   5
Being buried in
The dentist's and
The dustman's bin.

His hearing is a trifle slow;
And sometimes when   10
A quick thought springs
It goes again.

Yet he was once
My little boy, who
In life's darkness all   15
The sunlight drew.

And I remember dawns,
When, as he clambered to my bed

And snuggled down
His darling head, 20

He'd say, "I wish that it would rain!
Then we could lie and talk!"

(11 November 1941)   *Copy-text: FM   Collated states: AP 1955* (no variants)

R41   TEARS

1

Man wounds, who never
Means the least
Small hurt; then time,
The waiting priest,

His penance of 5
Remembrance lays
Upon the heart:
To ache always.

Who no remorse
Has ever known, 10
Has for a heart
A naked stone;

No lichen there
As memory grows;
The dew of tears 15
It never knows.

2

Under a stone,
Forever I
Have laid my heart
In pain to lie. 20

O lichen of
Love's memory,
Cover the stone
And ransom me!

3

There is a tomb I know.　　　　　　　25
No need for me to go
By the wood's path (or some
Sad ache of life) to come
To it, for it is in
My heart, and your last inn.　　　　30

4

"Who spoke?"
In sleep I heard the child,
Then woke,
And wept unreconciled.

(Pts 1, 2: 13 October 1947; Pt 3: 5 January 1948; Pt 4: 2 January 1948)　*Copy-text:*
FM　Collated states: None

R42　GRIEF

Where once we marked the silver seagulls flake the sky,
While wind-filled, hooded sails shuttled the harbour blue,
There, where the fountain flung its crystal arch on high,
Though you had come again to find me as you used to do,
And though it may be you had asked was my heart broken,　5
Only the poplars would have answered, only the willows
　　　spoken.

Past all misunderstanding, past all grief and pain,
There is but quiet now; nothing can hurt again.
Life, like the scent of the rose, knows naught of its mesh;
But on the petals are bruises, wounds in the flesh.　　　10

"We will still hold him, though he is gone," they said.
But I, who had given you freedom through all
Your days, I could not pursue you when dead,
Nor ask you to wait and answer my call!
Yet all my heart will follow you, star to star,　　　　15
Asking, in agony, if there you are.

There was an hour in which, as once we two had done,
I stood and watched the charcoal-burners bed the clay;
And memory, that blossom of the after years,
Rose like the scent of honey on a summer's day.   20

(Stanza 1: 24 November 1945; Stanza 2: 28 November 1945; Stanza 3: 12 February 1948;
Stanza 4: 12 July 1950)[1]   *Copy-text: FM*   *Collated states:* None
5 may be *Ed.*] maybe *x*

---

[1] In ML 7/1, an original numbering of parts (which correspond to the stanza divisions
of R42) is struck out, establishing the form found in the copy-text. The dates given to
these parts are repeated in a number of the MSS at other locations.

R43   THEY CALLED HER SUNSHINE

She lived, we knew not how,
    We knew not why,
Save that undrawn the lot[1]
    That she must die;

Save that, what cruelty   5
    Befell, no part
In hate was hers. She had
    The laughing heart.

She loved all things; the sheen
    Of leaves, the grass   10
Whose tussocks gleamed like
    Palaces of glass;

While deeps within her welled
    If but a mote,
Riding a sunbeam, set   15
    Its gold afloat;

(19 July 1951)   *Copy-text: FM*   *Collated states: Jindy* (1951) (*A*)   Wright2 (*B*)
7 In] Of *A*   hers. She] hers . . . she *A*   **16** afloat;] ~! *A*

---

[1] I.e. chance (or fate) had not decided – adapts the ancient custom of settling an outcome
(e.g. of disputes or competitions) by placing lots, markers bearing the name of those
involved, in a receptacle and drawing one out at random.

And when a little ant,
    In running stood
And feelered at her hand,
    Joy rose in flood.   20

Maybe the world had need
    Of her, whose art
Knew naught of hate. . . . *She had*
    The laughing heart.

17 ant,] ~ *A*   18 running] ~, *B*   20 flood.] ~— *A*   22 her,] ~ *A*
23 naught] nought *A*   hate. . . . *She*] ~—/ ~ *A*   ~ . . . ~ *B*

R44   A MEMORY

I

All wounded things were hers!
There was no need of plan or chart
For these to find
That mother-hungry heart.

Once as she played she found   5
A tiny frozen bird, and wept
In dreams, its pain
Still hers although she slept.

2

And once, a child not seven,
The Sunday shepherd of her flock,   10
She stood between her brothers and
A pawing bull—fearful,
And yet not craven.

(25 February 1940)   *Copy-text: FM   Collated states: SMH*, 16 March 1940, p. 13 (*A*)
Not otherwise recorded: A presents each part as a single stanza.
2 plan] ~, *A*   chart] ~, *A*   5 Once] ~, *A*   played] ~, *A*   8 hers] ~, *A*
10 her] the *A*   12 bull—fearful,] bull. *A*   13 And . . . craven.] *Om. A*

There in her pink-sprigged frock,
Trembling and small, I saw her stand.   15
Through all these years I see her still.

14–16 There . . . still.] So through the years I see her stand,/ Trembling and small,/
There in her little pink, sprigged frock. *A*

R45   THE MOTHER-HEART

1

Child-bound I stay, who would away!
Far would I go, but this says *No*!
Up from the marsh there comes the harsh
Cry of a bird, and I, deep stirred,
Think long of how, on its first bough,   5
Ancestrally sat what was I.

Whence the bird's wing? The hard, dry thing
Once ooze made earth, and earth made dearth
Save where came change to widen range!
So the finned grew to wings and flew,   10
But blind as man, who, in his span,
Knows not of Thither, yet asks of Whither.

Child-bound, unfree, no wing helps me,
Though all the powers, that once were ours,
In life's still deep recessive[1] sleep.   15

2

Fall kind, O Sun, upon my baby's head.
Shine friendly on his path where'er his feet may tread!
So small he is, and so defenceless come,
Where man is, writhing, shaped beneath life's potter thumb.

[cont. overleaf

(Pts 1, 2: 30 August 1947; Pt 3: 16 August 1950; Pt 4: n. d.; Pt 5: 3 February 1946)   *Copy-
text: FM   Collated states: SMH*, 13 May 1944, p. 7, Pt 4 only, as LOSS (*A*)   *Bn*, 10 April
1946, p. 15, Pt 5 only, as FOUNDATIONS (*B*)

(**0.1–49.1**) 1 . . . 5] *Om. B*   **0.1–35.1** 1 . . . 4] *Om. A*

[1] See I130 n. 1.

Unbruised he lies where all are bruised and hurt,   20
Who from his velvet sleep is waked: the loud alert
Of life to be forever in his ears,
No matter what his lot may be, or what the years.

O Life as need! O strange, bewildering
Change from babe to man! How can we women dare to fling 25
So soft a thing into this dreadful reel
Of clay, save that eternal storge² compels the wheel!

                    3

There was no idolatry at my child's birth*
Only the wind blew and the rains fell;
No cannon roared in worship when my baby came,   30
Nor did any church pray, or ring me its bell.

There were no Archbishops and no Cardinals;
No pomp, and no idolatry at all;
Only the floods were our baptismal font,
And our Jordan-water³ was the rain in its fall.   35

                    4

She was a simple soul,
Just a woman who swept
And dusted house: patched, sewed,
Did shopping, ate and slept.

She died. There was a child,   40
Her daughter's child, who room
To room wandered, and wept
That woman in her tomb.

Now where the slow feet trod,
I hear the questing beat,   45

---

38 house:] ~, *A*   39 ate] ~, *A*   **44–7** Now . . . feet.] *Om. A*

² Natural affection, usually that of parents for their offspring.
³ Reference to the baptism of Christ in the river Jordan (see Matthew 3. 13–17): water collected from the river was sometimes used in baptisms, even into the twentieth century.

Each day above my head,
Of those small, anxious feet.

Grief spares no age. The tears
Of childhood need no years.

5

All life is one;   50
It knows nor high nor low!
So, like the mother-hen
That turns the eggs she sits upon,
Before my pillow I uncover,
Into the children's room I go,   55
And turn my babies over.[*]

* During the floods on the Hunter River, a girl wife had her baby with
only her husband and a friend to attend her.
[*l. 56] When I was little no mother ever thought of going to bed without
turning all the smaller children. Elder ones got the order, "Turn over
on your other side", and did it.   n5

(49.1–56) 5 . . . over.] *Om. A*   51 low!] ~. *B*   52 So,] ~ *B*   mother-hen] mother
hen *B*   53 she] it *B*   (n1–5) *During . . . it.] *Om. A*   n1–2 *During . . . her.]
Om. B   n3 little] a child *B*   n4 order,] ~ *B*   over] *Om. B*   n5 side",] ~," *B*
it] it almost without waking *B*

R46   LIFE[1]

1

Leaf, leaf on the tree, no measure of me
Are you, where you break to bud and awake!

[*cont. overleaf*

(Pt 1: 6 October 1945; Pt 2: 23 November 1945; Pt 3: 10 May 1950; Pt 4: 3 October
1942; Pt 5: 13 November 1940; Pt 6: 8 January 1945; Pt 7: 25 April 1952)   *Copy-text:*
FM   *Collated states: SMH,* 4 January 1941, p. 9, Pt 5 only, as IF ONLY . . . (*A*)   *Bn,* 5
June 1946, p. 2, Pt 1 only, as THE LEAF (*B*)   *AP 1946,* Pt 1 only, as THE LEAF (*C*)

Not otherwise recorded: In *B* and *C* the last five syllables of each line are set as a new
line, with the first word capitalised. *B* is in italics throughout.
(0.1–40.1) 1 . . . 5] *Om. A*   0.1 1] *Om. B C*   2 you,] *you B*   ~ *C*

[1] Musical setting of Pt 2 by Dorothy Hodges is held in ML 3/M.

No measure? The last year's leafage is past,
And, as I too must, is mouldered to dust.

While the fresh new leaf knows naught of the brief,   5
Bright thing that was seen in the last year's green!

For only the tree endures; and as we,
(This leafage is man) you know but your span.

And yet though you fall, though none may recall
Where broken you drift, life still is your gift.   10

But life never yours! What moulder endures,
In root or in sap, is an unknown hap.[2]

2

Something there was dropped to a tree,
Lighter than mist, or spume at sea.
There, as it sat, its lifted throat   15
Sang of its joy, in note by note.

Somebody said,
It was a bird;
But it was life,
Was life I heard.   20

3

I watch the doves,
That, in the cold,
With bent knees rest
Above their hearts,
And brood. And, as   25
I watch, I think

---

4 I too] *I, too,* B   ~, ~, C   dust.] *dust,* B   ~, C   **6** the last year's] *its mantling* B
its mantling C   green!] *green.* B   ~. C   **7** endures;] *Endures,* B   Endures, C
and] *and,* B   ~, C   **9** recall] *recall,* B   ~, C   **10** drift,] *drift* B   ~ C   **11** But]
But, B   ~, C   life] *oh,* B   oh, C   yours!] *yours!...* B   ~!... C   endures,]
endures B   ~ C   **12** sap,] *sap* B   ~ C   (**12.1–63**) 2 ... Alway!] *Om.* B C

---

[2] Happening, chance event.

How man, for all
His might, is but
A feathered bird,
Where life keeps warm,   30
Breasted upon
Its heart.

4

He had not known as he came down,
Cantering on his way to town,
That he should see, upon the line,   35
Her little smock so white and fine.[*]

Scarcely he dared, as he rode by,
To see it float the wind on high;
And yet his eyes and heart were drawn
Toward that web of lace and lawn.   40

5

If only we could speak! Or if
We could but let each other know
Out of what rich and steadfast deeps
The living tides of friendship flow!

Ever the heart essays, the lips   45
Refuse—silent lest some word rend
A veil long usage held, and we,
Fearing the lover, lose the friend.

6

What if comes loss! Quickened to flame,
Love once was lit upon a name.   50

So through the years, though all is ash,
Remember, still, that living flash.

Too cold the heart that has no keep,
Where memory may sometimes weep.

7

How shall I, 55
Who have eaten the dry
And unsalted bread of grief,
Eat the sweet loaf
Of another day?

Though it were in my mouth, 60
I should remember
That other bread—
Alway!

[*] Manners and morals change with time, and today a smock is just an overall and no longer a shift or chemise. So people openly stand and look at things in shop-windows that once not only were never shown, but, if mentioned, were named almost in a whisper.

As late as the '70s, where there was a family the clothes-lines were n5 put up behind the kitchen, and no male visitor, coming or going, ever rode or drove round that way. I remember Mrs John Stinson, of Kindra Station,[3] with a voice of outrage telling her husband that she would never have a certain young man at the house again, as he had committed the unpardonable sin of riding past the clothes-lines, when the washing had n10 not yet been brought in.

The rule was to hang sheets, towels, tablecloths and napery on the first line near the kitchen, especially where there was a man cook, whether white or Chinese. The feminine wear, protected by this, went on the next or middle line, and the "coloureds" and boys' wear on the third or n15 back line. Thus the middle line was shielded from sight. No man who knew manners ever rode by those lines.

The blacks had similar taboos. Whenever they camped, the women's side of the place was forbidden to the men. If a man trespassed he could be banished to the Ngaviah-Vas (Never-Nevers),[4] or killed as a breaker n20 of tribal law.

Father once ordered a man off the station he managed because he had ridden into a camp on the women's side, quite regardless of their feelings. "Only that the blacks know me," father furiously said, "you might have had us all killed!" n25

(n1–25) §Manners . . . killed!"] *Om. A–C*   n10–11 had not *Ed.*] not not X

[3] See G12 line 11 and G28 n. 3.
[4] See R65 author's note, lines 27–30.

R47   FROM THE DUST

Silver is the dust in the heat,
Un-marked even by the little feet
Whose need must back
And forward track.

So, till the sunset will it lie,   5
As the harsh hours of day go by!
Then will the snake
His slow trail make,
And the fat, dumb
Lizard will come;   10
The echidna's plaiting feet,
Patterning will meet
The plover and the quail;
All these, and more, will trail,
Forced, even as man, to go,   15
Man knows not where—but these do know.

These are the un-burdened, whose one care
Is life. They do not bear
The weight of things
Like man, who brings   20
Out of the blind
Wells of the mind,
Even as God,
The constant rod
Of the created, which   25
Makes man poor though it enrich.

[*cont. overleaf*

(n. d.)   *Copy-text: FM   Collated states: Boh* (August 1939), p. 2 (*A*)

Not otherwise recorded: A's text is in italics throughout.

1 Silver] (For "Bohemia").// *Silver A*   **2** Un-marked] *Unmarked A*
3 Whose] *Where A*   **5** So,] *So A*   lie,] *lie A*   **6** As] *While A*   by!] *by; A*
12 Patterning] *Patterning, A*   **13** quail;] *quail— A*   **14** will] *in A*
15 Forced,] *Drawn A*   man,] *man A*   go,] *go A*   **16** Man] *He A*   where—but]
where. But A   these do] *all these A*   **17** un-burdened] *unburdened A*   **20** Like]
As A   **22** the] *his A*

Life's freedom in the dust still lies,
Yet but the burdened and the unfree rise.

27 lies,] *lies. A*   **28** unfree] *un-/ free A*

R48   STOIC

The road before me,
The door behind,
Closed with the darkness
Of a blind.
Which shall I choose,   5
If choose I must? One
With its vision,
One with none? . . .

Only the flesh we love;
The spirit is no more   10
Than lone birds flying
On a distant shore!

(25 February 1949)   *Copy-text: FM   Collated states: Sy* 11.2 (1950), p. 83 (*A*)
2 The] A *A*   **3** the] *Om. A*   **4–5** blind./ Which] ~.// ~ *A*   **6** One] one *A*
8 none? . . .] ~? *A*   **9** love;] ~, *A*   **12** shore!] ~. *A*

R49   THE FLESH

I die? I, that from the dust arose
And saw the stars? The stars
Were nameless but for me!
For I am eye and ear to man in all
That measures where life's universe is mind,   5
Or worlds outside the mind.

(9 October 1949)   *Copy-text: FM   Collated states: Bn,* 28 March 1951, p. 12 (*A*)   Moore
(*B*)
3 me!] ~, *A B*

Let the soul have its hour! Give it its cold eternity
Where no sense asks the rose of love to bloom,
Life's fire to warm, its joy to sing,
Or in the sky the moon to be   10
The loveliness of night!
But I, I the poor perishable,
In one brief moment can declare
All these to man, and bring to him
His utmost depth and reach. Even the soul   15
Itself I give, for wanting me, no soul
Found man in whom to house.

And I alone give man his child—
Give him his own recording self,
Father to son, and son to son again.   20
What is the soul beside all this?
What can it give to man who lived in me,
And by me saw the stars?

9 joy] joys *B*   10 Or] And *A B*   11 loveliness] butterfly *A B*   16 wanting]
without *A B*   me,] ~ *A B*   17 man] man in whom to be, *A B*   house.] ~! *A B*
18 child—] ~, *A B*

R50   THE LOOM

1

Life is the leafage of a tree
Which time has named eternity.

Leaf talks to leaf; then death distrains.
Only eternity remains.

2

Lovely the growing wheat,   5
Lovely its golden yield!
                                        [*cont. overleaf*

(2 December 1950)   *Copy-text: FM   Collated states: Bn*, 21 March 1951, p. 12 (*A*)
0.1 1] *Om. A*   2–3 eternity.// Leaf] ~./ ~ *A*   3 leaf;] ~, *A*   then death
distrains] and then—refrains *A*   4.1 2] *Om. A*

This is the bread we eat,
Whereby we till the field.
Then in the dust we lie.
Above, the wheat is high.   10

                    3
Clouds, that serve earth, from earth must rise.
In conquest over death, life dies.

Then, as again the rain is cloud,
The dust makes grass its living shroud.

Life is a cycle which life breeds,   15
Where ever on itself it feeds.

9 lie.] ~; *A*   10.1 3] *Om. A*   11 rise. *A*] ~ *X*   12–13 dies.// Then] ~./ ~ *A*
14–15 shroud.// Life] ~./ ~ *A*   16 Where] ~, *A*   itself] ~, *A*   feeds.] feeds.//
When I from you depart,/ Still hold me in your heart—/ Not quite forget! Only/
The unremembered know/ How dark where we must go./ But if, within your
heart,/ You keep me one small room,/ The friendliness of flesh/ Will weave me in
its loom. *A*

                    R51   RADAR[*]

They have been lonely for so long,
For they have lost the olden tie
Of flesh through which to call, and feel
Its radar answer to their cry!

The void lies deep between.   5
Within that dark unseen,
Maybe the arrow, prayer,
Is all that reaches there.

[*] In regard to human radar (aura or wave-length) I think I may claim
to be the first to state, with evidence, that it can be, and is, inherited. I
did this first over the air in about 1950, and later on in an article in the
Melbourne *Argus* 14th September 1951. In this I pointed out, first, that
no one had ever seen a nude ghost, and that, therefore, the clothing,   n5
accoutrements, horses, dogs, chains, etc., which have accompanied the
recorded ghosts, are immortal too. From this I went to miracles, and then

to the natural miracles of aura or human radar. This, I said, if measured,
could help to do away with divorce, as it would define a basis of the
complementary for marriage. Also I considered it would be a better proof   n10
of parentage than blood tests. A second article on the subject appeared
in the Sydney *Sunday Telegraph* 24th August 1952.

(15 December 1950)   *Copy-text: FM   Collated states:* None

R52   IN THE GARDENS

How boundless distance makes dimension where
    Worlds undimensioned lie,
As when some faint, untensioned mist becomes
    A floating cloud on high.
How white the cloud! How shapely fair within   5
    The far tenuity
We call the sky! God, Who gave chaos form,
    In this same way we see.

So man an idol makes, and sets
    It on an altar-stone,   10
That he may sometimes find, through it,
    Him, the Immeasurable One.

(5 March 1952)   *Copy-text: FM   Collated states: Presb*, 5 September 1952, p. 3 as THE
VISION (*A*)

1–2 dimension where/ Worlds] dimension/ Where the *A*   **2** lie,] ~! *A*
3 faint,] ~ *A*   3–4 mist becomes/ A floating] mist/ Lies like a *A*   **4** on high]
within the sky *A*   **5** white] still *A*   5–6 fair within/ The] fair/ within that *A*
7 sky] void *A*   chaos] Chaos *A*   8–9 see.// So] ~./ ~ *A*   **10** an altar-stone,]
a sacred stone *A*   **11** find, through] see, in *A*

R53   ON ONE-TREE HILL[*]

Old Bill and I,
On One-tree Hill,

(1 August 1952)   *Copy-text: FM   Collated states: Boh* (September 1952), p. 11 (*A*)
2 On] From *A*

Looked on the plain
Where all was still.

Nothing was there,   5
Where, once, the larks
Rose in a cloud
Of singing sparks.[1]

Nothing was there,
Twixt earth and sky,   10
Save One-tree Hill,
Old Bill and I.

[*] This is a reminder of the millions of ground larks which once nested
in the tufts of grass on every open plain of Australia. They had to build
where and as they did, because, when startled, they rose almost vertically
into the air.

Nesting in the grass they were the first victims of the bushfire, the   n5
plough and the pasturing stock. Yet they once glittered like sparks in
the sun, as they mounted and sang in their myriads.

In about 1874 there was a small half-acre plain at Houlaghan's Creek
near Wagga. One day my father excitedly came home saying that the
larks were coming back again, because in that small space he had counted   n10
a hundred nests. To protect them from the hoofs of cattle and horses
he put up a dog-leg fence round the spot. The grass thickened and the
larks multiplied. Then travellers put their horses in on the grass. These
trampled the nests and eggs, so there was nothing hatched, and again
the larks died out. After that father went by a different road to town.   n15
He had loved the larks, and they were gone. As to the fence, it became
a neighbour's firewood.[2]

---

3 the] a *A*   6 Where, once,] ~ ~ *A*   8 sparks.] ~! *A*   11 One-tree]
One-Tree *A*   n1–17 *'This . . . firewood.] *Om. A*

---

[1] Cf. Q10 lines 1–4.
[2] Of R53, MG commented to Douglas Stewart on 4 August 1953: 'I'm glad I lived when
I did, & had the father I had' (*Letters* 289).

R54   NOT MINE THE SEA!

Not mine the sea, although it holds
Me like a moon-drawn tide,
But mine the inland plains, for which no far
Horizon is too lonesome or too wide.

Give me to see again the burning sun, 5
The dry air bright as sparkling wine,
The distant cloud of evening where
It lies above the west in lines
Of living gold, which, long ago,
Old Womerah named as stepping stones divine.[*] 10

There walked Arunta's gods in journeying,[1]
But no gods walk the sea-made cloud;
For, though the very sky itself is bowed
Above some thunder-head in mass,
The night, in coming, makes it but a shroud. 15

There are no stars reflected in the deep
Like those that lit the Old Man Plain,[*]
As there the swagman made his homely bed,
The sky his roof, the very universe
A choir to sing his eyes to sleep— 20
As I, a child, so often slept,
Or watched the running moon slip through a cloud!

Nothing can dim the wonder of those years,
When from the mother-earth a living power arose
Through me no ocean ever gave, not though 25
(As some strong magnet holds the steel that clings,)
The sea-tide draws me to it, as its own
Immensity is drawn toward the sky.

[*] The long, pebble-ended lines of clouds so often seen in the clear
above the far horizon were called by the aboriginals the stones on which
their Gods walked when journeying from one place to another. I was so
small when this was first told to me that I imaginatively saw the Gods
journeying, the father God in front, the mother next, the children n5
tagging along behind, all with bundles on their backs and each dressed
in Biblical fashion. That the blacks were unclad, and their Gods naturally
the same, was then quite beyond my ken. But this is, none the less, the
measure of the average man's belief as to heavenly wear, even today.

(8 April 1952)   *Copy-text: FM*   *Collated states:* None

[1] Dreamtime divinities, including Womerah (line 10), in a role more often given to
Biami (see I4 n. 2); for Arunta, see Preface, p. xxxiv.

[*l. 17] I have forgotten the aboriginal word for the Old Man Plain, but   n10
my father explained it as meaning "venerable, old, and vast in being
rather than in area".

"Old Man Kangaroo" came from a similar root. In the native speech
its name means the wise old father who looked like an anxious and
careful man, as he watched for danger when his flock was feeding. He   n15
was described as one who knew the moment when the embryo was about
to be born, and who at once rose on guard. As the young matured, he
made the stripling males feed apart from the young does. Again and
again I have seen the Old Man of a kangaroo group suddenly stilt up
on his stiffened tail above his normal height, as some young doe made   n20
a short spurt apart, and, stooping her head between her hind legs, with
her lips remove the just-born from the inner side of the tail, and then
with her paws open the pouch and put the infant kangaroo on the teat.[2]
Not till the young mother returned to the group would the Old Man
relax his tense, high pose.   n25

The blacks never killed the female of any animal or bird unless in a
last extremity and in order to save life. As a matter of fact, the taste of
female flesh was repugnant to them. They would spear a bullock or a
steer, but never a cow. Not in our time. As the kangaroos fed, the mothers
in the middle, the young does on one side and the young males on the   n30
other, it was easy to single off and work a young male out, then stun or
spear it without disturbing the others. But at the slightest sound or a
foreign scent, at an instant sign from the Old Man the whole lot would
instantly be off.

n22 remove *Ed.*] removed *x*

[2] Perhaps the doe's intensive licking of the pouch and opening before and after the
birth: the new-born receives no assistance from the mother as it makes its way to the
pouch.

R55   JINDRA[*][1]

Inscribed to A. H. Chisholm[2]

They heard the plovers cry[*] the night that I was born,
And when they christened me a thistle-seed had wings;

(19 May 1952)   *Copy-text: FM   Collated states: Trib*, 9 July 1952, p. 5 as "JINDRA" (*A*)[3]
Not otherwise recorded: In *A*, MG's first note is set under the title, the others are set in
columns. Headings corresponding to the copy-text lemmas are bullet-pointed, bold
and without quotation marks; and inset quotations and enclosing quotation marks are
in boldface. Wherever copy-text has 'aboriginal/s', *A* has 'Aboriginal/s'.
2 thistle-seed] thistle seed *A*

How then can I sit in quiet by a hearth,
And never hear the wind blow through the yarran till it sings.[*]

Beside the Murrumbidgee, in the long ago,[*]   5
At eve the lubras tented grass above my head;
And there as in a nest all night I lay, as warm
As slept the gentle wallaby within his bed.

A child, I loved all things that moved on earth or air—
The butterfly, the beetle, and the singing bird;   10
The possum's race[*] was mine, and roads the forage-ants,[*]
Through length and breadth, swept clear of every shred and
    sherd.

Nothing might mar their roads, not even when they crossed
The powdered summer-dust on tracks the teamsters made—
A dust the ants must raise as walls on either side,   15
Each uncemented mote in perfect balance laid.[*]
(No man, no matter what his tools, such walls has made.)

And, oh, how rapt I watched the spiders spin their webs,
Or when, as captives caught, they folded up their knees,
And lay, like tiny painted stones,[*] within a palm   20
Whose wistful fingers used to mother even these.

The very cows I fed lowed soft and warm to me,
And little foals came trotting up to see me pass;

3 How then] ~, ~, *A*   sit] ~, *A*   6 eve] ~, *A*   7 there] ~, *A*   12 Through]
Through all their *A*   every] *Om. A*   13 their] these *A*   14 summer-dust]
summer dust *A*   15 walls] ~, *A*   18 And, oh,] ~ Oh *A*   23 pass;] ~, *A*

[1] Probably Jindera, s. of Wagga Wagga – not MG's birthplace, but one of the places, perhaps only a property, to and from which the Cameron family moved during her early childhood: see *Letters* 276 and volume 1, Introduction, p. xxxiii.
[2] MG's friendship with Alec Chisholm (1890–1977), newspaper editor and naturalist, dated from her publication of his article 'Save the Birds' on the Women's Page of *Wr* (25 February 1909). Her letter of 9 July 1952 telling him that JINDRA is inscribed for him has a postscript: 'I should have put lyre bird. But I kept the lark, as it *was* the lark, as an end' (*Letters* 276).
[3] *Trib* has a prefatory note: 'TRIBUNE is proud to publish this autobiographical poem and notes by Mary Gilmore, the "Grand Old Lady" of Australian literature. She sent it to us "to give a good Australian send-off" to our new magazine section.'

For I belonged to that rich fellowship can bend,
The wonder held, above a lark's nest in the grass.   25

All things I loved. . . . My father heard a plover cry
The night that I was born,[*] and thistle-seed had wings
The day they christened me.
How then shall I sit in quiet by a hearth,
And never hear the wind blow through the yarran till it sings. 30

[*] The aboriginal meaning of the word Jindra, is "where the plovers
nest".[4]

[*l. 1] "They heard the plovers cry." In aboriginal folk-lore the plover
itself and its cry symbolized one who would walk-about, mentally and
physically, i.e., one who had wings to the mind.   n5

[*l. 4] "The yarran tree." The name meant, "The tree that sings when
the wind blows through it." My father used to take us as children to hear
it sing, pointing out the small slender leaves which were more dense than
in the boree, myall, or gidyea, and which gave a silken or singing sound
in the wind. All the names of native trees, like mulga, myall, gidyea,   n10
wilga, mallee, and boree, had poetic yet descriptive meanings according
to their type. There was a reference to the blossoms of the yarran but I
have forgotten that now. Yarrangerry Station near Temora had its name
from the groves of yarrans which grew there.

[*l. 5] "Beside the Murrumbidgee." As a small child after serious illness,[5]   n15
the aboriginals told father I would not live unless I was fed, not on
our overcooked and "long dead" food, but in the native way. So he,
knowing the value of their knowledge, let me go to live with the tribe
on the bank of the Murrumbidgee. Every native child had a star. The
lubras showed me mine. They called it Jiembra, the dancing star. It   n20
was the evening star to which they pointed. I was told I was like it, and
that I was to look for it every evening and say I wished to be like it.

---

24 can bend] which bends *A*   26 loved. . . .] ~ . . . *A*   29 How then] ~, ~, *A*
sit] ~, *A*   n1–2 ⁵The . . . nest".] (*"Where the plovers nest," Aboriginal.*) *A*
n3 folk-lore] folk lore *A*   n4 symbolized] symbolised *A*   n6 yarran tree]
Yarran Tree *A*   meant,] ~ *A*   "The] the *A*   n7 it."] ~. *A*   n10 wind. All]
~. *P* ~ *A*   n11 mallee,] ~ *A*   n12 blossoms] blossom *A*   n13 near Temora]
Om. A   n14 yarrans] *yarran A*   n15 Beside the Murrumbidgee] **When**
to build up my health *A*   n17 overcooked *A*] over-/ cooked *X*   n19
Murrumbidgee. Every] ~. *P* ~ *A*   n20 Jiembra,] *Om. A*   the] "~ *A*   star.]
~." *A*

---

[4] Uncorroborated, as are the translations in author's notes for lines 1, 4 and 5. On the
yarran, see K23 n. 1; on myall, see I25 n. 1; and, on wilga, see K7 n. 1. *Mulga, gidyea,*
mallee and *boree* are derived respectively from Kamilaroi *malga*, Yuwaalaraay *gijirr*,
Wembawemba *mali* and Wiradjuri and Kamilaroi *burrii* (Dixon). See also R70.
[5] Cf. K20 author's note.

Strangely enough my mother remembered a verse of her childhood, which belonged to the white people, and which ran:

> Starlight, star bright, first star I've seen tonight,   n25
> Wish I may, wish I might, get the wish I wish tonight.

This shows an affinity of belief and custom belonging equally to black and white people.

For my bed, a couple of large tussocks would have a nest made between them, in which I slept nose to knee like a black child. The lubras would   n30 draw the tops of the grass together as a tent, to keep me dry in the dew, and against the wind. I could see the stars through the grass, but almost before I saw them I was asleep, only waking in the morning when hot food, a small bird or fish just caught and baked in its clay envelope, would be brought to me. When I think of that food and what is served in our   n35 hospitals to the sick, I realize where curative knowledge of food lay!

[*1. 11] "The possum's race." This is the meaning of the aboriginal word. The possum always went full gallop up the tree to his nest, leaving upward-going claw marks in the bark.

[*1. 11] "The forage-ants." The forage- or night-ants were in large colony   n40 nests. Some of their roads were two or three inches wide. No black ever wantonly destroyed anything. Everything was regarded as a protector to man, either as a food-giver or as a scavenger. The blacks told father that the forage-ants protected man by cleaning up dead matter. Their roads were kept as clean as if swept by a broom. One Sunday morning,   n45 finding such a road with walls of dust on either side where it crossed the inches-deep dust of "a travelling road", as white children would we kicked it to pieces. All day it lay in ruins, but next morning it was there without a sign of destruction. Father caught us before the kicking could begin again. From then on we knew not to destroy anything just   n50 for destruction's sake.

[*1. 16] "In perfect balance laid." Wherever man has built great temples of uncemented stones, as with the Maya civilization of South America, the walls have been perpendicular. If sloping the building was of clay, or cement was used as in the case of the pyramids. The walls on the roads   n55 of travelling ants, when going through thick dust, sloped upwards from the inside of the path. Each grain of dust had to hold its place against the direct pull of gravity, and resist the wind as well.

---

n28 people.] people. *P* The dancing star was called Jiemba, and Jiemba from that time was my name amongst the blacks. *A*   n31 together] ~, *A*   as] like *A* n32 wind. I] ~. *P* ~ *A*   n35 me. When] ~. *P* ~ *A*   n36 hospitals] ~, *A* realize] realised *A*   n40 forage-] forage *A*   n41 or three] *Om. A*   n43 man,] ~ *A*   scavenger. The] ~. *P* ~ *A*   n44 that] *Om. A*   forage-ants] forage-ant *A* n45 broom. One] ~. *P* ~ *A*   n47 would] ~, *A*   n49 destruction. Father] ~. *P* ~ *A*   n52 Wherever] ~, *A*   n52–3 man . . . America] as with the Maya civilisation of South America, man has built great temples of uncemented stones *A* n55 cement] mortar *A*   used] ~, *A*   n56 travelling ants,] travelling-ants *A* dust,] ~ *A*   n57 inside] side *A*   n58 and] and had to *A*

[*l. 20] "Like tiny painted stones." We had no fear of anything but the death adder. We gathered the small earth and tree spiders as we gathered   n60
flowers; the brown and grey, the green, the striped and the spotted. It was always a mystery where, when held in the hand, their legs went, so that they looked like little pebble-stones.

[*l. 27] "The night that I was born." I have mentioned the plover in native folk-lore. My father, according to the custom of the Scottish   n65
Highlands at that time, was nursed by a woman from Skye, to whom her folk-lore was more real than the ground she walked on. I have written in one of my earlier books that father always said that the aboriginal myths and legends were the equal of the Greek. He also regarded their folk-lore as equal to that of the Highlands. Though I was born in the afternoon,   n70
he always declared that he heard a plover cry in the distance.

In keeping with this, in later years, when asked by the chief of the Waradgeri tribe to allow my brother George (born in 1872) to be sung in the Emu totem, he had this done.[6]

It was about this time (1872–3) that father one day came home saying   n75
he had heard the most beautiful love-song he had ever known. It was an aboriginal woman's song to her distant lover. He said it equalled anything Sappho wrote. The only words I now remember of his version are the burden of the cry, "Our shadows meet together in the moon", and two lines in his words: n80

> The moon is high,
> And yet I am alone.

If you look at the full moon you will see the two shadows quite plainly.

What Sappho wrote (I quote roughly) was: n85

> It is the noon of night,
> And yet I lie alone.[7]

This song I never heard again till Mr William Harney brought it to me,

---

n59 tiny] *Om. A*   n60 and tree] *Om. A*   n61 the green, the] green, red or black *A*   n62 went,] ~ *A*   n63 pebble-stones] pebble stones *A*   n65 folk-lore] folklore *A*   father] Father *A*   n66 time,] ~ *A*   n67 folk-lore] folklore *A* n68 father] Father *A*   n69 folk-lore] folklore *A*   n71 declared that] said *A* n72 In keeping with] More than *A*   later years] years later *A*   n74 totem,] ~ *A* this] it *A*   done.] done. This brother, I might add, was our best family lepper and runner. *A*   n75 father] Father *A*   one day] *Om. A*   n76 love-song] love song *A*   n78 of his version] *Om. A*   n80 in his words:] *Om. A*   n82 alone.] alone." *A*   n84–5 plainly. *P* What] ~. ~ *A*   n88 Mr] Mr. *A*

---

[6] See R64. See also entry for n74: 'lepper' means *leaper*.

[7] On Sappho, see R35 n. 1. In *The Poems of Sappho*, translated by Edwin Marion Cox (London: Williams & Norgate Ltd, 1925), Fragment 48 is given literally as: 'The moon has set, and the Pleiades; it is midnight, the time is going by and I recline alone'. MG could have had access to other translations.

not far from Riverina where I had first heard it, but from the Northern
Territory. Instead of the quantitative measure father used, Mr Harney   n90
adopted an ordinary English beat, and instead of father's "Our shadows
meet together in the moon" he has "My lover's shade is in the moon".[8]
Father's version: "The moon is high, and yet I am alone", is indicated
in Mr Harney's book, *Songs of the Songmen*, in two different wordings.
But in Mr Harney's version of the poem there is something else of the   n95
utmost importance, and that is the aboriginal couplet heading the verse.
This couplet is:

> *Mid baia gi a ri ri mana yana*
> *Min bai yin gu mada mana.*

Only a very ancient and long-used language could have built up such   n100
an intricate and concentrated assonant and consonant rhyme system.
The tragedy is that no Australian or European critic has considered it
in relation either to the Celtic in its forms, to the Red Indian and the
Aurancanian[9] of America, or even to modern literature.

---

n89 far] *Om. A*   where . . . it] *Om. A*   **n90** father] Father *A*   used,] ~ *A*
Mr] Mr. *A*   **n91** father's] Father's *A*   **n92** moon"] ~", *A*   *n93* version: "The]
~:/ "The *A*   *n93* high, and] high,/ And *A*   *n93* alone", is] **alone.**"/ ~ *A*
n94 Mr] Mr. *A*   **n95** else,] *Om. A*   **n97** is] runs *A*   *n99 mada*] yada *A*
n100 long-used] long used *A*   **n103** Celtic] ~, *A*   **n103-4** to the Red . . .
America,] *Om. A*

[8] On Harney, see Preface, p. xxxv. He uses the line quoted by MG as the title of his
translation of 'A Tjarada of the Wagaitj Tribe' in *Songs of the Songmen: Aboriginal
Myths Retold* (Melbourne: F. W. Cheshire, 1949). The 'aboriginal couplet' (n98–9) he
translates as 'Behold our shades are there within the moon' and the separation of the
lovers is expressed in 'I think of you afar; behold the moon' (line 4) and 'The world is
glad today; yet I'm alone' (line 26).
[9] The Amerind (Mapuche) language once spoken over most of central Chile and across
Argentina and still in widespread use.

R56   THE WHINNYING MARE OF BRONTE[1]

I

So deep I slept I had not known how fleet
The feet of time upon its endless shore;
So sweet was sleep I turned and asked for more,
That, rounded out, the hour might be complete.

---

[1] On Bronte, see E73 n. 1. Other place names refer to MG's childhood memories: on
Brooklyn (line 11), see F152 and L7; on Malebo (line 24), see I30. Cartwright's Hill (line
13) appears under its earlier name of Pulvers Hill in H63 author's note for line 17. Two

But, in a sudden nickering down the street,   5
Came that which shook all being to the core—
A clear high whinny that the night wind bore,
The wrench of bitten grass, a mare's light feet.

And there it seemed as though again I heard,
On other nights which frost made white and still,   10
By Brooklyn hedges where the sound half-blurred,
Upon the metalled road the sudden ring
Of cantering hoofs come over Cartwright's Hill,
And one late rider all his full heart sing.

                            2

I rose, and musing looked across the Bay,   15
Hearing the world's wide ocean whisper low,
And marked the moonlight, like a broken bow,
Lie on the water in a lace of spray.
Yet I was in a dream-world far away,
Seeing great oleanders all a-blow,   20
Where, like tall candles, lilies, row on row,
Bloomed where the hot night matched the burning day.

And as I stood, I saw no more the Main,
But looked on Malebo and all her pines,
The lanes that wound between the glistening vines,   25
The golden river, and the fields of grain;
And time was driven backward where it ran,
And I a child again where I began.

                            3

And then I turned to watch the wave uprear
In mantling crest, and leap in sudden shock   30

of the MSS in NLA 727 3/6/2.1 are annotated: 'English eludes me! I am sure my natural
speech is Gaelic – something that sings itself with the song. English is not like that; it may
chant, but for singing it has to be broken up and re-made – or used in olden forms made
fixed by singing – handed down to us in song.' Another MS (same location) concludes:
'I had so much to express & language was always on the other side of the fence from true
experience. I handle language better now, but I never control what I want, nor what best
expresses. M. G.'

Upon the cliffy barrier of rock
As though some self within had flung it there!
Once I had thought it matched with man—a snare
By which at life's realities we mock,
For now I stood, a prisoner in life's dock,   35
With reason challenged by a whinnying mare.

We make no answer to the sea, the sun!
But all the common cries of life are one.
There is no life-call but has human range,
And so, though maybe some will think it strange,   40
The sound of that thin whinny by the sea,
All day among the streets it followed me.

(17 November 1920)   *Copy-text: FM*   *Collated states:* None

R57   JOB xxviii, 7, 8[1]

Dark woman of long grief,
    Whither go you today?
I go, she said, where the winds go,
    Though the earth bids me stay.

I go where the winds go,   5
    A path no man hath trod;
The vulture's eye hath not seen it,
    But the keeper is God.

By it no lion walks,
    And no young lions stray;   10
Only the wind goes with me there,
    Though the earth bids me stay.

Life's combat I have loved,
    Full harvest have I sown,
And I have loved my kind: who go   15
    On that strange path alone.

[1] Job 28. 7–8: 'There is a path which no fowl knoweth, and which the vulture's eye hath not seen: The lion's whelps have not trodden it, nor the fierce lion passed it by.'

The cup I held was full,
    Ever it brimmed in crown;
It is not empty yet (she said),
    But I have laid it down.   20

(23 April 1940)   *Copy-text: FM*   *Collated states:* None

R58   WORD-HELD[1]

When the last door is shut, not from the dust
That mounts within the tomb will time rebuild
That which was I! But in the field I tilled
Gleaners will find some little word upthrust
Above the shallow of convention's crust,   5
And from it they will bind in sheaf (word-willed,
Word-held) this very self that once was filled
With all the vehemence of life's high gust.[2]

How many, whom the noisy world disdains,
Conquer by words the very world that spurns!   10
For, though worms may devour, the word remains,
The wick by which man's flame immortal burns.
And, whether fame the brighter grows or wanes,
Only by words a man to earth returns.

(19 October 1924)   *Copy-text: FM*   *Collated states: Wr,* 25 March 1925, p. 5 as OF
WORDS (*A*)

1 ˢWhen the last door is shut] This I . . . when I am dead *A*   2 That mounts
within] Within *A*   time] any man *A*   3 I!] ~. *A*   4 find . . . upthrust] gather
of each word that thrust *A*   6 And] ~, *A*   from . . . bind] straw by straw, bind
me *A*   sheaf (word-willed] ~: ~ *A*   7 Word-held)] ~, *A*   this . . . once] that
which at one far time *A*   8 gust.] ~! *A*   9 many,] ~ *A*   disdains,] ~ *A*
10 by] through *A*   that] which *A*   spurns!] ~— *A*   11 may] shall *A*
remains,] ~: *A*   12 The] A *A*   by which man's] whereby the *A*   burns.] ~! *A*
13–14 And . . . man] Ah, though deface the word life's dusty stains,/ But by it
each *A*   14 earth] earth again *A*

----

[1] See R10 n. 1.
[2] Energy, vitality; cf. *gusto.*

R59   LOVE'S WINTERED HEARTH

Not death we weep, for death is but the change[1]
Of wandering life from here to unknown there!
Not death, O friend, but all the hours to share
No more; familiar ways no more to range
Companionly; life's wintered hearth; the strange   5
Dark stillness of the house, so cold and bare
Since the beloved went alone to face
The path that life itself must soon estrange!

O, never death we weep! But the dear head
That leaned, the hands so quick and warm, the look   10
That sought the answering look, and as a book
Beneath the reader's hand reveals as read
Some pictured page, so did it too reveal!
Here are the wounds not time itself can heal.

(8 May 1933)   *Copy-text: FM   Collated states: SMH,* 20 May 1933, p. 9 (*A*)

1 Not . . . change *A*] Not death, O friend, but all the hours to share *X*   **2** here]
Here *A*   there] There *A*   **3** hours] honurs *A*   **4** familiar . . . more] no more
familiar ways *A*   **6** bare] ~, *A*   **7** beloved] belov-ed *A*   face] fare *A*   **8** life]
love *A*   **8–9** estrange!// O,] ~./ ~ *A*   **9** But] but *A*   **10** look] ~. *A*
11 look,] ~ *A*   and] that *A*   **13** pictured] picture *A*   reveal!] ~. *A*   **14** Here
. . . heal.] These do we weep when death on them sets seal. *A*

---

[1] A compositor's error appears responsible for a duplication of line 3 as line 1. *A*'s
reading, which is supported by all MS readings, is adopted here.

R60   IN TESTAMENT

To earth I leave my bones, to friends my name,
To bury or to keep as they may choose,
Uncaring what remembrance I may lose
Where the world's hucksters[1] scatter noise as fame!

[*cont. overleaf*]

(18 July 1922)   *Copy-text: FM   Collated states: Wr,* 26 July 1922, p. 5 (*A*)[2]

1 bones,] ~: *A*   **2** bury] buy *A*   choose,] ~— *A*   **3** Uncaring] Careless of *A*
4 scatter] patter *A*   fame!] ~. *A*

Slow for the good deed done, but quick to blame,   5
These body-snatchers of post-mortem news,
I see them wait—ghouls of the lesser muse—
Poor penny-a-liners paid per inch of shame.
Dead, to be sport of such as these? The meat
They tear? My very bones held up to view   10
Lest some last shred of being yet remain
Untorn? Ah, friends, when in the narrow sheet
Of death I lie, should one kind heart and true
Remember me, these wolves would wait in vain!

5 Slow] Slack *A*   the] a *A*   but] and *A*   to] for *A*   6 These] The *A*   news,]
~. *A*   7 wait] stand *A*   8–9 shame./ Dead] ~!// ~ *A*   9 these? The]
~?—the *A*   10 tear? My] ~—my *A*   11 last] sad *A*   being] flesh should *A*
12 Untorn] Untouched, untorn *A*   Ah,] O *A*   12–14 when . . . vain!] to sleep is
sweet—/ To sleep in one kind heart and know it true!/ Give me your heart: Keep
there my fame, my name. *A*

---

[1] Pedlars or hawkers, usually with the pejorative implication that their goods are
worthless.
[2] *A* is identified as written in St John of God's Hospital, Goulburn, where MG
underwent treatment for heart and blood pressure problems March–September 1922:
cf. composition date.

R61   VERDICTS

[1]   "ANGRY PENGUINS"[1]

You who have moved so long
In a contorted world of form,

(Pt 1: 11 January 1947; Pt 2: 31 November 1944; Pt 3: 1 January 1945; Pt 4: 6 October
1944; Pt 5: 13 December 1946; Pt 6: 4 March 1949; Pt 7: 14 July 1950; Pt 8: 4 August
1947; Pt 9: n. d.; Pt 10: 16 November 1950; Pt 11: 27 December 1950; Pt 12: 11
March 1949)   *Copy-text: FM   Collated states: Sy* 9.2 (1948), p. 98, Pt 1 only, as ANGRY
PENGUINS (*A*)   *Boh* (February 1951), p. 32, Pt 11 only (n. t.) (*B*)[2]

(0.1–86.1) s"ANGRY . . . ROAD] Om. *B*

---

[1] The name of the radically modernist literary quarterly (1944–46, mostly edited by
Max Harris) and of the group of writers and artists associated with it and its 1946
supplement the *Angry Penguins Broadsheet* – ventures ended by the notorious Ern
Malley hoax (see Michael Heyward, *The Ern Malley Affair*, 1993). Many members
continued to espouse avant garde positions.
[2] *B* has an editorial heading 'DAME MARY'S LATEST VERSE'.

For whom no single chord
Can bring a tuneful song,
Who, in some dark land of Heth,[3]   5
Storm and Chimera[4] ask,
How will your hearts endure
The simpleness of death?

[2] SOME MODERNISTS

Eyes fixed they sit and stare—
Brooders, not even dreamers—   10
Seeking to bring gold from a shadow,
And fruit from a passing wind.
"Ours are the mountains of thought," they cry,
"In us dwells the all-comprehending mind!"
But only their own kind talk to them,   15
Or use their idiom.

[3] SOME CRITICS

When the little men of today
Have finished praising
The little men whom they call great,
Maybe someone will remember you,   20
And say, "We had no idea
He had so much in him!"
But today they are so full
Of the little men,
It is only the little men   25
They can see.

[4] VALUES

If you have heard the wind whispering in the trees,
And the trees whispering back again,

---

3 single] trembling *A* **4** a] its *A* **5** in] of *A* (8.1–98) ⁵SOME . . . rend.] *Om. A*

[3] In Genesis, part of the land of Canaan, here implying an Old Testament world of passion and conflict.
[4] In Greek mythology, a fire-breathing creature synonymous with all fantastic monstrous beings, and also with vain imaginings.

If you have thought of these as force and entity
Till you have deemed yourself too small   30
For even God to see,
Maybe you will ask, "Do these things think of me?"
And know that entity and force are nothing,
Wanting thought.

[5]   THE THUMB

"Intellect" said one, "is the world's builder!"   35
But from the prehistoric and the dumb
Came this: "Not intellect, but memory!"
And, lifting up its thumb,
It said: "The first remembered movement made by this
Was man's first step towards the skies."   40

[6]   TODAY

Today we stand, amazed,
To watch some far plane ride
The altitudes of space
Man's living thought defied

Yet in infinity   45
Where universes breed,
Beyond all sight move stars,
At what terrific speed!

[7]   THE CALL

Where at low tide the jagged rocks emerge,
And the slow tumble of the seas asperge,[5]   50
Here, as I stand and watch across the bay
Where moonglades lengthen and the ripples play,
Adventure calls, and with its olden urge
Beats these bent shoulders with its living scourge.
Maybe the cherubim and seraphim,[6]   55
As with veiled faces bowed they worship Him
Who boundless is, speak man's nostalgic cry
To break the bondage of this narrow verge,

---

[5] Sprinkle, spray.   [6] See J23 n. 3 and C58 n. 2.

And with the endless vast of time to merge,
Ageless, unbroken, where Nirvanas[7] lie.   60

And yet man more than mollusc is.
Adventure, even in death, is his.

[8]   FREEDOM

Words give us freedom of the mind,
And yet mind is their prisoner,
For in their limit thought is bound.   65
But, when the fitting word we find,
The mind, as king and conqueror,
Rides all creation on that sound.[8]

[9]   WORDS

Life has no words;
Life has but cries;   70
Love, hate and pain,
As these arise.

But words have life;
They stand like men,
Linked or alone,   75
Fleshed by the pen.

[10]   THE LAST WORD

The world looks at me,
And I look at the world;
And as I look I ask,
"What has the world done for me?"   80
Then the world
Looks at me and says,
"What have you done for me?"
After which there is nothing to say,
For the world is so vast,   85
And I am so small.

---

[7] In Buddhism, the culmination of the individual's quest for liberation from the phenomenal world and from the desires of ego-centred consciousness; the plural form here casts it as only one of a number of similar projects.
[8] For Parts 8 and 9, cf. R10 and n. 1.

[11]   THE ROAD

He who rides the ass of faith
Rides in easy travel;
He who walks on his two feet
Finds the road is gravel.   90

[12]   AUTUMN LEAVES

Gathered in page by page,
Where once we bound in sheaves,
The little songs of age
Come as our autumn leaves.

The old volcanoes sleep.   95
But sometimes, ere the end,
Out of the quiet deep
Some thought will rise and rend.

87 faith] ~, *B*   89 feet] ~, *B*   (90.1–98) ᵛAUTUMN . . . rend.] *Om. B*
98 rend. *Ed.*] ~ *X*

R62   FRAGMENTS

I

Gulls tossed in the wind like a flutter of leaves,
Recovered, divided, and then made on
As their ancestors did through millions of years;
But the winds were there or ever the ancestors came,
And the winds will be there when the last gull goes.   5
Only the things without will are eternal.

Then I thought of the earth when the last green leaf
And the last white bird had gone,

(Pts 1, 3, 7: 9 October 1944; Pt 2: n. d.; Pt 4: 27 October 1945; Pt 5: 6 July 1947; Pt
6: 10 November 1945; Pt 8: 23 November 1947)   *Copy-text: FM   Collated states: AP
1945*, Pts 1 and 3 only, as REMEMBERING (*A*)

2 divided,] ~ *A*   on] ~, *A*   3 years;] ~. *A*   4 or ever] before *A*   came] were *A*
5 the winds] they *A*   6 Only . . . are] The thing without Will is *A*   8 And . . .
had] That had Will would be *A*

When only the wind would remain
And the long grey reaches of desolate sand,   10
And I saw that the will is a leader to death.
Only the things without will are eternal.

2

Year by year to the old Strathdownie swamps[1]
The ibises come, and they make their camps[*]
As the first flight did when the bogs, now peat,   15
Were of emerald green, and the curlew's cry,
And the grey snipe's bleat, and the bittern's boom
                    (*Doom!   Doom!   Doom!*)
Rose on the air from each reedy leat.

And though swan and pelican now are but ghosts,   20
Still the ibises come in their endless hosts,
And down from their day-long flight, in the height,
They drop at the night to the reeds
And the ooze. And there, till the season ends
And the pools recede, they feed   25
Where the sedges are thick with the water breeds,
While their sentinels sit on the tree-tops nigh,
And utter their strange, harsh, warning cry,
Should danger appear.
Then, when the leaders rise for the flight,   30
Our hearts move with them, although
We know not the end, nor the way they go.

3

What lovely things were mine! For I have seen
The pelicans move like a river where they fished the full
            lagoons,

9 remain] ~, *A*   10 sand,] ~. *A*   11 And . . . that] *Om. A*   the will] The Will *A*
death.] ~, *A*   12 Only] And only *A*   will] Will *A*   12.1–32 2 . . . go.] *Om. A*
32.1 3] II *A*   33–8 For . . . showers] I who am/ Now like an old tree whose roots
claw on a rock,/ But which remembers how once its topmost branches/ Caught the

---

[1] On Strathdownie as a regional area, see I29 n. 4; on the stations (East and West
Strathdownie) referred to at n19, see N1 n. 29; and cf. Pt 2's theme with K17 and
M29.

The swans in all their beauty cover billabong and lake,   35
And parrots in the grass like twittering fields of green,
While to the tree-tops, from the sky,
The cockatoos would fall like showers of silver hail.

4

By day the sea is a thing of light,
The waves lift as though beneath them   40
Feet were walking to the shore.
But in the night
The sea is dark;
Prone on its face it lies,
With its back humped up to the sky.   45

5

Noon, and the void without a cloud!
And suddenly I was aware
Of motion that no movement made
That any touch of cheek or hand could feel,
And yet some inner self   50
Perceived it as a sound,
Mighty and vast: the sound of atmospheres
Drawn upward toward the sun.

6

Out on a bough till the end of time!
But he saw the sky as a silver arch, and the grass   55
Like a sea in the world beneath;
He measured how seed-time and harvest come,
With the bees like a mantle on forests of bloom.
And he heard no whining in all that he saw,
Though the great drought came and the tempests roared,   60
For, facing its loss, life still moved on,
Till death was the last thing left to defeat.

---

sun! For when I was young/ I saw the pelicans like rivers/ Where they sailed the
dark lagoons,/ And swans that in their beauty covered swamp and lake,/ While on
the earth parrot and parakeet/ Moved like a living field of grass,/ And from the sky
the cockatoo/ Fell like a shower *A*

38 hail.] hail . . . . *A*   **38.1–83** 4 . . . satellite.] *Om. A*

7

Only the vines were alive in the sun,
All else was asleep, though the wind
Went by with a rippling run,   65
Or a whirlwind leap.
Only the vines were alive in the sun,
As he, in his lengthened span,
On earth as his anvil beat,
Till the flashes leapt from the leaves   70
Like sparks from a forge;
And there, in the sweat of toil,
Was wakened the might of man.

8

Let time run forward as it will,
The backward look still keeps   75
What time would leave behind!
Mark how the water rimples where
Upon the face of ocean shines
The moon, and how her rays make visible
The unillumined, all-embracing deep!   80
So on the waves of life's fantastic sea
Shines memory—
The mind's reflecting satellite.

[*] We are told that the twenty million ibis which still nest on the
Macquarie Marshes each year are living "on borrowed time".
    In a few years, when the construction of new dams will involve
the draining of the marshes, the ibis will have to find fresh breeding
grounds or perish. These birds live on frogs, yabbies, small fish and   n5
insects. Scientists have found as many as two thousand grasshoppers in
the stomach of one ibis. The birds nest in huge colonies; often several
species breed amicably side by side. Local inhabitants assess the ibis
population of the Macquarie Marshes at twenty million. Ornithologists
have counted 240,000 birds in one colony. Ibis make big, rough nests of n10
sticks near a swamp, and usually lay five eggs. Each November the trees
in and around the marshes are a mass of these crude nests.
    The Macquarie Marshes (officially Roubaix Swamp) are a chain of
waterholes stretching for forty-six miles off the Warren-Corinda road,

(n1–27) ⁵We . . . gone.] *Om. A*

and eighty-six miles from Warren. We are told that altogether they   n15
cover 44,000 acres. The whole area has been declared a bird sanctuary,
in which the local graziers act as rangers to protect the birds because of
their value in keeping down grasshoppers.

In the old Strathdownie Marshes, on one of the first stations taken
up in western Victoria by my father's cousins soon after Sir Thomas   n20
Mitchell had explored it, in 1905, even after we came back from South
America there seemed to be nests in every tree, and if a shout or a shot
startled the birds, the massed sound of their cries, and the flapping of
rising wings, would almost deafen one. The coming of the ibis to these
rookeries took about three weeks, the sky never being quite empty of a   n25
trail looking like a black kite with a long tail. Then, as they came, so they
went, the air aching with the silence after they had gone.

n21 it, *Ed.*] ~ x A

ABORIGINAL VERSIONS

R63   ICHABOD[1]

We were the unarmed race,
Naked the land we trod,
Now are we Ichabod,
Held by the harsh embrace
That evermore evokes   5
The burden of two yokes.

One is the yoke race-deep
Within our hearts, that yearn
For what is lost, and mourn
What memory would keep,   10
Sacred and undefiled,
As though it were a child.

One is the pressure by
The hard, relentless hand
Laid heavy on the land   15
Once ours in tribal tie.
Through this we long have wept
Justice that died—or slept.

In the old days, when earth
Was ours in commonage,   20
We took but hunter's wage,
And there was none knew dearth;
Freedom to all we gave,
And none with us was slave.

When came the white man's guns,   25
The world that saw us pass
Heard no loud cry "*Alas!*"

[1] Implying moral or cultural decline: after the Philistines captured the ark of the Covenant, the dying wife of an Israelite captain called her newborn son Ichabod ('inglorious'), saying 'the glory [*kabod*] of Israel is departed' (1 Samuel 4. 19–22).

Where, as a tree we once
Stood high. Stricken, denied,
Beneath their hands we died.   30

Pity we do not ask,
Yet may God's judgment stand,
And, with an even hand
Advancing to its task,
Bid the great balance fall,   35
Equal on one and all.

Not ours a conquered past.
In all the world, alone,
One flesh was ours, one bone!
In our closed women's caste   40
No alien ruler's blood
Mingled its impious flood.

Nor made we savage creeds.
We worshipped as the high
Gods ordered from the sky;   45
Our offerings were deeds.
Now are we compound-penned,
And all our ways condemned.

Never our language cried,
As yours, how conqueror   50
And conquest overbore,
And ruled![2] We kept our pride;
None patched upon our speech
A tyrant's alien reach.

But now, should someone ask   55
How from afore-time sprung
Our once unmingled tongue,
No answer comes; a mask
Of loss, where fragments speak,
Covers the lore men seek.   60

[2] For two centuries after the Norman Conquest (1066), French displaced English as the second official language (after Latin). English regained its position but its Germanic nature was changed by Romance vocabulary and grammar.

Still, in the far-off deeps
Of forest where the white
Man dare not come, the might
Of racial passion keeps
Its ancient law. We roam   65
There free; the dead come home.

Today, hunted and shamed,
Torn and bespattered by
Pursuing hate, the lie
About us the acclaimed   70
As truth, we, the bereft
Of hope, have nothing left.

Yet of your mercy, if
That mercy be no more
Than some small dendroglyph[3]   75
Set for us on the shore
Where once we walked the proud,
Yield us at last that shroud.

(13 October 1938)   *Copy-text: FM*   *Collated states:* None

[3] Tree carving of geometric patterns, found in NSW and used to mark burials and initiation grounds.

R64   SINGING THE KNEES[*]

THE EMU CEREMONY[1]

Be strong, be strong, little knees!
Strong is the bird,

(n. d.)   *Copy-text: FM*   *Collated states: Mjn* [1].9 (1942), p. 6 as SINGING THE KNEES/
(THE EMU TOTEM) (*A*)[2]

Not otherwise recorded: Wherever copy-text has 'emu', *A* has 'Emu'.
1 be . . . knees] little knees, be strong *A*

[1] See R55 author's note for line 27.
[2] See O13 n. 1 on *Meanjin*. On Longfellow and "Hiawatha" in *A* (see entry for n1–22), see H65 lines 13–20 and n. 3.

The emu bird,
Be strong as the bird, little knees.
Swift, swift, be swift, little knees!   5
Swift is the bird,
The emu bird,
Be swift as the bird, little knees.

Wise, wise is the bird,
The emu bird;   10
Be wise like the bird, little knees,
Be wise.

In the day's march be strong,
Through the wide rivers be strong,
Climbing the mountains be strong,   15
In the long stalking of foeman or quarry
Be strong! Endure as the bird, little knees,
Endure as the bird.

I have sung you,
Sung you the song of the bird;   20
As the voice of the emu bird
I have sung you to strength,
Endure and be strong, little knees.

3 bird,] ~—*A*   4 Be] Be as *A*   knees. *Ed.*] ~ X   5 Swift, swift,] ~—~—*A*
7 bird,] ~—*A*   9 Wise,] Wise—wise—*A*   17 strong!] ~. *A*   19 you,]
you—sung you—*A*   22 to] his *A*   strength,] ~; *A*   23 Endure] ~, *A*
n1–22 [8]In . . . practices.] AMONG the aboriginal mystery ceremonies is that of
Singing the Knees for a man-child when he is about to stand up and begin walking.
The ceremony or invocation refers to the time of the half-gods, or the "between-
time" of the aboriginals, when men still remembered their descent from birds and
animals. The singing is done by the Medicine Man, so that the child may be strong
as the animal or bird or reptile of the totem to which the boy belongs. In other
words, that he will be a man, not only of strong legs, but of undefeatable legs. The
song is according to a universal Australian custom. I might add that the Waradgery
tribe on the Murrumbidgee, of which my father was made a blood brother, asked
father as a special courtesy to him to allow my brother George, then a baby, to be
"sung." I have ventured to do as Longfellow did for the Red Indian in "Hiawatha,"
i.e., I have used our own language and European verse form to interpret for our
own people the manner, meaning, and custom of the native whom we refused to
interpret when we should and could have done it fully, and with justice. *A*

---

[3] See K20 n. 1.

[*] In 1872, when my brother George was about six months old, the leader of the Waradgeries,[3] the remnant of the tribe being near us at Houlaghan's Creek[4] out of Wagga Wagga, said that as a special favour to father, because he had not only protected the blacks but had been made blood-brother to them, he would ask the last of the medicine-men   n5 to perform the Emu ceremony over the baby (father called it "singing the knees") as it would make him strong to run and jump, and also enduring.

The child was to be fully fed after a good sleep and his other physical requirements attended to so that he would be at ease, and there would   n10 be no taint or urgency about him during the ceremony, in which there must be neither hindrance nor disturbance by any need of the child. At the time named, with the baby fed and washed, in a clean plaid frock, his hair combed and tied up in a roach,[5] father went to the appointed place. My mother wanted to go too, but father had to tell her she would   n15 be put to death if she even went near the locality, as it was a man's observance and no woman could be allowed to approach or see it. It was a long ceremony, taking nearly three hours, and the curious thing was that, as had been foretold, this boy became the best runner and "lepper"[6] of the family.   n20

Father never told anything of what took place, except to say that it was very impressive, and in some things similar to Masonic practices.

---

[4] See H21 and, on Wagga Wagga, G36, H63, K17 and n. 1 and R65 author's note, line 43.   [5] Topknot.   [6] Cf. R55 n. 6.

R65   NGCOBBERA[*]

Now was he NGCOBBERA, a man while yet a youth. No pain
a man might endure had daunted him, nor any fear that he
must face had shaken him. So as he sat alone and apart he
worked upon the warrior-spear he shaped; and as he worked
his mind within him made a song, and the words were the   5
song of the spear.

When he had finished shaping and polishing the wood, he
bound upon the shaft the flint already dressed; then, rising up,
he turned toward the place of his initiation. When he had come
to it, standing before the spot where his hidden CHURINGA[1] lay,   10

(12 February 1932)   *Copy-text: FM*   *Collated states:* None

---

[1] See I23 author's note and n. 4.

he made incantation, and the words of the incantation were old as the origin of the CHURINGAS and his people.

All night he kept his vigil, the sky above him, the earth beneath, the unseen world of his tribal past about him. None succoured him, none came near him. In the long hunger and thirst of his initiation he waited. Then, when the morning came, he stood as a man, serene and calm. Facing toward the sun as it rose over the height, he took his homeward way. But now, as he went he made the song of the woman-drawer.[2]   15

[*] The word *ngcobbera* in the Riverina tribe at Wagga Wagga meant an initiate. With other tribes it was *kebbera*.[3]

Mrs C. Bede Maxwell, who wrote *Wooden Hookers* and *The Cold Nose of the Law*,[4] once told me that in looking up material at the Mitchell Library she found the word *cobra* as meaning "wife", and that the top   n5 of the hill in what is now Macquarie Street was the burial place of the *cobras*.

The first time *ngcobbera* was changed to the Australian word "cobber" was on Cowabbee Station near Wagga Wagga, then managed by my father for Mr Joseph Hannah. Like all children of that day I loved the   n10 woodheap, especially in the evening, for then it was the men's forum. There one heard all sorts of strange and interesting things. The hands one evening were greasing stirrup-leathers, girths, etc., as father had ordered a round-up of all outside cattle for next day. Tom Giddings was head stockman; my mother's brother, Joshua, was second in charge,   n15 with several less trained youths as helpers. A native guide was needed for these, and the senior men said to get an *ngcobbera* (or initiate) as, being still young, he would not have the bitter memories of the older men in regard to the white man's desecration of their women and little girls and therefore could be trusted. The pronunciation of the   n20 native word being attempted several times without accuracy, my uncle impatiently exclaimed, "Call it cobber! Everyone will know what it means!" So cobber, a trusted guide or mate, went all over Australia. It was in common use while the blacks were plentiful. When they were killed off it languished for a time. Then suddenly it sprang up again with   n25 all its old force during the 1914 war.

[2] See K9, its author's note and n. 1.
[3] Cf. *kubura:* young man who has attended a bora (Ridley), i.e. an initiate; on *bora* see I21 and n. 1. Derivations in n5–7 have not been corroborated, nor the transition to English *cobber* (n8–23, repeated in R69 author's note to *A*: see entry for n15–16) and *Never-Never* (n27–31). The unpublished 'Ngava-Ngava' (1932?) in ML 6/10 and NLA 8766 10/6/2 and 8766 10/7/4 has similar notes.
[4] Published 1940 and 1948 by Angus & Robertson; born Violet Spool in 1901, she also wrote *Surf: Australians against the Sea* (1949).

Another word of the same early period was what our men called "Ngava-Ngava", or in another form, "ngaviah-vas"; this being the imperfect more or less phonetic spelling of an ill-recollected aboriginal word, which we turned into "Never-Nevers". And once again it was at the woodheap on Cowabbee that I first heard it.   n30

The *ng* sound in Aboriginal is almost the same as the old Irish *gnah* which John McCormick brought back to the concert-platform.[5] The aboriginal word described and named the arid, inhospitable centre of Australia, to which evil-doers fled, and lesser law-breakers were   n35
banished. It was a place of horror to the tribes, and was spoken of in a lowered voice, for there men killed each other, and broke marriage totems because there was neither tribe nor tribal law, each man being a potential enemy or victim of every other. Even in time of famine (and this to the blacks was the foulest thing) without repulsion they ate strangers, and   n40
one another when there was nothing else to eat.

The doubling of a word deepens and widens its meaning, as in names like Wagga Wagga, Tilba-Tilba, Gol-Gol, Bool-Bool, Gin-Gin (hard g) and so on.

In Gogeldrie the two gs are soft. Also we must have put the v sound   n45
into Ngava-Ngava, as the blacks had no v, it being one of several of our letter sounds not known to them.[6]

To come to later times, Woolloomooloo was "Wulla Mulla",[7] and when the new pronunciation was adopted, I had to count the "oos" on my fingers to learn it. Eunonyhareenyah, "the breeding place of   n50
the Emu", was changed in pronunciation to Eunonaareena[8]—and again I had trouble with the change. The original Cootamundra ended in *derra*, then it became Cooroomundry, and finally Cootamundra. Returning to Woolloomooloo, it meant "the feeding place of the young kangaroos", the old marsh producing fine soft reeds, and the hillside a   n55
tender grass. Father used to take us, when little, to see the young ones feeding there.

---

[5] Probably John McCormack (1884–1945), renowned Irish tenor; he regularly included Irish folk songs in recital performances.

[6] Neither Dixon nor Thieberger include *v* in their sound lists for Aboriginal languages.

[7] Reed gives it as from *wullaoomullah*, a young kangaroo; for 'Cootamundra' (line n52), see I18 n. 1.

[8] Eunonyhareenyah school is located at Eunony, n.w. of Goulburn (place name listed as 'unofficial' in the *Australian Gazetteer*).

R66   THE GREAT SNAKE[1]

Into a hole in the ground he went,
Into a hole and the darkness before him;
Into the hole he went, and the dark
About him; into the hole he went,
And the dark behind him.   5

No light of moon or sun
Was with him there;
Then with a rock earth closed him in.

Forever he sleeps, save that
Sometimes in dreams he turns.   10
Then the mountains are shaken.

(26 September 1940)   *Copy-text: FM   Collated states: Sy* 3.2 (1942), p. 22 as
ABORIGINAL/ (THE GREAT SNAKE) (*A*)   *Trib*, 5 May 1954, p. 8, headed "ABORIGINAL VERSIONS"
(*B*)

3 went,] ~ *A*   **4** went,] ~ *A*   **7** Was] Went *A*

[1] In Aboriginal belief, the Rainbow Serpent, a Dreamtime creation figure, sleeps under
the surface of the land and natural disasters follow any disturbance of that sleep.

R67   AN ABORIGINAL SIMILE[*][1]

There was no stir among the trees,
No pulse in the earth,
No movement in the void;
The grass was a dry white fire.
Then in the distance rose a cloud,   5
And a swift rain came:

(revised 7 April 1947)   *Copy-text: FM   Collated states: Trib*, 5 May 1954, p. 8, headed
"ABORIGINAL VERSIONS" (*A*)

Not otherwise recorded: Lines 7–8 are set in bold in *A*.
3 void] sky *A*   **6** came:] came. It came *A*

[1] Musical setting by Dorothy Hodges is held in ML 3/M.

> Like a woman running,
> The wind in her hair.[2]

[*] Besides the simile "a woman running, the wind in her hair," when a solid dark shower ran in the distance across the sky, the aboriginals called it "a leg of rain". Sometimes there would be one leg only, sometimes several, each after the other. These were legs running. This was also said of waterspouts, one or more.

n5

---

n1–5 ˢBesides . . . more.] *Om. A*

[2] Cf. W. E. Harney's 'The Rain Comes' (in *Songs of the Songmen*: see R55 n. 8):

> Young Tamataka sighs and speeds overhead.
> Her tears fall down on this thirsty ground;
> Her hair streams out behind her, so 'tis said,
> As on she speeds with rain-clouds swirling round. . . .
> Those misty trailing clouds in midst of dearth
> Are Tamataka's hair, ending the 'dry.'

R68   AN ABORIGINAL BELIEF[1]

> Sun like a burning coal,
> Grass like a water-flame,
> While, in the height above, no breast of white
> Sits like a nested bird.
> But on the far horizon lie
> Long, pebble-ended lines of cloud.
> These are the stones whereon,
> In journeying, walk the Gods.[2]

5

(revised 7 April 1947)   *Copy-text: FM   Collated states: Trib*, 5 May 1954, p. 8 as WHERE THE GODS WALK, headed "ABORIGINAL VERSIONS" (*A*)

Not otherwise recorded: Lines 7–8 are set in bold in *A*.

3 breast of white] cloud *A*   **5–6** on . . . cloud.] far, upon the distant sky-line,/ Mark where, each after each,/ Lie the long, pebble-ended banks of grey. *A*

---

[1] Musical setting by Dorothy Hodges is held in ML 3/M.
[2] See R54 author's note for line 10.

R69 IN THE BLOSSOM TIME[*]

At the nesting of the waterfowl,
When the reeds are full of sound
And the fish spring for the gnat,
I will make ready, for the moon
Of flowering grass is drawing near,   5
And life moves in the blood.

Then I shall swing the woman-drawer,
The calling *Narmi*,[1]
And in that time of blossom,
You will come to me.   10

[*] As other early peoples did, and as we still do in the words "honeymoon" and "harvest-moon", the aboriginals of Australia in their native condition marked the year by natural phenomena, and held festival at the full moon. So there was the period or moon of the nesting of the waterfowl, the moon of the growing grass, the moon of the red quandong, of the   n5 blossoming of the kurrajong, and so on.

    The name Morangorell, an early station on the Bland belonging to my father's people,[2] meant "the nesting place of the waterfowl"; and in the

<hr />

(10 August 1940)   *Copy-text: FM*   *Collated states:* Sy 2.3 (1941), pp. 22–3 as ABORIGINAL (*A*)[3]

Not otherwise recorded: Line n7 does not begin a new paragraph in *A*.

1 ˢAt the nesting] In the moon *A*   **2** sound] talk *A*   **3** spring] springs *A*
4 ready] walk-about *A*   **5** flowering] growing *A*   drawing near] here *A*
6 life moves] the life wakes *A*   **7–8** Then . . . *Narmi*,] By the women's mi-mi/
I will swing the calling *narmi*/ In the dusk—the woman-drawer/ That will speak
for me— *A*   **9** that time] the moon *A*   blossom,] ~ *A*   **10** to me] *Om. A*
n1 other] all *A*   did, and] ~ (~ *A*   do in the words] keep in reminder in
expressions like *A*   "honeymoon"] honey-moon *A*   **n2** "harvest-moon"] ~) *A*
Australia] ~, *A*   native] primitive *A*   condition] ~, *A*   **n3** phenomena,] ~ *A*
n5 grass,] grass, or (as I have heard my father say) *A*   quandong,] quandong, or *A*
n6 kurrajong,] currajong. *A*   and so on.] *Om. A*   **n7** The name] *Om. A*   my]
Om. A   **n8** "the] "The *A*   waterfowl";] ~", *A*   **n8–9** in the 6os and 7os]
Om. A

<hr />

[1] On the woman-drawer, see I26 n. 2, K1 author's note for line 19, K8 and K9.
[2] Susannah Cameron, cousin of MG's father (*CG* 20–1), married Dugald Cameron McGregor at Goulburn in 1844; in 1848 he was gazetted as occupying Morangorell on Bland Creek (near Temora, NSW).
[3] On 'cobber' in *A* (see entry for n15–16), see R65 n. 3; on 'churinga' (entry for n17–24), cf. I23 author's note and n. 4.

60s and 70s the coming of the then self-governed blacks to the station
was as regular as the coming of the birds and their moon. The moon   n10
being male, or father, the feasting of the period of promiscuity for the
ngcobberas (initiates of a certain age) began when it was full, and usually
lasted three nights. Father always forbade any of his men to go near the
tribe at this period. In this I refer to the time when the blacks along the
Darling and down to the Murray were still tribal, and were allowed to   n15
keep their own laws.

The aboriginal year cycle had not twelve fixed months as with us. It
was measured by blossom or seeding time among plants, and breeding
time among animals, birds and fish. Also by animal or bird migrations.
Whatever names the periods had were those of what was plentiful. I have   n20
a haunting feeling that father, comparing their mode with ours, put it
as possibly ten moons, the moon being their real unit of measure. I do
remember him saying that if they measured by the moon their method
did not require a leap year, and was therefore more exact than ours.

---

n9 then self-governed] *Om. A*   **n10** coming of the] *Om. A*   birds] ~— *A*
their] the *A*   **n11** or father,] *Om. A*   **n12** *ngcobberas*] ~, *A* (initiates] or
initiates *A*   age)] ~, *A*   when it was full,] at the full moon *A*   **n12–13** usually
lasted] lasted for *A*   **n13** of his] white *A*   **n14** tribe] tribes *A*   In this] *Om. A*
to the] to a *A*   **n15** Murray] Murray (these being the only ones I knew) *A*
n15–16 tribal . . . laws.] allowed in many places to remain tribal, and were permitted
to keep and practise their own native ritual. *P* Men going alone out back, or
on strange country not yet settled, preferred the *ngcobbera* as a guide, as he was
young, more easily frightened of a gun, and, as I have heard the men say, not
having the harrowing memories of outrage that the elder men had, was less likely
to attack. On all the stations I recollect *ngcobbera* was shortened to *cobber* by the
white stockmen.   **n17–24** The aboriginal . . . ours.] The *narmi* was the tiny or
miniature *churinga* (if it really were a *churinga* in the stricter sense) and was a means
of courtship. The boy would stand unseen and swing it. It had a sharp sound, that
almost was a whistle. I remember my mother asking how, if the boy had to keep
out of sight of the women, the girl he wanted would or could know she was the one
meant, and father replied that there were always ways, and that the elder women, if
they were satisfied with the boy, would give the girl the sign, or pretend they were
too busy to notice what was going on. At the Sydney Museum I was astounded to
find that the woman-drawer (as the word translated) was in every case marked "toy
churinga". And when I asked why, I was told that it was *"because it was small"*! *A*

R70   IN THE BEGINNING

Myall, boree, and gidyea,[1]
These are the trees of the land;

---

[1] See R55 n. 4.

The Gods made them and gave them;
Life from the earth they draw.

Boomerang, womerah, spear,   5
These were the weapons we shaped,
With shields to carry in battle,
And stout nulla-nullas[2] to throw.

Yet more than these I have named
The high Gods gave to the elders.   10
Forests they sowed as the sea,
Grass and the wonder of blossom.

Birds they formed as the winged;
Mulgan[3] the eagle they fashioned;
Boomerang of the sky was he,   15
In the height he was king.
In islands of space in the trees
Set they the wide-spinning spider;
Red in the sun was his body,
Gold in the light was his web.   20

Strong as the sinews of men
Was the silk that he spun,
He the sun-lover,
He the bird-killer;
Lines for the fishing of eels   25
The white man twined from his thread.

(1 August 1940)   *Copy-text: FM*   *Collated states:* None

---

[2] Clubs or other heavy weapons.
[3] From Wiradjuri *malyan*: eaglehawk (Thieberger), *mullyan* (Parker, Reed).

R71   TO HELEN CAMERON ROBERTS[*]

She who was one with them,
    Who knew their lore
And loved them as her friends,
    Once asked an ancient of his tribe,

"How did your people learn to make   5
   The swift, returning boomerang?"

"We watched the new moon in the sky,"
   The old man said;
"We watched it go, and saw
   That it returned. From it   10
We made the boomerang."

[*] Mrs Roberts' father was "Christison of Lammermoor", and a relative
of my father, his mother being one of our Camerons. Mrs Roberts is the
second daughter. The eldest one, Mrs Bennett, wrote his life.[1] The book
is of outstanding literary value. So much so that I remember that great
critic, Mr A. G. Stephens,[2] wondering if a woman could have written   n5
it. But Mrs Bennett did. She inherited her power and her quality from
her father, whose articles in the Melbourne Press on early Victorian
racehorses and racing if reprinted could be read now as eagerly as they
were in his own day. He was associated with the owner of an invincible
racehorse and steeplechaser of early Victoria, called from his clumsy   n10
shape the Camel.

Mrs Roberts' Queensland story of the boomerang is different from
two told to us in New South Wales, the first of which I remember well,
the second only in part.

In the first of mine, the sons of Biamai[3] having grown up rebelled   n15
against their father as being old. He, hearing of it, called them together,
and so that all would be fair he arranged for a contest of skill in which
the one who did the greatest thing would take his place. However, he
stipulated that he was to be the last in the contest. All having done their
feat (I omit these for want of space) Biamai stooped down, picked up his   n20
boomerang, which all through had lain at his feet, and without fuss or
ado threw it into the sky. It stayed there. He had out-done all his sons
and remained chief God.

The crescent moon is the boomerang as thrown and fixed in the sky.
As it increases in size it is the boomerang whirling round and round, and   n25
returning to the earth. It never falls, but at a certain point of nearness in
space it turns and goes back. This movement is repeated for ever.

The second story deals with the origin of the boomerang and the
raising of the sky. (And here it may be noted that in all the great body

---

[1] Biography (London: Alston Rivers, 1927) of Robert Christison (1837–1915), explorer,
pioneer and owner of Lammermoor station in n. Queensland, by Mary Montgomerie
Bennett (née Christison, 1881–1961), author of several polemical works on Aborigines,
including *The Australian Aboriginal as a Human Being* (London: Alston Rivers,
1930).
[2] See K44 n. 10.   [3] Also Biami; see I4 n. 2.

of aboriginal lore there is a constant hint of evolution.) There was a time   n30
when all things were lowly and crept or sat close to the earth. This was
before the sky was "heaved up". (We parallel this in the word "heaven",
heaven being the "lift", the "heft", or the "heaved up".) When the sky
was lifted, man, bird and beast stood up, i.e., evolved. But the things
asleep woke up too late and remained unevolved and as they were. These   n35
are the reptiles, fish, and other creeping things. For lifting the sky a pole
from a magic pool had to be used. The lift was so great that the pole
bent. This became the boomerang.

In his reproduction of raising the sky Mr Byrom[4] Mansell has made
what I consider the world's first important painting of aboriginal culture   n40
and modern art fused as one. Hitherto these have been separate. Here
they are merged, and without one destroying the other. I think this is
the first time that modern art has done this. I know of no instance of
this merging either with Aurancanian,[5] Red Indian, or African primitive
paintings. Sculpture and carving are different. I do not include them   n45
here.

(24 July 1948)   *Copy-text: FM   Collated states:* None

[4] In Fryer copy of *FM*, 'Byrom' is corrected to 'Byram'. William Arthur Byram Mansell
(1894–1977), artist and textile designer, began incorporating Aboriginal motifs into his
work in 1948, inspired by Sir Baldwin Spencer's Aboriginal art collection.
[5] See R55 n. 9.

R72   "EVIL DESTROYS ITSELF"[*]

Evil destroys itself. Yet we
Who were not evil were destroyed.

Once out of time long gone,
A whirlwind came that wrenched and tore
In ruthless, onward force, until   5
The very trees were broken by
Its all destroying might!
We were the trees, the broken trees!
And still we answer out of grief,
"Evil destroys itself."   10
Goodness alone is the eternal.
Evil is life's moulting time.

[*] I first heard this phrase from my father in Riverina in 1874. In about
1934 Mr William Harney[1] brought it back to me from the Northern

Territory. This, as well as an aboriginal woman's love song of which I have told in the notes to "Jindra"[2] shows how homogeneous in spite of tribal differences the natives were, and is an indication of unity of origin. Moreover it shows an unconquered people. See stanza vii in "Ichabod".[3]

Today we are told that the aboriginals probably spoke the oldest living language in the world, and that in their painting they have the world's oldest art, which, thanks to them, is still living art.

In the 60s or 70s they told father the story of how they came to Australia from a far happier and more fertile land. This is too long to write here, but it will be found in full in the *Labour Daily*, a copy of which I sent to Sir Colin MacKenzie,[4] as it gave affirmation to his statement of the age (and identity) of an aboriginal woman's skull found in a dilly-bag beside the skeleton of a long dead lubra near Jerilderie.[5]

As I have written, father always said the lore of the aboriginal was the equal of the Greek, and in some stories paralleled it. But till lately no one bothered to collect the deeper lore or the equally profound philosophic teaching of this people.

n5

n10

n15

n20

(16 December 1947)   *Copy-text: FM*   *Collated states:* None

[1] See Preface p. xxxv and R55 n. 8.
[2] See R55 author's note for line 27 and nn. 7 and 8.   [3] See R63.
[4] (1877–1958, knighted 1929), orthopaedic surgeon and comparative anatomist.
[5] Riverina township, NSW.

R73   ENVOI

I have given to life, I have served its day,
    I have not eaten my bread apart;
And now I have come to the end of the way,
    By the gate of the lonely heart.

(20 August 1947)   *Copy-text: FM*   *Collated states:* None

SECTION S
Verse for Children (1955)[1]

[1] Composition dates in *VC* range from 1915 (S14) to 1942 (S8), but most were written during MG's tenure of *Wr* Women's Page: see volume 1, Introduction pp. xli–xlii and lix. The MS collections in ML and NLA show that a collection of children's verse was a persistent ambition, finally achieved in 1955. See volume 1, Appendix for manuscript locations and descriptions.

S1 ONE SNAIL, TWO SNAILS

One snail and two snails
Had a little talk;
One snail and two snails
Went a little walk.
They came to a garden   5
And climbed up a tree,
Where a jolly old kookaburra
Gobbled up the three.

(10 December 1917)   *Copy-text: VC   Collated states:* None

S2 THERE WERE THREE LITTLE SHEEP

There were Two little sheep,
And Three little sheep,

(20 November 1916)   *Copy-text: VC   Collated states:* Bkfw, 15 July 1920, p. 147 as THREE LITTLE SHEEP (*A*)

Not otherwise recorded: In *A* some words and syllables are marked with a slash (/), perhaps for accentuation, or to guide recitation; these indications do not correspond to the capitalisation in the copy-text.[1] Only 'Hush' (line 10), 'It's' (line 15) and line 28 have internal capitals in *A*. *A*'s final stanza is not in italics.
1 sheep,] ~ *A*   2 sheep,] ~ *A*

---

[1] Early MSS show MG experimenting with different systems for marking pitch and stress, and her comments indicate that these were meant as an aid to oral delivery.

Came to see why Baby
Wouldn't go to sleep.

They Peeped in the window,   5
And they Entered at the door,
And their Hard little hoofs
Tap-Tapped on the floor.

Said the First little sheep,
"O Hush-a-bye-bye!   10
You will Waken all the lambs
In the fold if you cry!"

And the Second little sheep,
With a shake of his Head,
Said, "It's High Time babies   15
Were all Away to bed."

But the Third little sheep
Never said a word,
For Baby cuddled up
Like a Tired little bird.   20

Then the Three little sheep,
In the Turning of a pin,
Tap-Tapped out,
As they tap-tapped In.

Hush-a-bye Baby,   25
    Hush-a-bye-bye!
Hush-a-bye Baby,
    Bye-Bye-Bye . . .

---

5 window,] ~ *A*   **6** door,] ~ *A*   **9** sheep,] ~ *A*   **13** sheep,] ~ *A*   **14** Head,]
head *A*   **15** Said,] ~ *A*   **17** But the] The *A*   **20** Tired] sleepy *A*
21 sheep,] ~ *A*   **22** pin,] ~ *A*   **23** out,] ~ *A*   **26** *Hush-a-bye-bye!*] Hush-a-
bye-bye, *A*   **27** *Baby,*] baby. *A*   **28** *Bye-Bye-Bye . . .*] Bye—Bye—Bye. *A*

s3   RUN LITTLE BETTYKIN

Run, little Bettykin,
    Run, run, run!
Silver stars a penny,
    And thrippence[1] for the sun!
But better than the sun   5
    Is the nice new moon;
If Betty eats her porridge
    She shall have it for a spoon.

(9 September 1917)   *Copy-text: VC   Collated states:* None

───────

[1] Small coin worth three pennies.

s4   BONES IN A POT

Little Billy Button
Said he wanted mutton;
Miss Betty Bligh
Said she wanted pie;
But young Johnny Jones   5
Said he wanted Bones—
Bones in a pot,
    All hot!

(10 December 1917)   *Copy-text: VC   Collated states:* None

s5   PULLING THE SHEETS[*][1]

Draw the sheet, draw the sheet,
Draw the sheet and over;

───────

[1] A working song or chant for women folding sheets after laundering (i.e. a 'linen cry', author's note).

We made the cloth of linen thread,
And bleached it in the clover.[2]

Draw the sheet, turn the sheet,   5
Fold the edges under;
We saw the bud upon the flax,
And watched it in a wonder.

We saw the blue, the bonny blue,
And then the blue was over;   10
We hulled the flax that made the sheet,[3]
And bleached it in the clover!

[*] *Draw the sheet* was an old linen cry in Ireland.

(24 March 1923)   *Copy-text: VC   Collated states: Wr*, 13 February 1929, p. 5 as
PULLING THE SHEET (*A*)

Not otherwise recorded: Refrain lines 1–2 and 5–6 are not italic in *A*.
3 the cloth of] it of the *A*   thread,] ~ *A*   **5** *turn*] draw *A*   **7** flax,] ~ *A*
11 hulled . . . made] pulled the stalk to make *A*   sheet,] ~ *A*   **12** And] We *A*
it in] upon *A*   clover!] ~. *A*   **11** *Draw . . . was*] *Om. A*   an] An *A*

[2] White bed-clothes, table-linens etc. were often spread on grass ('clover') to be bleached
by sunlight.
[3] Stripped the outer covering of the flax plant (to use its fibres in making linen).

s6   THE BEETLE

"Hum . . . Drum! Hum . . . Drum!
    Beetle where are you?"
"I caught a little cold,
    As I walked in the dew!
So I flew in a doorway,   5
    And found a little toe,
Peeping through a window
    In a little shoe!"

(10 December 1917)   *Copy-text: VC   Collated states:* None

s7   SINGING THE MOON

The lovely shearer of the sky
Sets out to tend her flocks on high,
Where, as she moves across the night,
She parts the fleeces, left and right,
And all her sheep have stars for eyes,   5
As o'er the heavenly marge they rise.

When at the full she sharps her edge,
And slices through the silver fledge,[1]
How bright the rainbow nimbus shows
That marks the way her shearing goes!   10
How white and fine her fleeces are,
As on she flies from near and far!

Sometimes a small and wayward sheep
Out of the flock will darting leap,
And we who watch from here below,   15
"A falling star!" will whisper low.
"Nay, not a star," she softly says,
"It is a little lamb that strays!"

A child, I watched that pointed arc
Hang o'er the forest dim and dark,   20
I watched it broaden out and fill,
I watched it full—I watch it still.
O, if that shining blade, above,
Could shear out hate and leave but love!

(15 February 1940)   *Copy-text: VC*   *Collated states:* None

---

[1] Fleece (by extension from the feathers of a newly fledged bird).

s8   THE KOOKABURRA

When the little brown knees of the spider are folded in sleep,
And she hangs on her web in a tiny round heap,

Kookaburra will wake,
And his head he will shake,
And laughing will sing,   5
"Kook-kook-kooka-burra, burra-burra.
Kookaburra-burra! Kookaburra-burra!"
And down from his branch will float on his wing.

Then the wee spotted snake in the grass will be shaken
      with fright,
And he'll hope that a tussock may hide him from sight,   10
But the bird, in the air,
Will exclaim, "I declare!"
And chuckling will sing,
"Kook-kook-kookaburra, burra-burra!
Kookaburra-burra! Kookaburra-burra!"   15
And up to his tree the snake he will bring.

"But why did you do it?"
    A little boy said.
"Because," laughed the bird,
    "I had to be fed!"   20

(26 September 1942)   *Copy-text: VC*   *Collated states:* None

s9   LULLABY

Summer shall not wake,
    Winter shall not sleep,
The bud shall not break,
    And harvest shall not reap,
Not while a blink   5
    In my little baby's eye,
Makes his mother think
    Her baby wants to cry!

The lamb shall not bleat,
    The sky not be blue,   10
The wrens shall not fleet
    The bramble bushes through,

Not while a blink
In a little baby's eye,
Makes his mother think   15
Her baby wants to cry!

(8 September 1924)   *Copy-text: VC   Collated states:* None

S10   THE WIND

As the sun looked over the fence
To see if the day could pass,
A light little wind of morning
Came tripping along the grass.

"Good morning, Sun!" cried the wind,   5
"Good morning, Wind!" said the sun,
"Have you brought a nice day?" asked the wind,
"It's a beautiful day," said the sun.
"Then I think I'll go on," said the wind.

But first on a cobweb some dewdrops he pinned,   10
And then he went off with a run.

(n. d.)   *Copy-text: VC   Collated states:* None

Not otherwise recorded: From line 5 the layout, which in *VC* is dictated by an illustration,
has been editorially aligned with stanza 1 and a line-break inserted after line 9.

S11   THE BOLD BUCCANEER

A Buccaneer he was, a Buccaneer bold,
And the rings in his ears were the good red gold;
His sword was like silver, and his strong talk ran
On the things he would do
When he got to Japan.   5

O, the Buccaneer bold, he sailed down the Bay,
With his drums rat-a-tan and his fifes so gay,

But his bold bad mind like a nor'-easter ran
On the things he would do
When he got to Japan.   10

When he got to the Heads, where a big wind blew,
He called on the bos'n[1] to pipe up the crew,
And he talked to them there (as a Buccaneer can)
Of the things he would do
When he got to Japan.   15

Then that Buccaneer cove, he tramped up and down,
As brassy as the Mayor of his own Borough town;
And he flipped out his sword as a lady might her fan,
Just to show what he'd do
When he got to Japan.   20

Now the bos'n so bold was a Buccaneer, too,
But he didn't half like what the captain would do;
And before two jiffs, a battle there began
Of the things they *wouldn't* do
When they got to Japan.   25

Just then, in the cabin of the bold Buccaneer,
A demijohn[2] of rum hit a demijohn of beer!—
And you never saw the like, for the two of them ran,
And forgot what they'd do
If they got to Japan.   30

(*c.* 1927)   *Copy-text: VC   Collated states:* None[3]

---

[1] See Q11 n. 4.
[2] Large bottle with narrow neck and bulging body, of 10–15 gallons (approx. 45–67 litres).
[3] All MSS are annotated: 'Appeared December 1927', but no published version has been sighted.

s12 SAID THE CAT TO THE KITTEN

Said the cat to the kitten,
"Will you find my little mitten,
    That I wore when visiting the Queen?"
    Said the kitten to the cat,
"It is underneath the mat,   5
In the place where it always has been!"

Said the old cat, then,
"Before I count ten,
    Can you find the hat I wore
    When visiting the Queen?"   10
Said the little kitty-cat,
"You cannot have the hat,
    For it's many, many years
        Since the old thing was seen!"

Then the old pussy-cat   15
Sat down upon the mat,
    And cried for the hat
    She wore to see the Queen,
While the naughty little kitten
Stole the last lone mitten,   20
    And played it was a mouse
        She found upon the green.

(3 August 1927) *Copy-text: VC Collated states: Wr*, 7 September 1927, p. 5 as FOR THE CHILDREN, signed MARY GILMORE. (With apologies to A. A. Milne.) (*A*)

Not otherwise recorded: A divides the poem into six 3-line stanzas. Lines 9–10, 13–14, 17–18 and 21–2 each correspond to a single line in *A*.

3 visiting] I went to look at *A*   **5** underneath] under *A*   **6** been!] ~. *A*
8 "Before . . . ten] To the little kit-ten *A*   **9** Can you find] "I'd like *A*
9–10 wore/ When visiting] wore when I went to see *A*   **10** Queen?"] ~. *A*
11 kitty-cat] kitty kat *A*   **13** many,] years and *A*   **13–14** years/ Since] ~ since *A*
14 seen!] ~. *A*   **15** pussy-cat] pussy cat *A*   **17** And] And bitterly she *A*
17–18 hat/ She wore to see] hat had seen *A*   **18** Queen,] ~; *A*   **19** While] But *A*
20 last lone] lonely, only *A*   **21–2** mouse/ She] ~ she *A*

s13   THE QUICKEN TREE[1]

'Twas all beneath the Quicken Tree
Miss Dollie danced a spring with me,
And there we met with pipers three—
Whirly—whirly—jig-ma-jee!

The first he played a dancing reel   5
Of heel and toe, and toe and heel,
Whip and clip, and feather and wheel—
Whirly—whirly—jig-ma-jee!

The next he piped an Irish jig,
His cheeks blew out, his chest was big;   10
And then, he cut the strangest rig—
Whirly—whirly—jig-ma-jee!

The third one was a kilted man,
He stamped and strode as he began,
He screeched and skirled, till off we ran—   15
And that's the end o' the jig-ma-jee!

(15 April 1922)   *Copy-text:* VC   *Collated states:* Wr, 23 August 1922, p. 5 (*A*)

Not otherwise recorded: The collation for lines 8 and 12 is identical to line 4.

2 Miss . . . spring] My love she stepped awhile *A*   **3** with] three *A*   pipers] ~, *A*
4 Whirly—whirly—] Whirley, whirley, *A*   **5** played] piped *A*   **7** wheel—] ~, *A*
9 jig,] ~. *A*   **10–11** His . . . rig] Bedad! he cut the strangest rig!/ His cheeks blew
out, his chest was big *A*   **13** one] he *A*   kilted] gombeen *A*   **14** stamped and
strode] seized the pipes *A*   began,] ~; *A*   **15** skirled,] ~ *A*   ran—] ~, *A*
16 And . . . o' the] Whirley, whirley, *A*

---

[1] A folk name for the rowan (or mountain ash) – sacred to the Druids, which may explain
the Celtic association here.

s14 HUSH-A-BYE-BYE[1]

The pinky-pinks are all asleep,
The stars are out, their watch to keep;
Mothers sing softest lull-a-bies,
And all good babies shut their eyes.
Hush, little baby! Hush-a-bye!   5

The last white lamb is in the fold,
Close to his mother against the cold;
The tented daisy hangs her head,
And all good babies go to bed.
Hush-a-bye, baby! Hush-a-bye!   10

Hush! Hush! Hush-a-bye!
All the minutes go marching by!
One, Two, Three, Four—
Sleep! Sleep! and hear no more!
Hush-a-bye, baby! Hush-a-bye!   15

(30 August 1915)   *Copy-text: VC*   *Collated states:* None

---

[1] Intended to be sung: NLA 727 2/2/4 is annotated: 'Air. From The Mistletoe Bough (adapted)' – a ballad (London: Cassell, [191?]), words by Thomas Haynes Bayly (1797–1839), music by Henry R. Bishop (1786–1855).

SECTION T
Uncollected Poems 1954–1962

T1 THE KISS

Not the kiss at the door,
That simple thing,
Which, like a wing,
Touches and is no more!
But in the written word;   5
Nested
Like some warm-breasted bird.

(23 September 1953)   *Copy-text: AP 1954*, p. 71   *Collated states:* None

T2 IMMORTAL

Ponder the line that Euclid[1] drew,
Primal, and yet for ever new,

Which, point to point of Einstein's arc,[2]
In outer space still finds its mark.

Though to the height we pyramid,   5
Euclid in high or low is hid,

And it may be, in these bare lines,
Some ghost of his great hand defines.

[1] See O4 n. 1.
[2] In physics, *arc* is a term for the measurement of space–time. By defining space as curved, Albert Einstein (1879–1955), in his *General Theory of Relativity* (1910), addressed observed discrepancies between arc seconds in planetary movements, as predicted by Newtonian physics. Euclid's definition of a straight line as the shortest distance between two points was retained in modified form: objects moving in curved space–time follow the straightest possible line.

Radar of thought,[3] from man to man
Still runs the line, as it began.   10

(23 September 1953)   *Copy-text: Mjn* 13.4 (1954), p. 573   *Collated states:* None

[3] See R51 and author's note.

T3   THIS MIDGET, MAN

Man like an emmet[1] runs his roads,
   As here and there they pass,
His roads no more than ants might make
   Amid the tufted grass.

At times, with tiny telescope,   5
   He sweeps the endless skies,
Hoping to sight a comet's path,
   Or see new suns arise—

And then this midget, man,
   Upon his back a hod,[2]   10
Builds him a little church,
   And there he measures God.

(1 August 1954)   *Copy-text: Mjn* 13.4 (1954), p. 573   *Collated states:* None

[1] Ant.
[2] Container used in building for carrying mortar or plaster upon the shoulder.

T4   VERSE

A pharisee[1] builded a famous church,
   Where he in the front seats sat; the poor
Were given a place at the back,
   Where the wind came in at the door.

[1] In the New Testament, the Pharisees were a politically influential Jewish sect criticised by Christ as merely outwardly religious, rather than inwardly observant of the Law, (e.g. Matthew 23. 1–31); their name has become synonymous with spiritual arrogance and hypocrisy.

Alone in his pride the pharisee sat,   5
  Empty the seats from the front, apart,
For the poor they prayed, as all men may,
  In the church of the heart.

(n. d.)   *Copy-text: Ovld* no. 4 (1955), p. 8   *Collated states:* None

T5   OUR FLEECE UNBOUND

Old Father Parramatta rolling to the sea,
Flings backward to the sun each shining ray
That falls upon his homely face, while we,
His children, walk beside him as he goes, or lie
In peaceful ease upon his breast.   5
What shall we write if not this land of ours—
This land that is our life, these rivers that
So nurture us, these mountain tops, these plains!
Here those we wanton slew, their myths, their stories told,
Back to the dim "afore-time," long ere Rome was born.   10
And our Old Parramatta rolling to the sea
What has the Tiber more than he?[1]
Longfellow wrote Red Indian myths in words of gold[2]
Homer wrote Ilium—a village built
Upon the spot where someone's cow was lost and found.[3]   15
But we, who have the place, the ancientry, the need,
Our tale is still untold, our fleece unbound.[4]

(14 October 1955)   *Copy-text: SMH,* 29 October 1955, p. 10   *Collated states:* None
9 stories *Ed.*] storie *X*

---

[1] Cf. lines 11–15 with H65 and I135 for the common aspiration for a mythology to give resonance to a national literature.
[2] See H65 lines 13–20 and n. 3.
[3] MG refers to that version of the founding of Troy in which Apollo instructs Ilus to build a city on the spot at which he finds the lost cow he is seeking: see Robert Graves, *The Greek Myths*, vol. 2 (Harmondsworth: Penguin Books, 1960), p. 261.
[4] I.e. our (cultural) riches (alluding to Jason and the golden fleece, and paralleling Australia's economic riches derived from rural exports) that are not yet written and published (*bound*).

T6   BUSH BRED

The wind comes in at the door,
The rain down the chimney falls,
The drips, blown under the eaves,
Flip through cracks in the walls.

Once in the city I lived,   5
With bricks and mortar and stone;
But here I'm back in the bush,
And at home to the bone.

Let mortar and stone and brick,
Unchanged, their centuries span!   10
But, in age, an old bark hut
Turns grey, like a man.

(26 December 1955)   *Copy-text: Ovld* no. 6 (1955–56), p. 5   *Collated states:* None

T7   TIME THE ETERNAL NOW

We measure out a day
And think we measure time—
Time the eternal now!
Like birds upon a bough
We sit and talk a while,   5
And then we are away.
But time, the bough, remains.

Now is but all man has,
For yesterday is gone,
Tomorrow is not yet.   10
Lose now, and all is done.
Time, his eternal now,
Man rests upon
As on a bough.

Then off he flies   15
And only time remains.
Time, life's eternal now.

(7 October 1956)   *Copy-text: Ovld* no. 8 (1956), p. 8   *Collated states:* None

T8   THE SOUL[1]

I am the soul.
I am that which is immortal.
Nor joy,
      nor suffering has part in me.

I am that which has no child.   5
I have
      no title-deeds to life;
I but a tenant am.

I am the intangible.
Nothing in me has memory—   10

Only I am.[2]

(9 January 1957)   *Copy-text: AP 1957*, p. 89   *Collated states:* None

[1] One of the MSS in ML 7/5 is annotated: 'Dear Mr Editor in enclosing "The Soul", owing to a good Presbyterian upbringing I hesitate, having no wish to be damned for blasphemy. But is it? In any case it may not pass your eye *as poetry*, Yours Sincerely, Mary Gilmore'. See volume 1, Appendix for manuscript locations and descriptions.
[2] Only the soul, in being of and from God, may share in the quality of complete Being expressed in 'I am': see I140 n. 1.

T9   YEA AND NAY

This was the cry of one I early knew:
One who had chewed the bitter bread
Of life until he made it sweet.

Lord! when it comes my time to go,
Let me not linger on like some dead bough   5

That hangs quite unresponsive to the air,
Before it falls. But let me be still fresh
And quick; still like a cup held out
To catch some word, some thought might feed
This ever hungry, ever wakeful mind!   10

The bough no feeling has. Only it hangs.
No bird upon it lights, no nest is there,
No sudden, friendly movement in it stirs.
But, oh, give me, ere my last sands run out
To take one long, remembering, backward look   15
Of love for all I knew. Then let me fall.

(n. d.)   *Copy-text: SMH*, 5 January 1957, p. 10, signed DAME MARY GILMORE   *Collated*
states: None

T10   THE UNION MEN[1]

One voice to speak,
One step to take,
A thousand men as one—
        As like a wall
        Lest one should fall   5
        They stand till all is won.

These are the men
Who, foot by foot,
Beat down the might of wrong,
        And now hold fast   10
        In case the past
        Should rise again, still strong.

No evil dies,
It only lies

---

[1] Calls for co-ordinated union action in Australia had been made from the 1880s. In 1947
the newly named Australian Council of Trade Unions strove to strengthen the power of
the movement by a policy of a single union in each industry or sector. Attempts to curb
union power through extensions of penal clauses into the Commonwealth Arbitration
Act resulted in industrial disputes becoming a major issue by 1957. T10 contrasts with
MG's criticism of unionists' lapses in A24 and A25.

In silent, seeming sleep,   15
    Waiting the hour,
    Once more in power,
    Over the world to sweep.

A thousand men,
No two alike,   20
And yet they stand as one!
    While so they stand
    No alien hand
    Can bring them down undone.

(n. d.)   *Copy-text: Trib*, 16 April 1957, p. 6   *Collated states:* None

T11   THE PROUD

Within the citadel of self they stand
And face the world—who bore the shock
Of hate that struck them as they rose, the tongue
Of slander, and the sneer of all the lesser breeds.
But with some went the loneliness of those   5
In whom the dream fulfilment never knows.

Only the proud are free. Pride is the power,
Can wait release, can pause and poise, and when
The forward moment comes, march on again.

(9 June 1957)   *Copy-text: SMH*, 3 August 1957, p. 17   *Collated states:* None

T12   HE WILL REMEMBER

Though the joy of the day is over and gone,
He will remember the coming of dawn
In the spring, when the heart,
Like an opening flower,
Awakes to the sun!   5

Now winter is come, and the dark
Will lengthen the tape of the hours
Till only endurance is left.
Yet, even then, he will remember
The coming of dawn in the spring,   10
And the glory of light. . . .
The glory of light.

(13 June 1957)   *Copy-text:* Mjn 16.3 (1957), p. 264   *Collated states:* None

T13 THE RENTAL

I lived within a little house
With broken pane and creaking door;
When down the chimney came the wind,
The ash was blown across the floor.

And it was life itself, not I,   5
Which fixed the rent that I must pay,
For I had but a tenancy
Renewed at will from day to day.

Out by the gate there ran a street
Where tired people came and went.   10
I set a rose beside my door,
And in that setting paid my rent.[1]

(n. d.)   *Copy-text:* Ovld no. 10 (1957), p. 22   *Collated states:* None

[1] See T18, which refers to this poem.

T14 THE ANVIL

Yours is the anvil, his the harp—,
  But let not grief be yours for this!
Where all is heard, together one,
  Even the gnat a singer is.

> *There is an Ear that hears all things*   5
> *And in His heart the anvil sings—*

(18 January 1958)   *Copy-text: Presb*, 7 February 1958, p. 4   *Collated states:* None

T15 A MEMORY[1]

Last night, as on my balcony I stood,
There was a sound that caught upon my ear,
And as I turned I thought what was it, there,
The years were asking me to hear.

Rap, rap, it came, nor fast nor slow,   5
As toward me on the street it shaped its course,
And I stood, struck, in sudden loneliness,
Hearing the trotting of a harnessed horse.[*]

[*] The trotting of a harnessed horse is different from that of one ridden.
The bush remembers, the city forgets; but it is the difference between
what is pulled and what is carried.

(7 January 1958)   *Copy-text: Quad* 1.2 (1958), p. 7   *Collated states:* None

[1] Cf. R56 lines 1–10.

T16 THE HALF OR THE WHOLE

O Man! who, through the flesh,
Measured Creation's might,
Drove through the rimless air,
Bade time and space unite;[1]

Who, the unknowing, brought   5
Out of the darkness life,

(2 July 1957)   *Copy-text: Sy* 19.1 (1958), p. 10   *Collated states: AP 1959*, p. 34 (*A*)

[1] Cf. T2 n. 2.

And gave that bringing strength
Through conquest born of strife;

Are you no more than these,
The engines you have made,   10
Which piece to piece you bent,
Which, formed, your will obeyed?

As you these engines toil,
As you they must be fed.
But it is you, not they,   15
Who multiplied and bred.

7 And] Then *A*   14 fed.] ~; *A*

T17   WORDS

Words are the makers of the world,[1]
Vocabularies build;
Trowel in hand they lay the bricks,
By them the fields are tilled.

Lawless is man where no words build;   5
Without them he remains
The stagnant water of a marsh,
A stream no bank retains.

Words give man rule. A King upon
His throne is there because   10
Words put him there—the servant of
The words that are his laws.

Wolves make no aeroplanes, and dogs
No telescopes. The whale
That spouts the ocean lacked the word   15
Bid man erect the sail.

(n. d.)   *Copy-text: Sy* 19.4 (1958), p. 205   *Collated states:* None

[1] See R10 and n. 1.

T18   TO THE AUSTRALASIAN BOOK SOCIETY[1]

Life lent to me a house,
(I wrote of this before.)[2]
I set, to pay my rent,
A rose beside the door.

Today the house is old,   5
But yet, as you may see,
The rose is still a rose,
And pollened for the bee.

So in this verse I send
A bud that bloomed today;   10
Its heart is full and warm—
A rent to you I pay.

For you a house gave me,[3]
And there, as long as time
My name remembered keeps,   15
My rose will climb.

(27 September 1957)   *Copy-text: Ovld* no. 11 (1958), p. 27   *Collated states:* **None**

---

[1] A cooperative publishing company set up in Victoria in 1952 by left-wing literary figures uneasy with the literary policies of the Communist Party of Australia. Although wound up in 1981, the Society's journal *Overland* survives.

[2] See T13.

[3] This second 'house' refers to the controversial William Dobell portrait of MG commissioned by the Australasian Book Society (completed 1957). T18 appeared on the same page of *Ovld* as Elizabeth Vassilieff's article ' "A Sort of Grandeur": Dobell's Portrait of Dame Mary Gilmore'. Cf. MG's scathing reaction to Eric Saunders's portrait of her: 'It was a travesty, the eyes were marbles & the nose a log . . . The fur was well painted' (letter to George Blakemore, 28 March 1953, in Charles Sturt University Regional Archives RW 114/2-a).

T19   INFINITY

Within the vault of heaven
Weaving their far Euclidean circles[1]
In the height, on their untiring wings,
In endless flight the eagles moved.
So, questing, moves the mind of man   5
This speck amid infinities.

(20 February 1958)   *Copy-text: Presb*, 13 February 1959, p. 2, signed *Dame Mary Gilmore   Collated states:* None

---

[1] See O4 n. 1. An (unpublished) author's note intended for T19 reads: 'I remember that when at about eight father began to teach me the simplicities of Euclid, he took me out to watch the eagles circling in the sky. Planes take a straight line. But dots, circles, immensity and a little book called Euclid still live with me' (AMS in ML 4/4).

T20   NIGHT

'The moon is gone,' the old man said,
As he looked at the sky,
And I, at his word,
Was back in the bush again,
When the world was young   5
And the moon was a measure of time.

The sun might quarter the day,
But the moon made months,
And the months made years;
The earth and the tides were hers.   10
With the man in her lap
She seemed like a friend,
But the sun was always alone
      And afar.

'The moon is gone,' the old man said,   15
And time was snapped like a broken thread;

(26 September 1958)   *Copy-text: Quad* 2.2 (1959), p. 37   *Collated states:* None
10 hers. *Ed.*] ~ X

Though I sat by a hearth I too was alone,
Only the pitiless dark remained,
   The dark—and the night.

T21   THIS MARVEL

I mulled above a word,[1]
   One that we often find,
And wondered why it was
   It speaks from mind to mind.

Grunted in ages past,   5
   When man first spoke as man,
The speech of all the world
   In that first word began.

(21 May 1959)   *Copy-text: Ovld* no. 16 (1959), p. 34   *Collated states:* None

[1] ML copy of MS sent to *Ovld* 22 July 1959 adds: 'I hope you know that old word "Mull," or "Mulled", as meaning to puzzle over and work out the meaning. Haven't heard or seen it for years'.

T22   THE ROOM

I closed the door on grief and faced the sun,
Lest what life asked of me were left undone
When all life's debt I paid in lose or win.
Then I unlocked that door and entered in.

(7 June 1960)   *Copy-text: Boh* (August 1960), p. 3   *Collated states:* None
2 undone *Ed.*] ~. x

T23 ARROWS

1

Why gibe
That woman is a woman?
As man
She, too, is human;
So human   5
That, since time began,
She gives her son
What makes him man.

2

Since from the boundless
To the limited life came,   10
Prayer is the cry of man
For oneness with the Infinite
Again.

3

Save that by memory
Man's reason lives,   15
For all we see or do,
Lives are but sieves.
If memory went
What would remain?
Only the scattered chaff   20
Without the grain.

4

Not life but memory makes man.
Life leaves no mark on time;
But memory has given us words.
Words are the steps by which we climb.[1]   25

(Pts 1, 2: 15 July 1960; Pt 3: n. d.; Pt 4: 11 September 1959)   *Copy-text: Mjn* 19.4 (1960),
p. 357   *Collated states:* None

---

[1] See R10 and n. 1.

T24   TO X

1

Life lends us (from eternity)
A rosebush with a thorn,
And sometimes when we pluck a bud,
We find our fingers torn.

But though the thorns may lacerate,   5
The pain forgotten goes;
And though the petals all may fall,
Their scent retains the rose.

2

Though happiness with pain is yoked,
As tares with seedlings grow   10
Life gives us still, as our reward,
The happiness we sow.

3

My songs, dear lad, are songs of age,
Yours are of life and hope.
I watch death, sitting face to face;   15
You: with a telescope.

(9 May 1961)   *Copy-text: Ovld* no. 21 (1961), p. 21   *Collated states:* None

T25   WHEN I AM GONE

When I am gone I ask
No mighty ones to follow me;[1]
No lions, tigers, elephants or tall giraffes
But just the little ants—
The little folk   5
Who, day and night,

---

[1] See volume 1, Introduction, p. lxxii.

Carry the burden of the small,
And save the world—
These were my friends in life;
In death they will remember me.   10

(n. d.)   *Copy-text: Trib*, 5 December 1962, p. 1   *Collated states: Boh* (February 1963),
p. 3 (*A*)

10 remember] remeber *A*

SECTION Z
Unverified Press Clippings 1893–1943[1]

[1] See volume 1, Introduction, p. lxxvii, but note that the number of unverified poems has, since the time of writing, reduced from sixteen to fourteen.

z1   [SOME MEN OF OLD AUSTRALIA][1]

Some men of Old Australia
Are sour as they can be,
As hand in hand,
A sturdy band,
We're ready to cross the sea.   5

These men of Old Australia
Shrink back from a righteous strife,
And, cow'ring, shirk
The up-hill work
Of leading a manly life.   10

And these men of Old Australia
Are the men who always like
The inside place
In life's rough race,
And care not whom they strike.   15

"They dearly love to eat the fruit
Which other people grow,"
Their only toil
To seize as spoil
What other people sow.   20

[cont. overleaf

(n. d.) *Copy-text source:* Print clipping in NLA 727 11/9/1, signed MATTIE DICK
Attributed publication: Junee, March 1893[2]

1 Old *Ed.*] old X

[1] In addition to the versions of THE MEN OF THE NEW AUSTRALIA collated under A12, the sheet of print clippings in NLA 727 11/9/1 contains a parody of A12 signed

These men of Old Australia
Grind the poor from shore to shore:
Their creed is "Might
The only Right;"
They preach Christ's creed no more.   25

O, these men of Old Australia
Are mad they've lived to see
The masses band
And claim that land
Should be, to all men, free;   30
That no lazy drone
Has right to own
Another man's life as fee.

They fatten on rents from city slums,
From the frontage lands of our rivers;   35
To them it bodes an evil hour,
This sharing alike, e'en a pint of flour—
The sharers alone being givers.

'REPUBLICAN' (see below) and Z1, a response embedded in a Letter to the Editor (of
Junee) from MG as 'MATTIE DICK'. (See volume 1, Appendix for manuscript locations and
descriptions.) The letter, which is damaged in the clipping and has some badly blotted
ink over-writing, reads: '[SIR, It is] with extreme diffidence that I [lift] my little pipe in an
endeavour to parallel the mighty clarion blown by "Republican;" and, if I have failed in
my attempt, I trust he will look leniently upon that failure, and remember that it is but
where "Might is the only Right" that one can hope to succeed—having taken what is
another's. Further, I crave pardon of "Republican" wherein I may have offended by taking
what was his, and, without due acknowledgment, used it as though it were mine.'

PARODY

The Men of New Australia,
Whoever they may be;
Have formed a band
And hand in hand
Are ready to cross the sea.

For the Men of New Australia
Have turned from a hopeless strife,
Of trying to shirk
That manly work
Which leads to a truer life.

Yes the Men of New Australia
Are the sort who never like
To take their place

In life's hard race,
But dearly love to "strike."

They dearly love to eat the fruit
Which other people grow,
To share the spoil
But never toil,
Nor either plough or sow.

The Men of New Australia
Will go to a foreign shore,
And claim the right,
As a guiding light,
To live, but work no more.

Then the Men of Old Australia,
Will be glad that they lived to see,
That motley band,
Get off the land,
And leave this country free
Of each lazy drone,
Who claims to own
A right to a worker's fee.

They are gathering out from the slums,
And out from the bends of the rivers,
To them it was an evil hour
When squatters stopped the pint of
   flour
They were wont to beg from the givers.

[2] The relevant period is not covered by the broken and limited run in the sole holder of *Junee*, the State Library of NSW.

z2   [I REMEMBER WHEN I WAS A CHILD]

I remember when I was a child,
   And lived on the drouthy Merool,[1]
In the days when the place was wild,
   And no one heard tell of a school,
That a little old man called Murray   5
   Was always around and about,
And the Quandary[2] bar couldn't empty
   While Jimmy had jink for a shout.[3]

And, dear sir, if you'd send me a scrawl,
   To say if he still is around,   10
I would prize it far higher than all
   The letters that litter me round
From this one, and that one, and t'other,
   Who don't care a curse for a chap,
Unless he is loaded with money,   15
   Or knows the last method of snap.[4]

[cont. overleaf

(2 May 1893)   *Copy-text source:* Print clipping in ML 3 VN/1, headed ORIGINAL POETRY (FROM A VALUED CORRESPONDENT), signed J. CAMERON   *Attributed publication:* *TemI*, 13 May 1893

3 was *Ed.*] was a X

[1] Merool Creek, near Wagga Wagga, prone to drying up in times of drought.
[2] Riverina township, in the shire of Temora.
[3] Money (coins) to buy a round of drinks for other pub patrons (slang).
[4] Simple card game, metaphorically (as in lines 17–24) a scheme for snapping up other people's money.

Now, I say that the practice called snap
   Is simply an orthodox way
Of deceiving a fair-dealing chap
   At his expense making your hay;   20
And I think the fellow who does this
   Should never be reckoned as straight,
That he, who would swindle another,
   Ain't fit to be anyone's mate.

Well, as Jimmy ain't one of that sort,   25
   I'd like to find out if he's well,
And show that I give him a thought,
   As I did when I wasn't a swell.
So would you call round to J. Harmon,
   And ask him to say if he's heard   30
If Murray is still on Quandary,
   And oblige by sending me word.

31 Quandary *Ed.*] Quadary *x*

z3   "ME AN' ROME WE COME TO TOWN"

Me an' Rome[1] we come to town, it might be Monday week,
But when we struck the office we wuzn't fit to speak,
Fur there wuz Larry Petrie,[2] alookin' quite at home
(Which of course he wuz, boys, as wuz known to me an' Rome).

(22 October 1893)   *Copy-text source:* Print clipping in NLA 727 11/9/1, signed M.J.C.
Attributed publication: Wr, 28 October 1893[3]

[1] See I90 n. 1.
[2] Union activist Larry Petrie is rescued from death in the bush in A10; for the protracted government action against him and the Seamen's Union (lines 10–14 and 18), see A10 n. 2.
[3] W. H. Wilde's description of Z3 as unpublished in '"The Crows Kept Flyin' Up": Old Bush Song or Mary Gilmore Ballad' (*Australian Literary Studies*, 10 (1981), 105–11) is based on the AMS in ML 4/9, annotated '22 October 1893' and 'Worker'. The only surviving copy of *Wr* for this date has missing pages. A print cutting of Z3 is preserved (with several other early *Wr* poems) in NLA 727 11/9/1; it is annotated by MG '28 October 1893', which suggests that '22 October' is a composition date. As the *Wr* copy for 28 October is also imperfect, publication is unverifiable.

Lookin' quite at home, boys, with a twinkle in his eye 5
That made us think o' nights when the twinkles in the sky
Seemed like God asmilin' at some true, unselfish deed
Done to help another in an hour of bitter need.

He smiles at me an' Rome, like the honest hearted mate
We alwuz knew he wuz, boys, in spite of what the State 10
Wuz pleased to say he might be a little while ago
When the Seamen's Union struck against an under-tow

That sucked 'em down, sucked 'em down, an' left 'em weak
          and wore,
When at last they struggled out upon a barren shore.
Well Rome he wags his tail, boys, an' looks in Larry's face, 15
'S if to say, "We're glad ye're back afillin' of yer place;

"We're glad to see yer home, with yer spirit still unbroke,
   Spite o' legal Justice doin' slowest Gov'ment stroke."[4]
An' then he turns to me, boys, an' wags at sich a rate,
I knew that he wuz sayin', "It's Larry, man an' mate." [5] 20

Fur Rome he mostly knows just the thing I'd like to say,
An' alwuz ups an' sez it, the best an' shortest way.
But that is how it wuz, boys, we wuzn't fit to speak,
When first we struck the office—it might be Monday week.

8 an *Ed.*] an' *x*   9 an' *Ed.*] 'an *x*   20 man *Ed.*] ~, *x*

---

[4] Colonial slang for very slow-going physical labour, typically used of convict road-gangs, here transferred to the workings of the justice system. Cf. C60.
[5] Echoes the concluding phrase of A10.

z4   WE ARE SO WEARY[1]

We are so weary we could lay
   Our arms about each others' necks;

(4 March 1894)   *Copy-text source:* Print clipping in NLA 727 11/9/1, headed BY NIGHT
AND DAY, signed M.T.C.[2]   *Attributed publication: Wr* [1894]
1 lay *Ed.*] ~, *x*

---

[1] One of a sequence on contemporary social conditions: see A30 n. 1.

And weep, or turning Godward, pray,
 That Death would take us in the night.

And yet, if it did chance that light   5
 Of day should fall across our poor,
Dead faces, where we lay, we might
 Not sleep as soundly as we would.

We might half start and sigh, because
 That it was day. If you but knew   10
How sad we are, you would not pause,
 To laugh our words, you would not turn

Away with curling lip, or shrink
 Because our ways are rude and rough,
Our faces marked with lines that sink   15
 Through skin and flesh to meet the bone.

We have no time to trim our speech,
 And mend our untaught, awkward ways—
No time to learn—no one to teach—
 No time for anything but work.   20

Oh, if but somewhere we might go
 Where we could face the day unlinked
With work—somewhere, where we could know
 That we were free, we would go out,

And hiding in the cool of long,   25
 Green grass, with aching eyes down pressed
Against rough roots, that smelled so strong
 Of growing earth, lie down and rest.

3 Godward, *Ed.*] ~ *x*   6 day *Ed.*] ~, *x*   should *Ed.*] shonld *x*

---

[2] The print clipping in NLA 727 11/9/1 shows Z4 as the first of three un-numbered
poems in a single column, the other two corresponding to Pts III and IV of B136. On
the publication date, see B136 n. 1. See also Z5.

Z5   WE WHO ARE CRYING

If only I could sleep! All day
    I work and work, and never cease,
Who long to lie at rest upon
    The fresh green grass and be at peace.

Who long for light, and pure, sweet air,   5
    For love of God, for hope, for all
That makes life beautiful, and bids
    No sorrow wait upon its call.

If only I could sleep, perhaps,
    The day itself would seem more kind,   10
The work less hard and life less sad;
    And, may be, I one day would find

That life was sometimes sweet, that love
    Was something more than shadows set
In dreams, to stir our hearts an hour,   15
    And make us weep—till we forget.

If only I could sleep! Dear God,
    The hours of work are long, so long;
And, oh! the hours of night are short,
    We who are crying are not strong.   20

Our eyes are dim, our heads fall down
    Upon our breasts, our muscles creep;
When night comes down, we are so tired,
    We lie awake, who ask to sleep.

(2 March 1894)   *Copy-text source:* Print clipping in NLA 727 11/9/1, headed BY NIGHT
AND DAY. IV, unsigned[1]   *Attributed publication: Wr* [1894]

---

[1] See Z4 nn. 1 and 2: 'IV' in Z5's heading suggests that I–III applied to the three un-
numbered poems that included Z4.

z6   TO MY BROTHER*[1]

"Some day I shall go to the holy land of history."

Pursued by one long thought he inly held,
He sat and mused, a boy of dreaming years;
He did not see the leaves that whirled in spheres
By the wind's lightness lifted and impelled,
He did not heed the outward hours that knelled,   5
Nor hear the rustling in the hollow spears
Where the lone cricket clipped the grassy ears,
Or marked him silent there, and inly spelled.

Only he heard the clash of mighty arms,
The shout of conquest by the victors raised,   10
The sound of tumult dying out afar,
The sudden rush of feet in sharp alarms;
For in another world he moved and gazed,
Seeing Darius in his golden car.[2]

* H.B.M. Consul in Roumania. His first (Australian) thought on
receiving notice of the appointment was "Now I shall have a horse—
"a Tartar of the Ukraine breed."[3]

(31 March 1921)   *Copy-text source:* Print clipping in NLA 727 11/9/2[4]   *Attributed
publication: ArgL*, 8 April 1921 (reprinted from *SnMH)*

4 wind's *Ed.*] winds *x*   **10** victors *Ed.*] victor's *x*

[1] MG's younger brother, John Cameron (1869–1949), writer, newspaper editor, Boer war
correspondent and member of the British diplomatic service, hence H[er] B[ritannic]
M[ajesty] in author's note.
[2] Darius the Great, ruler of ancient Persia from 521–486 BC, celebrated for extensive
military campaigns and the splendid trappings of his kingdom, especially its chief city
Persepolis.
[3] Descended from horses of the Turkic and Mongolian peoples of central Asia (Tartars)
who invaded e. Europe in the Middle Ages; regarded as particularly strong and fiery,
and bred as a cavalry mount for the Russian army.
[4] An editorial note reads: 'Reprint from the Goulburn S. M. Herald by request of
authoress.—Ed. A.L.' No copy of *ArgL* or of *SnMH* for 1921 has been found: the
SnMH microfilm catalogued in the State Library of NSW as covering 1921–23 contains
only 1923.

Z7   HOW BROOKFIELD DIED[1]

Tell it abroad, tell it abroad,
   Tell it by chapel and steeple,
How in the height of his manly prime
   Brookfield died for the people!

Here was the station, there was the train,   5
   And women and children crying;
And thick as a gallop of fiery rain
   The madman's bullets came flying.
And there, in his own old quiet way,
   Brookfield stepped to the breach—   10
And a man might wait for a thousand years
   For a lesson like this to teach.

. . . Blood for blood, says the law; and blood
   For blood on the earth was spilled,
As the rattling shots died, thud by thud,   15
   And hell for a moment stilled!—
Was it for this that the Lord God made,
   And gave to his heart its bent?
Only we know, at call, unafraid,
   Brookfield answering went.   20

[*cont. overleaf*

(n. d.)   *Copy-text source:* Print clipping in NLA 8766 12/10/2[2]   *Attributed publication:*
BM, 28 April 1921[3]
12 teach. *Ed.*] ~ X

[1] On Brookfield and the Barrier (line 21), see F77 n. 1 and n. 3.
[2] Despite an identical title, Z7 is distinct from F77, published in *Wr* on 31 March 1921.
An editorial heading, 'HISTORY IN RHYME', refers to an accompanying letter from MG.
In this, she explains that she has sent Z7 and Z8 as 'two pieces of verse for recitation',
suitable for teaching children that 'Broken Hill has a figure all its own, fit to be set by
any other in the history of unselfishness . . . They are not only part of my contribution
to the Brookfield Memorial, but, I hope, a contribution to the Labor movement itself,
as one of the means of touching the enthusiasm of the people – since enthusiasm and
growth go together.'
[3] Unverified: microfilm copies of *BM* held in NLA and the State Library of NSW are
unpaginated, refer variously to a Latest News Edition or a Sporting Edition and appear
to be incomplete (also for Z8).

But where the Barrier women wept,
    And its men thought tears no shame,
The child shall ask, ere it turns to sleep,
    The story of Brookfield's fame.
And on, through the years, forever he stands   25
    A man among men, my brothers,
Who gave to the full of his kind, strong hands,
    And died, as he lived, for others!

So tell it abroad, tell it abroad,
    Tell it by chapel and steeple,   30
How, in the height of his manly prime,
    Brookfield died for the people!

22 shame, *Ed.*] ~. x

z8   O, CAPTAIN OF THE HOST

O, Captain of the Host,
    O, clansman of the brave,
Dost hear the ancient foeman boast,
    And thou within thy grave?

Come, rise! And lead us forth again   5
    As in the olden days,
For now, as then, the call for men,
    Across the night we raise!

Oh, then among the graveyards,
    And from the musty tomb,   10
There was a sound of stirring,
    Of voices from the gloom;
And by the shadowed highways,
    And in each darkening street,
There came, in columns marching,   15
    The tread of ghostly feet!

"Now, who are ye?" the foeman cried,
    "That meet us from the dark;

And who are ye upon the street
    Whose footsteps leave no mark;   20
And who is this who leads the way,
    As one who will not yield?"
"We are," they said, "the Fighting Dead,[1]
    Who follow the brave Brookfield!"[2]

    There was a sound   25
    Within the night,
    A sound that has no name,
    As out of the grave, to left and right
    The massed battalions came;
    There was a sound,   30
    A sound that grew,
    That throbbed along the ground,
    As though an army's feet had found
    A place in that review.

From where they stood the dead men spoke,   35
    They spoke in a speech of flame,
Till those who slept in their beds awoke
    And answered them name by name,
Until an army of living men
    Stood, rank and regiment there,   40
And met the foe, and broke the foe,
    And drove him back to his lair!

Oh! out of the dust shall rise the dead,
    And out of the dust the word,
As memory wakes to answer a call   45
    That never goes by unheard;
And ever The Fighting Dead shall lead,
    And their flag fly, fold by fold,
As long as a Barrier[3] father keeps
    The story of Brookfield told!   50

(n. d.)   *Copy-text source:* Print clipping in NLA 727 11/9/2   *Attributed publication:*
BM, 9 May 1921[4]

37 awoke *Ed.*] awok[. . .] X

---

[1] Cf. I38.   [2] See F77 n. 1.   [3] See F77 n. 3.   [4] See Z7 n. 3.

z9   [UNTIL SWEET PITY STIRS]

Until sweet pity stirs
All we would say,
For all poor prisoners
Here let us pray.

But one brief hour they stand   5
Where His kind sun[1]
Leans like a Father's hand
There on each one.

But one small grating shows
Where His bright star   10
Ever serenely glows,
And his saints are . . .

Moons in the night look down
And, dews impearled,
Let thy dear light still drown   15
All their strange world!

Ah! for all prisoners,
Here let us pray;
But that His mercy stirs,
We were as they.   20

Gold is the aspen tree;
And, like a sword,
Yonder tall poplar see
Point heaven toward.

(24 May 1921)   *Copy-text source:* Print clipping in NLA 727 11/9/2   *Attributed publication: SnMH*[2]
6 kind sun *Ed.*] Kind Son *x*

[1] See entry for line 6: emendation is based on a revision made in MG's hand on the print clipping, linking line 6 to the nature imagery that follows.
[2] Z9 is part of a letter to the Editor advocating prison reform in response to an earlier *SnMH* article on the Goulburn gaol and signed 'MARY GILMORE. Hotel Imperial, 24/5/21'.

But in the prison cell,   25
    No leaf, no stem;
Only the walls that spell
    Shadow to them.

Set for us all—though far—
    Give back the moon,   30
Give back the loving star,
    The sun at noon!

Light in a narrow bound
    Sends forth no ray;
Life in a narrow round   35
    Faints by the way.

Pray for all prisoners—
    Whose loss must be
All the sweet lavenders
    Of memory.   40

210   GOONDAWYA,[*] FELLOW TRAVELLER

"You and I we drink together"—[1]
    Shades that through the forest pass—
Stooping to the self-same rivers,
    Kneeling on the self-same grass;

"You and I we drink together"—   5
    O, ye early ones who were,
First in all her dawning ages,
    Pilgrims of the plain and spur!

[cont. overleaf

(5 January 1923)   *Copy-text source:* Print clipping in NLA 8766 9/6/6   *Attributed publication:* None[2]

3 Stooping *Ed.*] Stopping *X*

---

[1] AMS dated 5 January 1923 in NLA 727 2/3/14 has as its epigraph: "'Wee gnallen yicoba jaleeba maroomba. Goondawya!' (Aboriginal for "You & myself drink together; good. Goodbye!")'; cf. author's note.
[2] The clipping (perhaps from *WDA*), sent to her by Eileen Day, Grammar School, Wagga Wagga, is annotated by MG: 'Chosen for Eisteddfod she said' and 'Have forgotten I ever wrote this! 3. 10. 44'.

Cup the hands, take up the waters,
As the whispering rivers flow,   10
Where the first men of Australia
Saw the summer come and go.

Cup the hands, take up the waters,
Drinking where they used to drink;
Past and present bound together   15
In one long unending link.

Goondawya! Goondawya!
Lift the proud hands in salute:
Hush! the shadowy tribes are passing,
Footsteps noiseless, voices mute.   20

Goondawya! Goondawya!
. . . Faintly, from the utmost bound,
Echo whispers out of distance,
Dies the shadow of a sound!

[*] Goondawya means Good-bye.

Z11   WAITIN' FOR A LASSIE

(SPECIALLY WRITTEN FOR THE WENTWORTH MAGAZINE.)

O Johnny, was it you then,
    And you then, and you then,
Was it you came a courtin'
    To bonnie Bessie Lee?
For I saw the lassie standin',   5
    Ribboned up an' faldalled,[1]
An' I knew she wasn't lookin'
    For a boy as old as me.

Was it you I saw at gloamin',
    Walkin' down the loamin',[2]   10

[1] Decked out with finery: cf. H67 line 1.
[2] Rhyming nonce word, from *loam* as the ground, earth.

With a big bunch of buttercups
   Gathered on the way?
I was makin' for the short cut
   Along the tedded hay,[3]
But I hit the other track   15
   As if I couldn't stay.

O Johnny, O Johnny, was it
   You then, and you then,
Or was it just an old man
   Lookin' backward through the years?   20
For it seemed as if I saw
   A lad who wasn't you, John,
Waitin' for a lassie that
   I couldn't see for tears.

(11 May 1927) *Copy-text source:* Print clipping in NLA 727 11/9/2 *Attributed publication:* WMag (July? August? 1927)[4]

---

[3] Grass cut and strewn out to dry as hay.
[4] *WMag* holdings are incomplete. Z11 and Z12 are taken from a single page of print cuttings (in NLA 727 11/9/2), which also contains a version of I96. MG's annotations of Z11 and Z12 show uncertainty as to the month of publication.

Z12   EYES OF THE HEART[1]

(SPECIALLY WRITTEN FOR THE WENTWORTH MAGAZINE.)

She: If I dyed my hair,
       And painted my face,
    It was that I might
       In your eyes find grace.

He: Not the painted face,   5
       Nor the hennaed hair,
    Could hide from my heart
       The woman was there.

(16 August 1920, revised 4 May 1927) *Copy-text source:* Print clipping in NLA 727 11/9/2 *Attributed publication:* WMag (July? August? 1927)[2]

---

[1] See H14 n. 1.   [2] See Z11 n. 4.

z13   TO GINGER MEGGS AND HIS CREATOR[1]

Mark where he goes, so much a part of all of us,
    This valiant Ginger Meggs with red and flaming hair!
He is our youth, dreaming its dream continuous,
    Fresh as of old, and with its own familiar air.

He is Australia's son, this Ginger Meggs, who looks   5
    At us across the years so much what we were once,
That we again bend down with him about his books—
    Anxious, sincere, and yet at end the wilful dunce.

How oft we filled with wrath, as he has filled, to find
    "The best-laid schemes of mice and men gang oft agley",[2] 10
Because came buttin' in, some fool who had no mind,
    And made a tragedy of what we planned as play.

And O the longing we too had that justice might,
    If but an hour, sit down with us and be our friend;
And then the bitter grief that rent us in the night   15
    Because injustice was our portion to the end!

O full of plans! O lad so rich in all that makes
    The boy! Though but an artist's dream I take your hand,
While, from the heart's hot-deep, the warm tear, risen, breaks,
    In fellowship with that red head Bancks gave our land.   20

(2 August 1931)   *Copy-text source:* Print clipping in NLA 727 11/9/2   *Attributed publication:* None

10 oft *Ed.*] aft *x*   **19** heart's *Ed.*] hearts *x*   breaks, *Ed.*] ~. *x*

[1] Ginger Meggs first appeared in 1921 in the comic strip 'Us Fellers' in the children's section of the *Sunday Sun*; within a year the strip was a major feature and its creator, James C. Bancks (1889–1952), became at one time the highest paid cartoonist in Australia. On MG's enthusiasm for Ginger Meggs, see also R24 n. 1.
[2] From 'To a Mouse on Turning Her Up in her Nest with the Plough, November 1785': *The Poems of Robert Burns* (1896).

z14   PRO PATRIA[1]

A Squawk Machine[2] squealed loud and long,
    It squealed to friend and foe,
"There's a great big Convoy just arrived,
    And I am letting you know!"
The painted girls came hurrying in,   5
    Sweating disease and sin,
Till soldiers, sailors, and shore-men
    Were sheep within their pen.

The Squawk Machine went squealing on,
    Disease came boldly forth,   10
And marched along with the Services,
    To west, and east, and north;
And as the Squawk the louder squealed,
    A spy with listening ear,
Cried "Ha! Ha-ha! How good it is   15
    That friendly Squawk to hear!"

"For waste of men comes where it squeals,
    Disease where mass in groups
The painted girls who work for me
    To decimate the troops;   20
Though guns are dear, the girls are cheap,
    And cheaper still disease,
So I shout 'Banzai!'[3] for the Squawk Machine,
    So good to the Japanese."

                        [cont. overleaf

(26 April 1943)   *Copy-text source:* Print clipping in NLA 727 11/9/2, signed Patriot[4]
Attributed publication: KCT, 29 April 1943

7 shore-men *Ed.*] ~, x

[1] See P1 n. 1.
[2] Instrument for making ugly noise: here, metaphorical for careless gossip threatening wartime security (see composition date).
[3] Commonly regarded as a war cry but its literal sense of 'ten thousand years (of life)' makes it also a popular expression of happiness or congratulation – here, ironic.
[4] MG has marked up the clipping with revisions and added the publication reference and her initials against the signature.

And was spread from mouth to mouth,   25
  Maybe to a submarine,
The news of a Convoy starting out,
  Or of Leave-men just come in.

APPENDIX

COMPOSITION DATES OF THE POEMS

A S THE Preface explains, composition dates can be important for the interpretation of Gilmore's poems. Accordingly, this Appendix provides a list of all of her published poems in the chronological order of their composition.

Composition dates given are the earliest recorded. They are established by:

- Gilmore's annotations to MSS, print clippings, and the occasional date added to journal-published poems, although this is cited only if not ante-dated by a MS; or
- publication, whether in a journal or collection, as this provides a terminal date, indicated here as, for example, 'By 1910'.

Gilmore commonly provided composition dates on first drafts and kept that date on revised MSS. Two factors complicate the reliability of these annotations. It is not always possible to be sure whether the annotated date refers to composition, publication or the sending of a poem out for publication (although such dates are usually preceded by 'Published' or 'Sent' and the name of the relevant publication). When preparing to deposit her papers in library collections she sometimes annotated retrospectively and imprecisely, for example, '1880s' (B62) or '*c.* 1887' (A3). A further complication is that when preparing a final typescript for publication Gilmore usually removed the composition date. In the absence of other MS resources, notably with *The Wild Swan*, poems can be dated only by year of publication. In ordering this list, as elsewhere, all year dates are treated as being the first day of the year; poems dated only by the month are treated similarly.

Revision dates on MSS are very rare (see volume 1, Introduction, n. 98). For instance, MSS of B16, R67 and R68 bear a revision date but no composition date; B93, M67 and Z12 bear both: all cases are noted.

1880s, B62

c. 1887, A3
1 March 1887, A1

1888, A4, A5
November 1888, A2

1892, B103
9 April 1892, B20
30 July 1892, B128
14 August 1892, B106
18 September 1892, A6

By 1893, Z1
29 April 1893, B16 (rev.), B98
2 May 1893, A7, Z2
1 September 1893, B35
By 2 September 1893, A8, A9
2 September 1893, A10
12 September 1893, A11
19 September 1893, B5
2 October 1893, B99
22 October 1893, A21, Z3
December 1893, A13

January 1894, A14, A15, A20, A22, B127
17 February 1894, A19
By 24 February 1894, A16
24 February 1894, A17
26 February 1894, A30
28 February 1894, B136 Pt I
1 March 1894, B136 Pt II
2 March 1894, Z5
4 March 1894, Z4
11 March 1894, B24
By 24 March 1894, A18
1 April 1894, B136 Pt III
15 April 1894, B17, B38
By 13 October 1894, A23
14 October 1894, B102

1895, A27, B60
June 1895, B49
20 July 1895, A25
By 31 August 1895, A26
26 November 1895 (rev. 24 February 1906), B93
30 November 1895, A30b, A47
2 December 1895, B61
4 December 1895, A42
9 December 1895, B63
18 December 1895, A29, B27, B131
19 December 1895, B76

1896, B1, B22, B72
14 February 1896, B74
20 February 1896, A33
21 April 1896, B75
By 24 April 1896, A28

By 10 April 1897, A30a
By November 1897, A31

1898?, A35
c. 1898, A36
1898, B71
By February 1898, A32
6 February 1898, B101
22 April 1898, A34
16 August 1898, B83

1899, B10

1901, B80
12 July 1901, A38
21 September 1901, A39

1902, B105
July 1902, B59
17 August 1902, B2, B81
18 August 1902, B68
20 August 1902, B54, B79

27 August 1902, B32
31 August 1902, B21, B123
14 September 1902, A37
By 4 October 1902, B11
13 November 1902, B46
By 22 November 1902, B25
24 November 1902, B86
6 December 1902, B69
14 December 1902, A40

1903, B89, B92
By 3 January 1903, B30
By 14 February 1903, B33, B125
4 March 1903, A41, B70
13 March 1903, B41, B66
17 March 1903, B64
21 March 1903, B29
By 28 March 1903, B78
18 April 1903, B15, B114
20 April 1903, B3, B8, B91
22 April 1903, B23
26 April 1903, B7
29 April 1903, B112
30 April 1903, B43, B44
17 June 1903, A52
18 June 1903, B115
20 June 1903, A44, B31
25 June 1903, B36
1 July 1903, B52
4 July 1903, B39, B73, B77
8 August 1903, B53
3 September 1903, B19
14 September 1903, B55
2 October 1903, B48
By 10 October 1903, A43
12 October 1903, B6
23 October 1903, B56
4 November 1903, B14

12 February 1904, B37
11 April 1904, B85
19 April 1904, B87
By 7 May 1904, B28
15 May 1904, B88
2 June 1904, B82
5 June 1904, B51, B67

By 13 July 1904, A46
By 16 July 1904, B26
19 July 1904, B42

1905, B100
17 April 1905, B133
5 June 1905, B13, B90, B116
20 June 1905, B18
By 1 July 1905, A48
By 23 December 1905, A49

1907, B96
11 February 1907, B120
2 March 1907, B135
30 March 1907, B47
3 April 1907, B40, B84
4 April 1907, B111
11 April 1907, B113
7 May 1907, B110
5 June 1907, B95, B109
6 June 1907, B94
7 October 1907, A50
8 October 1907, B58

1908, B107
By 2 January 1908, A51
5 June 1908, B97
22 June 1908, B34
By September 1908, B126
26 December 1908, A53

19 January 1909, B45
17 February 1909, B50, C4
17 July 1909, B108, B124
7 September 1909, B57
16 September 1909, B130
21 September 1909, B4
22 September 1909, B65, B117
24 September 1909, B118, B121
25 September 1909, B119
27 September 1909, B12
30 September 1909, B122
By December 1909, B104

By 1910, B9, B132, B134, B136 Pt IV
9 January 1910, B129

12 March 1910, C5
23 March 1910, B137
24 March 1910, C10
25 March 1910, E48
26 March 1910, C1
20 July 1910, C3
21 July 1910, M59
27 July 1910, C6
By 10 November 1910, C2

9 May 1911, D4
14 July 1911, C7
13 September 1911, E12
17 September 1911, E74
21 November 1911, C9

27 September 1912, C12
6 October 1912, E79
By 12 December 1912, C8

1–3 January 1913, E53
10 January 1913, C11
21 January – 2 February 1913, E51
25 January 1913, C31
4 March 1913, C19
10 March 1913, C15
14 March 1913, C33, E59
22 March 1913, C20, C24, E9, E52
23 March 1913, C25
30 March 1913, D3
April 1913, C17
1 April 1913, C30
3 April 1913, C14
7 April 1913, E78, E79
By 10 April 1913, C13
16–17 April 1913, C32
By 15 May 1913, C16
25 June 1913, E73
By 17 July 1913, C18

2 January 1914, C21
4 January 1914, E33
5 January 1914, E84
17 January 1914, C29, E56
By 5 February 1914, C22
8 February 1914, C52

16 March 1914, C23, C26
22 March 1914, E40
23 March 1914, E46
5 April 1914, E45
14 April 1914, E55
21 May 1914, C28
22 May 1914, E22
By 11 June 1914, C27
1 July 1914, E24
18 October 1914, E63
10 November 1914, C37

14 February 1915, C36
16 April 1915, C35
By 29 April 1915, C34
By 15 May 1915, E60
27 May 1915, E18
June 1915, C38
13 July 1915, C48, E65
By 15 July 1915, C39
15 July 1915, E44, F64
16 July 1915, C47
28 July 1915, C42
30 August 1915, S14
4 September 1915, C51
17 September 1915, C40
28 October 1915, C46
29 October 1915, C44
22 November 1915, C41
27 November 1915, C43
29 November 1915, C57
By 30 December 1915, C45

1916, E87
18 March 1916, E3
2 April 1916, K61
17 July 1916, C49
21 July 1916, C50
11 August 1916, E19
13 August 1916, E6
15 August 1916, E16
15–16 August 1916, E90
3 September 1916, C54
4–5 September 1916, E66
5 September 1916, E83
6 September 1916, E23, E77

9 September 1916, E64
21 September 1916, C53
By 2 November 1916, E80
4 November 1916, E21 Pt VI
8 November 1916, E21 Pts II, III
9 November 1916, E21 Pts I, VII
12 November 1916, E21 Pt VIII
13 November 1916, E34
15 November 1916, E21 Pts IX, X
20 November 1916, E38, S2
23 November 1916, E28
26 November 1916, E21 Pt V
1 December 1916, F41
23 December 1916, C55
26 December 1916, E14
28 December 1916, E36

By 1917, D1, D2
8 January 1917, I105
11 January 1917, C56
14 January 1917, E39
22 January 1917, E72
26 January 1917, E71
2 February 1917, E86
15 March 1917, E47
16 March 1917, F1, K90
30 June 1917, E58
1 July 1917, E68
17 July 1917, E13
18 July 1917, F75
August 1917, E10, E27, E89, F82
8 August 1917, E67, F73
10 August 1917, C58
11 August 1917, E2
22 August 1917, C65
30 August 1917, F74
By 2 September 1917, E92
By 6 September 1917, C59
9 September 1917, S3
10 September 1917, F80
18 September 1917, E25, E26
25 September 1917, F4, K89
By 27 September 1917, C60
3 October 1917, E75
12 October 1917, C61
21 October 1917, E31

23 October 1917, E62
By November 1917, C63
November 1917, C62
1 November 1917, E1 Pts III, IV, H95
3 November 1917 , E1 Pts V–VII
4 November 1917, E82
11 November 1917, E61
14 November 1917, E76
21 November 1917, C64, F12
22 November 1917, C66, F3
26 November 1917, J72
By December 1917, C63
1 December 1917, E37
8 December 1917, F48
10 December 1917, E15, E69, S1, S4,
    S6
15 December 1917, J68

By 1918, E1 Pt II, E17, E21 Pt IV,
    E32, E42, E57, E93, E94, E95, E96,
    E97, E98, E99
3 January 1918, F78
4 January 1918, E43
By 10 January 1918, F2
14 January 1918, E29
By 24 January 1918, E88
By February 1918, E54
2 February 1918, F5
14 February 1918, E11
20 February 1918, E4, F10
28 February 1918, E41
By March 1918, F6
8 March 1918, E5
10 March 1918, E91
24 March 1918, F7
31 March 1918, E7
3 April 1918, F8
7 April 1918, E1 Pt I
17 April 1918, F11
14 May 1918, E30
By 16 May 1918, F9
17 May 1918, F14
25 May 1918, E70
21 June 1918, E8
2 July 1918, E35
6 July 1918, E85

7 July 1918, E21
27 July 1918, E50
By 1 August 1918, F13
3 August 1918, F47
4 August 1918, E49
By 15 August 1918, F15
27 September 1918, I139
By 24 October 1918, F16,
By November 1918, F17
By 7 November 1918, F18
12 November 1918, F19
By December 1918, F20
By 5 December 1918, F21
18 December 1918, F25
By 19 December 1918, F22
29 December 1918, M91, P1 (rev. 19
    February 1933 and 11 April 1940)

By 16 January 1919, F23, F24
2 February 1919, F51 Pt II
By 20 February 1919, F26
26 February 1919, F29, F30
By March 1919, F27
2 March 1919, F28
5 March 1919, K86
By 10 April 1919, F31
25 April 1919, G28
27 April 1919, I84
By 1 May 1919, F32
3 May 1919, K113
7 May 1919, F102
8 May 1919, F39
10 May 1919, K97, K112, M110
11 May 1919, K107
12 May 1919, F40
By 15 May 1919, F33
17 May 1919, F35
18 May 1919, F45
By 22 May 1919, F34
25 May 1919, F43
28 May 1919, F36, F37, K111
1 June 1919, F38
3 August 1919, F42
14 September 1919, F44
26 October 1919, F49
12 November 1919, M69

23 November 1919, F52
24 December 1919, F53

By 1920, M19
1920, F46
4 January 1920, F50
17 January 1920, K83
By February 1920, F51 Pt I
4 February 1920, F54
7 February 1920, I85
10 February 1920, F88
18 February 1920, F65, G15
19 February 1920, F66, K37
28 February 1920, K44
2 March 1920, F149
7 March 1920, K94
16 March 1920, F55
29 March 1920, I72
31 March 1920, G38
2 April 1920, F122
25 May 1920, F57, F58,
By 3 June 1920, F56
4 June 1920, F59
11 June 1920, F61
13 June 1920, F60
2 August 1920, K35
16 August 1920, Z12 (rev. 4 May
    1927)
22 August 1920, K115
23–25 August 1920, J21
25 August 1920, J26
23 September 1920, F62
26 September 1920, J86
27 September 1920, K55
7 October 1920, F71
21 October 1920, F63, F76
24 October 1920, F68
26 October 1920, M60
1 November 1920, F67, F70
5 November 1920, K56 Pt II
11 November 1920, F91
14 November 1920, J65
17 November 1920, F97, R56
18 November 1920, J46
19 November 1920, I115, J14
20 November 1920, F87, M112

21 November 1920, M37
24 November 1920, M101
26 November 1920, M118
2 December 1920, F69

1921, F79
26 February 1921, K56 Pt 1
By March 1921, F72
23 March 1921, F77
26 March 1921, F92
29 March 1921, F81
31 March 1921, Z6
By April 1921, Z7
2 April 1921, M56
17 April 1921, J8
By May 1921, Z8
1 May 1921, F83
2 May 1921, F85
10 May 1921, F84
18 May 1921, J62
19 May 1921, J70
24 May 1921, Z9
By 26 May 1921, F86
5 July 1921, F89
11 July 1921, M20
18 July 1921, J94
19 August 1921, H26
11 September 1921, J63
12 September 1921, F90
1 October 1921, K84
2 October 1921, J54
9 October 1921, F103
11 October 1921, J48
12 October 1921, J79
23 October 1921, M119
11 November 1921, F94
12 November 1921, F99
28 November 1921, G16
29 November 1921, F98
By 1 December 1921, F93
1 December 1921, J71
20 December 1921, J16
22 December 1921, J3
24 December 1921, J9
25 December 1921, J4
26 December 1921, J76

By 5 January 1922, F95
By 19 January 1922, F96
24 January 1922, F144
2 February 1922, F133
7 March 1922, F100
8 March 1922, F107, F108, K29
9 March 1922, F101
12 April 1922, J23
15 April 1922, S13
23 April 1922, J15
9 July 1922, F104
18 July 1922, R60
24 July 1922, F105
27 July 1922, M38
29 July 1922, F109
By September 1922, F106
30 September 1922, F160
12 October 1922, F113, F116
14 October 1922, F115
15 October 1922, M39
23 October 1922, F123
29 October 1922, F110, G12
30 October 1922, I90
1 November 1922, M121
11 November 1922, G8
14 November 1922, G11
16 November 1922, F112
By 22 November 1922 F111
5 December 1922, J81
By 6 December 1922, F114
6 December 1922, J69

1923, F138
By 3 January 1923, F117
5 January 1923, Z10
8 January 1923, F119
20 January 1923, F121
By 31 January 1923, F118
c. February 1923, K54
5 March 1923, F120
7 March 1923, J18
23 March 1923, J25
24 March 1923, S5
25 March 1923, L5
4 April 1923, F131, F132
8 April 1923, F126, F141, G18

9 April 1923, F128, G10, H16
16 April 1923, H72 (rev. 11 October
      1927)
17 April 1923, G9
18 April 1923, G26
20 April 1923, F124, J17
21 April 1923, F129, J50
22 April 1923, I140
25 April 1923, J97
26 April 1923, F125
29 April 1923, M92
7 May 1923, F127
8 May 1923, I2
11 May 1923, M120
By June 1923, M116
By 13 June 1923, F130
17 June 1923, J33
23 June 1923, J37
24 June 1923, F135, I111, J91, J92
28 June 1923, F140
2 July 1923, J88
3 July 1923, J90
14 July 1923, F139
16 July 1923, J29
21 July 1923, F136
24 July 1923, F134, F154
26 July 1923, J39
27 July 1923, I64
1 August 1923, J22
2 August 1923, J36
6 August 1923, J45
By 22 August 1923, F137
30 August 1923, F143
20 September 1923, G24
1 October 1923, J41
3 October 1923, G22, G23
6 October 1923, G2
By 10 October 1923, F142
11 October 1923, M117
30 October 1923, F145
3 November 1923, I110
5 November 1923, M16
6 November 1923, I145
7 November 1923, J85
8 November 1923, K93, K108
9 November 1923, F147

10 November 1923, I67, J31
11 November 1923, F146
12 November 1923, I10
14 November 1923, J35
16 November 1923, L2
18 November 1923, K52
19 November 1923, H34
20 November 1923, J43
21 November 1923, F148
22 November 1923, F167, J27
6 December 1923, J5
7 December 1923, J10
8 December 1923, G43
11 December 1923, G33
14 December 1923, J75
17 December 1923, I144
21 December 1923, J73, J80
29 December 1923, G24

1924, J77 (rev. 15 September 1930)
3 January 1924, J58
5 January 1924, G32
10 January 1924, J2
13 January 1924, J52
22 January 1924, F150
25 January 1924, K76
26 January 1924, F153
30 January 1924, K25
20 February 1924, J42
26 February 1924, J66
27 February 1924, G36
28 February 1924, G17
1 March 1924, G21
8 March 1924, I7, J74
12 March 1924, F155
16 March 1924, I120, I122
17 March 1924, G29
18 March 1924, G1, G31, J95
21 March 1924, I74
27 March 1924, F151
29 March 1924, G20
31 March 1924, F152
1 April 1924, G19
2 April 1924, G35
8 April 1924, G39
9–12 April 1924, I29

19 April 1924, G5
20 April 1924, J67
By 16 May 1924, F156
17 May 1924, K59
By 21 May 1924, F157
1 June 1924, F159
8 June 1924, F158
8 July 1924, F161
12 July 1924, F162
30 July 1924, J89
2 August 1924, J96
5 September 1924, K53
6 September 1924, J47
7 September 1924, F163
8 September 1924, I121, S9
10 September 1924, K57, M51
17 September 1924, F166
19 September 1924, F164
22 September 1924, H1
25 September 1924, H30
28 September 1924, K42, K65
30 September 1924, G13
By October 1924, I113
1 October 1924, G37, K43
4 October 1924, H38
7 October 1924, F171
By 11 October 1924, I92
By 18 October 1924, F165
19 October 1924, R58
6 November 1924, J87
7 November 1924, F169
18 November 1924, F168
23 November 1924, J98
30 November 1924, J44
By December 1924, I114
1 December 1924, F170
7 December 1924, J6
16 December 1924, H24
By 17 December 1924, J11
17 December 1924, H2
By 18 December 1924, F172
19 December 1924, H10
20 December 1924, K78
22 December 1924, M76 Pt III

By 1925, G6, G27, G40, G41

2 January 1925, H4
By 21 January 1925, G30
10 February 1925, H3
By 12 February 1925, G14
By 28 February 1925, I138
By March 1925, J13
By 7 March 1925, I112
28 March 1925, H5
April 1925, M76 Pt II
5 April 1925, G7, H18
19 April 1925, J20
23 April 1925, H7, H9
25 April 1925, H6
By 2 May 1925, I32
13 May 1925, J24
24 May 1925, H12
27 May 1925, H14
29 May 1925, H8
By 1 July 1925, G4
By 7 July 1925, H11
7 July 1925, G34
13 July 1925, H19
20 July 1925, I25
22 July 1925, H13
23 July 1925, G42
26 July 1925, H15, J93
By 31 July 1925, I42
31 July 1925, G3
11 August 1925, J34, J64
21 August 1925, I26
By 5 September 1925, I33
5 September 1925, M82
11 September 1925, H21
By 25 October 1925, I19
By 18 November 1925, H17
By 21 November 1925, I35,
30 November 1925, J57
16 December 1925, I3
19 December 1925, K72

January 1926, H22
By 9 January 1926, I13
By 13 January 1926, H20
25 January 1926, I118
27 January 1926, H37
By 17 February 1926, H23

3 October 1927, M41 Pts I and II,
    M42, M43
8 October 1927, H71
14 October 1927, H80
By 19 October 1927, I143
By 29 October 1927, I22
November 1927, H66
By 12 November 1927, H65
22 November 1927, K91
By December 1927, I78, I79, I80,
    I96
6 December 1927, K64
By 8 December 1927, J28
By 17 December 1927, I128
19 December 1927, M26
21 December 1927, M107 Pt III
26 December 1927, H70
By 31 December 1927, I97

1928, H87
16 February – 15 June 1928, H90
By 7 March 1928 , I57
7 March 1928, H74
By 10 March 1928, I99
By 14 April 1928, I40
19 April 1928, I51
20 April 1928, H82
By 25 April 1928, H75
By 19 May 1928, I100
29 May 1928, H77
By 13 June 1928, H76
By 25 July 1928, H78
By 28 July 1928, I133
By 15 August 1928, I101
19 August 1928, H81
21 August 1928, H79
By 29 August 1928, I71
By September 1928, I125
6 September 1928, J12
9 September 1928, J84
16 September 1928, K96
By 26 September 1928, I132
4 November 1928, H86, J59
6 November 1928, H84
12 November 1928, K73
17 November 1928, K15

By 21 November 1928, H85,
16 December 1928, J1
By 19 December 1928, I31
21 December 1928, J53
23 December 1928, J56
By 26 December 1928, H88
26 December 1928, J99
31 December 1928, H92

By 2 January 1929, H89
6 January 1929, J32
13 January 1929, I136
By 17 January 1929, J40
By 2 February 1929, I98
3 February 1929, K74
By 23 February 1929, I20
25 February 1929, K102
27 February 1929, K101, K106
1 March 1929, K104
13 March 1929, K38
6 April 1929, K19
By June 1929, I91
By 19 June 1929, H91
19 August 1929, I1, K39, M23
27 August 1929, K105
31 August 1929, K27
7 September 1929, L7
18 September 1929, H94
20 September 1929, K51
25 September 1929, K88
26 September 1929, K110
7 October 1929, K99
By 9 October 1929, H93
16 October 1929, H97
By December 1929, I70
By 4 December 1929, H96
By 18 December 1929, I149

By 1930, I4, I5, I6, I8, I9, I11, I14,
    I15, I16, I23, I24, I30, I34, I36,
    I41, I43, I44, I46, I47, I48, I49,
    I50, I52, I53, I54, I55, I58, I59,
    I60, I63, I65, I66, I68, I69, I73,
    I75, I76, I77, I81, I82, I83, I86,
    I87, I88, I89, I93, I94, I95, I102,
    I104, I106, I107, I108, I116, I119,

I123, I128, I130, I134, I135, I141,
I142, I146, I150, I151, I152
By 22 January 1930, I148
By February 1930, I61
20 February 1930, K87
By March 1930, I56, I131
By 5 March 1930, I147, L1
23 March 1930, K80
7 April 1930, K103
24 April 1930, L3
By June 1930, I124
10 June 1930, K67, K68
12 June 1930, K66
15 June 1930, K82
By 25 June 1930, L4
29 June 1930, K81
13 July 1930, J7
31 August 1930, K47
8 September 1930, K36
20 October 1930, K50
18 November 1930, K114
26 November 1930, K100
27 November 1930, M14
2 December 1930, K11
3 December 1930, K17
7 December 1930, K5
10 December 1930, K1
14 December 1930, K3
15 December 1930, K6

By 1931, J49, J55
1 January 1931, L6
9 January 1931, K46
25 January 1931, K70
31 January 1931, K63
14 March 1931, K13
6 April 1931, K4
8 April 1931, K7, L8
15 April 1931, K22
24 April 1931, K60
30 April 1931, K26
6 May 1931, K40
7 May 1931, K33
9 May 1931, K9
12 May 1931, K69
21 May 1931, K28

3 June 1931, K8
7 June 1931, K10
2 August 1931, Z13
7 August 1931, K24
5 October 1931, L14
18 October 1931, M115
24 October 1931, K41
28 October 1931, K20
13 November 1931, K31
15 November 1931, K34, K109
2 December 1931, K15
6 December 1931, K32

By 1932, K2, K12, K16, K48, K49,
K58, K62
21 January 1932, K23
23 January 1932, L10
12 February 1932, R65
9 March 1932, K21
24 March 1932, M36
2 April 1932, L12
9 April 1932, M95
16 April 1932, L20
23 April 1932, M8
6 May 1932, M55 Pt IV
7 May 1932, M107 Pt II
10 May 1932, K75
20 May 1932, M81 Pt II
11 June 1932, M71
23 June 1932, L11
2 July 1932, M21, M73
9 July 1932, M17
16 July 1932, M29
18 July 1932, M67 (rev. 13 March
1936)
23 July 1932, M107 Pt I
24 July 1932, L15
15 November 1932, M66
29 November 1932, M98
14 December 1932, M52 Pt II
17 December 1932, M49

6 January 1933, M9
26 February 1933, M54
8 May 1933, R59
11 June 1933, M62 Pt VIII

15 July 1933, M11
13 August 1933, M104
By 29 August 1933, L13
28 November 1933, M58

1934, L16
21 January 1934, M94
22 January 1934, L21
16 February 1934, M33
By 15 September 1934, M63
24 September 1934, M25
9 December 1934, M32 Pt II
15 December 1934, M106

c. 1935, M96
26 January 1935, M44 Pt II
By 22 March 1935, M13
7 April 1935, M74
26 October 1935, O7
30 October 1935, M108 Pt III

By 1936, M62 Pts I–IV
1936, M47, M61
18 January 1936, L17, L18
17 February 1936, M93 Pt II
29 February 1936, M113
13 March 1936, M2
21 May 1936, M48
25 July 1936, M1
28 July 1936, M7
By 13 August 1936, L19
30 August 1936, M76 Pt IV
11 October 1936, M72
17 October 1936, M62 Pt V
28 October 1936, M99, M102
21 November 1936, M41 Pt III,
    M52 Pt I
10 December 1936, M55 Pts I, II
    and V
12 December 1936, M53
16 December 1936, M15

1937, M3
1 January 1937, M22 Pt I
26 January 1937, M76 Pt I
29 January 1937, M28 Pt II

11 February 1937, M22 Pts II and III
23 April 1937, M68
24 April 1937, M46
10 May 1937, M80
24 August 1937, M24
25 September 1937, M18
3 November 1937, M45
By 6 November 1937, M34
20 November 1937, M93 Pt I
By 18 December 1937, M31
18 December 1937, M30

9 March 1938, M5
19 March 1938, M27
3 July 1938, M12 Pt I
12 August 1938, M109
18 August 1938, M108 Pt I
19 August 1938, M105
20 August 1938, M44 Pt I, M100
2 September 1938, M50, M77
3 September 1938, M86
4 September 1938, M12 Pt II, M65
5 September 1938, M79
13 October 1938, L23, R63
23 October 1938, R22
31 October 1938, M114
5 November 1938, L22
10 November 1938, R2
15 November 1938, M83
11 December 1938, M84
16 December 1938, M6

By 1939, M28 Pt I, M32 Pt I,
    M55 Pt III, M62 Pts VI and VII,
    M70, M78, M81 Pt I, M85
2 January 1939, M87, M88
3 June 1939, R35 Pt 7
By 12 July 1939, O1
By August 1939, R47
2 December 1939, O4

c. 1940, O9
1940, O5, R13
3 January 1940, O3
8 January 1940, R23
15 February 1940, S7

3 February 1946, R45 Pt 5
1 March 1946, R25
6 June 1946, R35 Pt 5
14 June 1946, R28 Pt 1
13 December 1946, R61 Pt 5

10 January 1947, R35 Pt 6
11 January 1947, R28 Pt 2, R61 Pt 1
7 April 1947 (rev.), R67 and R68
By 25 June 1947, Q2
6 July 1947, R62 Pt 5
4 August 1947, R61 Pt 8
20 August 1947, R73
30 August 1947, R45 Pts 1 and 2
16 September 1947, Q12
13 October 1947, Q3, R41 Pts 1 and 2
23 November 1947, R62 Pt 8
16 December 1947, R72
28 December 1947, R27
29 December 1947, Q8

1 January 1948, R39
2 January 1948, R41 Pt 4
5 January 1948, R41 Pt 3
8 January 1948, Q11
26 January 1948, R1
29 January 1948, R24
12 February 1948, R42 (Stanza 3)
21 February 1948, R7
27 May 1948, R14 Pt 1
29 May 1948, R14 Pts 2 and 3
15 June 1948, R5
24 July 1948, R71
1 November 1948, R28 Pt 4

21 January 1949, R35 Pt 1
25 February 1949, R48
4 March 1949, R61 Pt 6
11 March 1949, R61 Pt 12
By April 1949, Q4
21 May 1949, R10 Pt 1
15 July 1949, R10 Pt 2
16 July 1949, R10 Pt 3
9 October 1949, R49

4 January 1950, Q6
3 March 1950, R11
19 April 1950, Q5
10 May 1950, R46 Pt 3
12 July 1950, R42 (Stanza 4)
14 July 1950, R61 Pt 7
16 August 1950, R45 Pt 3
16 November 1950, R61 Pt 10
2 December 1950, R50
15 December 1950, R51
27 December 1950, R61 Pt 11

19 July 1951, R43
29 December 1951, R21

5 March 1952, R52
8 April 1952, R54
25 April 1952, R46 Pt 7
2 May 1952, Q7
19 May 1952, R55
1 August 1952, R53
By 6 August 1952, Q9
19 August 1952, Q10
29 November 1952, Q16
By 17 December 1952, Q14

10 January 1953, R32
19 September 1953, Q17
23 September 1953, T1, T2
6 October 1953, Q18

By 1954, R9, R16, R35 Pt 2, R61 Pt 9, R62 Pt 2
1 August 1954, T3

By 1955, S10, T4
14 October 1955, T5
26 December 1955, T6

7 October 1956, T7

By 1957, T13
By 5 January 1957, T9
9 January 1957, T8
By 16 April 1957, T10
9 June 1957, T11

13 June 1957, T12
2 July 1957, T16
27 September 1957, T18

By 1958, T17
7 January 1958, T15
18 January 1958, T14
20 February 1958, T19
26 September 1958, T20

21 May 1959, T21
11 September 1959, T23 Pt 4

By 1960, T23 Pt 3
7 June 1960, T22
15 July 1960, T23 Pts 1 and 2

9 May 1961, T24

By 2 December 1962, T25

INDEX OF FIRST LINES

THIS is a first-line index of poems in Volumes 1 and 2. Poems are identified by their alphanumerics, e.g. 'B2' is the second poem of section B. Volume 1 contains sections A–H. Volume 2 contains I–T and Z, and A30a and A30b in the Corrigenda and Addenda.

All Souls' to-night! All Souls' to-night, F82
All talk is good talk, R26
All that he was behind him lies, K69
All that was I, I gave, E64
All wounded things were hers, R44
All yesterday she sat with her lost youth, M97
Alone in her own lost land, M67
Alone she sat upon her horse, H26
Along the street I see him go, H22
Although the Lord mayn't speak to-day, A22
Always they run behind, behind, H71
A man may strike, in his lordly pride, H1
Amen, Amen, and they went, J12
And it's whistle, whistle, whistle, B49
A pharisee builded a famous church, T4
A piper at the door, L1
Are these our people's leaders? These, R8
A robin redbreast on a fence, F158
"Art lonely, lad, now the earth covers thee, M8
A sailor man, I loved the sea, Q11
A scandal I heard, unexpectedly sprung, F153
Ascending on the written word, M53
A scuttering wind, K60
A shadow lies upon the hill, A3
As I came down from the mountain tops, K16
As Joseph was a-walking, J97
As light is measure of the sun, J71
A Squawk Machine squealed loud and long, Z14
As Simon leaned upon the bar, G14
A star shall be the candle-light, F47
As the soft gloaming fell, I61
As the sun looked over the fence, S10
As weeds grow out of graves and vaults, K42
A sweeping wind and a blinding rain, B19
As when some blundering one, Q18
A thousand faces cross my sight, F149
At the nesting of the waterfowl, R69
Attuned, they mused and spoke, F113

Baggage of thought and tents of dream, E43
Balkis of Sheba came, L12
Bare-armed, strong-thewed, and hardened out by toil, K106
Beautiful are they, that, ranging on the mountains, I133
Beauty was here that now is gone away, I52
Beauty without a peer, I48
Because a bird sings in a tree, B57

Can't find my stud, C22
Child-bound I stay, who would away, R45
Clear at even sinks the sun . . ., F80
Clo'es Props! Clo'es Props, E71
Cold in thy little bed, M47
Come again, Little Heart, C21
Come along, come along, come along, Johnny, G39
Come! Let me now confess it all, C32
Come not again, lone wandering by the shore, I23
Come soon, Summer, come soon! For cloud, K57
Come with me, my delight, K13
Coming down the street, M5
Common of pasture in Thy field, J42
Contest is ended in surrender, I82
Creep thou up to my shoulder, I120
Crossing Hyde Park, to take the morning air, F68
Cupid lost himself to-day, B3

Dame Nature, spinning in the sun, E53
Dark was the night, but bright the star, M60
Dark woman of long grief, R57
Day gives her radiant face whereon, B64
D' children, Lord, d' children, dey's weepin' all day long, B42
Dead, O God, B73
Dear messenger of Spring, I116
Death came and took away my friend, F44
Death comes to serfs and kings, L17
Death hath its beauty, too, I51
Deep in the meadow grass, I33
Deeply respectable are we, F5
Deformed, he waited on the kerb, E59
Dere's a little boy, B41
Did ye ever be hearin' of Mary McNab, G24
Does the poet sing his deed, F14
Do I mind poverty? Never, I106
Donald says, "Hold up your head, B46
Donal, my father, M23
Down by the Lepers' Squint (the Town Hall gate), F54
Down by the polder, where, I94
Down, down, E90
Down in a chapel by the sea, C24
Down in a quiet corner, B78
Down the pathway, C44
Down through the ages mark the blind men go, F76
Draw down the blind, B79
Draw near to beauty as it sleeps, I124

How life pupates through chrysalids of Time, F71
How many wander leaderless, F96
How oft we stalked a leaf and thought it you, I13
How shall the children sing of the strong, G42
How shall their longing tell itself aloud, K77
How splendidly the sun (his last, H89
How strangely life, forever asked to eat, K104
How that old Satan, who, M54
How wonderful is man, I58
"Hum . . . Drum! Hum . . . Drum, S6
Humpin' bluey on the track, A26
Husha-husha-bye, I123
Hush, Child Gesu! Hush Thee, then, C3
Hush, hush, little babe, O hush thee, K81
"Hush in my arms, my dear, my little child, F130
"Hush! it is Eastertide!" . . . "Be still! Be still, J25
Hush! O, my babe, B120
'Hush, thee, hush, A49

"I am growing too old to be wise, H84
I am he whom I sing, H53
I am not very patient, E41
I am poor, I am shabby—unashamed, H87
I am that man, who, in an hour of grief, K67
I am the freeman, E72
I am the idle, bone-idle I lie, R23
I am the Maker, R10
I am the mother of dreams. For I, C65
I am the Ploughman of the Moon, E50
I am the soul, T8
I am the woman-drawer, K9
I am Thy fugitive, who, path to path, J41
I, a poor singer, send out song, I45
I asked of God the truth, A46
I asked of winter what would he bring me, M55
I ask nor wealth, nor length of days, E10
I bid you come but once, sweetheart, B128
I buried a child I loved, to-day, O14
I climbed up Ben Buckler, F101
I closed the door on grief and faced the sun, T22
Ideas die for want of words, F144
I die? I, that from the dust arose, R49
"I do not hear the clock!" she said, J50
I don't know whether 'tis well to love, B61
I draw a-near you in your sleeping city, M17
I dreamed I was up in Heaven, A39

It's mighty fine to spout, an' say, A16
It's O the loving ways of him, B21
It's singin' in an' out, B1
It's us two when it's morning, B22
It's who will pound my mate, A32
I turned the pages of an old, old book, E36
It wailed. The night-air shivered at, H39
It was a long time going, R7
It was "Annie! Annie!" I heard him call, A30b
It was himself that came to me, G22
It was, it was a Fairy man, D4
It was my love complained, I79
It was O'Shea, the singer, sang, H5
I've pity for all writers, F118
I waited for my dear, F98
I wait in a garden sweet, B13
I walked abroad one summer's day, M48
I want the little homely ways, C11
I was good friends with Death while he was far away, C9
I was not sufficiently rebel, O2
I was one born to love, L16
I was the prodigal, O7
I waz trampin' from the 'Umbug to get to Murril Crick, A8
I who am I, E39
I who no beauty had, I46
I will arise and go to my Father, J21
"I will be strong, C42
"I win," says Life; "I win," says Death, C64
I wish I was back in Cosme ahuskin' of the corn, A33
I wisht I was unwed again, H59
I wonder if (when I am dead), F125
I would go back again if I could, E77
I write not flowering words, O1

Jessie Mackay, E13
Jesu, the wind that softened as it neared Thee, M58
John Curtin stood at the door, O11
Joy is lord of the earth, C43

Kangaroo and Wallaroo, Wallaby, Bandicoot, O9
Keekin' out d' winder, A52
Keep me, within thine heart, B107
Keep watch, O God, B100
Kings to their tombs, M113
Kisses on the dimpled arm, B112
Kissin', kissin', kissin', B59

Not Europe, crater of the newer world, C66
Not for me the silver word, G43
Not hers the noisy world, R32
Nothing endures but change, R14
Nothing to me is man, R11
Not his to be to-day acclaimed, F161
Not in crabbed words, F13
Not India the gem, H75
Not mine the sea, although it holds, R54
Not of ourselves are we free, E44
Not the kiss at the door, T1
Not till the hands are slack, and all the hot, K109
Not till the Lord of the House, J63
Not to be storm, H58
Not what we know but what we apprehend, J34
Now comes the final hour and we must part, F123
Now comes the hour in which I say farewell and go, M11
Now comes this Falcon of the South, L6
"Nowell!" rang the great bell, J1
Now God be my shield, J87
Now is the evening hour, C33
Now let all meanness die, Q12
Now lifteth the ice its pack, I69
Now may the Lord, Who fashioned me, and made, F90
Now they are gone, and I am come, M7
Now turned toward its doom, I64
Now wakes the Spring, when all the little flowers, H96
Now was he NGCOBBERA, a man while yet a youth, R65
"Now who be you, my foreign man, I44
Now you are gone, M14

O Babylon! thou mother of brave dreams, F79
O, beauty of beauty, I50
O Beauty that is praise, I47
O braiding thought move out—move on, M3
O'Brien was an Irishman, Q1
O but my heart was sad, Q6
O, Captain of the Host, Z8
O cloud that fliest o'er the stricken waste, C30
O Columbine, my Columbine, M112
O, could we weep, I87
O, Death, thou hast no charm for me, B117
O Durramela, hear, L11
O dusty words we find, K33
Of all the Pots the Potter made, C47
Of Christ, my Redeemer, I asked for a word, J81

O! for my children, F17
Of pride will I sing, in a song, I60
Oft have I stood to see the failing, I100
O glorious day, exultant to the end, H10
O God! how sweet it is to hear, B44
O, ha'e ye seen my bonnie love, B47
O heart, be a timbrel, O lips be a lute, J94
O holy land of home, H74
"Oh hush!" she says, "Do you not hear, M25
Oh, I could draw from you, C52
Oh, John, for old faith in you, F89
Oh, let us call again, J48
Oh, Sydney Town is my town, E38
Oh, the little children, where knowledge comes too soon, H8
Oh! The men of the New Australia, A12
Oh, 'tis many a year since I went down, F59
Oh, when you touch me, sweeps, M19
O, in what loveliness, K26
O Johnny, was it you then, Z11
O Joy! take up the silver cord, C1
O Keeper of the Sheep, C8
Old and poor, a pensioner, G16
Old Bill and I, R53
Old Father Parramatta rolling to the sea, T5
Old Forthright lived in a dell they called for his name, R13
Old friends, the years spilled "ifs," and "ands, F100
Old Granny on the hill, I57
Old John, C59
Old Sam Smith, M86
Old she is, with the children grown, G19
O! Life, beat not so heavy with thy flail, I103
O Life, I called to thee, E9
O life, thou battle-ground! O blood, of tides, K102
O, little Honey-Sweet, B70
O little song, A48
O Love the withered, wasted years denied, E79
O Man! who, through the flesh, T16
O, many birds are in the bush, B106
O, Me, I saw the Cross, B119
O memories in flood, H2
O Memory, mopoke of the heart, I71
O men, tread softly as you pass, K71
O Minadong! My Minadong, H42
O Mother Riverina! Mother, listen, H56
O movement of the dust above decay, I110

Once again a Battle-Cry is flung across the world, C38
Once e'er she slept, M96
Once from her Council Chamber door, B121
Once high I sprang, and then declined in drouth, F167
Once I came as a ghost, R19
Once in a dark hour of the soul, F4
Once in a garden walking, B90
Once, in an hour of talk, one said, H11
Once, I remember, when to some poor home, J82
Once like an ocean ran, I86
Once, long ago, A41
Once there was Nineveh, and there was Troy, H86
Once, to this venturer, M87
Once two went back, dreaming old love would wake, F63
One in the Never Never, J46
One sees an action only with the eyes, E52
One shall come walking, M57
One snail and two snails, S1
One voice to speak, T10
One will write with a golden pen, C15
Only above the grave of murdered faith, E3
Only eternal things, F168
Only the children of Mirrabooka, K3
Only the ruined know, R36
Only to know is not enough, J53
"On the Grampian heights the snow is white, F3
O pillow, dusty, fusty, old, H97
O prodigal of self, M100
O Sea! Mighty: Majestic: Wonderful, M37
O, singer in brown, B52
O, singer unafraid, F159
O swan, cry out in the night, K24
O, sweet is summer on the land, but sweeter far to me, G28
O sweet the bells of Easter-tide, J78
O, that again I might go back, H60
O that I too might make, K34
O that the blind would see! O that the deaf would hear, H65
O that thy heart confederate were with mine, M117
O, there will come a day, J8
Others may tune the pipe, may wander idly blowing, H14
O the ungathered that decay has stolen, I136
O the voice of her, and the face of her, B36
O, the wild winds that over it blow, H7
O thou bright bird! I watch thee to and fro, L4
O thou great ocean on, I131

Said the cat to the kitten, S12
Say, if you're goin' to Paraguay, A14
Say, it's mighty easy gassin', A25
Say now, Horatio, has language hours, K97
Says he, "I saw Frank Gulson down the street, H3
Says she, "I've got me Glory-box, G5
Say to him: "She is sad!" and leave, M99
Seeming as though the storm, M32
See where they sit and tap their thumbs, F33
Send the call across the sea, O17
Senorita Marie, A30a
Set thy light on a mountain, E40
Shall man say beauty passes, M71
Sharp wind and sleety rain, Q7
She beat upon the pavement, E25
She died—she died before her child was born, K79
She dwelt serene, as though apart, K75
She grew, but he remained where he began, M121
She had an innocence no time effaced, K43
She had the loving heart, M79
"She isn't the thing!" they said, G10
She laid her shoes out side by side, H92
She lived, we knew not how, R43
She's one and she's many—shadow and sun, F124
She stood alone, and yet I heard her sing, F1
She took her staff within her hand, J96
She was a bird, a thistledown, H35
She was Kate when first I knew her, F164
"She was so strong," they said, K74
She weeps and no one heeds, B38
She went on, who once was here, K51
She who was one with them, R71
Shivery, shivery, shaky, O, B29
Shut fast, shut fast the door, B124
Silver is the dust in the heat, R47
Singing down the meadow way, B53
Sing, O sing, B108
Sing, sing i' th' morning, B31
Sing sweet, little bird, sing sweet, sing sweet, B15
Sing the song o' pizen snaix, A13
Sleep and forget, C49
Sleep, hushling, sleep, I122
Sleep my baby sleep, A31
(Sleep! Sleep! Sleep!), B88
Sleep, with thy veiling hands lean over me, E47

There was a garden long ago, F87
There was a man—a man once lived in this our town, M36
There was a sweetness in that place, F152
There was great beauty in the names her people called her, K6
There was him, an' Jim, and Billy and I, A44
There was no hunted one, M40
There was no stir among the trees, R67
There was singing at earliest dawn, C63
There were three old divils set out one day, R30
There were Two little sheep, S2
The river goes a-winding down, B23
The road before me, R48
The road broke under the wheels, I63
The roar of constant traffic flies, L10
The Rue Tree is the tallest tree, J7
The rug that the woman had made, A35
The sea has soddened the baby clothes, B35
The sea he loved has taken him, F46
These are life's treasurings, E11
These are the little shoes that died, M114
These are the men whom peace obeys, I42
These have said many things to me, F21
The shadow creeps across the street, B104
The singers sang the mighty Dust, E69
The Sleep-Sea calls, A53
The soldier he lies on his back on the hill, F155
The son shall love his mother first, J16
The stars of night, M43
The striker stands where the boats go out, C13
The summer held it dear, H30
The sun drew it and made it, E87
The sunlight falls where the Harbor waters run, H48
The sun moves north; too swift, I54
The sun shines on the tomb, J28
The sun still lights the quandong leaves, M65
The swart Mahommedan, they say, F29
The tide is at the full, A47
The time you came you sat awhile and talked, M12
The tired man, the tired man, G2
The untilled fields they grew no wheat, H72
The voices of children, stifling, A7
The wattle is a lady, H38
The wind came slithering down the hill, C17
The wind comes in at the door, T6
The wind is sighing in the west, A1

We are the judges; behold in us, F23
We are the souls that cannot stay, H19
We are the trees, F22
Weary He came, and in His mother's lap, L2
We come from "clouds of glory" to the earth, F70
We dared not say farewell, M88
We did not think, did we, B131
We dwell not among the women as the white men do, M62
Weep not for me that I soon went, K68
We found it as the hunt went by, K27
We found the fox, we found the fox, I31
We have been strangers all these many years, E28
We have come at last from the gentile's land, L20
We have no words to speak our woe, A29
We live in many worlds, C61
We may blow about the country, A15
We measure out a day, T7
We only saw the road, Q16
We've a land we can measure with any that's seen, F61
We've been married, now, these thirty-odd years, H73
We were the unarmed race, R63
We who have wandered shall come back again, F85
We who look outward to the sun, E54
We would be kind, but we miss the way, A38
What are we but the vision of a thought, K40
What art thou whom I seek but a wind, I93
"What be you a-lookin' at, Emily Ann, R18
"Whatever ye sow, C23
What had the bloody hands of war for these, F25
What have I heard in the wilga, K7
What have we left of all the long, long years, I21
What is this magic men have praised, K64
What loveliness in leaves, R28
What loveliness lies shaped in stone, K32
What part has cruelty in God's good plan, K100
What shall I say to God, F53
What's in a name, H28
What's the good of wishin' for things, G11
What though I follow love, B130
What though thou should'st declare, I102
What was it, in thy heart, that made, M115
What wind of death has threshed the corn, E4
What years since last I heard the trotting hoof, L7
Wheesht! Wheesht, my bairn! not yet for you, M68
When at last I shall stand, K38

INDEX OF TITLES

This is a title index of poems in Volumes 1 and 2. Poems are identified by their alphanumerics, e.g. 'B2' is the second poem of section B. Volume 1 contains sections A–H. Volume 2 contains sections I–T and Z, and A30a and A30b in the Corrigenda and Addenda.

824 COLLECTED VERSE

CORRIGENDA AND ADDENDA
FOR VOLUME ONE

Corrigenda for volume 1

The following in volume 1 require correction:

- Chronology (entry for 'Early 1879'): *for* Woomargana *read* Woomargama
- p. lxiv line 4: *for* O9 *read* O10
- p. lxxi line 11: *for* on the page *read* on the line
- p. 193 n. 1: *for* C24 n. 1 *read* C24 n. 2
- p. 417 F82 n. 1: *for* evening *read* eve (*twice*)
- p. 484 n. 1: *for* L8 *read* L7
- p. 654 n. 5: *for* Vikings:p *read* Vikings:
- Stanza divisions should be removed after the following lines: in A12 (lines 4 and 16), A29 (8), A33 (4, 8, 16), E2 (16), F45 (10), F84 (12), F124 (6) and E49 (34; with 35–6 realigned)
- Stanza divisions are required after the following lines: in F104 (line 22), F124 (8) and H60 (39)

Appendix: The manuscripts

During the editing of volume 2, the original L14 was identified as a collated state for M85. Its removal from the L sequence means that manuscript information in volume 1's Appendix should now read at page 709:

L14	Buf 169/40			NLA 727 2/4/15††
L15	Fryer 2/3087	NLA 727	L18	Buf 172/15/71
	2/4/13$^{+\Delta}$			Fryer 2/2975†
L16	NLA 727 1/I	727 2/4/13		ML 6/3 6/5
L17	Buf 172/15/64			NLA 727 2/4/15††
	Fryer 2/2975†		L19	None sighted
	ML 6/3 6/5		L20	Buf 172/14/27

Fryer 2/2954
ML 4/5   6/2   6/3   6/10
L21   Fryer 2/2969   ML 6/2
6/3   6/9   6/10   7/2   7/3
NLA 727 1/O   727 2/4/13
8766 10/6/1   8766

10/6/2   8766 10/6/3$^+$
L22   ML 6/10   NLA 727
1/C   727 2/4/17$^+$
L23   Buf 172/14   ML 6/10
NLA 727 2/4/17$^+$

Similarly, late verification of the publication of O1 meant it could be transferred from the 'unverified' Z sequence (it was originally Z13) and that a newly identified poem (O8) could be incorporated. Two other poems however (the original O1 and O13) were removed when identified as collated states of, respectively, R35 and R3. Manuscript information from O8 onward and for Z13 and Z14 should now read at pages 712–13 and 717:

O8   ML 6/6   NLA 727 2/2/3
7272 2/4/19   727 2/5/1
O9   ML 6/6   NLA 727 2/
4/19   727 2/5/1$^+$
O10   ML 6/9   7/3   NLA 8766
10/6/1$^+$ 8766 10/6/3$^+$
O11   ML 7/3$^+$ NLA 727 2/
4/19$^+$ 727 2/5/2   8766
10/6/2   8766 10/7/4$^+$
O12   ML 7/4   NLA 727 2/
5/1$^+$
O13   ML 6/9   6/10   7/3   7/4$^+$
NLA 727 2/5/1   727
3/6/2.1   8766 10/6/1$^+$
8766 10/6/2   8766 10/6/3$^+$

O14   727 2/5/2$^+$ 727 3/6/2.3
8766 10/6/1
O15   ML 6/9   7/3   7/4
NLA 727 1/T   727 2/5/2
727 2/5/3   8766 10/6/1$^+$
8766 10/6/2   8766 10/6/3$^+$
O16   None sighted
O17   ML 6/9   7/3   NLA 727
1/S$^+$ 8766 10/6/1   8766
10/6/2   8766 10/6/3$^+$
8766 10/7/4
O18   NLA 727 2/5/3$^+$

Z13   Buf 168/36
Z14   NLA 727 2/5/3

Addenda for volume 1

The following two poems (A30a and A30b) were drawn to my attention by Rosemary Campbell. They have publication dates falling between those of A30 and A31. They were among those sent to W. A. Woods from Paraguay: see volume 1, Introduction, p. xxxix and A30a n. 1. A30b appears to have been written during the voyage there: see A30b's composition date and n. 1.

A30a   SENORITA MARIE

Senorita Marie,
   In the golden days,
When above the river
   Swung the summer haze,
Did you dream, O sweetheart,   5
   Of the time to be?—
One upon the river,
   One upon the sea.

Did you dream, my darling,
   As we watched the flow   10
Of that mighty torrent
   Drifting out so slow,
That I should remember
   In the time to be,
One upon the river,   15
   One upon the sea.

Think a little, Marie,
   When the summers wake,
Think a little of me
   For the dear old sake.   20
Think a little of me
   In the time to be,
One upon the river,
   One upon the sea.

Senorita Marie,   25
   When the days are long,
When the river murmurs
   To a summer song;
When the nights lie waiting
   In a shining veil,   30
And the splendid moonlight
   Makes the stars grow pale;
When Orion nightly
   Sees the White Cross set

> You may half remember,   35
> I can not forget.

(n. d.)   *Copy-text: Clip*, 10 April 1897, p. 4[1]   *Collated states:* None

---

[1] Appeared under a column heading 'WOMEN'S SCRAP BOOK', with the editorial comment:
'If there is no objection we'll start to-day with some song words sent me by our old
friend and correspondent "M.J.C."'

A30b   NO MORE

> It was "Annie! Annie!" I heard him call,
> But I made him answer never a word;
> And the sea grew hoarse as the moon went down,
> And the fog went drifting across the town;
>   And I knew he would think I had not heard   5
>   When I let him go with never a word.
>
> And then, "Annie! Annie!" it came again,
>   But I turned away for I would not hear,
> I steeled my heart and I set my lips—
> (God pity the women who watch the ships,   10
> For the sailing time is the time of Fear
> With the women praying that God be near—).
>
> But I knew if he called once more I'd go,
> Though the dead from their graves had shouted "No!"
> But he called me no more, no more, no more,   15
> And the ship went down within sight of shore.
>
>   *   *   *   *
>
> And the sea at the dawn sank moaning down,
> And the fog went drifting away from town.

(30 November 1895)   *Copy-text: Clip*, 8 May 1897, p. 6[1]   *Collated states:* None

---

[1] Editorial note reads: 'Several correspondents write approvingly of the song words
"Senorita Marie" published in this column [see A30a n. 1] lately. And they want some
more. Well, what about this from the same pen:—'.

Volume 1, Appendix: The manuscripts
The following entries should be added at page 683:

A30a   Not sighted   A30b   ML 4/9   NLA 8766 10/8/13

POEMS WITH STANZAS BROKEN
AT FOOT OF PAGE

GILMORE experimented with stanza lengths and sometimes varied them within the same poem. Although she usually ended stanzas with terminal punctuation, it will be occasionally unclear, for the purpose of quotation, whether the last stanza on a page is complete or whether, for layout purposes in this edition, it has been completed on the next page. The latter situation occurs in the following poems. (If necessary, the relevant page number is given; prose poems are unaffected.)

Volume One

A1, A3, A4, A7, A11, A12 (pp. 19, 20), A13, A18, A21, A22, A23, A26, A29, A33, A42 (p. 51), A47, A51 (p. 58), A52

B34, B35, B38, B46, B47, B48, B67, B74, B92, B106, B111, B113, B121 (p. 158), B132, B135, B136 (p. 170)

C6 (pp. 176, 177), C13 (p. 183), C14, C26, C44, C46, C50, C58, C59, C61

E1 (p. 232), E3, E4 (pp. 236, 237, 238), E7, E8, E10, E16, E17, E19 (p. 253), E20, E21 (p. 257), E25, E26, E27, E28, E35, E39, E42, E44, E45 (pp. 281, 282), E47, E48, E49 (pp. 285, 286), E51 (pp. 290, 291), E52, E53 (p. 294), E56, E59, E60 (p. 302), E66, E67, E69 (p. 311), E70, E76, E77, E81, E85 (p. 326), E86, E87, E88, E90, E91, E92, E94, E95, E99

F2, F3, F8, F11, F15, F16, F19, F20, F27 (p. 361), F29 (p. 364), F30, F36, F37, F42, F44 (pp. 379, 380), F45, F46, F47, F48, F49, F55, F56, F57, F59, F69, F72 (p. 407), F81 (p. 415), F82, F84, F86, F90, F91 (p. 426), F95 (pp. 430, 431), F100, F101, F102, F103, F104, F105 (pp. 441, 442), F114, F118, F119, F122, F124, F125, F127, F128, F129, F134, F139, F140, F145, F148, F150 (pp. 481, 482), F152, F153, F154, F157, F159 (pp. 490, 491), F160 (p. 493), F163, F165 (pp. 497, 498), F166, F167, F170, F171

G1 (pp. 507, 508), G2, G4 (pp. 511, 512), G5 (p. 514), G6, G8, G9 (p. 518), G10, G12 (p. 525), G15, G16, G17, G20, G21 (p. 539), G26, G29 (pp. 550, 551), G30 (p. 352), G31,